Managing Bank Risk

An Introduction to Broad-Base Credit Engineering

Managing Bank Risk

An Introduction to Broad-Base Credit Engineering

Morton Glantz

With Contributions by Moody's-KMV
and Johnathan Mun, Decisioneering Inc.

ACADEMIC PRESS
An Elsevier Science Imprint

Amsterdam   Boston   London   New York   Oxford   Paris
San Diego   San Francisco   Singapore   Sydney   Tokyo

Academic Press
An Elsevier Science Imprint
525 B Street, Suite 1900, San Diego, California 92101-4495, USA
http://www.academicpress.com

Academic Press
84 Theobalds Road, London WC1X 8RR, UK
http://www.academicpress.com

Library of Congress Catalog Card Number: 2001099439

International Standard Book Number: 0-12-285785-2

PRINTED IN THE UNITED STATES OF AMERICA

02 03 04 05 06 07 **MM** 9 8 7 6 5 4 3 2 1

TO MARK WINICK

The glow from his light fills us, still

CONTENTS

FOREWORD

The new economy did not arrive in the way some pundits predicted at the end of the last century. Instead of perpetual economic growth and the death of business cycles, we are in the midst of rapidly evolving markets and rapidly changing corporate structures. It is the pace at which companies appear and disappear that marks our new economy. However, many of the old economic problems remain: the correlation of corporate failures rises during the worst of economic times; financial institutions periodically face crises; and borrowers of all sizes fail to meet their obligations.

Over a decade ago, the Basel committee produced guidelines for determining bank regulatory capital. The objective of this accord was to level the global playing field for financial institutions and protect us all against systemic risk in the financial system. As markets evolved, the accord became irrelevant. An army of investment-banking professionals regularly create collateralized structures designed to circumvent regulatory capital requirements. A bank may find itself with too much exposure to a particular class of assets not paying the kind of returns needed to justify the regulatory capital allocated to these assets. A collateralized loan obligation (CLO) is the answer. The assets are placed in the CLO and presto, the regulatory capital requirement disappears. Oddly enough, most of these deals are done in a way so that the bank continues to hold the equity piece of the CLO—effectively retaining the credit risk on the assets. All that has happened is the assets are moved off the bank's balance sheet; the bank continues to hold the credit risk. In fact, the current accord when not circumvented, distorts lending behavior (e.g. lending to a AAA reinsurer requires more regulatory capital than lending to a sub-investment grade OECD bank.)

Over time, regulators have figured out the Basel accord needs to be substantially revamped. In recent years, arduous debates over how best to regulate financial institutions has hampered the release of a new accord. The markets, however, are not waiting for Basel. Financial institutions continue to build portfolios and periodically fail. In the case of Japan, an entire financial system sits on the brink of collapse. Technology and deregulation have enabled non-bank financial institutions to enter the credit markets in unprecedented ways. The result is a constellation of credit instruments ranging from credit sensitive notes to credit default swaps.

In the midst of these tumultuous times, Professor Glantz's book fills an expanding void around understanding practical implementation of new and more efficient credit portfolio engineering. Historically, banks held a near monopoly on the provision of credit. The opaque nature of the dealer-controlled markets in corporate bonds has hampered the development of liquidly traded debt markets. The world is changing. The internet has given birth to an assortment of credit exchanges. Theories once relegated to academia have facilitated rigorous modeling of credit instruments. Active management of credit portfolios has become the mantra of bankers and regulators, alike. New market participants ranging from large asset managers to CFOs managing account receivable portfolios portend a global market for credit where risk can be more sensibly managed. Market data and credit models become much more important in this new environment. This book provides the context for understanding these issues.

At one time a bank loan officer only had to track the fortunes of a handful of large, well known companies. The skills needed for this kind of analysis centered on understanding the qualitative aspects of a business. While fundamental analysis continues to have a place in understanding an obligor's credit quality, the nature of the credit business has changed. Narrowly focused, simplistic stand-alone credit analysis is no longer enough. To stay competitive, financial institutions must look to more sources of information and adapt sophisticated tools: cash flow computer modeling, time series / regression, simulation analytics, stochastic optimization, and interactive credit risk rating systems, to name a few. And information sources should cover the entire spectrum of obligors—not just the large, higher quality firms. In fact, portfolios of many small, risky companies may be safer than similarly sized portfolios of a few large, safe companies. This conclusion is not always intuitive or easily discerned. Portfolio analytics are needed to compare these two very different kinds of portfolios. This book will introduce you to these analytics.

Market-observable data are playing an increasingly important role in credit modeling. Equity-based measures of default probability such as the EDF™ credit measure developed by KMV can provide a framework to leverage credit analysts already doing fundamental analysis. Equity data provides a means to develop a forward-looking view of a company's credit risk. While lenders and credit analysts may have access to private information on a company, these private data are sometimes misleading and it is not always clear how to compare data across companies. Rigorous models of credit can be used to place all information in a common framework facilitating more meaningful comparisons across a large universe of obligors.

Debt markets also provide forward-looking and objective data. Unfortunately, debt-based measures still suffer from data quality problems. The corporate bond and loan markets are much less transparent than the equity markets. Nonetheless, efforts are underway to improve disclosure in the publicly traded debt markets. As the data from debt markets improves, we will have another source of information to estimate both expected default probabilities and expected recovery in the event of default. From a modeling perspective, bond and loan instruments typically embed both a default option and a pre-payment (or call) option. Combined with a liquidity risk premium, sorting out each piece of the credit puzzle in a loan or bond can be difficult without analyzing another instrument such as equity. The best strategy is to develop a comprehensive view of an obligor analyzing all data—both fundamental and market-- and integrate it into a portfolio framework that treats all instruments similarly. This book fills in the details of this analytical process.

Given these various trends, institutions that can simultaneously implement robust risk management procedures and strategies for uncovering credit risk investments with the highest return per unit of risk will be rewarded with higher market valuations. This orientation requires characterization of the correlation among the exposures in a portfolio. Once identified, strategies utilizing instruments such as credit derivatives can be used to improve a portfolio's return per unit of risk and minimize the probability of insolvency. This method of credit portfolio management requires an understanding of the analytics underlying valuation, correlation, and risk inherent in credit-risky instruments. In recent years, these types of analytics have highlighted many examples of mis-pricing in the debt markets. Many obligors still do not have a clear, objective understanding of their own level of riskiness. Since many participants (ranging from bank loan originators to corporate bond traders) in the debt markets suffer from a similar lack of understanding, the markets for credit periodically exhibit inefficiencies. Market-based measures of risk clear up this picture facilitating much more efficient pricing of debt. Institutions originating and trading credit that understand these market-based, credit portfolio analytics will hold a considerable advantage as credit markets evolve.

The 20th century has been punctuated by financial crises at different times in different countries. The U.S. experienced serious problems in its banking industry starting in the 1970s continuing into the 1980s. Once the seas had calmed, the emergent financial system reflected a tough market orientation with the government less inclined to bail out mismanaged institutions. Today we face a similar financial crisis in Japan. Tomorrow it will be some other country. The common current in these crises is the tendency of financial institutions to create highly concentrated portfolios without the discipline of regularly marking these portfolios to market. Developing this discipline underlies much of the rhetoric among regulators; whether the new Basel accord will encourage this discipline remains to be seen. Regardless, the tools and analytics described in this book can be implemented to meet the demands of whatever the Basel committee finally agrees upon. Satisfying regulators, however, should not be a portfolio manager's focus. Regulations should be viewed as a constraint within which portfolio managers must operate to maximize the value of the equity held by the portfolio's shareholders. The most competitive institutions will implement the analytics and technology necessary to facilitate market-oriented portfolio management. The market is an ocean of powerful waves that can harass or be harnessed. Institutions without this market focus will capsize or be rescued as has been particularly apparent in the bank failures and bank consolidations during the past decade. We will continue to see tidal waves of change in the financial industry. The ideas and strategies described in this book can be a compass for navigating these challenging currents.

Dr. Jeffrey R. Bohn
Managing Director, Moody's-KMV

PREFACE

This book as the title suggests, is concerned with the characteristics and analysis of individual credit exposures, as well as with the theory and practice of combining these exposures into portfolios, pricing them with appropriate credit insight, and optimally allocating capital. I've written *Managing Bank Risk* book for both bank practitioners and students of banking. My book was also drafted for readers involved with banking who want to develop additional analytical and marketing opportunities, or simply yearn to move a bit closer to the (credit) heartbeat. This group includes educators, entrepreneurs, accountants, investors, consultants, turnaround specialists, financial engineers and executives, investment bankers, research and ratings personnel and portfolio managers.

Managing Bank Risk focuses on myriad regulatory concerns presented in the September 2000 consultative document issued by the Basel Committee on Banking Supervision, Principles *for the Assessment of Banks' Management of Credit Risk,* This important position paper established broad guidelines for bankers so they might establish a sound credit risk environment, operate under sound credit granting processes, maintain appropriate administrational, and monitoring credit policies, and ensure that adequate controls over credit risk are part and parcel credit-management .

Employing the essence of "Principles," the book's two sections, *New Approaches to Fundamental Analysis*, and *Credit Administration* deal with recent developments in bank risk management. We focus on how connectivity between credit engineering and more traditional methods works as seamless partners. The art of banking is, after all, a matter of knowing how to balance scales. This involves assimilating into the lending blueprint disciplines that include statistics and simulation driven forecasting, risk adjusted pricing, credit derivatives, ratios, cash flow computer modeling, distress prediction and workouts, capital allocation, credit exposure systems, computerized loan pricing, sustainable growth, interactive risk rating models and probabilistic default screening.

This last concept is covered in Chapter 14, EDF™ Credit Measure, written by Moody's-KMV, the world's leading provider of market-based quantitative credit risk products. Moody's-KMV maintains one of the largest and most accurate databases of corporate default experience internationally.

What does *Broad-base Credit Engineering* mean? The concept involves utilizing appropriate risk-measuring tools that ensure credits are made in accordance with bank policy and regulatory requirements, and to provide bankers with a solid platform to judge asset quality and value. Effective analysis—on two fronts: micro and macro, not only helps detect poorly underwritten credits, it also serves to prevent weak credits from being granted, since credit personnel are likely to be more diligent if they know their analysis will be subject to review by bank examiners and senior management.

Serving this end, bankers need courage and wisdom to take reasonable risks: booking loans falling within defined parameters, and meeting risk-adjusted return goals set by a sound loan policy. Even with the best techniques, though, credit issues need definition and prioritization, solutions must be structured to fit specific deals, and a proper balance struck between credit engineering and good old-fashioned common sense.

Failure to follow prudent loan policies and procedures has led to asset quality problems, disappointing performance, numerous bank failures and intensified regulatory exams. When lending areas fail to master their craft, two things increase—portfolio risk and the probability of taking sizable hits to earnings. For these reasons, bankers need *new* analytic guidelines that spell the difference between successful banking and chaotic, lax lending infrastructures.

Creditors should be prepared to handle complex problems, understand strategic management goals set by the bank's corporate clients, and make crucial decisions involving millions of dollars of their company's money. Finally, even with the best techniques, it is important to define and prioritize credit issues, to modify analysis to fit specific circumstances, to strike a proper balance between quantitative analysis and qualitative credit concerns, and to evaluate individual credits and loan portfolios insightfully and creatively.

PEDAGOGY

Managing Bank Risk was developed on an intermediate to advanced level providing readers with abundant hands on approach. Each chapter includes a brief introduction and is then partitioned into several sections, with exhibits and tables numbered and titled to facilitate a systematic reading. Chapters are reinforced with end-of-chapter questions and, where appropriate, appendices and case studies. Noteworthy equations are highlighted. The derivations for equations are provided but are differentiated or appear in appendices. The reader who is not mathematically inclined can skip quantitative passages with no loss of qualitative ideas. *A References and Suggested Readings* section follows most chapters, as well. A special section in *References and Suggested Readings* catalogues important Internet links whereby readers can access additional sources and/or download software cognate to chapters.

CD-ROM

The book contains a CD that includes a collection of banking and risk models and related software. We are especially pleased to announce the publication of a new software tutorial: the author's interactive ten-point risk rating model. The program contains over 1300 lines of macro coding. It is a self-contained, spreadsheet-based tool allowing readers to learn risk rating in a self-study environment. The author also designed the program to allow easy adoption into the portfolio system.

The CD also includes:

- Enron Corporation comprehensive cash flow decomposition model
- Decisioneering's Crystal Ball software risk analysis demos including simulation, time series/regression, stochastic optimization and real options
- Stochastic net borrowed funds pricing model
- Trial versions of WizSoft data mining systems: a data mining analyzer and predictor and a data mining business rules detector for data auditing
- Asset based lending models, courtesy of the Federal Reserve Bank
- The Uniform Financial Institutions Rating System (CAMELS)
- Two portfolio optimization software models

- A library of documents and manuals from the International Swap Dealers Association, the Basel Committee on Banking Supervision, the Federal Reserve Bank, and others

ACKNOWLEDGEMENTS

I am especially indebted to Jeffrey R. Bohn a senior official at Moody's-KMV. Dr. Bohn and Peter J. Crosbie authored Chapter 13, Portfolio Management of Default Risk and Chapter 14, EDF™ Credit Measure.

One expert, Robert Kissell, was particularly helpful. Rob helped design the new risk rating tutorial. His broad expertise in finance and modeling was also an important source of wise counsel on many issues raised in this book.

I wish to offer a special word of thanks to Johnathan Mun, Ph.D. Vice President of Analytical Services Decisioneering, Inc., who contributed Real Options Analysis Toolkit trial software and the Bankers Primer on Real Options. Larry Goldman, a product expert at Decisioneering played an integral role in the chapter on forecasting and simulation. I am grateful to Dr. Abraham Median and Irina Sered, executives at Wizsoft, for contributing to the chapter on global exposure systems and most importantly providing WizRule and WizWhy trial software. I would like to thank Edward Feltmann, Karen Marx, Mike Bloomquist, and Craig Leiderman, my Fordham GBA students who offered valuable comments and provided fine research. Joseph Blake, a financial expert offered excellent insight.

I am indebted to a number of persons for their interest and encouragement in the preparation of this manuscript. In particular, my appreciation goes to J. Scott Bentley, Ph.D. Executive Editor Academic Press who first suggested the writing of this book, Brad Bielawski, production manager and Karen Carriere, editor for their patience and skill. This does not mean, however, that those listed above or others who were helpful are responsible for errors or omissions; the author must assume them. I have acknowledged every source I have been able to identify in footnotes and bibliographies, but some writers and sources may have been missed unintentionally.

Finally, my beautiful, patient and inspirational wife, Maryann, for sacrificing many hours so that I could devote time to this book, deserves the flower of all credits.

1

INTRODUCTION TO BANK RISK MANAGEMENT

Unlike Mark Twain's cat, which once sat on a hot stove lid and would never again sit even on a warm one, bankers should always be careful to get from an experience just the wisdom that is in it—no more, no less. Banks need a sense of caution in a liberal credit environment, but they also need the courage and wisdom to take reasonable risks when credit is tight. Financial institutions succeed as long as the risks they assume are prudent and within defined parameters of portfolio objectives. This means policies and procedures must ensure that exposures are properly identified, monitored, and controlled, and that loan pricing, terms, and other safeguards against nonperformance or default are commensurate with the levels of risk that banks assume.

Bank failures are the result of lax credit standards, ineffectual portfolio risk policies, risks assumed beyond limits of a bank's capital, misreading performance barometers and neglecting technological upgrades (both system wide and specific), loan exposure, and ineffective risk rating systems. As we shall see, banks have come under increased regulatory scrutiny with many incurring losses on loan write-offs. An internationally known bank surveyed its problem loan portfolio and came up with a pattern of root causes (Table 1.1).

TABLE 1.1   Major Bank's Survey: Root Causes of Problem Credits

Compromise of credit principles—that is, granting loans carrying undue risks or unsatisfactory terms with full knowledge of the violation of sound credit principles	Timidity in dealing with individuals having dominating personalities or influential connections or friendships, or personal conflicts of interest involved	Dependence on oral information furnished by borrowers in lieu of reliable financial data
Extension of credit on an unsound basis to directors or large shareholders	Being influenced by salary incentives and bonuses based on loan portfolio growth	Ignoring warning signs pertaining to the borrower, economy, region, industry, or other related factors
Earnings factor permitted to outweigh that of soundness	Credits representing undue risks or unsatisfactory repayment terms are granted	Poor selection of risks
Incomplete credit information	Failure to obtain or enforce repayment agreements	Loans for the speculative purchase of securities or goods
Loans granted without a clear agreement governing repayment	Lack of adequate supervision of old and familiar borrowers	Technical incompetence
Loans wherein the bank advances an excessive proportion of the required capital relative to the equity investment of the borrowers	Optimistic interpretation of known credit weakness based on past survival of recurrent hazards and distress	Collateral loans carried without adequate margins of security

Between 1980 and 1994, more than 1,600 banks insured by the Federal Deposit Insurance Corporation (FDIC) were closed or received FDIC financial assistance—far more than in any other period since the advent of federal deposit insurance in the 1930s (see Figure 1.1).

The rise in the number of bank failures in the 1980s had no single cause or short list of causes. Rather, it resulted from a concurrence of various forces working together to produce a decade of banking crises. Economic, financial, legislative, and regulatory conditions established the preconditions for the increased number of bank failures—for example, a structure of banking laws that inhibited competition. Second, a series of severe regional and sectoral recessions hit banks in a number of banking markets and led to a majority of the failures. Third, some of the banks in these markets assumed excessive risks and were insufficiently restrained by supervisory authorities, and as a result they failed in disproportionate numbers. Management attitude was impaired and reflected the managerial sentiment and regulatory provisions of the relatively benign pre-1980 environment for banking, when failures were rare.

During the 1980s, of course, performance ratios weakened and profitability declined and became more volatile, while loan charge-offs rose dramatically (Figure 1.2). Large banks assumed greater risk in order to boost profits, as indicated by the sharp rise in the ratio of loans and leases to total assets for these

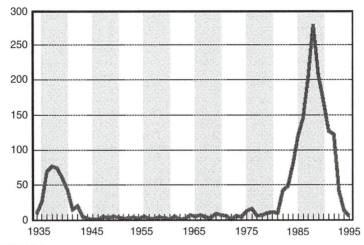

FIGURE 1.1   Number of Bank Failures 1934–1995

banks. In contrast, equity ratios increased over the period, particularly for large banks, in line with increased regulatory capital requirements and perhaps in response to market concerns about distress in the banking system.

POOR LENDING PRACTICES

What people remember most about the banking crises of the 1980s was the failure of Continental Illinois National Bank and Trust Company (CINB) in 1984, which turned out to be the largest bank failure in U.S. history. The Continental disaster is noteworthy because it focused attention on bank policy issues, most notably the effectiveness of supervision. During the time Continental was facing difficulties, Congress questioned whether bank regulators could adequately assess risk within an institution. Worse was the fear that the failure of such a large bank might cause the public to lose confidence in the bank examination and supervisory process. In addition, Continental was a particularly telling example of the problem that bank regulators faced when attempting to deal with safety-and-soundness issues in an institution that had already been identified as taking excessive risks but whose performance had not yet been seriously compromised.

Continental's problems started in 1981. The bank's second quarter earnings fell 12%. Some of Continental's corporate customers began to have severe problems. Nucorp Energy lost more than $40 million, with Continental holding a large percentage of the company's debt. Continental had also lent $200 million to near-bankrupt International Harvester.

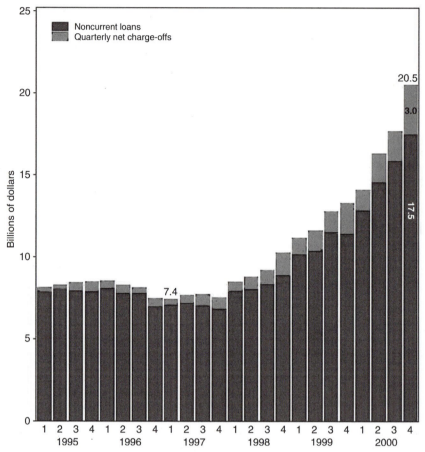

FIGURE 1.2   Credit Quality Commercial and Industrial Loans from Commercial Banks, 1995–2000

Though the banking environment improved in the 1990s, banks still came under increased regulatory scrutiny with many incurring loan write-offs. For example, Bank of America wrote off $1 billion in uncollectible loans. Banc One went through a similar problem, as did many other banks. Regulators feared that if companies failed to repay loans during good times, many more defaults would occur during a recession (Figure 1.3). Some lenders approved marginal deals believing that economic expansion lasts forever. When the competitive environment turned markedly less favorable along with policy actions like deregulation and tax changes, the number of bank failures increased. In a highly demanding environment, the difference between survival and failure is often determined by an individual bank's circumstances, particularly variations in the levels of risk it

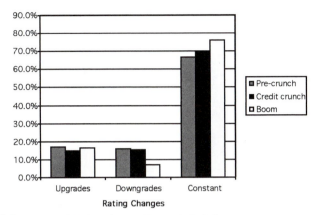

FIGURE 1.3   Grade and Rating Changes: Economic Periods

assumed, its access to capital, and, of course, management quality.

Through much of the 1990s, a sustained period of economic growth produced improving commercial loan credit quality. This trend reversed itself in 1998 when banks began experiencing a steady rise in nonperforming and delinquent commercial loans. Problems were related to weakening international economic conditions. The collapse of Asian currency exchange rates and default by the Russian government on its sovereign debts led to higher levels of problem foreign loans in 1998. Domestic industries that were highly dependent on exports (steel, for example) were also adversely affected by the fallout.

> As of September 30, 2000, noncurrent commercial and industrial loans held by commercial banks stood at $15.6 billion, a 46% increase over the previous year. Roughly 9% of this increase is attributable to the rise in nonaccrual and delinquent credit to U.S. domiciled borrowers. Through the first three quarters of 2000, annualized commercial and industrial loan loss rates reached 0.64%, up from 0.58% in 1999. The last time banks saw C&I loss rates this high was in 1993 (0.74%).
>
> Source: FDIC.

Larger banks, which have the greatest exposures to large- and middle-market corporate credits, have been hardest hit by the turnaround in business conditions (Figure 1.4). Steven Burton, FDIC Senior Banking Analyst noted:

> Much of the recent deterioration in banks' business credit quality is attributable to the seasoning of credits underwritten during a period of relaxed lending standards. Each of the three bank supervisory agencies has recognized and warned about the potential impact of loosened loan underwriting standards in the event of a slowdown in the economy. For example, just over a year ago, the Office of the Comptroller of the Currency (OCC) issued a warning to banks about the "…cumulative effect of the past four years of

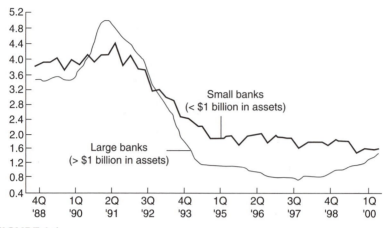

FIGURE 1.4

easing standards..." for commercial loans. The shift toward more liberal credit standards from 1996 to 1999 was fueled by various factors, including a robust economy, intense competition to originate syndicated credits, and an increased appetite for risk. During this period, a number of banks moved aggressively into non-investment-grade lending to combat narrowing interest margins and declining investment-grade yields. According to a recent Standard & Poor's commentary, several banks have acknowledged the role of 1997 and 1998 vintage credits in producing higher levels of problem loans.[1]

The deterioration in credit quality has resulted in, and will continue to be the aftermath of, bank closings. Recently, regulators shut down the Malta National Bank in Malta, Ohio. The failed bank had engaged in unsafe and unsound practices, and it had incurred significant losses with losses expecting to continue. The East Texas National Bank was shut down after regulators found the bank "critically undercapitalized," meaning tangible equity capital was less than 2% of total assets. Poor credit underwriting and loan administration practices by management and inadequate supervision by the bank's board of directors caused deterioration in asset quality. Loan losses and subsequent provisions depleted the bank's remaining capital and eventually led to a critically undercapitalized balance sheet.

As the FDIC has pointed out, rating agencies have also been active in reporting increased credit quality problems with major global banks taking a hit. Many of these banks found themselves servicing customers with higher agency ratings than the banks had themselves. Some customers even went so far as to question the common sense of carrying on a relationship with banks that were suffering a range of problems. Relationship managers from troubled banks were put on the

---

[1] FDIC Regional Outlook, First Quarter 2001, *Credit Problems for U.S. Businesses Continue to Increase.*

defensive as corporate clients consolidated banking, moving their accounts to stronger institutions. As noted by the Basel Committee on Banking Supervision:

> In order to maintain a sound credit portfolio, a bank must have an established formal evaluation and approval process for the granting of credits. Approvals should be made in accordance with the bank's written guidelines and granted by the appropriate level of management. There should be a clear audit trail documenting that the approval process was complied with and identifying the individual(s) and/or committee(s) providing input as well as making the credit decision.[2]

> An effective evaluation process establishes minimum requirements for the information on which the analysis is to be based. There should be policies in place regarding the information and documentation needed to approve new credits, renew existing credits, or change the terms and conditions of previously approved credits. The information received will be the basis for any internal evaluation or rating assigned to the credit, and its accuracy and adequacy is critical to management making appropriate judgments about the acceptability of the credit.
>
> Source: Basel Committee on Banking Supervision.

Lending policies that ignore basic principles of analysis are mostly responsible for debacles like Continental, Malta National Bank, and East Texas National. What does that boil down to? Forming the essential components of credit risk management structures are fundamental analysis or the return to basics and the ongoing stress testing that helps to predict the borrower's ability to repay. Regulators found these two attributes of sound credit management to be lacking, causing otherwise qualified bankers to turn from sound lending.

The "fundamental return to basics" apothegm is not as easy as it looks and is anything but fundamental. Many systems and models are available to lenders; some are advanced and we'll review a few of these in later chapters. But for now we'll return to basics, factors apparently lacking in the portfolio risk policies of failed banks. Bank regulators have also continued to maintain that many banks experiencing asset quality problems in the 1990s lacked an effective credit review process (indeed, many banks had no credit review function). The purpose of credit review is to provide appropriate checks and balances to ensure

Sampling of Advanced Credit Models
Aggregative versus structural models including internal credit rating systems, bottom-up credit risk models, default-mode and mark-to-market paradigms, current and future values of loans (mark-to-market type models), and model validation including back-testing and stress testing.

---

[2] Basel Committee on Banking Supervision, Basel, July 1999.

that credits are made in accordance with bank policy and to provide an independent judgment of asset quality that is uninfluenced by relationships with the borrower.

Effective credit review not only helps to detect poorly underwritten credits, it also helps prevent weak credits from being granted, because credit officers are likely to be more diligent if they know their work will be subject to review.

The model we use represents the core of credit risk management. It is called PRISM, an acronym for *perspective, repayment, intention, safeguards, and management.* In using the PRISM model, it is important to note that the thoroughness of your analysis will depend largely on the borrower's credit grade or Standard & Poor (S&P) rating. Highly rated borrowers require little mental activity; lowly rated borrowers often require the combined attributes of exhaustive analytics and introspection to properly process requests for credit.

We examine *management* first. This PRISM component centers on the "big picture"—what the borrower is all about, including history and prospects. Within the PRISM acronym, *management* is like contours of a decision tree: solutions in one sector lead to solutions further along—in the four more analytical sections. Next we probe *intention* or loan purpose. Purpose serves as the basis for *repayment. Repayment* focuses on internal and external sources of cash. Internal operations and asset sales produce internal cash, whereas new debt or equity injections provide external cash sources. We learn how conversion of temporary balance sheet assets provides the primary payment source of short-term loans, while long-term loans are paid from internally generated cash flow.

Internal *safeguards* originate from the quality and soundness of financial statements, while collateral guarantees and loan covenants provide external safeguards. The final component, *perspective,* pulls other sections together: the deal's risks and rewards and the operating and financing strategies that are broad enough to have a positive impact on shareholder value while enabling the borrower to repay loans.

Let's apply the PRISM model to the following case incorporating the author's suggested solutions.

CASE STUDY   Rose Jelly Corporation (RJC)

Situation

As a vice president in charge of a large branch of Your National Bank, you have been approached by RJC's vice president of finance, who is seeking a $500,000 increase (to $2,000,000) in the company's existing unsecured line of credit. In light of attractive compensating balances and a relationship dating from

1968, the company has requested that pricing on the line of credit be maintained at the prime rate. You have the fiscal audited statements dated June 30, 2001, for review. It is now March 2002. Management informed the bank that the purpose for borrowing was to support seasonal assets. Accordingly, the line will be retired at the conclusion of the season.

Business

Dating back to 1895, RJC manufactures and distributes boxed jellies and candy through approximately 300 company-owned retail stores and some 2,000 franchised dealers including 30 department stores. Sales are concentrated in the Northeast with recent expansion into the South and West. The primary selling season extends from Christmas through Valentine's Day to Easter. Rose receives 30-day terms from its suppliers and extends the same terms to its franchised dealers. Inventory is protected by refrigeration with buildups liquidated through special sales.

Management

Howard Rose II succeeded his father as chairman and president two years ago. At the time, Malcolm Singer, whose entire business career has been in the candy field (most recently as treasurer of Crochet Candy Corp, a New York–based candy manufacturer), succeeded Howard Rose II as vice president of finance and operations. Your National Bank maintains operating accounts for members of the Rose family.

Financial Reporting

PriceWaterhouseCoopers prepared the June 30, 2001, fiscal report and gave a standard short-form opinion. Inventory cost is on a first in, first out (FIFO) basis, and the company uses straight-line depreciation for both tax and reporting purposes.

Banking Relationship with Your National Bank

Account opened	1968; borrowed unsecured since 1969
Present facility	$1,500,000 line reaffirmed 9/23/01
Proposed facility	$2,000,000 unsecured line
Borrowing high point	$2,000,000
Outstanding	$1,500,000
Rate	prime rate
Fee	not applicable
12-month average outstanding	$1,229,000
12-month affiliated outstanding	0
Last cleanup	4/7/01 to 6/25/01
12-month average balances	$464,000
12-month affiliated balances	$200,000
No other banks involved	

Other: Company requests that if line is approved, deposit $500,000 availability into account.

Rose Jelly Monthly Borrowings ($000s omitted)

	J	F	M	A	M J	J	J	A	S	O	N	D
1999							1,250	1,750	1,750	1,750	1,750	1,750
2000	$1,000	1,000	500	500	0	500	500	1,000	1,500	1,500	1,500	1,500
2001	$1,000	1,000	500	500	0	500	1,000	1,000	1,500	1,750	2,000	2,000
2002	$1,500	1,500	1,500									

Zarchen Securities Corporation

Zarchen is a holding company that owns a 63% interest in RJC and maintains a nonborrowing relationship with Your National Bank. Balances in recent years have averaged $100,000. Zarchen's most recent fiscal year-end statement, dated December 31, 2001, shows a tangible net worth of $28 million with operations consistently profitable. Rose Jelly Corporation's credit file contains a memorandum, dated May 11, 1999, which states that the bank expects Zarchen to maintain Rose's working capital at $3 million. Attached to the memo is Zarchen's keepwell agreement to this effect, as Zarchen would not commit to a guarantee.

EXHIBIT I   Rose Jelly Corporation Income Statement
($000s omitted in dollar amounts)

	6/30/99	% Sales	6/30/00	% Sales	6/30/01	% Sales
Gross sales	$17,994	100.1	$18,379	100.1	$18,386	100.3
Less:						
Returns & allowances	18	.1	20	.1	54	.3
Net sales	17,976	100.0	18,359	100.0	8,332	100.0
Cost of goods sold	14.022	78.0	14.596	79.5	15.032	82.0
Gross profit	$3,954	22.0	$3,763	20.5	$3,300	18.0
Selling and administration expenses	3.728	20.7	3,238	17.6	3,094	16.9
Operating profit	$ 226	1.3	$ 525	2.9	$ 206	1.1
Depreciation & amort.	410	2.3	391	2.1	$ 384	2.1
Interest expense	54	.3	49	.3	69	.4
Other income (expenses)	(28)	.2	34	(.2)	22	(.1)
Net income (loss)	**$ (266)**	**(1.3)**	**$ 119**	**.7**	**$ (225)**	**(1.2)**

Candy and Confectionery Industry Average Results 2001

	% Sales
Gross profit margin	22.0
Operating expenses/sales	20.2
Net margin (adjusted)	0.9
Return on equity (adjusted)	4.5

EXHIBIT II   Rose Jelly Corporation Balance Sheet ($000s omitted)

Assets	6/30/97	6/30/98	6/30/99	6/30/00	6/30/01
Cash	$ 710	$ 802	$ 841	$ 750	$ 626
Accounts receivable (net)	392	383	404	432	472
Inventories	2,879	4,160	3,365	4,067	4,577
Other current assets	314	102	84	216	188
Current assets	**$4.295**	**$5.447**	**$4.694**	**$5,465**	**$5.863**
Property, plant, equipment (net)	2,667	2,347	2,105	1,935	1,870
Intangibles	58	40	40		
Other assets	737	851	699	713	6811
Total assets	**$7.757**	**$8.645**	**$7,498**	**$8,153**	**$8,454**
Liabilities and equity					
Notes payable	$ 0	$1,000	$ 0	$ 500	$ 500
Accounts payable	541	223	324	583	995
Taxes & accruals	836	789	821	613	741
Current portion long-term debts	14	13	15	16	15
Current liabilities	**1,391**	**2,025**	**1,160**	**1,712**	**2,251**
Noncurrent liabilities	146	133	117	101	88
Total liabilities	**$1.537**	**$2,158**	**$1.277**	**$1.813**	**$2.339**
Capital stock	1,400	1,400	1,400	1,400	1,400
Paid-in capital	290	290	290	290	290
Retained earnings	4.530	4.797	4.531	4,650	4.425
Total equity	**$6.220**	**$6.487**	**$6.221**	**$6.340**	**$6.115**
Total	**$7.757**	**$8.645**	**$7.498**	**$8.153**	**$8.454**

EXHIBIT III   Rose Jelly Corporation Accounts Receivable Aging Schedule

	6/30/99	%	6/30/00	%	6/30/01	%
Less than 30 days	$154,328	38.2	$152,928	35.4	$139,712	29.6
30–59 days	145,036	35.9	164,592	38.1	199,184	42.2
60–80 days	93,324	23.1	103,248	23.9	120,360	25.5
90 days and over	11, 312	2.8	11,232	2.6	12.744	2.7
Total net receivables	**$404,000**	**100.0**	**$432,000**	**100.0**	**$472,000**	**100.0**
Provision for doubtful accounts	40,000	9.9	35,000	8.1	41,000	8.7

EXHIBIT IV   Key Ratios ($000s omitted in dollar amounts)

Year (6/30)	Working capital	Current ratio	Quick ratio	Inventory turnover
1997	$2,904	3.08X	0.8X	5.4X
1998	3,422	2.69	0.6	5.1
1999	3,534	4.05	1.1	4.2
2000	3,753	3.19	0.7	3.6
2001	3,610	2.60	0.5	3.3
Industry average 2001		1.60	.5	4.6

Year (6/30)	Net worth	Debt/worth	Interest expense	Net profit
1997	$6,220	25%	N/A	$(546)
1998	6,487	33	N/A	(30)
1999	6,221	21	$ 54	(266)
2000	6,340	29	49	119
2001	6,115	38	69	(225)
Industry average		120		

EXHIBIT V   Rose Jelly Corporation Working Capital Schedule
($000's Omitted in dollar amounts)

	1997	1998	1999	2000	2001
Sources of funds:					
Net income (loss)	$(546)	$268*	$(266)	$119	$(225)
Depreciation	565	437	410	391	384
Amortization of deferred charges	60	60	60		
Disposals	n/a	n/a	34	36	21
Gain (loss) on disposals and abandonment of equipment sales of leasehold				(12)	29
Decrease in misc. assets	14	(117)	92		
Total	**$ 93**	**$ 648**	**$ 330**	**$ 534**	**$ 209**
Uses of funds:					
Cash dividends	$140				
Capital expenditures	164	$ 117	$ 201	$ 245	$ 368
Decrease in long term debt	14	13	17	16	14
Increase in other assets				54	(32)
Total	**$318**	**$130**	**$218**	**$315**	**$350**

Net change in working capital	$(225)	$518	$112	$219	$(141)
Working capital	$2,904	$3,422	$3,534	$3,753	$3,612
Volume/working capital	6.1:1	5.2:1	5.1:1	4.9:1	5.1:1
Volume/fixed assets	6.7:1	7.6:1	8.5:1	9.5:1	9.8:1

* Includes nonrecurring gains from sale of real estate of $244M and adjustment of prior years' federal income taxes of $54M; excluding these items there was a $30M loss.

PRISM ROSE JELLY ANALYSIS

PRISM: Management

Business Operations

Certain business attributes provide bankers with an image of their borrowers. These qualities result from of a number of factors: the number of years the firm has been in business, the firm's reputation and performance record, and, of course, the firm's willingness and ability to repay debt. Longevity means staying power and is very important to customers, vendors, competitive markets, and financing sources. A long business life also imparts reputation—for some, the most important attribute of all. Past performance is a good indicator of future success.

You begin the information flow with the following facts:

Company Information

- History of the business including any predecessor companies, changes in capital structure, present capitalization, and any insolvency proceedings.
- Description of products, markets, principal customers, subsidiaries, and lines of business.
- Recent product changes and technological innovation.
- Customer growth, energy availability, and possible ecological problems.
- List of the company's principal suppliers, together with approximate annual amounts purchased, noting delinquencies in settlement of suppliers' accounts.
- Market segmentation by customer type, geographic location, product, distribution channels, pricing policy, and degree of integration.
- Strategic goals and the company's track record for meeting or missing goals.
- Number and types of customers broken down in percentage sales/profit contribution. Note the extent the borrower is over dependent on one or a few customers.

PRISM: Management
1. Business Operations
2. Management
3. Bank Relationship
4. Financial Reporting

- Government contracts.
- Capital equipment requirements and commitments.

Industry Information

- Industry composition and, in particular, recent changes in that composition.
- Image of the company and its products and services compared to industry leaders.
- Number of firms included in the industry and whether that number has been declining or increasing.
- Borrower's market share and recent trends.
- Recent industry merger, acquisition, and divestiture activities, along with prices paid for these transactions.
- Recent foreign entrants.
- Suppliers power versus buyers' power.
- Bases of competition.
- Industry's rate of business failure.
- Industry's average bond rating.
- Degree of operating leverage inherent in the industry.
- Industry reliance on exports and degree of vulnerability.
- Names of bank industry specialists you should communicate with for help in developing projections and other industry analysis.
- Trade organizations, consultants, economists, and security analysts that can help you with forecasts.
- Adverse conditions reported by financial, investment, or industry analysts.
- Extent litigation that will affect production or demand for industry products (case in point, Firestone tires).
- The effect of government regulations and environmental issues on the industry.
- If publicly traded, the exchanges on which the stock is traded, the dealer making markets for over-the-counter stock, institutional holdings, trading volume, and total market capitalization.

Analysis of Rose Jelly's Business Operations

Rose Jelly Corporation has been manufacturing quality boxed jellies and candy since 1895. With more than 100 years of service in the confection industry, Rose has proven staying power as a family-run business. Another strong indicator of RJC's entrenchment in the jelly business revolves around its distribution network. Presently, sales are concentrated mainly in the Northeast region of the United States to approximately 2,000 franchised dealerships and 300 company-owned outlets, along with 30 department stores. In addition, in the works is an ambitious expansion project targeting the South and West. This is particularly interesting since Rose may be in the mature (or declining) phase of its business cycle and is attempting to revitalize its market share.

The banker typically examines details of company operations. Each type of business has its own idiosyncrasies that set it apart from other industries. How economically sensitive is the business to new products, competitors, interest rates, and disposable income? How has the borrower fared in good markets as well as bad when benchmarked against the rest of the industry? Is the company seasonal?

Rose Jelly Corporation is a seasonal business selling its top-of-the-line holiday jelly products from Christmas through Valentine's Day to Easter. With this type of operation, it is not only important to identify the selling season but also to realize that seasonal industries are traditionally undercapitalized. If these two elements are factored incorrectly, the firm's level of risk and capacity to repay debt may be misinterpreted. During the fiscal year, a seasonal company's balance sheet will go through expansion and contraction. At the high point or most active part of the season, sales are closely in sync with manufacturing, while collections are probability slow. Based on Rose's previous borrowing patterns, debt and assets increase July through December, expanding the balance sheet. At the low point or least active part of the season, the last of the receivables are converted into cash in the form of a "cleanup." At this juncture, RJC's balance sheet contracts January through June as debt is retired.

Since Rose won't specify what the additional funds are for, it can be assumed that the money will be used to increase working capital to support expansion plans in the South and West.

Zarchen, a holding company, owns a 63% interest in Rose Jelly and maintains a nonborrowing relationship with Your National Bank.

The bank may ask for a Zarchen Securities Corporation guarantee. We'll evaluate this possibility in the PRISM section title "Safeguards."

Management

Banks need to understand to whom they are granting credit. Therefore, prior to entering into any new credit relationship, a bank must become familiar with the borrower or counterparty and be confident that it is dealing with an individual or organization of sound repute and creditworthiness. In particular, strict policies must be in place to avoid association with individuals involved in fraudulent activities and other crimes. This can be achieved through a number of ways, including asking for references from known parties, accessing credit registries, and becoming familiar with individuals responsible for managing a company and checking their personal references and financial condition. However, a bank should not grant credit simply because the borrower or counterparty is familiar to the bank or is perceived to be highly reputable.[3]

---

[3] *Principles for the Management of Credit Risk.* Consultative paper issued by the Basel Committee on Banking Supervision, Basel, September 2000.

Who are the key players and what contributions are they making? It's a good idea to prepare a brief biographical summary for each senior manager so you are better able to evaluate overall management philosophy. The human factor in decision making is hugely significant because a single error in judgment can cause serious and unpredictable problems.

We break management into two parts: (1) the ability to guide the corporation into a new and better future and (2) the willingness to repay during hard times. In turn, the key to effective management deals with, again, two dimensions: (1) responding to changes in the external environment and (2) creatively deploying internal resources to improve the competitive position of the firm.

Integrity deals also with communication. Since the majority of information comes from management, lenders must have confidence in that information. The amount and quality of information you obtain from management will depend on the requirements of the deal and, of course, the type of information management is willing to supply. Keep a simple rule in mind: the lower the credit grade, the more information management is asked to supply. For example, the bank may require that management supply some of the following forms of information or may take these factors into consideration:

- List of officers and directors, along with affiliations, ages, and number of years in office.
- Names, addresses, and contacts of the company's professional advisers, including attorneys, auditors, principal bankers at other banks, and investment bankers.
- The number of people employed and major areas of activity.
- Strategies management is using to increase market share and profitability.
- The intelligence demonstrated in taking advantage of changes in the marketplace and environment.
- Overview of management's problem-solving and decision-making abilities to ensure that the right decisions are made at the appropriate level.
- Management's basic philosophy—for example, is management entrepreneurial?
- Information about the work environment.
- How management and subordinates work as an effective team. Management can be smoothly intergraded or crisis prone.
- Ratio of officer salaries to net revenues. Is compensation reasonable when compared to results?
- Whether or not executives prevent problems from arising, or use valuable time to work out the same problems over and over.
- The reputation of present owners, directors, management, and professional advisers gathered from industry journals, periodicals, and a good Internet browsing.

- Adequacy of quantitative and statistical information including strategic and tactical plans, effective policies and procedures, adequate management information systems, budgetary control and responsibility accounting, standards of performance and control, management, and human resources development.
- An organization chart, mission statement, business plans, and strategic plan (short term and long range).
- Whether the business objectives and strategies are well thought out and represent genuine management tools or have been presented only for show.

Not much management information is supplied in the case, so we will have to make do with what we have. Having succeeded his father two years ago, Howard Rose II resides as chairman and president of RJC. Malcolm Singer, an executive with extensive experience in the candy field, was hand-picked by Howard Rose II to fill his vacated position as vice president of finance and operations. Rose Jelly Corporation has maintained a favorable rating with the bank based on its ability to meet all short-term obligations. Both executives are responsible for the current state of affairs, raising questions as to their qualifications and ability to repay the loan. Management's final evaluation rarely shows up here; instead we view management quality in perspective when all other PRISM sections are complete.

Bank Relationship

If the relationship is an existing one, how solid has it been? Obviously, a loyal customer with a strong history receives better treatment than someone who walks through the door for the first time.

Rose Jelly has had an account at National Bank since 1969. The account has been entirely satisfactory.

Account opened	1968; borrowed unsecured since 1969
Present facility	$1,500,000 line reaffirmed 9/23/01
Proposed facility	$2,000,000 unsecured line
Borrowing high point	$2,000,000
Outstanding	$1,500,000
Rate	prime rate
Fee	not applicable
12-month average outstanding	$1,229,000
12-month affiliated outstanding	0
Last cleanup	4/7/01 to 6/25/01
12-month average balances	$464,000
12-month affiliated balances	$200,000
No other banks involved	

Rose Jelly requests that if the line is approved, deposit $500,000 availability into the company's account. The 12-Month Average Balances/Outstandings = $664,000/$1,229,000 = 54%. This means that the borrower effectively borrows over half its own money. There is also something peculiar about Rose's credit request. If its borrowing requirements fall between July and December, why is the firm requesting an increase in its line in March?

Financial Reporting (see Chapter 2)

Naturally, banks evaluate the accounting firms that prepare financial statements. Reputation is important. Are financials liberal or conservative? Do they provide an accurate picture of the borrower's condition? Following are a few good pointers for banks to adhere to:

- Obtain audited financial statements, including registration statements (if they exist) and comparative financial results by major division.
- Procure recent unaudited quarterly statements, including sales backlog information and a description of accounting practices.
- If possible, secure tax returns for the past five years, IRS reports, schedule of unused loss, carry backs, and investment credit carryforwards.
- Ask the client to submit projected operating and financial statements.
- Obtain any SEC filings and a shareholder list, if available.
- Form an opinion about the overall credibility and reliability of financial reporting. Check if an independent accounting firm audited the books and investigate the accountant's reputation.
- If financial reporting is overly complex (Enron: case in point) don't be afraid to ask questions.
- Check bank records. Auditors who submitted falsified reports on other deals will end up in the database.
- Review the adequacy and sophistication of the client's internal auditing systems.
- Find out what the auditor's major recent findings were and the company's disposition of those findings. Determine whom the internal auditing department reports to.

Accounting Watch List
- Excessively liberal accounting judgment calls: inappropriate provisions for sales returns, obsolete inventories, or contingent liabilities, hiding operating costs in order to fix aggerate earnings (WorldCom: case in point)
- Expenses being paid by stockholders directly or through bargain pricing
- Product liability
- Unfunded past service costs of pension plans
- Cutbacks in discretionary expenses: advertising, personnel development, and maintenance
- Stockholder-managers drawing excessive compensation
- Adoption of less-conservative accounting policies
- Sales subject to warranty and service guarantee
- Inaccurate interim reports

- Assess the adequacy of internal accounting controls along with the company's attitude toward strong controls making sure of the extent earnings were managed.
- Assess the strength of the financial management and controllership function.
- Determine how often internal reports are issued, how soon after the end of the period the reports are available, and, if they are used, whether the internal reporting timetable and content are consistent with the auditor's monthly closing requirements.
- Find out whether subsidiaries have autonomous accounting departments that may not be functioning uniformly and, if so, how overall control is exercised.
- Check to see if long-range plans reflect competitive reactions and include alternative strategies.
- Determine if objectives are described so achievement can be monitored.

The accounting firm of PriceWaterhouseCoopers is respected and well known. The bank's confidence in the quality of Rose's financial statements will be quite high. Inventory cost is on a FIFO basis, and the company uses straight-line depreciation for both tax and reporting purposes.

PRISM: Intention (Purpose)

Banks must operate under sound, well-defined credit-granting criteria. These criteria should include a thorough understanding of the borrower or counterparty, as well as the purpose and structure of the credit, and its source of repayment.[4]

PRISM: Intention
1. Support/Replace Assets
2. Support/Replace Creditors
3. Replace Equity

The bank must pin down what the loan's real *intention* is—real as opposed to fanciful. "Fanciful" is what troubled clients offer as the reason for needing the loan. Sometimes this stated intention is what the company would like the bank to believe, other times it is down and out fabricated. Behind *intention,* there are three reasons why firms borrow. The first deals with asset purchases—short term to support seasonality and long term to support growth. Loans used to acquire seasonal assets are repaid once inventory is worked down and receivables collected. Companies seek loans to finance fixed assets as well as nonseasonal current assets.

Second, firms borrow to replace other creditors. For example, management usually anticipates suppliers 2/10 net 30-day terms to take advantage of trade discounts.

On the downside, short-term loans approved to replace creditors may be symptomatic of problems if agency reports, such as Dun & Bradstreet, reveal tardiness. Late payments to suppliers often point to slow-moving inventory or

---

[4] Consultative paper issued by the Basel Committee on Banking Supervision, Basel, September 2000.

receivable problems. Loan requests to replace creditors (recycling debt) means, perhaps, another financial institution is offering better rates or service.

Third, firms borrow to replace equity—stock buybacks (e.g., buying up a partner's share in the business), acquisitions, leveraged buyouts, employer stock option plans, and so on. Equity replaced with debt can easily dislodge the debt-to-equity ratio and cash flow coverage putting the remaining equity at risk. One reason lenders prepare pro forma (what-if) financial statements is to ensure that the equity is not impaired.

The firm's management told their bankers the loan would be used to support normal seasonal activities. Be very careful. Management may be lying. The real reason for the firm's visit to the bank in all likelihood is to request monies to support stale inventory, replace suppliers not paid promptly, and restore cash flow that was depleted because of the firm's poor operating performance. **The red flag should have become evident as you examined the "bank relationship" section of PRISM: the *management phase*.** First, why is Rose requesting an increase in its line during the period the firm should be liquid? The balance sheet should be contracting in March 2002, since it is in the least active part of the season. Receivables should have converted leaving the firm cash flush to repay. On the contrary, RJC has little cash to support excessive inventory and weakening accounts receivable aging.

What evidence supports this hypothesis? Inventory levels increased 21% and 13% over a two-year period. During the same period, gross sales posted little or no increases. A large inventory may reflect on an investment with little or no internal rate of return.

The aging indicates a weakened accounts receivable position. Perhaps annoyed vendors are in no hurry to send in checks. Returns and allowances have increased as well, supporting our stale inventory hypothesis. Hypotheses often change to facts in the repayment phase of the PRISM model. Let's see what liquidity and leverage ratios reveal.

PRISM: Repayment

Firms can raise cash primarily in two ways, (1) through business activities and (2) with new monies from debt and equity sources. Asset liquidations bring in cash as well, but they are normally used as a secondhand source (Figure 1.5).

The conversion/contraction process influences short-term *internal* repayment sources. Say a company borrows to support its seasonal manufacturing operations. Assets and liabilities increase spontaneously. The seasonal high point begins as inventory is sold, creating receivables. When receivables convert to cash, the balance sheet contracts and the company retires its debt. As a result, the seasonal conversion process becomes the primary source of repayment.

Seasonal loans provide the short-term working capital needs of eligible small businesses by financing the seasonal increases in the trading assets (receivables and inventory), the liquidation of which repays the loan at the end of each

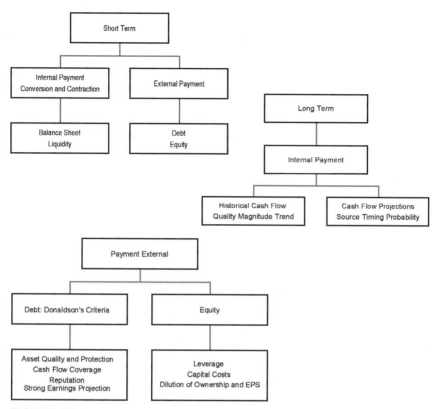

FIGURE 1.5 Debt Repayment

Short-Term Loan Facilities

Own paper borrowing implies that lenders evaluate each request on its own merit. These short-term, unsecured borrowings do not fall under a line of credit.

Lines of credit, unlike own paper borrowings, are usually established with a bank letter stating the approved advances and maximum amount allowed. The amount borrowed may be repaid and reborrowed up to line. While banks are not legally obligated to honor loan requests against lines of credit, arbitrarily canceling lines is the fastest way to alienate customers and lose business. Hence, lines are generally limited to high-quality customers and thus have little chance of failing.

---

season. A seasonal loan is taken out only for seasonal needs and is repaid when inventory and receivables are partially converted into cash at the end of the seasonal upsurge. It is, then, a self-liquidating loan, its repayment dependent on the conversion of other current assets into cash.

For many small and medium-sized firms, the true essence of seasonal lending emerges as an infusion of working capital to support operating activities stimulated by demand. Companies classified as seasonal in nature are traditionally undercapitalized, requiring short-term financing to support temporary current assets. In a broader sense, however, any short-term loan supporting temporary levels of accounts receivable or inventory is referred to as a seasonal loan if it is satisfied through the conversion of these assets.

Commercial banks grant short-term loans with the understanding that loans are retired at the low point of the seasonal cycle or the end of the cash conversion cycle. During the fiscal year, a seasonal company's balance sheet goes through expansion and contraction. At the high point or most active part of the period, debt and assets increase to support seasonal activity, thus expanding the balance sheet. During this phase, sales emulate the manufacturing cycle, the result of which is the conversion of inventory into accounts receivable. At the low point or least active part of the period, the manufacturing cycle has ebbed, leaving the firm with the responsibility to "clean up" outstanding short-term debt. This is accomplished through the conversion of account receivables to cash or deposits. Once all short-term debt has been satisfied, the firm's balance sheet will contract back to its normal level. Any excess cash on hand is usually designated for temporary current asset investments next season.

If the balance sheet fails to fully convert, a company may seek external sources to cover exposures in the form of new outside debt or equity injections. Bankers thus evaluate a borrower's debt capacity. The key attributes to acquiring new monies are the borrower's reputation, existing capital structure, asset quality, profit-generating abilities, and economic value.

Internal repayment of long-term loans is directly related to historical and projected cash flow quality, magnitude, and quality. Historical cash flow analysis provides a track record of the company's past performance. The main question to be

> **Intermediate Term Loans**
> Unlike confirmed lines of credit, revolving credits (R/Cs) and term loans (T/Ls) involve a *legal commitment* on the part of the issuing bank. The loans (commitments) are made under a written loan agreement that sets down the terms and conditions of advances. Commitment fees are computed on the average daily unused portion of line, generally $\frac{1}{4}$ to $\frac{1}{2}$%. Commitments require a loan agreement containing restrictive covenants.

> **Revolving commitments,** known as revolving credits or R/Cs, authorize discretionary borrowing up to a specific amount for periods of at least one year. R/Cs typically convert into term loans at the end of a specific period, as specified in the agreement. Revolving credits are useful financing vehicles for new projects not expecting to produce immediate cash flows. The expiration of revolving credits (and conversion to a term loan) can be timed to coincide with the project's expected cash flow, matching cash inflows and outflows.

answered is does the company have the cash flow to support fixed asset investment(s)? This can be determined by breaking down the historical cash flow into three areas: quality, magnitude, and trend.

The quality of historical cash flow is analyzed by looking at the firm's gross operating cash flow (net income plus noncash charges less noncash credits). If the gross operating cash flows are composed of primarily non-cash items such as depreciation, deferred taxes, or asset write-downs with a relatively small amount of cash being generated on the income statement, then the quality of the operating cash flow may not be sufficient to repay credit. As stated earlier, profits and the sale of assets play a major role in retiring debt requirements, so it is imperative that bank analysts identify what accounts for the firm's cash flow.

> **Term loans** refer to nonrevolving commitments with maturities beyond one year. These loans generally contain periodic (annual, semi-annual, or quarterly) amortization provisions. Term loans involve greater risk than do short-term advances, because of the length of time the credit and is outstanding. Because of the greater risk factor, term loans are sometimes secured. Loan agreements on such credits normally contain restrictive covenants during the life of the loan. These loans have assumed increasing importance in recent years. Term loans generally finance capital expenditures needed by the firm to maintain low production costs and improve its competitive superiority. Term loans also finance new ventures and acquisitions such as new product procurement or vertical/horizontal mergers.

The magnitude of historical cash flow relative to growth plans will help to identify the external financing requirements facing the firm. The smaller the cash flow, the greater the debt load required to support long-term growth plans. If, for example, the income statement is not producing enough cash flow to service its loans year after year, the firm is in jeopardy of defaulting on its loans and going bankrupt. Astute loan officers should question why funds are being funneled into a company in the first place if it cannot buy assets to produce a decent level of profits to pay back debt.

Historical cash flow trends enable the creditor to determine if the firm's cash flows support the decision to go for growth. This is determined by evaluating the company's viability. A healthy company is able to fund a good part its expansion internally. On the other hand, a company suffering from declining cash flows requires the helping hand of debt to expand.

Projections are not intended to predict the future perfectly, but to see how the borrower will perform under a variety of situations. It is up to the lender to ascribe an expected probability to each set of projections and to determine a most likely scenario on which to evaluate the borrower's *repayment* ability. Projections quantify expectations but can never replace a banker's judgment and experience; the mental ability to perceive and distinguish relationships is naturally a PRISM hallmark.

Let's look at *external* repayment of long-term (e.g., cash flow) loans. Repayment often depends on whether or not funding sources are readily available. Consider these questions: What will be the company's comfort level of debt? To what degree will operating cash flow protect debt service? Will the borrower continue to generate good asset quality in order to attract debt? Will the company sustain its overall reputation?

Some credit wells run dry during downturns. If the bank's approval depends solely on an external take out, beware. Consider what Federal Reserve examiners have to say:[5]

> Over-reliance on continued ready access to financial markets on favorable terms can come in many ways, including:
>
> 1. Explicit reliance on future public market debt or equity offerings, or on other sources of refinancing, as the ultimate source of principal repayment, which presumes that market liquidity and appetite for such instruments will be favorable at the time that the facility is to be repaid;
> 2. Ambiguous or poorly supported analysis of the sources of repayment of the loan's principal, together with implicit reliance for repayment on some realization of the implied market valuation of the borrower (e.g., through refinancing, asset sales, or some form of equity infusion), which also assumes that markets will be receptive to such transactions at the time that the facility is to be repaid;
> 3. Measuring a borrower's leverage and cash coverage ratios based solely on the market capitalization of the firm without regard to "book" equity, and thereby implicitly assuming that currently unrealized appreciation in the value of the firm can be readily realized if needed; or
> 4. More generally, extending bank loans with a risk profile that more closely resembles that of an equity investment and under circumstances that leave additional bank credit or default as the borrower's only resort should favorable expectations not be met.

Rose Jelly's Internal Repayment: Liquidity Ratios Exhibit IV

Year (6/30)	Current Ratio	Quick Ratio	Inventory Turnover
1997	3.08X	0.8X	5.4X
1998	2.69	0.6	5.1
1999	4.05	1.1	4.2
2000	3.19	0.7	3.6
2001	2.60	0.5	3.3
Industry Avg. 2001	1.60X	.5X	4.6X

The **current ratio** (current assets/current liabilities) is the most commonly used measure of short-term solvency providing an estimate of the borrower's ability to satisfy short-term liabilities. Bankers try to peak behind the ratio since magnitude means little if the numerator consists of poor quality assets. Although Rose's current ratio is higher than the industry benchmark, it would be incorrect to assume automatically that higher is better. Besides, the ratio appears to be in steady decline.

---

[5] Source: Federal Reserve Bank Mem.

The **quick ratio or acid test** (current assets less inventory/current liabilities) is more conservative than the current ratio because liquidity is measured without inventory reliance. The quick ratio, while on par with the benchmark, is also declining. If this borrower operates under a "business as usual" game plan, by next year the ratio might disappear altogether.

Inventory turnover is a reliable tool for determining inventory quality and salability. It took us a while, but the "hypothesis" we established in the *intention* phase is about to be validated. A sharply declining inventory turnover bears out the facts. The firm is building up perishable stock with no end in sight. To sum up, the deteriorating turnover points to inept inventory management or worse— fundamental and sustainable structural problems.

External Repayment: Debt Capacity

Year(6/30)	Debt/Worth
1997	25%
1998	33
1999	21
2000	29
2001	38
Industry Average	120%

The firm's relatively low leverage ratio is no guarantee that another bank will approve a takeout loan. Debt to equity depends on a number of factors (see Chapter 3, "Multivariate Ratio Analysis: A Banker's Guide"). Likewise, how high leverage may increase without undermining the borrower's financial structure depends on numerous factors including asset quality, cash flow coverage (of debt service), debt mix (short term versus long term), and sustainable operating and financial factors like revenue growth and equity market values.

It's apparent from leverage factors and liquidity trends that this borrower will be unable to borrow from other financial institutions to retire the $2 million pro- posed line.

External repayment is the ability and willingness to inject equity capital or subordinated debt. The bank will likely contact the parent, but it is unlikely the parent will provide additional equity.

PRISM: Safeguards

What *safeguards* or protection does the bank have against default? If a bank is to extend credit to a firm, the level of risk influences the degree of protection lenders generally require. Safeguards can be internal, external, or a combination of both (Figure 1.6). Internal safeguards refer to financial analysis, whereas col- lateral, personal guarantees, and loan covenants provide external protection. Although external safeguards are popular, they are usually not considered before internal protection. Internal protection relates to the borrower's cash power depending on whether the *intention* of the loan is short term or long term. Recall

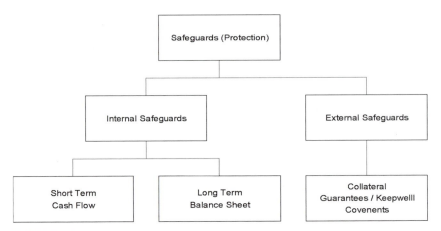

FIGURE 1.6   Safeguards against Default

that the primary source of internal repayment for short-term loans is balance sheet liquidity, the result of the season's cash conversion cycle. Internal safeguards of seasonal loans relate to the quality magnitude and trend of cash flows/income statements. The bank just wants to make sure a seasonal *temporary* problem does not become a *structural* cash flow problem in the years ahead.

External safeguards can come from a variety of sources, such as those listed here:

- Collateral
- Guarantees
- Covenants
- Syndications and participations
- Credit derivatives

Collateral

Collateral is defined as property pledged as security for the satisfaction of a debt or other obligation. Credit grades assigned to secured loans depend on, among other things, the degree of coverage, the economic life cycle of the collateral versus the term of the loan, the possible constraints of liquidating the collateral, and the bank's ability to skillfully and economically monitor and liquidate collateral. What is the collateral's value compared to credit exposure? What is its liquidity, or how quickly may its value be realized and with what certainty? What presumed legal right does the borrower have to the collateral?

Guarantees

A guaranty is a written contract, agreement, or undertaking involving three parties. The first party, the *guarantor*, agrees to see that the performance of the second party, the *guarantee*, is fulfilled according to the terms of the contract, agreement, or undertaking. The third party is the *creditor*, or the party to benefit by the performance.

Loan Covenants

Covenants of a loan agreement lay the framework for the financial plan jointly agreed on by the borrower and the lender. The number and detail of the covenants will largely depend on the financial strength of the enterprise, management's aptitude, and the length of the proposed loan.

Internal Safeguards

Up to this point, Rose's conversion cycle appears to be very weak. The important question is whether the firm's problems are structural/permanent or temporary? The borrower's working capital schedule (Exhibit V) shows no profits available to retire debt. Rose is dependent on depreciation expense as the major source of operating cash flow. The borrower appears to have serious structural problems.

In a manufacturing business like candy, companies are capital intensive. Depreciation greater than capital expenditures likely means a capital expansion slowdown. Combine this with increased manufacturing costs, lower quality products, technical (quality) problems, escalating downtime, and rising labor costs, and the results are a steady stream of operating losses.

External Safeguards

Collateral: Accounts receivable: limited value; inventory: no value.

Guarantee: Zarchen Securities, owner of 63% of Rose's stock, refused to provide the bank with a full, unconditional, and uncontested guarantee stating that it would not be able to convince stockholders to approve the guarantee.

Other options: None

As things stand now, RJC cannot repay a $2 million line at the conclusion of next season. The bank has no assurances that, if the debt obligation is postponed, the loan will ever be paid back.

PRISM: Perspective

What is the deal's *Perspective* or "conclusion(s)"? The *Perspective* section decomposes into the following:

1. Risk/reward analysis
2. Operating and financing strategies that the banker believes might improve performance and go a long way adding to shareholder value
3. Decision and pricing

Rewards

1. RJC owes $1.5 million now. Declining the credit may cause the company to go bankrupt, jeopardizing the entire exposure.
2. This is an old and profitable banking relationship.
3. This is an old, established business.

First Level: Risk/Rewards

Perspective marshals together the main points worked out earlier.

The firm has positive but many negative qualities. Positive qualities include: old established company with a one-time excellent reputation.

Risks
1. Inventory problems
2. The business is unprofitable

A family-run business since 1895, Rose Jelly Corporation has proven staying power in the confectionery industry and the endorsement of its competitors. The banking relationship dating back to 1968 has been strong with various members of the family maintaining operating accounts. Account balances, 53% of average outstandings, are excellent. The firm employs a top-notch, highly respected accounting firm to handle books.

Howard Rose II came to the bank requesting a credit extension to finance seasonal working capital, never stating the true loan purpose. The bank should have realized that the loan supports stale inventory and was set up to replace depleted cash flows brought on by losses. Rose should be liquid in March. During the company's "cleanup" period, short-term debt is paid as the balance sheet contracts. Not so here. This is the time for reduced renewals or flat out cleanup, not increases in outstandings. It was clear, earlier in the case, that the balance sheet, flush with stale inventory, and payables out of line with what they should be clearly signaled inventory problems.

Both Howard Rose II and Malcolm Singer may have extensive overall experience, but they seem out of sorts in both the candied jelly business and in financial management. In an industry that manufactures perishable goods, high inventory usually means stale output. The upshot? Unless a turnaround comes quickly, the firm will likely wipe out its customer base. The next step is likely bankruptcy.

Second Level: Operating and Financial Strategies

Capital-intensive industries like jelly manufacturing take advantage of accelerated depreciation for tax purposes. The method earns additional income by delaying future tax payments. With expansion, a company will use accelerated depreciation to help fund capital expenditures. If a borrower like Rose fails to use accelerated depreciation for tax purposes, or if an inspection of the cash flow statement reveals depreciation consistently in excess of capital investments, chances are plant facilities have been cut back or downright eliminated. Rose's cash flow problem may be attributed to major cutbacks in capital projects.

From the decline in the gross profit margin, we deduce that RJC has not succeeded in passing on increased manufacturing costs to customers. The firm's "sweets" are produced using either machines or labor. What factors up to this point indicate whether Rose is machine or labor intensive? Decreasing capital expenditures is a good indication of reduced operating leverage, and often results in an increase in variable (labor costs). Thus, lower operating leverage results in higher costs that must be passed on to the buyer. Marginal prices increases higher than the competition will at first not have any affect on sales. But if they get too high, which is the case with Rose, the product is priced out of the market and sales disappear. Compound this with poor forecasting and inventory control and you have a real mess on your hands. Consider the pricing policies of RJC and the firm's major competitors:

Year	Selling Price: Rose Jellies Corp.	Selling Price: Competitors
1997	$7.50	$7.50
1998	$8.25	$8.00
1999	$9.65	$8.25
2000	$10.26	$8.49
2001	$12.98	$9.20
2002	$14.50	$9.35

Third Level: Alternatives and Decision

The three alternatives are (1) status-quo—do nothing and lend as usual; (2) force a liquidation and collect what you can; (3) encourage the firm to restructure the business.

Status-quo Alternative

The bank followed this strategy for so long, why not continue? Actually, "status-quo" is not an acceptable option.

Liquidation Alternative

Liquidate or restructure? That's the $1.5 million question. Is it worth sinking more money into this company hoping it eventually returns to profitability, or should the bank simply cut its losses? After all, not only is the bank's exposure at risk, but additional millions may be in jeopardy if an effort were made to jump-start this company. Risks associated with trying to salvage $1.5 million outstanding could be quite low compared to the additional millions that may be required to save Rose. If a restructuring plan is chosen, there is no guarantee that cash flow levels would ever be attained again or that new customers could be found to replace the ones lost. To save the bank from further financial chaos, perhaps the most appropriate decision would be for bankers to liquidate the firm and collect what they can when the bankruptcy court distributes assets.

Restructuring Alternative

Argument: the long-standing favorable reputation of this jellied candy manufacturer might support a restructuring program. Reorganization of the management team is essential and should be

> The power for decision making by existing management must be ended. The team responsible for the firm's troubles is not the team to lead it out of the jungle.

effected through the counsel of a qualified consultant approved by the bank. But the company, not the bank, should decide this. If a restructuring effort is launched, the right goals and strategies must be established, and guidelines toward reaching these goals should be implemented by qualified managers.

This loan will likely be classified. The turnaround specialist will coordinate efforts with the bank's workout staff until the loan either is declassified or liquidated. If efforts are to continue, the bank will require frequent cash budget updates and will compare budget forecasts to actual figures when they arrive. Large variances between projected and actual results will be interpreted as meaning the reorganization is not working.

THE BASEL[6] COMMITTEE CONSULTATIVE PAPER AND THE PRISM MODEL

Both the *Consultative Paper* (Appendix 1.2 and CD) and the PRISM model offer an effective analytical structure. PRISM offers specific lending guidelines. Financials, management structure, and ability to repay are thoroughly analyzed. Basel does not act as a model per se but rather as a foundation of procedures lending institutions require to justify the approval process. The Basel Report and PRISM work hand in hand to outline risk management. PRISM offers bankers a better understanding of credit risk, case by case, while Basel focuses on general credit risks *and* risks of an entire credit portfolio.

The Basel Report acknowledges that financial institutions have faced difficulties partly owing to an absence of effectively defined and implemented credit standards and policies. Their argument is: banks need to closely monitor and control their own credit risk. In doing so, a lender must create the appropriate credit risk environment and initiate processes that minimize unacceptable exposures.

While the Committee Report provides a large format that aims to identify proper risk management controls, PRISM can be visualized as a subset model, under a specific aspect of the larger Basel document. The section titled, *"Operating under a Sound Credit Granting Process"* reveals what the PRISM model can achieve when executed properly.

What does operating under a sound credit granting process mean? A lender needs to analyze the purpose of the loan, source of repayment, integrity of the borrower, proposed terms and conditions of the credit, safeguards, and finally the risk profile of the borrower and its sensitivity to external conditions (perspective).

---

[6] Consultative paper issued by the Basel Committee on Banking Supervision, Basel, July 1999. See Appendix 1 to Chapter 1 and the CD. The Basel Committee on Banking Supervision is a committee of banking supervisory authorities that was established by the central bank Governors of the Group of Ten countries in 1975. It consists of senior representatives of bank supervisory authorities and central banks from Belgium, Canada, France, Germany, Italy, Japan, Luxembourg, the Netherlands, Sweden, Switzerland, the United Kingdom, and the United States. It usually meets at the Bank for International Settlements in Basel, where its permanent secretariat is located.

While PRISM is a powerful tool at assessing the creditworthiness of a particular customer, further analysis determines covariance (portfolio) risk, industry concentrations, capital adequacy, liquidity, availability of funds, and so on.

For example, a bank with a lending portfolio consisting of conservative, low-risk clients will be more likely to approve a risky loan. A bank with a high percentage of risk-laden borrowers will be more cautious taking on additional risk. PRISM does not account for this sort of portfolio-wide analysis.

Credit limits for particular customers and the dangers of loan concentrations are two important attributes of portfolio management. First, client credit limits are made based on financial strength against risks associated with financial distress. Second, limits, in smaller banks at least, are sometimes affected by the covariance of a single exposure vis-à-vis the portfolio. It is important to ensure with the proper hedge strategy—loan derivatives to syndications to securitizations—that a single exposure, or for that matter a specific industry concentration—will not overwhelm a portfolio to the degree that default by one customer puts the entire portfolio at risk. Again, PRISM focuses on establishing the creditworthiness of particular customers, not the general portfolio.

A further point is that the Basel Report advances the notion that banks should set standards dealing with documentation of credit policies and procedures, adequacy of risk monitoring systems, role of supervisors, and, most important a proper system of checks and balances. These standards should be instituted to ensure the integrity of daily operations.

Attempts to ensure safe lending procedures are supported by strict regulatory standards and the practice of using outside auditors to inspect systems in place. Additionally, improved technology allows banks to implement global risk systems that can analyze all credit lines and portfolios to a higher degree of accuracy.

> In considering potential credits, banks must recognize the necessity of establishing provisions for expected losses and holding adequate capital to absorb risks and unexpected losses. The bank should factor these considerations into credit-granting decisions, as well as into the overall portfolio monitoring process.[7]

The statement relates to the PRISM step *safeguards*. As we saw earlier, internal safeguards require analysis of cash flow or balance sheet liquidity, depending on the deal. These tools limit exposure to low credit grades while ensuring a definitive stop loss if a lending situation threatens to get out of hand.

REVIEW QUESTIONS

1. How can a banker supervise old and familiar borrowers?
2. Should a bank ever make exceptions to its established evaluation and approval process for the granting of credit? Why or why not? If yes, in what cases should exceptions be made?

---

[7] Ibid.

3. Describe the significance of each letter in PRISM. Why is PRISM used?

4. Why must a banker analyze industry information as part of the business operations section of the letter "M" in PRISM?

5. Based on its financial statements, why does Rose Jelly Corporation need an increase in the existing unsecured line of credit? What factors indicate this?

6. Describe the seasonal conversion/contraction process. How does it relate to repayment?

7. What are the potential benefits/risks of both the liquidation alternative and the restructuring alternative in the Rose Jelly Corporation case?

8. As a bank officer viewing a loan for the first time, what would you think is a more important to safeguard: internal or external controls?

9. What elements of PRISM allow the loan officer to take a proactive rather than reactive stance to the bank's investment?

To answer the next three questions, read Appendix 1.2.

10. What is the importance of the Basel Committee and why is it trying to help banks set institutional guidelines for credit?

11. How can PRISM be viewed as a tool to reach Basel Committee standards?

12. The Basel Committee set out to form capital adequacy requirements for all international financial institutions. If a bank holds a portfolio of strong investment grade loans, will the capital adequacy requirements be lower or higher for this portfolio and what is the reasoning behind this? Also, do you think the aforementioned bank would take on a higher risk loan to its portfolio and why?

SELECTED REFERENCES AND READINGS

Abeyratne, S. (2001). *Banking and debt recovery in emerging markets: The law reform context.* Aldershot: Ashgate.

American Bankers Association. Research Council. (1940). *The rise in bank lending activity: A study of the volume and number of loan transactions of American commercial and mutual savings banks, January 1, to December 31, 1939.* New York: Research Council American Bankers' Association.

American Savings and Loan Institute. (1971). *Lending principles and practices.* Chicago: American Savings and Loan Institute Press.

Bird, G. R. (1989). *Commercial bank lending and Third-World debt.* Houndmills, Basingstoke, Hampshire: Macmillan.

Brady, T. F., and Interagency Task Force on Small Business Finance (U.S.). (1982). *Commercial bank business lending by size of loan.* Washington, DC: Interagency Task Force on Small Business Finance.

Counts, A. (1996). *Give us credit.* New York: Times Books.

Darity, W. A., and Board of Governors of the Federal Reserve System (U.S.). (1985). *Loan pushing: Doctrine and theory.* Washington, DC: Board of Governors of the Federal Reserve System.

Devinney, T. M. (1986). *Rationing in a theory of the banking firm.* Berlin; New York: Springer-Verlag.

Dewey, D. B., Bankers' Association of the State of Illinois., *et al.* (1896). Address before the Bankers' Association of the state of Illinois at Springfield, IL, Oct. 15, 1896.

Donaldson, T. H. (1979). *International lending by commercial banks.* London: Macmillan.

Donaldson, T. H. (1983). Understanding corporate credit: The lending banker's viewpoint. New York: St. Martin's Press.

Fabozzi, F. J. (1998). Bank loans: Secondary market and portfolio management. New Hope, PA: Frank J. Fabozzi Associates.

Glassman, C. A., P. L. Struck, *et al.* (1982). *Survey of commercial bank lending to small business.* Washington, DC: Interagency Task Force on Small Business Finance.

Hayes, D. A. (1977). Bank lending policies: Domestic and international. Ann Arbor, MI: Division of Research Graduate School of Business Administration University of Michigan.

Onugu, B. A. N. (1979). *A survey and critical analysis of credit risk evaluation methods used by Massachusetts banks:* 190 leaves.

Pirok, K. R. (1994). *Commercial loan analysis: Principles and techniques for credit analysts and lenders.* Chicago, IL: Probus Pub. Co.

Prochnow, H. V. (1981). *Bank credit.* New York: Harper & Row.

Robert Morris Associates. (1978). *The bank commercial loan officer's credit decision: Process, information needs, and the implications for financial reporting.*

Saunders, A. (1999). *Credit risk measurement: New approaches to value-at-risk and other paradigms.* New York: Wiley.

Sauve, P., and Institute for Research on Public Policy. (1984). *Private bank lending and developing-country debt.* Montreal: Institute for Research on Public Policy.

Savage, D. T., and Interagency Task Force on Small Business Finance (U.S.). (1981). *American commercial banking structure and small business lending.* Washington, DC: Interagency Task Force on Small Business Finance.

Scanlon, M. S., and Interagency Task Force on Small Business Finance (U.S.). (1981). *Relationship between commercial bank loan size and size of borrower.* Washington, DC: Interagency Task Force on Small Business Finance.

Seiders, D. F., and Board of Governors of the Federal Reserve System (U.S.). (1982). *Interest rates and terms on construction loans at commercial banks.* Washington, DC: Board of Governors of the Federal Reserve System.

Shull, B., and Interagency Task Force on Small Business Finance (U.S.). (1981). *Changes in commercial banking structure and small business lending.* Washington, DC: Interagency Task Force on Small Business Finance.

United States. Congress. House. Committee on Banking Finance and Urban Affairs. (1981). *An analysis of prime rate lending practices at the ten largest United States banks: Staff report for the Committee on Banking, Finance, and Urban Affairs.* House of Representatives, 97th Congress, first session. Washington United States. Congress. House. Committee on Banking Finance and Urban Affairs. Subcommittee on Consumer Credit and Insurance and United States. Congress. House. Committee on Banking Finance and Urban Affairs. Subcommittee on General Oversight Investigations and the Resolution of Failed Financial Institutions. (1994). *Credit availability in the inner city: Joint field hearing before the Subcommittee on Consumer Credit and Insurance and Subcommittee on General Oversight, Investigations, and the Resolution of Failed Financial Institutions of the Committee on Banking, Finance, and Urban Affairs.* House of Representatives, One Hundred Third Congress, first session, August 10, 1993. Washington, DC: U.S. G.P.O.

United States. Congress. House. Committee on Government Operations. Commerce Consumer and Monetary Affairs Subcommittee. (1993). *The credit crunch and regulatory burdens in bank lending: Hearings before the Commerce, Consumer, and Monetary Affairs Subcommittee of the Committee on Government Operations.* House of Representatives, One Hundred Third Congress, first session, March 17, 23, and 24; and May 10, 1993. Washington, DC: U.S. G.P.O.

United States. General Accounting Office. (1993). *Bank regulation regulatory impediments to small business lending should be removed: Report to congressional committees.* Washington, DC: Gaithersburg, MD (P.O. Box 6015, Gaithersburg, MD 20884-6015)

Wood, J. H. (1975). *Commercial bank loan and investment behaviour.* London; New York: Wiley.

Credit Risk Measurement: New Approaches to Value at Risk and Other Paradigms (Wiley Frontiers in Finance) by Anthony Saunders (Preface) Hardcover—(September 1999) 226 pages

Managing Credit Risk: The Next Great Financial Challenge (Wiley Frontiers in Finance) John B. Caouette, et al/Hardcover/Published 1998

Banking Strategy, Credit Appraisal and Lending Decisions: A Risk-Return Framework. Hrishikes Bhattacharya/Paperback/1999

Credit Risk Modeling: Design and Application; Elizabeth Mays (Editor)

Corporate Credit Analysis (Risk Management Series); Alistair Graham/Hardcover/2000

Credit Concentrations: The Management Process Arthur H. Stampleman/Paperback/1994

Credit Risk Management: A Guide to Sound Business Decisions; Hal A. Schaeffer/Hardcover/2000

A Credit Risk-Rating System; Nancy Welsh (Editor)/Paperback/1994

Credit Risk: Models and Management; David Shimko/ Hardcover/1999

Framework for Credit Risk Management; Hardcover/2000

Perspective on Credit Risk; P. Henry Mueller/Paperback/1988

Strategic Credit Risk Management; John E. McKinley, John R. Barrickman/Paperback/1993

Active Bank Risk Management: Enhancing Investment and Credit Portfolio Performance; Globecon Group

Management Strategies: A Special Collection from the Journal of Lending & Credit Risk Management; Edward E. Furash

Commercial Bank Examination Manual Board or Governors of the Federal Reserve System Division of Banking Supervision and Regulation, Washington D.C.

SELECT INTERNET LIBRARY AND CD

CD includes

Federal Reserve Board Manuals including (1) Supervision Manuals, (2) A User's Guide for the Bank Holding Company Performance Report, (3) Bank Holding Company Supervision Manual, (4) Bank Secrecy Act Examination Manual, (5) Commercial Bank Examination Manual, (6) Consumer Compliance Handbook, (7) Examination Manual for U.S. Branches and Agencies of Foreign Banking Organizations, (8) Trading and Capital-Markets Activities Manual

Internet Library

Bank for International Settlements Publications
http://www.bis.org/publ/pub_list.htm
Link to download pdf file: Principles for the Management of Credit Risk; Basel Committee on Banking Supervision; Basel; September 2000
http://www.bis.org/publ/bcbs75.pdf
The Federal Reserve Bank of NY: The Credit Process: A Guide for Small Business Owners

Table of Contents: Introduction, Sources and Types of Funding, The First Step: Preparing Your
Business Plan and Loan Request, What the Lender Will Review, Resources and How to Use
Them, If Your Application Is Not Approved, Glossary, Information Guide.

http://www.ny.frb.org/pihome/addpub/credit.html

Bank for International Settlements, Publications and Statistics

BIS Papers, Conference Papers (1996—2000), Policy Papers (1996—2000), Economic Papers
(1979—1997), Committee Publications, Publications of the Basel Committee on Banking
Supervision, Publications of the Committee on the Global Financial System (CGFS),
Publications of the Committee on Payment and Settlement Systems

Working Papers, International Financial Statistics, Other Publications, Historical Data and
Methodology, Other BIS Publications, Group of Ten, Reports on the International Financial
Architecture, BIS/Centre for Economic Policy Research, BIS Review: Articles and Speeches of
Central Bankers

http://www.bis.org/publ/index.htm

The Credit Risk Resource

http://www.geocities.com/WallStreet/8589/credit.htm

Important Federal Reserve Bank PDF and HTM Links

http://www.bog.frb.fed.us/pubs/feds/2000/200039/200039pap.pdf. (See Table 4: Summary Statistics
from Bank Examinations over Time on page 46).

Division of Bank Supervision and Structure, Federal Reserve Bank of Kansas City Basics for Bank
Directors 113 Pages. "In recent years, bank profits have set records. Asset quality is strong.
Reserves and capital are high. In this environment, it is tempting for bank directors to relax their
bank oversight. Yet, experience has taught us that the seeds of future misfortune are often sown
in the fertile soil of today's prosperity. Because of this, it is extremely important that bank directors continue their strong oversight even in the best of times."

http://www.kc.frb.org/BS&S/PUBLICAT/PDF/dirbasics.pdf

The Federal Reserve Board Supervision Manuals

A User's Guide for the Bank Holding Company Performance Report; Bank Holding Company
Supervision Manual; Bank Secrecy Act Examination Manual; Commercial Bank Examination
Manual; Consumer Compliance Handbook; Examination Manual for U.S. Branches and
Agencies of Foreign Banking Organizations; Trading and Capital-Markets Activities Manual

http://www.federalreserve.gov/boarddocs/supmanual/

Important FDIC Link

Federal Deposit Insurance Corporation

Resolutions Handbook: A compilation of the lessons that the FDIC learned as it managed the banking crisis of the 1980s and 1990s.

Historical Statistics on Banking: Year-by-year statistical information on the banking industry
(beginning in 1934 for commercial banks and in 1984 for savings banks and savings institutions). Historical Statistics on Banking provides comprehensive lists of individual banks and
thrifts that failed or received financial assistance from the FDIC or the Federal Savings and
Loan Insurance Corporation (FSLIC).

Bank Failures & Assistance: A chronological list of financial institutions that have failed or received
FDIC assistance from 1991 to the present. Briefly describes the size and type of each transaction.

History of the Eighties: A detailed analysis of the complex economic, financial, legislative, and regulatory causes of the extraordinary number of bank failures in the 1980s and early 1990s.

Managing the Crisis—The FDIC and RTC Experience 1980–1994.: Proceedings of a 1998 symposium on strategies used by the FDIC and the Resolution Trust Corporation in resolving and liquidating the 1,617 banks and 1,295 thrifts that failed between 1980 and 1994.

A Brief History of Deposit Insurance: A 76-page document prepared for the International
Conference on Deposit Insurance in Washington, D.C., in September 1998. Describes FDIC's
role and the history of deposit insurance in the United States.

S&L Crisis: A Chrono-Bibliography: A timeline linked to pertinent bibliographical references, describing events that coincided with and in some cases contributed to the savings and loan crisis.

Government Studies on Deposit Insurance and Bank Failures: A listing of major U.S. government studies related to deposit insurance and bank failures as compiled by the FDIC Library. Many of the studies touch upon issues related to depositor protection including the causes of bank failures, "too-big-to-fail," and moral hazard.

http://www.fdic.gov/bank/historical/index.html

LOAN STRUCTURE STRUCTURING LOAN AGREEMENTS

Loan agreements offer a considerable amount of protection for banks involved in term lending by providing periodic review and renewal of a credit. Protection for the lender is based on two perceptions: (1) the longer a borrower has the money, the more likely a downturn in the business or economic environment will occur and (2) the plans on which the borrower based its financial plan will change. The loan agreement is normally prepared by the bank's legal counsel and reviewed by the borrower's attorney. A loan agreement defines the conditions under which lenders have the right to review the bank's credit decision. This should be at a point and on a level where the customer's condition has not slipped beyond retrieval. In other words, the lender can still step in while the borrower has enough flexibility left to solve problems not anticipated in the original projections.

The term loan agreements are tailored to each specific situation, but usually contain provisions under each of the following headings:

1. Preamble
2. Amount and term of the loan

3. Representations and warranties
4. Conditions of lending
5. Default provisions
6. Description of collateral
7. Covenants of the borrower
8. Miscellaneous

PREAMBLE AND DESCRIPTION

The preamble sometimes does little more than name lenders and borrowers, stating that an agreement has been entered into. Also, a statement of purpose may be included, as well as commitment fees, interest rates, prepayment rights, and a definition of terms used in the agreement.

AMOUNT AND TERM OF THE LOAN

As implied, this portion of the agreement sets forth the amount of the loan, the manner in which the borrower may draw down amounts, the interest rate, fees, maturity dates, and the provisions relating to prepayments. If the commitment agreement supports a term loan, it will call for periodic equal payments. However, provisions are sometimes made for a balloon payment or bullet payment at maturity. Balloon payments require periodic, equal payments made with a larger lump sum payment due at the end of the term loan. Similar to a balloon payment, a "bullet payment" sometimes includes a provision requiring cash flows from operations or asset sales above a predetermined amount to be earmarked for loan amortization to reduce the balloon or bullet portion of the loan. Banks do not generally impose a fee for the prepayment of an installment or for the early retirement of the entire loan if the funds are derived from current operations, from funding the debt, or from the sale of assets. However, if prepayment is the result of loans from another bank, a penalty is prescribed.

In cases where the loan is a revolving credit with provision for changing the credit into a term loan, a commitment fee can be charged. The bank is permitted to assess a fee for unused but committed funds since they must be readily available for the borrower's use. The bank will not feel free to invest these funds in high-earning assets such as other loans of intermediate maturities.

REPRESENTATIONS AND WARRANTIES

Generally this section refers to the possession of adequate licenses, patents, copyrights, trademarks, and trade names to conduct business in addition to the economic, financial, and legal circumstances prevailing at the time the original credit decision was made. The representations and warranties specify the borrower

1. Is legally incorporated.
2. In good standing.
3. Has the power to make the agreement, execute the notes, and to perform according to the agreement.
4. Submits financial statements that are correct and reflect the borrower's true financial condition.
5. Is permitted to borrow under the borrower's charter and by laws, governmental regulation, and other agreements as authorized by the board of directors.

This section may also include statements that the business and properties of the company have not in any way been materially or adversely affected since its latest audit and have no federal income tax liability in excess of the amount shown on the company's balance sheet.

Finally, the representations and warranties should include a paragraph dealing with any material pending litigation. This will ensure that the outcome of such litigation will not materially impair the ability of the borrower to perform under the agreement.

CONDITIONS OF LENDING

This article is concerned with the conditions that must exist and the representations that must be delivered to the lender in order to make the commitment binding. Before disbursing any monies under the loan, legal counsel must be satisfied with the documents submitted by the borrower, which include the following:

- Charter and by laws
- Resolutions adopted by the company's board of directors authorizing the contemplated transaction, together with any other required resolutions (for example, authorizing hypothecation of collateral, insurance, or guarantees)
- Certificates of good standing from those jurisdictions where the major properties of the borrower are located or a substantial portion of the borrower's business is transacted
- Copies of all consents and approvals that might have had to be obtained
- Copies of other debt instruments to which the borrower might be subject

A review of all the required documentation should enable legal counsel for the lender to determine if everything is legally acceptable. In most instances, corporate affairs of borrowers are far from simple and counsel for the lender should not be expected to become familiar with all the ramifications of the business of the borrower, guarantor, or any other party to the agreement. For that reason, opinions should be obtained from the borrower's counsel (preferably independent) stating that all necessary legal actions have been taken and that no provisions of charter, bylaws, or other applicable agreements have been violated.

It should also be noted that the loan agreement and any notes to be issued in connection with it are valid and binding obligations of the borrower. That way they will be enforceable in accordance with the terms of the loan and all other instruments (guarantees, for example) are similarly valid and enforceable.

On the financial side of the conditions precedent, it is obvious that the lender should have obtained a signed copy of the loan agreement and note(s) to be issued. In those instances where collateral is to be pledged, appropriate instruments should have been executed and, if applicable, the collateral should be in the hands of the lender. A similar consideration evolves around the execution and delivery of guarantees. Certifications should also be obtained when a contemplated loan is part of a larger financing program involving the raising of additional capital funds, the discharge of other indebtedness, or the prior investment of the borrower's own funds in a venture to be financed partly by the contemplated loan.

Finally, as a condition precedent, the lender will require two additional documents:

1. An incumbency certificate listing the names and signatures of the officers (with their respective titles) having the power to act for the borrower
2. A certification by a responsible officer that the representations and warranties contained in the agreement are true and correct as of the closing date

DEFAULT PROVISIONS

All term loans have default provisions under which the long-term lender has the right to accelerate the payment of the loan. This is mandated with an acceleration clause which states that if certain conditions are not met, the total loan is immediately due, or, at the very least, gives the bank the right to renegotiate the terms. If such a clause is excluded from the agreement, the bank is obliged to wait until each installment is due before legal action can be taken against the borrower. The fact that the right exists does not mean that it is always used, but it does give lenders flexibility at a time when they need room to maneuver.

Several default provisions are ordinarily included in term loan agreements. Probably the most important act of default relates to bankruptcy, reorganization, and nonpayment of indebtedness. Lenders must have the right to call in their outstanding loans or be relieved of any obligation to make further loans in the case of voluntary bankruptcy or reorganization proceedings. If lenders have not reserved for themselves the right to accelerate under the foregoing conditions, the lender might be in the awkward position of not having matured claims to present to the bankruptcy trustee. This, in turn, might stop them from proving their claims and/or recovering claims in full.

Another act of default is the misrepresentation of financial information presented in financial statements, the recent Enron and WorldCom debacles cases in point. This not only indicates financial trouble, it also raises the question of management's moral and perhaps legal integrity. Since financial statements are one of the principal means by which management is measured, misrepresentation is a clear indication that the borrower is not of high moral character. In this instance, it would be best for all parties concerned to dissolve the relationship. The failure to perform or observe any of the terms of the agreement is also a default.

The argument against acceleration is that nonpayment could precipitate bankruptcy. This, however, might or might not be the case and the holder of other unpaid indebtedness might rewrite the obligation in such a way that it is repaid over the near term (just keeping the debtor out of bankruptcy) or the creditor might take security to protect its interests. To what extent these possibilities are serious threats depends to a large degree on the strength of the covenants. Certainly in any lending arrangement where term loans are made with only a few covenants, the acceleration of other indebtedness should cross-accelerate the subject loan.

The Next Group of Defaults

These defaults relate to such things as material falsity or representation and warranties, default under negative covenants, or default under covenants contained in other debt instruments. Certainly if a representation on which a lender has based its decision should prove to be false in a material respect, the lender should have the right to review its decision. At times this can protect the lender from serious problems, especially if the contemplated loan is in violation of other agreements or statutory regulation.

DESCRIPTION OF COLLATERAL

When the loan is a secured loan, the agreement sets forth a detailed description of the collateral and how it is to be handled. If the collateral consists of securities, the agreement normally specifies who is to receive the interest or dividends, who is to have the right to vote the stock, under what conditions the securities are to be sold, and if sold, who is to receive the proceeds from the sale.

LOAN COVENANTS

This is a very important part of the loan agreement. The covenants of a loan agreement lay the framework for the financial plan jointly agreed upon by the borrower and the lender. The number and detail of the covenants will largely depend on the financial strength of the enterprise, management's aptitude, and the length of the proposed loan. For example, if the borrower is financially solid and has strong management, the number of covenants will be less than that for a borrower who is only moderately strong in both categories. Some of largest, best-managed companies borrow term money without restrictive covenants and with only certain basic events of default. With smaller companies in the prime commercial group, lenders are often content to set broad covenants limiting debt to an overall ratio of tangible net worth, prohibiting secured debt, and providing for the maintenance of a certain minimum working capital.

In actuality, the basic covenants in every term loan agreement should he constructed around these four principles:

1. Limitation of other indebtedness
2. Prohibition of secured obligations or of obligations ranking ahead of the commercial term loan
3. A provision for the maintenance of a certain minimum working capital.
4. Furnishing financial statements

Covenants can also be viewed as being negative or affirmative, primary, secondary, or tertiary.

AFFIRMATIVE COVENANTS

Affirmative covenants are good general business practices that management may not have control over. However, they remain obligations imposed on management. One of the most common affirmative covenants is the requirement that the bank be furnished with financial statements periodically with any relevant information as requested. This alerts the bank to any financial deterioration the borrower may be experiencing. It is common practice to require unaudited statements for the first three quarters of the borrower's fiscal year, in addition to audited statements at the year-end. Term loan agreements generally require, also, that the borrower carry insurance satisfactory to the bank to reduce those risks that are insurable.

Many term loan agreements require the borrower to maintain working capital at or above a stated amount. Some bankers consider this one of the most important provisions, since it requires the borrower to maintain a specific amount of liquidity. For obvious reasons, it also provides a measure of protection for other creditors as well. However, this provision may not provide as much protection as some people think. Why? It would be possible for a business to maintain the working capital requirements while carrying large investments in inventory and accounts receivable.

To say the least, a company in this situation is not very liquid. Therefore, a close check must be kept on the quality of current assets and current liabilities. Nevertheless, the working capital requirement is an influential force since it gives the bank the right to declare the borrower in default should working capital drop below the agreed level.

In some instances, an affirmative covenant incorporated in term loan agreements may require management that is satisfactory to the bank. This is another important provision since management is closely tied to the success of a firm. The provision means that if the management should change due to resignation, death, or other causes, the bank must give its blessing before new personnel are hired. Banks often require that insurance be carried on those people in responsible positions who cannot be readily replaced.

Negative Covenants

The objective of negative covenants is to prevent a dissipation of assets that would weaken the firm's financial strength and the assumption of obligations (definite or contingent) that might reduce the borrower's ability to repay the loan. Negative covenants are particulars the borrower agrees not to do during the life of the loan unless prior consent is obtained from the lending bank. This is usually satisfied with an amendment to the term loan agreement or by letter. Some negative covenants are those that in each case will take a definite management decision to violate.

For example, if a borrower agrees not to pay dividends, it cannot happen by accident that dividends are paid. Financial ratios are usually treated as negative covenants even though conscious management decisions are not always required to break these covenants. For instance, losses caused by adverse trading conditions may lead to the breach of the working capital minimum, or even a specified debt-to-equity ratio, even though management was not consciously trying to do this.

In negotiation, certain exceptions will be agreed upon, including, for instance, that overseas subsidiaries may pledge their assets to support their own borrowing, that prior existing secured debt is excluded, or that certain minimal monetary amounts can be raised on a secured basis annually without having the lender's specific approval. In limiting indebtedness, lenders should include limitations on leases and contingent liabilities other than normal product warranties.

A common negative covenant is the negative pledge clause usually found in unsecured loans where the borrower agrees not to pledge assets as security to other lenders, and not to sell receivables. Even though this clause may be included if the loan is secured, its importance is probably lessened since other lenders would be reluctant to loan sizable amounts to a firm that has already pledged most of its assets. Such a covenant assures the bank that other lenders will not be placed in a more favorable position than it occupies.

Prohibitions regarding merger and consolidation, except with the approval of the bank, are also generally included for the bank's protection. To assure that the productive ability of the concern remains intact, a prohibition is usually included against the sale or lease of substantially all of the borrower's assets. Term loan borrowers also usually agree not to make loans to others or to guarantee, endorse, or become surety for others. Such a prohibition reduces the possibility of cash withdrawals, a weakened financial position, and the assumption of contingent liabilities, which can become a heavy responsibility.

RESTRICTIVE CLAUSES AND/OR SECONDARY COVENANTS

Restrictive clauses and/or secondary covenants seem similar to negative covenants but are basically different. Negative covenants in general prohibit certain acts of management, while restrictive clauses permit certain acts but restrict their latitude. For example, a negative covenant may prohibit a term loan borrower from mortgaging plant and equipment during the life of the loan, while a restrictive clause may limit the amount of dividends the borrower is permitted to pay. These clauses may be required even if the primary covenants are tight. This is because a lender does not want all earnings in excess of debt requirements and fixed asset maintenance expenditures to be diverted into unknown or unspecified uses. The further out in time a loan runs, the more questionable it becomes that the original credit and financial tests will adequately protect the lender. These covenants include the following:

1. Prohibition of the sale, discount, or other disposition of accounts receivable with or without recourse.
2. Prohibition of changes in other debt instruments.
3. Limitation of prepayment or redemption of other long-term debt. The purpose of such a provision is to prevent the bank from being the last to be repaid. It also prevents the firm from using the bank's funds to pay off some other lender. If a borrower owes long-term debts to others, a limitation may be placed on the amount that may be retired annually without also retiring a portion of the term debt owed to the bank.
4. Prohibitions on mergers or consolidations, asset sales, and acquisitions.
5. Prohibitions on investments in other enterprises.
6. Limitations on capital expenditures. The purpose of this limitation is to prevent the firm from overextending itself. The amount that can be invested will vary considerably but may be limited to the company's annual depreciation charges.

7. Limitations may also be placed on salaries, bonuses, and advances to officers and employees, as well as to others. The limitation on salaries and bonuses is a way of forcing a borrower to "tighten his belt" until the borrower has adequate capital funds.
8. Limitations on dividends. The restriction on dividends may be in terms of a certain percentage of cumulative earnings, or it may be specified that dividends not be allowed to reduce retained earnings below a certain level.
9. Limitations on treasury stock purchases to prevent a weakening of the firm's financial strength.
10. Restrictions on the purchase of securities, with the usual exception of United States government obligations. This limitation is designed to prohibit speculation in securities.

THE MISCELLANEOUS SECTION

The final section sets forth any matter to be specified that does not logically fall in one of the previous sections. It includes where notices to borrowers or lenders shall be sent, what law governs the agreement, the duties of the agent bank in syndicated loans, and the borrower's agreement to pay certain expenses.

ABSTRACT OF THE BASEL COMMITTEE'S PRINCIPLES FOR THE MANAGEMENT OF CREDIT RISK[1]

THE MAIN ISSUES

1. While financial institutions have faced difficulties over the years for a multitude of reasons, the major cause of serious banking problems continues to be directly related to lax credit standards for borrowers and counterparties, poor portfolio risk management, or a lack of attention to changes in economic or other circumstances that can lead to a deterioration in the credit standing of a bank's counterparties. This experience is common in both G-10 and non-G-10 countries.

2. Credit risk is most simply defined as the potential that a bank borrower or counterparty will fail to meet its obligations in accordance with agreed terms. The goal of credit risk management is to maximize a bank's risk-adjusted rate of return by maintaining credit risk exposure within acceptable parameters. Banks need to manage the credit

---

[1] Source: Consultative paper issued by the Basel Committee on Banking Supervision, Basel, September 2000. Reprinted with permission. Full Adobe text is included on the CD.

risk inherent in the entire portfolio as well as the risk in individual credits or transactions. Banks should also consider the relationships between credit risk and other risks. The effective management of credit risk is a critical component of a comprehensive approach to risk management and essential to the long-term success of any banking organization.

3. For most banks, loans are the largest and most obvious source of credit risk; however, other sources of credit risk exist throughout the activities of a bank, including in the banking book and in the trading book, and both on and off the balance sheet. Banks are increasingly facing credit risk (or counterparty risk) in various financial instruments other than loans, including acceptances, interbank transactions, trade financing, foreign exchange transactions, financial futures, swaps, bonds, equities, options, and in the extension of commitments and guarantees, and the settlement of transactions.

4. Since exposure to credit risk continues to be the leading source of problems in banks worldwide, banks and their supervisors should be able to draw useful lessons from past experiences. Banks should now have a keen awareness of the need to identify, measure, monitor, and control credit risk as well as to determine that they hold adequate capital against these risks and that they are adequately compensated for risks incurred. The Basel Committee is issuing this document in order to encourage banking supervisors globally to promote sound practices for managing credit risk. Although the principles contained in this paper are most clearly applicable to the business of lending, they should be applied to all activities where credit risk is present.

5. The sound practices set out in this document specifically address the following areas: (i) establishing an appropriate credit risk environment; (ii) operating under a sound credit granting process; (iii) maintaining an appropriate credit administration, measurement and monitoring process; and (iv) ensuring adequate controls over credit risk. Although specific credit risk management practices may differ among banks depending upon the nature and complexity of their credit activities, a comprehensive credit risk management program will address these four areas. These practices should also be applied in conjunction with sound practices related to the assessment of asset quality, the adequacy of provisions and reserves, and the disclosure of credit risk, all of which have been addressed in other recent Basel committee documents.

6. While the exact approach chosen by individual supervisors will depend on a host of factors, including their on-site and off-site supervisory techniques and the degree to which external auditors are also used in the supervisory function, all members of the Basel Committee agree that the principles set out in this paper should be used in evalu-

ating a bank's credit risk management system. Supervisory expectations for the credit risk management approach used by individual banks should be commensurate with the scope and sophistication of the bank's activities. For smaller or less sophisticated banks, supervisors need to determine that the credit risk management approach used is sufficient for their activities and that they have instilled sufficient risk-return discipline in their credit risk management processes.

7. The Committee stipulates, in Sections 11 through VI of the paper, principles for banking supervisory authorities to apply in assessing bank's credit risk management systems. In addition, the appendix provides an overview of credit problems commonly seen by supervisors.

8. A further particular instance of credit risk relates to the process of settling financial transactions. If one side of a transaction is settled but the other fails, a loss may be incurred that is equal to the principal amount of the transaction. Even if one party is simply late in settling, then the other party may incur a loss relating to missed investment opportunities. Settlement risk (i.e., the risk that the completion or settlement of a financial transaction will fail to take place as expected) thus includes elements of liquidity, market, operational, and reputational risk as well as credit risk. The level of risk is determined by the particular arrangements for settlement. Factors in such arrangements that have a bearing on credit risk include the timing of the exchange of value, payment/settlement finality, and the role of intermediaries and clearing houses.

THE MAIN PRINCIPLES

- Establish an appropriate credit risk environment
- Operate under a sound credit granting process
- Maintain an appropriate credit administration, measurement, and monitoring process
- Ensure adequate controls over credit risk
- Establish the role of supervisors

ABSTRACT

Establishing an Appropriate Credit Risk Environment

Principle 1:The board of directors should have responsibility for approving and periodically reviewing the credit risk strategy and significant credit risk policies of the bank. The strategy should reflect the bank's tolerance for risk and the level of profitability the bank expects to achieve for incurring various credit risks.

Principle 2: Senior management should have responsibility for implementing the credit risk strategy approved by the board of directors and for developing policies and procedures for identifying, measuring, monitoring, and controlling credit risk. Such policies and procedures should address credit risk in all of the bank's activities and at both the individual credit and portfolio levels

Principle 3: Banks should identify and manage credit risk inherent in all products and activities. Banks should ensure that the risks of products and activities new to them are subject to adequate procedures and controls before being introduced or undertaken, and approved in advance by the board of directors or its appropriate committee.

Operating under a Sound Credit-Granting Process

Principle 4: Banks must operate under sound, well-defined credit-granting criteria. These criteria should include a thorough understanding of the borrower or counterparty, as well as the purpose and structure of the credit and its source of repayment.

Principle 5: Banks should establish overall credit limits at the level of individual borrowers and counterparties, and groups of connected counterparties that aggregate in a comparable and meaningful manner different types of exposures, both in the banking and trading book and on and off the balance sheet.

Principle 6: Banks should have a clearly established process in place for approving new credits as well as the extension of existing credits.

Principle 7: All extensions of credit must be made on an arm's-length basis. In particular, credits to related companies and individuals must be monitored with particular care and other appropriate steps taken to control or mitigate the risks of connected lending.

Maintaining an Appropriate Credit Administration, Measurement, and Monitoring Process

Principle 8: Banks should have in place a system for the ongoing administration of their various credit risk-bearing portfolios.

Principle 9: Banks must have in place a system for monitoring the condition of individual credits, including determining the adequacy of provisions and reserves.

Principle 10: Banks should develop and utilize internal risk rating systems in managing credit risk. The rating system should be consistent with the nature, size, and complexity of a bank's activities.

Principle 11: Banks must have information systems and analytical techniques that enable management to measure the credit risk inherent in all on- and off-balance sheet activities. The management information system should provide adequate information on the composition of the credit portfolio, including identification of any concentrations of risk.

Principle 12: Banks must have in place a system for monitoring the overall composition and quality of the credit portfolio

Principle 13: Banks should take into consideration potential future changes in economic conditions when assessing individual credits and their credit portfolios, and should assess their credit risk exposures under stressful conditions.

Ensuring Adequate Controls over Credit Risk

Principle 14: Banks should establish a system of independent, ongoing credit review and the results of such reviews should be communicated directly to the board of directors and senior management.

Principle 15: Banks must ensure that the credit-granting function is being properly managed and that credit exposures are within levels consistent with prudential standards and internal limits. Banks should establish and enforce internal controls and other practices to ensure that exceptions to policies, procedures, and limits are reported in a timely manner to the appropriate level of management.

Principle 16: Banks must have a system in place for managing problem credits and various other workout situations.

The Role of Supervisors

Principle 17: Supervisors should require that banks have an effective system in place to identify, measure, monitor, and control credit risk as part of an overall approach to risk management. Supervisors should conduct an independent evaluation of a bank's strategies, policies, practices, and procedures related to the granting of credit and the ongoing management of the portfolio. Supervisors should consider setting prudential limits to restrict bank exposures to single borrowers or groups of connected counterparties.

COMMON SOURCES OF MAJOR CREDIT PROBLEMS

Most major banking problems have been either explicitly or indirectly caused by weaknesses in credit risk management. In supervisors' experience, certain key problems tend to recur. Severe credit losses in a banking system usually reflect simultaneous problems in several areas, such as concentrations, failures of due diligence, and inadequate monitoring. This appendix summarizes some of the most common problems related to the broad areas of concentrations, credit processing, and market and liquidity-sensitive credit exposures.

Concentrations

Concentrations are probably the single most important cause of major credit problems. Credit concentrations are viewed as any exposure where the potential losses are large relative to the bank's capital, its total assets, or, where adequate measures exist, the bank's overall risk level. Relatively large losses" may reflect not only large exposures, but also the potential for unusually high percentage losses given default.

Credit concentrations can further be grouped roughly into two categories:

- Conventional credit concentrations would include concentrations of credits to single borrowers or counterparties, a group of connected counterparties, and sectors or industries, such as commercial real estate, and oil and gas.
- Concentrations based on common or correlated risk factors reflect subtler or more situation-specific factors and often can only be uncovered through analysis. The recent disturbances in Asia and Russia illustrate how close linkages among emerging markets under stress conditions and previously undetected correlations between market and credit risks, as well as between those risks and liquidity risk, can produce widespread losses.

Credit Process Issues

Many credit problems reveal basic weaknesses in the credit-granting and monitoring processes. While shortcomings in underwriting and management of market-related credit exposures represent important sources of losses at banks, many credit problems would have been avoided or mitigated by a strong internal credit process.

Many banks find carrying out a thorough credit assessment (or basic due diligence) a substantial challenge. For traditional bank lending, competitive pressures and the growth of loan syndication techniques create time constraints that interfere with basic due diligence. Globalization of credit markets increases the need for financial information based on sound accounting standards and timely macroeconomic and flow of funds data. When this information is not available or reliable, banks may dispense with financial and economic analysis and support credit decisions with simple indicators of credit quality, especially if they perceive a need to gain a competitive foothold in a rapidly growing foreign market. Finally, banks may need new types of information, such as risk measurements, and more frequent financial information, to assess relatively newer counterparties, such as institutional investors and highly leveraged institutions.

The absence of testing and validation of new lending techniques is another important problem. Adoption of untested lending techniques in new or innovative areas of the market, especially techniques that dispense with sound principles of due diligence or traditional benchmarks for leverage, have led to serious problems at many banks. Sound practice calls for the application of basic principles to new types of credit activity. Any new technique involves uncertainty about its effectiveness. That uncertainty should be reflected in somewhat greater conservatism and corroborating indicators of credit quality. An example of the problem is the expanded use of credit-scoring models in consumer lending in the United States and some other countries. Large credit losses experienced by some banks for particular tranches of certain mass-marketed products indicate the potential for scoring weaknesses.

Some credit problems arise from subjective decision making by senior management of the bank. This includes extending credits to companies they own or with which they are affiliated, to personal friends, to persons with a reputation for financial acumen or to meet a personal agenda, such as cultivating special relationships with celebrities.

Many banks that experienced asset quality problems in the 1990s lacked an effective credit review process (and, indeed, many banks had no credit review function). Credit review at larger banks usually is a department made up of analysts, independent of the lending officers, who make an independent assessment of the quality of a credit or a credit relationship based on documentation such as financial statements, credit analysis provided by the account officer and collateral appraisals. At smaller banks, this function may be more limited and performed by internal or external auditors. The purpose of credit review is to provide appropriate checks and balances to ensure that credits are made in accordance with bank policy and to provide an independent judgment of asset quality, uninfluenced by relationships with the borrower. Effective credit review not only helps to detect poorly underwritten credits, it also helps prevent weak credits from being granted, since credit officers are likely to be more diligent if they know their work will be subject to review.

A common and very important problem among troubled banks in the early 1990s was their failure to monitor borrowers or collateral values. Many banks neglected to obtain periodic financial information from borrowers or real estate appraisals in order to evaluate the quality of loans on their books and the adequacy of collateral. As a result, many banks failed to recognize early signs that asset quality was deteriorating and missed opportunities to work with borrowers to stem their financial deterioration and to protect the bank's position. This lack of monitoring led to a costly process by senior management to determine the dimension and severity of the problem loans and resulted in large losses.

In some cases, the failure to perform adequate due diligence and financial analysis and to monitor the borrower can result in a breakdown of controls to detect credit-related fraud. For example, banks experiencing fraud-related losses have neglected to inspect collateral, such as goods in a warehouse or on a showroom floor, have not authenticated or valued financial assets presented as collateral, or have not required audited financial statements and carefully analyzed them. An effective credit review department and independent collateral appraisals are important protective measures, especially to ensure that credit officers and other insiders are not colluding with borrowers.

In addition to shortcomings in due diligence and credit analysis, bank credit problems reflect other recurring problems in credit-granting decisions. Some banks analyze credits and decide on appropriate nonprice credit terms, but do not use risk-sensitive pricing. Banks that lack a sound pricing methodology and the discipline to follow consistently such a methodology will tend to attract a disproportionate share of under-priced risks. These banks will be increasingly disadvantaged relative to banks that have superior pricing skills.

Many banks have experienced credit losses because of the failure to use sufficient caution with certain leveraged credit arrangements. As noted above, credit extended to highly leveraged borrowers is likely to have large losses in default. Similarly, leveraged structures such as some buyout or debt restructuring strategies, or structures involving customer-written options, generally introduce concentrated credit risks into the bank's credit portfolio and should only be used with financially strong customers. Often, however, such structures are most appealing to weaker borrowers because the financing enables a substantial upside gain if all goes well, while the borrower's losses are limited to its net worth.

Many banks' credit activities involve lending against real collateral. In lending against real assets, many banks have failed to make an adequate assessment of the correlation between the financial condition of the borrower and the price changes and liquidity of the market for the collateral assets. Much asset-based business lending (i.e. commercial finance, equipment leasing, and factoring) and commercial real estate lending appear to involve a relatively high correlation between borrower creditworthiness and asset values. Since the borrower's income, the principal source of repayment, is generally tied to the assets in question, deterioration in the borrower's income stream, if due to industry or regional economic problems, is likely to be accompanied by declines in asset values for the collateral. Some asset-based consumer lending (i.e., home equity loans, auto financing) exhibits a similar, if weaker, relationship between the financial health of consumers and the markets for consumer assets.

A related problem is that many banks do not take sufficient account of business cycle effects in lending. As income prospects and asset values rise in the ascending portion of the business cycle, credit analysis may incorporate overly optimistic assumptions. Industries such as retailing, commercial real estate and real estate investment trusts, utilities, and consumer lending often experience strong cyclical effects. Sometimes the cycle is less related to general business conditions than the product cycle in a relatively new, rapidly growing sector, such as health care and telecommunications. Effective stress testing which takes account of business or product cycle effects is one approach to incorporating into credit decisions a fuller understanding of a borrower's credit risk.

More generally, many underwriting problems reflect the absence of a thoughtful consideration of downside scenarios. In addition to the business cycle, borrowers may be vulnerable to changes in risk factors such as specific commodity prices, shifts in the competitive landscape, and the uncertainty of success in business strategy or management direction. Many lenders fail to "stress test" or analyze the credit using sufficiently adverse assumptions and thus fail to detect vulnerabilities.

Market and Liquidity-Sensitive Credit Exposures

Market and liquidity-sensitive exposures pose special challenges to the credit processes at banks. Market-sensitive exposures include foreign exchange and financial derivative contracts. Liquidity-sensitive exposures include margin and collateral agreements with periodic margin calls, liquidity backup lines, commitments and some letters of credit, and some unwind provisions of securitization. The contingent nature of the exposure in these instruments requires the bank to have the ability to assess the probability distribution of the size of actual exposure in the future and its impact on both the borrower's and the bank's leverage and liquidity.

An issue faced by virtually all financial institutions is the need to develop meaningful measures of exposure that can be compared readily with loans and other credit exposures. This problem is described at some length in the Basel Committee's January 1999 study of exposures to highly leveraged institutions.

Market-sensitive instruments require a careful analysis of the customer's willingness and ability to pay. Most market-sensitive instruments, such as financial derivatives, are viewed as relatively sophisticated instruments, requiring some effort by both the bank and the customer to ensure that the contract is well understood by the customer. The link to changes in asset prices in financial markets means that the value of such instruments can change very sharply and adversely to the customer, usually with a small, but nonzero probability. Effective stress testing can reveal the potential for large losses, which sound practice suggests should be disclosed to the customer. Banks have suffered significant losses when they have taken insufficient care to ensure that the customer fully understood the transaction at origination and subsequent large adverse price movements left the customer owing the bank a substantial amount.

Liquidity-sensitive credit arrangements or instruments require a careful analysis of the customer's vulnerability to liquidity stresses, since the bank's funded credit exposure can grow rapidly when customers are subject to such stresses. Such increased pressure to have sufficient liquidity to meet margin agreements supporting over-the-counter trading activities or clearing and settlement arrangements may directly reflect market price volatility. In other instances, liquidity pressures in the financial system may reflect credit concerns and a constricting of normal credit activity, leading borrowers to utilize liquidity backup lines or commitments. Liquidity pressures can also be the result of inadequate liquidity risk management by the customer or a decline in its creditworthiness, making an assessment of a borrower's or counterparty's liquidity risk profile another important element of credit analysis.

Market- and liquidity-sensitive instruments change in friskiness with changes in the underlying distribution of price changes and market conditions. For market- sensitive instruments, for example, increases in the volatility of price changes effectively increase potential exposures. Consequently, banks should conduct stress testing of volatility assumptions.

Market- and liquidity-sensitive exposures, because they are probabilistic, can be correlated with the creditworthiness of the borrower. This is an important insight gained from the market turmoil in Asia, Russia, and elsewhere in the course of 1997 and 1998. That is, the same factor that changes the value of a market- or liquidity-sensitive instrument can also influence the borrower's financial health and future prospects. Banks need to analyze the relationship between market- and liquidity-sensitive exposures and the default risk of the borrower. Stress testing—shocking the market or liquidity factors—is a key element of that analysis.

2

ACCOUNTING STANDARDS, FLAGS, AND DISTORTIONS

ACCOUNTING STANDARDS: A LENDER'S GUIDE

A new International Accounting Standards Board was appointed early in 2001 with the stated purpose of producing coordinated accounting standards within a few years. The hope is that several major accounting standards will be agreed upon within three years and will be accepted by accounting regulators in leading countries. Coordinated accounting standards will make it easier for lenders and investors to compare companies in different countries because such standards would put more responsibility on the "Big" international accounting firms that audit most companies around the world. The Big *Four* would have to determine not just whether the accounting met specific rules, but whether it complied with a principle.[1]

International accounting has long been troubled by conflicting rules in different countries, with some U.S. regulators believing that American standards are consummate vis-à-vis international standards that offer ways for companies to

---

[1] Floyd Norris, "Fewer Borders for Global Accounting," *New York Times,* January 26, 2001. C1, C5.

avoid rigorous auditing standards. "The Securities and Exchange Commission turned away efforts to allow major foreign companies to sell securities in the United States without adapting their accounting to American standards."[2] But as pressure grew for international standards, the U.S. position evolved to a less stringent level, which is that coordinated efforts to develop adept accounting standards will gain wide acceptance. A big improvement over past practices, the whole issue of accounting standards has raised great concern especially during periods of unrest in the financial markets, and certainly because of the Enron and WorldCom mess, to name a few. From the standpoint of bankers, the issue is equally important because comparative, rigorous auditing standards mean better measuring tools to evaluate individual deals along with the general loan portfolio. Consider the following Basel Committee quote:

> Banks should have methodologies that enable them to quantify the risk involved in exposures to individual borrowers or counterparties. Banks should use measurement techniques that are appropriate to the complexity and level of the risks involved in their activities, based on *robust data*, and subject to periodic validation.[3]

Note that the adjective *robust* was used to describe the noun *data*. It's clear: the ability of bankers to understand exposure risk will not move forward without a reckoning of both the terminology and conventions established by international accounting standards. How *should* auditors address these standards?

The Auditor's Role

The accountant's role centers around preparation of **independent** reports based on properly conducted audits, supported by all tests necessary to verify the accuracy of data under scrutiny, and most importantly free from conflicts of interest. While financial reports *can never* alone end as credit decisions, they play a major role within a much broader context called *lending due diligence*. That's because bankers need plenty of ancillary information before they begin to understand the borrower's *real environment*. As we saw in Chapter 1, credit decisions are founded on a banker's interpretation of real values, such as the earning power of assets, and never *just* on historically based financial reports. Real values are generally absent from the auditor's report. That said, scant few documents are more crucial to the art of lending than good, old-fashioned and we hope, *truthful* financial statements. In today's complex lending environment set against elaborate accounting standards, the significance of the auditor's work and its impact on the usefulness and credibility of financial statements cannot be overstated. The auditor bears a great responsibility for fostering the usefulness of financial statements, now more than ever, post Enron, et al. Through standards adopted by the

---

[2] Ibid.

[3] *Principle 11,* from the July 1999 consultative paper, issued by the Basel Committee on Banking Supervision.

accounting profession, as well as those imposed both by government and private business sources, the vast majority of members of the accounting profession seek to perform their work with one primary objective—to increase the reliability and usefulness of audits.

Auditors are members of independent accounting firms meeting prescribed professional standards and are licensed to practice in the country or state of clients. The auditor, on the basis of his or her independent judgment formed against the background of appropriate accounting standards and procedures, attests to the fairness of financial statements presented by management. Auditors are responsible to the reader for the proper exercise of judgment in two main areas: (1) that statements are presented fairly in accordance with generally accepted accounting principles and (2) that there is adequate disclosure.

The Comptroller of the Currency (OCC), and the Federal Deposit Insurance Corporation (FDC) closed The First National Bank of the Panhandle in Panhandle, Texas, when it found that First National was critically undercapitalized, having less than 2% tangible equity capital. The bank's financial troubles were due primarily to alleged fraudulent lending activities committed by a former senior officer. Insufficient application of the bank's credit controls and procedures allowed these practices to remain undetected. As a result, First National incurred huge loan losses that depleted substantially all of its capital.

Although auditors undertake assignments for fees, it is the accountant's responsibility, not management's (no matter how prodigious the fee), to decide—good or bad—what information will be disclosed. However, the terms of an accountant's engagement determine to a large degree the extent of the audit, the number and detail of schedules, and the amount of verification work completed. Also, the adequacy of the audit and the experience and reputation of the accountant are weighed against the size and financial condition of the borrower. Nonetheless, accountants have a fiduciary responsibility to clarify all data bankers want clarified that have been included in audits of publicly traded companies. If stock is privately held, banks requiring additional schedules, exhibits, or other information that have been withheld from publication will usually require the borrower's permission before accountants release the desired information.

Financial reports are expected to present fairly, clearly, and completely the borrower's economic, financial, and operating condition. In preparing financial reports, it is perhaps naïve to think that accounting (like any communication process) is immune to threats of bias, misinterpretation, error, and evasiveness. To minimize these dangers and to render financial statements that are industry comparable and consistent from period to period, the accounting profession has developed a body of conventions—both generally accepted and universally practiced.

Without this body of accounting conventions, each auditor or chief financial officer would have to develop a unique theory structure and individualistic set of practices. In this hypothetical and somewhat ridiculous setting, bankers would be required to know every company's anomalous accounting method, a nigh impossible task. Today there is almost universal adoption of a common set of accounting concepts, standards, and procedures under the heading of generally accepted accounting principles (GAAP) and international accounting standards (IAS).

Although accounting standards and principles have provoked debate and healthy criticism, international business recognizes this far-reaching body of theories, methods, and practices as the fundamental bonding of finance and banking. There is little to substitute in the way of conventional auditing standards as the alternatives are often quite bleak, Russia being a good case in point. Russia's access to the international capital markets and overall economic well-being was delayed until the country fashioned a system of business and contract law and a foundation of accounting standards.

International Accounting Standard No. 1 (IAS 1), "Disclosure of Accounting Policies," includes the following guidelines for financial reports:

- Fair presentation
- Accounting policies
- Going concern
- Accrual basis of accounting
- Consistency of presentation
- Materiality and aggregation
- Offsetting
- Comparative information

IAS 1 prescribes the minimum structure and content, including certain information required on the face of the financial statements:

- Balance sheet (current/noncurrent distinction is not required)
- Income statement (operating/nonoperating separation is required)
- Cash flow statement (IAS 7 sets out the details)
- Statement showing changes in equity. Various formats are allowed:

   1. The statement shows (a) each item of income and expense, gain or loss, which, as required by other IAS Standards, is recognized directly in equity, and the total of these items—examples include property revaluations (IAS 16, Property, Plant and Equipment), certain foreign currency translation gains and losses (IAS 21, The Effects of Changes in Foreign Exchange Rates), and changes in fair values of financial instruments (IAS 39, Financial Instruments: Recognition and Measurement)—and (b) net profit or loss for the period, but no total of (a) and (b). Owners' investments and withdrawals of capital and other movements in retained earnings and equity capital are shown in the notes.
   2. Same as above, but with a total of (a) and (b) (sometimes called "comprehensive income). Again, owners' investments and withdrawals of capital and other movements in retained earnings and equity capital are shown in the notes.
   3. The statement shows both the recognized gains and losses that are not reported in the income statement and owners' investments and withdrawals of

capital and other movements in retained earnings and equity capital. An example of this would be the traditional multicolumn statement of changes in shareholders' equity.

The report of an independent accountant may be a complete, detailed audit implying attempts to verify all items and transactions or it may simply be a book audit concerned only with the maintenance of mathematical accuracy in transferring the general ledger and other schedules onto reported statements. Between these extremes are special-purpose audits and limited audits. In the latter, the auditor's report usually indicates that some items are incorporated with insufficient verification because of restrictive circumstances or because of management's insistence that certain figures be accepted without complete checking. For a book audit in such cases, accountants protect themselves and avoid misleading users as to the extent of the verification by noting in the report's certificate limitations imposed on the examination. Accounting standards are governed by reporting thresholds called *opinions*. Let's examine the underlying principles behind accountant's opinions.

Certified Opinions

An accountant's summary opinion may be worded something like this: "In the opinion of this auditor, generally accepted accounting principles have been followed, they have been applied on a basis consistent with that of the preceding year, and the financial statements present fairly the firm's financial condition." Eastman Kodak's opinion, written by the firm's auditors, is an example of a certified audit:

Report of Independent Accountants

To the Board of Directors and Shareholders of Eastman Kodak Company

In our opinion, the accompanying consolidated financial statements appearing on pages 35 through 55 of this Annual Report present fairly, in all material respects, the financial position of Eastman Kodak Company and subsidiary companies at December 31, 1999 and 1998, and the results of their operations and their cash flows for each of the three years in the period ended December 31, 1999, in conformity with accounting principles generally accepted in the United States. These financial statements are the responsibility of the Company's management; our responsibility is to express an opinion on these financial statements based on our audits. We conducted our audits of these statements in accordance with auditing standards generally accepted in the United States, which require that we plan and perform the audit to obtain reasonable assurance about whether the financial statements are free of material misstatement. An audit includes examining, on a test basis, evidence supporting the amounts and disclosures in the financial statements, assessing the accounting principles used and significant estimates made by management, and evaluating the overall financial statement presentation. We believe that our audits provide a reasonable basis for the opinion expressed above.

Rochester, New York
January 18, 2000

The letter of transmittal in which the accountants reported the results of Kodak's audit is termed the *certificate*. The certificate may be a relatively brief "short form" or it may be a more expansive "long form" document. In general, the short-form certificate describes the scope of the work in general terms, noting exceptions to usual practice or procedure and expressing the opinion that the schedules prepared fairly and correctly present the results of operations for the period reported and the actual financial condition of the concern on the date of the statement. The long-form letter is made in connection with all material assets (and liabilities), besides including standard phrases used in the short certificate. Bankers almost always deal with the short certificate. The short certificate covering a detailed audit usually assures the client and the creditors of Eastman Kodak of the following:

1. Kodak's accounting records were audited for the period indicated.
2. The examination was made in accordance with generally accepted auditing standards.
3. Such tests of the accounting records and other auditing procedures were made as were necessary under the circumstances.
4. The major assets and liabilities were confirmed or checked, with exceptions noted if there were any.
5. In the opinion of the PricewaterhouseCoopers (PWC), the facts and figures reported fairly present the affairs of Eastman Kodak and were arrived at in conformity with generally accepted accounting principles, which were applied in a manner consistent with that of the preceding year.

The importance of the last statement is such that its absence from the report of an independent accountant invariably should be questioned. This phrase gives assurance that, in the absence of notice to the contrary, no changes have been made from one year to another in method of evaluation or in determining depreciation charges and reserves, and that income statement items have not been shifted from one category to another. Thus, PricewaterhouseCoopers has put its reputation on the line. Here's another example of a short-form certificate:

> We have examined the consolidated balance sheet of A. B. Morris Textile Corporation and its subsidiary companies as of December 31, 1999, and the related consolidated statements of income, stockholders' equity, and changes in financial position for the year then ended. Our examination was made in accordance with generally accepted auditing standards and accordingly included such tests of the accounting records and such other auditing procedures as we considered necessary in the circumstances.
>
> In our opinion, such financial statements present fairly the financial position of the companies at December 31, 1999, and the results of their operations and the changes in financial position for the year then ended, in conformity with generally accepted accounting principles applied on a basis consistent with that of the preceding year.

There are lower threshold opinions. Auditors sometimes render qualified opinions, adverse opinions, or disclaim an opinion.

Qualified Audit

A qualified audit stipulates that overall the financial statements provide a fair representation of the firm's condition, but that certain items need qualification. Exceptions outlined in this opinion are not serious enough to negate the report. If so, the audit would contain an adverse opinion. Events that result in opinions other than the standard unqualified short form include following:

1. The examination has limited scope or constraints placed on the audit.
2. Financials depart from that required to present fairly the firm's financial position or its results of operations due to a digression or lack of conformity with generally accepted accounting principles and standards or inadequate disclosure.
3. Accounting principles and standards are not consistently applied.
4. Unusual uncertainties exist concerning future developments, the effects of which cannot be reasonably estimated or otherwise resolved satisfactorily.

Example: A Critical Look at Sunbeam—Changes in and Disagreements with Accountants on Accounting and Financial Disclosure[4]

On November 20, 1998, the audit committee recommended and Sunbeam's board approved the appointment of Deloitte & Touche as its independent auditors for 1998, to replace Arthur Andersen, Sunbeam's former auditor. On June 25, 1998, Sunbeam announced that Arthur Andersen would not consent to the inclusion of its opinion on Sunbeam's 1997 financial statements in a registration statement Sunbeam planned to file with the Securities and Exchange Commission (SEC). On June 30 that same year, Sunbeam announced that the audit committee of its board of directors would conduct a review of Sunbeam's prior financial statements and that those financial statements should not be relied upon. Sunbeam also announced that Deloitte & Touche had been retained to assist the audit committee and Arthur Andersen in their review of Sunbeam's prior financial statements.

Sunbeam announced that the audit committee had determined that Sunbeam would be required to restate its financial statements for 1997, the first quarter of 1998, and possibly 1996, and that the adjustments, while not then quantified, would be material. On October 20, 1998, Sunbeam announced the restatement of its financial results for a six-quarter period from the fourth quarter of 1996 through the first quarter of 1998. On November 12, 1998, Sunbeam filed a Form 10-K/A for the year ended December 28, 1997, which contains an unqualified opinion by Arthur Andersen on Sunbeam's restated consolidated financial statements as of December 29, 1996, and December 28, 1997, and for each of the three years in the period ended December 28, 1997.

---

[4] Adapted from the December 31, 1999, annual report.

Arthur Andersen's report on Sunbeam's financial statements for Sunbeam's two fiscal years ended December 28, 1997, contained no adverse opinion or disclaimer of opinion and was not qualified or modified as to uncertainty, audit scope, or accounting principles. In connection with its audits for those periods and through November 20, 1998, there were no disagreements with Arthur Andersen on any matter of accounting principles or practices, financial statement disclosure, or auditing scope or procedure, which disagreements if not resolved to the satisfaction of Arthur Andersen would have caused Arthur Andersen to make reference thereto in its report on the financial statements for such years.

It was reported in the firm's annual report that Sunbeam had not consulted with Deloitte & Touche on any matter that was either the subject of a disagreement or a reportable event between Sunbeam and Arthur Andersen. In connection with the restatements referred to previously, in a letter dated October 16, 1998, Arthur Andersen advised Sunbeam the following conditions existed which Arthur Andersen believed to be material weaknesses in Sunbeam's internal controls: "In our opinion, [Sunbeam's] design and effectiveness of its internal control were inadequate to detect material misstatements in the preparation of [Sunbeam's] 1997 annual (before audit) and quarterly financial statements."

As part of its audit of Sunbeam's 1997 consolidated financial statements, which led to the restatement of these financial statements, Arthur Andersen was required to consider Sunbeam's internal controls in determining the scope of its audit procedures. In November 1998, Arthur Andersen advised management of its concerns regarding Sunbeam's internal controls. Management has substantially addressed these concerns and has implemented additional internal controls surrounding accounting processes and procedures and financial reporting. In a candid statement, management stated that the company's internal control structures would detect material misstatements in the annual and quarterly financial statements.

Adverse Opinion

An adverse opinion is required in any report in which the exceptions of fair presentation are so material that in the independent auditor's judgment a qualified opinion is not justified. Adverse opinions are rare, because most enterprises change their accounting to conform to auditor's desires. A disclaimer of an opinion is normally issued for one of two reasons: (1) the auditor has gathered so little information on the financial statements that no opinion can be expressed or (2) the auditor concludes on the basis of the evaluation that the ability of the company to continue on a going-concern basis is highly questionable because of financing or operating problems.

The following adverse opinion raised substantial doubt about the company's ability to continue as a going concern:[5]

---

[5] Extracted from the December 31, 1999, annual report.

Board of Directors and Shareholders
The Great American Golf Works, Inc.

We have audited the accompanying balance sheets of The Great American Golf Works, Inc. (a Delaware corporation), as of December 31, 1999 and 1998, and the related statements of operations and comprehensive income, changes in shareholders' equity and cash flows for each of the years then ended. These financial statements are the responsibility of the Company's management. Our responsibility is to express an opinion on these financial statements based on our audits.

We conducted our audits in accordance with generally accepted auditing standards. Those standards require that we plan and perform the audits to obtain reasonable assurance about whether the financial statements are free of material misstatement. An audit includes examining, on a test basis, evidence supporting the amounts and disclosures in the financial statements. An audit also includes assessing the accounting principles used and significant estimates made by management, as well as evaluating the overall financial statement presentation. We believe that our audits provide a reasonable basis for our opinion.

In our opinion, the financial statements referred to above present fairly, in all material respects, the financial position of The Great American Golf Works, Inc., as of December 31, 1999 and 1998, and the results of its operations and its cash flows for each of the years then ended, in conformity with generally accepted accounting principles.

The accompanying financial statements have been prepared assuming that the Company will continue as a going concern. As discussed in Note A to the financial statements, the Company is dependent upon its majority shareholder to maintain the corporate status of the Company and to provide all nominal working capital support on the Company's behalf. **Because of the Company's lack of operating assets, its continuance is fully dependent upon the majority shareholder's continuing support. This situation raises a substantial doubt about the Company's ability to continue as a going concern.** The majority shareholder intends to continue the funding of nominal necessary expenses to sustain the corporate entity. The financial statements do not include any adjustments that might result from the outcome of this uncertainty.

S.W. Hatfield, CPA
Dallas, Texas

Compilation

A compilation is actually management's report. For a compilation, a CPA prepares monthly, quarterly, or annual financial statements. However, he or she offers no assurance as to whether material, or significant, changes are necessary for the statements to be in conformity with generally accepted accounting principles (or another comprehensive basis of accounting, such as the cash or tax basis). During a compilation, the CPA arranges the data in a conventional financial statement format and does not probe beneath the surface unless he or she becomes aware that the information management provided is in error or is incomplete. A compilation is sufficient for many private companies. However, if a business needs to provide some degree of assurance to outside groups that its financial statements are reliable, it may be necessary to engage a CPA to perform a review.[6]

The following compilation report was prepared for Quadratech Inc.:[7]

> To the Board of Directors and Stockholders of Quadratech, Inc.
>
> I have compiled the accompanying balance sheet of Quadratech, Inc. (a Nevada Corporation), and its subsidiaries as of June 30, 2000, and the related consolidated statement of operations and accumulated deficit, and cash flows for the three and six months then ended, in accordance with Statements on Standards for the Accounting and Review Services issued by the American Institute of Certified Public Accountants.
>
> A compilation is limited to presenting in the form of financial statements information that is the representation of management. I have not audited or reviewed the accompanying financial statements and, accordingly, do not express an opinion or any other form of assurance on them.
>
> The accompanying consolidated financial statements have been prepared assuming that the Company will continue as a going concern. As discussed in Note 11 to the consolidated financial statements, the Company's operating losses in prior years and accumulated deficit raise doubts about their abilities to continue as a going concern. The consolidated financial statements do not include any adjustments that might result from the outcome of this uncertainty.
>
> The December 31, 1999, financial statements were audited by me and I expressed an unqualified opinion on them in my report dated May 3, 2000. I have not performed any auditing procedures since that date.
>
> s/ W. William Cary
>
> W. William Cary, CPA
> Temecula, CA

In view of the basic assumptions of accounting, what principles or guidelines must the accountant follow in recording transaction data? The principles basically relate to how assets, liabilities, revenues, and expenses are to be identified, measured, and reported.

Historical Cost

Historical costs are real and once established are fixed for the life of the asset or as long as the asset remains on the company's books. For example, when a company purchases a building, the purchase price or historical cost is recorded on the company's balance sheet. However, if that building appreciates in value, the asset is still recorded at the historical cost, less depreciation. This accounting practice often results in assets that are carried at significantly off-market prices. Bankers should note that historical costs might overstate or understate asset value.

---

[6] AICPA Web site: http://www.aicpa.org/members/tools/brochure/under.htm "Understanding Compilation Review and Audit" AICPA—The CPA. Never Underestimate the Value. Communications Division American Institute of Certified Public Accountants—1121 Avenue of the Americas, New York, NY 10036.

[7] Extracted from the 10QSB filed on September 14, 2000.

In a slightly different context, the accounting principal of recording assets at historical cost may lend itself to manipulation as noted in the following trading example. A company with a trading position that is out the money (money is lost if the position is closed) may be inclined to roll over that position and either postpone (recognizing the loss) or hope the market changes and turns the position into a gain.

Accounting Standards as Applied to Revenue Realization

This is one facet of reporting practice that lenders pay particular attention to. Revenues, cash received for merchandise sold or services rendered, are generally recorded at the time of sale or completion of the service. However, two conditions must be met before revenue can be recorded. First, the earnings process must be substantially complete. Second, the collectability of the revenue must be estimated. The earnings process is not substantially complete under the following conditions:

1. The seller and buyer have not agreed on the price of the merchandise or service.
2. The buyer does not have to pay the seller until the merchandise is resold.
3. The merchandise is stolen or physically destroyed, and the buyer does not have to pay the seller.
4. Intercompany transactions exist—the buyer and seller are related parties.
5. The seller must continue to provide substantial performance or services to the buyer or aid in reselling the product. If, however, substantial performance has occurred and the collectability of the revenue can be estimated, the sale of the product or service can be recorded.

Revenue recognition, while consistent with applicable accounting standards, may be derived from sources other than operating cash flows. For example, some firms turn retiree medical plans into a source of profit. Financial Accounting Standard No. 106, introduced in the early 1990s, requires companies to report their total anticipated retiree health care coverage costs. Companies had two incentives to overstate their anticipated costs: (1) excessive costs provided a rational basis to reduce employee benefits and (2) if the excessive costs proved to be wrong (i.e., too excessive), then the companies could recognize a paper gain by reducing their retiree liability.

Consider this example: "In its latest fiscal year, Procter & Gamble's retiree medical program boosted corporate pretax income by $336 million. Altogether, since 1994 the retiree medical plan has contributed $909 million to pretax income."[8] As another example, Walt Disney took a $202 million pretax charge to

---

[8] Ellen Schultz and Robert McGough, "Health Advisory: Investors Should Do a Checkup on Firms That Use Medical Plans to Lift Profits," *The Wall Street Journal,* October 25, 2000, C1, C21.

reflect retiree-health liability after its 1993 change in accounting standards. With its large liability, Disney dramatically reduced by more than half its related expenses in the following year. As the estimate of the benefit liability began to be excessive, the company began to book paper gains—$90 million from 1995 through 1998.[9]

The Matching Principle

The popularity of the calendar year as a fiscal period is partly due to the collection of federal income taxes on a calendar-year basis. However, the Internal Revenue Service permits filing tax returns on the basis of a business year instead of a calendar year. GAAP recognizes the concept of matching under the accrual method. The intention is to determine revenue first and then match appropriate costs against revenue. If a financial statement is prepared on another basis of accounting, a statement must be made that the presentation is not in conformity with GAAP. Many small businesses have chosen this method. By preparing their financial statements on an income tax basis, many of the complexities, such as calculating deferred taxes, are avoided. Thus, the cash method of accounting can be used when preparing a compilation or review of a financial statement.[10] Note the following two examples:

> March 5, 1999
> A compilation prepared for Trilogy International, Inc.[11]
>
> To the Board of Directors
> Trilogy International, Inc.
> Palm City, Florida
>
> I have compiled the accompanying statement of assets, liabilities and equity–income tax basis of Trilogy International, Inc. (a corporation), as of December 31, 1998, and the related statement of revenue and expenses–income tax basis from the period of inception (August 7, 1998) through December 31, 1998, in accordance with Statements on Standards for Accounting and Review Services issued by the American Institute of Certified Public Accountants. The financial statements have been prepared on the accounting basis used by the Company for income tax purposes, which is a comprehensive basis of accounting other than generally accepted accounting principles.
> A compilation is limited to presenting in the form of financial statements information that is the representation of management. I have not audited or reviewed the accompanying financial statements and, accordingly, do not express an opinion or any other form of assurance on them.
> Management has elected to omit substantially all of the disclosures ordinarily included in financial statements. If the omitted disclosures were included in the financial statements, they might influence the user's conclusions about the Company's assets, lia-

---

[9] Ellen Schultz, "This Won't Hurt: Companies Transform Retiree-Medical Plans into Source of Profits," *The Wall Street Journal,* October 25, 2000, A1, A14.

[10] Sally A. Wahrmann, NST, CPA, "A Change in Accounting Method from Cash to Accrual," *The Tax Advisor,* February 1993.

[11] Extracted from the 8-K filed by AMERINET Group Com Inc. on December 16, 1999.

bilities, capital, revenue and expenses. Accordingly, these financial statements are not designed for those who are not informed about such matters.

Nora F. Catano, CPA, PA

The independent auditors' report for Twin Trees Apartments, a limited partnership, is as follows:[12]

> We have audited the accompanying statements of assets, liabilities, and partners' capital–income tax basis of Twin Trees Apartments, a Limited Partnership as of December 31, 1994 and 1993, and the related statements of revenues and expenses–income tax basis, changes in partners' capital (deficit)–income tax basis, and cash flows)–income tax basis for the years then ended. These financial statements are the responsibility of the Partnership's management. Our responsibility is to express an opinion on these financial statements based on our audits.
>
> We conducted our audits in accordance with generally accepted auditing standards. Those standards require that we plan and perform the audit to obtain reasonable assurance about whether the financial statements are free of material misstatement. An audit includes examining, on a test basis, evidence supporting the amounts and disclosures in the financial statements. An audit also includes assessing the accounting principles used and significant estimates made by management, as well as evaluating the overall financial statement presentation. We believe that our audits provide a reasonable basis for our opinion.
>
> As described in note 1(b), these financial statements were prepared on the basis of the accounting the Partnership uses for income tax purposes, which is a comprehensive basis of accounting other than generally accepted accounting principles.
>
> In our opinion, the financial statements referred to above present fairly, in all material respects, the assets, liabilities, and partners' capital of Twin Trees Apartments, a Limited Partnership as of December 31, 1994 and 1993, and its revenues and expenses, changes in partners' capital, and cash flows for the years then ended on the basis of accounting described in note 1(b).
>
> [Signature of KPMG Peat Marwick LLP]
>
> February 10, 1995

Consistency

While consistency means applying identical methods from fiscal year to fiscal year, firms are free to switch from one method of accounting to another, but with restrictions. Firms and their accountants need to demonstrate to bankers and investors that the newly adopted principle is preferable to the old. Then the nature and effect of the accounting change as well as the justification for it must be disclosed in the financial statements for the period in which the change is made.

Disclosure

Adequate disclosure calls for revealing facts significant enough to influence the judgment of a knowledgeable reader. Sufficient disclosure includes more

---

[12] Extracted from the 10K filed by Freedom Tax Credit Plus on July 2, 1996.

descriptive explanations, acceptable presentation, and succinct but meaningful footnotes—or example, detailed disclosure of financial obligations, current accounts such as inventory breakdown and method of pricing, and whatever additional disclosure is required to prevent the audit from becoming a guessing game. Auditors can add one or more paragraphs to an unqualified report if they feel that the information is important for the reader to know. This addition is known as the emphasis of a matter paragraph and is usually added before the standard opinion paragraph of an unqualified report. Obviously, the paragraph should not include mention of the emphasized matter and should instead refer to the footnotes.

Objectivity

Notwithstanding an audit disclaimer, it is imperative that bankers be assured that information in financial reports is factual and impartial. While no disclosure is totally objective, the process must be based on the auditor's sound judgment, diagnostic good sense, and an irrefutable background. Reliable estimates must be made of depreciation charges, deferrals, and accruals, along with revenue items, equity earnings, restructuring charges, and deferred tax credits. Estimates are deemed objective if the audit process is founded on adequate information and data that can be authenticated by independent parties. Most important, if there is any doubt, "objectivity" should favor conservatism. Schilit suggests that financial statement readers favor firms that present conservative accounting policies.

> Companies that fail to use conservative accounting methods might demonstrate a lack of integrity in their financial reporting process. Indeed, many analysts place a premium on companies that use conservative accounting policies. In searching for excellent companies, for example, the widely respected analyst and shenanigan buster Thornton O'Glove offers the following advice: Look for companies that use very conservative accounting principles. In my experience, if a company does not cut corners in its accounting, there's a good chance it doesn't cut corners in its operations. You know you've got your money with a high quality management.[13]

Frequency of Statements

Annual Statements

For purposes of credit analysis, the date of the annual statement is important in order to relate the figures to the stage or level of seasonal operations and to the closing date of the income tax statement. The date of the statement filed with the income tax return occasionally differs from that published for trade use. Bankers usually consider this when observing the provisions for income taxes.

Interim Statements

The Securities and Exchange Commission requires filing of quarterly sales data by all concerns listed on an exchange. Many of these concerns issue midyear

---

[13] Howard M. Schilit, *Financial Shenanigans* (New York: McGraw-Hill, 1993).

and even quarterly statements for the benefit of creditors, investors, and potential stock subscribers. Some small-cap firms, attempting to comfort suppliers and other credit sources, issue quarterly statements or trial balance figures covering very short interim periods, including monthly. Since the trial balance serves as a source of valuable interim information, its use in credit analysis is increasing (analysis of the trial balance will be discussed in Chapter 4, which is devoted to seasonal loans). Interim reports are unaudited or are at most subjected to a limited review. Short-term lenders may request cash budgets prepared by the borrower's financial team and completed with only peripheral help from accountants.

FOOTNOTES: AN ASTUTE LENDER CAN BE NO LESS AN ASTUTE AUDITOR

Smart lenders read their client's annual report cover to cover in order to pay heed to small print items. After all, there is more to a financial report than just numbers. We find the chairperson's optimistic statement, a historical record of three or more years, pictures of smiling employees, the latest hot products, charts that Andy Wahol would proudly have molded into museum quality, and wonderfully vivid graphs. Of course, there are the footnotes, where *real* information is to be found.

Footnotes are integral to financial statements but are often overlooked because they tend to be somewhat technical and frequently appear in small print. Footnotes are the accountant's way of disclosing details about crucial data. Restrictions imposed by footnotes provide bankers with a wealth of information for assessing the financial condition of borrowers and the quality of reported earnings.[14] Schilit reminds us that the footnotes detail such issues as "(1) accounting policies selected, (2) pending or imminent litigation, (3) long-term purchase commitments, (4) changes in accounting principles or estimates, (5) industry specific notes, and (6) segment information showing healthy and unhealthy operations."

On the whole, credit analysts see footnote disclosure as a step above core financial data. As Kenneth Fisher in Forbes noted: "The back of the report, the footnotes is where they hide the bad stuff they didn't want to disclose but had to. They bury the bodies where the fewest folks find them—in the fine print."[15] The Accounting Principles Board (APB), in Opinion No. 22, "Disclosure of Accounting Policies," concluded, "information about the accounting policies adopted and followed by a reporting entity is essential for financial-statement users in making economic decisions."

---

[14] Schilit, *Financial Shenanigans.*

[15] This insightful quote was restated by Schilit, *Financial Shenanigans,* pg. 22.

Read Everything but the Commercials

As an integral part of financial reports, a statement identifies accounting policies adopted and followed by the reporting entity. The APB believes disclosure should be given in a separate "Summary of Significant Accounting Policies" statement preceding the notes to the financial statements or as the initial note. After carousing the disclosure of accounting policies, wise bankers look for information that may negatively impact borrowers, like contingencies. The complete disclosure of material contingencies is an important property of financial statements according to International Accounting Standards guidelines because of the uncertainties that may exist at the conclusion of each accounting period.[16]

For example, standards governing accounting for loss contingencies require accrual or note disclosure when specified recognition and disclosure criteria are met. Gain contingencies generally are not recognized in financial statements but can be disclosed. Reporting criteria center around the high probability that a change in the estimate will occur in the near term. Here are examples of the types of situations that may require disclosure in accordance with Statement of Position (SOP) 94-6:

1. Specialized equipment subject to technological obsolescence
2. Valuation allowances for deferred tax assets based on future taxable income
3. Capitalized motion picture film production costs
4. Inventory subject to rapid technological obsolescence
5. Capitalized computer software costs
6. Deferred policy acquisition costs of insurance enterprises
7. Valuation allowances for commercial and real estate loans
8. Environmental remediation-related obligations
9. Litigation-related obligations
10. Contingent liabilities for obligations of other entities
11. Amounts reported for long-term obligations such as pensions
12. Expected loss on disposition of a business or assets
13. Amounts reported for long-term contracts

Under Financial Accounting Standards Board (FASB) Statement No. 5, an estimated loss from a loss contingency must be charged against net income as soon as the loss becomes probable and estimable. In addition, now that the use of prior period adjustments has been extremely narrowed by FASB Statement No. 16, "Prior Period Adjustments," almost all such loss accruals must be charged against current income. Another impact of FASB Statement No. 5 on earnings is that accrual of contingency losses is prohibited unless it is probable that an asset has been impaired or a liability has been incurred and that the loss is estimable.

---

[16] Financial Accounting Standards Board Statement No. 5, "Accounting for Contingencies."

This means that firms cannot provide reserves for future losses through yearly income statement adjustments. The reason is to prevent earnings volatility, the result of guesswork.

Classification of Contingencies

1. Probable: likely to materialize.
2. Reasonably possible: halfway between probable and remote.
3. Remote: slight chance of materializing.

To review, while some contingencies are disclosed in footnotes, bankers should recalculate certain balance sheet ratios in figuring possible losses. That's because creditors focus on a possible accounting loss associated with financial instruments, including losses from the failure of another party to perform according to contract terms (credit risk), the possibility that future changes in market prices may render financial instruments less valuable (market risk), and the risk of physical loss.

Likewise, a financial instrument has off-balance sheet risk if the risk of loss exceeds the amount recognized as an asset or if the obligation exceeds the amount recognized in the financial statements. Bankers are particularly watchful of general loss contingencies.

General Loss Contingencies

General loss contingencies may arise from risk of exposure to the following:

1. Product warranties or defects
2. Pending or threatened litigation
3. Risk of catastrophe (i.e., losses)
4. Direct guarantees—guarantor makes payment to creditor if debtor fails to do so
5. Claims and assessments
6. Preacquisition contingencies

Financial Instruments with Off-Balance Sheet Risk

While management may claim that off-balance sheet financial instruments reduce risks, these instruments can function as speculative tools. Borrowers anticipating a harsh fiscal year may capitalize on positive changes in the value of financial instruments to improve results—results unattainable through normal operating activities.

1. A recourse obligation on receivables or bills/receivable sold
2. Interest rate and currency swaps, caps, and floors
3. Loan commitments and options written on securities; futures contracts
4. Obligations arising from financial instruments sold short
5. Synthetic asset swap, which might result in an unwind if the bond goes into default
6. Obligations to repurchase securities sold

Product Warranties or Defects

A warranty (product guarantee) is a promise, for a specific time period, made by a seller to a buyer to make good on a deficiency of quantity, quality, or performance in a product. Warranties can result in future cash outlays, *frequently significant additional outlays*. Although the future cost is indefinite as to amount, due date, and even customer, a liability—an estimate of costs incurred after sale and delivery associated with defect correction—does exist and experienced lenders ask accountants or management to quantify the downside effect.

Litigation Contingencies

Publicly traded companies are required to disclose litigation contingencies when eventual loss from a lawsuit is possible. Studies were done on the classification of predisposition years (which refers to years before the year of court adjudication or settlement). It was found that 47.6% of surveyed companies showed unsatisfactory disclosure with no mention of the litigation in financial statements or a strong disclaimer of liability did not accompany mention of the litigation. Legal action includes antitrust, patent infringement, fraud or misrepresentation, breach of contract, and other noninsurable lawsuits.

This survey represents a banker's bona fide red flag if ever there was one. Contingencies such as product lawsuits losses can show up from nowhere, are often explosive, and can finish off an otherwise profitable company in the process. The best hedge against litigation contingencies is preparation that often means a present value analysis. This means placing values on material lawsuits by determining present value. Minor lawsuits, on the other hand, are usually irrelevant; an adverse opinion will not affect equity, debt service, or the borrower's sustainable cash flows. On the contrary, if we have a Firestone on our hands, can litigation be settled? If so, when and for how much? This brings up other questions:

- If litigation cannot be settled, when will the court hear the case?
- What are the probabilities the court will render an adverse opinion?
- If the opinion is adverse, will there be grounds for appeal?
- If so, when will the appeal be heard?
- What are the probabilities the appeal will collapse?
- Given the time value of money and the joint probabilities of adverse opinions including appeals, what is the expected present value of the product lawsuit (use face amounts, not expected reduced awards)?
- What are the pro forma expected losses on fiscal spreadsheets? Is the financial structure strong enough to absorb expected losses?
- Related to the previous question, how do adjusted (pro forma) debt and cash flow coverage ratios stack against the industry or benchmarks? Has the borrower's industry quartile ranking deteriorated? What is the anticipated impact on bond ratings or the bank's credit grade?

Environmental Contingencies

Environmental protection laws pose many dangers for unwary lenders. To avoid potentially unlimited liability that may result from environmental violations, prudent bankers try to extract expected present values and adjust financials accordingly. Environmental trouble spots include, but are not restricted to, the following:

- Transportation of hazardous substances
- Real property
- The disposition of hazardous substances
- Manufacturing processes that involve use, creation, or disposition of hazardous wastes
- Petroleum or chemicals stored on the premises
- Underground storage tanks
- Equipment used to transport hazardous materials
- Pipes leading to waterways

CIT Corporation, a leading commercial finance company, prepared a checklist regarding a client:

1. Are toxic or otherwise hazardous or regulated materials, such as used machine oil, handled at any stage of the production process?
2. Request a copy of the borrower's Environmental Protection Agency (EPA) plan, if any.
3. Does the client have above or belowground tanks and when were they last inspected for environmental impact purposes?
4. Are there paint shops on the property?
5. What was the previous use of the property prior to our client owning it and how long has our client been at this property?
6. Have there been past or are there present EPA violations against the property? Provide copies of those violations to our marketing representative?
7. Are there any waterways on or near the property? If so, where are they located in proximity to the property?
8. What is the specific use of the property (i.e., what kind of process or processes are being done on the property)?
9. Does our prospective client stock drums of solvents or fluids on the property? What is the exact nature of those solvents or fluids and where are they located?
10. What is the nature of the uses on adjoining and neighboring properties? Do they appear to create environmental risk?

Risk of Catastrophic Losses

It might be a good idea if bankers worried more about the possibility that some borrowers may face the risk of catastrophic loss. Two criteria must be met to classify a gain or loss as an extraordinary item (both criteria must be met before a company can classify a gain or loss as extraordinary):

- *Unusual*: The event is one that is unrelated to the typical activities of the business.
- *Nonrecurring*: The event is one that management does not expect to occur again.

Natural disasters meet the definition of unusual (unrelated to the typical activities of the business). For example, a corn farmer in Kansas hit by a drought would not classify the loss as nonrecurring and thus could not be considered extraordinary. On the other hand, a flood in Phoenix would give rise to an extraordinary loss. The criteria of "unusual" and "nonrecurring" must be considered from the standpoint of the firm's geographical location and business.

Direct and Indirect Guarantees

Direct guarantees, representing a direct connection between the creditor and the guarantor, warrant that the guarantor will make payment to the creditor if the debtor fails to do so. In an indirect guarantee, the guarantor agrees to transfer funds to the debtor if a specified event occurs. Indirect guarantees connect directly from the guarantor to debtor but benefit the creditor indirectly.

FASB 5 requires that the nature and amount of the guarantee be disclosed in the financial statements. Guarantees to repurchase receivables or related property, obligations of banks under letters of credit or standby agreements, guarantees of the indebtedness of others, and unconditional obligations to make payments are examples of the types of guarantee contingencies that must be disclosed even if they have a remote possibility of materializing.

Recourse Obligations on Receivables or Bills Receivables (B/Rs) Sold

A widely used method of financing transactions involving small, high-ticket items, notably furs and fine jewelry, has been the presentation of B/Rs or notes receivable for discount or as security to demand loans. A B/R is an unconditional order in writing addressed by one person (or firm) to another, signed by the person giving it, requiring the person to whom it is addressed to pay on demand, or at a fixed or determinable future time, a sum certain in money to order or to bearer. A B/R evidences indebtedness arising out of the sale of goods by the bank's customer in the normal course of business. B/Rs are endorsed over to the bank with *full recourse* to the bank's customer. These are off-balance sheet contingencies and should be pro forma back on the balance sheet by an amount equal to the expected loss.

Asset Securitization

If an asset can generate cash flow, it can be securitized. When a company securitizes its assets, those assets are sold as a "true sale" and are no longer assets of the company. In fact, many times that is precisely the reason companies securitize assets (i.e., to get them off their balance sheet so as to improve their profitability ratios). However, some have argued that securitization may inadvertently cause adverse selection for the company's remaining assets—that is, the company securitizes its best assets (the assets most marketable and easiest to securitize) and retains its poorer assets thereby causing an adverse selection.

Creditors face little risk in the event of bankruptcy because assets can be liquidated quickly. In exchange, however, the creditors receive a lower return on their investments. In addition, if these creditors liquidate the securitized assets, the company will be further unable to recover from a financial crisis and will put its general creditors at even greater risk. Other risks beside credit/default include maturity mismatch and prepayment volatility. As a side note, bankers and investors can reduce contingency risks by using computer software containing models and structural and analytical data for asset securitizations, including commercial loan securitizations, whole (loan and senior) subordinated securities, as well as home equity loans.[17]

Futures Contracts

A commodity such as copper used for production may be purchased for current delivery or for future delivery. Investing in commodity futures refers to the buying or the selling of a contract to deliver a commodity in the future. In the case of a purchase contract, the buyer agrees to accept a specific commodity that meets a specified quality in a specified month. In the case of a sale, the seller agrees to deliver the specified commodity during the designated month. Hedging against unexpected increases in raw material costs is a wise move; speculating in commodity futures, with the bank's money, is another story. There is a large probability that the firm will suffer a loss on any particular purchase or sale of a commodity contract.

Management may purchase a contract for future delivery. This is known as a long position in which the firm will profit if the price of the commodity, say copper, rises. Also management may enter into a contract for future delivery (short position). These long and short positions run parallel to the long and short positions in security markets.

Pensions

Pension expense represents the amount of money management should invest at the end of the year to cover future pension payments that will be made to employees for this additional year's service. Accounting records reflect management's best guess as to real pension costs. Accountants try to measure the cost of these retirement benefits at the time the employee earns them, rather than when the employee actually receives them. A multiplicity of pension assumptions needs to

---

[17] Ron Unz, "New Software Can Provide Risk Models, *American Banker,* August 25, 1992, 12A (1).

be compiled to come up with the required pension amount. These include the following:

- Interest invested funds are expected to earn
- Number of years an employee is expected to live after retirement
- Salary of employee at retirement
- Average years of service of an employee at retirement

Beware of unfunded projected benefit obligations since this liability indicates that pension investments fall short of future pension benefits. Borrowers that continuously fund less than current pension expense or incorporate unrealistic assumptions in their pension plan could find themselves embedded in a thicket of thorns in the not-too-distant future.

Companies with defined benefit pension plans must disclose three items: (1) the pension discount rate, (2) the expected rate of future compensation increases, and (3) the projected long-term rate of return on pension assets. Understanding what these figures mean provides insight into, for example, whether a merger candidate's pension liabilities make it worth less than meets the eye, and how companies use perfectly legal (but fairly sneaky) accounting gimmicks to inflate profits.

Discretionary Items

Some expenditures are discretionary, meaning they fall under management's control. These include the following:

- Repair and maintenance of equipment
- Research and development
- Marketing and advertising expenditures
- New product lines, acquisitions, and divestitures of operating units

Management might forgo timely equipment repairs to improve earnings, but the policy could backfire over the longer term.

Research and Development

In its Statement of Financial Accounting Standards No. 2, "Accounting for Research and Development Costs" (October 1974), the Financial Accounting Standards Board concludes, "All research and development costs encompassed by this Statement shall be charged to expense when incurred." The FASB (Statement No. 2) mandated all companies to expense R&D outlays. The FASB reached its conclusion as a result of a reasoning process in which several preliminary premises were accepted as true.

- Uncertainty of future benefits. R&D expenditures often are undertaken when there is a small probability of success. The FASB mentioned that the high degree of uncertainty of realizing the future benefits of individual research and development projects was a significant factor in reaching this conclusion.

- Lack of causal relationship between expenditures and benefits.
- R&D does not meet the accounting concept of an asset.
- Matching of revenues and expenses.
- Relevance of resulting information for investment and credit decisions.

An incontrovertible solution for avoiding problems dealing with overstating R&D expenditures is to expense costs associated with the acquisition of assets where some significant probability exists that the asset will be worth less than cost. This so-called conservative approach is consistent with guidelines dealing with expensing R&D.

BASIC ELEMENTS OF FLAGS, GIMMICKS, AND PROBLEMS: A FEW WORDS CAN BE WORTH A THOUSAND PICTURES

Change in Auditors

When firms frequently change auditors, particularly if downtiering occurs, bankers want to know why. Management may cite high auditing fees as the motive for the change, but there may also be adverse credit implications foretelling lower quality disclosures, conflict of interest, and less validation effort. The downtiering in auditors may have been brought on by a difference of opinion between the auditor and management regarding treatment and certification of material items. The bank may also check with other bankers sharing the credit or the firm's suppliers. At the very least, the bank must compare the present accountant's certificate with that of the previous auditor to ensure any variances are understood.

Creative Accounting

Creative accounting is any method of accounting that overstates revenues or understates expenses. Creative accounting is a sure sign that something is amiss. Bankers view it as a smoke screen to hide real operating results in order to prolong the company's credit standing and to confound investors. It's been a long-standing tradition for borrowers on an economic downspin to pass off inflated financial results in an attempt to fool bankers into thinking performance was better than it actually was. For example, companies might choose to inflate income or navigate around accounting rulings governing revenue recognition, inventory valuation, depreciation, and treatment of research and development costs, pension costs, disclosure of other income, or any number of other accounting standards. We certainly do not need to be reminded that there has been a marked increase in the number of large restatements of financial results because select *major corporations* and their auditors failed to heed accounting standards.

A major international bank's regulators criticized the institution for inflating its reserve accounts. The regulators forced the bank to reduce some of its reserves because it was believed that they were intentionally inflated so that the bank could draw on them when losses arose. This would artificially create more stable earnings, which was clearly the bank's motive, since analysts and investors were punishing it for volatile earnings. The regulators insisted that reserve accounts are not meant to smooth future earnings; rather they should reflect an allocation that relates to problems or potential problems with current assets.

According to the bank's 1998 10K, federal regulators required the bank to provide detailed components of the allowance for credit losses itemized by category. This breakdown of the allowance at each year-end reflected management's best estimate of possible credit losses and did not necessarily indicate actual future charge-offs. The bank informed its stockholders that due to a multitude of complex and changing factors that were collectively weighed in determining the adequacy of the allowance for credit losses, management expected that the allocation of the total allowance for credit losses would be adjusted as risk factors change.

Investors can be fooled as easily as bankers. Any investor or banker who thinks accounting results are tangential should think again. Consider the sharp effect earnings "perception" had on Emulex's stock price. In August 2000, Emulex Corporation, a producer of fiber-channel adapters, was the victim of an earnings-reporting hoax. A report sent out on the wire warned of an earnings restatement. In less than two hours, Emulex refuted the news, but not before the Nasdaq stock plunged 60%, cutting the firm's market value by $2.45 billion to $1.62 billion. Emulex later recovered most of those losses, but not before sending the company on one of the wildest rides an individual stock has taken in recent years—all because of earnings misperception.

When Sunbeam Corporation's earnings accounting practices (discussed earlier in the chapter) came under attack, the stock fell to a year low, though the firm denied income statement accounting gimmicks. *Barron's* published a sharply critical article suggesting that Sunbeam's 1997 profits of $109.4 million were largely due to improper shifting of costs, write-offs, and revenues. On July 2, 1998, the SEC informed Sunbeam that it was commencing a formal investigation of the company, certain officers, directors, employees, and other entities pertaining to possible violation of federal securities laws and regulations.

Specifically, Sunbeam may have caused these suspected violations by filing or causing to be filed inaccurate reports with the SEC; failing to maintain accurate books, records, and accounts; failing to create or maintain adequate internal accounting controls or circumventing such controls; recklessly making false or misleading statements in reports filed with the SEC or in other public statements; and making false or misleading statements to an accountant in connection with audits or examinations of the company's financial statements or reports filed with the SEC.

MicroStrategy Inc., a Vienna software maker, reported that the SEC started an investigation related to its restatement of past financial results. In recent disclosures, MicroStrategy reported that it has been losing money for the past three years, instead of making money as it had previously reported. The company also overstated past revenue, from the $205.3 million originally reported for 1999 to a revised figure of $151.3 million. Since MicroStrategy disclosed its accounting problems, its stock has lost 92.4% of its value.

Rent-Way Inc., an operator of rent-to-own stores, investigated "possible accounting irregularities" that will cause it to restate its financial results during the last fiscal year.[18] The company's controller was suspended and the chief operating officer relinquished his operating responsibilities. An assistant controller and others brought discrepancies that had been covered up to the attention of the chief financial officer and chairman of board of directors.[19] After this news, Rent-Way's share price plunged to $7 from more than $23.

In 1997, Oxford Healthcare Inc. experienced unanticipated software and hardware problems arising in connection with the conversion that resulted in significant delays in the company's claims payments and group and individual billing, which therefore adversely affected claims payment and billing. Oxford recorded a $291 million loss in 1997. The problem was so severe and made such an impact on its operations that the company's stock plummeted from a high of $89 in the third quarter of 1997 to a low of $13.75 in the fourth quarter of 1997, according to the company's 10K report.

Mitsubishi Motor Company allegedly hid 64,000 customer complaints about its vehicles dating back two decades. Government inspectors found the complaints hidden in a company locker room. Japanese automobile manufacturers are required to report consumer complaints to the Transport Ministry. Japanese police raided the company's headquarters to investigate this coverup of customer complaints. The raid caused the company's share prices to fall 12.4%. Managers trying to avoid a humiliating recall apparently hid the letters. The car defects were fixed directly and were not reported to Mitsubishi management, as required, according to an internal investigation reported by Mitsubishi's president Katsuhiko Kawasoe.[20]

An independent audit by PricewaterhouseCoopers in 1998 revealed that Alphatec, once a star on Thailand's stock exchange, overstated profits by at least $164 million between 1994 and April 1997, a period when the audit report says the company should have been reporting significant losses. Revenue was said to

---

[18] Eleena DeLisser, "Rent-Way Probes Accounting, May Restate Its Results," *The Wall Street Journal,* October 31, 2000, A6.

[19] Ibid.

[20] BBC News, "Police Raid Mitsubishi Headquarters," August 28, 2000. [online].

be six to ten times as high as it actually was, according to employees familiar with Alphatec's true numbers. PricewaterhouseCoopers also found the firm had transferred at least $160 million of corporate funds to companies controlled by the CEO, without board approval. And PricewaterhouseCoopers discovered Alphatec maintained two sets of widely divergent accounting books. How such questionable dealings have brought Thailand's preeminent high-tech company to rock bottom is a parable to the supremacy of accounting standards or, depending on one's viewpoint, a testimonial to the decay of business ethics.

Core earnings have always served as a key benchmark of corporate well-being. Alphatec had a choice—report transparent, real earnings—but the firm worked with an agenda that went far beyond straightforward revenue/expense disclosure. Worse still, management thought they could get away with it. While numbers tweaking has been around for ages, some firms metamorphose profits into a new art form. Let the banker beware—accounting opaqueness is no friend of prudence.

As *The Wall Street Journal* noted, "Mutual fund investors know NAV as the abbreviation for the daily Net Asset Value at which fund shares are bought and sold. But there are some cases where it might seem to stand for Not Accurately Valued."[21] Oftentimes, the securities being valued are not very liquid—that is, they may have low trading volumes and limited investor interest. Sometimes, the securities are not traded, such as private company stock, syndicated bank loans, and high-yield, unrated municipal bonds. Therefore, the price assigned to them may be somewhat arbitrary. As an example, *The Wall Street Journal* noted that "Heartland High-Yield Municipal Bond Fund and Heartland Short Duration High-Yield Municipal Fund tumbled 70% and 44%, respectively, in a single day when the funds slashed the values at which they were carrying certain bonds in the portfolios."[22]

A routine review of director loans conducted during a federal bank examination of a relatively small savings bank revealed a pyramiding scheme whereby the bank was making additional interest-only loans to an affiliated person who was never required to pay down principal. When the interest payments were becoming past due, the bank would issue another interest-only loan, the proceeds of which paid the past due payments on other loans. Specifically, the initial loan review revealed satisfactory underwriting and documentation. In fact, it was the thorough documentation that revealed the use of the proceeds. Included in the loan closing documents was a bank ticket indicating a credit to another bank account. Upon further investigation, it was discovered that the other account was another interest-only loan with the same borrower that was in arrears. Essentially, the bank was issuing new loans to this director to pay the interest payments of this borrower's other loans that had fallen into delinquency.

---

[21] Karen Damato, "Subtle Fund Peril: The Fuzzy NAV," *The Wall Street Journal,* October 27, 2000, C1.
[22] Ibid.

During an internal audit of a money center bank, auditors discovered a disguised or misnamed account with a debit balance. Some unclaimed corporate actions were diverted into this account, as opposed to the proper unclaimed dividends account, for example. Interestingly, the manager of the unit did not create this scheme to directly gain financially. Instead, this maneuver was crafted as a slush fund that would be used if the unit mistakenly missed a corporate action. In other words, since the unit missed the corporate action and its client was due money, the client would be paid from this fund instead of by the issuer.

In 1998, Waste Management's financial reporting forced the corporation to restate its earnings retroactive to 1992. The adjustments included a $3.5 billion pre-tax charge. The accounting gimmicks involved overstating earnings by inflating the value of trucks, recycling facilities, hazardous waste plants, engineering operations, and landfills.

WorldCom's CFO used an aberrant technique to account for charges paid to local telephone networks to complete calls. According to WorldCom, the company transferred more than $3.8 billion in "line cost" fees to its capital accounts. However, line costs consisted principally of access and transport charges and should have been charged to operating expenses in the year incurred. One of accounting's most basic rules is that capital costs must be connected to long-term investments, the purchase of a building, for example. In other words, expenditures are classified as capital costs only if assets purchased increase future revenues (every child knows the difference between daddy painting the house and daddy buying a new house). WorldCom's Herculean accounting shenanigan provided billions of dollars to the income statement, effectively turning a fiscal 2001 loss and the first quarter, 2002 into a profit (WorldCom Group's fiscal 2001 profits were $2.3 billion). The inevitable financial restatement will be one of the largest in corporate history—six times that of Enron Corp.

DUBIOUS ACCOUNTING: ENRON CORPORATION 2001 [23]

On December 2, 2001, Enron Corporation, the energy trading giant based in Houston, Texas, filed for the largest Chapter 11 bankruptcy in U.S. history. The events that led up to the bankruptcy, which appeared to have happened in a mere six weeks, capped a tumultuous plummet of Enron's shares and sent its creditors and trading counterparties into a financial panic. How could the seventh largest U.S. company in 2000, with revenues of more than $100 billion and assets of $61.7 billion, disintegrate so rapidly following its third quarter earnings statement on October 16, 2001?

[23] The author wishes to thank Edward A. Feltmann for authoring this section. Mr. Feltmann is a credit officer for Bayerische Landesbank assigned to U.S. Utilities. Submitted with permission.

To recap, on October 16, 2001 Enron announced that it would take a $1.01 billion in after-tax nonrecurring charge to its third quarter earnings to recognize asset impairments in its water and waste water service unit, restructuring costs in its broadband services, and losses associated with other investments including a retail energy service. These charges occurred in ventures outside its core businesses in wholesale energy and transportation and distribution services. The $644 million net loss Enron took for the quarter was its first reported quarterly loss since the second quarter of 1997. In a conference call from the company on October 16, Enron also revealed that it would declare a reduction to shareholder equity of $1.2 billion related to the company's repurchase of its common stock. This repurchase was tied to the performance of several special-purpose entities operated by the private investment limited partnership, LJM2 Co-Investment, L.P. (LJM2). LJM2 was formed in December 1999 and was managed until July 2001 by Enron's CFO, Andrew Fastow. On October 22, the Securities and Exchange Commission (SEC) began an investigation of these transactions. Following an overwhelming loss of investor confidence in the company, Fastow was fired on October 24. Enron's share price declined over 80% for the year by the end of October.

Prompted by SEC inquiry, Enron filed a Form 8-K to the commission on November 8, revealing that it would restate its financial statements from 1997 to the first two quarters of 2001 with net reductions totaling $569 million for the four and one-half years—roughly 16% of its net income over the period. Enron also announced that accounting irregularities had occurred in previous financial periods, and as a result three unconsolidated special-purpose entities (SPEs including LJM2) should have been consolidated in the financial statements pursuant to U.S. GAAP. During the initial capitalization and later in ongoing transactions with the SPEs, Enron issued its own common stock in exchange for notes receivable. The company then erroneously increased both notes receivable and shareholder's equity on its balance sheet in recognition of these transactions. However, GAAP requires that notes receivable culminating from transactions containing a company's capital stock be presented as deductions from stockholder's equity and not as assets,[24] which is not how Enron and its auditor, Arthur Andersen, had booked the transactions. These overstatements happened twice, resulting in $1 billion in overstated shareholder's equity, and combined with a purchase of a limited partnership's equity interest in an SPE in the third quarter of 2001 that reduced equity an additional $200 million, resulting in the $1.2 billion total reduction in shareholders' equity.

Characteristic of the firm in its prime, during which little of the company's complex financial maneuvers were adequately explained, minimal information was provided in Enron's public financial statements to indicate to investors and lenders the loss potential connected to the extensive portfolio of SPEs. Buried in

---

[24] EITF Issue No. 85-1, "Classifying Notes Received for Capital Stock," and SEC Staff Accounting Bulletin No. 40, Topic 4-E, "Receivables from the Sale of Stock."

the footnotes of the 1999 annual report under "Related Party Transactions" (which is destined to become a highly popular section to be read by energy-sector credit analysts interested in job security) is mention of the company's transactions with LJM2 partnership, that a senior member of Enron was a managing member of LJM2, and that transactions with the partnership involve Enron common stock going to the partnership in return for notes receivable. The partnership was mentioned again in the footnotes of quarterly statements and in the 2000 annual report, but few details were disclosed about the vehicles and the complicated transactions behind them. Because LJM2 and other Enron SPEs, like JEDI and Chewco, were considered off-balance sheet entities, extensive financial information did not have to appear in the financial statements of Enron. Among the steps to satisfy GAAP requirements for off-balance sheet treatment of the partnerships, at least 3% of the company's capital had to be contributed by outside investors; while this was originally considered to be achieved, evidently this was not the case. It was not until the filing of the 8-K on November 8, 2001, that Enron and its auditor, Arthur Andersen, determined that three unconsolidated entities were mishandled in previous financial statements and should have been consolidated. The extent of the losses associated with these vehicles and the full scope of financing Enron used in off-balance sheet transactions were effectively obscured to the outside lending community until this disclosure. Meanwhile, the energy company's on-balance sheet levels of debt, debt-to-equity, and interest expense coverage ratios did not look noticeably unhealthy before the third quarter of 2001.

Not only has Enron's accounting practices come under serious scrutiny following its meltdown, but Andersen's reputation was considerably challenged as well. Serving as Enron's auditors since 1985, Andersen, one of the Big Five auditing firms, stood by the financial reports of its client until November's restatements. Of particular interest from an accounting standpoint is Andersen's treatment of Enron's off-balance sheet entities and its mark-to-market accounting practices on its energy-trading contracts. Briefly, mark-to-market accounting on energy-trading contracts (whether forwards or spot-market transactions) allows companies to include earnings in current periods for contracts that have yet to be settled. Currently, GAAP does not specify how to derive the fair value of these contracts and allows energy companies ample discretion in calculating their value. Enron required substantial liquidity and an investment-grade credit rating to maintain its energy-trading operations. Much of the liquidity was obtained from lenders satisfied with its impressive revenues and seemingly healthy levels of reported debt. Thus, the treatment of its off-balance sheet debts and mark-to-marketing practices on its trading contracts were critical to the operations of the energy company. Given the extent (Enron had more than 100 off-balance sheet partnerships) and complexity of off-balance sheet activities at Enron, it may prove that Andersen was not capable of accurately and thoroughly auditing all the transactions that Enron conducted. In addition, the method of the mark-to-market accounting used by Enron, a firm that attributed over 90% of its earnings in 2000 to energy trading, had a major bearing on the impression of Enron's strong operating performance. Andersen's treatment of these issues and the financial data provided by its client call into question the value of Enron's financial statements that were critical to lending decisions. Ongoing disclosures of knowledge of accounting improprieties at Enron and the destruction of Enron documents did not bode well for Andersen's efforts to maintain its own credibility and financial health as well as bolstering evidence to the increasing use of creative accounting at major U.S. corporations in recent years.

Even after taking a $1.01 billion after-tax nonrecurring charge to its third quarter earnings and restating earnings from previous quarters, Enron's quarterly 10-Q reports suggested that the firm still made a profit through the first nine months of 2001. The company's problems with corporate governance, aggressiveness in its investments outside of its core operations, and even its explosive revenue growth, among other things, were strong indications for lenders to Enron of the increased risks involved in transactions with the company. It stands now, along with the WorldCom debacle, as one of the greatest lessons in U.S. history to bankers and many other financial participants.

CHAPTER SUMMARY: THE TIE BETWEEN BANKERS AND AUDITORS

In spite of the development of the accounting profession internationally, there appears to be a lack of uniformity in both training and experience. Those who rely on certificates of auditing firms must know more about the firms performing audits, meaning the license the individual auditor or firm holds and the requirements necessary to obtain the license. If this is not enough, even the professional organizations of CPAs do not claim equivalence of competence for respective members—the same can be said for professional organizations of lawyers or doctors.

How then does a lender judge the auditor? The best call is by relying on (1) an objective appraisal that comes with a banker's knowledge of the requirements the auditor has met in securing his or her professional title and (2) a subjective appraisal through personal knowledge and reputation. This usually requires the lenders to have a personal acquaintance with the auditor. These direct dealings may occur through discussions relative to specific borrowers' financial statements, bank reference (CPA files)[25] files denoting experience with different auditors, discussion with other bankers who have knowledge of the particular auditor's work, and the local or national reputation of the auditor. In any case, bankers should judge auditors against the highest standards of the profession, and auditors should meet the following requirements:

[25] Data mining software is a wonderful tool with which to accumulate CPA experience via a CPA central file. The accounting shenanigans Howard Schilit so expertly defines can accrue on the bank's Intranet system in real time—a record of discredit exposed to the entire lending cadre.

- Possession of the CPA certificate
- Membership in state and national associations
- Interest in the profession implied by active participation in professional organizations

It is impossible, of course, to document every area in which differences of interpretation or disagreement in opinions can arise between the banking and accounting professions. After all, financial reports are dynamic, breathing documents. Because good audits are precursive to credit and breathes life into the banking profession, the arts of credit and accounting operate as sides of the same coin in much the same way as pharmaceuticals relate to the art of doctoring. Most loan officials do not view financial statements as inanimate, repetitive, or detached objects. As for the rest, these bankers have only themselves to blame when their deals hit fire and the Office of the Comptroller of the Currency uses its authority to close up their shop.

REVIEW QUESTIONS

1. What is the meaning of *qualified audit*? Name some events that might result in opinions other than the standard short form.
2. Describe the accounting standards for revenue recognition. Explain the principle that should be followed to match the appropriate costs against revenue.
3. What kind of information should a banker seek in the contingency section or notes? Is it possible to assess the probability that those contingencies materialize?
4. How does a lender judge the auditor? Name three of the standards you would expect your auditor to fulfill.
5. Financial reports are expected to present fairly, clearly, and completely the borrower's economic, financial, and operating condition. To what extent is the auditor responsible for the accuracy of the financial statements in the case of an audit, a qualified audit, and a compilation?
6. Regarding the Sunbeam case—specifically the changes in and disagreements with accountants on financial disclosure, how did the company's internal control over misstatements in financial statements affect the findings of Arthur Andersen, Deloitte & Touche, and lastly the SEC?
7. Give key examples of information found in the footnotes of financial statements. What is the significance of such material?
8. Why would a change in auditors or examples of creative accounting be considered a red flag? What do such flags suggest about a company's current situation?

9. Many companies try to manipulate their performance ratios by securitizing their assets in an effort to get them off the balance sheet. How might such actions negatively affect the firm?

SELECTED REFERENCES AND READINGS

Alexander, D., and S. Archer (1995). *European accounting guide*. San Diego, CA: Harcourt Brace.

American Institute of Certified Public Accountants. (1986). *Other comprehensive bases of accounting*. New York: American Institute of Certified Public Accountants.

Berton, L., and J. B. Schiff. (1990). *The Wall Street Journal on accounting*. Homewood, IL: Dow Jones-Irwin.

Carey, J. L., and W. O. Doherty. (1966). *Ethical standards of the accounting profession*. New York: American Institute of Certified Public Accountants.

Centre on Transnational Corporations (United Nations). Intergovernmental Working Group of Experts on International Standards of Accounting and Reporting and United Nations Conference on Trade and Development. (1994). *Conclusions on accounting and reporting by transnational corporations*. New York: United Nations.

Choi, F. D. S. (1991). *Handbook of international accounting*. New York: Wiley.

Choi, F. D. S. (1997). *International accounting and finance handbook*. New York: Wiley.

Chorafas, D. N. (2000). *Reliable financial reporting and internal control: A global implementation guide*. New York: Wiley.

Contact Committee on the Accounting Directives (European Commission). (1996). *An examination of the conformity between the International Accounting Standards and the European Accounting Directives*. Luxembourg, Lanham, MD: Office for Official Publications of the European Communities; UNIPUB <distributor>.

Gore, P. (1992). *The FASB conceptual framework project, 1973–1985: An analysis*. Manchester, UK; New York: Manchester University Press. Distributed exclusively in the USA and Canada by St. Martin's Press.

International Accounting Standards Committee. (2000). *International accounting standards explained*. New York: Wiley.

Ma, R. (1997). *Financial reporting in the Pacific Asia region*. Singapore; River Edge, NJ: World Scientific: Singapore Institute of Management.

Miller, M. A. (1999). *Miller GAAP implementation manual*. San Diego, CA: Harcourt Brace Professional.

Miller, M. A. (2000). *Miller international accounting standards guide*. San Diego, CA: Harcourt Brace Professional.

Miller, M. A., and L. P. Bailey. (1994). *Miller GAAS guide*. San Diego, CA: Harcourt Brace Professional.

Mueller, G. G., H. M. Gernon, and G. K Meek. (1994). *Accounting: An international perspective*. Burr Ridge, IL: Business One Irwin.

Nobes, C. (1999). *International accounting and comparative financial reporting: Selected essays of Christopher Nobes*. Cheltenham, UK; Northampton, MA: Edward Elgar.

Ordelheide, D., and KPMG International. (2001). *TRANSACC: Transnational accounting*. Hampshire, England; New York: Palgrave.

Riahi-Belkaoui, A. (1998). *Critical financial accounting problems: Issues and solutions*. Westport, CT.: Quorum.

Schilit, H. (1993). *Financial shenanigans*. New York: McGraw-Hill

United States Federal Accounting Standards Advisory Board and United States Office of Management and Budget. (1993). *Accounting for inventory and related property*. Washington,

DC: Executive Office of the President Office of Management and Budget. For sale by the U.S. G.P.O. Supt. of Docs.

United States Federal Accounting Standards Advisory Board and United States Office of Management and Budget. (1996). *Accounting for revenue and other financing sources and concepts for reconciling budgetary and financial accounting.* Washington, DC, Executive Office of the President, Office of Management and Budget. For sale by the U.S. G.P.O. Supt. of Docs.

United States Office of Management and Budget. (1998). *Amendments to accounting for property, plant, and equipment: Definitional changes, amending SFFAS no. 6 and SFFAS no. 8, Accounting for property, plant, and equipment and supplementary stewardship reporting.* Washington, DC: The Office of Management and Budget: For sale by the U.S. G.P.O. Supt. of Docs.

Van Riper, R. (1994). *Setting standards for financial reporting: FASB and the struggle for control of a critical process.* Westport, CT: Quorum Books.

Wallace, R. S. O. (1995). Research in accounting in emerging economies (Vol. 3). Greenwich, CT: JAI Press.

SELECT INTERNET LIBRARY AND CD

Basel Committee on Banking Supervision, Bank for International Settlements, Ch-4002, 7 April 2000

Basel Committee review of international accounting standards

The growing interdependence of international financial and banking markets necessitates transparent and comparable published financial statements.

http://www.bis.org/press/p000407.htm

International Accounting Standards Board, Standards and Interpretations

IASC publishes its standards in a series of pronouncements called International Accounting Standards (often abbreviated IAS). Standards are numbered sequentially IAS 1, IAS 2, etc.

http://www.iasc.org.uk/frame/cen2.htm

Financial Accounting Standards Board

Mission is to establish and improve standards of financial accounting and reporting for the guidance and education of the public, including issuers, auditors, and users of financial information.

http://accounting.rutgers.edu/raw/fasb/

US Security Exchange Commission Accounting Archives

http://www.sec.gov/cgi-bin/srch-edgar?accounting

APPENDIX **2.1**

A REVIEW OF ELEMENTAL FINANCIAL STATEMENTS

A financial statement is a "picture," and most financial analysts frequently refer to it as such. If the analogy is pursued further, the balance sheet may be referred to as a "still picture," in that it "freezes" a moving process or business phenomenon at a stated place and at a stated time. By the same token, a wise person noted, the profit-and-loss statement may be likened to a "motion picture," intended to show business history in the making and between balance sheet dates. The still shots, set up side by side, may be thought of as portraying the condition of a given business at stated intervals. However, taking a picture of little Felise only on her birthdays will not explain such developments as physical growth, changes in features, or personality changes. Sole reliance on the snapshots will cause the observer to miss such occurrences as Felise's summer at the beach or the time when a tendency toward Mozart first occurred. Aside from general knowledge as to how well or poorly she was eating in that period, such changes in little Felise could not accurately be accounted for except through a "motion picture" record of the whole period. Furthermore, when Felise is seen riding her bike, whistling with her hands in her pockets, crying over an injury, or winning all the games in the neighborhood, she will become something real, vital, and functional; and the observer's attitude toward her, because of increased familiarity with her activities and interest in them, becomes greatly enlivened.

Since ratio, cash flow and projection analysis employs financial data taken from the firm's financial statements, it is helpful to begin with a review of these accounting reports. For illustrative purposes, we shall use data taken the financial statements of Trudy Patterns Inc., a case study developed further in Chapter 3.

Sections of the financial statements are highlighted in Exhibit I:

EXHIBIT I   **Trudy Patterns, Inc. Company Balance Sheet Year Ended December 31 ($ thousands)**

Assets		1998	1999	2000
1.	**Current assets**			
2.	Cash and cash items	$15,445	$12,007	$11,717
3.	Accounts and notes receivable, net	$51,793	$55,886	$88,571
4.	Inventories	$56,801	$99,087	$139,976
5.	**Current assets**	**$124,039**	**$166,980**	**$240,264**
6.	Property, plant, and equipment	$53,282	$60,301	$68,621
7.	Accumulated depreciation	$(8,989)	$(13,961)	$(20,081)
8.	**Net fixed assets**	**$44,294**	**$46,340**	**$48,539**
9.	**Total assets**	**$168,333**	**$213,320**	**$288,803**

Liabilities and equities		1998	1999	2000
10.	**Current liabilities**			
11.	Short-term loans	$10,062	$15,800	$55,198
12.	Accounts payable	$20,292	$31,518	$59,995
13.	Accruals	$10,328	$15,300	$21,994
14.	**Current liabilities**	**$40,682**	**$62,618**	**$137,187**
15.	Long-term bank loans	$19,125	$28,688	$28,688
16.	Mortgage	$8,606	$7,803	$7,018
17.	**Long-term debt**	**$27,731**	**$36,491**	**$35,706**
18.	**Total liabilities**	**$68,413**	**$99,109**	**$172,893**
19.	Common stock (no par value)	$69,807	$69,807	$69,807
20.	Retained earnings	$30,113	$44,404	$46,103
21.	Stockholders' equity	**$99,920**	**$114,211**	**$115,910**
22.	**Total liabilities and equity**	**$168,333**	**$213,320**	**$288,803**

TRUDY'S BALANCE SHEET

The balance sheet is a statement of assets, liabilities, and stockholders' equity at the close of business on the date indicated. The balance sheet represents a given point in time in a company's life cycle. Divided into two sides, the left side of the balance sheet represents all items owned by the business that have a monetary value. The right side reports liabilities and equity, which represent the claims of the creditors and owners (stockholders) against the firm's assets. Both sides must always be in balance. Since the claims of creditors take preference over those of owners or stockholders, the interest of the latter is determined by subtracting the liabilities from the assets. Another common way of stating the balance sheet equation, therefore, is assets minus liabilities equals stockholder's equity $(A - L = E)$.

Assets

Current assets represent cash and other assets or resources, which are reasonably expected to be realized in cash or sold or consumed during the normal operating, cycle of the business, typically less than one year. These assets are mostly working assets in the sense that they are in a constant cycle of being converted into cash. Inventories, when sold on credit terms, convert into accounts receivable; receivables when collected, turn into cash; cash is then used to pay the supplier or bank debt that financed the inventory and production costs that began the operating cycle.

5. Current assets	$240,264

Cash and Cash Items

Cash represents bills and coins in the till and on deposit at the bank. Cash and marketable securities should be combined, since marketable securities represents near transaction cash rather than term investments. If Trudy had disclosed restricted cash, the bank's computer would have footnoted the item or listed it separately. Examples of restricted cash include cash held in a collateral trust account or cash held by a foreign subsidiary not available to pay the firm's debt. The inclusion of funds other than those freely available for withdrawal to meet current obligations results in an overstatement of both the working capital and current ratio position of the company. It is also important to note that cash transferred into the United States from foreign subsidiaries may also be subject to a heavy foreign tax.

2. Cash and cash items	$11,717

Accounts Receivable

Receivables represent amounts due from trade customers within the period of one year or less on open accounts known to be collectible. Customers are usually granted credit terms of generally 30 days in which to pay for their purchases. The amount due from customers of Trudy Patterns is gross $98,210. However, some of Trudy's customers will fail to pay. To reflect expected receipts, the total is net, after a provision for doubtful accounts. Failure to exclude bad debt and to provide for an adequate allowance for doubtful accounts and notes receivable overstates assets and current earnings.

Notes receivable represent a contingency until honored by the maker at the date of maturity. Trudy may be able to discount its notes at the bank. Since the endorser is liable if the maker refuses payment at maturity, disclosure of this information will help you appraise the current asset position of the company and its ability to pay short-term debt. If Trudy's balance sheet had listed "Receivables from Affiliates, Officers, or Subsidiaries," the bank would have considered these amounts as noncurrent assets. Advances to subsidiaries or management may represent funds transferred out of the core business.

3. Accounts and notes receivable net	$88,571

Inventories

Inventory represents assets held for sale in the ordinary course of business. Inventory consists of raw materials used in production, work in process, goods in process of manufacture, and finished goods ready for shipment. Inventory is normally reflected in the financial statements at the lower of cost or market. The general tendency in times of rising prices is for inventory values on the balance sheet to be less than replacement costs. We should break out Inventory components that are material or change significantly.

4. Inventories	$139,976

Property, Plant, and Equipment

Property, plant, and equipment represent assets not intended for sale over the normal course of business. However, these assets are considered essential to the production, distribution, or warehousing activities of the company. This asset category includes land, buildings, structures, machinery, and equipment. These items are shown at aggregate cost under a single figure with a single aggregate deduction of allowances for depreciation and depletion.

6. Property, plant, and equipment	$68,621
7. Less: Accumulated depreciation	$(20,081)
8. Net fixed assets	$48,539

All of these items added together produce the figure listed on Trudy Pattern's balance sheet as total assets.

9. Total assets	$288,803

Liabilities and Equities

Current liabilities include all obligations that are owed within one year. The classification is intended to include obligations for items that have been entered into during the operating cycle. Examples include payables incurred for the purchase of materials and supplies or in providing services to be offered for sale; and debts, which arise from operations directly, related the operating cycle, such as wages incurred but not yet paid. Other current liabilities, whose ordinary liquidation is expected to occur within a year, include short-term debt and current maturities of long-term obligations.

14. Current liabilities	$137,187

Short-Term Loans

Short-term credit in the form of bank loans, for example, may be either unsecured or secured. Unsecured debt includes all debt whose "security" is the cash-generating ability of the firm.

11. Short-term debt	$55,198

Accounts Payable

Accounts payable are incurred when a firm like Trudy purchases goods or services on credit from suppliers. It is analogous to a charge account for a consumer. By accepting cash payments at some future date rather than immediately following the sale, the supplier assumes the role of a lender. Nearly every firm uses trade credit to finance inventory.

12. Accounts-payable	$59,995

Accruals

The firm also owes salaries and wages, interest on funds borrowed, fees to accountants and attorneys, pension contributions, insurance premiums, and similar items. To the extent that the amounts owed and not recorded on the books are unpaid at the financial statement date, these items are grouped as a total under accruals. Income tax payable is usually stated separately because of the amount and importance of the tax factor.

13. Accruals	$21,994

Long-Term Liabilities

The category "long-term liabilities" is used to include all obligations not classified as current. The most important items included are notes and bonds payable with maturities of over one year. Notes and bonds are normally valued at face value. Of all the methods by which to raise long-term capital, long-term debt is the most widely used.

17. Long-term debt	$35,706

Long-Term Bank Loans

Long term obligations must be retired after the current fiscal year. Such obligations may include bonds that are outstanding and long-term bank loans. In the financial statements, a breakdown of the various debt issues may be footnoted after the body of the financial statement. If subordinated debt appeared on the company's financials, the bank's computer would include it under capital funds. Subordinated debt is junior to senior creditors in the event of asset liquidation.

15. Long-term bank loans	$28,688
16. Mortgage	$7,018

Stockholder's Equity

21. Stockholders equity	$115,910

Common Stock

All corporations issue common stock. It is the first security to be issued and the last to be retired. Common stock represents the chief ownership of the company and has the greatest voting rights. Common stockholders have the last claim on earnings, since all other claims must be paid first. Trudy's common stockholders also stand to benefit the most from the success and profits reported by the firm; other stakeholders, such as bond holders, have fixed claims and do not participate in earnings over and above such claims.

19. Common stock	$69,807

Retained Earnings

Retained earnings delineate profits, income, and various adjustments from the date of incorporation after deducting dividends and transfers to capital stock accounts. Retained earnings accumulate as the firm earns profits and reinvests profits into productive assets.

20. Retained earnings: Beginning balance	$44,404
34. Net income for the year	$1965
35. Less: All dividends	$(266)
20. Retained earnings: Ending balance	$46,103

EXHIBIT II   Trudy Patterns Inc. Income Statement Year Ended December 31 ($ millions)

		1998	1999	2000
23.	Net sales	$512,693	$553,675	$586,895

24.	Cost of goods sold	$405,803	$450,394	$499,928
25.	**Gross profit**	**$106,889**	**$103,281**	**$86,967**
	Cost and expenses:			
26.	Selling, administration, and general expenses	$38,369	$46,034	$50,643
27.	Depreciation	$4,781	$4,973	$6,120
28.	Miscellaneous expenses	$6,082	$10,672	$17,174
29.	**Total costs and expenses**	**$49,233**	**$61,678**	**$73,937**
30.	**Earnings before interest and taxes (ebit)**	**$57,658**	**$41,602**	**$13,030**
	Less interest expense:			
	Interest on short-term loans	$956	$1,683	$5,470
	Interest on long-term loans	$1,913	$2,869	$2,869
	Interest on mortgage	$779	$707	$636
31.	Total interest expense	$3,648	$5,258	$8,974
32.	**Earnings before taxes**	**$54,010**	**$36,343**	**$4,056**
33.	Income taxes	$26,068	$17,589	$2,091
34.	**Net income**	**$27,943**	**$18,754**	**$1,965**
35.	Dividends on stock	$7,062	$4,463	$266
36.	Additions to retained earnings	$20,883	$14,291	$1,699

THE INCOME STATEMENT

Net Sales

The first item on the income statement (Exhibit II) is usually gross sales or operating revenues. If other sources than sales of merchandise are important (such as commissions earned or rents received), disclosure of the amount from each of these sources is essential (10% or more of the combined total for either source is considered significant under Rule 5-03 of Regulation SX of the Securities and Exchange Commission). Lenders usually distinguish between sales and extraneous income like interest income, equity earnings, and other revenue not related to the primary business.

23. Net sales	$586,895

Cost of Goods Sold

In a manufacturing company such as Trudy Patterns, the cost of goods sold represents costs involved in manufacturing; these costs are key to the company's operation. Production costs consists of raw material, labor and overhead. Overhead costs, while not traceable to finished goods, are usually significant and need to be controlled. Examples of overhead costs are plant rent, depreciation, maintenance, and repairs. A reasonably detailed disclosure of the composition of cost of goods sold, including opening and closing inventories, together with an explanation of the basis used in inventory valuation is essential to any revealing analysis of the production cycle. A rapid rate of change in cost of goods sold relative to sales means that production costs cannot be passed along to consumers, and thus the firm faces a structural problem in its operations.

24. Cost of goods sold	$499,928
25. Gross profit	$86,967

Cost and Expenses: Selling, Administration, and General Expenses

For the most part, these expenses are controllable and may vary with the level of gross sales (variable expenses) or be a fixed component regardless of sales levels. Selling expenses include salaries and other expenses of the sales department. General and administrative expenses include salaries of Trudy's officers and other administrative employees, research and development costs, insurance, and rent allocated to operations.

26. Selling, administration, and general expenses	$50,643
28. Miscellaneous expenses	$17,174
27. Depreciation	$6,120
29. Total costs and expenses	$73,937

Earnings before Interest and Taxes (EBIT)

Earnings before interest and taxes (EBIT) is a measure of the strength of the firm's operations, or the cash generated from operations. Cash generated from operations includes earnings, as well as other noncash expenses such as depreciation.

30. EBIT	$13,030

Less Interest Expense

Interest expense is the cost for borrowed funds, whether the borrowing is for short-term or long-term purposes. Borrowing funds to finance the company's operations or capital purchases imposes a burden on the company, as the loan plus interest on the borrowed funds will need to be repaid from cash generated from operations.

Interest on short-term loans	$5,471
Interest on long-term loans	$2,869
Interest on mortgage	$636
31. Total interest expense	$8,975
32. Earnings before taxes	$4,056

Income Taxes

Corporations are taxed at the federal and in some cases the state and local levels on the profits they earn. U.S. corporations must pay a tax on their earnings at a statutory rate of 34% of their pretax profit.

33. Income taxes $2,091

Net Income

Net income is the profit generated by the company's selling activities less all applicable expenses for production, sales expense, general and administrative expenses, interest, and taxes.

34. Net income   . $1,965

3

MULTIVARIATE RATIO ANALYSIS

A Banker's Guide

INTRODUCTION AND OVERVIEW

Ratios were originally developed at the turn of the twentieth century from credit relationships businesses had with each other and with lenders. When the first comprehensive system of ratio analysis was introduced in 1919, it was totally from the creditor's viewpoint. Ratio analysis helps creditors evaluate a company's financial strengths and weakness, flagging any irregularities that may affect repayment of debt. For purposes of examining potential credit serviceability today, financial managers analyze internal operations in much the same way. But ratios don't tell the whole story; they offer clues, not direct answers. It is unreasonable to expect that the mechanical calculation of one ratio or a group of ratios will automatically yield critical information about a complex corporation. Bankers must interpret, compare, and look behind the numbers in order to form conclusions about a company's well-being.

Ratios serve as relative measures or interactions between numbers. They are used to (1) clarify the relationship between accounts or items appearing on financial reports (structural analysis), (2) match borrowers' performance against historical levels (time-series analysis), and (3) compare performance with benchmarks or industry averages (cross-sectional analysis). Ratios simplify absolute numbers down to a common scale. For example, a borrower may have expanded markets over the past few periods, so comparing gross profit, an absolute number, to historical levels will not be particularly useful. On the other hand, ratios eliminate the problem of trying to extract meaning through a vacuum of absolute numbers—gross profit, debt level, or, for that matter, revenue.

These are the basic tools to measure the size, trend, and quality of a company's financial statements and cash flow, as well as the extent and nature of their liabilities. We can use these tools to track a firm's historical performance, evaluate its present position, and obtain a relative value to compare with industry averages. Does the company earn a fair return? Can it withstand downturns? Does it have the financial flexibility to attract additional creditors and investors? Is management adroit in its efforts to upgrade weak operations, reinforce strong ones, pursue profitable opportunities, and push the value of common stock to the highest possible levels?

Limitations of Ratios

Ratios are not perfect. Time-series and cross-sectional analyses may be distorted by inflation or an unusual business climate. Time-series analysis tends to be distorted more by inflation than cross-sectional comparisons because all observations in a cross-sectional analysis is made in the same time period, with the same resource price structure. The banker's problem is to determine the nature of bias and, most important, the adjustments needed to make ratios generally more meaningful. Furthermore, because financial statements are routinely prepared for special purposes, such as reports to shareholders and bankers, financials may be more liberal than realistic. The bank's overall assessment of even the most detailed financial reports is important and should be standard practice before the first ratio is calculated.

Indeed, the application of ratio analysis necessitates comparable results between the standard and the ratio itself in order for the information to be usable. While reading this chapter, the following considerations should be kept in mind:

1. The ratios in this chapter apply to manufacturers, wholesalers, retailers, and service companies. We use different ratios to analyze banks, utilities, insurance, and finance companies. Divergent asset quality and capital structure make it necessary to employ other ratios.
2. Ratios concentrate on the past.
3. Some firms window-dress their financial statements to make them look better for credit analysts. For example, recently one firm sold its corporate aircraft for cash just before issuing a quarterly statement.
4. Benchmarks or industry leaders are better targets for high-level performance. The idea is to match customers against the solid performers—the average is not necessarily good.

5. Lack of quality and availability of data diminish the usefulness of ratios.
6. Ratios come from raw numbers derived from accounting data. International Accounting Standards (IAS) along with generally accepted accounting principles (GAAP), as we saw applied in the previous chapter, allow flexibility and, therefore, varied interpretation. It's more fact than fiction that differing accounting methods distort inter-company comparisons so banks should consider the impact of applying different methods for the following conditions:
   a. *Revenue recognition.* Certain types of companies, for example, contractors, may recognize revenue on a percentage of completion method for major projects to closely match the timing of costs and profits earned.
   b. *Inventory valuation.* Last in first out (LIFO) versus first in first out (FIFO).
   c. *Depreciation.* Even under GAAP, there is considerable latitude for depreciation schedules for various asset classes. Firms with large capital equipment requirements may benefit from accelerating depreciation to minimize taxes.
   d. *Bad debts.* Although GAAP requires that companies establish a reserve account or provision for doubtful accounts, there is room for interpretation on what percentage of problem accounts should be recognized or when a bad debt should be charged off. A good example of this was the banking industry in 1991. Federal regulators viewed the banks as under-reserved with respect to potential problem loans, particularly in real estate. The regulators encouraged banks to make huge additions to their reserves, resulting in large losses for the banks.
   e. *Capitalization of costs.* GAAP allows computer software companies to capitalize certain developmental costs over the expected life of the software. This technique can significantly affect a company's perceived profitability and cash flow.
   f. *Pension fund costs.*
   g. *Cost versus equity accounting for investments.* How an investment (for example, in another company) is recognized on the balance sheet can greatly affect the financial statements. Investments at cost remain on the balance sheet at the lower of cost or market. Provided that the value of the investment does not depreciate below cost, there will be no change in the carrying value of the investment. Under the equity method of accounting for investments, the company is required to reflect its percentage share of the profit or losses from the investment in each period. Suppose company A owns 35% of company B. Company A is required to report 35% of

company B's profit or losses in each period on company A's financial statements, though these are noncash events to company A.

h. *Seasonality and different fiscal years.* These factors also hinder intercompany ratio analysis.

i. *Mergers and acquisitions.* Plans to divest subsidiaries or acquire new business units often have a material effect on future performance. Smart bankers ask for details and use information supplied by borrowers to construct pro forma consolidated statements as if the divestitures or acquisition occurred during the last fiscal period.

Peer Group or Industry Comparisons

Comparative ratio analysis can be extremely informative. However, under certain circumstances, we might question the validity of comparative ratios, especially when we compare ratios to industry norms without knowing the history of the firm. In addition, the analyst must keep in mind the performances of the rest of the industry and suitable industrial averages against which the firm will be benchmarked. We begin to question comparative ratio analysis when a firm's position or business cycle differs from that of the rest of the industry. This often creates an illusion of poor or exaggerated ratios. For example, a firm with a high current or quick ratio may be viewed as liquid (as having the ability to convert current assets into cash quickly and meet expenses) when in reality the high current ratio may be due to an inefficient use of resources.

Analysts might find it difficult to compare a diversified firm's financial statement to industry averages. This is because they are not really comparing "like numbers"; the firm's ratios may be composed of figures from many industries because of its varied operations. Before jumping to conclusions about quality, magnitude, and ratio trends, the analyst needs to judge each company individually using insightful benchmark matches and asking, is the ratio composed of the "right stuff"?

A comparison of IBM with Cray Research in the early 1990s, for example, would not have easily yielded accurate information. IBM was so much larger than Cray at the time that the two firms had separate and diverse financial statements, even though they were in the same industry. Or consider Electric Boat. Electric Boat had a few very expensive submarines listed on its balance sheet and could greatly influence comparisons if management disposed one submarine just before or after the end of a fiscal period.

The type of assets leads to different levels of quality in the ratios. R. J. Reynolds, with its diverse number of divisions and product lines, could easily fit this category. RKO owns radio and television stations, makes movies, bottles soda, runs hotels, and holds a large stake in an airline company. If only the total business income figure is available for this conglomerate, there is no way to tell from the consolidated data the extent to which the differing product lines contribute to profitability and risk.

In the highly volatile capital markets industry, we might find it hard to establish a meaningful set of comparative industry averages. The various methods of classifying assets and liabilities in this business with market volatility add up to a comparison quandary. Companies that specialize in niche markets and cater to specialized markets pose still another problem. The Concord Jet, for example was the sole company in its market, so there was no other firm against which to compare it.

Companies vary in size within an industry, which could distort ratios, and some firms may straddle more than one industry. Some industries, such as biotechnology, are extremely volatile. Similarly, each firm has diverse contingencies such as patents, litigation, licensing agreements, and joint ventures that affect comparisons. Additional problems arise with the use of industry averages. Norms only represent the center, and therefore the actual position of the company within its peer group is often not clear. For example, IBM has a large bearing on the benchmark.

Geographic differences can affect companies in the same industry. For example, how can you compare two home-building companies? One firm may do business on the East Coast, while the other may operate on the West Coast. Both firms are grouped together into one broad industry group: regional home builders. Because of differences in local economies, cultures, and demographics, the East Coast builder can have drastically different financial ratios compared to the West Coast builder.

Another problem surfaces when we analyze a youthful firm or industry. New businesses lack history, making it difficult to track historical trends. Dot-com firms, for example, are in their infancy. Another industry that comes to mind from the not-so-distant past is software. It was not long ago when this industry was small and developing. The space industry and research and development firms further illustrate the difficulty in establishing meaningful benchmark comparisons.

Different accounting practices sometimes distort ratio comparisons, such as FIFO versus LIFO, leasing versus financing, accounts receivable provisions, capitalized expenses, differing depreciation methods, and research and development costs accounting. Since comparative financial ratios are based on accounting numbers, the possibility of different firms, or even different divisions within a company, using different accounting methods can lead lenders down the wrong path. Sometimes ratios are calculated that do not reflect ongoing operations, which might confound lenders when they compare the net margin to industry averages. Also, some firms use different year-ends, and this practice may alter financials and distort comparisons. Another difficulty lies in comparing international firms or foreign-owned companies. How do their accounting methods differ from the generally accepted accounting principles used in the United States? What influences might government regulation have on these entities?

One area of benchmark comparisons where ratio analysis is simply not enough is the seasonal business. Because the flows and contractions of seasonal businesses do not always coincide, lenders might find it hard to peg an industry average. This will, of course, depend on whether the lender calculates ratios before or after the peak season.

The material size differences among firms might make it hard to canvass an industry and pick the right benchmarks. Large firms tend to operate efficiently because of economies of scale and their high operating leverage. For example, IBM functions more efficiently than small computer companies. Industry comparisons might be inaccurate, however, because IBM has a sizable bearing on the benchmark.

Comparative ratios are guides. Analysts decipher ratios using good judgment. When bankers work with ratio comparatives, they should ensure it is reasonable to rank two companies, the company to the industry, and one industry to another. There may be unique characteristics that would cause valid differences in the comparison, meaning the relationship manager should know enough about an industry to select the appropriate benchmark. Where possible, industry averages should be avoided in favor or specific benchmarks. If a lender feels uncomfortable with averages, he or she should at least check to see if the firm's ratios fall beyond one standard deviation of the median. Above all, lenders should talk to people familiar with the industry. Accountants, consultants, suppliers, and industry specialists provide first-rate information.

Ratio Trends

Are financial trends consistent with the past, or do ratios reveal an unreasonable departure from historical trends? Trends can be correlated using industry comparisons, thus helping to validate the financial strength of borrowers.

Loan officers can probably furnish more stories than they would like to admit on cases where loans went bad because nobody picked up on the trends. Here is one example: a seasonal amusement park operator who was historically cash rich during the tourist season needed to borrow in the off season to pay expenses. Patterns in the interim reports depicted the expansion and contraction process. A newly assigned account officer noticed that the company's loan was fully extended in the middle of August, and the account officer began to ask questions. The outcome: the borrower diverted cash normally used to repay the bank loan into a new fledgling enterprise and couldn't repay the credit line.

There are several categories of financial ratios: liquidity ratios, activity or performance ratios, leverage or capital structure ratios, profitability ratios, and growth and valuation ratios. Specific examples of each ratio are presented in the following case study of Trudy Patterns Inc.

CASE STUDY   Trudy Patterns Inc.

The loan officer at First Central Bank was recently alerted to the deteriorating financial position of their client, Trudy Patterns Inc. If any ratio falls significantly below the industry averages provided by *Robert Morris Associates Annual Statement Studies,* computers flag deficiencies and produce exception reports. Loan terms require that certain ratios be maintained at specified minimum levels. When the bank ran an analysis on Trudy Patterns three months ago, after receiving the December 31, 2000 fiscals (Exhibit II), the firm's banker noticed that key ratios continued to trend down, falling below industry averages. The banker sent a copy of the computer output to management, together with a note voicing concern.

Initial analysis indicated that problems were developing, but no ratio was below the level specified in the loan agreement between bank and borrower. However, the second analysis, which was based on the data given in Exhibit I, showed that the current ratio was below the 2.0 times specified in the loan agreement.

EXHIBIT I   Trudy Patterns Inc. Ratio Trends

Ratio	1998	1999	2000	Industry
Current ratio	3.05	2.67	1.75	2.50
Quick ratio	1.65	1.08	0.73	1.00
Average collection period	37 days	37 days	55 days	32 days
Inventory turnover	7.1x	4.5x	3.6x	5.7x
Fixed asset turnover	11.7x	12.0x	12.1x	12.1x
Working capital turnover	6.2x	5.3x	5.7x	4.5x
Total asset turnover	3.0x	2.5x	2.0x	2.8x
Average settlement period	18 days	26 days	44 days	35 days
Gross profit margin	19.9%	17.7%	14.8%	18.0%
Selling, general, and administration expenses	8.7%	10.2%	11.5%	9.3%
Net profit margin	5.5%	3.4%	0.4%	2.9%
Return on total assets	16.8%	8.9%	0.7%	8.8%
Return on net worth	28.3%	16.7%	1.7%	17.5%
Dividend payout rate	25.3%	23.8%	13.5%	7%
Debt ratio (debt/assets)	40.6%	46.5%	59.9%	50.0%
Times interest earned	15.8x	7.9x	1.4x	7.7x

The loan agreement specified that under these conditions the bank could call for immediate payment of the entire bank loan, and if payment was not forthcoming within 10 days, the bank could call the loan, forcing Trudy Patterns Inc. into bankruptcy. The banker had no intention of actually enforcing loan covenants at this time, but instead intended to use the loan agreement to encourage management to take decisive action to improve the firm's financial condition.

Trudy Patterns manufactures a line of costume jewelry. In addition to its regular merchandise, Trudy creates special holiday items for the holiday season. Trudy finances its seasonal working capital requirements with a $300,000 line of credit. In accordance with standard banking practices, however, the loan agreement requires repayment in full at some time during the year, in this case by February 2001.

Higher raw material costs, together with increased wages, led to a decline in the firm's profit margin during the last half of 1999 as well as during most of 2000. Sales increased during both of these years, however, due to the firm's aggressive marketing program—this despite competition from shell and turquoise jewelry makers.

The company received a copy of the banker's ratio analysis, along with a letter informing management the bank would insist on immediate repayment of the entire loan unless the firm submitted a business plan showing how operations could be turned around. Management felt that sales levels could not improve without an increase in the bank loan from $300,000 to $400,000, since payments of $100,000 for construction of a plant addition would have to be made in January 2001. Although the firm had been a loyal customer for more than 50 years, management questioned whether the bank would continue to supply the present line of credit, let alone approve facility increases.

The banker examined exigent ratios with the client, centering on strengths and weaknesses revealed by the ratio analysis. He wanted to know specifically the amount of internal funds that could have been available for debt payment if fiscal performances were at industry levels, with particular focus on the two working capital accounts—receivables and inventory. After meeting with management, the bank reviewed alternatives and arrived at a credit decision.

EXHIBIT II   Trudy Patterns Inc. Balance Sheet, Year Ended December 31 (in thousands of dollars)

	Assets	1998	1999	2000
1.	**Current assets**			
2.	Cash and cash items	$15,445	$12,007	$11,717
3.	Accounts and notes receivable, net	$51,793	$55,886	$88,571
4.	Inventories	$56,801	$99,087	$139,976
5.	**Current assets**	**$124,039**	**$166,980**	**$240,264**
6.	Property, plant, & equipment	$53,282	$60,301	$68,621

7.	Accumulated depreciation	$(8,989)	$(13,961)	$(20,081)
8.	**Net fixed assets**	**$44,294**	**$46,340**	**$48,539**
9.	**Total assets**	**$168,333**	**$213,320**	**$288,803**
	Liabilities and equities	**1998**	**1999**	**2000**
10.	**Current liabilities**			
11.	Short-term loans	$10,062	$15,800	$55,198
12.	Accounts payable	$20,292	$31,518	$59,995
13.	Accruals	$10,328	$15,300	$21,994
14.	**Current liabilities**	**$40,682**	**$62,618**	**$137,187**
15.	Long-term bank loans	$19,125	$28,688	$28,688
16.	Mortgage	$8,606	$7,803	$7,018
17.	**Long-term debt**	**$27,731**	**$36,491**	**$35,706**
18.	**Total liabilities**	**$68,413**	**$99,109**	**$172,893**
19.	Common stock (no par value)	$69,807	$69,807	$69,807
20.	Retained earnings	$30,113	$44,404	$46,103
21.	Stockholders' equity	$99,920	$114,211	$115,910
22.	**Total liabilities and equity**	**$168,333**	**$213,320**	**$288,803**

Income Statement Year Ended December 31 (in thousands of dollars)

		1998	1999	2000
23.	Net sales	$512,693	$553,675	$586,895
24.	Cost of goods sold	$405,803	$450,394	$499,928
25.	**Gross profit**	**$106,889**	**$103,281**	**$86,967**
	Cost and expenses:			
26.	Selling, admin., & general expenses	$38,369	$46,034	$50,643
27.	Depreciation	$4,781	$4,973	$6,120
28.	Miscellaneous expenses	$6,082	$10,672	$17,174
29.	**Total costs and expenses**	**$49,233**	**$61,678**	**$73,937**
30.	**Earnings before interest and taxes (EBIT)**	**$57,658**	**$41,602**	**$13,030**
	Less interest expense:			
	Interest on ST loans	$956	$1,683	$5,470
	Interest on LT loans	$1,913	$2,869	$2,869
	Interest on mortgage	$779	$707	$636
31.	Total interest expense	$3,648	$5,258	$8,974

32.	Earnings before taxes	$54,010	$36,343	$4,056
33.	Income taxes	$26,068	$17,589	$2,091
34.	Net income	$27,943	$18,754	$1,965
35.	Dividends on stock	$7,062	$4,463	$266
36.	Additions to retained earnings	$20,883	$14,291	$1,699

LIQUIDITY RATIOS

Liquidity ratios measure the quality and capability of current assets to meet maturing short-term obligations as they come due. Acceptable liquidity levels depend on economic and industry conditions, the predictability of cash flow, and the quality of assets making up liquidity ratios.

Current Ratio

Defined as current assets/current liabilities, this ratio is a commonly used measure of short-term solvency and debt service. The company's current ratio at year-end 2000 is as follows:

Current ratio = Current assets/Current liabilities = $240,264/$137,187 = 1.75

1998	1999	2000	Industry average
3.05	2.67	1.75	2.50

Current assets	
Cash	11,717
Account receivables	88,571
Inventories	139,976
Current assets	240,264
Current liabilities	
Short-term loans	55,198
Accounts payable	59,995
Accruals	21,994
Current liabilities	137,187

The borrower's current ratio declined over the past three years, falling below the industry average. An accounts receivable buildup points to a worsening (accounts receivable) aging in addition to increased possibilities of bad debt write-offs. Furthermore, inventory has increased. While some financial writers maintain that "high is best," the current ratio's magnitude means little if receivable and inventory quality falls below acceptable levels.

Quick Ratio (Acid Test)

A more conservative liquidity measure, the quick ratio depicts the borrower's short-term repayment ability. This ratio is generally considered to be a more accurate assessment of liquidity than the current ratio since inventory reliance is lower.

Quick ratio = Cash and accounts receivable/Current liabilities = $11,717 + $88,571/ $137,187 = 0.73

1998	1999	2000	Industry average
1.65	1.08	0.73	1.00

The firm's quick ratio has also declined over the past three years, dropping below the industry average.

ACTIVITY OR TURNOVER RATIOS

Average Collection Period

The average collection period (ACP) measures the time it takes to convert receivables into cash. Accounts receivable policy is closely allied to inventory management, since these represent the two largest current asset accounts. Of approximately equal magnitude, together they comprise almost 80% of current assets and over 30% of total assets for manufacturing industries. The average collection period is influenced partly by economic conditions and partly by a set of controllable factors, which are called internal (management) factors. Internal factors include credit policy variables (liberal, balanced, or conservative credit policy), credit terms, sales discounts, and collection.

Average collection period = (Accounts receivable/sales) $\times$ 365 = $88,571/$586,895 $\times$ 365 = 55

1998	1999	2000	Industry average
37	37	55	32

Trudy Pattern Inc.'s average collection period has increased and is well above the industry average. A short ACP generally equates to acceptable receivable quality, but only a receivable aging will confirm this. In any case, the banker will determine the role management plays in influencing this ratio. For instance, if receivables slowed due of a sluggish economy, the industry average would be higher—not so here.

Bad Debt Expense/Sales

This ratio measures overall accounts receivable quality. The lender should take the following steps:

- Verify that the allowance for bad debt is seasonable.
- Request that the borrower furnish specific client information.
- Divide bad debt expense by sales.

- Compare the ratio over time. It may be that receivable problems are related to lax customer screening or the weak financial condition of the borrower's customers.

Inventory Turnover

How well does management control inventory? The inventory turnover measures the number of times inventory turns over from fiscal year to fiscal year and is always benchmarked to the industry. Inventory control is essential to the overall cycle of cash flows and debt service, since redundant inventory points to unproductive investments carrying unacceptable returns.

Inventory control (and analysis) presumes a basic understanding of the interrelationship between raw materials, work in process, and finished goods. Investments in raw materials depend largely on anticipated production, seasonality, and reliability of suppliers. If raw material inventories are salable and commodity-like, inventory is more liquid than, say, work-in-process inventory. However, a buildup indicates price increases or shortages.

Work-in-process inventory deals with the length of the production cycle. Particulars include equipment efficiency factors, engineering techniques, and maintenance of highly skilled workers. Bankers watch for production slowdowns and manufacturing inefficiencies.

Finished goods involve coordinating production with anticipated sales. A buildup here is especially worrisome. If the consumer market avoids production output, how will loans be repaid?

Inventory turnover (cost) = Cost of goods sold/Inventory = $499,928/$139,976 = 3.6
Inventory turnover (sales) = Sales/Inventory = $586,895/$139,976 = 4.2

1998	1999	2000	Industry average
7.1	4.5	3.6	5.7
9.0	5.6	4.2	7.0

Inventory turnover is substantially below the industry average and is trending downward, suggesting (1) too much inventory is on hand, (2) actual liquidity may be worse than indicated (by the current ratio), and (3) inventory is obsolete and may have to be written off.

Fixed-Asset Turnover

Directing the firm's capital equipment policies is central to management's goal of maximizing shareholder's wealth. Investment in fixed assets decreases cash flow in periods investments are made. As a result, cash generated by productive assets must offset initial investment outflows, producing a positive net present value. In other words, this ratio influences the sustainability of the firm's cash flow.

Fixed asset turnover = Sales/Net fixed assets = $586,895/$48,539 = 12.1

1998	1999	2000	Industry average
11.7	12.0	12.1	12.1

Trudy Pattern Inc.'s fixed asset turnover is level to the industry. Let's review some clues that point to *efficient* fixed asset management. Large ratios suggest the following:

- The firm's efficient use of property, plant, and equipment has resulted in a high level of operating capacity.
- Merger and divestment activity has changed to the composition and size of fixed assets on the consolidated balance sheet.
- The firm has increased its plant capacity, utilizing more of the machines already in place.
- Management has planned expansion programs carefully, using up-to-date capital budgeting techniques.
- Fixed assets required to maintain a degree of operating leverage and production efficiency were divested.

However, a high turnover may also indicate the borrower is not replacing deposed or depreciated assets.

Working Capital Turnover

Working capital, as defined by the literature, is the excess of current assets over current liabilities—that is, cash and other liquid assets expected to be consumed or converted into cash within the accounting period over obligations due within the same period. Working capital is a general measure of liquidity and represents the margin of protection short-term creditors expect. Working capital is essential for a company to meet its continuous operational needs. Its adequacy influences the firm's ability to meet its trade and short-term debt obligations, as well as to remain financially viable.

Working capital turnover = Sales/Working capital = $586,895/103,077 = 5.7

1998	1999	2000	Industry average
6.2	5.3	5.7	4.5

Total Asset Turnover

Total asset turnover suggests how efficiently borrowers utilize capital or how many dollars of turnover is generated by each dollar of investment.

Total asset turnover = Sales/Total assets = $586,895/288,803 = 2.0

1998	1999	2000	Industry average
3.0	2.5	2.0	2.8

In 2000, asset turnover for Trudy Patterns dipped significantly below the industry average, implying the borrower employed more assets per sales dollars versus the industry. A decline in this ratio points to lower asset productivity. With *fixed* assets turnover equal to the industry average, problems in this business can be traced to poor current asset management and planning.

The Average Settlement Period (ASP)

The ASP measures the length of time a company takes to pay creditors, or the number of times trade payables turn over in one year.

Average payment period = Accounts payable/Average purchases per day

The lower the ratio, the shorter the time period between purchase and payment. If, for example, the firm's payables turned slower than the industry average, likely causes would be disputed invoices, received extended terms, deliberately expanded trade credit, or cash flow problems.

The average settlement period or day's payables ratio yields the average length of time trade payables are outstanding.

Accounts payable turnover = Cost of goods sold/Accounts payable
Average settlement period (ASP) = (Accounts payable/Cost of good sold) × 365 =
$59,995 /$499,928 × 365 = 44 days

1998	1999	2000	Industry average
18	26	44	35

PROFITABILITY RATIOS

Management's success in expense control, the ability to counter economic and industry downturns, plus a number of hybrid factors (such as quality, trend, and magnitude of the ratio's residual components) make up this important ratio group.

Gross Profit Margin

The gross profit margin measures production success and is an integral part of the lending toolbox because it is especially adept at differentiating between temporary and structural problems. Were higher production costs successfully passed on to consumers? Are raw material costs adequately controlled? Is the labor/machine mix optimal? Do production policies and methods measure favorably against benchmark firms? What is the degree of operating leverage? Operating leverage is an important constituent of this ratio. For example, to a physicist, *leverage*, implies raising a heavy object with a small force using a lever. In business, a high degree of operating leverage implies that relatively small changes in sales result in large changes in operating income.

Gross profit = Net sales − Cost of goods sold (Net sales = Gross sales −
Returns, allowances, discounts)
Cost of goods sold = Beginning inventory + Purchases + Factory labor + Overhead +
Factory depreciation + Freight in − Ending inventory
Gross profit margin = Gross profit/Net sales = $86,967/$586,895 = 14.8%

1998	1999	2000	Industry average
19.9%	17.7%	14.8%	18.0%

The gross profit margin for Trudy Patterns Inc. has fallen sharply and is significantly below the industry average. This may have resulted from a weak pricing policy, high production costs, or a combination of both. Gross profit troubles can usually be traced to poor asset management policies and operating leverage problems, likely the case here.

Selling General and Administration Expenses/Sales

The ratio measures management's ability to control costs not associated with production. Expenses that are higher than historical levels may be justified if expenses are accompanied by strong product demand. For example, outlays for advertising, promotion, and research expenditures promote sustainability of cash flows and thus directly influence shareholder value.

Selling, general, administration plus miscellaneous expenses/Net sales = $50,643 +
$17,174/$586,895 = 11.5%

1998	1999	2000	Industry average
8.7%	10.2%	11.5%	9.3%

Expenses, including miscellaneous expenses to sales, are much higher than the industry norm. The firm's accountant included interest cost, meaning Trudy Patterns' failure to reduce short-term debt has resulted in higher miscellaneous expenses.

Effective Tax Rate

The provision for income taxes excludes excise, social security, and sales taxes. You may want to compare this rate to the statutory tax rate and to the prior year's effective tax rate.

Effective tax rate = Income taxes/Earnings before taxes = $2,091/$4056 = 51.6%

1998	1999	2000
48.3%	48.4%	51.69%

Net Margin

This important yardstick of success depicts the percentage of each sales dollar remaining after all expenses and taxes have been deducted.

Net margin = Net income/Net sales = $1,965/$586,895 = 0.4%

1998	1999	2000	Industry average
5.5%	3.4%	0.4%	2.9%

The borrower's low margin reflects rising costs accompanied by lower than proportional increases in revenue. As a first step toward improving profitability, Trudy Patterns should attempt to increase revenue or decrease costs. If demand would allow higher prices, profitability could be increased through selective price increases. Otherwise, the firm would have to attempt to cut costs. The relatively high inventory might be responsible for greater storage costs, larger losses from trend changes, and other factors. Operating expenses might also be cut back. Second, the low turnover indicates that this borrower is not utilizing assets efficiently. If higher sales cannot be produced to bring current assets into line, the firm should consider reducing assets, particularly inventory, which is twice as large as the industry average.

Return on Net Worth

The measure provides the per-dollar yield on investment to the equity holder. The ratio can be expressed as a function of the return on assets, the profit margin, and leverage. If returns are consistently below the risk-free rate of return, why is the business operating?

Return on net worth = Reported net income/Net worth = 1,965/$115,910 = 1.7%

1998	1999	2000	Industry average
28.3%	16.7%	1.7%	17.5%

Trudy Patterns' return to shareholders has fallen significantly and is far below the average for the industry.

Return on Total Assets

Also called return on investment or ROI, this ratio measures how effectively a company employs its total assets.

Return on total assets = Reported net income/Total assets = 1,965/$288,803 = 0.7%

1998	1999	2000	Industry average
16.8%	8.9%	0.7%	8.8%

While the ratio calculates profitability of assets, it ignores asset composition and quality and debt-to-equity mix. However, it appears that weak current asset productivity is the primary cause of a continuously deteriorating return on total assets.

Dividend Payout Ratio

This ratio indicates the percentage of earnings paid out in dividends.

Dividend payout ratio = Total cash dividends/Net income = $266/1,965 = 13.5%

1998	1999	2000	Industry average
25.3%	23.8%	13.5%	27%

Dividends affect the relationship between debt and shareholders' equity. Leverage will increase if a high dividend payout rate is financed by large debt infusions. Because dividends represent a use of cash (we'll see how this works in the chapter on cash flows), bankers target this ratio when debt levels become too high. For example, a historically profitable borrower serving the entertainment industry began paying large dividends financed by bank loans. When the inevitable recession occurred, the firm lacked the cash reserves and debt capacity to survive. The firm reduced its dividend but perhaps should withhold distribution until liquidity and operating problems are resolved.

LEVERAGE RATIOS

This family of ratios depicts the relationship between shareholders' funds (and reserves) and the total value of loans and other forms of debt made to them. The higher the leverage (or gearing), the greater the proportion of borrowed money to the firm's "own" money. Highly leveraged borrowers, depending on industry demographics, face greater risk if profits abruptly dissipate, because interest and principle must be paid whether or not profits are produced. How high leverage may increase without undermining the borrower's financial structure depends on numerous factors, including asset quality, cash flow coverage (of debt service), debt mix (short term versus long term), and sustainable operating and financial factors such as revenue growth and equity market values.

Unlike activity and profitability ratios, financial leverage is not something management necessarily wants to maximize, though asset returns or tax benefits may run higher. Strategic plans, at least the sound ones, aim at striking the right balance between the benefits of debt and the cost of risk.

Debt-to-Equity and Debt-to-Total-Assets Ratios

The debt-to-equity ratio and debt to total assets determines the relative use of borrowed funds. Debt levels vary according to the industry. For example, it is not uncommon for firms with highly liquid assets, such as banks, to boast 9:1 debt-to-equity ratios. On the other hand, manufacturers tend to position leverage below 100%.

Total debt/Equity = $172,893 /$115,910 = 149.1%
Total debt/Total assets = $172,893/$288,803 = 59.9%

1998	1999	2000	Industry average
40.6%	46.5%	59.9%	50.0%

The debt levels for Trudy Patterns Inc. have increased to above the industry average. Taken in isolation, this is usually not a concern. However, this borrower's questionable asset quality together with an apparent imbalance between current and noncurrent liabilities, weak cash flow coverage, and unquestioned low equity value (in real terms) may well have pushed leverage beyond acceptable tolerance levels.

Take, for example, the case of Bijou Furniture, a borrower that consolidated operations with a competitor to broaden market share. Based on sales projections, Bijou was able to finance the acquisition with loans. When sales dropped unexpectedly, the firm defaulted on its loans and was forced to sell assets at liquidation value to meet partial payments. The firm's banker might have avoided this headache had he or she considered the underlying mechanics of leverage ratios in general and the interdependence of leverage, return, and productively allied to this acquisition.

Times Interest Earned

This ratio measures how far earnings drop before interest is not covered. The ratio is not as useful as the fixed charge and cash flow coverage ratios.

Times interest earned = Earnings before interest and taxes/Interest = $13,030/$8,974 = 1.4

1998	1999	2000	Industry average
15.8	7.9	1.4	7.7

The firm covers interest costs with only 1.4X earnings. It appears that profits will not be available to make much of a dent toward paying down principle.

The Fixed Payment Coverage Ratio

The fixed charge coverage ratio is very similar to times interest earned. Adding the cost of annual long-term lease obligations to earnings before interest and taxes (EBIT) and dividing this number by the sum of interest charges plus lease obligations produces the result.

Fixed payment coverage ratio = Income before taxes + Interest charges + Lease obligations/Interest charges + Lease obligations[1]

---

[1] We have not determined the ratio for Trudy Patterns Inc.

This ratio can be particularly important for bankers lending to companies that negotiate long-term leases, since lease payments are both fixed and long term.

Debt Affordability Ratio

Cash inflows and outflows are two important determinants of debt affordability. Cash inflows equal operating income plus noncash expenses, while cash outflows pertain to financing costs.

Debt affordability ratio = Cash inflows/Cash outflows

When debt affordability falls below one, the firm might have taken on too much debt.

Cash Flow Coverage[2]

One of the most important ratios in credit analysis, cash flow coverage describes the number of times operating cash flows cover debt service. Debt service means interest and principle payments. The example (Exhibit III) illustrates how computer simulations and cash flow coverage work together.

A builder took his construction plans to Hanover Multifactor Bank requesting $3 million of permanent financing at 9% interest for a 12-year term with a balloon payment due at the end. The constant payment including interest and principal would be 10.23%. The bank stipulated that the building's *operating cash flow* must be sufficient to cover *debt service* of $306,900 with *no less than a 98% probability*. While the builder's net worth statement revealed some liquidity, the bank did not feel comfortable that enough external funds were available to supplement the project's expected cash flow coverage ratio. Extracting the cash flow coverage section from the simulation output, the bank determined that because cash flow coverage was good to only an 82.6% probability, short of the 98% required by Hanover Multifactor Bank, collateral and an escrow deposit were required. The customer agreed to the conditions and the bank approved the loan.

EXHIBIT III   Simulation Result of the Builder's Debt Service Coverage

Forcast: Cash flow from operations summary

Certainty level is 17.40%	This means that there is 17.4%
Certainty range is from $290,027 to $306,900	probability that operating cash flow
Display range is from $280,000 to $350,000	will not be sufficient to cover
Entire range is from $283,945 to $348,811	debt service.
After 1,000 trials, the standard error of the mean is $382	

---

[2] Not calculated for Trudy Products Inc.

GROWTH RATIOS

Although strong sales and profit growth rates are generally comforting to lenders, they may well be chimeric. Is growth real or illusionary? Are inflationary factors or noncash credits propelling fiscal results? Are revenues sustainable?

Sales Growth Rate

Sales growth rate = Sales $_t$ − Sales $_{t-1}$/Sales $_{t-1}$ = \$586,895 − \$553,675 /\$553,675 = 6.0%

1999	2000	Industry average
8.0%	6.0%	9.5%

Profit Growth Rate

Profit growth rate = Profit $_t$ − Profit $_{t-1}$/Profit $_{t-1}$ = \$1,965 − \$18,754/\$18,754 = −89.5%

1999	2000	Industry average
−32.9%	−89.5%	11.5%

VALUATION RATIOS

Valuation ratios extend beyond historical cost-based accounting offering a more realistic depiction of the real value of borrowers.

Book Value per Share/Market Range

If shares trade far below book value, a new equity offering may well result in dilution of existing shares. The question becomes, why is market perception of equity so low? Are book assets overstated in terms of their true net worth?

Book value per share = Common equity/Number of common shares outstanding

The market range is disclosed in annual reports, newspapers, or on the Internet.

Price/Earnings Ratio

The P/E ratio divides the stock price by earning for the previous four quarters. For instance, if a firm was trading at \$15 a share and \$1.00 in trailing earnings per share, the P/E is 15X:

\$15 share price/\$1.00 trailing EPS = 15 P/E

The P/E ratio is an important "loan" ratio because a borrower's stock "price" centers on the markets perception of future performance, whereas reported earnings are tied to the past and are influenced by the opinions of auditors. There are many permutations of P/Es using forecasted or trailing 12-month earnings.

Borrowers may report low earnings yet produce impressive values because they are engaged in extensive research and product development or are recent entrants in high-growth industries. It is important to establish industry homogeneity since industry distortions can and do occur.

Price/Sales

The price/sales ratio takes the current market capitalization of firms and divides the result by the trailing revenues of the previous 12 months. The market capitalization is the current market value of a company, arrived at by multiplying the current share price times the shares outstanding.

Liquidation Valuation Approach

One of the most important measures in any banker's ratio toolbox, the liquidation valuation approach focuses on the relationship between market value and liquidation values. Management's decision to divest a business unit can often be tied to these spreads. Hax and Majluf are proponents of the market value/liquidation value ratio.[3] They suggest that business units destroy value if liquidation value consistently remains above ongoing cash flow value and corporate resources could be better served elsewhere. Operations like this represent "cash traps" that end up draining recourses from other more successful business segments. Under such conditions, divestiture might be the most logical choice if the bank's exposure is to be salvaged.

STATISTICAL ANALYSIS OF RATIOS

Decomposition Analysis

Decomposition analysis builds on the notion that little in finance is left to chance. Management is constantly faced with exogenous forces tugging at their firms and must continuously shift assets and financial resources to counter these forces and preserve cash flow equilibrium. It is the extent, or magnitude, of statistical "shifting around" that corroborates decomposition. Equilibrium relationships in business organizations, suggested Baruch Lev, are usually the result of economic optimality criteria designed to improve efficiency and maximize value. Thus, for every level of activity there exists "optimal relationships between labor and capital inputs, inventory and sales, cash and short term securities, debt and equity

---

[3] Arnolodo C. Hax, professor of management, Sloan School of Management, MIT.

capital."[4] Management allocation decisions in the face of exogenous economic and market forces are reflected in financial statements.

Decomposition made it possible to measure the degree of stability firms have been able to sustain in an often volatile marketplace—inherent in the mix and volatility of their financial statements over time. Variations over time in the relationship among financial statement items shadow significant business events, planned and unplanned, and are thus crucial to lenders engaged in assessing future performance. Lev studied the implication of decomposition analysis to a wide range of administration and social science areas including economics, sociology, psychology, and accounting. Statistical decomposition of financial reports is especially suited for the analysis of mass data such as large computer files of financial statements.

The application of decomposition analysis to Trudy's balance sheet is discussed next.

	Absolute value			Relative value		
	1998	1999	2000	1998	1999	2000
Cash and cash items	$15,445	$12,007	$11,717	0.092	0.056	0.041
Accounts receivable, net	$51,793	$55,886	$88,571	0.308	0.262	0.307
Inventories	$56,801	$99,087	$139,976	0.337	0.464	0.485
Net fixed assets	$44,294	$46,340	$48,539	0.263	0.217	0.168
Total assets	$168,333	$213,320	$288,803	1.000	1.000	1.000

Lev designates the earlier relative values by pi, $i = 1...n$. In Trudy's case for 1999, p1 (cash/total assets) = .056, p2 (receivables/total assets) = .262, and so on, and $n = 4$. The corresponding values of a latter financial statement is qi, where q1 = .041, q2 = .307, and so on. The asset composition measure is defined by Lev as follows:

$IA = {}_n\Sigma i = 1, qi \log qi/pi$

Trudy's decomposition measure for 1999/2000 was calculated as follows:

IA = .041 loge .041/.056 + .307 loge .307/.262 + .485 loge.385/.464 + .168 loge.368/.217 = 0.01252 nits[5]

Asset Decomposition Measures (In 10^{-4} Nits)

	1996/97	1997/98	1998/99	1999/00
Trudy Patterns	352	392	372	125
Industry average (assumed)	125	165	140	153

---

[4] *Finanical Statement Analysis: A New Approach.* Baruch Lev, Prentice-Hall Contemporary Topics in Accounting Series, 1974, p. 49.

[5] The base of the logarithm is left for the analyst to decide. When natural logarithms are used as in the example, the unit of measurement is denoted as a nit.

The instability of assets during 1999/2000 as depicted by the sharp departure from previous asset decomposition numbers reflects, once again, Trudy's serious inventory and accounts receivable problems. That decomposition measures reflect the occurrence of important events worthy of investigation is supported by several studies, which empirically established an association between certain key business events and decomposition measures. The point remains, according to some studies, financially distressed firms had, for at least five years before bankruptcy, substantially larger balance sheet decomposition measures (shifts) than those of comparable solvent firms.

FIRST CENTRAL BANK'S CREDIT DECISION

While Trudy Patterns Inc. has been a customer of the bank for some years, the operations have deteriorated over the past three years. If the trend continues, the company could end up insolvent with First Central Bank writing off its investment. The bank would not retreat to a status quo position of inaction, but instead would cajole management into correcting operating and liquidity problems.

Trudy Patterns has the potential for raising an additional $37,118 by liquidating redundant accounts receivable and $52,269 through reduction of inventories. Reductions in these working capital accounts could not be achieved overnight, but assuming inventories are salable and the accounts receivable collectible, it should be possible for the firm to generate cash from these sources and reduce the bank's exposure.

First Central first estimated the dollar amount of excessive receivables by (1) setting the average collection period (in the formula) equal to the industry average, (2) including the firm's fiscal sales, and (3) solving for accounts receivable. The result was pro forma receivables, assuming collections had been industry efficient. The difference between year-end and pro forma receivables represents additional cash that could have been used to pay down the loan as depicted by the following accounts receivable pro forma analysis:

1. Determine the additional cash inflows likely by reducing the ACP
2. Average collection period = (Accounts receivable/Sales) × 365
3. Insert the industry collection period into the formula = 32 days in formula 32 = (Accounts receivable)/$586,895) × 365
4. Solve for accounts receivable in (3)

Accounts receivable = $51,453

5. Determine pro forma cash available

Fiscal accounts receivable	$88,571
Less pro forma accounts receivable	$51,453
Cash available by reducing collection time	
Industry average	**$37,118**

In addition, if inventories could be reduced to the average level for the industry, this would provide the firm with approximately $52,269 in receivables or cash as seen in the inventory pro forma analysis:

Fiscal inventory turnover (cost) = Cost of goods sold/Inventory = $499,928 /$139,976 = 3.6

Industry Average: 5.7

1. Set the Inventory Turnover to the industry average; include Trudy's cost of goods sold and solve for Inventory:

Industry inventory turnover (Cost) = Cost of goods sold/Inventory 5.7 = $499,928 /Inventory;

Pro forma inventory = $87,707

2. Solve for Inventory to obtain pro forma inventory:

Fiscal inventory	$139,976
Receivable and cash available to firm	
If inventory is converted as fast as industry average	$87,707
Additional cash or accounts receivable available	**$52,269**

The bank decided to extend the full amount of the credit but placed a lien on receivables and enforced a tight repayment plan. Trudy Patterns Inc. agreed to reduce inventories and accounts receivable to inventory levels over the 12 months. The plan called for selling off inventories by cutting sale prices and increasing advertising expenditures while, at the same time, cutting back production. The company agreed to follow a "get tough" policy on collecting tardy receivables, while improved production control measures were enacted immediately to help the gross profit margin recover. These practices paid off, and the company met scheduled loan payments.

SOURCES OF COMPARATIVE RATIOS

Robert Morris Associates (RMA) Annual Statement Studies

RMA's Annual Statement Studies is the only source of comparative financial data derived directly from more than 150,000 statements of commercial bank borrowers and prospects. These financial statements come directly to RMA from the association's member institutions, who get their data straight from the customer.

RMA offers 16 "classic" financial statement ratios along with common-size balance sheets and income statements. Six balance sheet and income statement line items are presented in common-size format in 600 industries at the four-digit SIC level and at the six-digit North American Industry Classification System (NAICS) level. Data are arrayed by asset and sales size with six different asset and sales size categories presented. RMA statement studies are available in book form, CD-ROM, or on the Internet.

D&B Dun's Financial Profile

D&B provides an overview of the financial condition of firms or an entire industry, complete with industry benchmarking of an organization's key business ratios and financial and payment performance. The report provides a narrative analysis of the company and displays a line-by-line report of up to three years of financials, with common-size percentages and industry comparisons.

Standard & Poor's COMPUSTAT Global Database

This database provides financial and market data on more than 12,000 international companies in 70 countries around the world. It includes each company's annual income statement, balance sheet, cash flow and supplementary data with up to 12 years of history, industry-specific data sets for financial services companies, daily downloads for key balance sheet and income statement data, and non–North American industrial company cash flow items and economic sector information.

The list of U.S. and Canadian public companies and indexes includes 10,300 active and 9,400 inactive companies, 900 Canadian companies, 600 indexes including the S&P 500, S&P midcap 400, S&P small-cap 600, 332 annual fundamental financial data items, 128 quarterly fundamental financial data items, financial data items specific to the financial services industry, industry and geographic segment information, 20 years of annual information, 20 years of monthly information (with data to 1962 available on tape products), and daily updates available on more than 50 data items. All other data items are updated weekly or monthly.

OneSource Information Services Inc.

OneSource provides Web-based business and financial information to banking professionals who need quick access to reliable corporate, industry, and market intelligence. Its Business Browser product line provides news, trade press, executive biographies, analyst reports, company financial results, stock quotes, and industry statistics. OneSource integrates business and financial information on more than 1 million global public and private companies from more than 25 information providers drawing on more than 2,500 sources of content.

Thomson Financial Services

The FIRST CALL Fundamentals Database offers access to five years of pricing and valuation data including projected fundamentals and key financial ratios. This database is updated weekly, with price-dependent items updated daily. Quarterly and annual income statement and balance sheet items are included with footnotes. Thomson's segment, Sheshunoff Information Services, offers the

Sheshunoff(r) Self-Paced Financial Statement Analysis. This tool addresses elements of financial statement analysis, with coverage of individual creditworthiness, ratio analysis, and cash flow analysis.

SUMMARY

Ratios are only diagnostic tools. Like electrocardiograms measuring changes in the heart's electrical activity, ratios catch irregularities in a business. Just like diagnostic tools in medicine, analysts must interpret, compare, and look behind the numbers. Mechanical, unthinking ratio analysis is dangerous—just ask the folks in load workouts. However, when used intelligently and with good judgment, ratios provide insights into a firm's operations and into the riskiness of cash flows.

1. Describe the advantages and disadvantages of using a ratio analysis. Can important financial information be gained simply by performing a ratio analysis? What types of information cannot be interpreted from a simple ratio analysis?
2. Describe the concept of benchmarking. When is benchmarking appropriate? When is it inappropriate? What would you do if the client were a unique company with no obvious peers or industry to benchmark against?
3. What significance do geographic difference play when comparing companies in the same industry? What adjustments would you make when comparing Proctor & Gamble, a U.S. consumer goods company, to Unilever, a European consumer goods company.
4. Describe how differences in international accounting practices can distort financial comparisons.
5. List some methods that can be used by the bank to determine if Trudy Patterns might be having trouble paying its suppliers. What insights can be gleaned from analyzing Trudy's financial statements and most recent trial balance? What are some facts that cannot be fully understood from that analysis?

SELECTED REFERENCES AND READINGS

Bueno, R. A. (1976). *Performance and sensitivity analysis of the generalized likelihood ratio method for failure detection.* Cambridge, MA: Electronic Systems Laboratory Dept. of Electrical Engineering and Computer Science, Massachusetts Institute of Technology.

Chow, E. Y., and Massachusetts Institute of Technology, Electronic Systems Laboratory. (1976). *Analytical studies of the generalized likelikhood ratio technique for failure detection.* Cambridge, MA: Electronic Systems Laboratory, Massachusetts Institute of Technology.

Fridson, M. S. (1995). *Financial statement analysis: A practitioner's guide.* New York: J. Wiley.

Gates, S. (1993). *101 business ratios: A manager's handbook of definitions, equations, and computer algorithms: How to select, compute, present, and understand measures of sales, profit, debt, capital, efficiency, marketing, and investment*. Scottsdale, AZ: McLane.

Gupta, L. C. (1983). *Financial ratios for monitoring corporate sickness: Towards a more systematic approach*. Delhi: Oxford University Press.

Helfert, E. A. (1994). *Techniques of financial analysis*. Burr Ridge, IL: Irwin.

Ketz, J. E., R. K. Doogar, and D. Jensen. (1990). *A cross-industry analysis of financial ratios: Comparabilities and corporate performance*. New York: Quorum Books.

Kiers, H. A. L., and International Federation of Classification Societies, Conference. (2000). *Data analysis, classification, and related methods*. Berlin; New York: Springer.

Miller, B. E., and D. E. Miller. (1991). *How to interpret financial statements for better business decisions*. New York: Amacom.

Sanzo, R. (1977). *Ratio analysis for small business*. Washington, DC: Small Business Administration (Office of Management Information and Training). For sale by the Supt. of Docs. U.S. Govt. Print. Off.

Troy, L. (1997). *Almanac of business and industrial financial ratios*. Englewood Cliffs, NJ: Prentice Hall.

Tyran, M. R. (1986). *Handbook of business and financial ratios*. Englewood Cliffs, NJ: Prentice Hall.

Viscione, J. A. (1983). *Analyzing ratios: A perceptive approach*. New York: Publications Division of the National Association of Credit Management.

Wallin, J., and Svenska Handelshögskolan (Helsinki, Finland). (1985). *Financial ratio analysis and mathematical programming: Pattern recognition models for default risk assesment*. Helsingfors: Swedish School of Economics and Business Administration.

Westwick, C. A. (1987). *How to use management ratios*. Aldershot, Hants, England: Gower.

4

CREDIT ANALYSIS OF SEASONAL BUSINESSES

An Integrated Approach

Lenders deciding to approve or renew seasonal loans weigh the obligor's financial condition, bank relationship (including deposit balances), and payment history. Most seasonal loans are unsecured; risks include the borrower's inability to meet scheduled maturities, the loss of principal and interest, and the possibility of conversion to "evergreen credit," which locks the bank into the credit for many years.

Seasonal loans are self-liquidating and provide short-term working capital needs by financing seasonal increases in receivables and inventory (see Chapter 5, "Asset-Based Lending"). The liquidation or cash conversion/contraction process retires the loan at season's end, which is one good reason banks actively seek seasonal loans. Seasonal firms typically finance seasonal working capital by purchasing raw materials on credit from suppliers, creating accounts payable and thus easing cash needs.

EXAMPLES OF SEASONAL BUSINESSES

1. Jewelry retailers, bookstores, and toy distributors increase sales markedly just before the holiday season. Retail department stores and candy retailers follow the same pattern. Garden outlets, sporting goods stores, and home lumber dealers experience peak sales during warm spring and summer months.
2. Retail businesses use seasonal loans to support swings in sales activity. Clothing stores anticipate increases in volume in the spring and again in the fall as new lines arrive. Retail firms borrow heavily during the Christmas and Easter seasons to carry increased inventories and accounts receivable.
3. Steel operations on the Great Lakes usually build iron ore inventories during summer months to supply their needs during winter when lake freighters cannot transport raw materials because of inclement weather.
4. Swimsuit manufacturers start producing bathing suits in fall for spring distribution to retailers. During the manufacturing phase, inventories build along with labor, overhead, and other product costs. In the spring, swimsuits are sold. Shortly thereafter, receivables fall due with proceeds providing the annual (loan) cleanup.
5. Building contractors achieve higher levels of production when weather is favorable.
6. Forest products producers build substantial log inventories to keep manufacturing plants supplied with raw materials during seasons when logging operations make little headway.
7. Coal and fuel oil dealers build inventories in during summer months, running them off steadily in fall and winter to a low point by early spring.
8. Food processors use short-term lines to finance crops grown and shipped at distinctive seasons. Short-term financing supports fertilizer and other production costs and the harvesting season for distribution and marketing of the crop (see Chapter 5).
9. Securities firms involved in investment banking, commission brokerage, and security trading are large borrowers of short-term funds from commercial banks. As investment bankers, these firms require short-term funding to support underwriting and distribution activities.
10. Fish canneries must do their processing as the fish are caught, which often results in the accumulation of substantial inventories (see Chapter 5).

THE SUCCESSFUL SEASONAL CYCLE

The typical seasonal company goes through five stages (Figure 4.1):

1. *Buildup period.* During the buildup period, demand deposits drop, whereas loan balances, trade payables, and inventory increase. At this point, the balance sheet begins to expand.
2. *High point.* As a company reaches its high point, inventory, bank debt, and trade payables reach a peak. The need for liquidity bottoms out, and receivables remain low. The balance sheet reaches expansion limits.
3. *Conversion cycle begins.* Inventory decreases and receivables increase as product demand strengthens. Payables and bank debt remain steady or decline slightly. The balance sheet moves in tandem with the reduction in liabilities.
4. *Conversion cycle intensifies.* Shipments accelerate causing inventory to decline quickly and receivables to build further. Demand deposits rise, but at a slower rate as some receivables convert to cash. Payables and short-term loans begin to fall faster as collections are converted into cash. Balance sheet contraction moves in tandem with cash conversion.
5. *Conversion cycle subsides.* The low point approaches. Firms ship very little merchandise. Inventory is already at low levels and receivables decline quickly, since the conversion process causes deposits to swell. The balance sheet fully contracts to its low point as trade payables and bank debt are retired or cleaned up. After the traditional 30 days have passed, renewed debt replenishes cash in preparation for the next season.

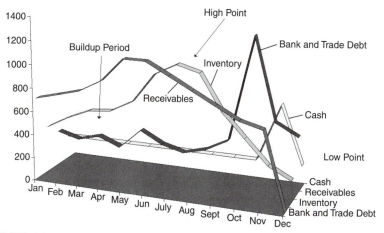

FIGURE 4.1 Successful Seasonal Conversion

Sometimes things go wrong and inventories have not been sold. At season's end these obligors may not have cash available to zero out credit lines. The process generally follows a repetitive pattern (Figure 4.2):

1. *Buildup period.* Demand deposits drop and loan balances, trade payables, and inventory increase. The balance sheet starts expanding. So far, so good.
2. *High point period.* As the firm reaches its high point, inventory, bank debt, and trade payables peak. Liquidity requirements abate, receivables remain low, and the balance sheet reaches expansion limits. Still there are no signs of problems.
3. *Conversion cycle fails.* Surprise of surprises—books are canceled, goods are shipped late, production break downs, and consumer demand evaporates. As a result, inventory is stuck at high levels. Receivables and cash remain at low levels, the result of the impeded conversion cycle. With low cash balances, the borrower finds it difficult or impossible to repay suppliers and short-term lenders.

In part due to heavy inventory requirements during peak season, seasonal borrows are traditionally undercapitalized. Acme Toy Company typically receives orders for the bulk of its sales during the summer months. Shipments of orders are expected in October, November, and December, just in time for the start of the holiday rush. Since Acme manufactures most of its product line before the shipping period, short-term bank loans are used to finance raw material buildup. As toys are delivered to retailers during the fall months, the firm experiences higher receivable levels as inventory is sold. After the holiday season has ended, inventory and receivables decline as deposits increase. Cash is

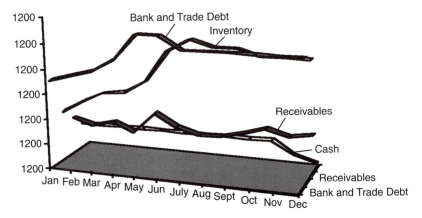

FIGURE 4.2 Unsuccessful Seasonal Conversion Process

used to pay down short-term bank loans and payables. As long as the firm sells inventory, debt and equity levels normalize by fiscal close. The firm's short-term undercapitalized position is only that—*temporary.*

Gem Lawn Furniture closes its books on August 31. During late summer and fall, Gem purchases raw materials, the bulk of which are forest product derivatives, and seasonal borrowing begins. Labor and other manufacturing costs increase in late fall and early winter, pushing borrowings to a high point. By late winter, demand accelerates with products shipped from warehouses to distribution channels. Inventories reduce while receivables increase. With production at or near a low point, Gem's credit line levels off. By early summer, receivables and bank debt begin running off, the result of cash collections. At the close of books on August 31, inventories and receivables are reduced to their annual low point and seasonal debt is retired.

The successful conversion contraction flow experienced by Gem may not have occurred if short-term debt were used to finance long-term, or core assets (as opposed to working capital assets) because the firm would be forced to use cash to pay two short-term loans simultaneously. Long-term, or core assets ordinarily are financed with long-term debt (match funding) to preserve the working capital required for the annual seasonal cleanup. Core assets (nonseasonal) are, in actually, a firm's nerve center—its most direct route to sustainable cash flows and shareholder value. Again, *core assets should be supported by liabilities of similar duration—short-term debt used to finance core assets could easily result in seasonal liquidity problems.*

SEASONAL LENDING TECHNIQUES

Cash Budgets

One of the most effective tools used to derive peak short-term financing requirements are cash budgets. Cash budgets usually span short periods—monthly, quarterly, semiannually, or annually, but management will also use cash budgets to help focus on long-term horizons—two, five, or ten years. Short-term budgets pinpoint both borrowings required and timing of repayments. Cash budgets do the following:

1. *Provide lenders with a way to monitor seasonal activity.* For example, if *actual* cash receipts fall below *planned* receipts, bankers may assume that management either missed revenue targets or goals were unrealistic to begin with.

2. *Help determine appropriate credit lines or loan ceilings.* Lenders typically set credit lines roughly equal to the highest cash deficit revealed in the budget.

3. *Spot the months bankers can reasonably expect loan reductions.* If additional drawdowns replace loan repayments—watch out; inventory likely did not sell.

4. *Identify wayward deployment of seasonal advances.* For example, if a borrower suffered a fiscal loss and anticipates payment of substantial dividends, the loan may be used to line investors' pockets *and not* to finance seasonal working capital. Firms have also been known to fund the activities of affiliates or management-sponsored investments out of loans bankers intended for the purchase of inventory.

5. *Work as quasi-marketing tools.* For instance, capital expenditures normally call for considerable cash outlays during the budget period. If the bank spots these anticipated outlays early enough, it can sponsor term loans or other facilities before the client approaches another bank or leasing company.

PREPARING A CASH BUDGET

Refer to Acme's Cash Budget in Table 4.1 and on the CD (Models_Demos/ Chapter 4).

1. Set up a matrix that includes both historical and forecast sales by month. Data can be extracted from the obligor's projected sales budget, which projects the expected monthly sales in units and selling price per unit.
2. Next calculate credit sales as a percentage of total sales. Acme sells 80% on credit.
3. Subtract credit sales from total sales to arrive at cash sales.
4. Next, develop an accounts receivable aging from historical experience and expectations. For example, Acme expects 25% of the present month's credit sales to be collected in the current month and 5% of the prior month's credit sales to be collected in the current month.
5. Enter expected collections in the budget you've developed from the aging.
6. Enter total cash inflows.
7. Develop the cash disbursement for purchases schedule following the same method we used to find cash receipts from sales.
8. Enter total cash inflows.
9. Juxtapose total cash inflows with outflows.
10. Complete the Cumulative (Financial Needs) Surplus Zero Balance Account Matrix. This schedule assumes that the firm keeps no minimum balance and that First City Bank will automatically finance all overdrafts.
11. Complete the cash budget, assuming Acme requires a minimum $900 transactions cash in its demand deposit account at all times.

TABLE 4.1 Acme's Cash Budget

Acme Toy Company
Cash Budget
31-Mar-94
(in 000's up to decimal point)

		Actual Sales				Forecasted Sales					
		December	January	February	March	April	May	June	July	August	September
Total Sales		900.00	900.00	1,800.00	2,250.00	2,700.00	3,600.00	5,400.00	5,400.00	2,700.00	1,800.00
Credit Sales		45.00	63.00	90.00	180.00	225.00	450.00	1,575.00	1,575.00	135.00	45.00
Cash Sales						2,475.00	3,150.00	3,825.00	3,825.00	2,565.00	1,755.00
First Month (A)						56.25	112.50	393.75	393.75	33.75	11.25
Second Month (B)						9.00	11.25	22.50	78.75	78.75	6.75
Third Month(C)						36.90	73.80	92.25	184.50	645.75	645.75
Fourth Month (D)						5.67	8.10	16.20	20.25	40.50	141.75
Total Cash Receipts Forecasted from Sales						2,582.82	3,355.65	4,349.70	4,502.25	3,363.75	2,560.50
and Collections											
(A) Percent of Current Month's Credit Sales	25.00%										
(B) Percent of Prior Month's Credit Sales	5.00%										
(C) Percent of Second Prior Month Credit Sales	41.00%										
(D) Percent of Third Prior Months Credit Sales	9.00%										
Total Cash Receipts Forecasted from Sales and Collections						2,582.82	3,355.65	4,349.70	4,502.25	3,363.75	2,560.50
Cash Dividends Received						45.00			45.00		
Disposals								540.00			
Interest						9.00	9.00	9.00	9.00	9.00	9.00
Total Cash Inflow						2,636.82	3,364.65	4,898.70	4,556.25	3,372.75	2,569.50
Cash Disbursements for Purchases											
		Actual Purchases				Forecasted Purchases					
		December	January	February	March	April	May	June	July	August	September
Total		2,700.00	2,700.00	1,350.00	900.00	900.00	900.00	450.00	225.00	225.00	270.00
Credit		1,800.00	1,800.00	1,350.00	900.00	900.00	900.00	225.00	45.00	45.00	90.00
Cash						0.00	0.00	225.00	180.00	180.00	180.00
Payment											
First Month (A)						225.00	225.00	56.25	11.25	11.25	22.50
Second Month (B)						558.00	558.00	558.00	139.50	27.90	27.90
Third Month (C)						148.50	99.00	99.00	99.00	24.75	4.95
Fourth Month (D)						27.00	20.25	13.50	13.50	13.50	3.38
Total Cash Disbursements Forecasted from Purchases						958.50	902.25	951.75	443.25	257.40	238.73
(A) Percent d Current Month's Credit Purchases	25.00%										
(B) Percent of Prior Month's Credit Purchases	62.00%										
(C) Percent of Second Prior Month'c Credit Purchases	11.00%										
(D) Percent d Third Prior Months Credit Purchases	1.50%										
Total Cash Disbursements						April	May	June	July	August	September
Selling Expenses						958.50	902.25	951.75	443.25	257.40	238.73
General and Administration Expenses						765.00	900.00	1,080.00	1,080.00	540.00	360.00
Taxes: Income						1,350.00	1,620.00	1,530.00	1,350.00	1,350.00	1,350.00
Taxes: Withholding						126.00			126.00		
Pensions						90.00	90.00	90.00	90.00	90.00	90.00
Dividends						45.00		45.00		45.00	
Funded Debt Payments						63.00			63.00		
Total Cash Outflow						450.00		450.00			
						3,847.50	3,512.25	3,696.75	3,602.25	2,282.40	2,038.73
Juxtaposing Total Cash Inflows to Total Cash Outflows:											
						April	May	June	July	August	September
Total Cash In						2,636.82	3,364.65	4,898.70	4,556.25	3,372.75	2,569.50
Total Cash Out						3,847.50	3,512.25	3,696.75	3,602.25	2,282.40	2,038.73
Net Cash Available						(1,210.68)	(147.60)	1,201.95	954.00	1,090.35	530.78
Cummulative Cash Available						(1,210.68)	(1,358.28)	(156.33)	797.67	1,888.02	2,418.80

Thus, Acme Toy Company will require $1,210,680 in cash in April and $147,600 in May, looking to its own cash and marketable securities account. This assumes that the cash and marketable securities account on March 31, is $900 and the firm needs $900 in cash to operate. It is obvious that the firm does not need a credit line of $7.5 million originally as requested. A credit line of $1.5 million to 2 million appears to satisfy the requirements of the budget. ATC needs to borrow from utside sources as follows:

						April	May	June	July	August	September
Net Cash Available						(1,210.68)	(147.60)	1,201.95	954.00	1,090.35	530.78
Cash Balance Available (Balance March 31)						900.00	(310.68)	(458.28)	743.67	1,697.67	2,788.02
Cummulative (Financial Needs) Surplus Zero Balance Account						(310.68)	(458.28)	743.67	1,697.67	2,788.02	3,318.80
Mininum Cash Balance						900.00	900.00	900.00	900.00	900.00	900.00
Cummulative (Fancial Needs) Minimun Balance Account						(1,210.68)	(1,358.28)	(156.33)	797.67	1,888.02	2,418.80

Trial Balance and Break-Even Inventory

Trial balances take "snapshots" of general ledger accounts for assets, liabilities, and owner's equity during any point in the season. Lenders, to detect liquidity problems that compromise repayment, use the break-even inventory method, derived from a trial balance. Liquidity problems stem from inventory devaluations (write-downs), and trouble can surface quickly—two or three months down the season—often on the heels of disappointing bookings. At this point in time, inventory value usually falls below recorded book value.

Trial balances are associated with the *periodic* inventory method, inventory counted and valued at the lower of cost or market "periodically," as opposed to the *perpetual* inventory system, inventory counted and valued frequently. Because ending inventory determines cost of goods sold and ultimately profits, *bankers should know inventory value throughout the season.* Examples of perpetual inventory include items scanned into the computer a shopper sees at cash registers and high-ticket items painstakingly monitored. Of the two methods, periodic inventory is more uncertain, rendering seasonal analysis indefinable at best if not nigh impossible unless break-even techniques are effectively employed.

Though accountants have not appraised inventory value, assuming periodic inventory, management certainly has—how could they not know if inventory is reduced to fire sale values? Thus, lenders derive *break-even inventory* by first asking management for estimated *lower of cost or market inventory* values. They then figure spreads between the two—break-even and estimated. For example, if inventory *required* to break even is $700,000 while management's *estimated* inventory is $300,000, net loss for the period is derived at $400,000. *Interim losses caused by large devaluations reduce chances of a debt cleanup.* The logic is that write-downs follow production problems, poor strategic planning, stockpiling, canceled orders, overly optimistic sales projections, and flawed cash budgets.

Seasonal Ratio Analysis

Seasonal ratios (reviewed in the Finn Coat case study presented later in this chapter) are analyzed on a comparative basis and summarized in the write-up.

(Cash + Accounts receivable)/(Short-term bank debt + Trade payables)

Near the seasonal low point, cash and receivables should be sufficient to reduce short-term debt and trade payables.

Returns and allowances/Gross sales

High ratios may be due to merchandise allowances, defective lines, or a missed season. Have returns been reshipped on a timely basis? Holdover goods post-season are usually written down.

Purchases/Sales

A high ratio point may be due to saturated inventory, or may just be the result of normal gearing up in anticipation of strong orders.

Break Even Shipments (BES)

BES derives shipments (gross sales) needed to break even. Shipments must be sufficient to cover production and operating expenses for both shipping (forecast) periods and buildup (historical) months in order for the obligor to produce fiscal profits. BES is best used a few months before season's end since minimal sales occur early in the cycle. Some successful seasons are chronicled by late, brief selling, culminating in excellent shipping months just prior to fiscal. Christmas ornament manufacturers, for example, ship very late in the season with profits during seasonal months offsetting losses that come with production. The following equation derives break-even shipments:

$$Sb = \frac{Ei}{(Gi)(1 - Ri)}$$

where Sb = Break-even shipments
         Ei = Estimated expenses
         Gi = Interim gross profit margin, which can be derived from the break-even inventory method
         Ri = (Returns + Allowances + Discount on sales)/Gross sales

Sb must be compared to Se, the value of shipments the company expects to ship over the period being analyzed.

If $Se > Sb$, results will be profitable
If $Se < Sb$, losses will result
If $Se = Sb$, the company breaks even

EXAMPLE: BREAK-EVEN SHIPMENTS

A firm provides the following information for the month of April. Can we expect a profit or loss based on the data given?

- Estimated gross profit margin is 35%
- Estimated shipments are $ 500,000
- Returns allowances and discounts are 10% of gross sales
- Expected expenses are $ 200,000

The solution can be calculated as follows:

$$Sb = \frac{Ei}{(Gi)(1 - Ri)}$$

$$Sb = \frac{200,000}{(.35)(1 - .10)}$$

$$Sb = 634,921$$

Compare Sb to Se. Since estimated shipments (Se) of 500,000 fall below the break-even point (Sb) of 634,921, the firm can expect a loss during the month of April.

Review Early Warning Signs of Trouble

While storm signals come in all shapes and sizes, the big question is, are problems temporary or structural? As the lender, you must be the judge. The following situations warrant your attention:

1. Slow in-house orders in comparison to corresponding periods in previous years.
2. Factory operating well below capacity.
3. Changes in the manner payables are paid.
4. Owners no longer take pride in their business.
5. Frequent visits to the customer's place of business reveals deteriorating general appearance of the premises. For example, rolling stock and equipment has not been properly maintained.
6. Loans to or from officers and affiliates.
7. Management does not know what condition the company is in and the direction in which it is headed.
8. The lender did not examine the obligor's cash budget and as a result overestimated seasonal peaks and valleys thereby approving an excessive loan.
9. An inability to clean up bank debt or cleanups effected by rotating bank debt.
10. Unusual items in the financial statements.
11. Negative trends, such as losses, weak gross margins, slowness in accounts receivable, and decrease in sales volume.
12. Intercompany payables/receivables are not adequately explained.
13. Cash balances are substantially reduced or are overdrawn and uncollected during normally liquid periods.
14. Management fails to take trade discounts because of poor inventory turnover.
15. Cash flow problems and very low probabilities that operating cash flows will cover debt service.
16. Withholding tax liability builds as taxes are used to pay other debt.
17. Frequent downtiering of financial reporting sparked in an effort hire a more "liberal" accountant.
18. Changes in financial management.

19. Totals on receivables and payables aging schedules do not agree with amounts shown on the balance sheet of the same date.

20. At the end of the cycle, creditors are not completely paid out. The bank sometimes can be paid out when the borrower leans on the trade. (This often gives bankers a false sense of security, but the company may be unable to borrow from the trade for the next buildup of inventory.)

21. Sharp reduction in officers' salaries brings a lower standard of living to company managers and might suggest a last ditch effort to save a distressed business. Alternatively, reduced salaries might signal a concerted effort to make headway.

22. Erratic interim results, signaling a departure from normal and historical seasonal patterns.

23. The lender does not allow enough cushion for error. If the seasonal loan is not repaid and there is no other way out but liquidation of collateral, the lender is taking possession of collateral at the worst possible time. It is the end of the season, and if the obligor cannot sell, how will the bank?

24. Financials are submitted late in an attempt by managers or their accountants to postpone unfavorable news.

25. Unwillingness to provide budgets, projections, or interim information.

26. Suppliers cut back terms or request COD.

27. Changes in inventory, followed by an excessive inventory buildup or the retention of obsolete merchandise.

28. The borrower changes suppliers frequently, or transient buying results in higher raw material costs.

29. Increased inventory to one customer or perilous reliance on one account.

30. Changing concentration from a major well-known customer to one of lesser stature, pointing to problem inventory. A good mix of customers is the best defense against "seasonal shock therapy."

31. The lender permits advances on the seasonal loan to fund other purposes, notably payments on the bank's own term debt. Indeed, the term debt is handled as agreed, but the seasonal loan goes up and stays up.

32. Company loses an important supplier or customer.

33. Concentrations in receivables and payables. Failure to get satisfactory explanations on these concentrations. Failure to conduct investigations on the creditworthiness of larger receivables.

34. The lender finances highly speculative inventory whereby the borrower is trying for a "home run."

35. Intangible signals, such as failure to look the banker in the eye, letting the condition of the business deteriorate, or taking longer to return calls.

36. Management orders three-pound lobsters during a banker's lunch because the bank is picking up the check. This weekend they won't be able to afford gourmet dining—the firm has just gone off the cliff.

DEFENSIVE MEASURES

Prudently structured credits fall back on a second way out, or, as the literature defines it, a good exit strategy. Temporary problems usually are not serious: the bank simply waives the annual cleanup. If conditions are precarious, the bank may decide to restructure the credit—that is, extend a term loan or revolver to be repaid over the next few years out of operating cash flows. A loan agreement, by virtue of its covenants and events of default, will give the bank greater control over the credit. Consider these important factors:

- *Cash flow.* Strong cash flows are crucial to debt service. If an established seasonal borrower boasts a solid track record, the bank can afford to be generous. This year's temporary problems may be corrected with strong cash flow returning over the next year or two. But if cash flow expectations are bleak, the banker can expect a series of chronic structural problems.
- *Equity injection.* Owners may be asked to inject cash in the form of subordinated debt, or straight equity if profits cannot sustain the capital structure or if assets are poorly utilized.

TABLE 4.2   The Arithmetic of Working Capital

Equation	Equation defined	Explanation
1	Assets = Liabilities + Equity	Basic accounting equation
2	Working capital = Current assets – Current Liabilities	Traditional definition of working capital
3	Current assets + Fixed assets = Current liabilities + Fixed liabilities + Equity	Equation 1 expanded
4	Current Assets – Current liabilities = Fixed liabilities + Equity – Fixed assets	Rearrange current accounts to the left of the equal sign and non current accounts to the right.
5	Working capital = Fixed liabilities + Equity – Fixed assets	Substitution: Equation 2 equals Equation 4
6	ΔWorking capital = ΔFixed liabilities + ΔFixed assets – ΔEquity	Increases in WC are a function of increases in fixed liabilities, increases in equity and decreases in fixed assets
7	Working capital + Fixed assets = Fixed liabilities + Equity	Equation 5 rearranged with fixed assets moved to the left side of the equal sign

- *Formula-based advances.* Such advances against confirmed orders, or asset liens, may work on a temporary basis (see Chapter 5).
- *Credit insurance.* Insurance against excessive losses may be assigned to the bank. However, if the business is in trouble, credit insurance will be unavailable or prohibitively expensive.

Working Capital as a Defensive Measure

Broadly defined, working capital is the excess of current assets over current liabilities. It is cash and other assets expected to be consumed or converted into cash over the accounting period less obligations due during the same period. Working capital is a generic measure of liquidity acting as the margin of protection short-term creditors look to, behind (the primary source of payment) conversion of current assets. In short, a basic understanding of working capital mechanics (and cash flow) provides lenders with a way to differentiate between temporary or structural problems.

Cash Flow versus Working Capital Analysis

A cash flow is more refined than a working capital analysis and should always be used to evaluate loans with maturities beyond one year. However, working capital concepts are much more direct and perfectly suited for seasonal—"What's my second way out?"—analysis.

The Mechanics of Working Capital

Simple, very useful working capital math (Table 4.2) crystallizes the flow funds approach and points the way to the second way out of the credit.

From Equation 6 we see that subtracting the noncurrent accounts of two balance sheets is equal to working capital. Thus, increases in noncurrent liabilities, increases in equity, and reductions in noncurrent assets represent sources of funds. Decreases in noncurrent liabilities, decreases in equity, and increases in noncurrent assets serve as uses of working capital.

Equation 7 is the core of working capital liquidity analysis, helping to answer the question, are these temporary or structural problems? The right side of Equation 7—long-term liabilities (generally funded debt) plus equity, is the firm's capital structure (or permanent financing). Equation 7 easily confirms that the capital structure supports both fixed assets and the firm's entire working capital position. For example, suppose you lent money to a business only to find out that because of structural problems (competitive pressures, eroding gross profit margin, etc.) the obligor will at best break even. Assuming no new stock is issued, the equity component of the capital structure decreases or stays constant.

Next, since a major attractor of debt capacity is continuous expansion of the equity base, the firm may find it difficult to attract debt capital. The right side of

Equation 7 will reduce or remain unchanged at best. Let's assume capital expenditures are bottlenecked—the major part of the capital expansion program the bank financed has been poorly deployed. If the fixed asset component (Equation 7) balloons upward while the capital structure stagnates or falls, lenders will likely not have liquidity protection—or they will find the preverbal second way out of the credit.

On the other hand, suppose the borrower promises strong, quality profits over the next few years. The firm will likely prosper and draw on its long-term financing sources. The capital structure will indeed expand, and if fixed assets are maintained at efficient levels, the working capital component in Equation 7 expands nicely. Liquidity flows into the business to finance innovative product lines, reduce debt levels, help fund acquisitions, and position the balance sheet for high yield restructuring, leveraged buyouts, treasury stock purchases, and so on. Equation 7 provides a straightforward methodology to working capital (funds) analysis. The mathematics of Equation 7 point to three factors that produce liquidity levels short-term lenders look to for protection:

1. Before you approve a seasonal loan, evaluate exit strategies. The best one, a surefire second way out, is *Equation 7 liquidity*. Make sure strong (high-quality) profits are attainable—and sustainable—and that sufficient profits are retained to fund debt service.
2. Encourage borrowers to borrow long term if funds are used to expand core assets (capital expenditures).
3. Ask for a capital budget, evaluate and authenticate it, and confirm that capital outlays produce industry-acceptable internal rates of return.

CASE STUDY   Finn Coat Manufacturing Corp.

On Ocotber 15, 20x8, Finn Coat Manufacturing reported its results ($000s) for the previous nine months (Exhibit I).

EXHIBIT I   Finn Coat Manufacturing 9/30/x8 Nine-Month Results Prepared By J. Smith, Treasurer

Account	9/30/x8	9/30/x7 (1)
Cash	15	125
Sales (gross)	3,080	3,600
Accruals	1,180	
Purchases	560	
Prepaid expenses	735	
Net plant and equipment	7,111	

Discounts on sales	187	200
Intangibles	140	
Equity	2,900	
Factory labor*	490	
Freight in*	80	
Short-term bank debt	1,000	200
Long-term debt	6,000	6,000
Factory depreciation expense	30*	
Officer salaries	28	70
Returns and allowances	153	135
Other assets	1,875	
Fiscal (beginning) inventory*	840	
Accounts receivable	1,100	1,150
Accounts payable	680	775
Factory overhead*	650	
Administration expense	280	
Selling expense	536	
Estimated tax expense	30	

*Cost of goods sold items.
(1) Only partial comparatives were available.

After analyzing the figures, you place a call to J. Smith, who informs you of the following details:

1. Inventory (cost or market) as of today (10/18/x8) is worth a good $650.
2. Due to an increase in foreign imports, coupled with temporary shortages, profit margins have been squeezed. However, margins should increase slightly in December and by next June the gross profit will approach the 12/31/x7 fiscal gross profit margin of 36%. (Fiscal 19x7 net sales were $4,700.)
3. Delivery and production schedules indicate that $400 will be shipped in October and $200 in November.
4. Expenses in October and November are expected to be $110 and $130, respectively.
5. Returns, allowances, and discounts to gross sales are expected to continue unchanged from the trial balance date.
6. The credit file indicates that more than 50 trade inquiries were received over the past two months versus historical levels of approximately 20 during the same time period.

Finn Coat Manufacturing Analysis

1. Derive a break-even (B/E) income statement and balance sheet. Compare break-even inventory with management's estimates. Determine the magnitude of profit or loss. Determine the interim gross profit margin.
2. Calculate seasonal ratios.
3. Derive break-even shipments.
4. Write up Finn's interim results incorporating break-even and ratio analyses.
5. Meet with Finn Coat's management and suggest follow-up.

As step 1 in Exhibit II shows, you will first need to derive a break-even income statement and balance sheet, comparing break-even inventory with management's estimate of inventory value (on the basis of cost or market value, whichever is lower). If the break-even point is higher than estimated inventory, the firm will suffer a loss measured by the nine-month difference between the two inventory values. In addition, determine the interim gross profit margin.

EXHIBIT II Finn Coat Manfacturing Break-Even Income Statement (9/30 x8) and Break-Even Inventory

Steps to derive break-even inventory	Trial balance information		
Step 4: Include sales *given*	Sales		3,080
Steps 5 and 6: Returns and allowances and discounts given	Returns and allowances	(153)	
	Discounts	(187)	(340)
Step 7: *Derive* net sales	Net sales		2,740
Step 8: *Calculate* break-even cost of goods sold			
	B/E cost of goods sold		(1,866)
Step 3: Let gross profit = expenses	B/E gross profit		874
Step 2: Include expenses *given*	Officers salaries		(28)
	Administration expenses		(280)
	Selling expenses		(536)
	Estimated taxes		(30)
Step 1: Profits assumed *break even*	B/E profit		0

Break-even inventory position

Break-even inventory	
Plus (fiscal) beginning inventory (given)	840
Plus purchases (given)	560
Plus labor (given)	490

Plus freight in (given)	80
Plus depreciation (given)	30
Plus overhead (given)	650
Less:	
Break-even cost of goods sold (derived as before)	(1,866)
Equals break-even inventory	784

Profit/Loss estimate

Management's estimated inventory	650
Less: Break-even inventory	784
Equals interim loss	**(134)**

Interim gross profit margin

Cost of goods sold	
Fiscal inventory	840
Purchases	560
Factory labor	490
*Freight in	80
Depreciation	30
Overhead	650
Less: Mgt. estimated inventory	(650)
Equals actual cost of goods sold	**2,000**

Measure actual interim gross profit margin
= Gross profit/sales
= 2740 – 2000 / 2740
= 27%

Break-even balance sheet*** 9/30/x8

Cash	15	Accruals	1,180
Accounts receivable	1100	Accounts payable	680
B/E inventory*	784	Short-term debt	1,000
Prepaid expenses	735	Long-term debt	6,000
Fixed assets	7111	Fiscal equity**	2,900
Other assets	1875		
Intangibles	140		
Total assets	**11,760**	**Liabilities and equity**	**11,760**

* Plug
** Equity remains unchanged from fiscal amounts (i.e., it breaks even).
*** Notice that the break-even balance sheet produces the same inventory as the break-even derived on the income statement.

Since Finn's estimated inventory is below the break-even point, the firm suffered a nine-month loss. The banker surmises the loss is due to an inventory write-down—just the thing to affect liquidity and seasonal ratios. Ratio analysis along with basic trial balance analysis will corroborate Finn's poor year:

Ratio	19x8	19x7
Cash + accounts receivable/Short-term debt + Accounts payable	.66	1.30
Returns and allowances/Gross sales	.049	.038
Short-term debt/Accounts payable	1.5	.26

- Officer salaries declined to $42 from $70.
- Nine-month gross sales declined 14%.
- Liquidity is low compared to last year.
- Short-term debt and payables have not reduced.
- Receivables increased substantially relative to sales.

As a final step, determine shipments required for the company to break even for the months of October 19x8 and November 19x8.

- Compare each month's break-even shipments to management's estimates of shipments.
- Determine if the firm will be profitable during each of the two months.
- Use the actual interim gross profit to find break-even shipments.

$Sb = Ei/(Gi)(1 - Ri)$

$Sb \text{ (Oct.)} = 110/(.27)(1 - .11) = 457 > 300 \sim \sim Loss$

$Sb \text{ (Nov.)} = 130/(.27)(1 - .11) = 540 > 200 \sim \sim Loss$

The Write-up

Nine-month 19x8 gross sales declined 14% to $3,080M from the corresponding period the previous year. Returns and allowances increased slightly to 4.9%. The gross profit margin, derived at 27%, was weak and reflected the high cost of linings associated with temporary shortages. Break-even inventory of $784 was well over management's estimate of $650M, suggesting an interim loss of around $134M.

The poor interim performance affected liquidity as cash and receivables were only 66% of bank and trade debt, versus 1.3X the previous year. Accounts receivable declined to $1,100M but moved faster than sales. Increased reliance on bank lines was evidenced by bank-to-trade debt of 1.5X versus .26, while two-month trade inquiries jumped to 50, a considerable increase over historical periods. Noteworthy was the decline in officers' salaries to $42M from $70M.

The firm's weak interim performance is not expected to improve over the next few months as only $400M and $200M will be shipped in October and November, significantly below the break-even level of $457M and $540M. As part of your evaluation of Finn Coat Manufacturing, you should arrange a meeting with management and the firm's accountant to discuss these results.

As the account officer, you should prepare a cash budget to pinpoint the inflow and outflow of funds. Check loan documentation to ensure it is current and in order.

If the problem is minor and expected to be temporary, then your bank may merely waive this year's cleanup. If the problem is more acute, other steps may have to be taken. The bank may decide to restructure Finn's loan by creating a loan to be repaid over months or years from internally generated cash flow (this presumes that future cash flows are expected). The loan agreement, by virtue of its covenants and events of default, will give the bank greater control over the borrower. Loans may also be put on a demand basis, although the effect on the borrower is largely psychological. Also consider (1) *cash-flow (strong cash flows are crucial), (2) equity injections, (3) formula-based advances including accounts receivable financing,* and (4) *collateral.*

Many firms unsuited for unsecured seasonal borrowings may meet financing needs by securing assets or changing over to accounts receivable financing. Chapter 5 examines collateral and accounts receivable financing in relation to the risk characteristics of the borrower, advantages to the borrower and the bank, credit and collateral analysis, documentation, and safeguards to ensure the authenticity and collectibility of assigned collateral. Collateral will not automatically assure payment—the bank will need to judge the overall risks of the credit by evaluating the quality and magnitude of collateral, the borrower's financial condition, management's strategic plans, cash flow, and debt servicing ability. But most important are the internal controls, policies, practices, and procedures of the bank itself.

5

ASSET-BASED LENDING

Many bankers would prefer to extend unsecured credit because unsecured loans entail lower overhead costs. Firms unable to borrow unsecured generally fall into these categories:

1. New and unproven business life cycle
2. Questionable ability to service unsecured debt
3. Year-round financing in amounts too large to justify unsecured credit
4. Working capital and profits insufficient to periodically clean up short-term loans
5. Working capital inadequate for sales volume and type of operation
6. Previous unsecured borrowings no longer warranted because of various credit factors
7. Loan amounts that fall beyond the borrower's unsecured credit limit

Secured borrowers can be categorized into two broad market segments: short- and long-term.

Banks can utilize collateral and guarantees to help mitigate risks inherent in individual credits but transactions should be entered into primarily on the strength of the borrower's repayment capacity. Collateral cannot be a substitute for a comprehensive assessment of the borrower or counterparty, nor can it compensate for insufficient information. It should be recognized that any credit enforcement actions (e.g., foreclosure proceedings) typically eliminate the profit margin on the transaction. In addition, banks need to be mindful that the value of collateral may well be impaired by the same factors that have led to the diminished recoverability of the credit. Banks should have policies covering the acceptability of various forms of collateral, procedures for the ongoing valuation of such collateral, and a process to ensure that collateral is, and continues to be, enforceable and realizable. With regard to guarantees, banks should evaluate the level of coverage being provided in relation to the credit quality and legal capacity of the guarantor. Banks should only factor explicit guarantees into the credit decision and not those that might be considered implicit such as anticipated support from the government.

Source: Basel Committee on Banking Supervision, Basel, July 1999.

MARKET SEGMENTS

Short-term secured borrowers	Long-term secured borrowers
Commodities	Real estate
Middle market and microbusinesses	Project finance
Finance companies	Leasing
High net worth individuals	Corporate finance
	Transportation and shipping
	High net worth individuals

When evaluating collateral, banks take into account the degree of coverage and economic life cycle of the collateral versus the term of the loan, constraints liquidating collateral, and the bank's ability to monitor and liquidate collateral, namely (1) collateral values matched to credit exposures, (2) liquidity (how quickly value can be realized), and (3) legal rights to pledged assets. Companies finance against receivables when existing credit facilities cannot finance expanding needs or when requirements fluctuate beyond acceptable norms.

Secured financing offers several advantages from the borrower's view:

- It is an efficient way to finance an expanding operation because borrowing capacity expands along with sales.
- It permits borrowers to take advantage of purchase discounts because cash is received immediately upon sales, permitting prompt payment to suppliers and thereby earning the company a good enough reputation to reduce the cost of purchases.
- It ensures a revolving, expanding line of credit.

Secured financing also offers advantages to the bank:

- Collateral loans generate a relatively high yield loan.
- Secured financing generates a depository relationship.
- It permits a continuing banking relationship with long-standing customers whose financial condition no longer warrants unsecured credit.
- It generates new business.
- It minimizes potential loss when loans are formula based—advances made against a percentage of acceptable collateral.
- Expansion of volume often requires additional financing as existing bank lines prove inadequate.

BASIC AXIOMS OF ASSET-BASED LENDING

Bankers generally look at collateral as cake frosting, the cake being cash flow. As we saw in the first chapter, collateral acts as the secondary means of repayment, with cash flow or asset conversion being the primary source. Borrowers are, after all, going concerns—they should not be in liquidation or restructuring nor should they be likely candidates for either at the time the bank considers taking collateral.

As such, banks should establish lending standards governing asset-based loans before obtaining collateral. These standards should be derived from well-defined loan policies and procedures. Peter Larr offers the following guidelines for successful asset based lending:[1]

Financial Analysis

This means a due diligence effort to follow the PRISM method from top to bottom—a thorough financial analysis, with analytic standards equal to unsecured deals.

Seniority

Seniority refers to placing a priority on obligor assets over other creditors via a legally protected claim on specific collateral, or it means that the bank is senior on unsecured claims against an asset pool to which no other creditor has a claim.

Protection

Defined as the net realizable value of the specific assets that, upon liquidation, the collateral should be adequate to cover a risk exposure (principal, accrued interest, and collection costs). Collateral protection includes five and possibly more links:

---

[1] Peter Larr was a senior vice president and risk asset review executive at Chase Manhattan.

1. *Value.* Value is associated with market price. How a market price is obtained depends on the nature of the collateral. Price quotations taken from a newspaper or from an electronic feed to a production system for listed securities are quite different from an appraiser's opinion of the value of a painting. Valuations of real estate present complexities because they are affected by capitalization rates and projected cash flow assumptions regarding leasing or sellout rates.

2. *Margin.* Margins should be sufficient to include coverage of the borrower's overhead for the period of time necessary for the borrower to liquidate the collateral on behalf of the lender. This is realistic since the borrower, even in financial distress, would likely be able to dispose of collateral faster, more easily, and more cheaply than the lender.

3. *Vulnerability.* Event risk and inherent volatility make up the risk of vulnerability.

4. *Marketability.* The ease and timeliness of liquidation, which can affect value and margin, are part of the marketability concept.

5. *Insurance.* Assets taken as collateral must be properly insured in order to protect value. If collateral is not fully insured, at least the value and the margin should be reassessed.

Control

Poor collateral control can lead to loss. If a bank is unable to ensure internal quality control, then the institution should not encourage collateralized exposures. See the Home Federal Savings & Loan case at the chapter's conclusion. Collateral monitoring requires two broad designs: management and auditing with the proper resources devoted to the management of both operations and systems supporting collateral. This means trained personnel must administer the collateral loan book to ensure collateral retains acceptable values.

SECURITY INTEREST

A security interest in loans arises when lenders receive something more tangible than traditional promises of repayment. Any asset allowing title transfer acts as a pledge to secured credit; upon default, banks have rights, senior to other creditors, to claim assets pledged.

If a borrower defaults on a secured loan and collateral is sold for less than the loan amount, the bank becomes a general or unsecured creditor for the balance. The last thing a secured lender wants is an unsecured loan position, since collateral was required to approve the deal in the first place. Therefore, banks want collateral with market values that are comfortably above loan exposures (i.e., the loan-to-value ratio is minimized) and pledged assets with durability (life span) in excess of loan terms.

Secured loans require documentation, generally known as *security* agreements. A bank's security interest in collateral is formalized with a security agreement signed by bank and borrower (the parties) and filed with a public office (usually the secretary of state) in the state the collateral is located. This filing gives public notice to interested parties that the lender has prior claim to collateral. Before approving loans, lenders search public records to determine if pledged assets are secured elsewhere. The *Uniform Commercial Code (UCC)* deals with lender protection on security interests. Bankers should be familiar with the UCC before they obtain a security interest in collateral.

Under Article 9 of the UCC, the bank must create a valid and enforceable security interest and "perfect" that interest. Once enforceable security interest is created, the secured party can always enforce it, on default, against the debtor, provided there is no superior third-party interest. If the holder of a valid and enforceable Article 9 interest takes the additional steps required under Article 9 "to perfect," it will defeat most such third parties. Sections 9-203 and 9-204 of the UCC require that the parties take four steps to create a valid and enforceable security interest:

1. Enter into a security agreement.
2. Reduce as much of that agreement to writing as is necessary to satisfy Section 9-203 (which also requires that the debtor sign this writing), or give possession of the collateral to the creditor.
3. Have the debtor acquire rights in the collateral.
4. Have the secured party give value.

Section 9-302(10) provides for automatic "perfection," without filing a financing statement, when any or all assignments to the bank do not transfer a significant part of the outstanding accounts of the borrower. However, in all other accounts' receivable security interests, the bank must file a financing statement to "perfect" its security interest. The law of the jurisdiction in which the debtor is located governs the "perfection" of the security interest. Location is determined by place of business, executive office, or residence if the debtor has no place of business in the state. Federal Reserve examiners focus on a multitude of issues during bank audits (see also Appendix 1 to Chapter 5, "Accounts Receivable Financing Key Points).

FEDERAL RESERVE AUDIT GUIDELINES: COLLATERAL[2]

The Commercial Bank Examination Manual suggests that leaders ask the following questions when evaluating collateral:

---

[2] *Commercial Bank Examination Manual,* Division of Banking Supervision and Regulation, The Board of Governors, Federal Reserve System. The entire 1,130-page manual is available in Adobe format on the CD: Subdirectory: Library/Federal Reserve Systems manuals.

1. Is negotiable collateral held under joint custody?
2. Has the customer obtained and filed for released collateral sign receipts?
3. Are securities and commodities valued and margin requirements reviewed at least monthly?
4. When the support rests on the cash surrender value of insurance policies, is a periodic accounting received from the insurance company and maintained with the policy?
5. Is a record maintained of entry to the collateral vault?
6. Are stock powers filed separately to bar negotiability and to deter abstraction of both the security and the negotiating instrument?
7. Are securities out for transfer, exchange, and so on controlled by prenumbered temporary vault-out tickets?
8. Has the bank instituted a system which ensures that security agreements are filed, collateral mortgages are properly recorded, title searches and property appraisals are performed in connection with collateral mortgages, and insurance coverage (including loss payee clause) is in effect on property covered by collateral mortgages?
9. Are acknowledgments received for pledged deposits held at other banks?
10. Is an officer's approval necessary before collateral can be released or substituted?
11. Does the bank have an internal review system that reexamines collateral items for negotiability and proper assignment, checks values assigned to collateral when the loan is made and at frequent intervals thereafter, determines that items out on temporary vault-out tickets are authorized and have not been outstanding for an unreasonable length of time, and determines that loan payments are promptly posted?
12. Are all notes assigned consecutive numbers and recorded on a note register or similar record? Do numbers on notes agree to those recorded on the register?
13. Are collection notices handled by someone not connected with loan processing?
14. In mortgage warehouse financing, does the bank hold the original mortgage note, trust deed, or other critical document, releasing only against payment?
15. Have standards been set for determining the percentage advance to be made against acceptable receivables?
16. Are acceptable receivables defined?
17. Has the bank established minimum requirements for verification of the borrower's accounts receivable and established minimum standards for documentation?

18. Are accounts receivable financing policies reviewed at least annually to determine if they are compatible with changing market conditions?
19. Have loan statements, delinquent accounts, collection requests, and past due notices been checked to the trial balances that are used in reconciling subsidiary records of accounts receivable financing loans with general ledger accounts?
20. Have inquiries about accounts receivable financing loan balances been received and investigated?
21. Is the bank in receipt of documents supporting recorded credit adjustments to loan accounts or accrued interest receivable accounts? Have these documents been checked or tested subsequently?
22. Are terms, dates, weights, description of merchandise, and other particulars, shown on invoices, shipping documents, delivery receipts, and bills of lading? Are these documents scrutinized for differences?
23. Were payments from customers scrutinized for differences in invoice dates, numbers, terms, and so on?
24. Do bank records show, on a timely basis, a first lien on the assigned receivables for each borrower?
25. Do loans granted on the security of the receivables also have an assignment of the inventory?
26. Does the bank verify the borrower's accounts receivable or require independent verification on a periodic basis?
27. Does the bank require the borrower to provide aged accounts receivable schedules on a periodic basis?

LOANS SECURED WITH ACCOUNTS RECEIVABLES

Accounts receivable financing is an arrangement whereby a bank or finance company either advances funds by *purchasing* invoices or accounts receivable outright over a period of time (*factoring*) or lends against receivables, using an assignment on receivables as primary collateral. Factoring is conducted on a notification basis (the client's customer is notified that the factor purchased receivables), whereas straight receivable financing is practiced on a non-notification basis.

Although accounts receivable loans are collateralized, bankers analyze the borrower's financial statements as if loans were unsecured. Financial statements are analyzed with particular focus on working capital trends. Even if collateral quality is solid and well in excess of the loan, borrowers must demonstrate they are creditworthy; collateral liquidation is an exit strategy of last resort (there may be court claims against collateral if the firm is in financial distress and the banker books the loan with prior knowledge of the borrower's condition).

Trade reports are reviewed, and agings of receivables and payables are scrutinized. Banks take only *acceptable receivables*, accounts that are current or not more than a given number of days past due (see Exhibit I, Accounts Receivable Audit Worksheet, and Exhibit II, Borrowing Base Analysis). The entire amount of receivables may be unacceptable if a certain percentage (e.g., 10%) is 90 days or more delinquent. Also, a limit is placed on the maximum dollar amount due from any one account debtor, since there is always the possibility of unforeseen and undisclosed credit failure or a return of merchandise. A common benchmark is for lenders to ensure that no more than 20% of assigned receivables are from one customer. To verify the authenticity of pledged collateral, banks institute a program of direct confirmation. This procedure is particularly important if receivables are pledged on a non-notification basis, since the bank does not have the same control of the debtor accounts as it does when the receivables are pledged on a notification basis.

The following factors should be considered in evaluating the quality of receivables pledged:[3]

• *The turnover of the receivables pledged and the borrower's credit limit.* If the turnover is decreasing, the quality of receivables may be deteriorating.

• *Aging of accounts receivable.* The bank should obtain a monthly aging of the accounts receivable pledged. The banker should note the percentage of accounts delinquent in relation to the total accounts pledged, concentrations if any, and those accounts with past due balances that also have current amounts due.

• *Concentration of debtor accounts.* A lender may be vulnerable to loss if a large percentage of the dollar amount of receivables assigned is concentrated in a few accounts. A list of concentrations should be prepared periodically showing the largest accounts.

• *Ineligible receivables.* Lenders should be aware of receivables, which, by their nature, should be excluded from the lending formula. The following receivables are examples:

- *Due from affiliated companies.* Although such receivables might be valid, the temptation for the borrower to create fraudulent invoices would be great.
- *Receivables subject to a purchase money interest, such as floorplan arrangements.* The manufacturer will frequently file financing statements when merchandise is delivered to the borrower. That filing usually gives the manufacturer a superior lien on the receivable. An alternative would be to enter into an agreement with the manufacturer whereby rights to the receivables are subordinated to the bank.

---

[3] Ibid.

Formula Basis Loans

Newly created receivables feed into a pool, while reductions flow from payments on account, returns and allowances, bad debts, and the charge-off of serious past due accounts. Rates are quoted as a spread over the prime lending rate. In addition to charging interest—two or three percentage points above prime—it is customary to impose a service charge amounting to 1% or 2% of the borrower's average loan balance. See Exhibit II, Borrowing Base Analysis. The model is available on the CD in the subdirectory Models_Demos/Chapter 5/An Audit: Borrbase.

The quality of financed receivables are influenced by a number of important factors:

- The credit standing of the borrower's customers
- Age and size of the receivable
- Merchandise quality
- Number of returns due to missed season or faulty merchandise
- General competitive positive of the borrower
- The amount of funds continuously generated in the account
- Credit policies

The Loan Agreement

Important items usually covered by a loan agreement for accounts receivable financing include the following:

- Duration of the lending arrangement.
- Right of the bank to screen the accounts presented to it by the borrower to determine which are acceptable as security.
- Procedure by which accounts held by the bank are to be replaced or the loan reduced if they become past due.
- Percentage that the bank will lend against the face amount of the receivables.
- Maximum dollar amount of the loan.
- Reports required from the borrower to indicate amounts owed by each customer. As additional sales are made, the borrower may be required to submit copies of invoices or other evidence of shipment.
- The responsibility of the borrower to forward directly to the bank payments received on assigned accounts.
- Authorization for the bank to inspect the borrower's books and to verify, through confirmation by a public accounting firm or other agency, the accounts receivable.

The Loan Formula Certificate

The bank usually requires a loan formula certificate, signed by an official of the company. This certificate, completed by the client, includes total receivables, eligible receivables, total inventory, eligible inventory, loan amount outstanding, and the amount of debt that is over or under allowed borrowings. Additional advances may be made if sufficient collateral is available. The debt is to be reduced if it is over the amount allowed as shown by the loan formula certificate.

Exposure Percentage

Except in special circumstances, advances are limited to 75% or 80% of outstanding accounts receivable. This does not include any accounts that are more than 90 days past due, any intercompany accounts or those from related businesses, or any accounts that have offsetting payables or prepayments. To derive the exposure percentage, divide accounts receivable advances into net collateral. Net collateral represents assigned receivable plus blocked cash accounts, less dilution and 90 days past due accounts. This information feeds into a computer and is plotted against the borrower's records. While minor differences are ignored, ledger accounts may reveal major discrepancies like unreported receipts. (See Exhibit II, Borrowing Base Analysis.)

The Loan Officer's Responsibilities

The loan officer's responsibilities follow designated policies and procedures to ensure the safety and integrity of assigned receivables. The affairs of the borrower, together with the status of the loan, are policed on a regular basis. Public filings are recorded properly, and state statutes are followed with regard to locale and number of filings needed to ensure a proper lien.

THE AUDIT: SCOPE AND DETAILS

To verify information supplied by the borrower, the bank will usually send bank personnel to the borrower's place of business to audit its books; but if the bank is small, the lender will sometimes commission the audit to outside financing agents. If this is the case, the cost of borrowing on the security of accounts receivable tends to be higher than the cost of an unsecured loan. The audit should occur several times a year and is usually performed on a quarterly basis. The scope of such an audit should include the preparation of balance sheets, profit and loss statements, a working capital analysis, agings of payables and receivables, an inspection of inventory and related records, and a determination that the debtor accounts are properly marked on the books as assigned to the bank. The audit also should include procedures to ascertain that all significant credit memos have been properly issued and reported by the borrower to the bank. If a bank decides to take a security interest in a company's seasonal collections, it will require a judicious and thorough audit of the financial statements.

The step-by-step approach to analyzing accounts receivable as a security is as follows:

Step 1: Financial Statements

Current information fundamental to a sound audit includes trial balances, interim statements, cash budgets, invoice copies, and ledger computer printouts. In all probability, a trial balance may be required if inventory is not valued on a perpetual basis (Chapter 4).

Step 2: Receivables (Overview)

Banks conduct a credit check on large positions. The three main sources of credit information include agency reports, banks, and trade debtors. Ratings are evaluated and recorded on the audit report, then classified as acceptable or not acceptable. Some minor accounts, while not considered prime paper, may be classified as acceptable due to their small size. Other measures of receivable quality, or lack of it, include the collection period, proximity to economically depressed areas, diversification, and balance of the portfolio.

Receivable concentrations are watched carefully because the danger of control looms large. For example, the client's customer may end up dictating unfavorable terms or threaten to cancel orders at the slightest provocation. Key points to consider when securing a portfolio of concentrated receivables are as follows:

1. Evaluate these receivables thoroughly in terms of account classification and aging. An aging schedule is discussed later.
2. Obtain credit reports and checkings on the largest accounts. Sources of information include agency reports, banks, trade journals, suppliers, and credit reporting agencies. Evaluate the information and record it in the audit report. Verify receivables with trade debtors and compute the collection period for each account.
3. Classify accounts into acceptable and unacceptable categories.
4. Keep an eye on other measures, such as (a) the collection period, (b) the delinquency ratio (past due receivables over credit sales), and the bad debt ratio (write-offs over net receivables).
5. Check the files of past due accounts for recent correspondence and the progress of the collection effort. Review large positions.

Step 3: Accounts Receivable Aging

A Dun and Bradstreet code (if rated) depicts approximate net worth. Receivables are listed in several categories: 1 to 30 days, 31 to 60 days,

Aging Schedule of Accounts Receivable		
Number of days outstanding	Amount	Percentage
0–30	$45,000	66.3%
30–45	$11,300	16.6%
45–60	$6,500	9.6%
60–90	$3,200	4.7%
90 or more	$1,900	2.8%
Total	**$67,900**	**100.0%**

61 to 90 days, and accounts over 90 days past due. Levels of concentration are measured by dividing the sum of the largest accounts receivable into total receivables. Accounts over 90 days are usually discarded from the net collateral figure. (See also Exhibit I, Accounts Receivable Audit Worksheet.)

Concentration is tested by the ratios: (1) acceptable receivables to total receivables and (2) average of the five largest receivables summed to total receivables. The average size of accounts is calculated to determine expense allocation. The larger the account, the more work is involved and the more the bank should be compensated.

Step 4: Credit and Collection Policies

The lender should review the following items:

- *Terms of sale.* This can vary by industry and can range from cash before delivery to extended seasonal dating.
- *Credit approval.* Firms having strict policies have fewer receivables exposed. Should the borrower have approved the order to begin with? See Exhibit III, Acceptance versus Rejection Cost Model.
- *Collection.* Policies are optimized: maximize collection while maximizing customer goodwill. Collection policies should be convincing without being harsh.
- *Average collection period (ACP).* The lender should analyze trends alongside the inventory. Interim ACP should be annualized and compared to similar periods, particularly if the client is a seasonal operation.

Step 5: Analysis of Delinquencies

Instead of supplying the borrower with additional funds as new sales are made, bankers may do the following:

1. Substitute new receivables for those no longer acceptable as collateral—that is, until delinquencies are corrected.
2. If delinquent receivables are large, the borrower is faced with the prospect of having to operate without funding from either the customers or the bank.

Step 6: Evaluation of Sales Policies

1. A breakdown of the client's sales record usually yields illuminating data. Sales trends may be developed if the client routinely conducts sales analysis on a weekly basis. Sales analysis enables the lender to probe and discover whether or not the borrower's marketing activities are fluid and, if not, isolate the problem(s).

2. A detailed analysis of the client's sales record is required in the initial audit. More than a few companies fail to appreciate the value of sales analysis, not realizing that omitting this step often leads to weak forecasting results. Valuable sales information is frequently buried in invoice files. There is no single method to analyze sales data. Typical methods will reduce sales into categories that include geographic analysis where sales are separated by location. The lender must determine the geographical distribution and concentration of the client's sales, while keeping the following factors in mind:

- Product analysis, size of package, and grade
- Class of trade
- Price
- Method: mail, telephone, and direct selling
- Terms: cash or charge
- Order size

It is important to keep in mind that although proper compliance with the UCC, in most instances, creates a valid and enforceable first lien, it does not insulate the bank from the need to police its collateral. By filing, the bank establishes the right to collect on only those receivables assigned to it, provided the following factors hold:

- The sales are legitimate.
- The merchandise has been delivered.
- The merchandise is as ordered.
- Sales were made without warranties.
- The merchandise was not shipped on consignment.
- The merchandise is not subject to offset (contra-accounts or liens).
- The receivable has not already been paid to the borrower.

Step 7: Product Analysis and Product Policies

Analysis should be directed to product planning where specific product objectives and policy are outlined. Also, since products have life cycles, it is essential that the product be defined in terms of its life cycle. In the first stage, promotion is important to nurture produce acceptance, while the growth stage marks introduction of competitors.

The first phase generally requires large-scale promotion in order to get the product off the ground and could cause enough of a cash drain to put the capital structure at risk. In the maturity stage, the entrance of new or improved competitors often causes products to decline (stage 4), while R&D of new or improved competitive products may trigger a new stage 1 or 2, startup or rapid growth. These concepts are developed further in Chapter 8, "Risk Management and Sustainable Growth." Product policies should be reviewed and generally include the following items:

- Sales volume
- Type and number of competitors
- Technical opportunity
- Patent protection
- Raw materials required
- Production load
- Value added
- Similarity to major businesses
- Effect on other products

Step 8: Inventory

If the audit includes an examination of inventory, lenders determine the amount and condition of inventory and the breakdown of inventory, including raw materials, work in progress, and finished goods. Merchandise quality is important since the higher the inventory quality, the fewer the returns and refusals to pay. The returns-to-gross-sales ratio can effectively monitor inventory quality. Lenders also should consider the following:

1. Economic order quantity models might easily identify order or carrying cost problems.

2. Decomposing each inventory segment is important in order to inventory build up problems. This is accomplished by dividing each component of inventory as a percentage of total inventory:

- *Check raw material inventory.* A large raw material inventory may mean stockpiling raw material.
- *Watch work-in-process inventory.* If out of line, this could signal a production problem.
- *Evaluate the finished goods inventory.* If this inventory climbs too fast, this may reveal demand problems. If inventory is not moved out on a timely basis, the borrower may liberalize credit standards, which may well reduce the quality of the bank's lien on receivables.

Step 9: Fixed Assets

This phase of the examination includes an evaluation of fixed assets and the depreciation methods in use.

Step 10: Analysis of Accounts Payable and Purchases

An absence of diversity is almost as risky as receivable concentrations. Payables represent purchases. Slow payables are a drag on the client's major supply sources, which could be cut off without warning. Without supplier support, goods cannot be produced. Bankers isolate large payable(s) and work out a payable concentration ratio—large payable to total payables. An accounts payable audit typically includes the following information:

- Classification according to creditor
- Dates of each payable
- Amount and maturity date
- Payables aging, which is compared to the receivables aging
- Listing of large or unusual payables

Step 11: Subordination Agreements

Creditors review subordination agreements often since these agreement funds boost working capital and the firm's capital structure.

Step 12: Analysis of Deposits in Cash Account

Analysis of the cash account can spot unauthorized sales of encumbered assets, withdrawal of funds for personal use, or fraudulent practices, such as unauthorized multiple assignments of receivables. Cash position determines if remittances have been diverted. Differences in unreported credits are recorded and explained.

Step 13: Bank Statement Audit

This section of the auditing procedure serves as a reminder for the lender to scrutinize the borrower's bank statement.

1. Confirm that collections have been earmarked to reduce loan balances.
2. Closely watch checks payable to subsidiaries (representing advances), because they represent a cash drain from the core business. In addition, the principals may be devoting excessive time to an outside venture unrelated to the core business.
3. Review bank statements and checks for large items and stale or unusual checks.
4. Diversion of credits to other uses may easily create an untenable cash position at some future date and drive the company out of business. Any prudent lending officer will question any large withdrawal, which usually shows up as a large-item check.
5. Record federal, withholding, and social security taxes and look over paid checks to verify that remittance to governmental agencies has

indeed been made. Nonpayment of these obligations might easily jeopardize the bank's collateral position. Also review paid checks to ensure that subordinated indebtedness remains intact.

6. Examine bank accounts at other financial institutions for updated credit stories. Other banks will likely not offer an unsecured loan because of your bank's lien against receivables.

Step 14: Analysis of Loans, Collateral, and Statistics

Statistics are maintained on a monthly basis. These data help the lender to gauge the firm's peak requirements and cash needs.

Step 15: Prebillings

Prebilling represents the assignment of invoices before goods are actually shipped. The prebilling audit involves matching invoice and delivery dates. If invoices are forwarded prior to the shipment date, this amounts to a storm signal. Bankers spot prebillings by comparing shipment dates to the assigned invoice dates. Prebilling practices are strongly discouraged, because invoices should not be forwarded to lenders before shipment.

Step 16: Check for Fraud

All accounts appearing in the general ledger should be of sufficient quality to minimize the risk of fraud. Lenders should be cognizant of two areas of concern regarding deceptive practices: (1) the nature of accounts receivable financing, which provides opportunities for dubious practices, and (2) the variety of fraud possibilities, which present opportunities for deceiving lenders. The varieties of fraud include the following:

- Assignment of fictitious accounts, accompanied by forged shipping documents
- Duplicate assignment of the same account
- Diversion of collections to clients use, otherwise known as personal withdrawals beyond a reasonable amount
- Failure to report chargebacks (returns and allowances)
- Submission of false financial information
- Forged shipping documents

Step 17: Record Comparisons and Ledgering Accounts

Lenders compare the borrower's records with the bank's records. Ledger accounts may reveal credit allowances or contra items such as bills receivable discounted. Major discrepancies must be noted, explained, and corrected.

In ledgering the accounts, the lender receives duplicate copies of the invoices together with the shipping documents and delivery receipts. Upon receipt of satisfactory information, the bank advances the agreed percentage of the outstanding receivables. The receivables are usually pledged on a notification basis. Under this method, the bank maintains complete control of all funds paid on all accounts pledged by requiring the borrower's customer to remit directly to the bank. The same application of payments is then used as an under-the-blanket assignment method.

LOANS SECURED BY INVENTORIES

If a borrower is considered a poor or questionable risk, lenders may insist on a blanket lien against inventory—assuming suppliers have filed no prior liens and will continue to ship based on the bank's lien. While blanket liens provide security against all inventories, borrowers are free to dispose inventory as long as funds are earmarked to reduce outstandings. Downside risk includes declining stock values or severe markdowns by borrowers in panic.

Marketability

Marketability means that pledged inventory can sell at prices at least equal to book value or replacement cost—this pertains to most auto tires, hardware goods, and footwear as opposed to high-tech items where a real chance of obsolesce exists. Marketability is associated with the inventory's physical properties as well. A warehouse full of frozen turkeys may be marketable, but the cost of storing and selling turkeys may be prohibitive.

Price Stability and Physical Properties

Standardized and staple durables are desirable since these ticket items have stable prices, ready markets, and no undesirable physical properties. *Perishability* creates problems for sellers and lenders for obvious reasons, as does specialized items. *Specialized* inventories are problematic if markets are thin—special-purpose machinery, fresh produce, and advertising materials, for example. Large, high-ticket items may not be desirable collateral if expenses associated with storage and transportation is high. Commodities and products such as grain, cotton, wool, coffee, sugar, logs, lumber, canned foods, baled wood pulp, automobiles, and major appliances are acceptable collateral, whereas refrigerators-in-process are usually worthless.

Trust Receipts

A trust receipt is an instrument acknowledging that the borrower holds goods in trust for the lender. The lien is valid as long as the merchandise is in the borrower's possession and properly identified. When lenders advance funds, borrowers convey a trust receipt for goods financed.

Goods can be stored in a public warehouse or held on the premises. The borrower receives merchandise with the lender advancing anywhere from 80% to 100% of cost. The lender files a lien on items financed. Documents include a list of each item along with its description and serial number. The borrower is free to sell the secured inventory but is "trusted" to remit to the lender immediately earmarked funds, which are used to repay advances plus accrued interest. In return, the lender releases the lien. The lender conducts periodic checks to ensure that the required collateral is still "in the yard." Inventory financing under trust receipts, for retail sale, is commonly called "floorplanning." For example, an automobile dealer may have arranged to finance the purchase of new cars with trust receipts.

Warehouse Receipts

Like trust receipts, field warehouse financing employs inventory as collateral. A warehouse receipt allows the lender to obtain control over pledged collateral, providing the ultimate degree of security. The costs of these loans are high due to the high cost of hiring third parties (warehouse firms) to maintain and guard inventory collateral. In addition to the interest charge, the borrower must absorb the costs of warehousing by paying the warehouse fee, which is generally between 1% and 3% of the loan.

Terminal Warehouse

A *terminal warehouse* is located within the borrower's geographical area. It is a central warehouse used to store the merchandise of various customers. The lender generally uses a terminal warehouse when secured inventory is easily and cheaply transported to the warehouse. When goods arrive at the warehouse designated by the lender, the warehouse official "checks in" the merchandise, listing each item on a warehouse receipt. Noted on the check-in list is the quantity, serial or lot numbers, and estimated value. After officials check in merchandise, the receipt is forwarded to the lender, who advances a specified percentage of the collateral value to the borrower and files a lien on all the items listed on the receipt.

Field Warehouses

Field warehouse financing is usually economical; the "warehouse" is established on the borrower's premises. Under a field warehouse arrangement, a lender hires a reputable field warehousing company to set up a warehouse on the borrower's premises or lease part of the borrower's warehouse. The warehousing company, as the lender's agent, is responsible for seeing that the collateral pledged is actually in the warehouse. There have been instances when warehousing companies have fraudulently issued receipts against nonexistent collateral. If this happens, and the borrower defaults, the lender ends up serving as an unsecured creditor.

Once inventory is isolated, it is registered with the warehouse receipt forwarded to the lender. The lender advances a specified percentage of collateral value and files a lien on the pledged security. A field warehouse may take the form of a fence around a stock of raw materials, a roped-off section of the borrower's warehouse, or a warehouse constructed by the warehousing company on the borrower's premises.

Regardless of whether a terminal or field warehouse is established, the warehousing company employs a security official to guard inventory. The guard or warehouse official is not permitted to release collateral without prior authorization, since lenders have total control over inventory. Only upon written approval of the lender can any portion of the secured inventory be released.

Although most warehouse receipts are non-negotiable, some are negotiable. This means that the lender may transfer it to other parties. If the lender wants to remove a warehouse receipt loan from its books, it can sell a negotiable warehouse receipt to another party, who then replaces the original lender in the agreement. In some instances, the ability to transfer a warehouse receipt to another party may be desirable.

Example of a Field Warehouse Loan Transaction

A canner of exotic fruits determines that its major requirements for bank financing occur during the canning season. To get the required seed capital to purchase and process an initial harvest of fruit, the canner can finance approximately 20% of its operations during the season.

As cans are put into boxes and placed in storerooms, the canner realizes that additional funds are needed for labor and raw material to make the cans. Without these funds, operations will come to a grinding halt. A seasonal pattern clearly forms here. At the beginning of the fruit harvest and canning season, cash needs and loan requirements increase and reach a maximum at the termination of the canning season. Because of the canner's modest worth and substantial seasonal financing needs, the firm's bank insists on acceptable security for the funds required to meet those needs. The bank obtains the services of a field warehouse company and a field warehouse is set up.

The field warehouse company notifies the bank that the boxes of canned fruit have been shipped and "checked in." At this point, the bank is assured of control over the canned goods upon which loans are based and can establish a line of credit under which the canner can draw funds. As the canner receives purchase orders, it sends them to the bank. The bank then authorizes the warehouse custodian to release the boxes of canned fruit associated with the purchase orders. When the high point of the season is over, the line of credit is diminished as the canner receives checks from the canner's distributors. This results in a borrowing low point, putting the canner in the low-debt position necessary before a new seasonal buildup occurs.

In certain instances, banks may permit outstanding seasonal loans to the canner to reach an amount many times the amount of the canner's own equity capital. The fruit growers, the canner, the canner's distributors, the field warehouse company, and the bank all join forces in working out a successful distributive process to everyone's advantage. If the run-off of cash isn't enough to retire seasonal loans and the canner's financial structure is sound, the bank will likely carry over the loan(s) until the next season. This should give the canner enough time to clean up the debt. The primary consideration for this arrangement is the fact that canned fruit is easily salable.

As discussed before, warehouse receipts may be negotiable or non-negotiable. Negotiable warehouse receipts are used to finance inventories in which trading is active, such as corn, cotton, and wheat. The major disadvantage of negotiable warehouse receipts is that they are easily transferred, are usually in large denominations, and must be presented to the warehouse operator each time a withdrawal is made. Therefore, banks prefer the use of non-negotiable receipts issued in the name of the bank for the simple reason that they provide better control of the pledged inventory.

LOANS SECURED BY MARKETABLE SECURITIES

A loan secured directly or indirectly by any stock or convertible security falls under Regulation U. Federal Reserve Regulation U governs extension of credit by banks for purchasing and carrying margin securities. Also included are loans used to purchase or carry margin stock. Margin stock is defined as follows:

- Listed or unlisted stock
- Securities convertible into a margin stock
- Most over-the-counter stock
- Rights or warrants
- Mutual fund certificates

Suggested Guidelines: Advances against the Market Value of Securities

Collateral	Advance
Stocks listed on major exchanges	70%
Over-the-counter stocks	50%
Listed bonds	80%
Unlisted bonds	Function of quality
U.S. government securities	90%–95%
Municipal bonds	Function of quality

Convertible securities	80% of call value and 50–70% of premium
Mutual funds	70%
Stocks selling below $5	Nominal advance
Stock inactively traded	Nominal advance

Definitions and Points to Keep in Mind

• Unregistered stock is sold as a block to a private investor and does not fall under the usual regulations. Letter stock cannot be broken up and is not passed through the market. The security represents a source of funds to the firm and can be more flexible concerning dividends, since it is off-market and non-voting.

• Bearer instruments should not secure advances unless the lender is convinced that the borrower owns the securities. Proof of ownership must be established by canceled checks, delivery tickets, and so forth, unless the borrower is well known at the bank.

• When hypothecated collateral (collateral owned by someone else) secures advances, extra caution is needed. Hypothecated collateral may cause problems in liquidation. The most effective way to preserve collateral integrity is for the lender to obtain a new hypothecation agreement when the loan is renewed.

• Stock splits involve the division of capital stock into a larger number of shares. The lender should ensure that additional shares are obtained, since the stock may fall to under-margined levels.

• Bond quotations should be reviewed regularly. Bond prices are inversely related to interest rates and might fall to under-margined levels during periods of rising interest rates.

A large international bank broke down collateral into three categories for the purpose of risk grading (Chapter 19):

Classification I: Highly Liquid and Readily Attainable Collateral
with Difference Secured by Other Less-Liquid Assets

1. Cash
2. Bankers acceptances or commercial paper
3. Top-investment-grade bonds

Classification II: Independent Audit/Valuation Required

1. Highest accounts receivable quality—liquid and diversified
2. Highest inventory quality—liquid and diversified
3. Fixed assets—prime and readily marketable
   a. Real estate—commercial
   b. Easily accessible by assignees or participants
   c. Voting rights on collateral not abridged

EXHIBIT 1 Accounts Receivable Audit Worksheet (CD:Models_Demos\ Chapter 5\Araudit)

Source: Federal Reserve Bank Loan Examination Manual and Other Sources	Accounts Receivable Audit Worksheet
Name Of Borrower	ABC Industrial Corporation
Address	222 Main Street, Chicago Ill. 12222
Date Account Opened	3/6/89
Account Officer	Michael Smith
Auditor	Bill Jones
Audit Date	7/1/99
Loan Exposure	$2,000,000
Accounts Receivable Line	$2,500,000
12 Month Average Balances	$900,000
Date of Last Statement (Fiscal or Interim)	406.95

1 Are any accounts receivable from goods on consignment?	No	$				
2 Foreign accounts?	No	$				
If yes name, location, amount and terms						
5 Do we receive delivery evidence?	Yes					
6 Delivery evidence inspected?	Yes					
7 What form?						
8 Do we receive purchase order evidence?	Yes					
9 Purchase orders inspected?	Yes					
10 Subsidiary or affiliated accounts:			Receivable	Payable	Payment Terms	
	Name		Amount	Amount	and Status	

11 Sales to related companies last 12 months?	Yes	Apex Manufacturing Co. wholly owned subsidiar	
If yes, percent of sales	0%		
Comments			
12 Unusual conditions peculiar to this type of business which might affect overall picture			
13 General terms of sales	45 days		
14 Average collection period	40 days		
15 Any recent change in terms of sales	No	If yes, explain:	
Returns and allowance last 12 months	0%		
16 12 months prior to above	4%		
17 Extended terms granted?	No	If yes, explain:	
18 Credit to cash sales	80%		
19 Customers pre-billed while goods are held?	No	If yes, explain:	
20 Does company trade on bills receivables, installments?	Yes	If yes, explain: High ticketed items are sold on 120 day rates which are discounted at the bank or presented on a demand rate basis.	
21 Status of this collateral?	Bank has approved a $500,000 secured line for notes presented on a demand basis. Outstandings are approximately $70,000. Notes have been paid promptly from high rated customers.		
22 Are agency reports obtained on concentrated receivables?	Yes		
23 Are collections reported promptly to bank?	Yes		
Amount of unreported collections	$2,000	Details: Smith Manufacturing Co. Reason: oversight in reporting to bank. Situation has been corrected.	
24 Are cash sales collections included in collections reported to bank?	Yes		

25 Accounts Receivable aging review

	Current				Prior			Prior
Aging		Amount	Percent	Aging		Amount	Percent	Aging
1 - 30 Days		1,200,000	61.5%	1 - 30 Days		900,000	30.4%	Date
31 - 60 Days		500,000	25.6%	31 - 60 Days		1,200,000	40.5%	
61 - 90 Days		200,000	10.2%	61 - 90 Days		800,000	27.0%	4/1/99
Over 90 Days		50,000	2.6%	Over 90 Days		60,000	2.0%	
Total		1,950,000	100.0%			2,960,000	100.0%	
Less Credit Balances		(40,000)				(120,000)		
Total Aging		1,910,000				2,840,000		
Less Ineligibles		(67,000)				(78,000)		
Total Eligible		1,843,000				2,764,000		

26 Is cross aging used to determine eligible receivables?	Yes	If yes, explain: C Stores with even one account 90 days past due are ineligible. Smith & Co. has been cross-aged. See analysis below.	

	Current			Cross Aging Analysis		
Aging		Amount	Percent	Amount	Percent	
1 - 30 Days		1,200,000	61.5%	20,000	20.0%	
31 - 60 Days		500,000	25.6%	40,000	40.0%	
61 - 90 Days		200,000	10.2%	30,000	30.0%	
Over 90 Days		50,000	2.6%	10,000	10.0%	
Total		1,950,000	100.0%	100,000	100.0%	
Less Credit Balances		(40,000)				
Total Aging		1,910,000				
Less Ineligibles		(67,000)				
Less cross aging Ineligibles		(100,000)				
Total Eligible		1,743,000				

27 Explain status of all accounts past due 90 days or more including disputes, attorney actions etc.	

28 Concentration of major accounts?	% Receivables	Summary					
29 Concentration details							
Name	% to total	Current	1-30	31-60	61-90	Over 90	
ABC Stores	15.0%	120,000		10,000			
Bill Williams Inc	10.0%	300,000	25,000	35,000			
Smith Retail Inc	12.0%		35,000	75,000			
Ace Furniture	20.0%					$0,000	
Totals	67.0%	620,000	60,000	110,000	10,000	$0,000	

Name	Terms	Agency Rating	
ABC Stores	30 days	A	
Bill Williams Inc	45 days	A	
Smith Retail Inc	45 days	B-	
Ace Furniture	30 days	C	

30 Monthly agings received?	Yes	If no, explain:		
31 Invoice payment follow up	Specific Invoice	X	Balance forward to older invoice	N/A
32 Agings accurate and complete?	Yes	If no, explain:		
33 Does borrower receive advance payments?	Yes			
34 Details on potential write-offs				
35 Bad debts expensed or is a reserve set up	80% Expensed			
36 If reserve set up, is it adequate?	Yes	If no, explain:		
Signatures shown on documents authorized and authentic	Yes	If no, explain:		
37 Are credit reviews accurate and complete regarding credit and collateral risk?	Yes	If no, explain:		
38 Has the loan been classified during previous examination?	No	If yes, complete the following:		
	Current Balance	Date Repaid		
39 Violations of laws and / or regulations?	No	If yes, explain:		
Contingent liabilities or environmental litigation				
40 (actual and potential)	No	If yes, explain:		
Audit summary				

EXHIBIT II   Borrowing Base Analysis (CD:Models_Demos\ Chapter 5\Araudit)

Borrowing Base Analysis Accounts Receivable Financing	
Accounts Receivable Analysis	
Accounts receivable balance last report	12,003,020
Plus new accounts receivable	3,400,345
Plus (minus) adjustments	(100,340)
Less deposits to cash collateral account	(567,666)
Less collections not deposited to cash collateral account	(900,900)
Total value of outstanding accounts receivable	13,834,469
Less accounts over 90 days per aging 7/31/95	(350,000)
Less other ineligible accounts	(650,500)
Net eligible accounts receivable for this period	12,833,959
Inventory Analysis	
Inventory balance last report	9,500,000
Plus inventory incoming	1,250,060
Less inventory outgoing	(1,550,000)
Plus (minus) adjustments	(35,500)
Less other ineligible inventory	(76,550)
Net eligible inventory for this period	9,088,010
Loan Request	
Loan Value Of The Accounts Receivable and Inventory Collateral	
Allowable advances against eligible receivables	70.0%
Allowable advances against eligible receivables	50.0%
Accounts receivable eligible against loan (borrowing base)	8,983,771
Inventory eligible against loan (borrowing base)	4,544,005
Collateral loan value for this period	13,527,776
Loan Balance Last Report	11,500,000
Less deposits in cash collateral account to be applied to loan	(2,555,550)
Less loan payments	(1,500,000)
Present loan balance	7,444,450
Excess (Deficit) collateral loan value over loan balance	6,083,326
Borrowers request for additional advances	5,000,000
Surplus (shortfall)	1,083,326
Advances to be approved	5,000,000

EXHIBIT III Acceptance versus Rejection Costs Model (CD:Models_Demos\ Chapter 5\Araudit)

ACCEPTANCE VS. REJECTION COSTS MODEL

Input Screen

	Enter Costs Below
Acceptance Costs	
Clerical Costs Associated With Opening Account	$30
Credit Investigation Cost	$40
Collection Costs	$130
Dollars Tied Up In Receivables (Sale Price)	$100,000
Probability of Non Payment	4.00%
Incremental Cost of Production and Selling	$60,000
Average Time in Days between Sale and Payment	45
Cost of Funds	15.00%
Rejection Costs	
Incremental Profit From Sale	$40,000
Probability of Non-Payment	96.00%

Output Screen

Acceptance Cost	$4,449
Rejection Cost	$38,400
Accept/Reject Credit:	ACCEPT CREDIT
Probability B/E	0.380

Output Screen formulas:

Acceptance Cost   equal-> $(G11 \times G12) + (+G10 \times (G13/365) \times G14) + SUM(G7:G9)$

Rejection Cost   equal-> $G18 \times G19$

Accept/Reject Credit: IF(B25>B23,"ACCEPT CREDIT","REJECT CREDIT")

Probability B/E = $(B18/(B18+B12) - ((B10 \times B13 \times B14)/365)/(B18+B12) - (B8+B9)/(B18+B12))$

EXHIBIT IV Inventory Evaluation Checklist (CD:Models_Demos\ Chapter 5\Auditinv)

Inventory Evaluation Checklist*

1 Name of Borrower
2 Period Covered
3 Is periodic or perpetual inventory system used
4 What is the valuation method?
5 Have there been changes in valuation or other accounting and what was the impact on current period income?

6 What are any accounting principles particular to this industry?

7 List the major amounts by major categories
  Raw materials

8 List the following amounts by top five product lines

9 List location of inventory if applicable, showing amounts at each location

10 List amounts pledged as collateral
11 Any writedows on inventory anticipated?

12 List any consignments

13 List appropriate physical damage insurance amounts and expiration dates

14 List imported components or goods

15 Discuss your analysis of potential shrinkage, obsolescence, perishability and overall condition based on your most recent visit to the company.

Marces Eyeglass Production Co. Inc.
January 31, 1995 to March 31 1995
Perpetual
FIFO

Company changed from LIFO to FIFO in February 1995. Inventory profits as a result of that changed were 250,000.

Inventory usually carried on Weighted Average Method

Category	Amount	% of Total
Raw materials	245,000	18.0%
Work in process	455,000	33.4%
Finished goods	650,000	47.7%
Other	12,000	0.9%
Total	1,362,000	100.0%

Product Line	Amount	% of Total
The Beauty Lens Line	27,000	2.0%
The Smart Eyeglass	45,500	3.4%
Marcho Man Frames	1,200,500	90.4%
Nerdsville Lenses	45,000	3.4%
Simple Style Frames	10,000	0.8%
Total	1,328,000	100.0%

Location	Amounts	Description
Miami Beach, Fla.	500,000	Approximately 400,000 of Marcho Man Frames + 45,000 of Nerdsville Lenses
Fire Island New York	27,500	The Beauty Lens line located here

Entire line   Yes   Approximately half of the Marcho Man Line will be written off unless a more effective promotion campaign gets under way soon

None

Product Line	Coverage	Expiration Date
The Beauty Lens Line	20,000	12/31/95
The Smart Eyeglass	50,000	12/31/95
Marcho Man Frames	5,000	Expires next month
Nerdsville Lenses	125,000	12/31/95
Simple Style Frames	50,000	12/31/95
Total	250,000	

Product Line	Amounts	Country
The Beauty Lens Line	2,500	Lima, Peru
The Smart Eyeglass	10,000	Tokyo, Japan
Marcho Man Frames	3,500	Berlin, Germany
Nerdsville Lenses	25,000	London, England
Simple Style Frames	23,060	Teheran, Iran
Total	64,060	

EXHIBIT V Inventory Audit Worksheet

Inventory Audit Worksheet
John Smith Coats and Garments Manufacturing Co. Inc.

	Date	Amount	Turnover Days	Returns
1. Last Inventory Examination	11/2/94	$1,500,000	45	3%
2. Date of This Exam	7/31/95	$3,200,000	120	14%

3. Last Physical Inventory	6/30/94	Write Ups/(Downs)
4. Method of Inventory Valuation	First In First Out	Amount ($500,000)

Inventory Breakdown and Trends

	12/31/91	12/31/92	12/31/93	12/31/94
Raw Materials	50.0%	30.0%	20.0%	10.0%
Work In Process	20.0%	25.0%	20.0%	20.0%
Finished Goods	30.0%	45.0%	60.0%	70.0%

5. Is Inventory aged and eligible vs. ineligible inventory determined? Yes — Inventory over 140 days old are considered ineligible
6. Is cross aging used to determine final eligible inventory Yes — Ineligible inventory deducted from borrowing base
7. Inventory Aging Schedule (Conservative) incorporating cross aging

Cross Aging Analysis

Inventory Holding Period	Amount	Percent	Amount	Percent
1 - 45 Days	300,000	20.0%	20,000	20.0%
46 - 90 Days	200,000	13.3%	40,000	40.0%
91 - 140 Days	800,000	53.3%	30,000	30.0%
Over 140 Days	200,000	13.3%	10,000	10.0%
Total	1,500,000	100.0%	100,000	100.0%
Less Returns	(50,000)			
Total Aging	1,450,000			
Less Ineligibles	(100,000)			
Less C/A ineligibles	(100,000)			
Total Eligible	1,250,000			

8. Inventory Condition — Inventory condition is satisfactory except for a slight (5%) increase in perishables
9. If Returns/Gross Sales Abnormal Give Reason — Increase in Cost returns (to 12% vs. 5%) due to late shipments
10. Does Company Plan To Reship? When? — Reshipment of the Coat line will not be possible unless the firm makes substantial writedowns
11. Frequently of Inventory Reports — Monthly
12. Date and Amount on Last Reported Submitted — 6/30/95
13. Describe Inventory Records/Audit — Periodic Inventory method for interims.
14. Describe Consigned Inventory — 15% of flower styled jackets consigned to Midwest Stores
15. Describe Consigned Inventory
16. Any Inventory Under Trust Receipt? — No
17. Any Evidence of Consigned Inventory In Borrowing Base Reports? — Yes
18. If Yes, Has It Been Included or Broken Out As Ineligible On — No. However adjustments will be made to correct eligible inventory
19. Does Inventory Total Balance to General Ledger? If Not Explain — There are small differences due to returns. This will be corrected in 30 days.
20. Borrowing Base — 70%
21. List Inventory Located Beyond 100 Mile Radius — F/S 12/31/94

Location	Amount	Percentage
Dallas, TX	$560,000	19.0%
Moscow, Russia	$300,000	10.0%
Tbilisi, Iraq	$5,000	0.2%

22. Spot Check of Inventory Contents Including Comments On Any Dormant, Perishable, or Obsolete Inventory: — Yes. 10% of inventory located in Dallas is obsolete. 90% of inventory located in Moscow is dormant
23. Describe Inventory (Wholesale, By Product, By Type of Raw Material, Status of Work's in Process, Finished Goods By Product Etc.
24. Current Backlog Firm Orders on Hand — $20,000
25. If Contract Work, How Much In Uncompleted Work In Process? — No
26. Does Backlog Reflect That Current Inventories Will Continue To Turn Successfully? — No
27. Does Backlog Reflect Sufficient Work To Equal or Surpass Latest Three Monthly Sales or Revenue? If Not, How Long? — 5 Weeks
28. Are Order and Carrying Costs Under Control? If Not, Explain — No. Carrying Costs are building due to identified obsolese problems.
29. Storage Area Protected At Night By:
    Alarm System — Yes
    Sprinkler System — Yes
    Guards — No
    Other Methods Of Protections — None
30. Insurance Coverage — ABC Insurance Co. New York City, NY
    Fire — $1,000,000
    Theft — $5,000,000

Classification III: Other Collateral (No Impact on Credit Grade)

1. Leasehold improvements
2. Stock of subsidiaries
3. Stock on pink sheets
4. Receivables—concentrated/questionable quality
5. Inventory—concentrated/questionable quality
6. Real estate—questionable quality and marketability

CASE STUDY   Collateralized Loans Gone Wrong: Home Federal Savings & Loan Association of San Diego, California: 1994[4]

Home Federal Savings & Loan Association, a once strong 59-year-old San Diego thrift shop, was placed under the care of the Resolution Trust Corp. (RTC) after problems surfaced in July 1992. All tolled, 134 branches with $4.7 billion in deposits were sold to four competing financial institutions led by Chatsworth-based Great Western Bank.

Some analysts blamed the government, citing the 1989 thrift bailout act that imposed tough new capital requirements and curtailed real estate development activities of the sort HomeFed S&L held in its portfolio. Other bank experts blamed the 1986 tax reform act. The act wiped out lucrative real estate tax shelters hurting the S&Ls that booked loans for income property.

"There is no question the government's takeover of HomeFed and subsequent actions have hurt the city's ability to bring itself out of this [1991–1992] economic recession," San Diego's mayor told the House Banking, Finance and Urban Affairs Committee at a hearing.[5] The local press commented that those who wrote the laws that governed HomeFed Bank, as well as those who enforced them, shared in the blame. Few disputed that the RTC committed some world-class blunders at HomeFed Bank, but the fact remained that San Diego's biggest lender self-destructed on bad loans and poor management control.

In its nearly six decades, HomeFed Bank contributed to the community in a major way. The bank financed homes for growing families, donated huge sums of money to local arts and charities, and was a pillar of the community. But the institution mushroomed to close to $20 billion in assets at its peak, in part by aggressively investing directly in real estate developments, loans for office buildings, and other nontraditional thrift activities.

During the boom years of the 1980s, the bank's construction lending strategy worked fine, and HomeFed prospered. But HomeFed had too many loans and projects in place, did not stress its portfolio to regulatory standards, and finally fell victim to a recession that started on the East Coast and rolled west. HomeFed

---

[4] Source SalomonSmithBarney stock analysis.
[5] San Diego newspaper report.

Bank's portfolio of bad loans and foreclosed real estate included holdings in Arizona, Texas, Florida, Washington, D.C., and other exotic locales far distant from the thrift's home base.

If HomeFed Bank hadn't already been fighting recessions elsewhere, perhaps it would have survived the one that hit California. All the same, the S&L was insolvent by late 1991. The errors committed by HomeFed Bank's management were compounded by those committed by the government agents who tried to clean up the bank's substantial problems. John Downey, deputy director of the Office of Thrift Supervision (OTS), acknowledged to the House Banking Committee that the cancer eating away at HomeFed Bank was not detected early enough. In retrospect, it seemed clear that decisive action was not taken quickly enough once the symptoms appeared.[6]

Government documents show that the OTS and Federal Deposit Insurance Corp. (FDIC) argued over whether to seize HomeFed Bank in late 1991 or give it more time. The FDIC favored an early takeover. It should be noted that the S&L had been insolvent for six months by April 1992 when the OTS finally offered a plan to sell HomeFed Bank with RTC financing as an inducement to potential buyers.

The thrift's management already had been shopping HomeFed Bank to various investors and other financial institutions and knew that no one wanted to buy it without the protection of government guarantees against taking losses on bad assets.

However, the rescue effort failed. Congress never passed the RTC funding bill that the agency said was needed to finish the industry cleanup, and frustrated regulators wound up seizing HomeFed Bank anyway. Along the way, the RTC broke its own rules when it hired contractors to help out at HomeFed Bank and failed to monitor these personnel, thus turning the project into an national scandal.

Ironically, the RTC earlier in 1992 learned it had $3 billion in reserves all along—enough money to sell HomeFed Bank, funding bill or not. The agency quickly announced plans to sell the S&L by fall. The California press called the episode a "comic opera." The reinvigorated sales effort itself turned into, again, a comic opera when the RTC put the effort on hold because the House of Representatives hung a rider on new funding to help minorities buy failed S&Ls. The reason for the delay, according to the RTC, was to make sure the HomeFed sale conformed to the minority bidding provision, which seemed sure to become law by the time the sale was completed.

But the bill languished in a House-Senate conference committee for weeks. The RTC, tired of waiting, resumed the bidding for HomeFed, which in turn whipsawed a local group that was hoping to buy the thrift. Whether the investor group led by a former HomeFed Bank executive could have put together a winning bid for the institution is unclear. The former banker said he could have counted on sub-

---

[6] See Chapter 11 on capital adequacy.

stantial financial backing, but the money melted away the longer the sale was stalled. The following chronology highlights HomeFed Bank's experience:

12/30/88	Merged a wholly owned subsidiary of HomeFed Corp. to effect merger into HomeFed Corp., a holding company- Nontaxable, Counsel's opinion. Treasury Department ruling requested.
	Per share Home Federal Savings & Loan common ($0.01 par).
	Convertible debenture 6 1/2s, 2011: Debentures now are joint obligations of Home Federal Savings & Loan and HomeFed Corp. Debentures are convertible into HomeFed Corp common at $43.75 per share. Conversion is apparently nontaxable.
	Holding company formed to acquire Home Federal Savings & Loan Association of San Diego.
09/05/89	Rights attached to common. Rights are exercisable for .01 share series. A junior preferred at $110 or, in the case of company's acquisition, for a number of acquiring company's common having a value twice the exercise price. Rights become exercisable only if a person or group acquires 15% or more of company's common, or makes a tender or exchange offer for at least 25% of company's common. No income results from receipt of rights, and rights apparently take a zero basis (Rev. Ruling 90-11). Rights expire 9/5/99 and are redeemable, at company's option, at $0.01 per right.
04/03/92	Company indicates that subsidiary bank, HomeFed Bank, FSB, will be sold by federal regulators in a financially assisted transaction per an "Accelerated Resolution Program." Company also indicates it is unlikely that shareholders and bondholders would retain any value in their investment in the bank.
06/25/92	Involuntary petition in bankruptcy filed against company by committee of bondholders.
10/22/92	Filed petition under Chapter 11 of the Federal Bankruptcy Code in U.S. Bankruptcy Court, San Diego, California. Note. Trading price of common was minimal with stock worthless in 1992.
04/17/96	Offered convertible debenture 6 1 /2s, 2011 at 100.
	Debenture 6 1/2s, 2011 are convertible (nontaxable) into common at $43.75 per share through 5-15-2011.
	Cash paid for fractions result in capital gain or loss, computed by comparing cash with basis of portion of debenture representing fraction.

HOME FEDERAL SAVINGS & LOAN ANALYSIS

In retrospect, HomeFed Bank's real estate portfolio carried both unique and common underwriting risks compounded by management's not fully understanding the portfolio's ability to repay (in times of stress) and values of underlying real estate collateral.

The bank adversely affected its financial condition by granting loans on ill-conceived real estate projects in locations far removed from its home base: Arizona, Texas, Florida, and Washington, D.C. Apart from losses stemming from unanticipated economic downturns in some areas, failure came as the result of lax underwriting standards and improper management of the bank's overall collated real estate loan portfolio.

A principal indication of unsound lending practices should have been revealed earlier: the apparent improper relationship between loan amounts and market values of the property (for example, high loan-to-value ratios in relationship to similar types of properties and failure to examine the portfolio's debt service ability). For commercial real estate loans, sound underwriting practices are critical for detecting problems such as unrealistic income assumptions, substandard project designs, potential construction problems, and poor marketing plans.

In short, HomeFed Bank did not have in place effective internal policies, systems, and controls to monitor and manage its real estate loan portfolio risk. An indication of improper management of the bank's portfolio was excessive concentration in loans to related borrowers and credit approvals for projects in geographic locations outside the bank's designated trading area, as mentioned earlier. Effective portfolio monitoring tools needed to evaluate important economic and business statistics in areas serviced by the bank were missing—for example, the ability to gather information on permits for and the value of new construction, absorption rates, employment trends, vacancy rates, and tenant lease incentives.

Weaknesses disclosed by monitoring statistics might have detected that the real estate market the bank serviced was experiencing severe problems, namely declining real estate values, and ultimately, troubled real estate loans. If bank managers had addressed the kinds of questions posed in Exhibit VI, they might well have prevented many of the bank's losses.

Other aspects of potential problems in the bank's real estate projects could have surfaced, including the following:[7]

1. An excess supply of similar projects under construction in the same trade area
2. The lack of a sound feasibility study or analysis that reflects current and reasonably anticipated market conditions
3. Changes in concept or plan (for example, a condominium project converted to an apartment project because of unfavorable market conditions)
4. Rent concessions or sales discounts, resulting in cash flow below the level projected in the original feasibility study, appraisal, or evaluation
5. Concessions on finishing tenant space, moving expenses, and lease buyouts
6. Slow leasing or lack of sustained sales activity and increasing sales cancellations that may reduce the project's income potential, resulting in protracted repayment or default on the loan
7. Delinquent lease payments from major tenants
8. Land values that assume future rezoning

---

[7] Source: *Federal Reserve System Commercial Bank Examination Manual,* March 1994, Section 2100.4; Real Estate Construction Loans; Internal Control Questionnaire.

9. Tax arrearages
10. Environmental hazards and liability for cleanup

EXHIBIT VI   Construction Loans: Federal Reserve Commercial Examination Guidelines

1. Personal guarantee from the borrower on construction loans?
2. Personal completion guarantees by the property owner and/or the contractor?
3. Construction borrower to contribute equity to a proposed project in the form of money or real estate?
4. Background information on the borrower's, contractor's, and major subcontractors' development and construction experience, as well as other projects currently under construction?
5. Payment history information from suppliers and trade creditors? Credit reports?
6. Detailed current and historical financial statements, including cash flow related information?
7. Land and construction costs?
8. Offsite improvement expenses?
9. Soft costs, such as organizational and administrative costs, and architectural, engineering, and legal fees?
10. Estimated cost breakdown for each stage of construction?
11. Computer cash flow worksheet?
12. Cost estimates of more complicated projects be reviewed by architect, construction engineer, or independent estimator?
13. Construction loan agreement reviewed by counsel and other experts in terms of building codes, subdivision regulations, zoning and ordinances, title and/or ground lease restrictions; health and handicap access regulations, known or projected environmental protection considerations?
14. Liens filed on non real estate construction improvements (i.e., personal property movable from the project)?
15. Limit the loan amount to a reasonable percentage of the appraised value of the project when there is no prearranged permanent financing?
16. Limit the loan amount to a percentage of the appraised value of the completed project when subject to the bank's own takeout commitment?
17. Limit the loan amount to the floor of a takeout commitment that is based upon achieving a certain level of rents or lease occupancy?
18. Unsecured credit lines to contractors or developers, who are also being financed by secured construction loans, supervised by the construction loan department or the officer supervising the construction loan?

19. Adequate procedures to determine whether construction appraisal or evaluation policies and procedures are consistently being followed in conformance with regulatory requirements and that the appraisal or evaluation documentation supports the value indicated in the conclusions?
20. Inspections conducted on a regular basis?
21. Inspection reports sufficiently detailed to support disbursements?
22. Spot checks?
23. Disbursements compared to original cost estimates, checked against previous disbursements, made directly to subcontractors and suppliers, supported by invoices describing the work performed and the materials furnished.
24. Counsel review takeout agreements for acceptability?
25. Obtain and review the permanent lender's financial statements to determine the adequacy of its financial resources to fulfill the takeout commitment?
26. Delinquent accounts report generated daily?

REVIEW QUESTIONS

1. Why would it not be practical for a typical retailer to use field warehouse to finance inventory?
2. Describe an industry that might be expected to use each of the following forms of credit and explain your reasons for choosing each one:
   a. Field warehouse financing
   b. Factoring
   c. Accounts receivable financing
   d. Trust receipts
3. What are the advantages of secured financing from the bankers point of view?
4. Indicated whether each of the following changes will raise or lower the cost of a firm's accounts receivable financing and explain why this occurs:
   a. The borrower eases up on its credit standards in order to increase sales.
   b. The borrower institute a policy of refusing to make credit sales if the amount of the purchase (invoice) is below a certain level.
   c. The borrower agrees to give recourse to the bank for all defaults.
5. Discuss the statement, Poor collateral control can lead to loss. If a bank is unable to ensure internal quality control, then the institution should not encourage collateralized exposures.
6. What four steps are required for bank to create a valid and enforceable security interest in collateral securing a loan?

7. What factors should be considered in evaluating the quality of receivables pledged?
8. The availability of secured bank credit is more important to small firms than to large ones. Why?
9. What is included in a loan formula certificate?
10. Explain the objectives of a bank audit of pledged assets. Discuss three out of the seventeen steps you feel are most important.
11. Explain the differences between terminal and field warehouse. Which would the bank prefer?
12. Discuss the statement: HomeFed Bank did not have in place effective internal policies, systems, and controls to monitor and manage its real estate loan portfolio risk.

SELECTED REFERENCES AND READINGS

Berger, A. N., and G. F. Udell. (1988). *Collateral, loan quality, and bank risk.* New York: Salomon Brothers Center for the Study of Financial Institutions Graduate School of Business Administration, New York University.

Berger, A. N., and G. F. Udell. (1993). *Lines of credit, collateral, and relationship lending in small firm finance.* New York: New York University Salomon Center Leonard N. Stern of Business.

Boot, A. W., A. V. Thakor, *et al.* (1991). Secured lending and default risk: Equilibrium analysis, policy implications and empirical results. *Economic Journal: The Journal of the Royal Economic Society* **101,** 458–472.

Fleisig, H. (1996). Secured transactions: The power of collateral. *Finance and Development, a Quarterly Publication of the International Monetary Fund and the World Bank* **33,** 44–46. Also published in Arabic, Chinese, French, German, Portuguese, and Spanish.

Gilmore, G., and D. Carlson. (2000). *Gilmore and Carlson on secured lending: Claims in bankruptcy.* Gaithersburg, MD: Aspen Law and Business.

Hilson, J. F., J. S. Turner, and P. H. Well. (1999). *Asset-based lending: A practical guide to secured financing.* New York: Practising Law Institute.

Karatzas, I., M. Shubik, and W. Sudderth. (1997). A stochastic infinite-horizon economy with secured lending, or unsecured lending and bankruptcy. *Cowles Foundation for Research in Economics, Yale University. Discussion Paper*, No. 1156, 1–34.

Lakin, L., and H. J. Berger. (1970). *A guide to secured transactions.* Mundelein, IL: Callaghan.

Siebrasse, N. (1997). *A review of secured lending theory.* Washington, DC: World Bank.

Sopranzetti, B. J. (1998). The economics of factoring accounts receivable. *Journal of Economics and Business* **50,** 339–359.

SELECT INTERNET LIBRARY AND CD

CD includes

Accounts Receivable Audit Worksheet; Borrowing Base Analysis for Accounts Receivable Financing; Acceptance versus Rejection Costs Model; Inventory Evaluation Checklist; Construction Loans: Federal Reserve Commercial Bank Examination Guidelines.

ACCOUNTS RECEIVABLE FINANCING EXAMINATION PROCEDURES[1] COMMERCIAL BANK EXAMINATION MANUAL, MARCH 1994

1. If selected for implementation, complete or update the Accounts Receivable Financing section of the Internal Control Questionnaire.
2. Based on the evaluation of internal controls and the work performed by internal/external auditors, determine the scope of the examination.
3. Test for compliance with policies, practices, procedures and internal controls in conjunction with performing the remaining examination procedures. Also, obtain a listing of any deficiencies noted in the latest review done by internal/external auditors and determine if corrections have been accomplished.
4. Obtain a trial balance of the customer liability records and:
   a. Agree or reconcile balances to department controls and general ledger.
   b. Review reconciling items foreasonableness.

---

[1] Excerpts from Commercial Bank Examination Manual Federal Reserve System Section 2160: Accounts Receivable Financing.

5. Using an appropriate technique, select borrowers for examination. Prepare credit line cards.

6. Obtain the following information from the bank or other examination areas, if applicable:
   a. Past-due loans.
   b. Loans in a non-accrual status.
   c. Loans on which interest is not being collected in accordance with the terms of the loan. Particular attention should be paid to loans which have been renewed without payment of interest.
   d. Loans whose terms have been modified by a reduction on interest rate or principal payment, by a deferral of interest or principal, or by other restructuring of repayment terms.
   e. Loans transferred, either in whole or in part, to another lending institution as a result of sale, participation or asset swap, since the previous examination.
   f. Loans acquired from another lending institution as a result of a purchase, participation or asset swap, since the previous examination.
   g. Loan commitments and other contingent liabilities.
   h. Extensions of credit to employees, officers, directors, principal shareholders and their interests, specifying which officers are considered executive officers.
   i. Extensions of credit to executive officers, directors, principal shareholders and their interests, of correspondent banks.
   j. A list of correspondent banks.
   k. Miscellaneous loan debit and credit suspense accounts.
   l. Loans considered "problem loans" by management.
   m. Shared National Credits.
   n. Specific guidelines in the lending policy.
   o. Each officer's current lending authority.
   p. Current interest rate structure.
   q. Any useful information obtained from the review of the minutes of the loan and discount committee or any similar committee.
   r. Reports furnished to the loan and discount committee or any similar committee.
   s. Reports furnished to the board of directors.
   t. Loans classified during the preceding examination.

7. Review the information received and perform the following for:
   a. Loans transferred, either in whole or in part, to or from another lending institution as a result of a participation, sale/purchase, or asset swap:
      - Participations only:
      - Test participation certificates and records and determine that the parties share in the risks and contractual payments on pro rata basis.

- Determine that the bank exercises similar controls and procedures over loans serviced for others as for loans in its own portfolio.
- Determine that the bank, as lead or agent in a credit, exercises similar controls and procedures over syndications and participations sold as for loans in its own portfolio.
- Procedures pertaining to all transfers:
- Investigate any situations where loans were transferred immediately prior to the date of examination to determine if any were transferred to avoid possible criticism during the examination.
- Determine whether any of the loans transferred were either nonperforming at the time of transfer or classified at the previous examination.
- Determine that low-quality loans transferred to or from the bank are properly reflected on its books at fair market value (while fair market value may be difficult to determine, it should at a minimum reflect both the rate of return being earned on such loans as well as an appropriate risk premium).
- Determine that low-quality loans transferred to an affiliate are properly reflected at fair market value on the books of both the bank and its affiliate.
- If low-quality loans were transferred to or from another lending institution for which the Federal Reserve is not the primary regulator, prepare a memorandum to be submitted to the Reserve Bank supervisory personnel. The Reserve Bank will then inform the local office of the primary Federal regulator of the other institution involved in the transfer. The memorandum should include the following information, as applicable:
  - Name of originating institution.
  - Name of receiving institution.
  - Type of transfer (i.e., participation, purchase/sale, swap).
  - Date of transfer.
  - Total number of loans transferred.
  - Total dollar amount of loans transferred.
  - Status of the loans when transferred (e.g., nonperforming, classified, etc.).
  - Any other information that would be helpful to the other regulator.
  b. Miscellaneous loan debit and credit suspense accounts:
  - Discuss with management any large or old items.
  - Perform additional procedures as deemed appropriate.
  c. Loan commitments and other contingent liabilities:
  - Analyze the commitment or contingent liability if the borrower has been advised of the commitment, and the combined

amounts of the current loan balance (if any) and the commitment or other contingent liability exceeding the cutoff.

d. Loans classified during the previous examination:
- Determine disposition of loans so classified by transcribing:
  - Current balance and payment status, or
  - Date loan was repaid and source of payment.
- Investigate any situations where all or part of the funds for the repayment came from the proceeds of another loan at the bank, or as a result of a participation, sale or swap with another lending institution.
- If repayment was a result of a participation, sale or swap, refer to step 7a of this section for the appropriate examination procedures.

e. Uniform Review of Shared National Credits:
- Compare schedule of credits included in the Uniform Review of Shared National Credits program to line cards to ascertain which loans in the sample are portions of shared national credits.
- For each loan so identified, transcribe appropriate information from schedule to line cards. (No further examination procedures are necessary in this area.)

8. Consult with the examiner responsible for the Asset/Liability Management analysis to determine the appropriate maturity breakdown of loans needed for the analysis. If requested, compile the information using bank records or other appropriate sources. Refer to the Instructions for the Report of Examination section of this manual for considerations to be taken into account when compiling maturity information for the GAP analysis.

9. Prepare line cards for any loan not in the sample which, based on information derived from the above schedules, requires in-depth review.

10. Obtain liability and other information on common borrowers from examiners assigned cash items, overdrafts, lease financing and other loan areas and together decide who will review the borrowing relationship.

11. Obtain credit files for each loan for which line cards have been prepared. In analyzing the loans, perform the following procedures:
a. Analyze balance sheet and profit and loss items as reflected in current and preceding financial statements, and determine the existence of any favorable or adverse trends.
b. Review components of the balance sheet as reflected in the current financial statements and determine the reasonableness of each item as it relates to the total financial structure.

    c. Review supporting information and consolidation techniques for major balance sheet items.

    d. Ascertain compliance with provisions of loan agreements.

    e. Review digest of officers' memoranda, mercantile reports, credit checks and correspondence.

    f. Review the following:
- Relationship between amount collected in a month on the receivables pledged as collateral and the borrower's credit limit.
- Aging of accounts receivable.
- Ineligible receivables.
- Concentration of debtor accounts.
- Financial strength of debtor accounts.
- Disputes, returns, and offsets.
- Management's safeguards to insure the authenticity and collectability of the assigned receivables.

    g. Analyze secondary support offered by guarantors and endorsers.

    h. Ascertain compliance with established bank policy.

12. Transcribe significant liability and other information on officers, principals and affiliations of appropriate borrowers contained in the sample. Cross-reference line cards to borrowers, where appropriate.

13. Determine compliance with laws and regulations pertaining to accounts receivable lending by performing the following steps for:

    a. Lending limits:
- Determine the bank's lending limit as prescribed by state law.
- Determine advances or combinations of advances with aggregate balances above the limit, if any.

    b. Section 23A, Federal Reserve Act (12 USC 371©)—Transactions with Affiliates:
- Obtain a listing of loans to affiliates.
- Compare the listing to the bank's customer liability records to determine its accuracy and completeness.
- Obtain a listing of other covered transactions with affiliates (i.e., acceptance of affiliate's securities as collateral for a loan to any person).
- Ensure that covered transactions with affiliates do not exceed limits of section 23A.
- Ensure that covered transactions with affiliates meet the collateral requirements of section 23A.
- Determine that low-quality loans have not been purchased from an affiliate.
- Determine that all transactions with affiliates are on terms and conditions that are consistent with safe and sound banking practices

c. 18 USC 215-Commission or Gift for Procuring Loan:
-   While examining the accounts receivable loan area, determine the existence of any possible cases in which a batik officer, director, employee, agent, (,.attorney may have received anything of value for procuring or endeavoring to procure any extension of credit.
-   Investigate any such suspected situation.

d. Federal Election Campaign Act (2 USC 441b)-Political Contributions and Loans:
-   While examining the accounts receivable loan area, determine the existence of any loans in connection with any political campaign.
-   Review each such credit to determine whether it is made in accordance with applicable banking laws and regulations and in the ordinary course of business.

e. 12 USC 1972-Tie-In Provisions:
-   While examining the accounts receivable loan area, determine whether any extension of credit is conditioned upon: Obtaining or providing an additional credit, property, or service to or from the bank or its holding company, other than a loan, discount, deposit, of trust service.
-   The customer not obtaining a credit, property, or service from a competitor of the bank or its holding company (or a subsidiary of its holding company), other than a reasonable condition to assure the soundness of the credit.

f. Insider Lending Activities. The examination procedures for checking compliance with the relevant law and regulation covering insider lending activities and reporting requirements are as follows (die examiner should refer to the appropriate sections of the statutes for specific definitions, lending limitations, reporting requirements, and conditions indicating preferential treatment):
-   Regulation 0 (12 CFR 215)-Loans to Executive Officers, Directors, Principal Shareholders, and Their Interests:
-   While reviewing information relating to insiders received from the bank or appropriate examiner (including loan participations, loans purchased and sold, and loan swaps): - Test the accuracy and completeness of information about accounts receivable loans by comparing it to the trial balance or loans sampled.
    -   Review credit files on insider loans to determine that required information is available.
    -   Determine that loans to insiders do not contain terms more favorable than those afforded other borrowers.
    -   Determine that loans to insiders do not involve more than normal risk of repayment or present other unfavorable features.

- Determine that loans to insiders, as defined by the various sections of Regulation 0, do not exceed the lending limits imposed by those sections.
- If prior approval by the bank's board was required for a loan to an insider, determine that such approval was obtained.
- Determine compliance with the various reporting requirements for insider loans.
- Determine that the bank has made provisions to comply with the disclosure requirements for insider loans.
- Determine that the bank maintains records of public disclosure requests and the disposition of the requests for a period of two years.
- Title VIII of the Financial Institutions Regulatory and Interest Rate Control Act of]978(FIRA)(12 SC]972(2))Loans to Executive Officers, Directors, and Principal Shareholders of Correspondent Banks:
  - Obtain from or request the examiners reviewing "Due From Banks" and "Deposit Accounts" to verify a list of correspondent banks provided by bank management, and ascertain the profitability of those relationships.
  - Determine that loans to insiders of correspondent banks are not made on preferential terms, and that no conflict of interest appears to exist.

g. Financial Recordkeeping and Reporting of Currency and Foreign Transactions (31 CFR 103.33)—Retention of Credit Files: Review the operating procedures and credit file documentation and determine if the bank retains records of each extension of credit over $5,000, specifying the name and address of the borrower, the amount of the credit, the nature and purpose of the loan and the date thereof. (Loans secured by an interest in real property are exempt.)

14. Determine whether the consumer compliance examination uncovered any violations of law or regulation in this department. If violations were noted, determine whether corrective action was taken. Extend test to determine subsequent compliance with any law or regulation, so noted.

15. Perform appropriate steps in the separate section, Concentration of Credits.

16. Discuss with appropriate officer(s) and prepare summaries in appropriate report form of:
    a. Delinquent loans, including breakout of "N" paper.
    b. Loans not supported by current and complete financial information.
    c. Loans on which documentation is deficient.

    d. Inadequately collateralized loans.

    e. Classified loans.

    f. Small Business Administration delinquent or criticized loans.

    g. Transfers of low-quality loans to or from another lending institution.

    h. Concentrations of credit.

    i. Extensions of credit to major shareholders, employees, officers, directors, and/or their interests.

    j. Violations of laws and regulations.

    k. Other matters concerning the condition of the department.

17. Evaluate the function with respect to:

    a. The adequacy of written policies relating to accounts receivable financing.

    b. The manner in which bank officers are conforming with established policy.

    c. Adverse trends within the accounts receivable financing department.

    d. Accuracy and completeness of the schedules obtained from the bank.

    e. Internal control deficiencies or exceptions.

    f. Recommended corrective action when policies, practices or procedures are deficient.

    g. The competency of departmental management.

    h. Other matters of significance.

18. Update the workpapers with any information that will facilitate future examinations.

6

CASH FLOW ANALYSIS

A Banker's Guide

Cash flow analysis well may be the most important tool used by commercial and investment bankers to evaluate loans and value companies. Cash flow is literally the cash that flows through a company during the course of a quarter or the year after adjusting for noncash, nonoperating events. Lenders rely on cash flow statements because cash flows reveal both the degree by which historical and future cash flows cover debt service and borrowers' chances for survival. Cash flow is literally the firm's lifeblood. The greater and more certain the cash flows, the lower the default probabilities. Volatile cash flow is associated with weak bond ratings and higher default rates.

While the cash flow statement provides a "PRISM" (see Chapter 1) by which lenders peer into the future, there really is no substitute for in-depth knowledge of the firm, the industry in which the borrower operates, and the quality of management. In the final analysis, historical cash flows are simply offerings set by accounting information and guidelines, and they come to life only through the diligence, alertness, and the creativity of the minds that perceive them.

CASH VERSUS ACCRUAL-BASED INCOME

Revenue and profits power cash flows; all else is ancillary. But be wary. For example, a clothing manufacturer may make several large shipments of finished products shortly before the end of the fiscal year. The anticipated payment for these goods is booked as a debit to accounts receivable and a credit to *revenue*. While this transaction is recorded on the company's income statement, the goods shipped may be subject to returns. This results in the manufacturer shipping out a "make good" in a subsequent period. In another case, if the goods are acceptable but the customers are marginal credit risks, a substantial portion of the payments may never be realized and may be written off. In both instances, accrued revenue may not bring cash to the company resulting in artificially inflated fiscal disclosure.

Take the case of Enron (see also Chapter 2). After reporting healthy profits for years, Enron imploded, fueled in part by illusionary earnings in energy services. The firm supplied power to a customer at a fixed rate and then would make rosy projections on electricity and natural gas prices for the full term of the deal, which could last as long as 10 years. In short, those prices would decline enough to produce substantial profits. Under GAAP, Enron was required to "mark to market" the value of its energy trades. However, this is difficult to do when no active market exists on "energy paper" as with stocks or bonds. Companies like Enron were allowed to use their own simulation models to estimate fair market value and use the derived value as the appropriate market value.

To complicate matters, many contracts dealt with customers in states that had not yet deregulated their power markets. Enron forecast when states would deregulate those markets and then projected what prices would be under the currently nonexistent deregulated market. Then, based on its projections, Enron would calculate its total profit over the life of the contract. After discounting that figure to account for the risk its customer would default and the fact that it would not receive most payments for years, Enron would book the profit immediately. You are encouraged to work through the Enron Bankers Cash Flow Tutorial. The workbook and users guide are on the CD in the subdirectory Models_Demos/ Chapter 6.

INTRODUCTION TO ANALYSIS: SFAS 95 AND IAS 7

Statements of Financial Accounting Standards (SFAS) No. 95 (United States accounting standards) and International Accounting Standards (IAS) No. 7 mandate that cash flow statements be included in annual reports. Following is a summary from IAS 7:

- The cash flow statement is a required basic financial statement.
- It explains changes in cash and cash equivalents during a period.

- Cash equivalents are short-term, highly liquid investments subject to insignificant risk of changes in value.
- Cash flow statements should break down changes in cash and cash equivalents into operating, investing, and financial activities.
- Operating: Cash flows may be presented using either the direct or indirect methods. The direct method shows receipts from customers and payments to suppliers, employees, government (taxes), and so on. The indirect method begins with accrual basis net profit or loss and adjusts for major noncash items.
- Investing: The following should be disclosed separately: cash receipts and payments arising from acquisition or sale of property, plant, and equipment; acquisition or sale of equity or debt instruments of other enterprises (including acquisition or sale of subsidiaries); and advances and loans made to, or repayments from, third parties.
- Financing: The following should be disclosed separately: cash receipts and payments arising from an issue of shares or other equity securities; payments made to redeem such securities; proceeds arising from issuing debentures, loans, notes; and repayments of such securities.
- Cash flows from taxes should be disclosed separately within operating activities, unless they can be specifically identified with one of the other two headings, financing, or investing activities.
- Investing and financing activities that do not give rise to cash flows (a nonmonetary transaction such as acquisition of property by issuing debt) should be excluded.

Looking at this from the banker's perspective, cash flow statements should be completed in sufficient enough detail to make it easier for analysts to measure the impact cash and noncash investments have on financial position, external financing requirements, reasons for variances between payments and income, and the ability to fund dividends and meet obligations. Prior accounting standards (specifically, Accounting Principles Board (APB) Opinion 19) allowed businesses to disclose information on either a working capital or cash basis. However, there are significant problems with accepting working capital as a proxy for cash. For example, working capital reports fail to take into account the composition of working capital. While absolute working capital may increase, liquidity could actually be compromised due to buildups of stale inventory.

The section on operating activities may be disclosed using either direct or indirect methods. Under either method, a reconciliation of net cash flow from operations to net income is required, and either method should result in the same cash flow from operations.

The direct method focuses on cash and the impact cash inflows/outflows have on the borrower's financial condition. By checking numbers carefully and comparing cash-based numbers to accrual results, bankers walk away with a better understanding of their client's cash flow. The indirect basis starts off with net income but makes the necessary adjustments to pull out noncash and nonoperating revenue and expenses to arrive at the correct operating cash flow.

Indirect Method of Cash Reporting: The Banker's Cash Flow

Most reported cash flow statements commingle working (capital) assets/liabilities with gross operating cash flow (GOCF), which is weak disclosure, at best. *Net operating cash flow* should break out working capital and not combine income statement accounts. GOCF represents the income statement's ability to provide the primary internal cash required for future growth. Two cash sources are available to finance growth: internal and external. We associate external financing with debt or equity injections, while internal sources originate from within firms themselves, namely from profits and net asset disposals.

For purposes of the banker's cash flow, internal cash flow or cash from the income statement is classified as *gross operating cash flow*. Thus, gross operating cash flow is introduced to the cash flow format. Gross operating cash flow is usually compared to cash provided by debt financing activities. This allows the lender to (1) check for any imbalance in internal versus external financing and (2) make comparisons in financial leverage trends (see Exhibit I).

EXHIBIT I   Revised "Banker's" Cash Flow

Company X for the Year Ended December 31, 19X8

Increase (Decrease) in cash and cash equivalents

Cash flows from operating activities:		
Net income	3,040	
Adjustments to reconcile net income to net cash provided by operating activities:		
Depreciation and amortization	1,780	
Provision for losses on accounts receivable	800	
Gain on sale of facility	(320)	
Undistributed earnings of affiliate	(100)	
Gross operating cash flow*		**5,200**
(Inc.) Dec. in accounts receivable	(860)	
(Inc.) Dec. in inventory	820	
(Inc.) Dec. in prepaid expenses	(100)	
Operating cash needs*		**(140)**
Inc. (Dec.) in accounts payable and accrued expenses	(1,000)	
Inc. (Dec.) in interest and income taxes payable	200	
Inc. (Dec.) in deferred taxes	600	
Inc. (Dec.) in other current liabilities	200	
Inc. (Dec.) other adjustments	400	

Operating cash sources*		**400**
Net cash provided by operating activities		**5,460**
Cash flows from investing activities:		
Proceeds from sale of facility	2,400	
Payment received on note for sale of plant	600	
Capital expenditures	(4,000)	
Payment for purchase of company S, net of cash acquired	(3,700)	
Net cash used in investing activities		**(4,700)**
Cash flows from financing activities:		
Net borrowings under line of credit agreement	1,200	
Principal payments under capital lease obligation	(500)	
Proceeds from issuance of long-term debt	1,600	
Net cash provided by debt financing activities*		**2,300**
Proceeds from issuance of common stock	2,000	
Dividends paid	(800)	
Net cash provided by equity and other financing activities		**1,200**
Net increase in cash and cash equivalents		**4,260**
Cash and cash equivalents at beginning of year	2,400	
Cash and cash equivalents at end of year	6,660	

*Category added to complete bankers cash flow format.

Direct Method of Reporting Cash

To form a better understanding of the intricacies of the cash flow statement, let's take a look at each section individually.

Investing Activities

The *Miller GAAP Guide* summarizes investing activities as including the following:

> Making and collecting loans and acquiring and disposing of debt or equity instruments and property, plant, and equipment and other productive assets; that is, assets held for or used in the production of goods or services by the enterprise (other than materials that are part of the enterprise's inventory).

Investment activities include advances and repayments to subsidiaries, securities transactions, and investments in long-term revenue-producing assets. Cash inflows from investing include proceeds from disposals of equipment and proceeds from the sale of investment securities (see Table 6.1). Cash outflows include capital expenditures and the purchase of stock of other entities, project financing, capital and operating leases, and master limited partnerships.

TABLE 6.1   Example of Investment Reconciliation

Cash flows from investing activities	
Proceeds from sale of facility	$2,400
Payment received on note for sale of plant	600
Capital expenditures	(4,000)
Payment for purchase of Company S, net of cash acquired	(3,700)
Net cash used in investing activities	$(4,700)

Properly, Plant, and Equipment (PP&E)

Cash flows associated with PP&E activities include fixed assets purchased through acquisitions and equipment purchases, capital leases, and proceeds from property disposals. Noncash transactions include translation gains and losses, transfers, depreciation, reverse consolidations, and restatements.

Lenders do not usually require borrowers to break out property expenditures into expenditures for the maintenance of existing capacity and expenditures for expansion into new capacity, though this would be ideal disclosure, since maintenance and capital expenditures are nondiscretionary outlays. However, due to the difficulty (and subjectivity) involved in differentiating between maintenance outlays from expansion, amounts assigned to maintenance accounts would likely prove unreliable.

Unconsolidated Subsidiaries

When companies acquire between 20% and 50% of outside stock, the purchase is denoted an "Investment in unconsolidated subsidiary" and is listed as an asset on the acquiring firm's balance sheet. Cash inflows/outflows include dividends, advances, repayments, and stock acquisitions and sales. Noncash events include equity earnings and translation gains and losses.

Investment Project Cash Flows and Joint Ventures

These include investments in joint ventures or separate entities formed for the purpose of carrying out large projects. Typically, new entities borrow funds to build plants or projects supported with debt guarantees furnished by companies forming the new entity. Cash flows generally are remitted (upstreamed) to owner firms as dividends. Bankers typically receive a through-and-through disclosure of the project's future cash flows. This is because endeavors like construction projects are governed by explicit accounting rules. Thus, it is often difficult for bankers to untangle cash flows hidden beneath noncash events such as equity earnings. In addition, the project's projections may not be useful if cash streams are masked in joint ventures while the loan that financed the project to begin with is disclosed on the borrower's consolidated balance sheet.

FINANCING ACTIVITIES

According to the *Miller GAAP Guide,* financing activities include the following:

> Obtaining resources from owners and providing them with a return on, and return of, their investment; borrowing money and repaying amounts borrowed, or otherwise settling the obligation; and obtaining and paying for other resources obtained from creditors on long-term credit.

Cash inflows from financing activities include new equity infusions, treasury stock sales, and funded debt such as bonds, mortgages, notes, commercial paper, and short-term loans. Cash outflows consist of dividends, treasury stock purchases, and loan payments.

Long-Term Debt

Bond proceeds represent the amount a company actually receives from a debt issue, while increases and reductions in long-term debt include amortization of bond discounts and premiums. Amortization of a bond discount reduces earnings (noncash charge), while the bond's *book* value increases accordingly. No cash was received or paid out via the bookkeeping entry in Table 6.2, yet debt levels were adjusted on financial statements. Thus, bond discounts are subtracted from debt increases to determine "true" debt increases. The amortization of a bond

TABLE 6.2   Example of Financing Activities

Cash flows from investing activities		
Net borrowings under line of credit agreement	$1,200	
Principal payments under capital lease obligation	(500)	
Proceeds from issuance of long-term debt	1,600	
Net cash provided by debt financing activities		$2,300
Proceeds from issuance of common stock	$2,000	
Dividends paid	(800)	
Net cash provided by equity financing activities		$1200
Cash flows from activites		$3,500

TABLE 6.3   **Coupon Rate below Market Rate**

Face value of bond	$1,000,000
Term	10 years
Interest paid annually	
Coupon rate	6 %
Market rate	10%
Solve for present value	$754,217

premium is subtracted from long-term debt reductions to determine the "actual" reductions. Let's review two short examples.

In Table 6.3, the bond proceeds are $754,217 because the bond sold at a discount. Proceeds from the issue are reported as $754,217. Each year the unamortized discount of $245,783, a contra liability against the bond, is amortized. As a result, book value debt increases in value to $1,000,000 at maturity. The entry represents a noncash debt increase. Consider the journal entries and the effects of a bond discount on the firm's financial statements (Figure 6.1).

Cash	$754,217	
Bond Discount	$245,783	
Bonds Payable		$1,000,000

Now let's assume $50,000 discount was amortized in the following year:

Amortization of Bond Discount (noncash expense)	$50,000	
Unamortized Bond Discount		$50,000

The amortization of bond discount reduced the unamortized bond discount to $195,783 (Table 6.4). Notice that the book value of bonds increased to $804,217.

Assume the firm borrowed $300,000 long term (as in the previous example) and had no other debt except for the bonds. While the increase in long-term debt is $350,000, actual proceeds are $300,000.

Let's examine a bond premium. Bond premiums arise when market rates are below coupon rates (Table 6.5). Proceeds from the bond sale in Table 6.6 are

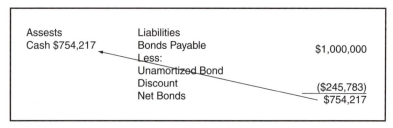

FIGURE 6.1   Balance Sheet Effect of Bond Amortization: Year 1 (initial period)

TABLE 6.4   Balance Sheet Effect of Bond Amortization: Year 2

Liabilities

Bond payable	$1,000,000
Less	
Unamortized bond	
Discount	(195,783)
Net bonds	$804,217
Debt issue increased	$50,000

$1,124,195, since the bond sold at a premium. Each year a portion of $124,195 of unamortized premium is set off as a noncash increase in income, while on the balance sheet debt is reduced (the unamortized bond premium decreases in value). At maturity, $1,000,000 will be due. As with the first example, amortization of the premium does not affect cash flows (Table 6.6).

Cash	$1,124,195		
	Bond premium		$124,195
	Bonds payable		$1,000,000

Assume $13,000 premium was amortized the following year:

Unamortized bond premium (noncash income)	$13,000	
Amortization of bond premium		$13,000

TABLE 6.5   Coupon Rate above Market Rate

Face value of bond	$1,000,000
Term	8 years
Interest paid annually	
Coupon rate	8%
Market rate	6%
Solve for present value	$1,124,195

TABLE 6.6   Balance Sheet Effect of Bond Premium: Year 1 (inital period)

Assets		Liabilities	
Cash	$1,124,195	Bonds payable	$1,000,000
		Plus:	
		Unamortized bond	
		Premium	124,195
		Net bonds	$1,124,195

The amortization bond premium reduced the unamortized bond premium to $111,195 (Table 6.7). The book value of bonds reduced to $1,111,195. Suppose the firm paid the $125,000 long-term debt in the previous example and had no other debt except for the bonds. While reductions in long-term debt amount to $138,000 ($125,000 debt payment and $13,000 bond premium amortized), the actual cash pay out was $125,000.

Keep in mind that the traditional interest-bearing bond is composed of the principal portion, which will be repaid to the holder of the bond, in full at maturity and the interest portion of the bond, consisting of coupon payments that the holder of the bond receives at regular intervals, usually every six months. On the other hand, zero coupons pay "zero" coupons, deferring the interest to maturity. The amortization required, because it is so large, increases reported debt levels, but no cash payout is made until maturity. Hence, the only time cash flow is affected is at maturity when payment is due investors. Bankers should always keep this in mind when evaluating disparate debt issues.

Conversion of debt to equity normally results in a substantial noncash transaction. However, conversion eliminates interest payments while reducing financial leverage. Financing activities also include preferred and common stock issues plus treasury stock inflows/outflows and options.

Dividends

Businesses grow by reinvesting current earnings. If stockholders withdraw earnings to support a lavish lifestyle, they put the cart before the horse. Most businesses experience cycles of good and bad times, growth and retraction. Without accumulating a "war chest," firms may not survive recessions or be liquid enough to repay obligations. Further, without reinvesting earnings, management cannot exploit opportunities by financing expansion internally. Exhibit II is an example of the most important source of internal cash flow, *operating activities*.

TABLE 6.7 Balance Sheet Effect of Bond Premium: Year 2

Liabilities	
Bonds payable	$1,000,000
Plus unamortized bond premium	111,195
Net bonds	$1,111,195
Debt issue decreased	$13,000

EXHIBIT II   Operating Activities

Cash flows from operating activities		
Net income	$3,040	
Adjustments to reconcile net income to net cash provided by operating activities:		
Depreciation and amortization	1,780	
Provision for losses on accounts receivable	800	
Gain on sale of facility	(320)	
Undistributed earnings of affiliate	(100)	
Gross operating cash flow		**$5200**
Increase in accounts receivable	$(860)	
Decrease in inventory	820	
Increase in prepaid expenses	(100)	
Operating cash needs		**(140)**
Decrease in accounts payable and accrued expenses	$(1,000)	
Increase in interest and income taxes payable	200	
Increase in deferred taxes	600	
Increase in other liabilities	200	
Other adjustments	400	
Operating cash sources		**400**
Net cash provided by operating activities		**5,460**

The *Miller GAAP Guide* defines operating activities as follows:

> All transactions and other events not defined as investing or financing activities. Operating activities generally involve producing and delivering goods and providing services. Cash flows from operating activities are generally the cash effects of transactions and other events that enter into the determination of income.

Gross Operating Cash Flow

Gross operating cash flow, an important feature of the cash flow statement, equals net income plus noncash charges, less noncash credits, plus or minus nonoperating events. This section depicts cash generated by operating income, routinely the borrower's dominant source of internal financing.

Noncash charges represent reductions in income not calling for cash outlays. Depreciation and amortization, provision for deferred taxes, asset write-downs, amortization of bond discounts, provisions, reserves, and losses in equity investments are familiar examples of noncash charges. Noncash credits increase earnings without generating cash and include equity earnings in unconsolidated investments, amortization of bond premiums, and negative deferred tax provisions. Nonoperating charges and earnings such as restructuring gains/charges, gains and losses on the sale of equipment, are adjusted as well, representing further refinements to reported earnings.

A typical interpretative problem area for lenders is disclosure of unconsolidated entities where cash inflows depend on dividend streams returned by projects or investment divestitures. Noncash profits can easily be managed by selecting liberal accounting methods or by simply manufacturing income. In one such case Enron, involved in a joint venture with Blockbuster, reported large profits even though the venture never attracted more than a few customers (see Enron cash flow, available on the CD).

Cash generated from nonrecurring items may artificially inflate the borrower's profits, but it usually cannot be depended on to provide cash flow to support long-term financing. Included are gains and losses from the sale of business units, judgments awarded to the company, and other one-time cash inflows.

One-time extraordinary expenses usually have little impact on long-term cash flows. For example, if XYZ Company settles a lawsuit over patent infringement that results in a one-time cash payout, the long-term health of the company may not be affected—that is, if XYZ Company can afford the settlement. On the other hand, consider a pharmaceutical company that loses a product liability suit, resulting in a cash settlement along with the recall of its best-selling drug. If the product is crucial to long-term survival, the borrower may end up financially distressed. Lenders should review nonrecurring items and their impact on credit decisions since it is core earnings that pay off loans, not phantom events or extraordinary income. Indeed, borrowing or capital stock issues may provide more funds than operations, but bankers count on business operations to provide the funds to finance ongoing operations, repay obligations, and distribute dividends.

Equity Earnings

Equity earnings show up on the income statement as increases to earnings. These often illusory earnings end up included in retained earnings, and because they are noncash items, leverage and coverage ratios are sometimes distorted. What's the story behind equity earning? Suppose your borrower owns between 20% and 50% of another firm's stock. Accountants say your borrower "influences" the firm's operations and so must include the prorated share of earnings into its financial statements. Thus, if the firm makes $1,000,000 profit, 25% of those profits (or $250,000) are included as equity earnings.

Suppose your borrower, company A, originally invested $1 million in company B in year 0, obtaining a 25% equity stake. By year 5, the value of this 25% stake may have grown to $2.5 million. The equity earnings from this investment would have been reflected on your borrower's (company A) income statement over the five-year period, but no cash has been received from the investment (assuming no dividends)—cash that might have paid loans. To adjust for the income statement distortion, banks pull this noncash credit from cash flows. The investment may be perfectly circumspect in a number of ways, but there is the danger that the investment could pay out ill-timed dividends or otherwise set the stage for financial maneuvering—siphoning funds, for example.

Deferred Tax Credits

Deferred tax credits cause earnings to increase but may not provide cash, nor offer a sustainable source of cash. Deferred tax credits often come about when previous provisions for deferred taxes are reversed.

Operating Cash Needs

Of approximately equal magnitude, accounts receivable and inventory typically constitute almost 80% of current assets for manufacturing industries. With such a large, relatively volatile working capital investment, operating cash needs deserve special attention. Accounts receivable and inventory levels reflect the borrower's marketing abilities and credit policies. Revenue from sales may have been reported for the period, but cash may have not been received. A rise in receivables represents a use of cash and is usually financed. A decrease in receivables is associated with cash inflows. Recall from the discussion of ratios in Chapter 3 that the volume of credit sales and the collection period determine the levels of receivables. The average collection period is influenced by economic conditions as well as controllable factors. Effective inventory policies like *just in-time* methods improve internal cash flows, while redundant inventory is often very costly.

Operating Cash Sources

The right side of the balance sheet supports assets. Large increases and decreases in current accounts represent substantial inflows and outflows of cash. Operating cash sources generally include non-interest-bearing current liabilities that tend to follow sales increases. Accounts payable represent inventory purchases on credit. Increases in accounts payable are a source of cash in the sense that they delay cash outflows into the future. While the borrower has use of this cash, it can utilize it for daily needs as well as for investment purposes. Eventual payment to creditors decreases accounts payable, converting them into a use of cash. Generally, decreases from one period to the next represent an amount paid to suppliers in excess of purchases expensed. Increases in accruals and taxes payable represent sources of cash, because items such as salaries, taxes, and interest are expensed but not paid out. Thus, cash is conserved for a limited period. A decrease in accruals arises from payments in excess of costs expensed. In the current period, therefore, the decrease is subtracted from the cash flow as a use of cash.

Net Operating Cash Flow

Net operating cash flow denotes the cash available from gross operating cash flow to internally finance a borrower's future growth (after demands on working capital demands are satisfied). One of the great things about the structure of the cash flow format is how pieces of information surface to offer compelling insights about company operations. For example, if gross operating cash flow is often lower than net cash flow from operations, traditional sources of working capital, accounts payable, and accruals have completely covered traditional working capital uses, accounts receivable, inventory, and so on. As a result, precious operating cash income need not be diverted to support working capital levels and can thus be rerouted to finance "growth" strategies included in investment activities—the lifeblood of shareholder value.

CASH FLOW WORKSHOP

The cash flow analysis is not a stand-alone document. It is used in conjunction with the balance sheet and income statement. As discussed earlier, cash flow is the sum of cash flowing in and out of firms. Before beginning our workshop, we consider transactions making up sources and uses of cash and how each is derived. The statement of cash flow is directly related to the balance sheet. To illustrate, behind two fiscal balance sheets are underlying transactions that make up all operating, investment, and financing activities. Subtracting two balance sheets will make it relatively easy to classify transactions that indeed end up on the banker's cash flow statement. Let's start with the basic accounting equation below in Exhibit III. Later on in the chapter we shall move the technique further along by decomposing and recreating the cash flow of a complex international company—Essar Steel, Mumbai, India. and, of course the cash flow of Enron Corporation, on the CD, has been dismantled and recreated.

EXHIBIT III   Steps to Derive Cash Flow Equation

Derivation of cash flow	Notes
Equation 1: Assets = Liabilities + Equity	Basic accounting equation
Equation 2: Cash + Accounts receivable + Inventory + Net fixed assets + Investments in unconsolidated subsidiaries = Accounts payable + Accruals + Short-term debt + Current portion long-term debt + Long-term debt + Equity	Extrapolate the basic accounting equation
Equation 3: Cash = Accounts payable + Accruals + Short-term debt + Current portion long-term debt + Long-term debt + Equity − Accounts receivable − Inventory − Net fixed assets − Investments in unconsolidated subsidiaries	Solve for cash
Equation 4: Δ Cash = Δ Accounts payable + Δ Accruals + Δ Short-term debt + Δ Current portion long-term debt + Δ Long-term debt + Δ Equity − Δ Accounts receivable − Δ Inventory − Δ Net fixed assets − Δ Investments in unconsolidated subsidiaries.	Multiply both sides of Equation 3 by delta (Δ)

Equation 5: $-\Delta$ Cash $= -\Delta$ Accounts payable $- \Delta$ Accruals $- \Delta$ Short-term debt $- \Delta$ Current portion long-term debt $- \Delta$ Long-term debt $- \Delta$ Equity $+ \Delta$ Accounts receivable $+ \Delta$ Inventory $+ \Delta$ Net fixed assets $+ \Delta$ Investments in unconsolidated subsidiaries	Multiply both sides of Equation 4 by by minus 1

Equations 4 and 5 prove that changes in cash are exactly equal to differences between cash sources and uses. Note assets, defined as uses of cash, depict negative deltas (Δ) preceding balance sheet changes, while liabilities and equity accounts, traditional sources of cash, are preceded by positive deltas. As we saw earlier, if a borrower, say company A, manufactures product X, sells it but has not paid for raw materials used in production, cash is conserved. This results in increases in accounts payable, a source of cash. Conversely, if the firm sells on terms, no cash is received at the time of the sale, resulting in the expansion of receivables, a use of cash. Cash sources and uses appear as follows:

Sources of cash include	*Uses of cash include*
Decreases in assets ($-\Delta$)	Increases in assets ($+\Delta$)
Increases in liabilities ($+\Delta$)	Decreases in liabilities ($-\Delta$)
Increases in equity ($+\Delta$)	Decreases in equity ($-\Delta$)

Let's get started with the workshop by reviewing the five steps to appraise the banker's cash flow statement:

- Step 1. Review the balance sheet and income statement.
- Step 2. Develop a control sheet.
- Step 3. Prepare reconciliations arising from your control sheet.
- Step 4. Complete the cash flow statement.
- Step 5. Develop your analysis.

Step 1: Review Wedgewood Corporation's Financial Statements for 1998 and 1999

Begin by examining the balance sheet and income statement for Wedgewood Corporation, the fictitious company we will use to study these five steps (see Exhibits IV and V).

EXHIBIT IV   Wedgewood Corporation Balance Sheet for Fiscal Year Ending December 31

	1998	**1999**
Cash	$110	$130
Accounts receivable	230	280

Inventory		200	220
Current assets		*$540*	*$630*
Gross property	$620		$800
Less: Accumulated depreciation	(180)		(250)
Net fixed assets		440	550
Investment in unconsolidated subsidiary		240	410
Total assets		**$1,220**	**$1,590**
Accounts payable		$300	$330
Wages payable		20	30
Taxes payable		10	10
Short-term debt		100	102
Current maturities		70	80
Current liabilities		*$500*	*$552*
Long-term debt		$330	$380
Deferred taxes		25	48
Other liabilities		15	90
Common stock		120	170
Paid-in capital		140	200
Retained earnings		130	180
Treasury stock		(40)	(30)
Liabilities and equity		**$1,220**	**$1,590**

EXHIBIT V   **Wedgewood Corporation Income Statement for Fiscal Year Ending December 31**

	1998	1999
Sales	1,370	1,400
Cost of goods sold	(885)	(880)
Gross profit	**485**	**520**
Depreciation expense	(84)	(90)
Operating expenses	(492)	(520)
Operating profit	**(91)**	**(90)**
Loss (gain) on sale of equipment	12	(10)
Equity earnings in unconsolidated subsidiary	201	230
Profit before taxes	122	130
Current taxes	2	(27)
Deferred taxes (credit)	45	(23)
Net profit	**$169**	**$80**

Additional Transactions Made in 1999

1. The company purchased new equipment for $250; cash received from disposals totaled $40.
2. Dividends received from investment in unconsolidated subsidiaries totaled $140; advances to unconsolidated subsidiaries were $80.
3. The company placed a new debt issue of $60.

Step 2: Develop the Control Sheet for Wedgewood Corporation

1. The next step will be to sort out the year-to-year cash changes employing the control sheet as follows (Exhibit VI).
2. Measure year-to-year balance sheet changes for each account.
3. Determine sources and uses of cash for each account. For example, Wedgewood's accounts receivable increased by $50 in 1999, reflecting a use of cash.
4. Total columns in order to identify the cash change. The change in cash is equal to the difference between sources and uses of cash.

EXHIBIT VI   Wedgewood Corporation Control Sheet, December 31, 1999

Item	Increase	Decrease	
Cash	20		
	Sources	Uses	Further development
Accounts receivable		50	Directly to cash flow
Inventory		20	Directly to cash flow
Net PP&E		110	Fixed asset reconciliation
Investment in unconsolidated subs	170		Investment reconciliation
Short-term notes	2		Directly to cash flow
Accounts payable	30		Directly to cash flow
Accruals	10		Directly to cash flow
Current portion long-term debt	10		Long-term debt reconciliation
Senior long-term debt	50		Long-term debt reconciliation
Deferred taxes	23		Deferred tax reconciliation
Misc. liabilities	75		Directly to cash flow
Common stock	50		Equity reconciliation
Additional paid-in capital	60		Equity reconciliation
Retained earnings	50		Equity reconciliation
Treasury stock	10		Equity reconciliation
Total	370	350	
Change in balance sheet accounts	20		
Proof: matches with change in cash	20		Directly to cash flow

Cash sources/uses appear as net changes, so reconciliations to balance sheet accounts are required to break out balance sheet differences. For example, Wedgewood Corporation's equity account changed, but the question is why. Was income the contributing factor, or was it cumulative currency translations, new equity, or dividends?

Step 3: Prepare and Analyze Reconciliations

Net Fixed Asset Reconciliation

Included are capital expenditures, depreciation, acquisitions, capital leases, proceeds from disposals of property, unrealized translation gains and losses, and transfers. Adding book gains or subtracting book losses derives proceeds from disposals. Translation gains and losses (FASB 52) earmark currency holding gains and losses. They are included so that bankers may distinguish between realized and unrealized fixed asset transactions (Exhibits VII and VIII).

EXHIBIT VII   An Example of the Fixed Asset Reconciliation

Net PP&E	(prior period)
Less: Depreciation and amortization of net fixed assets	(current period)
Less: Proceeds from disposals	(current period)
Less: Losses on sale of fixed assets	(current period)
Plus: Gain on sale of fixed assets	(current period)
Plus: Capital expenditures	(current period)
Plus: Acquired fixed assets	(current period)
Plus/(Less) translation gains (losses)	(current period)
= Derived net property plant and equipment	(current period)
Less: Actual net property plant and equipment	(current period)
= Increase/Decrease in net property plant and equipment	(current period)

EXHIBIT VIII   Wedgewood Corporation Fixed Asset Reconciliation

	Amount	Information	Source/Use	Category
Beginning balance	440	Balance sheet		
Less: Depreciation	(90)	Stmt cash flow	Source	Gross operating cash flow
Less: Disposals	(40)	Stmt cash flow	Source	Investment activities
Plus: Capital expenditures	250	Stmt cash flow	Use	Investment activities
Gain/loss on disposal	(10)	Stmt cash flow	Use/source	Gross operating cash flow
Derived ending balance	550			
Balance sheet ending balance	550	Balance sheet		
Increase/Decrease in fixed assets	0	Derived	Use	Investment activities

Depreciation, disposals, capital expenditures, gain/loss on disposal, and (increase) decrease fixed assets transactions equal balance sheet changes reflected on the control sheet. If derived ending balances do not match the balance sheet, derives the difference and label it "Increase/Decrease in net property plant and equipment" (Exhibit VII).

Investment Reconciliation

Equity investment transactions include equity earnings, dividends from subsidiaries, advances and repayments, purchase and sale of securities, translation gains/losses, consolidations, and deconsolidations. A summary financial statement may be included in the footnotes if the auditor determines that a more detailed explanation is warranted. Equity earnings are sometimes netted out against dividends. Dividends can be pulled out as the difference between undistributed equity and equity earnings. Project finance activities can also show up in investment schedules (see Exhibits IX and X).

EXHIBIT IX   An Example of the Investment Reconciliation

Investment in unconsolidated subsidiaries	(prior period)
Plus: Equity earnings	(current period)
Less: Cash dividends from subsidiaries	(current period)
Plus: Advances to subsidiaries	(current period)
Less: Repayment of loans	(current period)
Plus: Translation gains (FASB 52)	(current period)
Less: Translation losses (FASB 52)	(current period)
= Derived investment in unconsolidated. subsidiaries	(current period)
Less: Actual investment in unconsolidated subsidiaries	(current period)
= Increase/Decrease in investment in unconsolidated subsidiaries	(current period)

EXHIBIT X   Wedgewood Corporation Investment Reconciliation

	Amount	Information	Source/Use	Category
Beginning balance	240	Balance sheet		
Plus: Equity earnings	230	Income statement*	Use	GOCF
Dividends received	(140)	Income statement*	Source	GOCF
Plus: Advances	80	Stmt cash flow	Use	Investment activities
Derived ending balance	410			
Ending balance	410	Balance sheet		
Increase/Decrease in investments	0	Derived	Source	Investment activities

*Information also applies to the statement of cash flow and footnotes.

Deferred Tax Reconciliation

Tax expense includes both current and deferred taxes. Deferred taxes arise because of "timing differences"—for example, when income/expenses reported on financial statements differ from taxes reported to the IRS. Some common factors causing timing dissimilarities include different depreciation methods for financial statement and tax purposes, and recognition of income in different periods for book and tax purposes. For example, if taxable income exceeds book income (this occurs when prepaid cash is booked such as a subscription), deferred taxes are recorded as an asset. A negative provision increases income and reduces the deferred tax liability. Information on deferred tax is usually found in the tax footnote and is illustrated in Exhibits XI and XII.

EXHIBIT XI   The Deferred Tax Reconciliation

Deferred taxes	(prior period)
Plus: Deferred tax provision	(current period)
Less: Deferred tax credits	(current period)
= Derived deferred taxes	(current period:
Less: Actual deferred taxes	(current period)
= Increase/Decrease deferred taxes	(current period)

EXHIBIT XII   Wedgewood Corporation Deferred Tax Reconciliation

Deferred tax accounts	Amount	Information	Source/use	Category
Balance sheet beginning balance	25	Balance sheet		
Provision for deferred taxes	23	Income statement	Source	GOCF
Derived ending balance	48			
Balance sheet ending balance	48	Balance sheet		
Increase/Decrease in deferred taxes	0	Derived	Source	Investment activities

Equity Reconciliation

Comprehensive equity reconciliations are frequently organized in annual report footnotes and the cash flow statement. The equity reconciliation is actualized as follows:

- Equity accounts and opening balances appear as headings with total equity presented in the last column.
- Listed down columns are transactions corresponding to their respective equity account. Totals for each transaction, along the row, are recorded in the total equity column.
- After transactions are recorded, each column is totaled identifying the ending balance for each equity account. The ending balance equals year-end account balances.

- The total equity column should reconcile to the sum of the account balances across the bottom, thus maintaining the self-proving nature of the system.
- Transactions not affecting cash cancel out, so no number is carried to the total column and will not appear on the cash flow statement.

Examples include net income, cash dividends, proceeds from stock sale, the exercise of stock options, cumulative translation adjustments, and purchases and sales of treasury stock. Cash transactions affecting equity are carried to the cash flow statement. Equity transfers, like stock dividends, are excluded. The equity reconciliation and classification to cash flow accounts are recorded in Exhibit XIII.

EXHIBIT XIII   Wedgewood Corporation Reconciliation of Equity Accounts

	Common stock	Paid-in capital	Retained earnings	Treasury stock	Total
Equity accounts beginning balance	120	140	130	(40)	350
Net income (loss)			80		80
Cash dividend			(30)		(30)
Sale of treasury stock		60		10	70
Stock sale	50				50
Ending balance	170	200	180	(30)	520

Equity accounts	Amount	Source/(Use)	Category
Beginning balance	350		
Net income (loss)	80	Source	Gross operating cash flow
Cash dividends	(30)	Use	Financing activity: Equity and other
Sale of treasury stock	70	Source	Financing activity: Equity and other
Stock sale	50	Source	Financing activity: Equity and other
Ending balance	520		

By reviewing long-term debt schedules provided in the footnotes, we can figure out the decreases in debt issues and the addition of new debt (Exhibits XIV and XV.

EXHIBIT XIV   The Long-Term Debt Reconciliation

Current portion	(prior year)
Plus: Noncurrent portion	(prior year)
Plus: Increase in long-term debt	(current year derived from the issue-by-issue breakdown in the footnotes)
Less: Noncurrent portion	(current year)
= Reductions in long-term debt	(current year)

EXHIBIT XV   Wedgewood Corporation Long-Term Debt Reconciliation

	Source/(Use)	Category	
Current portion long-term debt, 1998	70		
Noncurrent long-term debt, 1998	330		
Plus: New debt issue, 1999	60	Source	Financing activity: debt
Less: Current portion long-term debt, 1999	(80)		
Less: Noncurrent long-term debt, 1999	(380)		
= Long-term decreases, 1999	0	Use	Financing activity: debt

Other Possible Reconciliations (absent from Wedgewood Corporation)

Intangible Reconciliation

Goodwill and intangible reconciliations are required when amortization of goodwill or intangibles is disclosed in the annual report (Exhibit XVI).

EXHIBIT XVI   The Intangible Reconciliation

Balance sheet beginning balance	(prior year)
Less: Amortization of intangibles	(current year)
Plus: Acquired intangibles	(current year)
Derived intangibles	(current year)
Balance sheet ending balance	(current year)
(Inc.)/Dec. in intangibles	(current year)

Minority Interest Reconciliation

Claims on the parent's income by minority shareholders is recognized as minority interest in earnings (income statement) and minority interest (balance sheet) (Exhibit XVII).

EXHIBIT XVII   Minority Interest Reconciliation

Balance sheet beginning balance	(prior year)
Plus: Minority interest in earnings	(current year)
Less: Dividends to minority interest	(current year)
Derived minority interest	(current year)
Ending minority interest	(current year)
Inc. (Dec.) in minority interest	(current year)

Step 4: Complete the Cash Flow Statement for Wedgewood Corporation (Exhibit XVIII)

EXHIBIT XVII Wedgewood Corporation Banker's Cash Flow, December 31, 1999

Cash flow accounts	Amount		Information transferred from
Net Income	80		Equity reconciliation
Plus/Less: Noncash Items			
Depreciation	90		Fixed asset reconciliation
Inc./(Dec.) deferred tax	23		Deferred tax reconciliation
Inc./(Dec.) equity earnings	(230)		Investment reconciliation
Gain/Loss disposals	10		Fixed asset reconciliation
Gross operating cash flow		**(27)**	
(Inc.)/Dec. net accounts receivable	(50)		Control sheet
(Inc.)/Dec. inventory	(20)		Control sheet
Operating Cash Needs		**(70)**	
(Inc.)/Dec. net accounts payable	30		Control sheet
(Inc.)/Dec. accruals	10		Control sheet
Operating cash sources		**40**	
Net cash provided by operating activities		**(57)**	
Capital expenditures	(250)		Fixed asset reconciliation
Dividends received from subsidiaries	140		Investment reconciliation
(Advances) net of repayments	(80)		Investment reconciliation
Cash received from sale of equipment	40		Fixed asset reconciliation
Net cash used in investing activities		**(150)**	
Long-term debt	60		Long-term debt reconciliation
Short-term debt	2		Control sheet
Cash flows from interest-bearing debt		**62**	
Cash dividends	(30)		Equity reconciliation
Sale treasury stock	70		Equity reconciliation
Misc. long-term liabilities	75		Control sheet
Equity	50		Equity reconciliation
Cash flows from equity and other financing activities		**165**	
Net change in cash items		**20**	Derived: Also matches control sheet

Step 5: Develop Your Analysis: Bullets and Points for Completing the Cash Flow Statement

Gross Operating Cash Flow

- Merchandise is sometimes shipped out at the end of the year to window-dress the financials. Be on the lookout for the following warning signs: unearned income; shifting sales to future periods via reserves; income smoothing gimmicks; creating gains and losses by selling or retiring debt; hiding losses inside discontinued operations; selling assets after pooling; moving current expenses to later periods by improperly capitalizing costs, amortizing costs too slowly, and failing to write off worthless assets.
- Analyze the quality, magnitude, and trend of earnings. Check quality of earnings in such areas as adequacy of reserves, nonrecurring items, and cash versus accrual-based income.
- When you analyze earnings trends, pay particular attention to the contribution of income to overall financing. If income is contributing less and less to overall financing, go back and check the strategic plans.
- Compare net income and dividends to each other. Are dividends large in proportion to net income? If so, why are they upstreamed?
- Compare depreciation with capital expenditures. If depreciation is greater than capital expenditures, assets may be running below optimal levels.
- Although reserves and write-downs such as inventory are add-backs to gross operating cash flow, they should be fully investigated.

Operating Cash Uses

- Beware of the following red flags: large overdue receivables; overly dependent on one or two customers; related-party receivables; slow receivables turnover (annualize this frequently); right of return exists; changes in terms, credit standards, discount or collections, or creating receivables through distortive accounting. For example, Enron issued its common stock in exchange for notes receivable. The company then increased both notes receivable and shareholder's equity in recognition of these transactions. However, accounting convention requires that notes receivable culminating from transactions containing a company's capital stock be presented as deductions from stockholder's equity and not as assets, which is not how Enron and its auditor, Arthur Andersen, had booked the transactions.
- If the average collection period has increased, determine the reason(s).
- Large increase when sales are flat; slow inventory turnover; faddish inventory; inventory collateralized without your signature; watch

unjustified LIFO to FIFO changes; insufficient insurance; change in divisional inventory valuation methods; increase in the number of LIFO pools; unreasonable intercompany profits; inclusion of inflation profits in inventory; large, unexplained increase in inventory; gross profit trends bad but no markdowns; inclusion of improper costs in inventory; capitalized instead of flow-through.
- Be sure to write down inventory if losses are sizable.

Operating Cash Sources

- The spread between loan pricing and an annualized 37% return associated with anticipating $^2/_{10}$ net 30 terms multiplied by the payable is nothing to sneeze at. Check to see if the payables manager takes advantage of trade discounts.
- Operating cash flow should be compared with accounts payable. A "bulge" in payables may indicate late payments, particularly if gross operating cash flow is not making an adequate contribution to investment activities, or the operating unit is highly leveraged.
- Determine if the cash conversion cycle contributes to increased payables balances and late payments.

Net Cash Provided by Operating Activities

- Net cash provided by operating activities is the line in the cash flow statement that provides cash to primary expenditures after working capital coverage.
- Working capital requirements can pull large amounts of cash from the business. This can cut into capital expansion programs, particularly if operating cash flow falls significantly below expectations.
- Keep in mind that one of the best ways to check the quality of earnings is to compare net income to net cash flow from operations. For example, if earnings consistently reach high levels but little remains to cover investment activities, then question what good is net income availability to pay debt service? For example, has net income been distorted and/or cannibalized by noncash credits, uncollectible receivables, or increases in unsaleable inventory? If so, little income will be left to finance both new investments and loan reductives.

Investment Activities

- Companies with volatile cash flow histories tend to invest less on the average than firms with smoother cash flows. They may also face stiffer costs when seeking funds from external capital markets.
- For firms with volatile cash flow patterns, business decisions are compounded by a higher tendency to have periods of low internal cash

flows that can distract managers and cause them to throw out budgets, delay debt repayments, and defer capital expenditures.

- Categorize investment activities into two groups: discretionary and nondiscretionary.
- Nondiscretionary investment activities refer to outlays required to keep a healthy gross margin on the operating-unit level. Say, for example, nondiscretionary investments are covered by the borrower's internal cash flow. From this you can assume that financing activities are discretionary and the firm has better control of its capital structure.
- Assets require continuous replacement and upgrading to ensure efficient operations.
- When depreciation expenses consistently exceed capital expenditures over time, this is an indication of a declining operation. Eventually, this will lead to a fall in earnings and profitability. Capital expenditures represent major nondiscretionary outlays.
- Watch out for outdated equipment and technology, high maintenance and repair expense, a declining output level, inadequate depreciation charges, changes in depreciation method, a lengthening depreciation period, a decline in the depreciation expense, and a large write-off of assets. Also watch out for distortions regarding currency translations.
- Check to see if deferred taxes are running off. Deferred taxes usually increase when capital expenditures accelerate.
- Download the most recent capital budgeting schedule. Focus on project cost, net present values (NPVs), and internal rate of return (IRR).
- Check to see if fixed asset turnover (sales/net fixed assets) increases sharply. As we saw in Chapter 3, this ratio measures the turnover of plant and equipment in relation to sales. The fixed asset/turnover ratio is really a measure of cash flow efficiency since it indicates how well fixed assets are being utilized.
- Determine if backlogs are increasing without a large pickup in sales. Unresolved backlogs unusually happen only once, and then customers go elsewhere.
- Determine if work-in-process inventory ties into a sharply deteriorating inventory turnover.
- Make sure the gross margin has not trended down over the past few years due to increased labor costs and decreased operating leverage.
- Always use real options criteria when applicable.

Investment Project Cash Flows and Joint Ventures

- Once the financial merits of a project have been examined, it must be discerned whether the project's cash flow is reasonably understood.

For example, if XYZ division fails to maintain property, plant, and equipment, a series of problems could easily ensue. The unit's aging or outmoded machinery would increasingly experience longer periods of downtime and goods produced could be defective. The operating unit will begin to fall behind its competitors from both a technological and opportunity cost standpoint. Worse, customers may perceive its products as inferior, of lower quality, or old fashioned compared to its competitors.

From a summary of IAS 31, a joint venture is a contractual arrangement subject to joint control. There are three types of joint ventures: jointly controlled operations, jointly controlled assets, and jointly controlled entities.

- The venture should recognize jointly controlled operations by including the assets and liabilities that it controls, the expenses that it incurs, and its share of the income that it earns from the sale of goods or services by the venture. Jointly controlled assets should be recognized on a proportional basis and jointly controlled entities should be recognized in consolidated financial statements, as outlined in the text box.
- The cost of capital should be appropriate. If it is artificially low, the project's NPV will be inflated.
- Look for a slow amortization period, a lengthening amortization period, a high ratio of intangibles to total assets and capital, and a large balance in goodwill even though profits are weak.
- Make sure the time frame to complete the project is realistic, rather than a "pie in the sky" scenario. Projects that take longer to complete than projected will invariably cost more than budgeted. This will lower the project's NPV and may lead to an eventual cash crunch for the company.
- Determine what, if any, contingencies have been made by the company in the event that the project costs or completion time exceeds the original estimate. If the business can raise additional capital without difficulty, this is a very positive factor from a lender's point of view.
- Watch for switching between current and noncurrent classifications, investments recorded in excess of costs, and investments.
- Determine the real value of projects and not just book values.
- Finally, savvy bankers should never cease questioning clients on off balance sheet projects not fully understood. What more eye-opening example eclipses the Enron projects disclosure (or lack of) reviewed in Chapter 2? Enron's Raptor partnerships were used to exaggerate profits by $1 billion over a period of months. Perhaps aggressive cash flow due diligence by bankers would have extracted this shenanigan from its Alice-in-wonderland milieu.

Financing Activities: Debt

- Increases in long-term debt should always be examined on a specific issue basis in order to ensure optimal financing.
- Optimal financing means financing that minimizes the cost of capital, maximizes equity value, and may prevent your borrower's credit grade or bond rating from downtiering.
- Make sure you distinguish real debt increases from accounting debt increases on the cash flow statement. For example, as we saw earlier, amortization of bond discount results in debt increases, but no cash inflow is involved.
- Decreases in long-term debt should be matched against increases in long-term debt along with the magnitude of gross operating cash flow. For example, in an expanding business, increases in long-term debt may exceed reductions. As long as leverage is within acceptable levels, internal cash flow is probably contributing its fair share to the overall financing of the business.
- Amortization of bond premiums distorts actual debt reductions. Find cash decreases by separating bond premiums from debt payments.
- Look for long-term debt conversions to equity. Conversion to equity may represent a substantial noncash exchange.

Equity and Other Financing Activities

- Review dividends to determine whether they are tied to income or are relatively constant.
- Examine financial leverage as well to verify that dividends are reasonable in light of future prospects. Determine whether an established partner exists in the business's capital expenditure program.

FINAL POINTS ABOUT CASH FLOW ANALYSIS

1. Cash flow statements retrace all financing and investment activities of a firm for a given period of time. This includes the extent to which cash has been generated and absorbed.
2. Today more and more lenders rely on the statement of cash flows as a measure of corporate performance because it "images" the probability distribution of future cash flows in relation to debt capacity.
3. The greater and more certain the cash flows, the greater the debt capacity of the firm.
4. SFAS 95 mandates segregating the borrower's business activities into three classifications: operating, financing, and investing activities. The

operating activities section may be presented using either a direct or indirect presentation.

5. The direct method focuses on cash and the impact of cash on the financial condition of the business.

6. Investing activities involve making and collecting loans and acquiring and disposing of debt or equity instruments and property, plant, and equipment and other productive assets—that is, assets held for or used in the production of goods or services by the enterprise.

7. Cash flows from unconsolidated subsidiaries include dividends from subsidiaries, advances and repayments, and the acquisition or sale of securities of subsidiaries. Noncash transactions include equity earnings, translation gains and losses, and consolidations.

8. Prudent bankers must obtain a full disclosure concerning the project's future cash flows since construction projects may report noncash earnings—construction accounting or equity earnings.

9. Investing activities involve obtaining resources from owners and providing them with a return on, and return of, their investment; borrowing money and repaying amounts borrowed or otherwise settling the obligation; and obtaining and paying for other resources obtained from creditors on long-term credit.

10. Operating activities include all transactions and other events that are not defined as investing or financing activities. Operating activities generally involve producing and delivering goods and providing services. Cash flows from operating activities are generally the cash effects of transactions and other events that enter into the determination of income.

11. Gross operating cash flow is often the most important line in the cash flow statement, representing net income plus all noncash charges less all noncash credits, plus or minus all nonoperating transactions.

12. Cash generated from nonrecurring items may artificially inflate earnings for a period, but it cannot be depended on to provide cash flow to support long-term financing.

13. Net income must be the predominant source of a firm's funds in the long run.

14. For the most part, current assets represent more than half the total assets of many businesses. With such a large, relatively volatile cash investment connected to optimizing shareholder value, current assets are deserving of financial management's undivided attention.

15. Net operating cash flow denotes the cash available from gross operating cash flow to internally finance a firm's future growth after working capital demands have been satisfied.

16. Sources of cash include decreases in assets, increases in liabilities, and increases in equity. Uses of cash include increases in assets, decreases in liabilities, and decreases in equity.
17. The control sheet shows that the change in the cash account is always equal to the difference between sources and uses of cash.
18. Sources and uses of cash are usually net changes, meaning the end result of many different transactions. Thus, reconciliations lie at the core of cash flow analysis.
19. The quality, magnitude, and trend of operating cash flow must be examined carefully since it should contribute a reasonable amount to financing. This is readily determined by the composition of the gross operating cash flow.
20. When depreciation expenses consistently exceed capital expenditures over time, this is an indication of a business in decline. Eventually, it will lead to a reduction in earnings and profitability.
21. If investment in unconsolidated subsidiaries represents a large item on the balance sheet, lenders should ask for financial statements of the unconsolidated subsidiary—or at least a full financial summary.

ANALYSIS   Essar Steel Limited, Mumbai, India

It's time to put our most important tool, cash flow, to use. We shall take the complex cash flow of an old and respected Indian company Essar Steel and rewrite it into a banker's format with help from the computer. The objective of this exercise is simply to "get to know our credit." Remember, the further down loan exposures appear on the grading scale—that is, the worse the rating—the greater the detail served at the table called due diligence—it's as simple as that. Readers who wish to study the Enron cash flow instead may do so. Open the files Enron CF2A and Enron User Guide located in the directory Models_Demos\Chapter 6\Enron. To complete this exercise we return to the Basel Committee principles, namely number 6, point 44:

> Each credit proposal should be subject to careful analysis by a credit analyst with expertise commensurate with the size and complexity of the transaction. An effective evaluation process establishes minimum requirements for the information on which the analysis is to be based. There should be policies in place regarding the information and documentation needed to approve new credits, renew existing credits and/or change the terms and conditions of previously approved credits. The information received will be the basis for any internal evaluation or rating assigned to the credit and its accuracy and adequacy is critical to management making appropriate judgments about the acceptability of the credit.

We require an Excel model to reconstruct Essar Steel Limited's cash flows included in the annual report in order to develop a broad analysis of the firm's operating, financing, and investing activities. Our Excel model, which is on the CD, will reshape the original cash flow into a transparent, and assuredly, more formal banker's document.

CASH FLOW RECONSTRUCTION

Step 1: Scan the Original Cash Flow into Excel

Essar cash flow statement	1998–99	Rs. in crores 1997–98
Net profit (loss) before taxes and extraordinary items	(496.45)	27.01
Adjustment for:		
Depreciation	326.22	292.32
Foreign exchange variation	(39.34)	55.61
Share issue expenses/deferred revenue exp. written off	41.89	32.79
Provision for doubtful debts	2.90	3.53
(Profit)/loss on sale of fixed assets	(52.96)	
Interest charges	502.40	461.57
Lease rent	44.97	39.72
Interest received	(88.89)	(124.13)
Dividend received	(1.11)	(0.84)
Income from investments.	(1.57)	(2.26)
Operating profit before working capital changes	*238.06*	*785.32*
Adjustment for:		
Trade and other receivables	(17.51)	(45.79)
Inventories	77.87	(184.93)
Trade payable	118.53	(21.94)
Cash generated from operations	416.95	532.66
Direct taxes paid	(27.46)	(14.62)
Net cash flow from operating activity	*389.49*	*518.04*
Cash flow from investing activities		
Purchase of property, plant, and equipment and other long-term assets	(146.41)	(213.70)
Sale proceeds of property, plant, and equipment and other long-term assets	0.21	0.52
Acquisition of equity of other company and interest in joint ventures	(0.10)	
Purchase of investments	(17.27)	(0.85)
Sale of investments	0.60	
Intercorporate deposit/loans given to companies	(39.25)	(150.68)
Receipt of intercorporate deposit loans given to companies	194.51	135.67

Interest received	40.17	82.64
Dividend received	1.11	0.84
Income from investments	1.57	2.26
Net cash from investing activities	*35.24*	*(143.40)*
Cash flow from financing activities		
Proceeds from long/short-term borrowings	633.11	491.90
Receipt of long-term advances from customers (net)	1185.35	
Repayment of long-term advances from customers (net)	(190.36)	
Repayments of amount borrowed (installments/short-term loans)	(279.58)	(954.56)
Interest and similar charges paid and charged to revenue	(395.95)	(517.69)
Interest and similar charges paid and capitalized	(207.22)	(299.80)
Lease rent liabilities paid	(28.84)	(89.26)
Dividend paid	(4.97)	(41.40)
Deferred revenue expenses	(33.43)	(39.50)
Net cash from financing activities	*(507.24)*	*(264.96)*
Net increase in cash and cash equivalents	**(82.51)**	109.68
Cash and cash equivalents opening balance (includes marketable securities of Rs. 1.51 crores, previous year as Nil)	159.61	49.93
Cash and cash equivalents closing balance (includes marketable securities of Rs. 1.54 crores; previous year 1.51 crores)	*77.10*	*159.61*

Before continuing, we delete subtotal and total rows and then add up columns to ensure the scan was completed correctly.

Disclosure issues on original cash flow appear as follows:

1. *Net profit (loss) before taxes and extraordinary items.* Profits are normally reported on an after-tax basis.
2. *Foreign exchange variation.* Does this label mean foreign exchange translations or transactions? If items are translations, they should be included in financing activities. If they represent transactions, they belong in operating expenses.
3. *Direct taxes paid.* This item was included below cash generated from operations. It belongs in income.
4. *Share issue expenses/deferred revenue expense written off.* Why are these items combined? The first appears to belong in financing activities. How did deferred revenue expense arise?
5. *Operating profit before working capital changes.* This category is useless to banks since operating profit does not pay loans. Gross operating cash flow does, but it is not included in Essar's cash flow.

6. *Adjustment for trade and other receivables, inventories, and trade payable.* These adjustments are combined when disclosure requires breaking out these working capital accounts into operating cash uses and operating cash sources.

7. *Purchase of property, plant, and equipment and other long-term assets and receipt of intercorporate deposit loans given to companies.* These are large items and should be broken out.

8. *Cash flow from financing activities.* This category includes combined debt issues that should be broken out.

9. *Interest and similar charges paid and charged to revenue and interest and similar charges paid and capitalized.* These items are bunched together and not specific to the financing instruments they represent.

We now develop the control sheet and reconciliations directly from the original cash flow statement. See the Bsreconcil Worksheet.

Step 2: Scan Essar's Balance Sheet into Excel

Balance Sheet as of March 31, 1999

Schedule	As of March 31, 1999	Rs. in crores as of March 31, 1999
Sources of funds		
Shareholders' funds		
Share capital	330.35	330.35
Reserves and surplus	1753.79	2083.83
Total shareholder finds	2084.14	2414.18
Loan funds		
Secured loans III	2848.27	2585.74
Unsecured loans IV	1539.60	1287.47
Total loan funds	4387.87	3873.21
Long-term advances from customer	1098.37	1288.72
Total	**7570.38**	**7576.11**
Application of funds		
Fixed assets V		
Gross block	5885.81	5434.60
Less depreciation	(1383.72)	(1042.02)
Net block	4502.09	4392.58
Capital work-in-progress		
(Refer to note 15 of schedule XXI)	336.34	1360.72
	4838.43	5753.30

Investments VI	298.21	281.55
Current assets, loans, and advances		
Interest accrued on investments	0.58	2.23
Inventories VII	690.73	768.60
Sundry debtors VIII	625.91	644.31
Cash and bank balances	75.56	158.10
Loans and advances X	1790.99	836.85
	3183.77	2410.09
Less: current liabilities and provisions		
Current liabilities XI	(1098.88)	(1062.36)
Net current assets	2084.89	1347.73
Miscellaneous expenditure X11	181.28	193.53
(to the extent not written off or adjusted)		
Profit and loss account XIII	167.57	
Total	**7570.38**	**7576.11**

Before continuing, delete subtotal and total rows and add up columns to ensure the scan was completed correctly.

Step 3: Set Up the Control Sheet (Color-coded cells requiring reconciliations are included in the Enron Steel model on the CD.)

	Control Sheet Increase	Decrease
Cash and bank balances	82.54	
	Source	**Use**
Share capital		
Reserves and surplus		330.04
Loan funds		
Secured loans III	262.53	
Unsecured loans IV	252.13	
Long-term advances from customer		190.35
Net block		109.51
Capital work-in-progress		
(Refer to note 15 of schedule XXI)	1024.38	
Investments VI		16.66
Interest accrued on Investments	1.65	
Inventories VII	77.87	
Sundry debtors VIII	18.40	

Loans and advances X		954.14
Less: Current liabilities and provisions		
Current liabilities XI	36.52	
Net current assets		
Miscellaneous expenditure X11	12.25	
(to the extent not written off or adjusted)		
Profit and loss account XIII		167.57
Total source/use	1685.73	1768.27
Proof change in chase	(82.54)	

Step 4: Match Reconciliations against Corresponding Numbers on the Control Sheet.

(Notice that the sum of transactions making up reconciliations equals its corresponding match on the control sheet.)

Instructions: Match each reconciliation against its corresponding numbers on the control sheet.

Reconciliations		
Reserves and surplus		
Beginning balance	2083.83	
Profit and loss account	(118.38)	
Transfers and others	(211.66)	
Ending balance	1753.79	(330.04)
Secured loans		
Beginning balance	2585.74	
Nonconvertible debentures	140.57	
Foreign currency loans—banks	7.50	
Rupee loans—banks	(74.40)	
Foreign currency loans fin. institutions	2.27	
Rupee loans—fin. institutions	(17.69)	262.53
Interest accrued and due	149.13	
Working capital loans from banks	55.15	
Ending balance	2848.27	
Unsecured loans		
Beginning balance	1287.47	
Floating rate notes	82.35	
Foreign currency loans: foreign banks	(37.52)	252.13
St foreign currency loan from bank	150.00	

Other unsecured loans	57.30	
Ending balance	1539.60	
Net fixed assets		
Beginning balance	4392.58	
Depreciation expense	(356.43)	
Disposals	(878.25)	109.51
Capital expenditures	1344.19	
Ending balance	4502.09	
Loans and advances		
Beginning balance	836.85	
Subsidiary company—unsecured	990.94	
Other loans	(57.22)	
Deposits and others	20.42	954.14
Ending balance	1790.99	
Current liabilities		
Beginning balance	1062.36	
Acceptances for goods and services	(102.73)	
Capital expenditures creditors	(48.78)	
Creditors for goods and expenses	228.48	36.52
Other current liabilities	(40.45)	
Ending balance	1098.88	
Profit and loss account		
Beginning balance	0.00	
Unexplained balance as per P&L account	285.95	
General reserve per contra	(118.38)	167.57
Ending balance	167.57	

Step 5: Make a Copy of the Worksheet BSReconcil Calling It EssarCF

You can now develop a first draft cash flow in your own format. Include labels only, leaving plenty of space for the following items to be filled in: net income, gross operating cash flow, operating cash needs, operating cash sources, net cash flow from operations, investment activities, financing activities, and change in cash. The computer will transfer all items listed on the control sheet and reconciliations onto your newly formatted cash flow.

Essar Steel cash flow (copy previous page and insert columns)

Net income	(118.38)	
Depreciation expense	356.43	
Gross operating cash flow		238.05

Interest accrued on investments	1.65	
Inventories VII	77.87	
Sundry debtors VIII	18.40	
Operating cash needs		97.92
Acceptances for goods and services	(102.73)	
Capital expenditures creditors	(48.78)	
Creditors for goods and expenses	228.48	
Other current liabilities	(40.45)	
Operating cash sources		36.52
Net cash flow from operations		372.49
Investment activities		
Disposals	878.25	
Capital expenditures	(1344.19)	
Loans/advances: subsidiary company—unsecured	(990.94)	
Other loans	57.22	
Deposits and others	(20.42)	
Long-term advances from customer	(190.35)	
Capital work in progress	1024.38	
Current and long-term investments	(16.66)	
Miscellaneous expenditure x11	12.25	
Total investment activities		(590.46)
Financing activities		
Secured loans		
Nonconvertible debentures	140.57	
Foreign currency loans—banks	7.50	
Rupee loans—banks	(74.40)	
Foreign currency loans—fin. institutions	2.27	
Rupee loans—fin. institutions	(17.69)	
Interest accrued and due	149.13	
Working capital loans from banks	55.15	262.53
Unsecured loans		
Floating rate notes	82.35	
Foreign currency loans: foreign banks	(37.52)	
Short-term foreign currency loan from bank	150.00	
Other unsecured loans	57.30	252.13
Financing activities		
Unexplained balance as per P&L account	(285.95)	
General reserve per contra	118.38	
Transfers and others	(211.66)	(379.23)
Change in cash	(82.54)	

Finally, we absorb information included in Essar's original cash flow that will enhance our final version, adjusting continuously and ensuring that change in cash is always correct. The final version appears in EssarCF2.

The final version

Revised cash flow and reconciliations		1998–1999
Operating activities		
Loss before taxes	(496.45)	
Direct taxes paid	(27.46)	
Net loss	*(523.91)*	
Depreciation expense	356.43	
Provision for doubtful debts	2.90	
Adjustments to amount to retained earnings	405.53	
Gross operating cash flow		**240.95**
Interest accrued on investments	1.65	
Inventories VII	77.87	
Sundry debtors VIII	15.50	
Operating cash needs		**95.02**
Trade payable	118.53	
Acceptances for goods and services	(102.73)	
Capital expenditures creditors	(48.78)	
Creditors for goods and expenses	109.95	
Other current liabilities	(40.45)	
Operating cash sources		**36.52**
Net cash flow from operations		**372.49**
Investment activities		
Disposals	878.25	
Capital expenditures	(1344.19)	
Loans/advances: subsidiary company—unsecured	(990.94)	
Other loans	57.22	
Deposits and others	(20.42)	
Long-term advances from customer	(190.35)	
Capital work in progress	1024.38	
Current and long-term investments	(16.66)	
Miscellaneous expenditure x11	12.25	
Total investment activities		**(590.46)**
Financing activities		
Secured loans increases		

Nonconvertible debentures	140.57	
Foreign currency loans—banks	7.50	
Foreign currency loans—fin. institutions	2.27	
Interest accrued and due	149.13	
Working capital loans from banks	55.15	
Secured loans decreases		
Rupee loans—banks	(74.40)	
Rupee loans—fin. institutions	(17.69)	262.53
Unsecured loans—increases		
Floating rate notes	82.35	
St foreign currency loan from bank	150.00	
Other unsecured loans	57.30	
Unsecured loans—decreases		
Foreign currency loans: foreign banks	(37.52)	252.13
Financing activities		
Unexplained balance as per P&L account	(285.95)	
General reserve per contra	118.38	
Transfers and others	(172.32)	
Foreign exchange variation	(39.34)	(379.23)
Change in cash		**(82.54)**
Correct change in cash per control sheet		**(82.54)**
Notes from CF annual report		
Repayment of long-term advances from customers (net)	(190.36)	
Repayments of amount borrowed (installments/short-term loans)	(279.58)	
Interest and similar charges paid and charged to revenue	(395.95)	
Interest and similar charges paid and capitalized	(207.22)	
Lease rent liabilities paid	(28.84)	
Dividend paid	(4.97)	
Deferred revenue expenses	(33.43)	

REVIEW QUESTIONS

1. What are the short-term and long-term effects of extraordinary items on the cash flow? Give examples of extraordinary items; categorize them into operating, investing, or financing activities, and discuss their impact on the cash flow.
2. Define cash and noncash events. Explain the process of amortizing bond discounts and premiums and the effect it has on the cash flow. What other are noncash items.

3. What are the differences between gross and net operating cash flow? What are the some of the operating cash sources and needs?

SELECTED REFERENCES AND READINGS

Bierlen, R., and A. M. Featherstone. (1998). Fundamentals, cash flow, and investment: Evidence from farm panel data. *Review of Economics and Statistics*, 427–435.

Comiskey, E. E., and C. W. Mulford. (2000). *Guide to financial reporting and analysis*. New York: Wiley.

Cotton, W. D. J., and M. Schinski. (1999). Justifying capital expenditures in new technology: A survey. *Engineering Economist* **4**, 362–376.

Dechow, P. (1994). Accounting earnings and cash flows as measure of firms performance. 3–42.

Emmanuel, C. B. (1988). Cash flow reporting, Part 2: Importance of cash flow data in credit analysis. *Journal of Commercial Bank Lending*, 16–28.

Falkena, H. B., and W. J. Kok. (1988). *Essays on financial risk management*. Basingstoke, England: Macmillan Press.

Gahlon, J. M., and R. L. Vigeland. (1988). Early warning signs of bankruptcy using cash flow analysis. *Journal of Commercial Bank Lending*, 4–15. Establishes that seven cash flow variables and suggested ratios capture statistically significant differences between bankrupt and nonbankrupt firms, on average, as much as five years prior to bankruptcy. These ratios and variables are thus strong candidates for inclusion in the early warning systems banks use for identifying potential credit problems.

Gentry, J. A., P. Newbold, *et al.* (1990). Profiles of cash flow components. *Financial Analysts Journal*, 41–48.

Helfert, E. A. (1991). *Techniques of financial analysis*. Homewood, IL: Irwin.

Jay, N. R., and T. M. Shank. (1997). Using cash flow metrics to differentiate rated bonds. *Journal of Financial Management and Analysis*, 23–32.

Kaplan, S. N., and R. S. Ruback. (1994). *The valuation of cash flow forecasts: An empirical analysis*. Cambridge, MA: National Bureau of Economic Research.

Kaplan, S. N., and L. Zingales. (2000). *Investment-cash flow sensitivities are not valid measures of financing constraints*. National Bureau of Economic Research, Working Paper Series: 1–5.

Kaplan, S. N., and L. Zingales. (1995). *Do financing constraints explain why investment is correlated with cash flow?* Cambridge, MA: National Bureau of Economic Research.

Kathuria, R., and D. C. Mueller. (1994). *Investment and cash flow: Asymmetric information or managerial discretion*. University of Maryland, Debt. of Economics, Working Paper (3): 1–[46].

Kiyotaki, N., and National Bureau of Economic Research. (1990). *Learning and the value of the firm*. Cambridge, MA: National Bureau of Economic Research.

Lamont, O. A. (1996). *Cash flow and investment: Evidence from internal capital markets*. Cambridge, MA: National Bureau of Economic Research.

Masonson, L. N. (1990). *Cash, cash, cash: The three principles of business survival and success*. New York: Harper Business.

Mills, R. (1998). Strategic value analysis. *Economic and Financial Computing* **8**, 153–198.

Myers, S. C., and National Bureau of Economic Research. (1989). *Signaling and accounting information*. Cambridge, MA: National Bureau of Economic Research.

Nordgren, R. K. (1986). Understanding cash flow: A key step in financial analysis. *Journal of Commercial Bank Lending*, 2–17.

Tracy, J. A. (1989). *How to read a financial report: Wringing cash flow and other vital signs out of the numbers*. New York: Wiley.

SELECT INTERNET LIBRARY AND CD

CD includes

EssarCF2: Essar Steel Cash Flow Model
EnronCF2A: Enron fiscal 2000 cash flow model
Enron User Guide: User Guide to help you work throught the Enron cash flow model.

Internet Library

International Accounting Standards

IAS 7: Cash Flow Statements:
http://www.iasc.org.uk/frame/cen2_17.htm

Financial Accounting Standards Board

Summary of Statement No. 95, "Statement of Cash Flows" (Issued November 1897)
http://accounting.rutgers.edu/raw/fasb/

7

PROJECTIONS AND RISK ASSESSMENT

One crucial issue in risk management deals with analyzing what could go wrong with individual credits and portfolios and factoring this information into the analysis of risk-adjusted returns, capital adequacy, and loan provisions. "What if" analysis can unveil previously uncovered areas of credit risk exposures and plays the vital role of locking into areas of potential problems. This chapter explains how to process scenarios through various forecasting techniques ranging from modified percentage of sales to advanced stochastic optimization analysis.

The Basel Committee on Banking Supervision has this to say about forecasting:

> In the final analysis banks should attempt to identify the types of situations, such as economic downturns, both in the whole economy or in particular sectors, higher than expected levels of delinquencies and defaults, or the combinations of credit and market events, that could produce substantial losses or liquidity problems. Stress test analyses should also include contingency plans regarding actions management might take given certain scenarios.

The emphasis on bank forecasts developed as loan demand increased to fund large and complex credits including mergers and acquisitions. These new deals represented a new class of borrowers who pushed their financial structure to exceedingly high debt levels. As a result, lenders began to work with a new breed of sophisticated forecasting and valuation models to predict expected default, financial needs, and shareholder value with a great deal more accuracy and insight.

Building projected financial statements around a set of critical assumptions or value drivers involves research, logic, and up-to-date predictive software. Computers, after all, do not make credit decisions. They merely quantify assumptions about the future, serving as another tool, albeit an important one, in the process of loan decision making. The real value of computers is that the technology facilitates rapid analysis of many alternatives, mimicking as realistic an environment as possible. Sometimes, when appropriate, the bank will run a "sensitivity analysis," examining the effect of changing key assumptions in any number of combinations to construct a range of outcomes from pessimistic to optimistic. However, we will see that simulation and optimization analysis are far more advanced methods of stress testing than running a borrower's forecast through various "sensitivities."

> Many banks do not take sufficient account of business cycle effects in lending. As income prospects and asset values rise in the ascending portion of the business cycle, credit analysis may incorporate overly optimistic assumptions. Industries such as retailing, commercial real estate and real estate investment trusts, utilities, and consumer lending often experience strong cyclical effects. Sometimes the cycle is less related to general business conditions than the product cycle in a relatively new, rapidly growing sector, such as health care and telecommunications. Effective stress testing, which takes account of business or product cycle effects, is one approach to incorporating into credit decisions a fuller understanding of a borrower's credit risk.
> Source: Basel Committee.

FORECASTING FACTORS

In determining the most suitable forecasting technique for a given situation, one of the first checks is to determine comparability between the forecast methods used and the quality/amount of data or, for that matter, the complexity of the facility or borrower being evaluated. It is apparent from the start that lenders should be aware of both the benefits and the pitfalls of each forecasting method before choosing one. It is not uncommon for a preferred forecasting method to offer incomplete, inaccurate results in one situation while producing okay results in another similar analysis.

Availability of comprehensive, historical data is the standard prerequisite for developing forecasts. Since different forecasting methods generally require various amounts of historical data, requirements for data quality (and quantity) may vary as well. Next comes accuracy—triple-A-rated firms usually require little data with accuracy hardly an issue (Enron Corporation not withstanding) while B-rated customers may require plenty of verifiable information. In the former case, risks are insignificant, financial statements are strong, and the firm operates in nonvacillating surroundings. A forecast error of 30% or more is irrelevant, whereas a forecast of error of 100 basis points may be enough to spell disaster for a borrower with a low rating.

STATISTICAL FORECASTING

Casual Forecasting

Casual models deal with forecast variables that exhibit a cause-and-effect relationship. For example, sales may be a function of market share, markup, promotion, competition, and economic sensitivities. Casual forecast models help lenders determine that relationship. So future sales can be more easily determined.

Causal (simple regression) is a special case of regression when lenders work with a single independent variable. In simple regression, as in multiple regression, lenders assume a linear association within historical data and allow models to estimate the relationship using the method of least squares. Simple regression is not limited to a time-series relationship. Rather, it predicts connections between any two variables, determining the value of one variable (dependent) as a function of the second variable (independent)—thus the name causal model. Mathematically, the causal is written as

$$Y = f(X)$$

The value of Y is a function of the value of X. When this is assumed to be a straight-line relationship, lenders write it as

$$Y = a + bX$$

Time-Series or Trend Forecasting Using Excel Functions

Time-series forecasting, on the other hand, predicts the future by expressing it as a function of the past (e.g., Sales = f(Time). Excel's functions =trend(draws a straight line through historical data, and =growth(draws a curve (see Table 7.1 and Figure 7.1).

Forecasting with Decisioneering's CB Predictor[1]

CB Predictor (www.decisioneering.com) analyzes the borrower's historical data for trends and seasonal variations. The software then predicts future values based

---

[1] The demo on the CD included with permission of Decisioneering. Readers are encouraged to download Decisioneering trial software used in this chapter.

TABLE 7.1 Historical Trend Function =trend(

Month	Sales	Trend
1	33,696	31,637
2	34,983	33,016
3	30,222	34,395
4	35,634	35,774
5	38,844	37,152
6	40,131	38,531
7	39,897	39,910
8	34,765	41,288
9	43,992	42,667
10	42,027	44,046
11	46,566	45,425
12	49,888	46,803
13	**Forecast**	**48,182**
14	**49,561**	
15	**50,940**	
16	**52,318**	
17	**53,697**	
18	**55,076**	
19	**56,454**	
20	**57,833**	
21	**59,212**	
22	**60,591**	

on this information. Lenders find it easier to answer questions like, "Will the firm's forecasted sales follow a historical pattern, or have they been inflated to make the firm seem more creditworthy? How much raw material will the borrower need to have on hand?" With CB Predictor, the bank will no longer have to pull these numbers out of thin air. Instead, lenders rely on robust, statistically proven techniques to create predictions. CB Predictor uses techniques of time-series and multiple linear regression categories. The model takes statistically complex methods of time-series forecasting and makes them easily available from a wizard-driven application within Excel. The CD contains a demonstration and tour of CB Predictor. You are encouraged to take the tour double clicking on CBPredQT located in the subdirectory Models_Demo/Chapter 7. For this demonstration you are a product forecaster for Tropical Hair Products Inc. You need to forecast unit sales of Regular Shampoo, Dandruff Shampoo, and conditioner for the next twelve months.

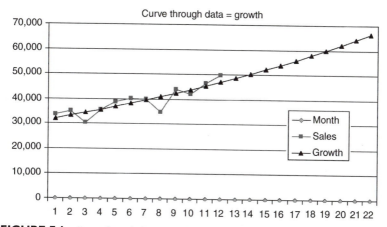

FIGURE 7.1   Curve through data=growth(

Simple Moving Averages

Simple moving averages start with the earliest period in the data and include the specified prices (open, high, low, close, midpoint, or average) for chosen number of periods. This total is then divided by the number of periods set in the Parameters menu of CB Predictor. Use the following formula

$$MA_t = \frac{(P_t + P_{t-1} + P_{t-2} + \ldots\ldots P_{t-n} + 1)}{n}$$

where n = number of bars, Pt = selected calculation price, Pt−1 = selected calculation price 1 period ago, and Pt−n = selected calculation price n periods ago. The moving average has distilled the trend from the daily price fluctuations (Figure 7.2).

Exponential Smoothing Averages

Since its development 50 years ago, exponential smoothing (ES) has become a popular method of forecasting among finance people. ES requires only a few data points to produce predictions and is well suited for large numbers or items. Exponential smoothing smoothes past values of a time series in a decreasing (exponential) fashion. This is achieved by the use of a formula embedded on a statistical model that derives exponentially decreasing weights associated with past observations, as shown in Figure 7.3.

Regression Curve Fitting—
The Exponential and Logarithmic Curve Fit

If the firm is undercapitalized, exponential (revenue) growth will stress capital. On the other hand, growth along a logarithmic curve (when sales increase at a

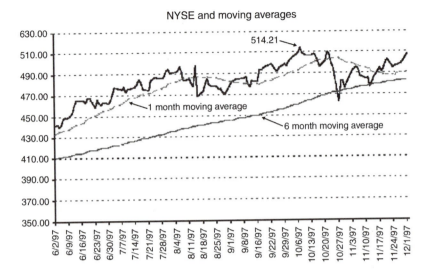

FIGURE 7.2 New York Stock Exchange and Moving Averages

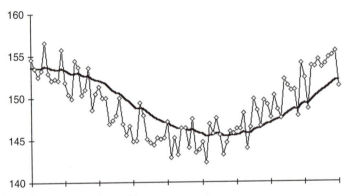

FIGURE 7.3 Exponential Smoothing

decreasing rate) attracts higher bond ratings, results in lower default risk, and usually produces stronger cash flows. We have seen exponential growth in hot Internet firms, in which revenues stretched across the projection horizon with increases compounded exponentially.

Exponential growth has been the focus of much discussion among researchers investigating food and raw material requirements. Some analysts argue for growth limits, because finite space and resources bind exponential increases. Others argue that stabilizing social and market mechanisms slow or stop exponential growth. As for business, most valuation experts argue that exponential growth retreats in the face of competitive markets when output becomes saturated in the marketplace, forcing down internal rates of return.

Whatever one's position, exponential growth may take place for extended periods of time, and that's the danger. Popular models, notably Excel's Trendline shown in Figure 7.4 functions, are effective tools that can spin data off into lower risk/higher risk curve fits. Let's examine sales data. We can see whether sales in the example appearing in Table 7.2 fits an exponential or logorithmetic curve (Figure 7.5).

Trendlines and Curve Fit Correlations in Excel

The R-squared statistic in Excel tells you what percentage of variation in the dependent variable (Y) is "explained" by changes in the independent variable. R^2 ranges from 1 (which means that the variation in the independent variable perfectly explains the variation in the dependent variable or that the relation between the two variables is very strong) to 0 (which means that there is no relationship between the variables). In general, the larger the R^2 value, the better changes in the independent variable explain variations in the dependent variable.

Multiple Regression

The idea of multiple regression is to predict a single variable from one or more independent variables. Multiple regression with many predictor variables is an extension of linear regression with two predictor variables. A linear transformation of the X variables is done so that the sum of squared deviations of the observed and predicted Y is a minimum. The computations are more complex, however, because the interrelationships among all the variables must be taken

TABLE 7.2   Sales to Inventory Matrix

	Year	Sales (X)
1	19X0	4.560
2	19X1	4.962
3	19X2	5.728
4	19X3	6.477
5	19X4	8.480
6	19X5	17.924
7	19X6	17.524
8	19X7	20.181
9	19X8	21.752
10	19X9	24.106

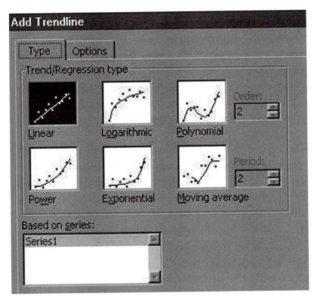

FIGURE 7.4   Excel's Add Trendline Option

into account in the weights assigned to the variables. The interpretation of the results of a multiple regression analysis is also more complex for much the same reason.

Here we find a lead/lag relationship between the dependent variable and a leading (independent) variable that could be used in predicting. From a practical view, the approach of paired indices is useful providing causal information. For example, you employ multiple regression and estimate *causal* relationships in data. This approach complements time-series forecasting. But be careful; you can run into problems. For example, to predict sales, you may decide that disposable income and television spots are two linking factors. However, future levels of that disposable income may prove not to be a viable link, nor can one be certain of the role television advertising plays in the future—that is, the "error factor" in the formula.

While a compelling relationship may appear between sales and disposable income/advertising, the association might yield limited value. Thus, forecasting issues are not necessarily resolved by identifying cause-and-effect relationships. Relationships between variables may change as as a firm moves through its economic environment, so casual forecasting is never used alone.

Multiple regression designates one variable as dependent (Y) and picks, via a step-wise operation, which variables are independent (X). You may elect to develop the regression apart from the step-wise method. For example, you may want to change one variable, measure another, then analyze the data with one or more of the standard statistical tests.

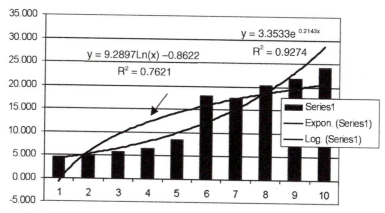

FIGURE 7.5   Exponential and Logarithmic Curve Fit and Correlations

The prediction of Y is accomplished by the following equation:

$$Y = \beta_0 + \beta_{1X1} + \beta_{2X2} + \beta_{3X3} + \beta_{4X4} \ldots + \textit{Random scatter}$$

If there is only a single X variable, then the equation is $Y = \beta_0 + \beta_{1X1}$, and the multiple regression analysis is the same as simple linear regression (β_0 is the Y intercept; β_1 is the slope).

SENSITIVITY FINANCIAL FORECASTING

Modified Percentage of Sales Method

Historical relationships that have held firm generally will not change much, at least into the near term. Finding relationships in historical statements improves forecast accuracy—it's as simple as that. If historical relationships, say accounts receivables to revenue, change significantly, the lender's ability to predict results becomes murky until he or she has identified and justified the new relationship.

That is where forecasting financial statements comes in. It is arguably the best way to complement or reinforce statistical methods.

One widely used technique is the *modified percentage of sales* method. This method is based on the premise that the balance sheet is correlated to changes in sales. Whether a firm restructures or just grows normally, variations in revenue generally require asset/liabilities adjustments. In the process of developing a forecast, the lender works with two important equations: the financial needs formula (F) and the projected percentage of sales externally financed formula (E):

$$F = A/S\,(\Delta S) + \Delta NFA - LI/S\,(\Delta S) - P(S)(1 - d) + R$$

The F formula determines the external financing needs of the firm. If used in conjunction with the percentage of sales method, both techniques render the same answer. The formulas are easy to enter into the HP 19BII Solver. 19BII Business Consultant's Solver creates menus of variables from equations you enter and lists those menus to run calculations. Equations are stored in the Solver's equation list. The equation list can include as many equations as you want, limited by the calculator's memory.

$$E = (A/S - L1/S) - (P/g)(1+g)(1-d) + R/\Delta S$$

F = Cumulative financial needs
A = Projected spontaneous assets
S = Projected sales
ΔS = Change in sales
ΔNFA = Change in net fixed assets
L1 = Spontaneous liabilities
P = Projected profit margin (%)
d = Dividend payout rate
R = Debt maturities
T = Targeted growth rate
L = Leverage
g = Sales growth rate

The E formula identifies the percentage of sales growth requiring external financing.

Setting up the Percentage of Sales Method: Do Financial Statements Make Sense?

Since balance sheet changes follow the income statement, the income statement is a logical point of departure. Internally generated sources of cash (payables, accruals, retained earnings, and so on) depend on revenue and margin assumptions. Assets (uses of cash) are tied to the income statement. See the Excel file BosProj.xls located in the Chapter 7 subdirectory on the CD and depicted in Table 7.3.

Current assets that are linked (or spontaneous) to sales include cash, receivables, prepaid expenses, and inventory. For instance, if accounts receivable historically run 30% of sales and next year's sales are forecasted to be $100 million, accounts receivable may project at $30 million. Fixed assets do not generally tie directly to sales.

On the right side are spontaneous liabilities—accounts payable and accruals move in tandem with sales. Liabilities independent of sales—all the funded ones representing financing activities—are excluded. Equity, including preferred and common, refers to financing activities and is not directly derived from variations in sales. The total for retained earnings is calculated by deducting the dividend payout from net profits. Before we go further, another important point to make is that you should estimate noncritical variables (not included in this exercise). You accomplish this by adjusting historical trends. Examples of noncritical variables include various prepaid assets and disposals (Exhibit I).

TABLE 7.3 **Input Screen Projection Assumptions**

	1999	2000	2001	2002	2003
Cash	2.0%	2.0%	2.0%	2.0%	2.0%
Receivables	15.1	15.1	15.1	15.1	15.1
Inventory	23.9	23.9	23.9	23.9	23.9
Fixed assets	8.3	8.3	8.3	8.3	8.3
Accounts payable	10.2	10.2	10.2	10.2	10.2
Accruals	3.7	3.7	3.7	3.7	3.7
Sales growth rate	6.0	6.0	6.0	6.0	6.0
Profit margin	1.0	1.0	1.0	1.0	1.0
Dividend payout	25.0	25.0	25.0	25.0	25.0
Loan amortization	$500.0	$500.0	$500.0	$500.0	$500.0

EXHIBIT I **Boston Widget Co. Inc. Balance Sheet, Year Ended December 31**

Assets	1996	1997	1998
Cash	$15,445	$12,007	$11,717
Receivables	51,793	55,886	88,571
Inventory	56,801	99,087	139,976
Current assets	124,039	166,980	240,264
Fixed assets	44,294	46,340	48,539
Total assets	168,333	213,320	288,803
Liabilities and equity			
Short-term debt	$9,562	$15,300	$54,698
Payables	20,292	31,518	59,995
Accruals	10,328	15,300	21,994
Current maturities	500	500	500
Current liabilities	40,682	62,618	137,187
Long-term debt	27,731	36,491	35,706
Total liabilities	68,413	99,109	172,893
Common stock	69,807	69,807	69,807
Retained earnings	30,113	44,404	46,103
Total liabilities and equity	168,333	213,320	288,803

1998 sales and profits were $586,895 and $5,869 respectively. Applying the modified sales percentage method to Boston Widget's 1998 financial statements, we see that the following accounts have been calculated as a percentage of 1998 sales and will be used as projection assumptions for the company's original five-year strategic plan (Exhibit II). (*Note:* This exhibit should be read along with Exhibit III.

EXHIBIT II   **Boston Widget Co. Inc. Projected Statements, Year Ended December 31**

	1999	2000	2001	2002	2003
Income Statement					
Sales * [Sales 1998(1+.06)]	$622,108.7	$659,435.2	$699,001.3	$740,941.4	$785,397.9
Profits [.01 ($622,108.7)]	6,221.1	6,594.4	6,990.0	7,409.4	7,854.0
Dividends [.25 ($6,221.1)]	1,555.3	1,648.6	1,747.5	1,852.4	1,963.5
Balance Sheet					
Cash [.02 ($622,108.7)]	12,442.2	13,165.2	13,955.1	14,792.4	15,680.0
Receivables [.151 ($622,108.7)]	93,885.3	99,518.4	105,489.5	111,818.8	118,528.0
Inventory [.239 ($622,108.7)]	148,374.6	157,277.0	166,713.7	176,716.5	187,319.5
Current assets	254,702.0	269,960.6	286,158.3	303,327.8	321,527.4
Fixed assets [.083 ($622,108.7)]	51,451.3	54,538.4	57,810.7	61,279.4	64,956.1
Total assets	306,153.3	324,499.1	343,969.0	364,607.1	386,483.6
Liabilities, Financial Needs, and Equity					
Short-term debt [not tied to sales]	54,698.0	54,698.0	54,698.0	54,698.0	54,698.0
Accounts payables [.102 ($622,108.7)]	63,594.7	67,410.4	71,455.0	75,742.3	80,286.8
Accruals [.037 ($622,108.7)]	23,313.6	24,712.5	26,195.2	27,766.9	29,432.9
Current maturity [not tied to sales]	500.0	500.0	500.0	500.0	500.0
Current liabilities	142,106.3	147,320.8	152,848.2	158,707.2	164,917.8
Long-term debt [not tied to sales]	35,206.0	34,706.0	34,206.0	33,706.0	33,206.0
Common stock [not tied to sales]	69,807.0	69,807.0	69,807.0	69,807.0	69,807.0
Ret. earn [1998 R/E + $6221.1 − $1555.3]	50,768.8	55,714.6	60,957.1	66,514.2	72,404.6
Financial needs * [Plug]	8,265.2	16,950.6	26,150.7	35,872.8	46,148.2
Liabilities and equity	306,153.3	324,499.1	343,969.0	364,607.1	386,483.6

* *Note:* Calculation carried out five decimal places to generate this projection.

Two outcomes occur as a result of applying modified percentage of sales: (1) projected liabilities and equity smaller than projected assets will produce financial needs (e.g., amount of additional funding required to obtain predicted sales) and (2) projected liabilities and equity larger than projected assets will produce a cash surplus.

You can see that Boston Widget requires additional debt or equity funding to meet sales targets in each of the four years projected.

Reintroducing the F and E equations, we can draw conclusions that go beyond the yields provided by a simple accounting projection. Let's begin by first examining the F equation:

$$F = A/S\ (\Delta S) + \Delta NFA - LI/S\ (\Delta S) - P(S)(1 - d) + R$$

$$F = .4094\ (35214) + 2912.3 - .1397\ (35214) - .01\ (622109)\ (1-.25) + 500 = 8244$$

The results yield identical financial needs as we see in the projected financial statements (allow for rounding errors).

We see the effect independent (X) variables have on Boston Widget's (Y) (i.e., financial needs after adjustments). The first test involves changes in spontaneous asset levels. Currently, Boston Widget's asset investments are projected at 49.2% of sales. If, for example, spontaneous assets levels decrease, the overall effect on financial needs, or F, will also decrease. Since inventory and accounts receivable usually make up 80% of current assets, it may be in the borrowers interest to hold the line to minimum levels to maintain optimal levels of working capital. When current assets operate at optimal points, the cash cycles becomes smooth and clean.

The second sensitivity variable is spontaneous liabilities. If Boston Widget's spontaneous liabilities increase from its current level of 14%, financial needs decrease. For example, by increasing accruals (a source of cash), financial needs will decrease as the company approaches or surpasses assets levels. What would be the overall effect if sales decreased? It makes sense that reduced sales projections require less financing and result in reduced external support. The same holds true for the dividend rate. By lowering the dividend payout ratio, additional funds will be funneled back into the company (retained earnings). With additional internal funds available to support future needs, cash requirements lower along with unsystematic risk. Stakeholders relax a bit. Now let's look at E:

$$E = .4921 - .1397 - .01\ /.06\ (1 + .06)(1-.25) + .014 = .234$$

Thus, 23.4% of Boston Widget's sales growth will be supported by external financing and 76.6% will be generated by internal cash flow (.234 × 35213 ≈ 8244, resulting in the same answer as calculated earlier). See Exhibit III.

EXHIBIT III   Deriving Financial Needs Using the "F" and "E" Equations Boston Widget Co. Inc.: Base Case Projection

		1999	2000	2001	2002	2003
F1	=	8,244.3	8,707.6	9,200.1	9,722.1	10,275.4
F	=	8,244.3	16,951.9	26,151.9	35,874.0	46,149.4
A/S	=	49.2%	49.2%	49.2%	49.2%	49.2%
T	=	6.0%	6.0%	6.0%	6.0%	6.0%
L1/S	=	14.0%	14.0%	14.0%	14.0%	14.0%
R/ΔS	=	1.4%	1.3%	1.3%	1.2%	1.1%
L	=	153.9%	158.5%	163.0%	167.5%	171.8%

Percentage of sales externally financed

$E = (A/S-L1/S) - (P/G)(1+G)(1-d) + R/\Delta S$ [Program this formula into the HP-19BII]

$E = .492122 - .1397 - .01\ /.06\ (1 + .06)(1-.25) + .014 = .234$

	1999	2000	2001	2002	2003
E =	23.4%	23.3%	23.3%	23.2%	23.1%

23.4% of Boston Widget's sales growth will be financed externally.

Proof	1999	2000	2001	2002	2003
E*ΔS =	8,244.3	8,707.6	9,200.1	9,722.1	10,275.4
Cumulative	8,244.3	16,951.9	26,151.9	35,874.0	46,149.4

Financials (F): (Note: fixed assets are included in A/S.)

$F = A/S(\Delta S) - L1/S(\Delta S) - P(S)(1-d) + R$ [Program this formula into the HP-19BII Business Consultant II]

$F = .4094\ (35214) + 2912.3 - .1397\ (35214) - .01\ (622109)\ (1-.25) + 500 = 8244$

As the formula implies, the E equation determines how much sales growth requires external financing. If E reaches 95% in the projection period, only 5% of sales growth will be internally financed—an immediate storm signal, if base year financial leverage is excessive.

Setting E to zero and solving for the sales growth rate, will give you a fast and efficient reading on the quality and magnitude of cash flows. Say, E is set to zero and the sales growth rate falls somewhere in the first industry quartile. This means sales growth rates are not only strong, but can be financed with internal cash flow. As another example, let's assume that base year leverage is high and you want to reduce leverage by internal financing levels set at 40%. Position the equation at 60% and solve for the capital output ratio (A/S).

The Cash Deficit Identifying the Borrower's Need

The cash deficit is the amount of external cash required from any source, bank or nonbank. The bank reviews the cash deficit to determine its causes. Perhaps the deficit is caused by the growth of core assets and capital expenditures or by nonproductive uses of dividends, treasury stock purchases, or large debt maturities. Most companies will show a combination of these uses. Another question: Can the borrower afford to grow? Are leverage, coverage, and liquidity ratios at reasonable levels, even during periods of financial stress? Coverage ratios may indicate that margins are too slim to support increased volume.

Table 7.4 summarizes the projection methods.

A SIMULATIONS APPROACH TO FINANCIAL FORECASTING

Standard forecasting models rely on single sets of assumptions, which usually lead to two outcomes—base case and worst. But static forecasting, base and worse cases, limit the variability of outcomes. It's difficult to know which of a series of strategic options the borrower will pursue without analyzing differences in both the range and the distribution shape of possible outcomes and the most likely result associated with each option.

TABLE 7.4   Projection Methods Summary

	Method	Advantages	Financial needs: First projection period	Cumulative financial needs
Projected financial statements	Computer	Provides forecasted financial statements	$8,244.3	$46,149.4
F equation	Calculator or computer	Derives financial needs quickly and allows you to perform accurate sensitivity analysis on the spot	$8,244.3	$46,149.4
E equation	Calculator or computer	Used with F formula, the E equation determines if the firm is generating sufficient internally generated fund	$8,244.3	$46,149.4

A simulation is a computer-assisted extension of sensitivity forecasting (as an add-on to Excel). Simulations help answer questions like these: "Will the borrower stay under budget if the bank finances the facility?" "What are the chances the project will finish on time and in the money?" "What are the probabilities that operating cash flow will cover debt service when all is said and done?" "Is multicollinearity a problem with the forecast?"

Introducing the technique known as Monte Carlo simulation, an entire range of results and confidence levels are feasible for any given forecast run. Monte Carlo simulation comprises real-world situations involving elements of uncertainty too complex to be solved with naive methods. The technique requires a random number generator set in the program. Crystal Ball and @Risk are two popular programs that generate random numbers for assumption cells you define. Using these random numbers, simulation programs compute the formulas in the forecast cells. This is a continuous process that recalculates each forecast formula over and over again. The CD includes a tour of Crystal Ball's demos. The demo, CBQD, is located in the subdirectory Models_Demos/Chapter 7.

Without simulation, sales as a value driver will reveal a single outcome, generally the most likely or average scenario (Table 7.5). Spreadsheet risk analysis uses both a spreadsheet model and a simulation to analyze the effect of varying inputs on outputs of the modeled system. As noted earlier, one type of spreadsheet simulation is Monte Carlo simulation, which randomly generates values for uncertain variables over and over to simulate a model (Table 7.6).

Monte Carlo simulation was named for Monte Carlo, Monaco, where the primary attractions are casinos containing games of chance. Games of chance, such

TABLE 7.5   The Piece of Cake Company Simulation Setup (open model on the CD)

Income statement		Percent sales	Formula	Distribution
Sales	1255.0			
Cost of goods sold	(510.2)	40.7%	=-B4*C5	Triangular
Gross profit	744.8			
Selling expenses	(200.8)	16.0%	=-B4*C7	Uniform
Administration expenses	(276.1)	22.0%	=-B4*C8	Normal
Profit before taxes	267.9			
Taxes	(93.8)	35.0%		
Net profit	174.1	Forecast variable		

Running a simulation produces a report which include a simulation summary and statistics shown in Table 7.9.

as roulette wheels, dice, and slot machines, exhibit random behavior. The random behavior in games of chance is similar to how Monte Carlo simulation selects variable values at random to simulate a model. When you roll a die, you know that either a 1, 2, 3, 4, 5, or 6 will come up, but you don't know which number will come up for any particular roll. It's the same with the variables that have a known range of values but an uncertain value for any particular time or event (e.g., interest rates, staffing needs, stock prices, inventory, or phone calls per minute).

SIMULATION CASE STUDY   Felrob Generator Products (FelrobGen[2]) Project Analysis under Uncertainty[3]

FelrobGen is a technology that is being developed to treat chronic Achilles' tendon pain. The device is used for adult patients who have had symptoms for a minimum of six months and have tried other standard methods of treatment. A device enclosed in a dome filled with medically treated water creates vibrating waves. During treatment, the dome is placed closely against the tendon so that the vibrating waves pass through the dome to the tendon. The treatment will involve a electrical current that travels through the surrounding water creating a vibration. Treatment is performed as an outpatient procedure.

During treatment, vibrating waves are focused on the point of maximal tenderness to be bombarded with high-intensity sound waves. Patients will not feel pain because the area is treated with local anesthesia. The theory is that the vibra-

---

[2] The product does not actually exist.
[3] This case was derived using a Crystal Ball example; clear view, on the CBQD demo.

TABLE 7.6   Simulation Summary and Statistics

Summary

Certainty level is 94.30% =94% probability that profits exceed 100; see next line

Certainty range is from 100.0 to +infinity

Display range is from 50.0 to 275.0

Entire range is from 66.6 to 268.3

After 1,000 trials, the std. error of the mean is 1.3

Statistics	Value
Trials	1000
Mean	173.9
Median	179.1
Mode	---
Standard deviation	42.0
Variance	1764.9
Skewness	-0.34
Kurtosis	2.45
Coeff. of variability	0.24
Range minimum	66.6
Range maximum	268.3
Range width	201.7
Mean std. error	1.33

Assumption: Cost of goods sold

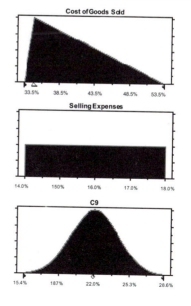

Triangular distribution with parameters:
Minimum	33.5%
Likeliest	35.0%
Maximum	53.5%

Selected range is from 33.5% to 53.5%

Uniform distribution with parameters:
Minimum	14.0%
Maximum	18.0%

Normal distribution with parameters:
Mean	22.0%
Standard Dev.	2.2%

Selected range is from -Infinity to +Infinity

tions will break up inflammation, which allows normal healing tissue to repair injury and alleviate pain.

The Food and Drug Administration (FDA) late last year approved a similar shock wave for adults who had been under treatment for at least six months with conservative methods and no relief. This device is similar to the sound wave treatment that has been used for years to break up kidney stones.

The Felrob Generator Project spreadsheet models a business situation filled with uncertainty. This new medical product could be developed and tested in time for release next year if the FDA approves this product. Although the technology works well for some patients, the overall success rate is marginal, and Felrob Generator Corp. is uncertain whether the FDA will approve the product. The firm has approached its bank requesting a $30 million five-year term loan. The project will raise $25 million in equity.

FelrobGen's banker, VP Anna Zarchen, has asked her lending team to run simulations using a spreadsheet application called Crystal Ball. She wants to determine whether the project is feasible, which will likely mean approval of the credit facility. The question is, should Zarchen approve the request as submitted, offer the client alternatives, or simply reject the project out of hand as too risky?

The bank received departmental estimates along with the project's income statement shown in Exhibit IV. A project estimate is an informed assessment of the likely project cost or duration. Informed means that the firm's department heads have an identified basis for the estimate and can communicate this to management who will take the results to the bank. The bank will consider the inherent uncertainty of project estimates, where every estimate is but one of many possible outcomes. Cost and duration measures are crucial and refer to the two major categories of estimates.

A few questions came up at initial meetings with the firm. Someone on Zarchen's team wanted to know if there were many possible outcomes, and if so, how will he recognize the outcome most likely? The answer is that the lender should not pick just one outcome but instead should identify the full range of possible outcomes. If the problem involves single point estimates and result A and result B are equally likely, there is a far greater chance that result A will be exceeded if the information, say a triangular distribution, is factored in. In addition, single point estimates tend to become self-fulfilling prophecies. Both the FelrobGen project manager and the person responsible for a critical (X) variable need to know its range dimension. For the most part, the distribution configuration isn't nearly as important as recognizing that there is a range of possible results. For example, in Table 7.6 cost of goods sold parameters were spread over a wide range.

Spreadsheet models only approximate a real-world domain. When building the spreadsheet models, the bank should be careful to refine the models until they approximate real-world conditions as closely as possible. To help accomplish this, Zarchen has asked the company to obtain a probability distribution assigned to each uncertain element in the forecast. The distribution describes the possible values variables could conceivably take on and states the probability of each value occurring. Next, the software randomly picks a value for each uncertain variable associated with an assigned probability distribution. The software will generate a set of financials based on the values selected. This creates one trial. Performing the last step many times produces a large number of trials. The output from a simulation is a table, or a graph, summarizing the results of many trials.

The lending group developed the Felrob Generator Project spreadsheet as a base case scenario (Exhibit IV). Zarchen has requested reports from various departments, along with projections and probability distributions. Information was received from the bank in a timely manner and distributed to the lending team. The lending team wanted a probability distribution assigned to each uncertain element in the forecast. The distribution describes the possible values the variable could conceivably take on, and it states the probability of each value occurring.

The various types of probability distributions provided by Crystal Ball include Beta, Binomial, Custom, Exponential, Extreme Value, Gamma, Geometric, Hypergeometric, Logistic, Lognormal, Negative Binomial, Normal, Pareto, Poisson, Triangular, Uniform, and Weibull. For now we'll review the lognormal distribution as an example of analytics required of the bankers (Figure 7.6). The lognormal distribution is widely used in situations where values are positively skewed (where most of the values occur near the minimum value) like in

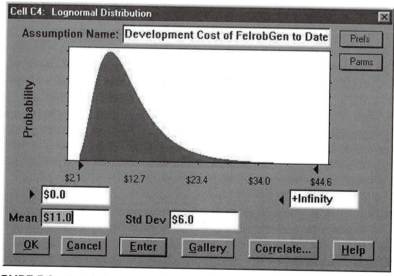

FIGURE 7.6 Cost: An Example of a Lognormal Distribution Development

financial analysis for security valuation or in real estate for property valuation. It is a continuous probability distribution. For example, financial analysts have observed that the stock prices are usually positively skewed, rather than normal (symmetrically) distributed. Stock prices exhibit this trend because the stock price cannot fall below the lower limit of zero but may increase to any price without limit. Similarly, real estate prices illustrate positive skewed since property values cannot become negative.

The parameters for the lognormal distribution are mean and standard deviation. The three conditions underlying a lognormal distribution are (1) the unknown variable can increase without bound, but is confounded to a finite value at the lower limit; (2) the unknown variable exhibits a positively skewed distribution; and (3) the natural logarithm of the unknown variable will yield a normal curve. From all the distribution choices available, the lending group settled on the following assumption cell definitions.

1. *Defining testing costs.* For this variable, testing costs, project designers felt any value between $6.6MM and $5.4MM has an equal chance of being the actual cost of testing. The budget will not allow costs over $4.4MM. Based on this information, management selected the uniform distribution to describe testing costs. The uniform distribution describes a situation where all values between the minimum and maximum values are equally likely to occur, so this distribution best describes the cost of testing the Felrob Generator.

2. *Defining marketing costs: The triangular distribution.* Management informed its bankers that the firm plans to spend a sizable amount marketing the Felrob Generator if the FDA approves it. Management expects to hire a large sales force and kick off an extensive advertising campaign to educate the public about this exciting new product. Including sales commissions and advertising costs, Felrob Generator Products expects to spend between $17.2MM and $19.8MM, most likely $18.0MM. Felrob Generator chooses the triangular distribution to describe marketing costs. The triangular distribution describes a situation where you can estimate the minimum, maximum, and most likely values to occur.

3. *Defining patients cured: The binomial distribution.* Before the FDA will approve the product, Felrob Generator Products must conduct a controlled test on a sample of 100 patients for one year. The FDA has stipulated it will approve the Felrob Generator if it completely corrects the problems of 20 or more of these patients without any significant side effects. In other words, 20% or more of the patients tested must show improvement after taking FelrobAGen for one year. Management is very encouraged by preliminary testing, which shows a success rate of around 20%.

For this variable, patients cured, management only knows that its preliminary testing shows a cure rate of 50%. Will the Felrob Generator meet FDA standards? Zarachen's staff picked the binomial distribution to describe the uncertainties, because the binomial distribution describes success number (20) in a fixed number of trials (100).

4. *Defining market penetration: The normal distribution.* The marketing department estimates that the corporation's eventual share of the total market for the product will be normally distributed around a mean value of 12% with a standard deviation of 1.20%. "Normally distributed" means that analysts expect to see the familiar bell-shaped curve with about 68% of all possible values for market penetration falling between one standard deviation below the mean value and one standard deviation above the mean value, or between 10.8% and 13.2%.

The low mean value of 12% is a conservative estimate that takes into account the side effects of the technology that were noted during preliminary testing. In addition, the marketing department estimates a minimum market share of 5%, given the interest shown in the product during preliminary testing.

Zarchen wants to know the certainty of achieving a profit. The final result is that FelrobGen can be 91% certain of achieving a profit (see the summary in Figure 7.7). The bank is encouraged by the forecast results. Forecast results are shown in Figures 7.7, 7.8, and 7.9.

EXHIBIT IV FelrobGen Income Statement Submitted to Bank Felrob Generator Products (FelrobGen) Project Analysis under Uncertainty

Costs (in millions)		Suggested distributions
Development cost of FelrobGen to date	$11.0	Lognormal
Testing costs	$6.0	Uniform
Marketing costs	$18.3	Triangular
Total costs	$35.3	
Drug test (sample of 100 patients)		
Improved by drug	20	Binomial
FDA approved if 20% or more patients helped	True	
Market study (in millions)		
Persons with chronic Achilles' tendon injuries	40.0	
Growth rate of injury	2.00%	Custom
Persons with disease after one year	40.8	
Gross profit on dosages sold		
Market penetration	12.00%	Normal
Profit per customer in dollars	$10.00	
Gross profit if approved (in millions)	$49.0	Forecast cell
Net profit (in millions)	$13.6	Forecast cell

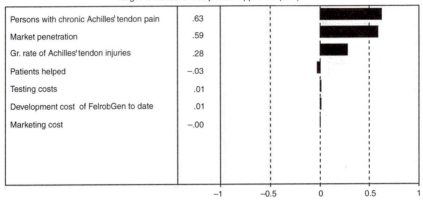

FIGURE 7.7   Sensitivity Chart

Summary

Certainty level is 9.10% that profits will be lower than zero
Certainty range is from infinity to $0.0 million
Display range is from ($15.0) to $40.0 million
Entire range is from ($35.3) to $37.9 million
After 1,000 trials, the standard error of the mean is $0.3

Statistics	*Value*
Trials	1,000
Mean	$12.4
Median	$12.6
Mode	—
Standard deviation	$9.1
Variance	$83.7
Skewness	-0.32
Kurtosis	3.71
Coeff. of variability	0.74
Range minimum	$(35.3)
Range maximum	$37.9
Range width	$73.1
Mean standard error	$0.29

The Sensitivity Chart

The Sensitivity Chart for FelrobGen (Figure 7.7) allows the bankers to judge the impact each assumption cell has on a particular forecast cell, in this case profit. During a simulation, Crystal Ball ranks the assumptions according to their importance to each forecast cell. The sensitivity chart displays these rankings as a bar chart, indicating which assumptions are the most important or least important ones in the model.

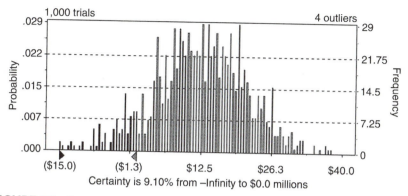

FIGURE 7.8   Forecast: Net Profit (MM)

Assumption: Testing Costs

Uniform distribution with parameters:
Minimum	$5.4
Maximum	$6.6

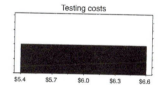

Assumption: Marketing Costs

Triangular distribution with parameters:
Minimum	$17.2
Likeliest	$18.0
Maximum	$19.8

Selected range is from $17.2 to $19.8

Assumption: Patients Cured

Binomial distribution with parameters:
Probability	0.4
Trials	100

Selected range is from 0 to +Infinity

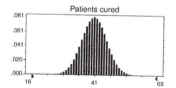

FIGURE 7.9   Distribution

A window opens displaying the sensitivity rankings of the assumptions in the simulation. The assumptions (and possibly other forecasts) are listed on the left side, starting with the assumption with the highest sensitivity. The middle column is a listing of either the rank correlations or contributions to variance of the respective assumption. The third section is a bar chart with assumptions appearing as

Assumption: Gr. Rate of Musculoskeletal Injuries

Custom distribution with parameters: <u>Relative Prob.</u>
Continuous range   -15.00% to -5.00%   0.250000
Continuous range   0.00% to   5.00%   0.750000
Total Relative Probability   1.000000

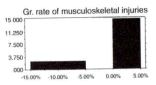

Gr. rate of musculoskeletal injuries

Assumption: Market Penetration

Normal distribution with parameters:
Mean   12.00%
Standard Dev.   1.20%

Selected range is from -Infinity to +Infinity

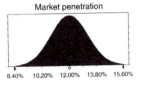

Market penetration

Assumption: Development Cost of Digoxin Drug to Date

Lognormal distribution with parameters:
Mean $11.0
Standard Dev. $6.0

Selected range is from $0.0 to +Infinity

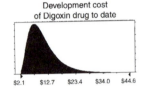

Development cost
of Digoxin drug to date

Assumption: Persons with Chronic Musculoskeletal Inj

Normal distribution with parameters:
Mean   40.0
Standard Dev.   4.0

Selected range is from -Infinity to +Infinity

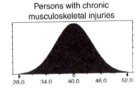

Persons with chronic
musculoskeletal injuries

green bars. The assumptions with the highest sensitivity ranking can be considered the most important one in the model. In this analysis, persons with chronic Achilles' tendon and market penetration are the two key variables in the forecast. The bankers will want to investigate this assumption further in the hopes of reducing its uncertainty, and therefore its effect on the target forecast. The assumption with the lowest sensitivity ranking is the least important one in the model.

The frequency counts appear in the frequency chart as shown in Figure 7.8 includes the start point and end point for each frequency range plus the number of trials that fell in that range and the probability of falling in that range. The assumptions output included in the Crystal Ball report includes the name, cell, and other types of information (Figure 7.9)

STOCHASTIC OPTIMIZATION

Optimization procedures are used to identify optimal maximum or minimum values subject to constraints. Today's optimization models are robust, solving problems with thousands and even millions of variables without disproportionately tying up the bank's computers. Any problem that has decision variables and an objective function to be maximized or minimized can be considered an optimization problem. If the problem is bounded by constraints, it is called constrained *optimization*; otherwise, the term used is *unconstrained optimization*. A factory may be limited in size, or able to produce only so much of a given product per day. Raw material may be in short supply, working capital sources limited, or work in process bottlenecked because of labor problems. Capital costs might be constrained by systematic and unsystematic risk factors. The question is, of course, how do you combine these thousands of constrained variables in a way that produces maximum value within these set boundaries?

Stochastic models can handle nonlinear relationships that are specifiable by the kinds of equations and formulas that are used in mathematical programming formulations. Conversely, deterministic optimization models like Excel's Solver do not apply to nonlinear problems other than those that can be expressed in "classical" mathematical programming form. One of the most important issues deals with the ability of stochastic models like OptQuest to solve a problem whose objective and constraining relationships can only be captured by means of a simulation, which, by definition, is beyond the capacity of any deterministic model to deal with. In addition, financial optimization in today's age of risk analysis should incorporate a combination of metaheuristic procedures from methods like tabu search, neural networks, and scatter search. Only the best stochastic model is vigorous enough to blend these technologies.

Stochastically driven optimization models allow you as the lender to more realistically represent the flow of random variables. Consider a credit problem whereby you try to maximize an objective function over a feasible region. Suppose the problem is very large, containing tens of thousands of variables, so it is unrealistic for you to run sensitivities. Obtaining these optimal values generally requires that you search in an iterative or ad hoc fashion. This entails running a simulation for an initial set of values, analyzing the results, changing more values, rerunning the simulation, and repeating this process until you find a satisfactory solution.

This process can be very tedious and time consuming even for small models, and it's not clear how to adjust the variables from one simulation run to the next, and so on. For example, a simulation run may contain only two decision variables. If each variable has 15 possible outcomes, trying each combination requires 225 simulation runs (15^2 alternatives). If each simulation takes only 1.7 seconds, then the entire process is completed using only two minutes of computer time. However, if instead of two decision variables, suppose you are running a problem containing five decision variables. Trying all combinations requires 769,000 simulations (15^5 alternatives), or five days of computer time. It is clearly possible that enumeration might take weeks, months, or even years to complete. This will not happen with well-designed stochastic models (e.g., Decisioneering's OptQuest). OptQuest employs combinations of metaheuristic procedures derived from systems like Tabu search, neural networks, and scatter search. Decisioneering has provided readers with a tour illustrating how bankers and their clients can make the best decisions through risk analysis with stocklastic optimization. The demo can be opened by double clicking on InsurQD located in the models_Demo/chapter 7 subdirectory on the CD. The Exacta Actuarial Consulting example has been designed to demonstrate optimization subject to uncertainty.

USE OF FORWARD-LOOKING TOOLS
IN THE APPROVAL PROCESS

Formal presentation of financial projections or other forms of forward-looking analysis used by the borrower are important for making explicit the conditions required for a loan to perform and for communicating the vulnerabilities of the transaction to those responsible for approving loans.[4] Technology-driven projections, rather than only describing single sets of "most likely" scenarios, characterize the kind of real-world events that might impair the loan. Confidence levels set around (1) probabilities that operating cash flows fail to cover debt service and (2) probabilities that a borrower's capital structure will fail to represent two major determinants of loan performance. Rigorous forecasting tools are central to initial approvals and for determining the adequacy of provisions and reserves.

Although it may be tempting to avoid running up simulations and optimizations for smaller borrowers, such as middle-market firms, these customers may collectively represent a significant portion of the institution's loan portfolio. Applying formal forward-looking analysis even on a basic level will help the institution identify and manage overall portfolio risk and pass the scrutiny of regulators.

Regulators stress that banks understand their customer's financial condition, ensure that credits are in compliance with existing covenants, corroborate that projected cash flows on major credits meet debt servicing requirements, affirm that the collateral in secured deals provides adequate coverage, and ensure that problem loans are classified on a timely basis. A common problem among troubled banks was their failure to monitor borrowers by neglecting to obtain periodic financial information and not stress-testing data sufficiently enough with modern tools. These banks failed to recognize early signs that loan quality was deteriorating and missed the opportunities to work with borrowers to stem their financial deterioration. As a result, poor and often naive loan monitoring led to a costly process by bank management to determine the dimension and severity of problem loans, resulting in large write-offs.

---

[4] FRB, Division of Banking Supervision and Regulation, SR 00-7 (Sup.), May 2, 2000. Subject: Lending standards for commercial loans.

REVIEW QUESTIONS

1. What advantages does a simple linear regression have over the percentage-of-sales method in financial forecasting?
2. What are the differences between casual and time series forecasting models and between two widely used time-series methods: simple moving averages and exponential smoothing? Under what condition might a lender choose any one of these forecasting methods?
3. Describe both the exponential and logarithmic curve fit. How do these curves help bankers determine whether a borrower's financial structure can support sales growth?
4. What is the rationale behind the modified percentage of sales forecast method? Describe essential elements behind this technique.
5. Evaluate the following statement: "Setting the percentage of sales growth that will require external financing (E) to zero, and solving for the borrower's projected sales growth rate (G), provides lenders with a quick but effective way to determine the magnitude of projected cash flows."
6. What are the major advantages of simulations over sensitivity forecasting methods.
7. Describe the differences among triangular, normal, and uniform distributions. Cite three examples of how each distribution might be used to describe the assumption variables of an income statement.

SELECTED REFERENCES AND READINGS

Books

Aiken, L. S., S. G. West, *et al.* (1991). *Multiple regression: Testing and interpreting interactions.* Newbury Park, CA: Sage.

Berry, W. D., and S. Feldman. (1985). *Multiple regression in practice.* Beverly Hills, CA: Sage.

Boyce, D. E., A. Farhi, *et al.* (1974). *Optimal subset selection: Multiple regression, interdependence, and optimal network algorithms.* Berlin; New York: Springer-Verlag.

Grimm, L. G., and P. R. Yarnold. (1995). *Reading and understanding multivariate statistics.* Washington, DC: American Psychological Association.

Härdle, W., T. M. Stoker, *et al.* (1988). *Investigating smooth multiple regression by the method of average derivatives.* Cambridge, MA: Sloan School of Management, Massachusetts Institute of Technology.

Heward, J. H., and P. M. Steele. (1973). *Business control through multiple regression analysis; A technique for the numerate manager.* New York: Wiley.

Launer, R. L., A. F. Siegel, *et al.* (1982). *Modern data analysis.* New York: Academic Press.

Rothman, P. (1999). *Nonlinear time series analysis of economic and financial data.* Boston: Kluwer Academic Publishers.

Shorter, J. (1982). *Correlation analysis of organic reactivity, with particular reference to multiple regression.* Chichester; New York: Research Studies Press.

Thomas, J. J. (1964). *Notes on the theory of multiple regression analysis.* Athens.

Wesolowsky, G. O. (1976). *Multiple regression and analysis of variance: An introduction for computer users in management and economics.* New York: Wiley.

Other Newspapers and Periodicals

Financial Forecasting at Atlantic Richfield Company. Baker, Al. (1992). *The Journal of Business Forecasting Methods & Systems* **11**(3), 9.

Financial forecasting at Rockwell International's Defense Electronics. Balmat, Robert E., III. (1992). *The Journal of Business Forecasting Methods & Systems* **11**(2), 3.

On the implications of specification uncertainty in forecasting. Benson, P. George and Christopher B. Barry. (1982). *Decision Sciences* **13**(1), 176.

Spreadsheet errors: Risks and techniques. Berglas, Anthony. (1999). *Management Accounting* **77**(7), 46 (London).

Group processes for forecasting. Brockhoff, Klaus. (1983). *European Journal of Operational Research* **13**(2), 115 (Amsterdam).

Improving financial forecasting: Combining data with intuition. Chopra, Vijay, and Kumar. (1996, Spring). *Journal of Portfolio Management* **22**(3) 97.

Networking capital forecasting at Dupont. D'Attilio, David F. (1992). *The Journal of Business Forecasting Methods & Systems* **11**(1), 11.

Faster financial forecasting. (1998, April). *Credit Management* 18, (Stamford).

Financial forecasting and the CPA. Fisher, Steven A. (1991). *The Journal of Business Forecasting Methods & Systems* **10**(1), 7.

Financial forecasting software. Fulford, James. (1996). *Accountancy Ireland* **28**(6), 30 (Dublin).

Using qualitative historical observations in predicting the future. Funkhouser, G. Ray. (1984). *Futures* **16**(2), 173 (Kidlington).

Financial forecasting for the rest of us. Hogan, Mike. (1995). *PC/Computing* **8**(1), 108.

Information technology. (1997). *Chartered Accountants Journal of New Zealand* **76**(3) 75, (Wellington).

Modeling financial decisions in construction firms. Lam, Ka Chi. (1999). *Construction Management and Economics,* **17**(5), 589 (London).

Financial forecasting at Teleport Communications Group. Martino, James P. (1993). *The Journal of Business Forecasting Methods & Systems* **12**(1), 7.

Model behavior. (1992). *Financial World* **161**(11), 74.

Financial modeling. Murray, Peter. (1992). *Australian Accountant* **62**(2), 51, (Melbourne).

Financial forecasting at Martin Marietta Energy Systems, Inc. Myhre, T. C. (1992). *The Journal of Business Forecasting Methods & Systems* (11) 1, 28.

New software speeds up financial forecasting. (1998). *Accountancy Ireland* **30**(2), 28 (Dublin).

Polishing the controller's crystal ball: Financial forecasting tips. Singhvi, Suren S. (1991).*Corporate Controller* **3**(6), 31.

Current approaches to time series forecasting. Snyder, Donald. (1982). *Business Forum* **7**(2), 24.

Financial forecasting for business and economics. Speight, Alan E. H. (1997). *International Journal of Forecasting* **13**(2), 293 (Amsterdam).

Pro-Forma Plus: The Financial Forecasting Model. Walkin, Lawrence. (1991).*CMA Hamilton* **65**(7), 28.

Financial forecasting for business and economics. Wells, Martin T. (1997). *Journal of the American Statistical Association* **92**(439), 1227.

SELECT INTERNET LIBRARY AND CD

CD Includes

CD includes the following links:
(1)Decisioneering's site *http://www.decisioneering.com*
(2)CB Predictor Model *http://www.decisioneering.com/cbpredictor/index.html*

(3) CD Models
Decisioneering's Crystal Ball Demo Tutorials in the 2000 Professional Edition.

Select Internet Library

Statistical Software for Forecasting

Provides 20 statistical programs for those who are interested in using the computer to make more profitable forecasting business decisions. It includes such programs as multiple correlation and regression, time-series analysis and decomposition, trend projections, and exponential smoothing for forecasting. A computer-assisted investment handbook, which also functions as the manual, lists and explains all the programs in detail. *http://business.software-directory.com/cdprod1/swhrec/017/214.shtml*

Forecasting Links

By Brian C. Monsell

Last update: October 23, 1999; business forecasting

Links to sites of interest to forecasters, including news, the international institute of forecasters, conferences, journals, and books for forecasters, FAQs, and other forecasting sites. Maintained by Fred Collopy. *http://www.cpcug.org/user/bmonsell/forecast.html*

Statistical Software on the Web

http://www.udel.edu/ASA/stats_software.html

Forecasting Bibliography and Links; Links to WWW sites on forecasting

International Association of Business Forecasters (IABF)

International Institute of Forecasters (IIF)

Forecasting E-Mail Discussion Groups

Institute of Business Forecasting (IBF)

http://www.autobox.com/links.html

California State University at Los Angeles has an extensive collection of links to other sites on the World Wide Web related to the statistical packages used most often at the university. *http://artemis.calstatela.edu/stats/statlinks.htm*

GLOSSARY OF
FORECASTING TERMS

- **Box and Jenkins** To create forecasts, you need to find a relationship between the variable being predicted, such as equity returns, and lagged values of predictive variables, such as dividend yield or earnings momentum. This ensures that forecasts are based solely on data available at the time the forecast is made, thereby avoiding the "look-ahead" bias. The autoregressive and moving average (ARMA) model, proposed by Box and Jenkins, predicts future values of a variable solely on the basis of its own past history. One of its sortcomings is that it ignores the role of other factors. ARMA models are often good at providing short-term forecasts, but they typically produce poor long-term forecasts.
- **Chi-Square Test** Nonparametric test for comparing the goodness of fit of a single sample distribution to a theoretical distribution or between any number of sample distributions. It is applicable only to nominal data in the form of frequencies in mutually exclusive categories and not to percentage data. There should also not be many categories with

- **Double exponential smoothing** Applies single exponential (SES) twice, once to the original data and then to the resulting SES data. CB Predictor uses Holt's method for double exponential smoothing, which can use a different parameter for the second application of the SES equation. CB Predictor can automatically calculate the optimal smoothing constants, or you can manually define the smoothing constants.
- **Double moving average** Applies the moving average technique twice, once to the last several periods of the original data and then to the resulting single moving average data. This method then uses both sets of smoothed data to project forward.
- **Exponential smoothing methods** Developed in the early 1950s. Since then they have become a particularly popular method of forecasting among businesspeople because they are easy to use, require little computer time, and need only a few data points to produce future predictions. These smoothing methods are well suited for short or immediate term predictions of a large number of items. They are suitable for stationary data or when there is a slow growth or decline over time. The method of exponential smoothing is based on averaging (smoothing) past values of a time series in a decreasing (exponential) manner. In Excel, for example, exponential smoothing averages the smoothed value for the previous period with the actual data for the previous data point. This feature automatically includes all previous periods in the average. You can specify how much to weight the current period.
- **F statistic** Tests the significance of the regression equation as measured by R^2. If this value is significant, it means that the regression equation does account for some of the variability of the dependent variable. The F test is similar to the t-test except that it tests the simultaneous significance of the variables in the regression equation. It is a statistical means of checking the hypothesis that the overall relationship between the dependent variable and all the independent ones is statistically significant. As a general rule, if $F > 5$ it means that there is a statistically significant relationship. The F test is the first statistic to examine in regression analysis. If it is greater than 5, then one can continue with the other tests. If it is less than 5, one must examine alternative models. If the F test is significant, one can examine each of the t tests and the R^2. If the F test is > 5, and each of the t tests > 2, then one can decide whether or not the R^2 is satisfactory. If it is, the remaining task is to check the regression assumptions. If R^2 is not satisfactory, it implies that there are other important factors that influence the dependent variable and that have not been included in the regression equation. It may be possible to identify these factors and increase the value of R^2 to some acceptable level.

- **Mean and variants of each variable** This information can be useful in understanding the sampling distribution of the mean of each variable and can be used in constructing confidence intervals. The mean (average) is a measure of central tendency in a frequency distribution, usually calculated as the arithmetic mean. The arithmetic mean is equal to the sum of observations divided by the number of observations. The geometric mean represents the nth root of the product of a set of n numbers, will always be less than the arithmetic mean unless all numbers are equal, and is usually used for averaging rates of change. The mode is a measure of central tendency equal to the most commonly occurring value in a distribution. It is generally only applicable to discrete data (e.g., integer values) because with continuous data (e.g., real numbers) it is highly unlikely that duplicate observations will occur. The median represents a measure of central tendency in a frequency distribution, very resistant and often used in exploratory data analysis (EDA), equal to the value in the distribution that divides the distribution into two halves of equal numbers of observations (50th percentile). If there is an even number of observations in the distribution, then the median is equal to the mean of the two adjacent values.

- **Moving averages** Eliminate randomness and smooth out a time series. This objective is achieved by averaging several data points together in such a way that positive and negative errors eventually cancel themselves out. The term "moving average" is used because, as each new observation in the series becomes available, the oldest observation is dropped and a new average is computed. The result of calculating the moving average over a set of data points is a new series of numbers with little or no randomness. The ability of moving averages to eliminate randomness can be used in time series analysis for two main purposes: (1) to eliminate trend and (2) to eliminate seasonality.

- **Percentage variation explained** Indicates what percentage of the overall variation in the dependent variable each one of the independent variables explains. The higher the percentage, the more influential is that variable. The sum of all percentage variations explained is $R2$.

- **Rsquared (R^2)** A measure of the adequacy of the fit. It indicates the percentage of the total variations of the dependent variable explained by variations in the independent variables. R^2 varies from zero to one. If it is zero, it means that the regression equation does not explain the variations in the dependent variable. If it is one, it means that the regression fit is perfect and that any changes in the dependent variable are accounted for by changes in the independent variables. Such a relationship is deterministic and forecasting will be perfect. Between these two extremes of zero and one, R^2 can serve as one indicator of

very low frequencies, and none with zero frequency, and if there are only two categories, both frequencies must be at least 5.

- **Coefficient of determination.** Indicates the percentage of the variability of the dependent variable that the regression equation explains. For example, an R^2 of 0.36 indicates that the regression equation accounts for 36% of the variability of the dependent variable and corrects R^2 to account for the degrees of freedom in the data. In other words, the more data points you have, the more universal the regression equation is. However, if you only have the same number of data points as variables, the R^2 might appear deceivingly high. This statistic corrects for that. For example, the R^2 for one equation might be very high, indicating that the equation accounted for almost all the error in the data. However, this value might be inflated if the number of data points was insufficient to calculate a universal regression.

- **Correlation coefficients** The correlation coefficients (or, alternatively, the simple correlation matrix, which is the aggregation of all correlation coefficients) show how all of the independent variables are correlated between themselves and the dependent variable. As a general rule, one does not want to include in a regression equation two or more independent variables that are highly correlated between themselves (i.e., more than .7), nor does one wish to include independent variables with low (i.e., less than .OS) correlation with the dependent variable.

The first case introduces multicollinearity, which is a computational problem causing the results to become unreliable. (It is like trying to divide 1 by .00000000001—the computer may not have enough significant digits to handle the division.) If there are two independent variables with a high correlation between them, no information is lost by removing one of them. Low correlations imply that there is no relationship between the dependent and the corresponding independent variables. Thus, if such an independent variable is included, it generally will add little in explaining variations in the dependent variable.

Looking at the correlation matrix of all variables, one can immediately exclude those independent variables having a low correlation with the dependent variable and then add independent variables that do not have a high intercorrelation between them. This can be achieved by starting with the independent variable with the highest correlation with the dependent variable, and then adding the independent variable with the next highest correlation with the dependent variable but with a low correlation with the previously included independent variable(s). (This information can be found by examining the correlation coefficients.) The correlation matrix allows one to exclude many variables (either high or low correlated), which makes the job of deciding on a final equation much easier.

how "good" the regression equation is. (However, an R^2 value of close to 1.0 does not necessarily indicate a good forecasting equation.)

* **Significance test** In hypothesis testing, a test that provides a criterion (probability associated with a particular sample or observation) for determining whether a difference between that observation and an expected value can be attributed to chance. The null hypothesis is either accepted or rejected by comparing the calculated probability with a critical value (such as 0.05).

* **Single exponential smoothing (SES)** Weights all of the past data with exponentially decreasing weights going into the past. In other words, usually the more recent data have greater weight. This largely overcomes the limitations of moving averages or percentage change models. Crystal Ball's CB Predictor can automatically calculate the optimal smoothing constant, or you can manually define the smoothing constant.

* **Standard deviation of each variable** A measure of dispersion of a frequency distribution standardized to sample size.

* **Standard error**: The term "standard error" is applied to various statistical measures (such as the mean) and gives the distribution within which that measure will fall when samples are drawn from any population or distribution. The standard error is dependent on the dispersion in the population and the size of the sample. The standard error for the arithmetic means is calculated as Standard error = SD of population/SR of number of units in the sample.

* **Sum of square deviations** The least squares technique for estimating regression coefficients minimizes this statistic, which measures the error not eliminated by the regression line. For any line drawn through a scatter plot of data, there are a number of different ways to determine which line fits the data best. One method for comparing the fit of lines is to calculate the sum of the squared errors (SSE) for each line. The lower the SSE, the better the fit of the line to the data.

* **t Statistic** A very important test, the statistic tests the significance of the relationship between the coefficients of the dependent variable and the individual independent variable in the presence of the other independent variables. If this value is significant, it means that the independent variable does contribute to the dependent variable.

* **The Durbin Watson test and homoscedasacity** Four assumptions are made in any application of regression: linearity, normality, independence of residuals, and constant variance. The first two are of little concern because they are almost always satisfied. For the last two, however, one must check to be sure they are not violated.

DISTRIBUTION TERMS AND GLOSSARY

TRIANGULAR DISTRIBUTION

Triangular distribution describes a situation where you know the minimum, maximum, and most likely values to occur. For example, we could describe the vacancy rate associated with the minimum, maximum, and most likely vacancy rate. Three conditions are required:

- The minimum number of items is fixed.
- The maximum number of items is fixed
- The most likely number of items falls between the minimum and maximum values, forming a triangular-shaped distribution, which shows that values near the minimum and maximum are less likely to occur than those near the most likely value.

Unlike the *uniform distribution* in which all values between the limits are equally likely, the triangular distribution peaks at a central value.

Example

Analysis of company X's property shows that the vacancy rate will not fall below 13% nor increase beyond 25%, with 15.4% the most likely rate.

The first step in selecting a probability distribution is to match your data with a distribution's conditions. Figure 7A.1 checks the triangular distribution:

- Minimum vacancy rate is 13.0%
- Maximum vacancy rate is 25.0%
- The most likely vacancy rate is 15.4%, forming a triangle.

Parameters: lower limit a, central value c>a, upper limit b>c
Domain: $a < = X < = b$
Mean: $(a + b + c)/3$
Variance: $[a^2 + b^2 + c^2 - ab - ac - bc]/18$

TRIANGULAR DISTRIBUTION FOR TYPE B UNCERTAINTY

Often all that is known about a process that contributes type B uncertainty is the maximum and minimum potential values and that central values are more likely to occur than extreme values. The uncertainty contribution from this process can be calculated from a triangular distribution.

NORMAL DISTRIBUTION

This is a continuous probability distribution that is used to characterize a wide variety of data types. It is a *symmetric distribution*, shaped like a bell, and is completely determined by its mean and standard deviation. The normal distribution is particularly important in statistics because of the tendency for sample means to follow the normal distribution (this is a result of the *central limit theorem*).

Most classical statistics procedures such as *confidence intervals* rely on results from the normal distribution. The normal is also known as the Gaussian distribution after its originator, Frederich Gauss. The normal distribution is the most important distribution in probability theory because it describes many natural phenomena, such as people's IQs or heights. Decision makers can use the

Assumption: Vacancy/Collections

Cell: B56

Triangular distribution with parameters:

Minimum	13.0%
Likeliest	15.4%
Maximum	25.0%

Selected range is from 13.0% to 25.0%

Vacancy Collections

13.0% 16.0% 19.0% 22.0% 25.0%

FIGURE 7A.1   Checks

normal distribution to describe uncertain variables, such as the inflation rate or the future price of gasoline. The three conditions underlying the normal distribution are as follows:

- Some value of the uncertain variable is the most likely (the mean of the distribution).
- The uncertain variable could as likely be above the mean as it could be below the mean (symmetrical about the mean).
- The uncertain variable is more likely to be in the vicinity of the mean than far away. Approximately 68% are within 1 standard deviation on either side of the mean. The standard deviation is the average distance of a set of values from their mean.

Example

You feel that the mean vacancy rate on the projected proposed by company X will be 15.4% with a standard deviation of 1.5%. This means that there is approximately a two-thirds probability that the vacancy rate will fall between 15.4% minus 1.5% and 15.4% plus 1.5%, or between 13.9% and 16.9%.

The first step in selecting a probability distribution is to match your data with a distribution's conditions. Figure 7A.2 the normal distribution.

Parameters: mean mu, standard deviation sigma>0
Domain: all real X
Mean: mu
Variance: sigma^2

LOGNORMAL DISTRIBUTION

The lognormal distribution is widely used in situations where values are positively skewed (most of the values occur near the minimum value)—for example, in financial analysis for security valuation or in real estate for property valuation. Stock prices are usually positively skewed, rather than normally (symmetrically) distributed. Stock prices exhibit this trend because they cannot fall below the lower limit of zero but may increase to any price without limit.

Assumption: Vacancy/Collections   Cell: B56

Normal distribution with parameters: Vacancy Collections
     Mean   15.4%
     Standard Dev.   1.5%

Selected range is from -Infinity to +Infinity

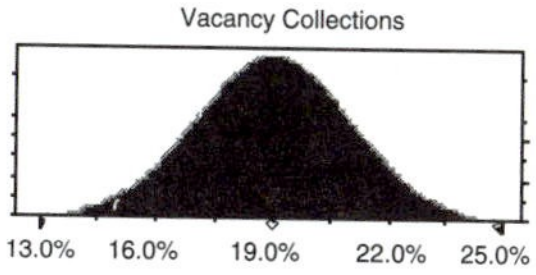

13.0%   16.0%   19.0%   22.0%   25.0%

End of Assumptions

FIGURE 7A.2   Assumptions Vacancy/Collections

Conditions

Real estate prices illustrate positive skewness, since property values cannot become negative unless it poses an environmental hazard.

The following three conditions underly the lognormal distribution:

- The uncertain variable can increase without limits but cannot fall below zero.
- The uncertain variable is positively skewed with most of the values near the lower limit.
- The natural logarithm of the uncertain variable yields a normal distribution.

Example

You assume that the lowest value vacancy rate can drop to zero. On the other hand, the project could end up with a vacancy of 100%. (Figure 7A.3).

UNIFORM DISTRIBUTION

This continuous probability distribution is useful for characterizing data that ranges over an interval of values, each of which is equally likely. It is sometimes called the rectangular distribution because of its shape when plotted. The distribution is completely determined by the smallest possible value, a, and the largest possible value, b. For discrete data, there is a related *discrete uniform distribution*.

The three conditions underlying uniform distribution are as follows:

- The minimum value is fixed.
- The maximum value is fixed.
- All values between the minimum and maximum are equally likely to occur.

Examples

The vacancy rate of at least 13% is expected, but not more than 25%. All values between 13% and 25% are equally likely to occur.

The first step in selecting a probability distribution is to match your data with a distribution's conditions. Figure 7A.4 checks the uniform distribution:

The minimum value is 13%, the value is 25%, and all values in between are equally possible. The conditions in this example match those of the uniform distribution.

Parameters: lower limit a,
upper limit b>a
Domain: a<=X<=b
Mean: (a+b)/a
Variance: (b-a) ^2/12

Assumption: **Vacancy/Collections**

Cell: **B56**

Lognormal distribution with parameters:
Mean 15.4%
Standard Dev. 1.5%

Selected range is from 0.0% to +Infinity

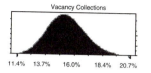

Vacancy Collections

11.4%   13.7%   16.0%   18.4%   20.7%

FIGURE 7A.3   Assumptions Vacancy/Collections

EXTREME VALUE DISTRIBUTION

A distribution used for random variables that are constrained to be greater or equal to 0. It is characterized by two parameters: mode and scale (Figure 7A.5).

Parameters: mode a>0, scale b>0
Domain: all real X
Mean: a-0.57721b
Variance: (3.14159265b)^2 /6

A COMPARISON OF DIFFERENT DISTRIBUTIONS APPLIED TO VACANCY RATE, SENSITIVITY, AND THE EFFECT ON THE COMPANY X PROJECT'S CASH FLOW COVERAGE

The income statement was left unchanged from the original (shown earlier). The only changes made were the shape of the distribution. Table 7A.1 has been set up to compare (1) certainty level (the probability that operating cash flow falls below debt service), (2) sensitivity by rank correlation, and (3) the run's statistics. The important message here is that the distribution selection you arrive at is as important as the underlying assumptions that form the variable itself.

Gamma Distribution

This distribution is used for continuous random variables that are constrained to be greater or equal to 0. It is characterized by two parameters: shape and scale. The gamma distribution is often used to model data which is positively *skewed*.

Assumption: Vacancy/Collections

Cell: B56

Uniform distribution with parameters:
Minimum 13.0%
Maximum 25.0%

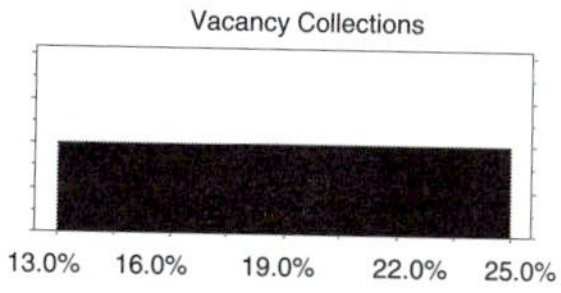

Vacancy Collections

13.0%   16.0%   19.0%   22.0%   25.0%

FIGURE 7A.4   Assumptions Vacancy/Collections

Cell: B56

Assumption: Vacancy/Collections

Extreme Value distribution with parameters:
Mode   15.4%
Scale   1.0%

Selected range is from -Infinity to +Infinity

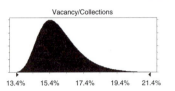

Vacancy/Collections

13.4%   15.4%   17.4%   19.4%   21.4%

FIGURE 7A.5   Assumptions Vacancy/Collections

The gamma distribution applies to a wide range of physical quantities and is similar to a host of other distributions: lognormal, exponential, pascal, geometric, erlang, poisson, and chi-square. The gamma distribution can be thought of as the distribution of the amount of time until the rth occurrence of an event in a Poisson process. It is used in meteorological processes to represent pollutant concentrations and precipitation quantities, and it has other applications in economics, inventory, and insurance risk theories. The parameters for the gamma distribution are location, scale, and shape.

Three conditions underly the gamma distribution:

- The number of possible occurrences in any unit of measurement is not limited to a fixed number.
- The occurrences are independent. The number of occurrences in one unit of measurement does not affect the number of occurrences in other units.
- The average number of occurrences must remain the same from unit to unit.

The sum of any two gamma-distributed variables is a gamma variable. The product of any two normally distributed variables is a gamma variable (Figure 7A.6).

Parameters: shape a>0, scale B>0
Domain: X>=0
Mean: aB
Variance: aB^2

Cell: C15

Assumption: Gr. Rate of Musculoskeletal Injuries

Gamma distribution with parameters:
Location   2.00%
Scale   1.00%
Shape   2

Selected range is from 2.00% to + Infinity

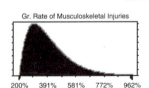

Gr. Rate of Musculoskeletal Injuries

200%   391%   581%   772%   962%

FIGURE 7A.6   Growth Rate of Musculoskeletal Injuries

TABLE 7A.1   Comparison of Select Distributions and Affect in Certainty Levels

Distribution	Summary	Sensitivity	Statistics	
Triangular	Certainty level is 17.40%	-.91	Trials	1,000
	Certainty range is from -Infinity to $306,900		Mean	$318,771
	Entire range is from $285,256 to $348,269		Median	$320,028
			Standard deviation	$11,656
			Skewness	-0.36
			Kurtosis	2.54
			Coeff. of variability	0.04
Normal	Certainty Level is 0.20%	-.80	Trials	1000
	Certainty Range is from -Infinity to $306,900		Mean	$328,875
	Entire Range is from $301,007 to $353,871		Median	$328,561
			standard deviation	$7,964
			Skewness	0.09
			Kurtosis	3.01
			Coeff. of variability	0.02
Lognormal	Certainty Level is 0.20%	-.79	Trials	1000
	Certainty range is from -Infinity to $306,900		Mean	$329,208
	Entire range is from $305,591 to $353,638		Median	$328,956
			Standard deviation	$8,349
			Skewness	0.08
			Kurtosis	2.82
			Coeff. of variability	0.03
Uniform	Certainty Level is 39.40%	-.96	Trials	1000
	Certainty Range is from -Infinity to $306,900		Mean	$313,684
	Entire Range is from $282,243 to $350,685		Median	$313,194
			Standard Deviation	$15,641
			Skewness	0.09
			Kurtosis	1.93
			Coeff. of Variability	0.05
Extreme Value	Certainty Level is 0.90%	-.72	Trials	1000
	Certainty Range is from -Infinity to $306,900		Mean	$326,663
	Entire Range is from $296,407 to $346,598		Median	$327,241
			Standard Deviation	$7,265
			Skewness	-0.42
			Kurtosis	3.47
			Coeff. of Variability	0.02

Binomial Distribution

This distribution gives the probability of observing X successes in a fixed number (n) of independent *Bernoulli trials*; p represents the probability of a success on a single trial.

For each trial, only two outcomes are possible. Trials are independent. The first trial does not affect the second trial and so on. The probability of an event occurring remains the same from trial to trial.

Example

You want to describe the number of defective items in a total of 70 manufactured items, 2% of which were found to be defective during preliminary testing.

There are only two possible outcomes: the manufactured item is either good or defective and the trials are independent

The probability of a defective item is the same each time:

Parameters: event probability $0<=p<=1$
Number of trials: $n>0$
Domain: $X=0,1,...,n$
Mean: np
Variance: $np(1-p)$

NEGATIVE BINOMIAL DISTRIBUTION

A discrete probability distribution is useful for characterizing the time between *Bernoulli trials*. For example, suppose machine parts are characterized as defective or non-defective, and let the probability of a defective part equal p. If you begin testing a sample of parts to find a defective, then the number of parts that must be tested before you find k defective parts follows a negative binomial distribution. The *geometric distribution* is a special case of the negative binomial distribution where k=1. The negative binomial is sometimes called the Pascal distribution.

Parameters

event probability $0<=p<=1$
number of successes k (positive integer)

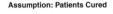

Assumption: Patients Cured   Cell: C10

Binomial distribution with parameters:
    Probability   0.25
    Trials   100

Selected range is from 0 to + Infinity

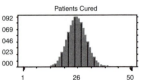

FIGURE 7A.7 Patients Cured

Domain: X=k,k+1,k+2,...
Mean: k/p
Variance: (1-p)/(p^2)

PARETO DISTRIBUTION

The Pareto distribution is widely used for the investigation of distributions associated with such empirical phenomena as city population sizes, the occurrence of natural resources, the sizes of companies, personal incomes, stock price fluctuations, and error clustering in communication circuits. This is a distribution used for random variables constrained to be greater or equal to 0.

Parameters: shape a>0
Domain: X>=1
Mean: a/(a-1) for a>1
Variance: [a/(a-2)]-[a/(a-1)] ^2 for a>2

GEOMETRIC DISTRIBUTION

A discrete probability distribution is useful for characterizing the time between *Bernoulli trials*. For example, suppose machine parts are characterized as defective or nondefective, and let the probability of a defective part equal *p*. If you begin testing a sample of parts to find a defective part, then the number of parts that must be tested before the first defective part is found follows a geometric distribution.

Three conditions underly the geometric distribution:

* The number of trials is not fixed.
* The trials continue until the first success.
* The probability of success is the same from trial to trial.

Example[1]

If you are drilling for oil and want to describe the number of dry wells you would drill before the next big gusher, you would use the geometric distribution. Assume that in the past you have hit oil about 10% of the time. The first step in selecting a probability distribution is to match your data with a distribution's conditions.

Checking the geometric distribution:

* The number of trials (dry wells) is not fixed.
* You continue to drill wells until you hit the big gusher.

---

[1] Source: Decisioneering's Crystal Ball Manual

The probability of success (10%) is the same each time you drill a well.

The geometric distribution has only one parameter: probability. In this example, the value for this parameter is .10, representing the 10% probability of discovering oil. You would enter this value as the parameter of the geometric distribution in Crystal Ball.

Parameters: event probability $0<=p<=1$
Domain: X=0,1,2,...
Mean: $(1-p)/p$
Variance: $(1-p)/(p^2)$

POISSON DISTRIBUTION

The distribution is often used to express probabilities concerning the number of events per unit. For example, the number of computer malfunctions per year or the number of bubbles per square yard in a sheet of glass might follow a Poisson distribution. The distribution is fully characterized by its mean, usually expressed in terms of a rate.

There are three conditions:

- The number of possible occurrences in any unit of measurement is not limited to a fixed number.
- The occurrences are independent. The number of occurrences in one unit of measurement does not affect the number of occurrences in other units.
- The average number of occurrences must remain the same from unit to unit.

Parameters: mean $B>0$
Domain: X=0,1,2,...
Mean: B
Variance: B

A BANKER'S PRIMER ON REAL OPTIONS

JONATHAN MUN, PH.D.[1]

Real options analysis applies financial options theory to capital investments, allowing bankers and their clients to evaluate capital investment strategies with a great deal more precision. Why is it a real option? It is "real" because real options deal with investments in operating capital and physical assets instead of financial assets. It is an "option" because management has the right, but not the obligation, to invest. The real options approach explicitly recognizes and incorporates the value of being able to defer investment, expand output, change technologies, or stop investing. Real options are used in situations where management has flexibility when making large capital budget decisions where high uncertainty exists. In other words, management can hedge capital expenditures by being able to make midcourse corrections downstream, when information becomes available and uncertainty becomes resolved. This way, management can reduce the risk of

[1] Dr. Mun is Director of Corporate Finance Development at Decisioneering, Inc. The author is grateful for this inclusion and the contribution of Decisioneering, the leader in development of advanced analytic tools, *www.decisioneering.com*

lump-sum investments while investing only under optimal conditions, navigating through a maze of uncertainty, and making upside risk a friend rather than viewing risk in its totality as a foe to be avoided completely.

For example, flexibility that is internal to the project allows management to modify capital expenditures as external conditions change. These include expansion, switching, contraction, or even abandonment options. Deciding to embark on a specific project makes possible a second project that was not feasible without the first. Some projects are engineered in such a way that production starts in later periods or is canceled altogether if events make production infeasible. Examples of business applications include investment banking, research and development projects, mergers and acquisitions, technology development, facility expansion, e-business and IT project prioritization, enterprise-wide risk management, business unit budgeting, licensing, contract valuation, and intangible asset valuation.

Applying real options methodology provides both bankers and borrowers with several advantages over traditional techniques:

- Leveraging existing static net present value analysis and adding layers of sophistication including dynamic simulation, real options analysis, and portfolio optimization of multiple interacting projects
- Providing framework for identifying, valuing, selecting, managing, and prioritizing the right projects for inclusion into a portfolio of multiple interacting projects
- Providing bankers with additional insights into strategic value and flexibility in the decision-making processes of borrowers and lenders alike
- Providing a view into correctly pricing and valuing financial contractual agreements with multiple clauses and options to extend or terminate
- Correctly evaluating the intrinsic value of bank-financed projects' and eliminating the possibility that management undervalued the strategic significance of certain projects, thereby allowing a framework for determining the synergistic or strategic value of projects previously only alluded to as management's "gut" feeling
- Identifying, framing, and valuing future strategic opportunities
- Giving a reliable, repeatable, and consistent process for decision making
- Allowing for the analysis of multiple decision pathways as opposed to not present value (NPV)'s single decision pathway and understanding full well management's ability to make strategic changes depending on external business conditions
- Incorporating new decisions over time as opposed to NPV's requirement of all decisions and assumptions defined at the outset

- Including Monte Carlo simulation of risk variables to enhance the decision-making process to include not only single-variable outputs but their respective range of probabilities of occurrences
- Minimizing the possibility of making detrimental decisions by selecting the wrong project or undervaluing a financial contract
- Solving problems that cannot be otherwise solved

TYPICAL EXAMPLES OF APPLICATIONS

Real options analysis has applications in numerous industries, including banking. In investment vehicles where interest rates play a major role in valuation, real options can be useful in identifying the true value of an asset that has an execution value tied to interest rate fluctuation. Other uses include providing analysts with a means for making decisions on facility expansions, evaluating geographical locations, valuing test markets, and extending into new types of financial vehicles and financial delivery mechanisms. It can also help analysts to value financial contracts filled with conditions, covenants, and extension or termination options. Analysts can then look at these financial projects in terms of a portfolio.

In the oil and gas industry, real options help firms in these industries make more informed decisions concerning exploration and production, optimal sizing of production facilities, and petroleum portfolio optimization. It can also help firms avoid undervaluing potentially lucrative projects.

Pharmaceutical research and development is fraught with risks. Real options help borrowers in this industry narrow the focus of research and development by finding the value of strategic options. This information allows companies to build optimal project portfolios and value options based on different phases of their R&D process. Management can identify the value of specific projects and prioritize them efficiently.

In manufacturing industries, real option analysis allows for increased flexibility in building and maintaining plants, allocating manufacturing resources, upgrading to new technological infrastructures, and optimally timing project implementation. This technique also helps these firms accurately value the information from market research, patents, and trademarks.

CRYSTAL BALL REAL OPTIONS: FLEXIBLE MODELING CAPABILITIES

Crystal Ball Real Options is a stand-alone application with direct linking and embedding to and from Microsoft Excel, providing significant flexibility in modeling. Preset templates allow banks and their borrowers to easily initiate analysis,

TABLE 7A.2   Project Analysis: Features, Functions, and Benefits

Feature	Function	Benefit
Traditional NPV analysis	Performs traditional NPV using discounted cash flow analysis	Starts the analysis with a methodology that management is fully aware of and comfortable using; is capable of performing a simple cost-benefit financial analysis
Monte Carlo simulation	Performs multiple scenarios with thousands of possible outcomes	Helps quantify risk and uncertainty, increases confidence in results, and provides probabilities of outcomes
Real options analysis	Quantifies the value of strategic options in projects	Helps identify hidden intrinsic value that are otherwise undervalued; provides a better and more precise valuation and decision-making framework
Portfolio optimization	Optimizes multiple projects in a portfolio of related projects	Models the interaction among projects or decision variables within projects to meet certain objectives—that is, a firm's multiple sets of interacting projects can be viewed as a rolled-up portfolio of projects, accounting for their risk diversification properties
Reporting	Easy-to-understand reports complete with powerful graphics and tables	Provides a clear understanding and precise interpretation of the analytical process and results
Wizard-based interface	Guides the user through the analysis process	Improves efficiency and ease of use

while the tree structure provides users with the flexibility to modify the analysis to fit a wide selection of problems.

Crystal Ball Real Options puts the power of real options analysis in an intuitive software environment (Table 7A.2). The model produces clear, concise, and easy-to-understand reports, complete with high-powered graphics and data tables. This capability allows results to be disseminated directly from the analyst's desktop to senior management and, where applicable, to the firm's investment and commercial bankers.

8

RISK MANAGEMENT
AND SUSTAINABLE GROWTH

Growth is important to financial health. But it is possible growth may be too rapid for a firm's own good, particularly if operations are small or if financial planning is deficient. The problem is that the more accelerated the growth rate, the greater the requirement for funds to support growth—particularly if growth is exponential and the borrower is saddled with high operating leverage. The resulting high debt ratios could easily cause financial problems, leaving the firm open to the flight of suppliers and customers. The sustainable growth model helps stave off excessive leverage problems by bringing to equilibrium the borrower's capital structure and targeted sales.

The sustainable growth rate is the maximum rate that sales can increase (over the foreseeable future) without depleting financial resources. In simple terms, operating units need money to make money. Sustainable growth solutions center on boosting equity when volume accelerates, thus maintaining the "right" balance between liabilities and equity. Industry benchmarks act as points of reference and reflect the cumulative decisions of management, lenders, suppliers, customers, and competitors. Whenever the relationship between liabilities and net worth is significantly below industry standards, questions arise about management competence and the firm's unsystematic risk control. Just look at the spreads between treasuries and the rates charged on corporate junk bond issues sitting in the lowest quartile of their respective industries.

The special case cash flow model we call sustainable growth measures the probability that sales increases within highly leveraged, rapid-growth companies stress out the financial structure. The model helps identify the proportion of growth fueled through internal versus external cash flow. The lender sets the results to different degrees of tolerance by manipulating specific variables to determine various levels of risk. Thus, sustainable growth acts as a telescope focused on the projected cash flow statement. For example, if the model reveals that 90% of sales growth targeted for the foreseeable future will be financed externally *while* the borrower is currently debt heavy, the situation could get out of hand, and fast.

We determine the sustainable growth rate by setting up (X) variables, including projected sales, assets, profit margin, dividend payout, and spontaneous liabilities, and solving for (Y), the sustainable growth rate. Again, sustainable growth runs are singularly important for highly leveraged, rapid-growth operations since their cash flows are often volatile and unpredictable. These units operate in an environment much riskier than any other period in a typical life cycle because unsystematic (company-specific) risks are unique and difficult to analyze. Let's see what this really means.

THE INDUSTRY LIFE CYCLE

Phase 1: Startup

Firms starting out face a high risk of financial distress: their higher risks require special types of financing. This led to the development of specialized venture capital sources. Venture capital companies, including commercial and investment banks, generally obtain an equity position in firms they finance. Venture capital loans call for higher risk premiums as well but are also supported by guarantees and are often structured with convertibles, warrants, or are tied in with the purchase of stock by the investment company. Because risks are so obvious (the startup phase requires initial asset investments in anticipation of sales), venture capital deals are priced with the appropriate spread over a base rate.

Phase 2: Rapid Growth

Following inception, a successful firm with good growth potential will enter phase 2 of its life cycle. The firm has achieved initial success and now may grow rapidly and start to earn profits. However, the small increment to equity generated by earnings retention is often trivial by comparison, too inconsequential to finance the insatiable appetite for new assets required by rapid growth firms. Creditors advancing funds at relatively low risk premiums often do not know if loans represent down payments for accelerating credit demands—until the firm implodes or whether loans can be successfully amortized through internal cash flow—the aftereffect of slower growth.

If rapid growth continues for long, the situation may further deteriorate, making it abundantly clear from the bank's standpoint that equity injections are required. Unsystematic risk (the debt-to-equity ratio) will exceed judicious limits, yet the firm may be reluctant to bring in outside capital because owners are unwilling to share control, give up tax benefits (of debt financing), or dilute earnings.

Phase 3: Mature or Stable Growth

The mature phase of a firm (or industry) life cycle is one in which growth rates for price, book value, earnings, and dividends are approximately the same and consistent with gross domestic product (GDP) growth. In the mature phase, operating activities throw off more cash, while growth requirements diminish sufficiently to lower investing activities, particularly in capital expansion areas. Financing requirements drop as more cash is generated than absorbed. The firm reduces debt levels with more ease while raising its dividend payout.

Phase 4: Decline

Sales decline and reduced profits are the consequence of heightened competition or changes in consumer demand. Thus, operating cash flow falls short of working capital and capital expenditures, though reduced investment activities provide limited cash flow because plant capacity is lowered. At this stage the firm should be paying down substantial amounts of debt and may engage in stock repurchases to further shrink its size. The firm may seek growth acquisitions to provide a longer lease on life.

THE SUSTAINABLE GROWTH MODEL

Successful firms move assets through operations efficiently, product lines produce healthy profits, and the equity base along with the rest of the capital structure strengthens. For a company in the rapid growth stage of its business cycle, this is a somewhat difficult task to attain. Characteristically, companies in this phase experience a rapid expansion in sales along with receivables, inventory, and fixed assets. Financial problems accelerate when a borrower's insatiable appetite for core assets and capital expansion overwhelms modest profit contributions to equity. The standard forecast model recognizes this:

$$F = A_1/S \, (\Delta S) + \Delta NFA - L_1/S \, (\Delta S) - P(S + \Delta S)(1 - D) + R:$$

$$E = (A/S - L_1/S) - (P/G)(1+G)(1 - D) + R$$

$$g^* = \frac{P(1 - D)(1 + L)}{A/S - P(1 - D)(1 + L)}$$

$$L^* = T((A/S) - P(1 - D)) - P(1 - D)/(P(1 - D)(1 + T))$$

Where
A = total assets projected
A_1 = projected spontaneous assets
D or d = dividend payout rate
E = projected percentage of sales growth externally financed
F = financial needs (−F = cash surplus)
G = sales growth rate (the same as T)
g*= sustainable growth rate
L = maximum leverage (historical)
L_1 = spontaneous liabilities
L* = equilibrium leverage
P = projected profit margin
R = debt maturities
S = projected sales
ΔS = change in sales
T = projected sales growth rate (targeted growth rate)
ΔNFA = change in net fixed assets

Consider the historical financial statements of Traude Inc. for the fiscal period ending December 31, 2000. This young growth company produces cable for the computer industry and is requesting a $50 million loan for plant expansion. The company needs the expansion program to raise operating leverage, reduce labor costs, improve production efficiency, and increase the gross profit margin. Management presented the historical and projected financial statements shown in Exhibits I through IV to the firm's bankers in support of its request for a loan.

EXHIBIT I   Traude Inc. Historical Balance Sheet, December 31, 2000 (in thousands)

		Percentage of sales
Cash	$2,000	.02
Accounts receivable	4,000	.04
Inventories	54,000	.54
Net plant and equipment	60,000	.60
Total assets	120,000	1.20
Accounts payable	20,000	.20
Accruals	6,000	.06

Long-term debt	44,000	Constant*
Capital stock	10,000	Constant*
Paid-in capital	10,000	Constant*
Retained earnings	30,000	Earnings retention
Total liabilities and equity	$120,000	

* Financing decision; does not vary with sales.

EXHIBIT II Traude Inc. Historical Income Sheet, December 31, 2000 (in thousands)

		Percentage of sales
Net sales	$100,000	1.00
Cost of goods sold	75,000	.75
Gross margin	25,000	.25
Expenses (including taxes)	23,000	.23
Net income	$2,000	.02
	Projected sales: 2001	$150,000

EXHIBIT III Traude Inc. Projected Balance Sheet, December 31, 2000 (in thousands)

		Percentage of sales
Cash	$3,000	.02
Accounts receivable	6,000	.04
Inventories	81,000	.54
Net plant and equipment	90,000	.60
Total assets	180,000	1.20
Accounts payable	30,000	.20
Accruals	9,000	.06
Long-term debt	44,000	Constant
Capital stock	10,000	Constant
Paid-in capital	10,000	Constant
Retained earnings	33,000*	Earnings retention
Available capitalization	136,000	
Financial needs	*44,000*	*Derived*
Total liabilities and equity	$180,000	

* $30,000 + .02 ($150,000) − 0 = $33,000

EXHIBIT IV   Traude Inc. Forecast Income Sheet, December 31, 2000 (in thousands)

		Percentage of sales
Net sales	$150,000	1.00
Cost of goods sold	112,500	.75
Gross margin	37,500	.25
Expenses (including taxes)	34,500	.23
Net income	$3,000	.02

As we saw in Chapter 7, the firm's financial needs can also be derived as follows:

$$F = A/S\,(\Delta S) - L_1/S\,(\Delta S) - P(S + \Delta S)\,(1 - d)$$

Thus,

$$F = 180{,}000/150{,}000\,(50{,}000) - 39{,}000/150{,}000\,(50000) - .02\,(150{,}000)\,(1 - 0) = 44{,}000$$

The percentage of sales increase that needs to be financed externally can be found by

$$E = (A/S - L_1/S) - P/G\,(1 + G)\,(1 - D)$$

Thus,

$$E = (180{,}000/150{,}000 - 39{,}000/150{,}000) - .02/.5\,(1 + .5)\,(1 - 0) = .88$$

Eighty-eight percent of sales growth will be financed externally. If Traude were leveraged at the end of its fiscal year, the projection period adds to leverage due to the imbalance between internal and external financing. Since sales growth is 50% in the first projection period, .88 (50,000) = 44,000, as before. While the E formula is efficacious for mature firms, we need a more powerful equation for Traude Inc. We shall use the sustainable growth model tailored for this specific lending deal.

Indeed, the forecast equations we derived in Chapter 7 serve as base equations for deriving the sustainable growth equations in this chapter.

As we can see from the equation, a firm's financial needs increase if asset efficiency, profits, or the retention rate $(1 - d)$ decline. On the other hand, reliance on trade credit or accruals will reduce external financing requirements. The sustainable growth model's powerful logic rests with the notion that the financial structure of a fast-growing, highly leveraged firm is already near a fixed saturation point. Increasing leverage beyond that point causes loan risk premiums to skyrocket following the change in unsystematic risk. The sustainable growth rate is estimated as follows:

$$g^* = \Delta S/S = \frac{P\,(1 - d)\,(1 + L)}{A/S - P\,(1 - d)\,(1 + L)}$$

We can easily derive the sustainable growth rate from the financial needs equation starting with a set of sustainable growth assumptions.

The standard assumptions of sustainable growth include the following:

1. No equity issues permitted while the company is in the sustainable growth mode
2. Constant dividend payout
3. Stable financial structure
4. Constant capital output ratio

In effect, we take a snapshot of the capital structure, stopping time in a mathematical manner of speaking. By withholding equity, we determine how the capital structure looks without equity injections—that is, can the firm sustain its financial health without additional equity inflows? Also, dividend payout, profit margin, and the debt-to-equity ratio are held constant as well—a requirement to set the math in place. We now regenerate the equation:

$$F = A/S\,(\Delta S) - L_1/S\,(\Delta S) - P(S + \Delta S)\,(1 - d)$$

by adding a lag variable (S + ΔS) and rearranging terms, assuming no equity financing except retained earnings:

$$A/S\,(\Delta S) = (F + L_1/S\,(\Delta S)) + P(S + \Delta S)\,(1 - d)$$

Where $A/S\,(\Delta S)$ equals incremental spontaneous assets, $(F + L_1/S\,(\Delta S))$ equals incremental external financing (all debt), and $P(S + \Delta S)(1 - d)$ equals profit retention (see Table 8.1).

Simplifying the term $F + L_1/S(\Delta S)$ with the given assumption of stable capital structure, we have $D/E = D/E$ and $\Delta D = \Delta E\,(D/E)$, where $D/E = L$. We can now substitute $\Delta D = \Delta E/(L)$. That is to say, an increase in equity (from retained earnings—remember our assumption) is followed by a proportional increase in

TABLE 8.1   Understanding Equation 1

This year's balance sheet	From equation 1	Next year's balance sheet	Assumptions
Assets	$A/S\,(\Delta S)$	Last year's assets plus the change in assets	
Debt	$(F + L_1/S\,(\Delta S))$	Last year's debt plus the change in debt	Financial needs—all debt plus incremental accounts payable and accruals (operating cash sources) (see assumption 1)
Equity	$P(S + \Delta S)(1 - d)$	Last year's equity plus the change in equity	Earnings retention only (see assumption 1).

debt. We now see that since ΔE can only come about as $P(S + \Delta S)(1 - d)$; we substitute for that term and obtain

$$\Delta D = P(S + \Delta S)(1 - d)L$$

We set the above back into the equation to obtain

$$A/S(\Delta S) = P(S + \Delta S)(1 - d)L + P(S + \Delta S)(1 - d)$$

We simplify as follows

$$S(\Delta S) = (P(S + \Delta S)(1 - d)L)/A + (P(S + \Delta S)(1 - d))/A$$

$$= P(S + \Delta S)(1 - d)(1 + L)/A$$

$$= P(S)(1 - d)(1 + L)/A + P\Delta S(1 - d)(1 + L)/A$$

$$\Delta S/S = P(S + \Delta S)(1 - d)(1 + L)/A$$

$$= (P(S)(1 - d)(1 + L))/A + (P\Delta S)(1 - d)(1 + L))/A$$

Thus,

$$\Delta S/S^2 = P(1 - d)(1 + L)/A + (\Delta S/S)(P(1 - d)(1 + L))/A$$

Finally, sustainable growth rate falls out as follows:

$$g * = \Delta S/S = \frac{P(1 - d)(1 + L)}{A/S - P(1 - d)(1 + L)}$$

The model may be adjusted to derive equilibrium leverage, L, given the firm's targeted growth rate (TGR), when the TGR is substituted for the sustainable growth rate, SGR.

The Two Conditions for Equilibrium Leverage ("L"): The Debt-to-Equity Ratio

The sustainable growth rate (g*) shows if the company is inundated with too much debt. If the *sustainable growth rate* (g*) falls below the *targeted growth rate* (T), excessive leverage will likely prevent the company from achieving its growth objectives. This is readily seen with two cases:

Case 1: Set "L," the debt-to-equity ratio, at the maximum levels the lender allows, a judgmental decision. The ratio may be set at the industry's unsystematic risk maximum, "bankruptcy" leverage, or simply at the lenders tolerance level.

Case 2: Set g* equal to the targeted growth rate, T, and solve for L to secure the debt-to-equity ratio in equilibrium with the borrower's targeted growth rate. The question, simply, is this: If the borrower continues its growth pattern, how high will leverage climb assuming the firm raises no new equity?

Formula: $T = \dfrac{P(1 - d)(1 + L)}{A/S - P(1 - d)(1 + L)}$

Example Case I

Here we see that the sustainable growth model identifies asset management, dividend payout, and operating and leverage imbalance.

Traude's lenders asked for new projections, citing that sales growth of 50% in the first projection period (just examined) was far too optimistic. Consequently, the firm met again with its bankers and presented a set of projections, insisting that while sales were pegged too high, improved manufacturing techniques would boost productivity and increase the net profit margin to 7%. Ratios were extracted from the new projections, including the net profit margin, dividend payout rate, assets to sales, and targeted growth rate. Projections include the plant expansion program related to the loan request (Figure 8.1).

Solving for the sustainable growth rate where:

A = projected assets
d = dividend payout rate
g* = sustainable growth rate
L = maximum leverage allowable by the bankers
S = projected sales

$$g* = \frac{P\,(1-d)\,(1+L)}{A/S - P\,(1-d)\,(1+L)}$$

$$g* = \frac{.07\,(1-.6)\,(1+1.50)}{1.8 - .07\,(1-.6)\,(1+1.50)}$$

= .04

This firm can sustain a 4% growth rate without increasing its debt-to-equity ratio above 150%. However, Traude's sales growth rate is already targeted at

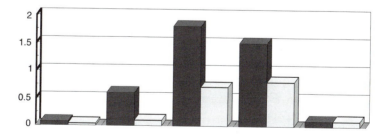

	Profit Margin	Dividend Payout	Capital Output	Leverage Limit	Target Growth
■ High Risk	7.0%	60.0%	180.0%	150.0%	10.0%
☐ Industry	4.0%	10.0%	70.0%	80.0%	10.0%

FIGURE 8.1   High-risk ratios versus the industry

10%. If the company grows at a higher rate than the sustainable growth rate, the firm's current debt-to-equity ratio will without question increase beyond the 150% leverage set by the lenders.

A 10% growth rate will have a negative effect on cash flow. Without adequate cash availability, operating leverage tends to increase as additional debt is raised to cover cash shortfalls. A high degree of both operating leverage and financial leverage may place the firm in jeopardy. If a firm has a significant degree of operating leverage, a high level of sales must be attained to reach its break-even point. Any changes in the sales level will have a substantial impact on earnings before interest and taxes (EBIT). Changes to EBIT directly affect net income, return on equity, and earnings per share. Financial leverage influences profits in much the same way—the higher the leverage, the higher the break-even point for sales and the greater the effect on profits from fluctuations in sales volume. Therefore, if Traude Inc. has a significant degree of both operating leverage and financial leverage, even minute changes in the level of sales will create wide fluctuations in net income, return on equity, and earnings per share. This is something the company cannot afford to deal with.

Will the firm need to revert to increased borrowings to finance differences between internal and external financing? Here, we are concerned with the effect recessions have on a company's financial condition. During a period of economic slowdown, sales may decrease sufficiently to cause cash flow streams to run dry. This means more money must be spent on new asset purchases, requiring a corresponding increase in sales and internal cash flow to match the assets purchases. The firm's bankers are well aware that without an adequate source of cash, the areas where debt funds are used (debt payments, etc.) run the risk of being in default, thereby putting the bank's investment in jeopardy. Traude's creditors can determine that an imbalance between internal and external cash flow will occur by comparing the firm's sustainable growth rate to its targeted growth rate.

Example Case 2

Set g* equal to the targeted growth rate T and solve for L to obtain the debt-to-equity ratio in equilibrium with the borrower's targeted growth rate.

$$g^* = \frac{P\,(1 - d)\,(1 + L)}{A/S - P\,(1 - d)\,(1 + L)}$$

$$.10 = \frac{.07\,(1 - .6)\,(1 + L)}{1.8 - .07\,(1 - .6)\,(1 + L)}$$

$$L = 4.84$$

Solving for L leaves a value of 4.84. Thus, leverage must increase to 484% for the sales growth and the financial structure to join in equilibrium. The firm's growth must be tied to its financial structure. Since the maximum allowable debt-to-equity ratio set originally by the firm's lenders was 150%, the deal, as presented, will not be approved. While high leverage might provide high returns for shareholders, this is not the bank's major concern. Levels of acceptable leverage are proportional to the reliability of Traude's projected cash flow. The characteristics of both the company and its industry, along with specifics of the transaction, are essential when management and its creditors set acceptable or tolerance leverage; leverage tolerance levels will be governed by sets of very specific factors that decide unsystematic risk.

For example, certain debt structures, such as having a layer of mezzanine capital subordinate to other creditor claims, might justify a higher tolerance level. Then again, if the company is in a very cyclical industry that is subject to rapid technological obsolescence making cash flow more difficult to predict, creditors might set a lower leverage tolerance.

Traude's profit margin is influenced by this firm's overall performance and its relationship to the industry. Within the analysis, operating trends will be carefully examined, as well as the company's position in the industry.

SOLVING SUSTAINABLE GROWTH PROBLEMS

Sustainable growth problems are resolved by equity infusions, reducing the capital output ratio (asset: sales), reducing dividends, and increasing profits. Pruning profits, which might include such strategies as selling off unprofitable divisions, is another solution to sustainable growth problems. Knowing when rapid growth levels off e.g., recognizing when the mature phase has begun) is interpreted as a solution as well. Once the firm reaches the mature phase of its life cycle, cash inflows pick up, overall financial and operating risk decreases, and working capital becomes more predictable.

If selling new equity is not feasible, a firm may reduce the dividend payout ratio or simply increase leverage. A cut in the dividend payout increases the sustainable growth rate by increasing the portion of earnings retained in the business, while increasing leverage raises the amount of debt the firm can add for each dollar of retained profits. As noted earlier, however, there are limits to the use of debt financing. All firms have a creditor-imposed debt capacity that restricts the amount of leverage the company can use. As leverage increases, the risks carried by owners and creditors rise, as do the costs of securing additional capital.

The most conservative solution to resolving sustainable growth problems is to simply reduce growth to a level compatible with the company's current dividend or financing policies. These solutions must be approached prudently. The timing of equity issues should be well planned so that serious share dilution is avoided. If a firm is willing and able to raise new equity capital by selling shares, its sustainable growth problems simply disappear.

Issue Equity

Although it is often beneficial for a company to issue equity, doing so may be difficult for a small firm with limited access to the venture capital market. Another factor to consider is that most countries do not have active, developed equity markets. Finally, recognize that new equity is expensive, dilutes ownership, and is likely to reduce earnings per share.

Define the Targeted Growth Period

By knowing with some degree of precision when rapid growth will end and a slower period expansion will take place, the company can reduce a sustainable growth problem. When actual growth exceeds sustainable growth, the first step is to find just how long the situation is likely to continue. If Traude's growth rate is likely to decline in the near term as the firm reaches maturity, the problem is temporary and can probably be solved by increasing leverage to feasible levels. Later, when actual growth falls below the sustainable growth rate, cash is generated, not absorbed, and loans can be repaid.

Improve the Capital/Output Ratio (Assets to Sales)

The assets-to-sales ratio is an important benchmark to measure sustainable growth problems. The ratio is set (in the equation) to represent the base (before profit retention) on which an appropriate and sustainable growth rate is calculated. If this rate exceeds a tolerable level, leverage will rapidly increase. Management largely decides capital output, as management policies give rise to expansion. Analyzing the effectiveness of these policies, we easily find a tolerable growth rate (for g*), set projected debt levels for L, and calculate an equilibrium assets-to-sales ratio. Covenants might be written to ensure that management administers the firm's asset portfolio to sustainable growth guidelines. If management fails to do this, problems show up in projections.

As noted earlier, unmanaged growth forces a firm to borrow from external sources with little restraint because the appetite for funds is enormous—resulting in a rising debt ratio. High debt levels reduce loan protection because they effectively block external equity infusions. In addition, as leverage increases within the sustainable growth universe, cash flows need to be channeled to debt service, cannibalizing operating cash flows. As mentioned previously, a company cannot sustain high financial and operating leverage. The upshot of all of this is that with cash flow volatility comes increased credit risk.

If, on the other hand, a firm's leverage is already too high, rather than using actual leverage in the model, the lender can use an industry average debt level and the same tolerable growth rate for g*. The derived equilibrium assets-to-sales ratio should be compared to the actual ratio of that firm to again decide the appropriateness of asset management policies.

But an asset-to-sales ratio in line with or lower than the industry norm depicts strong asset management practices. We can assume that asset utilization ratios provided in support of the loan agreement are being used efficiently and are growing at a pace that equity capital can support. In this case, if borrowers retire older debt uniformly and regularly, and if cash flows are predictable, credit risk is under control.

Increase Profit Margins

Improved profit margins reflect strategic, operating, and financing decisions. Strategies involve critically important decision areas such as choice of the product market areas in which the firm conducts its operations, whether to emphasize cost reduction or product differentiation, and whether to focus on selected product areas or seek to cover a broad range of potential buyers.

Reduce the Dividend Payout Ratio

Increases in both dividends and debt-to-equity ratios are potentially alarming because dividends reduce cash flow. On the other hand, earnings retention indicates a reinvestment commitment.

Prune Profits

When a firm spreads its resources across many products, it may not be able to compete effectively in all of them. It is better to sell off marginal operations and plow the proceeds back into the remaining businesses. Profitable pruning reduces sustainable growth problems in two ways: it generates cash directly through the sale of marginal businesses, and it reduces actual sales growth by eliminating some sources of the growth. Profit pruning is also available for a single-product company. The firm could prune out slow-paying customers or slow-turning inventory. This lessens sustainable growth problems in two ways: it frees up cash, which can be used to support new growth and it increases asset turnover.

A NEW STRATEGY: THE SOLUTION

1. The firm decided not to issue new equity, preserving ownership control. Instead, as agreed, subcontractors will produce and ship to Traude's customers. Because the use of subcontractors will squeeze profit margins, sales will continue to grow at 10% because Traude will absorb the higher costs of production.
2. Using subcontractors will lower inventory levels and reduce capital spending.

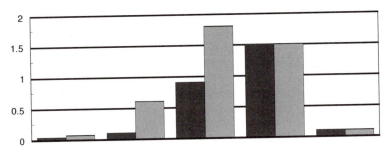

	Profit Margin	Dividend Payout	Capital Output	Leverage Limit	Target Growth
■ Revised Strategy	4.0%	10.0%	90.0%	150.0%	10.0%
▨ Original Strategy	7.0%	60.0%	180.0%	150.0%	10.0%

FIGURE 8.2   Revised strategy

3. Traude consents to a tight control of receivables.
4. Dividends must be reduced.
5. Leverage will not transcend the ceiling imposed by the firm's lenders (see Figure 8.2).

$$g* = \frac{P\,(1-d)\,(1+L)}{A/S - P\,(1-d)\,(1+L)}$$

$$g* = \frac{.04\,(1-.1)\,(1+1.50)}{.90 - .04\,(1-.1)\,(1+1.50)} = .11$$

The previous condition was as follows:

$$g* = (.07\,(1-.6)\,(1+1.50))/(1.8 - .07\,(1-.6)\,(1+1.50)) = .04$$

The sustainable growth rate is 11%. Thus, Traude Inc. can grow at 11% a year over the foreseeable future without increasing leverage beyond 150%, the leverage ceiling set by the firm's bankers. Since the firm's 10% targeted growth rate is less than its 11% sustainable growth rate, leverage will fall below the maximum level permitted by the firm's creditors. Poor asset management combined with an aggressive dividend policy proved to be root causes of the borrower's growth problem. Indeed, while profits declined under the revised strategies, sustainable growth rate actually increased.

CURVE FITTING

We all may have tried to draw a straight line through a maze of data plotted on an X-Y grid. The line, you hoped, would give you the general trend from the data and enable you to predict a Y value when you knew the X value. Although drawing lines to predict trends is easy, you can never be sure how well the lines fit the data. When Y depends on multiple sets of X, the problem becomes far too complex for hand-drawn lines.

Linear regression and multiple regression analyses are the most well-known methods of finding trends, predicting the near future, and calculating dependent or unknown values. Linear regression analysis uses a set of X and Y data to calculate a line with the least amount of error. Multiple regression analysis uses multiple sets of data to find a multidimensional plane with the least amount of error in predicting Y.

The Exponential Growth Regression Curve and the Sustainable Growth Model

Rapid growth rates, whether in nature or in business, usually can be described with an exponential curve. This type of growth happens in animal populations with plentiful food and little competition or predation. Such growth, we have seen, often occurs in the initial stages of rapidly expanding businesses. The *exponential curve fit* in Excel is an excellent tool for examining rapid or initial growth rates. We use it to examine growth rates as diverse as sales volume and tissue cultures. The key point is this: the sustainable model's capacity to red-flag thinly capitalized financial structures expands in proportion to the R square correlation score of growth rates and its regression line.

The Logarithmic Regression Curve and the Sustainable Growth Model

Industries and animal populations often grow rapidly at first, then decline with time. Limited resources, competition, or predation cause the slowdown. Populations (whether industry or animal) that are approaching the saturation point grow along a logarithmic curve. The logarithmic curve found easily in Excel along with the proper correlations illustrates a rapid growth, followed by a gradual decrease in the growth rate. After growth and resources balance out, growth may continue at the same rate at which resources increase. When industries grow, they eventually reach the saturation point; from that point on, replacements or population growth account for most new sales. Growth rates for industries that have reached this level are nearly straight lines.

A FINAL THOUGHT

The sustainable growth model teaches us that both quantitative and qualitative analyses call for judgment. Combined with the qualitative factors we consider, the objective of growth/leverage mathematics (e.g., sustainable growth) is to offer an infrastructure for lending decisions, pricing, and tight loan agreements.

REVIEW QUESTIONS

1. To reduce credit risk, what major elements should the company's financial planning include?
2. What is the sustainable growth model? What are the model's major assumptions?
3. What is the industry life cycle? Describe the funding requirements of borrowers along with the lender's primary credit risks in each stage of the life cycle.
4. Explain the meaning of the equations and the applications of the model.
5. Describe the techniques to solve sustainable growth problems. For a company like Traude Inc., what are the most important and perhaps the only way to solve the firm's sustainable growth problem?
6. How we use the exponential curve fit as an analyzing tool?

SELECTED REFERENCES AND READINGS

Clark, J. J., T. C. Chiang, *et al.* (1989). *Sustainable corporate growth: A model and management planning tool.* New York: Quorum Books.

Higgins, R. C. (1998). *Analysis for financial management.* Boston, MA: Irwin/McGraw-Hill.

Hofkes, M. W. (1996). Modeling sustainable development: An economy-ecology integrated model. *Economic Modeling* **13**, 333–353.

McFaddin, S., and M. Clouse. (1993). New model for sustainable growth in the energy industry. *Energy Economics* **1**.

9

FINANCIAL DISTRESS
Recognition and Diagnosis of Troubled Loans

Financial distress and insolvency are broad concepts: failure in economic terms usually follows cash flow decay—revenues not covering costs over defined periods. Economic failure also implies that investment rates of return have fallen short of hurdle rates (e.g., capital costs on a sustainable basis). Financial failure occurs when firms cannot meet current obligations when due, though book assets may exceed liabilities. However, when the market value of liabilities exceeds asset market values, the end result is insolvency.

Over the years, researchers have studied the factors that cause firms to fail. The general consensus is that one leading cause of failure is management incompetence—specifically, inexperience in dealing with industry demand/supply factors or new developments combined with a poor strategic approach to R&D planning, sales, finance, production, research, and cost containment. Well over three quarters of business failures can be attributed to management incompetence or a loss of ownership expertise (Figure 9.1).

In addition to management incompetence, the origins of many financial problems are infused in the fundamental changes that have occurred in an

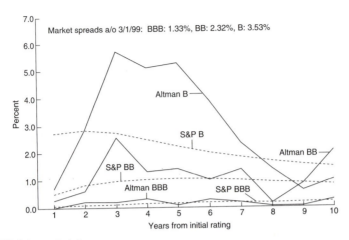

FIGURE 9.1   Default Rates
Source: "Managing Credit Risk: The Next Great Financial Challenge," *Mortality Losses by Original Rating—All Rated Corporate Bonds,* Caouette, John B., and Altman, Edward, and Narayanan, Paul (published by John Wiley & Sons, Inc., copyright 1998); *S&P Credit Week, January 28, 1998,* "Global Defaults Remain Low." *Note:* Recovery Rate Assumption = 0.58.

obligor's business, marketplace, economy, or industry months or even years prior to failure. They may be as systematic as changes in irreversible economic/industry demographics (the demise of shirt manufacturing in the United States, for instance) or company-specific changes, such as shifts in consumer purchases, loss of major contracts, expansion into consumer-adverse markets, accelerated growth without support of adequate capital, loss of key employees and customers, or an acquisition gone sour.

Sooner or later, these changes result in collapse and pose a series of crucial questions for lending institutions: Is financial collapse avoidable? What are the qualitative and statistical signals of distress? Can bankers detect signs early enough so that they can initiate a proper course of action before things get out of hand? The diagnostics that follow will serve bankers well in addressing the disease of financial collapse, as long as bankers take seriously the notion that to serve well is to learn well. Bankers must consider the warning signs:

- In-house orders are slow in comparison to corresponding periods in previous years.
- The factory is operating well below capacity.
- Changes are made in the manner payables are paid.
- Owners no longer take pride in their business.

- Frequent visits to the customer's place of business reveals deteriorating general appearance of the premises. For example, rolling stock and equipment have not been properly maintained.
- Unusual items appear in the financial statements.
- Negative trends become evident, such as losses or lower gross and net profits.
- Accounts receivable slows down.
- Sales volume decreases.
- Intercompany payables/receivables are not adequately explained.
- Cash balances are reduced substantially or are overdrawn and uncollected during normally liquid periods.
- Management fails to take trade discounts because of poor inventory turnover.
- Withholding tax liability builds as taxes are used to pay other debt.
- Financial reporting is frequently "downtiered" due to changes in financial management.
- At the end of the cycle, creditors are not completely paid out.
- Officers' salaries are sharply reduced.
- Interim results become erratic.
- Financials are late.
- Management is unwilling to provide budgets, projections, or interim information.
- Suppliers cut back terms or request COD.
- Changes in inventory are followed by an excessive inventory buildup or the retention of obsolete merchandise.
- The borrower changes suppliers frequently.
- Inventory to one customer increases.
- Concentration changes from a major well-known customer to one of lesser stature.
- The lender permits advances on the seasonal loan to fund other purposes.
- The company loses an important supplier or customer.
- Concentrations are in receivables and payables, and lender fails to get satisfactory explanations from the company on these concentrations.
- Loans are made to or from officers and affiliates.
- The principals of the company do not know what condition the company is in and the direction in which it is headed.
- The lender overestimates the peaks and valleys in the seasonal loan, thereby setting up a seasonal loan that is excessive.
- The company is unable to clean up bank debt, or cleanups are affected by rotating bank debt.

- The company fails to conduct investigations on the creditworthiness of larger receivables.
- The lender finances a highly speculative inventory position in which the owner is trying for a "home run."
- Product demand changes.
- Distribution or production methods become obsolete.
- The company has overexpanded without adequate working capital.
- The company has grown dependent on troubled customers or industries.
- There have been changes in senior management.
- The board of directors is no longer participating.
- Management lacks depth.
- Management is performing functions that should be delegated to others.
- Financial controls are weak.
- Improper pricing is detected.
- Investment in fixed assets has become excessive.
- The company has experienced unusual or extraordinary litigation and events not customarily encountered in the industry.
- Asset sales are used to fund working capital needs.
- The company begins to borrow against remaining unsecured assets.
- A profitable division is sold.
- Key personnel resign.
- There is an increase in large sales discounts or significant sales returns.
- The company is unable to make timely deposits of trust funds, such as employee withholding taxes.
- There are surprise losses and significant variances from expected or projected results when compared to actual results for the past several years without adequate explanation.
- Regular borrowing is at or near the credit limit or increased credit lines and borrowing inquiries begin to rise.
- Suppliers begin to request credit information late in the selling season or creditors become unwilling to advance credit.
- There is evidence of noncompliance with financial covenants or excessive renegotiation of broken loan covenants.
- Management cannot or will not explain unusual or complete off-balance sheet investments.

Financial Distress Models

The quantitative analysis of financial distress generally involves two statistical methods: regression and discriminant analysis. These methods are employed in predictive distress models. Regression analysis uses past data to forecast future values of dependent variables, while discriminant analysis produces an index that allows an observation to be classified into one of several a priori groupings. Bankers, auditors, management consultants, the legal profession, and a host of other users employ these database systems as important components of risk analysis and distress prediction. Of the statistical models popular today, ad hoc and otherwise, Edward Altman's Z-score model is probably the Johann Sebastian Bach of the genre.

Let's begin our study by examining the Z-score model. Altman's original data sample drew from 66 sample firms, half of which had filed for bankruptcy. All businesses in the database were manufacturers, and small firms with assets of less than $1 million were eliminated.

Altman's Z Score

The 1968 model used discriminant analysis to predict bankruptcy.[1] While the model was originally developed from samples of a closed industry environment (manufacturing), it is reported to provide a very high distress predictive confidence for up to two years prior to failure on nonmanufacturing firms as well. A number of other bankruptcy predictors have been published with some in use, but no distress model has been so thoroughly tested and widely accepted as this one. The discriminant function Z was found to be as follows:

$$Z = 1.2X_1 + 1.4X_2 + 3.3X_3 + 0.6X_4 + 1.0X_5$$

where

X_1 = working capital/total assets (as a percentage)
X_2 = retained earnings/total assets (as a percentage)
X_3 = EBIT/total assets (as a percentage)
X_4 = market value of equity/book value of debt (as a percentage)
X_5 = sales/total assets (times)

$Z > 2.99$: classified as financially sound
$Z < 1.81$: classified as financially distressed or bankrupt

The fabric of the model lies in the predictive power of what I call the *domino-multiplier syndrome* and the *asset management syndrome*. The *domino-multiplier syndrome* holds for high (operating) leverage firms engaged in the production of goods. A high degree of operating leverage implies that a relatively small change in sales results in a large change in net operating income. For example, airlines operate with high operating leverage, requiring seating in excess of a break-even load factor to cover fixed costs. Similarly, firms borrowing to

---

[1] *Journal of Finance,* September 1968.

expand their fixed asset base run the risk of not being able to cover fixed over-head if sales unexpectedly drop. The domino effect is propagated by large capi-tal expenditures followed by disappointing sales. Therefore, lenders should be extra cautious financing high operating leveraged borrowers unless convinced healthy *projected* sales will end up to be healthy *actual* sales. Stress testing by developing worst-case projections to establish that borrowers can safely with-stand recessions or sharp sales reductions is a must, particularly for lower rated credits.

The asset management syndrome implicit in the Z score clearly reveals that borrowers go bankrupt if assets such as inventory, receivables, and equipment grow out of control. Notice that total assets show up in the denominator of four out of five Z-score variables. It's clear that distressed companies hold too many assets on their balance sheets, well out of proportion with operating require-ments. The serious impact of redundant assets is brought out in sustainable growth rates as well. Sustainable growth mathematics and Altman's Z score link for this reason alone. The sustainable growth rate (see the discussion of the sus-tainable growth model in Chapter 8) compares a company's growth rate with its targeted growth rate to determine if the capital structure and growth are in equi-librium. Recall from Chapter 8, "Risk Management and Sustainable Growth," that the sustainable growth rate is defined thus:

$$g^* = \Delta S/S = \frac{P\,(1-d)\,(1+L)}{A/S - P\,(1-d)\,(1+L)}$$

F = Cumulative financial needs
A_1 = Projected spontaneous assets
S = Projected sales
ΔS = Change in sales
ΔNFA = Change in net fixed assets
L_1 = Spontaneous liabilities
P = Projected profit margin (%)
d = Dividend payout rate
R = Debt maturities
L = Debt-to-equity ratio e.g. leverage
R = Debt repayments
g^* = Sustainable growth rate

As implied in the denominator, if assets increase, the capital output ratio (A/S) increases, causing a decline in the sustainable growth rate. As noted in the chapter, if the sustainable growth rate drops below the targeted growth rate, the company is likely straining its capital. The relationship between assets and sales is an important benchmark of low-risk growth. It is positioned in the equation to represent the base (before profit retention) on which an appropriate and sustain-able growth rate is calculated. Recall from the previous chapter that if this rate exceeds a tolerable rate, leverage will increase rapidly. The assets-to-sales ratio is largely decided by management, as management policies give rise to asset expansion.

Let's take another look at a compelling variable in the financial needs formula (Chapter 7, "Projections and Risk Assessment"), capital output:

$$F = A_1/S\,(\Delta S) + \Delta NFA - L_1/S\,(\Delta S) - P(S + DS)(1 - d) + R$$

The A/S in the equation, which represents the net effect of low asset productivity (increased assets without a commanding increase in sales), will often lead to excessive borrowing and strained capital. Thus, cash flow, financial needs, sustainable growth, and Altman's financial distress equation are really members of the same HMO, providing similar clinical tests and offering only slightly different cures.

From this example we can readily see it is not so much the coefficients that produce Altman's Z score (though they too provide a great deal of different meaning), rather it's the model's connective attributes. Observing the operating leverage domino effect and taking each variable in order of importance, we draw the conclusions summarized in Table 9.1.

The following example depicts the income statement and balance sheet for the Specialty Group, a publicly traded manufacturer of specialty steel products. The totals presented in Exhibit I are for the year ending December 31, 2000. These abbreviated financial statements provide the data needed to use the discriminant Z function. Assume market value of equity is 109,554.

EXHIBIT I The Specialty Group

Net sales	281,242
Operating income	20,112
Current assets	114,101
Total assets	319,079
Current liabilities	73,425
Long-term debt	184,180
Deferred taxes	12,900
Common stock	47,353
Paid-in capital	100
Retained earnings	21,121
Total	319,079

Using the data in Exhibit I, the five key financial ratios required for function Z can be calculated. The Z value for the Specialty Group as of fiscal 2000 is as follows:

x_1 = working capital/total assets 12.8%
x_2 = retained earnings/total assets: 6.6%

TABLE 9.1 Comparing Z Score Variables in Terms of Importance: Relative Value of Coefficents and Domino Multiplies Syndrome

Importance: Coefficient relative values	Importance: Domino multiplier syndrome	Explanation: Domino multiplier syndrome
$3.3X_3$ EBIT/Total assets	$1.0X_5$ Sales/Total assets	Sale reductions force down the Z score. In addition, we have the beginnings of the domino effect. Sales declines also drives down x_3 (EBIT/assets) due to the negative effects of operating leverage.
$1.4X_2$ Retained earnings/ Total assets	$3.3X_3$ EBIT/Total assets	A drop in x_3 (EBIT/assets) knocks over a domino by driving down $1.4x_2$ (retained earnings/assets) as losses flow through.
$1.2X_1$ Working capital/ Total assets	$1.4X_2$ Retained earnings/ Total asset	Retained earnings are a component of working capital (along with increases in long-term obligations and reductions in fixed assets). Thus, x_2 (retained earnings/total assets) links to x_1 (working capital/total assets) and another domino falls.
$1.0X_5$ Sales/Total assets	$1.2X_1$ Working capital/ Total assets	What effect will our dominos have on x_4 (market value of equity/book value of debt)? Investors start dumping shares in panic selling, fearing that the firm's weak liquidity (caused by operating losses) makes it difficult or impossible to reduce debt.
$0.6X_4$ Market value of equity/Book value of debt	$0.6X_4$ Market value of equity/Book value of debt	Financial leverage reaches dangerous levels as the domino effect crosses its zenith.

x_3 = EBIT/total assets: 6.3%
x_4 = market value of equity/book value of debt: 40.59%
x_5 = sales/total assets: 88.1%

$$Z = 1.2(.1275) + 1.4(.0662) + 3.3(.0630) + .6(.4052) + .999(.8814) = 1.58$$

Recall the critical Z value is 1.81. The firm's 1.58 Z score falls below 1.81, placing it in the category of firms likely to go bankrupt. However, the firm's situation might not be as bad as the model suggests.

Can the traditional Z score be combined with traditional credit analysis? To fulfill a conceptual or intellectual objective, the answer is yes. But if the models use as part and parcel PRISM or support of credit reviews, then the answer is no. The problem with the Z-score model is industry homogeneity, as the generic 1968 Altman original was limited to a universe of manufacturers with less than $25 million in sales. Industries outside this industrial sector—financial institutions, telecommunications, service, utilities, and transportation—hardly fit the 1968 model. However, Zeta Services Inc. developed ZETA® credit scores, which enable users to appraise risk of a wide range of industries with data from financial statements yielding trends and warning signals. For companies that eventually fail, the score provides warning signs three to five years prior to bankruptcy, enabling users to take the necessary steps to reduce losses and maximize returns.

An uptrend in score signifies a company's increasing capacity to remain in business and service its debt. A downtrend may be followed by dividend cuts, asset liquidations, or bankruptcy. Zeta Services issues scores on more than 5,000 companies. The database covers most industrial publicly traded firms, service companies, and utilities. A sampling of variables include the following:

- x_1: *Return on assets*. This variable is measured by earnings before interest and taxes/total assets. It has proven significant in evaluating firm performance in several past multivariate analyses.
- x_2: *Earnings stability*. Zeta Services measures this variable by using a normalized measure of the standard error of estimate around a 10-year trend. The importance of this variable should not be surprising considering that earnings volatility and risk not only drive market returns but significantly influence bond ratings.
- x_3: *Debt service*. This variable represents the traditional interest coverage ratio.
- x_4: *Cumulative profitability*. This factor is measured by the firm's retained earnings/total assets. This ratio, which incorporates such factors as the firm's age, dividends, and profit accumulation, was found to be quite helpful in past studies.
- x_5: *Current ratio*. The famous current assets/current liabilities ratio, which tests liquidity, was found to be more informative in identifying failures.
- x_6: *Capitalization*. This is the common equity/total capitalization ratio. The updated model measures the capitalization ratio using a five-year average of market (not book) value. In addition, preferred stock is included at liquidation value.
- x_7: *Size of the business*. The firm's total tangible assets is the criterion used to measure this variable. Old, established businesses will generally be larger than new ventures, having built up their assets over extended periods of time. Statistically, newer businesses fail more rapidly than older, established ones.

---

[2] Edward I Altman, *Corporate Financial Distress and Bankruptcy,* New York: John Wiley & Sons, 1983.

Interestingly, Altman used an earlier version of the updated Zeta model, testing it against the original Z-score (1968) model:

> First, we compare the five year accuracy of each model using the particular sample of firms of each study. The newer ZETA model is far more accurate in bankruptcy classification in Years 2 through 5 with the initial year's accuracy about equal. The older model showed slightly more accurate non-bankruptcy classification in the two years when direct comparison is possible . . . the new seven variable model is, in some years, only slightly more accurate than the "old" five variable model when the data is comparable, that is, adjusted for more meaningful evaluation.[2]

Other Models

Several researchers influenced by the work of Altman (1968) on the application of discriminant analysis and explored ways to develop more reliable financial distress prediction models. Logit analysis, probit analysis, and the linear probability model are the most commonly used techniques as alternatives. Ohlson (1980) utilized the logit and probit analysis to estimate the probability of bankruptcy. The adjustments of estimation bias resulting from oversampling, such as weights based on prior probabilities in the estimation process and optimal cutoff point, are discussed in Zmijewski (1984). The problems of pooling data due to a small number of samples are addressed in Zavgren (1983).

Models that distinguish between financially distressed firms that survive and financially distressed firms that ultimately go bankrupt have been investigated as well. Sample firms were classified into bankrupt or nonbankrupt with classification probabilities estimated by the multinomial logit technique.

Wilcox, Santomero, Vinso, and others have adapted a gambler's ruin approach to bankruptcy prediction. Here, bankruptcy is probable when a company's net liquidation value becomes negative. Net liquidation value is defined as total asset liquidation value less total liabilities. From period to period, net liquidation values were increased by cash inflows and decreased by cash outflows. Wilcox combined cash inflows and outflows, defining them as "adjusted cash flow." All other things being equal, the lower the beginning net liquidation value, the smaller the company's adjusted (net) cash flow, and the larger the variation of the company's adjusted cash flow, the greater the probability of failure. Wilcox uses the gambler's ruin formula to show that a company's risk of failure is dependent on (1) the above factors plus (2) the size of the company's adjusted cash flow "at risk" each period (i.e., the size of the company's bet).

Another approach to distress prediction is founded on neural networks. Neural networks are computer systems and programs designed to process information parallel to the brain. These systems retain data in patterns and are able to learn from their processing experience.

Moody's Investors Service's RiskCalc Private Model is a Web-based program that estimates the probability that a private firm will default on a loan.

Various Industries Have Exhibited Negative Profitability Trends			
Industry	1998 to 1999 Average	1996 to 1999 Average	1994 to 1999 Average
Steel	(1237.9)%	428.6%	187.4%
Copper	(80.7)	65.5	13.2
Internet	43.2	42.7	(35.5)
Tires and rubber	(81.8)	(28.6)	12.7
Aluminum	(13.2)	13.9	156.4
Chemicals	(38.1)	(3.9)	18.4
Medical services and information systems	(48.2)	(2.5)	0.8
Property' casualty insurance	(3.9)	(2.0)	3.8
Recreational goods and services	0.5	2.5	17.1
Manufactured housing	2.5	10.4	3.3
Recreational vehicles	(9.8)	11.7	27.3
Agriculture	1.3	12.3	4.6
Wholesale trade	(8.8)	13.7	13.7
Cement and aggregates	1.2	21.6	60.5
Oilfield services and production	(373.7)	39.9	19.3
Airlines and freight	(13.2)	1085.5	666.5
All corporate people with inventory valuation and capital consumption	5.0	4.4	13.6

Source: U.S. Department of Commerce; Survey of Business Conditions.

Moody's uses a database of financial statements from 28,000 private firms and loan defaults from 1,600 private firms to isolate attributes common to distressed borrowers. A majority of private companies with $100,000 to $100 million of assets are not covered by private debt-rating firms, so there is no standard measure of their debt's risk level. There is no secondary market for that debt because without such benchmarking, securitization is impossible.

FROM RECOGNITION AND DIAGNOSIS TO CRITICIZED LOANS AND CLASSIFICATION STATUS

Financial Accounting Standards (FAS) Board Statement No. 114, "Accounting by Creditors for Impairment of a Loan," as amended by Statement No. 118, "Accounting by Creditors for Impairment of a Loan—Income Recognition and Disclosures," sets forth standards for estimating the impairment of a loan for general financial reporting purposes.[3] Regulators are instructed to follow FAS 114 *to the letter* in assessing the portion of the allowance for loan and lease losses, established for impaired loans in determining the amount of capital impairment (if any) and adequacy of the loan loss allowance. FAS 114, as amended by FAS 118 with regard to income recognition, establishes generally accepted accounting principles (GAAP) for use by banking organizations and other creditors when accounting for the impairment of certain loans.

According to FAS 114, a loan is "impaired" when, based on current information and events, it is probable that a creditor will be unable to collect all amounts due (principal and interest) according to the contractual terms of the loan agreement. The purpose of a loan review is, of course, to identify troubled loans, document findings, update credit grades, and, when necessary, criticize or classify exposures. Loan review includes discussing degrees of risk along with the likelihood of reorganization/liquidation with higher-level lenders including those assigned to workout areas and in-house attorneys. The worst thing a banker can do is to bury problems under the rug. Criticized assets fall into four categories.[4]

Special Mentioned Loans

Loans in this category are inherently weak. The Federal Reserve Bank (FRB) defines these exposures as to constitute an "undue and unwarranted" credit risk but not to the point of justifying a classification of substandard. Credit risks may be relatively minor yet may involve unwarranted risk. Credits may represent exposures the bank may be unable to properly supervise due to an inadequate loan agreement. In addition, they may include the poor condition or control over collateral and failure to obtain proper documentation or form other deviations apart from prudent lending practices. Future economic or market conditions may produce an adverse operating trend or cause imbalanced positions on balance sheets but will likely not reach a point where collateral liquidation is jeopardized.

Loans secured by assets carry certain risks, but to criticize these loans, it must be evident that risks are increased beyond a point where otherwise the original loan would not have been granted (e.g., crossing a credit grade threshold). Rapid increases in receivables, for example, without the bank knowing causative

---

[3] FAS 114 is effective for fiscal years beginning after December 15, 1994, and earlier application was permitted. FAS 118 is effective concurrently with FAS 114.

[4] *FRB Commercial Bank Examination Manual 1995,* Section 2060.1; Accounting, Reporting, and Disclosure Issues—Nonaccrual Loans and Restructured Debt Section 2065.1. Interagency policy statements and guidance, issued on March 1, 1991; March 10, 1993; and June 10, 1993, clarified supervisory policies regarding nonaccrual assets, restructured loans, and collateral valuation; SR-95-38; the reporting instructions for the bank call report and the FR-Y-9C, the consolidated bank holding company report; Division of Banking Supervision and Regulation SR 99-24 (SUP) September 29, 1999—Subject: Loan Write-Up Standards for Assets Criticized During Examinations.

factors, concentrations lacking proper credit support, lack of on-site audits, or other similar matters could lead auditors to rate the loan as a special mention. Assets in which actual, not potential, weaknesses are both evident and significant are likely candidates for more serious criticism.

A notable exception exists: an additional allowance on impaired loans may be necessary based on consideration of institution-specific factors, such as historical loss experience compared with estimates of such losses and concerns about the reliability of cash flow estimates, the quality of an institution's loan review function, and controls over its process for estimating its FAS 114 allowance.

Substandard Assets[5]

A substandard asset is inadequately protected by the obligor's financial condition or collateral pledged. Assets so classified must have well-defined weaknesses that jeopardize liquidation of the debt. They are characterized by the distinct possibility that the bank will sustain some loss if deficiencies are not corrected. Loss potential, while existing in the aggregate amount of substandard assets, does not have to exist in individual assets classified as substandard.

Doubtful Assets

An asset classified as doubtful has all the weaknesses inherent in one classified substandard with the added characteristic that weaknesses make collection or liquidation in full highly questionable. In some cases, auditors will determine a reasonable carrying value for a distressed asset and request a write-down through a charge to the loan loss reserve or a charge to the operating expenses, or they may look for an additional capital allocation. In addition, any portion of loan balances on collateral dependent loans exceeding the fair market value of the collateral and that can be identified as uncollectible is generally classified as a loss and promptly charged off.

Although the possibility of loss is extremely high, certain important factors may work to strengthen the credit and defer the downgrade classification to estimated loss at least temporarily. The borrower may be in the process of restructuring, an acquisition may be likely, capital injections forthcoming, or the bank may be in a position to obtain additional collateral.

Collateral-dependent loans are structured whereby repayment is predicated solely on the value of underlying collateral (no other reliable sources of repayment are available). Regulators do not automatically require additional allowances for credit losses for impaired loans over and above what is required on these loans under FAS 114. In addition, a collateralized loan that becomes

---

[5] See also Chapter 19, "Risk Rating Models: Design and Application."

impaired is not considered "collateral dependent" if repayment is available from reliable sources other than the collateral. Thus, any impairment on such a loan may, at the bank's option, be determined based on the present value of the expected future cash flows discounted at the loan's effective interest rate or, as a practical expedient, on the loan's observable market price.

Loss Assets

Banks are required to promptly charge off identified losses. Loans classified as losses are considered uncollectible and of such little value that their continuance as bankable assets is not warranted. This classification does not mean that the asset has absolutely no recovery or salvage value, but rather it is not practical or desirable to defer writing off what is clearly appraised as basically worthless. Losses are taken in periods this classification is acknowledged.

Partially Charged-Off Loans[6]

Exposures may have well-defined weaknesses that jeopardize collection in full, but a portion may be reasonably expected to be collected. When the bank has taken a charge-off in an amount sufficient that the remaining balance is being serviced and reasonably assured of collection—for example, with loans secured by readily marketable collateral—there may be no need to write down the remaining exposure.

A Word or Two on Income Recognition

FAS 118 amended FAS 114 to eliminate its income recognition provisions; thus, no FASB standard exists for income recognition on impaired loans. Since full collection of principal and interest is generally not expected for impaired loans, income accrual should normally be discontinued on such loans at the time they first become impaired.

The Classified Loan Write-up

Bank examiners file reports on classified exposures. These write-ups are often a lender's moment of truth, providing detail (as specified in the following list) sufficient to support a bank (or auditor's) classification.[7]

1. A general description of the obligation:
   a. Amount of exposure (both outstanding and contingent or undrawn)
   b. Location of obligor and type of business or occupation

---

[6] *FRB Commercial Bank Examination Manual* 1995, Section 2060.
[7] FRB memos and reports.

2. Description and value of collateral
3. Notation if the borrower is an insider or a related interest of an insider
4. Guarantors and a brief description of their ability to act as a source of repayment, especially if their financial strength has changed significantly since the initial guarantee of the credit facility
5. Amounts previously classified
6. Repayment terms and historical performance, including prior charge-offs, and current delinquency status
7. A summary listing of weaknesses resulting in classification or special-mention treatment
8. A reference to any identified deficiencies dealing with loan administration or violation comments elsewhere in the report
9. If management disagrees with the classification, a statement to that effect along with management's rationale
10. A concise description of management action taken or planned to address weakness in the exposure

FROM CLASSIFICATION STATUS TO WORKOUT

The goals of workout are twofold: to explain why the credit is not performing as agreed and to develop an analytical foundation for thinking about solutions to the problem. Generally, two choices are open to workout: loan restructuring or liquidation. We shall examine these alternatives more fully in the next section. For now, we assume a "go ahead" mode aimed at loan restructuring so the concepts might be developed more succinctly.

Loan problems, spotted both through monitoring systems like risk grading or by "traditional" PRISM analysis, should be summarily classified (as defined in the previous sections) and forwarded to loan workout. While line bankers know the borrower better than anyone at the bank, the workout department has more experience solving credit problems. Members of the workout department make decisions fast, usually without conferring with other departments (the legal department being the notable exception). The objective of the workout group is to correct problems that can be corrected and return the company to a traditional banking relationship. If that's infeasible, then the workout department's secondary objective is to maximize the potential for the ultimate collection of outstandings. The actions taken in this regard, if accomplished in a way consistent with prudent lending principles, can improve prospects for collection.

When a loan is transferred to the workout group, the relationship officer and workout officer meet to review all information dealing with the relationship. After reviewing the file, the workout officer schedules a meeting with the borrower and relationship officer. Legal counsel may also be present. The purpose of the meeting is to define the specific role of the workout group and its interaction with the borrower. The borrower will be informed that the new account officer is the workout officer.

The workout officer notes any additional sources of repayment or collateral that could be available from the customer. Arrangements are made for the workout banker to visit the company as soon as possible. Sound workout programs begin with full disclosure of relevant information and are based on a realistic evaluation of the abilities of both the borrower and the workout group to resolve problems. The workout officer and borrower should agree on the strategy aimed at resolving financial and operating problems, the course of which starts with a series of rhetorical questions:

1. Are 90-day cash budgets positive or negative?
2. Will the firm be able to extend trade terms?
3. Can the company file for an expedited tax refund to provide a quick injection of cash?
4. Can outside consultants be of assistance (accountants, investment bankers, turnaround specialists, outside counsel)?
5. Are there other sources of cash (e.g., guarantors, new equity)?
6. Is the company or any part of it viable, so that restructuring is a viable alternative?
7. Does the firm plan alternative legal moves that would prevent restructuring?
8. If a move isn't made quickly, will the delay cause a partial or full dissipation of assets, actions by other creditors, or increased carrying costs for the bank?
9. How should the bank treat new loans (new money)? Do advances enhance collateral value?
9. Is there a plan to repay new money within a reasonable time frame, and will a portion of the imbedded debt be repaid with it?
10. Will new money be LIFO and senior to embedded debt (a rule of thumb is that new money should not exceed one-third of embedded debt)?

Follow-up Procedures and Documentation

Obtain a Properly Signed Note

Obtaining a properly signed note, checked against borrowing resolutions, is essential to preserving the bank's position. It is also a good idea to make a copy of the note since the distressed borrower may claim there was never a properly executed note to begin with.

Review Subordination Agreements

One of the worst things that can happen to a lender is finding out that the subordination agreement executed by the principals has expired when it's most needed. This occurs when the documentation is not specific to continuing the subordination agreement past the cleanup period. In one case, the borrower signed a subordination agreement explicitly stating that the $1,000,000 lent to the business by the principles would not be paid until the loan was retired. The borrower cleaned up the $500,000 outstanding loan for one day, immediately signed a new note for the same amount, and withdrew the $1,000,000 falling under the subordination agreement. This action stripped the firm of underlying equity, causing it to go bankrupt shortly thereafter. The banker simply "forgot" to obtain a new subordination, when the loan rolled over.

Maintain a Complete Credit File

Workout officers will refer to memorandums of past meetings with borrowers, loan offering proposals, visits to companies, analyses of financial information, and ongoing records of due diligence and follow-up. It should be stressed that the loan officer's documentation in the file details both the original transaction and subsequent renewals. It is important, after learning that the financial condition has deteriorated, for the loan officer to write up credit file memos spelling out exactly what the bank officer's perception of the deterioration was along with a planned course of action. If the loan represents an initial transaction or renewal, the banker should write out who requested the loan, the individual's position in the company (making sure proper authorizations specified in the corporate resolution are in place and on file at the bank), and *if the guarantor, if any, approved it in writing*. The officer should also indicate who completed the signing of the note, the guarantee, the collateral, and the date.

The workout area requires complete and objective credit files to develop insight into projection assumptions, cash flows, and cash budgets, and if the borrower is a public firm, records of rating downgrades from agencies. It is not uncommon for financially distressed borrowers to inflate reality in order to appease the relationship manager and the workout group.

Make Sure Guarantees Are in Order and Completely Understood

The guarantor must have both the financial capacity and the willingness to provide support for the credit. Also, the nature of the guarantee should be worded so it provides support for repayment, in whole or in part, during the loan tenure. In addition, guarantees must be unconditional, uncontested, and legally enforceable. In a distress situation, the bank must have sufficient information in the credit file to support the guarantor's financial condition, liquidity, cash flow, contingent liabilities, and other relevant factors (including credit ratings, when available).

The bank will also note the number and amount of guarantees extended by a guarantor to determine if the guarantor has the financial capacity to fulfill the contingent claims that exist. If the guarantor was called on in the past to honor the agreement, information dealing with its ability and willingness to fulfill previous obligations should be available. In this case, the bank will note whether a previously required performance under a guarantee agreement was voluntary or the result of legal or other actions taken by the lender to enforce the guarantee.

Uniform Commercial Code (UCC) Filings

UCC filings should be reviewed to ensure that they have been properly filed and are up to date. In one case, the borrower gave the bank a security interest in receivables. The borrower asked the bank not to record the lien for 45 days. The account officer foolishly agreed, and the firm went bankrupt shortly thereafter. The failure to file a properly recorded lien caused the bank to lose its lien status in Chapter 7 bankruptcy proceedings.

The lender should check for the following unencumbered assets:

1. Accounts receivable
2. Inventory (placing liens can scare off trade credit)
3. Fixed assets (Do they offer equity value?)
4. Patents, trademarks, intellectual property
5. Stock of a subsidiary that is relatively debt free

Likewise, the lender should check that proper documentation for all collateral is in order:

1. Security agreements
2. Mortgages
3. Financing statements (UCCs)
4. Stock/bond powers
5. Federal filings (aircraft, intellectual property)

Because of the need for immediate and often tough action, the loan workout officer should not be unreasonably limited by committee and staff approvals. An open and frank relationship with the customer is of utmost importance at this point. Both relationship and workout officers should let the customer know how the situation is viewed and the actions he or she feels are necessary. Customers should be encouraged to be equally open and frank. The loan workout period is not the time to make enemies, as the disagreeable alternative might be a lender liability suit. We'll look at this possibility next, and offer a few pointers on how to avoid this hornet's nest.[8]

A Lender's Liability Help Line

The litigious nature of American society, coupled with the tenuous condition of many sectors of the country's economy, have combined to result in a plethora of liability suits against creditors. As shown in Appendix 1, these suits find their basis in imaginative uses of traditional state common law and federal statutory law. Of course, many defenses are available to lenders within this same body of law. Nevertheless, there is no substitute, legal or otherwise, for ordinary common sense on the part of lenders.

---

[8] Discussed more fully in Appendix 1.

Lenders can avert lawsuits, or mitigate their effects, if they follow a few basic, precautionary steps. These steps include avoiding any types of oral understandings with borrowers that are not in the loan documentation, avoiding any intrusion by the lender into the day-to-day operation of the borrower's business, avoiding any act or conduct that might lend support to a legal claim of malice or ill will, and giving to borrowers as much advance written notice as possible should the lender decide to terminate a loan or refuse further credit.[9] The proliferation of actions against lenders only underscores how important it is for lenders to use guidelines such as these (and those prescribed elsewhere in the chapter) and follow the basic precepts of caution and common sense in their lending and workout policies.

We offer a brief introduction to lender's liability, along with a few "pearls of wisdom." An old friend, Phil Z., an executive in the loan workout section of a major bank, compiled "A Lender Liability Help Line." Phil's colorful, direct manner has been left intact, and he'll be the first to assert that no guide can replace the sound advice of legal counsel.

Lender Liability Help Line: A Compliance List of Questions

Compliance with Agreements

1. Did the lender act in full compliance with the express terms of the documents governing the loans?
2. Were the terms of the document modified or waived by the subsequent writings, statements, or conduct?
3. Do loan documents unambiguously give the lender the right to terminate funding or to demand payments? Is this right consistent with the other terms of the loan?
4. Did the borrower breach any of the contractual covenants or conditions contained in the documents?
5. If so, can the breach be established by objective criteria?

Compliance with Duty of Good Faith and Fair Dealing

1. Assuming the lender terminated funding, did the lender give the borrower reasonable notice of its intent?
2. Was the borrower afforded a reasonable opportunity to obtain alternative financing?
3. Was the lender's action supported by objective criteria?
4. Was the lender's action consistent with its institutional policies for terminating funding?

---

[9] Granoff, "Emerging Theories of Lender Liability: Flawed Applications of Old Concepts," 104 *Bank. L. Journ.* **492**, 51315 (1987).

5. Did the lender cause the borrower to believe that additional funds would be forthcoming? Did the borrower act in reasonable reliance and to its determent on the anticipated financing?
6. Has a relationship of trust or confidence been established between the lender and borrower? Did the lender routinely offer advice or suggestions to the borrower? Is there a disparity of sophistication or bargaining power between the parties?

Domination and Control

1. If the terms of the loan give the lender broad power with respect to management and operations of the debtor, did the lender actually exercise such control in an improper fashion?
2. Has the lender's involvement merely consisted of its legitimate right to monitor the debtor's business and to collect its debt or has the lender, in effect, been running the debtor's operations?
3. Is the lender actively participating in the day-to-day management of the business or does the lender merely possess "veto power" over certain business decisions?
4. Is the lender the sole or primary source of credit for the borrower?
5. Did the lender wrongfully use threats in an attempt to control the borrower's conduct?
6. Does the lender have control over a substantial amount of the debtor's stock?
7. Do all factors indicative of control, taken together, constitute sufficient control to rise to the level of domination for the purpose of the instrumentality rule or the doctrine of equitable subordination?
8. If so, can the lender satisfy the higher standard of care required of fiduciaries?

Minimizing the Risk of Lawsuits

The lender should take the following steps to reduce the risk of a lawsuit:

1. Prepare memos to the file properly, leaving out epithets, vulgarisms, threats.
2. Make sure any deal struck is clearly understood by the parties, avoiding side agreements and oral "explications," if possible. It can be helpful to write a self-serving memo to the file, outlining the specifics.
3. Use appropriate documentation, reflective of the actual transaction.
4. Avoid the imposition of excessively harsh terms not intended for use (such as waiver of jury trial or management control provisions).
5. Review the bank's loan manuals and the borrower's credit evaluations, remembering either or both may be read to the jury.

6. Avoid personality conflict, immediately removing officers who could be accused of acting prejudicially or unfairly.
7. Pack up your troubles in an old kit bag, and leave them with the attorneys.

When the lender does find a problem loan, he or she should take the following steps before it's too late:

1. Review the file for all the facts.
2. Audit all loan documents.
3. Interview all the personnel involved.
4. Assess your borrower's motivation to settle rather than to sue.
5. Look for enforcement alternatives to filing a lawsuit. Will giving a little in a restructure gain a lot, such as collateral, new guarantees, or time to overcome adverse courses of conduct?
6. Review all waivers the bank might possibly have given, whether in writing or orally.
7. Provide ample notice of bank action (including demand, setoff), when that is at all practical. If working toward deadlines, make sure they are clearly understood by the borrower. Put them in writing if possible. When the deadlines are extended or modified, a written notice to the borrower should detail the new terms and conditions now applicable.
8. Work with good attorneys, called in as soon as practicable. Reliance on the advice of counsel may demonstrate good faith, adding to your chances of a successful defense.
9. Never sue for small sums or for spite. Consider the advisability of suing when the borrower can't pay.
10. Always be businesslike by avoiding abusive language, harshness, and table pounding.
11. Management changes can be effected, when necessary, but they require care to accomplish without liability.
12. Let the borrower and its advisers be the source of business plans, not the bank.
13. Finally, after making the climb up Loan Workout Mountain, you'll receive the Ten Commandments of the Workout Cycle.

The Ten Commandments of the Workout Cycle

1. Thou shalt watch for early warning signs of trouble.
2. Thou shalt get all of the facts.
3. Thou shalt bring a workout specialist to conduct the workout negotiations.
4. Thou shalt not waive any rights.
5. Thou shalt look at all of the alternatives prior to commencing workout discussions.

6. Thou shalt always look at both sides of the issue.
7. Thou shalt involve as many people as possible in workout discussions.
8. Thou shalt be honest.
9. Thou shalt not be arrogant.
10. Thou shalt take what you can get.

Loan Restructuring: A Workout Decision

For a formally restructured loan, focus is on the ability of the borrower to repay the loan vis-à-vis any modified terms. Classification follows a formally restructured loan if, after restructuring, weaknesses occur that threaten to jeopardize repayment set by modified terms. Clearly, a period of sustained performance is important in determining whether reasonable assurance of repayment exists. Due diligence might reveal an improvement in the borrower's condition that increase the chances of repayment. The borrower might win a sizable contract that significantly improves cash flow, financial leverage, and debt-service coverage. The loan may return to an accrual status (from a restructured basis), reasonably ensuring full repayment.

Regulatory reporting rules and GAAP do not require a banking organization that restructures a loan to grant excessive concessions, forgive principal, or take other steps not commensurate with the borrower's ability to repay in order to use the reporting treatment specified in Statement of Financial Accounting (SFAS) No. 15. Furthermore, the restructured terms may include prudent contingent payment provisions that permit an institution to obtain appropriate recovery of concessions granted in the restructuring, if the borrower's condition substantially improves.

FROM WORKOUT TO THE COURTS

Financial distress or default on some provision in the debt contract triggers the renegotiation of the firm's financial contracts. Bankruptcy law dictates the environment by which banks and other claimants bargain over the firm's assets. By imposing a particular structure on the bargaining between the claimants, bankruptcy law has a major effect on the outcome of renegotiations. Therefore, in examining bankruptcy law, we consider how the structure of the bargaining environment affects the outcome of renegotiations.

Chapter 11 Reorganization

Chapter 11 is the principal reorganization chapter of the Bankruptcy Code. It permits a borrower to be protected by the bankruptcy court while the firm tries to restructure. The formulation of a plan of reorganization is the principal purpose of a Chapter 11 case. The petition includes a list of assets and liabilities, and a detailed statement outlining current financial affairs along with financial and operating plans including the means for satisfying claims against and interest in the debtor—prior history and cause of the filing, assets and liabilities, income and expenses, treatment of creditors, liquidation analysis, projections of earn-

Retail and apparel companies that have filed Chapter 11 since 1992 with more than $50 million in liabilities upon their date of filing

Company	Date of filing	Status today
Macy (R.H.) & Co.	January 27, 1992	Acquired by Federated Department Stores an 12/19/94
* Leslie Fay Cos. Inc.	April 5, 1993	Emerged 6/4/97
Merry-Go-Round Ent.	January 11, 1994	Converted to Ch. 7, 3/1/96
Clothestime Inc.	December 8, 1995	Emerged 9/28/97
Lamonts Apparel Inc.	January 6, 1995	Emerged 1/31/98
Bradlees Inc.	June 24, 1999	Chapter 11
* Bidermann industries USA	July 17, 1995	Chapter 11
Caldor Corp.	September 18, 1995	Chapter 11
Petrie Retail Inc.	October 12, 1995	Chapter 11
Elder Beeman Stores	October 18, 1999	Emerged 12/30/97
Edison Brothers Stores	November 3, 1995	Emerged 9/26/97
Rickel Home Centers Inc.	January 10, 1996	Chapter 11
Color Tile	January 24, 1996	Chapter 11
Today's Man Inc.	February 2, 1996	Emerged 12/31/97
Lillie Rubin Affiliates	February 2, 1996	Acquired by Asher Fernsterheim
Rich's Department Stores	March 13, 1996	Converted to Ch. 7, 4/8/97
Braun's Fashions Corp.	July 2, 1996	Emerged 12/2/96
Barney's bar.	October 1, 1996	Chapter 11
County Seat Inc.	October 17, 1996	Emerged 10/1/97
* Buster Brown Apparel	November 25, 1996	Chapter 11
Strawberries Inc.	February 19, 1997	Chapter 11
Silas Creek Retail L.P.	June 11, 1997	Chapter 11
Montgomery Word	July 7, 1997	Chapter 11
Maidenform Worldwide Inc.	July 22, 1997	Chapter 11
Levitz Furniture Inc.	September 5, 1997	Chapter 11
Decorative Home Accents	September 29, 1997	Chapter 11
Wiz Inc.	December 16, 1997	Chapter 11
HomePlace Stores	January 5, 1998	Chapter 11
LA Geer Inc.	January 13, 1998	Chapter 11
Venture Stores Inc.	January 20, 1998	Chapter 11

* Apparel manufacturers

Source: Federal Filings Inc., a Dow Jones company

ings, tax consequences, and discussion of options. If it cannot formulate such a plan, the business may be forced into Chapter 7 liquidation.

The filing of a Chapter 11 petition also triggers the provisions of Section 362 of the Bankruptcy Code. Section 362 provides for an automatic stay of all attempts to collect prepetition claims from the debtor or otherwise interfere with the debtor's property or business. The plan also sets forth certain obligations that can be impaired or forgiven to allow the business to continue operations. Taxes, delinquent rent, mortgage arrearage, and so forth can be paid out over a period of time, usually five or six years, in order to improve the cash flow of the business.

The commencement of a Chapter 11 case creates an estate comprising all the legal and equitable interests of the debtor in property as of the date the petition is filed. Sections 1101, 1107, and 1108 provide that a debtor may continue to operate the debtor's business as a "debtor in possession" unless the Bankruptcy Court orders the appointment of a trustee. The debtors remain in possession of their property and continue to operate the business. A creditor's committee made up of the largest unsecured creditors may be appointed to provide additional input into the reorganization process.

Priority claims, including recent tax claims, are required to be paid in full, plus interest. Secured claims are required to be paid in full, also with interest. Unsecured nonpriority claims are required to be paid a dividend at least equal to that which they would receive if it were a Chapter 7 filing. Within these limits, there are an almost infinite variety of Chapter 11 plans, each based on the debtor's own financial situation.

Debtor-In-Possession Financing

In most cases, debtor-in-possession (DIP) financing is considered attractive because it is done only under order of the bankruptcy court, which is empowered by the Bankruptcy Code to afford the lender a lien on property of the bankruptcy estate or a priority position. The firm may possess receivables and other assets, which can be used as security for financing. Possibilities include receivable-backed lines of credit, factoring, equipment loans, inventory loans, and purchase order financing.

Conditions include (1) the obligor must have qualified commercial accounts receivable or other assets (e.g., prepetition), (2) the lender must have a first security position, and (3) the lender must file a post-petition, thereby gaining permission from the court to finance the assets (usually accounts receivable). As an example, the following services were offered by one financing source:[10]

- A continuous source of working capital during reorganization to enable a company to fill purchase orders, expand, and accelerate production

---

[10] The author would like to thank 1st National Assistance Finance Association for supplying a list of its services.

- A verified source of funding for suppliers, thus maintaining supply support throughout the reorganization
- A positive credit relationship with a financial institution, which could be utilized as a bridge to bank financing
- An accounts receivable management service
- Help in implementing a plan for reorganization

DEVELOPING A DIP ANALYSIS: THE DUE DILIGENCE PROCESS OF A LEADING COMMERCIAL FINANCE INSTITUTION[11]

1. Determine why the company is filing for Chapter 11.
   a. Overleverage only (i.e., Allied Stores).
   b. Operating performance problems.
   c. Lawsuits (Texaco, Manville).
   d. To get out of leases or contracts (Ames, Columbia Gas).
   e. Lack of alternative financing to buy inventory.
2. Evaluate depth and quality of management.
   a. Does management have the capacity and depth to focus on bankruptcy issues while ensuring that the management of the core business does not suffer?
3. Determine viability of the business.
   a. Will the negative publicity associated with the bankruptcy affect the company's operating performance?
   b. Will the borrower be able to emerge from Chapter 11?
   c. Asset values will be maximized if the company is a going concern; as a result there is less risk to a DIP lender.
4. Review the firm's prepetition liabilities.
   a. Review the most recent historical balance sheet.
   b. Determine secured and unsecured liabilities.
   c. If prepetition liabilities are unsecured, then interest will not have to be paid in Chapter 11.
   d. If prepetition liabilities are secured, interest may have to be paid during the Chapter 11 period.
5. Review of the company's prepetition assets.
   a. Look at most recent historical assets.
   b. Determine which assets are subject to a lien (encumbered) and which are not subject to a lien (unencumbered).
   c. If the asset is subject to a lien, the DIP lender will not realize the benefits of its super-priority status on this asset.

---

[11] Developed with the author when the author was providing seminars on the parent bank's behalf. Given with permission.

d. If the asset is not subject to a lien, the DIP lender will realize the benefits of its super-priority status in this asset.

   i. The single most important ingredient in evaluating whether DIP financing is feasible is the determination of the level of the debtor's unencumbered assets. To the extent that a substantial portion of the company's assets have not previously been pledged and that the lender designs a prudent borrowing base against the assets, the risks will be minimized. Highly liquid assets such as inventory and accounts receivable are preferred to assets such as real estate or equipment.

6. Analyze the company's projections.

   a. Detailed projections of earnings and balance sheet flows are necessary to develop month-by-month cash flow projections. Such projections will estimate borrowing needs and assets that will be available to support outstandings at any point in time.

      i. For a retailer, key assumptions include revenues, cash expenses, availability of credit from suppliers, inventory required to support sales levels, and capital expenditures.

   b. Reconstruct the balance sheet.

      i. Due to the automatic stay, which prohibits the payment of principal on all prepetition debt, all prepetition debt gives the appearance of equity and is renamed "liabilities subject to Chapter 11."

         1. This new liability account improves all leverage and tangible net worth covenants.

         2. Only true or live liabilities on the balance sheet are disclosed. Include the DIP financing line, all newly created administrative expenses (post-petition accounts payable), and prepetition secured debt that is getting interest in Chapter 11.

   c. Reconstruct the income statement.

      i. Develop a pro forma (what-if) statement from the previous year's performance and eliminate interest paid on prepetition debt, which no longer has to be paid.

      ii. Pro forma the previous year's statement and eliminate leases and contract obligations that were paid during the previous year but have now been rejected as a result of debtors rights in Chapter 11.

      iii. Include as a reduction to earnings extra expenses associated with the bankruptcy.

   d. Analyze collateral and liquidation.

      i. Determine which collateral is unencumbered and accrues to the benefit of the DIP lender (remember that liquid assets, inventory and accounts receivable, are preferred).

   e. Estimate the liquidation value of collateral.
- i. Compare this worst-case liquidation analysis to the amount of DIP financing required at any point in time.
- ii. The DIP loan should never be greater than a worst-case liquidation analysis of the available collateral.
- iii. A borrowing base will be computed based on a discount to the worst-case liquidation value of the asset.
- iv. In all retail situations it is important to determine the proceeds that could be realized (after expenses of a liquidation) in a going-out-of-business sale.
- v. It is important for the lender to hire consultants to determine the liquidation values of the asset in question.

   f. Audit the company's systems integrity.
- i. Review the company's control and monitoring systems and perform a quality audit of inventory and receivables.
- ii. It is important that the company's reporting is reliable and accurate because borrowing bases are generated off these reports.
- iii. For accounts receivable, the lender should be concerned with total outstandings, past-due accounts, and overall credit quality.
- iv. For inventory, the lender should be concerned with inventory mix, age, price points, gross margin, discounting practices, and shrink history.

Repayment of the DIP Loan

There are generally four ways for a lender to be repaid:

1. Cash flow from operations.
2. Liquidation of the collateral.
   - a. If the entity is no longer viable, a liquidation of the collateral will occur.
   - b. The bankrupt company will now be converted from a Chapter 11 proceeding to a Chapter 7 proceeding, in which the court presides over the liquidation of the company.
   - c. The DIP lender, with its super-priority status, will have first claim on the proceeds of the unencumbered assets.
   - d. If the borrowing base was conservative (as it should be), the DIP lender will be repaid in full.
3. The company emerges from bankruptcy and a new lender refinances the DIP loan.
   - a. The company emerges by filing for reorganization with the court.
   - b. This plan is voted on by the creditors.
   - c. After a negotiated settlement, creditors receive compensation for their claims.

d. The amount of settlement for each class of creditor depends on the priorities of their respective claims (i.e., senior secured debt may be repaid in full while senior subordinated debt may receive nothing).

e. It should be a condition in the DIP loan agreement that the DIP lender be paid in full before the courts will confirm any plan of reorganization.

4. Refinance of DIP loan by a new DIP lender.

Attributes of Firms While in Bankruptcy

1. Cash buildup

    a. In the year following bankruptcy, companies tend to generate large amounts of cash if the filing was due to overleverage of their balance sheets.

    b. The result of this buildup is due to most prepetition interest and debt service not having to be repaid.

    c. Another reason cash builds is due to working capital reductions as the company rationalizes its operations through the sale of noncore assets and or closing of marginal or unprofitable lines of businesses.

2. Trade support

    a. At the time of the bankruptcy filing, accounts payable and most accruals go to zero, with the former balances in these accounts reclassified as prepetition liabilities.

    b. Due to the administrative expense status of shipments made to a company after it files for Chapter 11, most companies have been able to obtain some trade support after the filing.

    c. For large bankrupt companies, quite often these companies are the vendors' best customer. The company retains significant buying power in bankruptcy because it is difficult for the supplier to quickly replace such a large customer.

Exhibit II shows the balance sheets of XYZ Corporation as recorded the day before filing for Chapter 11, the day after filing for Chapter 11, and one year after filing for Chapter 11.

EXHIBIT II   **Balance sheet of XYZ Corporation the day before filing Chapter XI, the day after filing, and one year after filing; Balance Sheets for XYZ Corporation Effects of a Bankruptcy Filing**

Balance sheet accounts in millions	Last day before filing	First day after filing	One year after filing	Change
Cash and equivalents	100	100	475	375

Accounts receivable, net	600	600	640	40
Inventories	900	900	800	(100)
Other current assets	80	80	110	30
Total current assets	*1,680*	*1,680*	*2,025*	*345*
Property plant and equipment	1,530	1,530	1,200	(330)
Other assets	80	80	55	(25)
Total assets	**3,290**	**3,290**	**3,280**	**(10)**
Accounts payables	550	0	245	245
Accruals	300	0	115	115
Current maturities of long-term debt	800	0	*0*	0
Other current liabilities	80	7	20	13
Total current liabilities	*1,730*	*7*	*380*	*373*
				0
Prepetition liabilities, frozen	0	2,983	2,983	0
Long-term debt	1,110	0	0	0
Long-term liabilities	*150*	*0*	*0*	*0*
Total liabilities	**2,990**	**2,990**	**3,363**	**373**
Shareholders' equity	300	300	(83)	(383)
Total liabilities and equity	**3,290**	**3,290**	**3,280**	**(10)**

Balance sheet trends	**XYZ Corporation**
Balance sheet account	**Explanation**
Assets	
Cash (1)	Builds
Other current assets	Largely unaffected by the bankruptcy
Long-term assets	May fall due to asset sales and rationalization of business
Liabilities	
Accounts payable	Only those payables incurred after the Chapter 11 filing
Accruals	Only those accruals incurred after the Chapter 11 filing
Total current liabilities (2)	Falls
Pre-petition liabilities (3)	Frozen
Long term liabilities	No new long-term liabilities are contemplated and would need court approval

1. Cash will build because
    a. All prepetition accounts payable are frozen.
    b. Most prepetition accruals are frozen.
    c. All unsecured liabilities are frozen so that no interest is paid.

2. Total current liabilities will fall because
   a. Only those current liabilities incurred after filing are included here.
3. Prepetition liabilities include
   a. Prepetition accounts payable
   b. Prepetition accruals
   c. Other prepetition unsecured liabilities
   d. Secured liabilities that are not secured by hard assets (which could include credit facilities secured by the stock of operating subsidiaries).

Examples of Recent Debtor in Possession Approvals[12]

Vencor Inc. Chapter 11: September 13, 1999

The U.S. Bankruptcy Court approved Vencor Inc.'s motion for an amendment to the company's debtor-in-possession financing to extend its maturity until October 31, 2000. The amendment also revised certain covenants and allowed the company to file its plan of reorganization through October 31, 2000. The court approved an amendment to the commitment letter among the company and certain DIP lenders to extend the date by which court approval must be obtained for the commitment letter to be effective through October 31, 2000.

AmeriServe Food Distribution Inc. Chapter 11: January 31, 2000

The U.S. Bankruptcy Court approved AmeriServe Food Distribution Inc.'s motion to enter into an information technology transition funding agreement with McLane Company Inc. and as well as an H-1B Visa transfer letter agreement with McLane Company Inc. The court also approved the company's motion to implement a transition plan and enter into a transitional funding agreement with Tricon Global Restaurants Inc. and McLane Company Inc. In a related order, the court approved the company's motion to extend the termination date of its post-petition debtor-in-possession financing facility. On October 4, 2000, the court approved the company's motion for an extension of its debtor-in-possession financing agreement through October 30, 2000.

Owens Corning Chapter 11: October 5, 2000

Owens Corning secured a $500 million debtor-in-possession financing commitment from Bank of America. The company also filed an emergency motion seeking a court order blocking bankruptcy lenders led by Credit Suisse First Boston from canceling the credit of the 109 affiliates that were not included in the Chapter 11 filing or from taking funds from these affiliates' accounts.

[12] New Generation Research Inc.

Factory Card Outlet Corp. Chapter 11: March 23, 1999

Factory Card Outlet Corp. (FCC) and its official committee of unsecured creditors entered into a nonbinding letter of intent with FCO Acquisition Corp. (FCOAC) regarding a potential transaction that could provide the company with funding to assist with its emergence from Chapter 11 protection. The letter outlines the general terms of a transaction and plan of reorganization in which FCOAC would invest $8 to $12 million in equity and subordinated debt. In exchange, FCOAC would receive notes and at least 85% of the common stock of the company upon its emergence from Chapter 11.

Safety Components International Inc. Chapter 11: April 10, 2000

The firm emerged from Chapter 11 protection. The company closed a three-year, $35 million credit facility with Congress Financial Corporation (Southern). The Congress facility has allowed the company to pay off its debtor-in-possession credit facility with Bank of America and is expected to provide adequate funding for Safety Components' ongoing global operating needs. In addition, the company also closed a two-year subordinated secured note facility with its prebankruptcy secured lenders for $20.9 million.

The Case of Sunbeam: Don't Let This Happen to You

In February 2001, the Sunbeam Corporation filed for Chapter 11 bankruptcy protection after a three-year effort to recover from an accounting scandal (see Chapter 2 for additional details) and a series of acquisitions that left it with $2.6 billion in debt and only $15 million in cash.

As part of the debtor-in-possession financing plan, which provided lenders first claim on a company's assets, the banks committed to lend $1.7 billion and agreed to provide another $285 million to allow Sunbeam to survive, at least for the present. Sunbeam's problems became apparent in 1998, when it was discovered that Albert J. Dunlap, a turnaround expert who was then the company's chief executive, had artificially bolstered sales by getting retailers to accept more goods than they could possibly sell.

At the same time, Sunbeam was struggling with high debt levels including a $1.7 billion bank loan it had taken on earlier that year after making three acquisitions. After Sunbeam's accounting irregularities became known, the banks were unable to sell portions of the loan to other lenders, as is customary with syndicated loans. Sunbeam's new CEO struggled to revive profits while negotiating with lenders to reduce exposures and facing shareholder lawsuits along with an investigation by the Securities and Exchange Commission.

While the firm restored some stability and repaired relationships with suppliers and discount retailers, Sunbeam's sales were still down 9.6% in the first nine months of 2000. The company blamed a weak economy. Both Bank of America and First Union said in the third quarter of 2000 that they expected to write down the value of a large corporate loan before the end of the year. While neither bank would identify the borrower, it is widely believed to be Sunbeam.

Since First Union and Bank of America were believed to have marked down the value of their Sunbeam loans, traders of bank debt have been anticipating that the banks will look to sell off portions of the loan. A few weeks before the filing, a $50 million tranche of the loan was sold off at an estimated price of 50 cents on the dollar. Soon after the loan sale, the value of the debt fell even further.

Chapter 7 Bankruptcy

In Chapter 7 bankruptcy, the borrower files a petition with the court, which includes detailed financial information about such factors as assets, liabilities, and income, plus a list of the assets claimed as exempt. The papers filed with the court are executed under penalty of perjury. The court process usually takes about three to four months.

The court appoints a trustee to review the bankruptcy filing, conduct the meeting of creditors, review the debtor's eligibility for a discharge, liquidate (sell) any nonexempt assets, and distribute the proceeds to creditors.

The obligor attends a meeting of creditors, which is usually held about one month after the filing. The debtor firm representative is put under oath, and the creditors have the right to ask the debtor about the debtor's assets and liabilities. Bankruptcy papers are reviewed for a true and accurate listing of all of the firm's assets and liabilities. If complications arise, such as litigation with a creditor or the trustee, the obligor may have to attend a court hearing or go through additional examinations and will receive such notice from the court or the firm's attorney.

REVIEW QUESTIONS

1. How can financial analysis be used to forecast the probability of a given firm's failure? If such analysis is properly applied, will it always predict failure? Explain.
2. What are the major sources of problem credits?
3. Why do creditors often accept a plan for financial rehabilitation rather than demand liquidation of the business?
4. How has the role of loan officers changed in terms of the way they evaluate loans? How has the use of computers affected their roles in recent years?
5. Describe how the Z-score model works. What do the results mean?
6. The Z-score equation used 5 particular financial ratios that contributed the most to the prediction model. Are these 5 ratios still effective analytical tools today? Give examples to support your answers.

7. What is the "domino-multiplier syndrome"? How does it relate the Z-score model? Why is that concept important for credit management?
8. Distinguish between a reorganization and a liquidation.
9. What are the two main goals of loan workouts? Describe each one.
10. Describe the process that a loan workout usually follows.
11. How could a bank minimize risk when doing a loan workout? What essential measures should be taken?
12. What are the main steps a workout officer should follow when a loan is transferred to the loan workout group?
13. Distinguish between Chapter 11 Reorganization and a Chapter 7 bankruptcy.
14. Comment on the following statement: "DIP financing is a very attractive piece of business for a bank because of the senior lien status provided by the court.
15. When a banker develops a DIP analysis cite at least five steps in the due diligence process.

SELECTED REFERENCES AND READINGS

Adams, C. F., R. E. Litan, and M. Pomerleano (Eds.). (2000). *Managing financial and corporate distress: Lessons from Asia*. Washington, D.C., Brookings Institution Press.

Aghion, P., O. Hart, *et al.* (1994). "Improving bankruptcy procedure." *Harvard Institute of Economic Research. Discussion Paper Series* 1–31. Attempts to provide an economic perspective on bankruptcy procedure. Argues that reorganization procedures like Chapter 11 are flawed because they mix the decision of who should get what with the decision of what should happen to the bankrupt company.

Altman, E. I. (Ed), (1981). "Bankruptcy and Reorganization." *Handbook of Corporate Finance* (Section 35). New York, John Wiley & Sons.

Altman, E. I. (1983). *Corporate Financial Distress and Bankruptcy: A Complete Guide to Predicting and Avoiding Distress and Profiting from Bankruptcy.* New York, (Wiley Finance Edition) John Wiley & Sons.

Altman, E. I. (Ed), (1984). "A Further Empirical Investigation of the Bankruptcy Cost Questions." *Journal of Finance* **39**, 1067–1089.

Altman, E. I. (Ed), (1986). "Bankruptcy and Reorganization." *Handbook of Corporate Finance* (Section 19). New York, John Wiley & Sons.

Altman, E. I. (1991). *Distressed Securities.* Chicago Ill., Probus Publishing Company.

Ang, J. S., J. H. Chua, and J. J. McConnell (1982). "The Administrative Costs of Corporate Bankruptcy: A Note." *Journal of Finance* (March 1982), pp. 219–226.

Aziz, A., and G. H. Lawson. (1989). Cash flow reporting and financial distress models: Testing of hypotheses. *Financial Management,* 55–63.

Bogdanoff, L. R. (1992). The purchase and sale of assets in reorganization cases—Of interest and principal, of principles and interests. *Business Lawyer* **4**, 1367–1459.

Brown, D. T. (1989). "Claimholder Incentive Conflicts in Reorganization: The Role of Bankruptcy Law." *Review of Financial Studies* **2**, 109–123.

Chatterjee, S., U. S. Dhillon, *et al.* (1996). Resolution of financial distress: Debt restructurings via Chapter 11, prepackaged bankruptcies, and workouts. *Financial Management,* 5–18.

Chen, Y., J. F. Weston, *et al.* (1995). Financial distress and restructuring models. *Financial Management,* 57–75.

Claessens, S., S. Djankov, and A. Mody (Eds.). (2001). "Resolution of Financial Distress: An International Perspective on the Design of Bankruptcy Laws." *World Bank Development Studies.* World Bank.

Coben, B. J. (1989). Global Chapter 11. *Foreign Policy* **75**, 109–127.

Cohen, B. J. (August 11, 1987). International chapter 11: Create an agency to aid third world debtors. *New York Times*, A23. Proposal for creation of an International Debt Restructuring Agency to negotiate resolution of debt-servicing difficulties on a case-by-case basis consistent with interests of creditors and debtors.

Dahl, H. (1992). USA: Bankruptcy under Chapter 11. *Revue De Droit Des Affaires Internationales/ International Business Law Journal* **5**, 555–566.

Denis, D. J., and D. K. Denis. (1995). Causes of financial distress following leveraged recapitalizations. *Journal of Financial Economics* **37**, 129–157.

Detragiache, E. (1992). Resolving financial distress: Does Chapter 11 help? *Johns Hopkins University. Dept. of Economics. Working Papers in Economics* **278**, 1–[33].

Franks, J. R., and W. N. Torous. (1994). Comparison of financial recontracting in distressed exchanges and Chapter 11 reorganizations. *Journal of Financial Economics* **35**, 349–370.

Gertner, R., and D. Scharfstein. (1991). "A Theory of Workouts and the Effects of the Reorganization Law." *Journal of Finance* **46**, 1189–1222.

Gilson, S. (1989). "Management Turnover and Financial Distress." *Journal of Financial Economics* **25**, 241–262.

Glover, S. I. (1992). Structured finance goes Chapter 11: Asset securitization by reorganizing companies. *Business Lawyer* **47**(2), 611–646.

Hendel, I. (1996). Competition under financial distress. *Journal of Industrial Economics* **44**, 309–324.

Ho, R. Y. W. (1996). The prediction of corporate financial distress and bank credit decisions: Hong Kong empirical evidence. *Savings and Development* **20**(2), 225–240. Examines the predictive ability of a distress classification model that is distinct from the models based on multiple discriminant analysis and that is simple and easy to use and can be applied to firms of all sizes and in different industries.

Hotchkiss, E. S., and R. M. Mooradian. (1998). Acquisitions as a means of restructuring firms in Chapter 11. *Journal of Financial Intermediation* **7**, 240–262.

Islam, S. (1989, February 3). Chapter 11 workouts for Latin debtors. *Wall Street Journal*, A14.

Johnsen, T., and R. W. Melicher. (1994). Predicting corporate bankruptcy and financial distress: Information value added by multinomial logit models. *Journal of Economics and Business* **46**, 269–286.

Kaiser, K. M. J. (1993). *An international view of bankruptcy laws: Summary and implications for corporations facing financial distress.* Fontainebleau, France: INSEAD.

Kupetz, D. S. (1998). The Bankruptcy Code is part of every contract: Minimizing the impact of Chapter 11 on the non-debtor's bargain. *Business Lawyer* **54**(1), 55–92.

Lasfer, M. A., P. S. Sudarsanam, *et al.* (1996). Financial distress, asset sales, and lender monitoring. *Financial Management* **25**, 57–66. Examines "the differing reactions of the stock market to divestments by financially distressed and healthy firms, and the impact of lender monitoring on that reaction."

Li, K. (1999). Bayesian analysis of duration models: An application to Chapter 11 bankruptcy. *Economics Letters* **63**(3), 305–312.

McLeay, S., and A. Omar. (1996). The sensitivity of distress prediction models to the nonnormality of bounded and unbounded financial ratios. *University College of North Wales. School of Accounting, Banking and Economics. Research Paper Series* **96**(23), 1–24.

Myers, S. C. (1977). "Determinants of Coorperate Borrowing." *Journal of Financial Economics* **5**, 147–176.

Nogler, G. E., and K. B. Schwartz. (1987). Choosing the best alternative in a Chapter 11 case. *Journal of Commercial Bank Lending* **70**, 48–53.

Opler, T., and S. Titman. (1993). Determinants of leveraged buyout activity: free cash flow vs. financial distress costs. *Journal of Finance* **48**, 1985–1999.

Opler, T. C., and S. Titman (1994). Financial distress and corporate performance. *Journal of Finance* **49**: 1015–40.

Popiel, P. A. (1987). Financial institutions in distress: Causes and remedies. *International Journal of Development Banking* **5**, 31–45.

Pulvino, T. C. (1999). Effects of bankruptcy court protection on asset sales. *Journal of Financial Economics* **52**(2), 151–186. This paper explores whether prices obtained from asset sales are greater under Chapter 11 reorganization than under Chapter 7 liquidation using commercial aircraft transactions.

Queree, A., and J. Matthews. (1993). *DIP in the financial services industry.* London: Banking Technology Ltd.

Suarez, J., and O. Sussman (1999). Financial distress and the business cycle. *Oxford Review of Economic Policy* **15**(3), 39–51.

Venkataraman, S. (1996). Financial distress and the role of capital contributions by the owner manager. *Federal Reserve Bank of Chicago, Working Paper Series, Issues in Financial Regulation* **96–22**, 1–31.

Warner, J. B. (1977). "Bankruptcy Costs: Some Evidence." *Journal of Finance* **32**, 337–347.

Weiss, L. A. (1990). "Bankruptcy Resolution: Direct Costs and Violation of Priority Claims." *Journal of Financial Economics* **27**, 285–314.

Weiss, L. A. (1996). *The impact of incorporating the cost of errors into bankruptcy prediction models.* Fontainebleau, France: INSEAD.

White, M. (1983). "Bankruptcy Costs and the New Bankruptcy Code." *Journal of Finance* **38**, 477–488.

Wilcox, J. W. (1976). "The Gambler's Ruin Approach to Business Risk." *Sloan Management Review* (March 1976).

Wruck, K. H. (1990). Financial distress, reorganization, and organizational efficiency. *Journal of Financial Economics* **27**, 419–444.

U.S. LENDER LIABILITY LITIGATION THROUGH 1992[1]

There is no scarcity of scholarly and legal writings on the subject of lender liability.[2] This appendix, rather than adding new research to the already vast quantity of materials, attempts only to provide an overview of the legal basis for the proliferation of lawsuits against lenders in the United States through 1992. It serves up a rigorous warning—bankers beware. The issue is the message, not so much recent rulings or court cases that might have been handed down since 1992.

Lender liability claims have arisen as a part of a "new, growing consumerism against banks"[3] that manifests itself in a conflict between the interests of the

---

[1] The author owes a special debt of gratitude to Bertram G. Kaminski, a litigation attorney who researched and prepared this appendix.

[2] Readers can find cases and commentaries by reference to computer search facilities at law libraries.

[3] Davis, "The Case against Juries in Lender Liability," *ABA Banking Journ.* at 184 (October 1987).

lender and those of the borrower and its owner.[4] The increase in the number of lawsuits brought against lenders has been traced to a fragile economy, favorable verdicts and large monetary judgments.[5] A weak economy, for example, has the effect of prompting banks to protect their own financial position by calling in loans and refusing to extend credit to marginal borrowers, and causing those same marginal borrowers to sue the banks when the loans are called or credit not advanced.[6]

Although borrowers have won only one case in nine against lenders,[7] those that borrowers have won tend to result in large jury verdicts against lenders.[8] Additionally, a review of lender liability cases demonstrates that borrowers are not only being released from their obligations to the lenders, but are also being awarded, by judge and jury alike, both compensatory and punitive damages.

Generally, lender liability litigation arises from the conduct of lenders in negotiating and administering loans, rather than from mistakes contained in the loan documents themselves.[9] The conduct of lenders commonly serves as a factual basis for legal action when (1) lenders become highly involved in the management and operations of the borrowers' businesses,[10] (2) lenders fail to honor loan commitments or impose new terms,[11] (3) lenders commence litigation against borrowers for nonmonetary defaults,[12] (4) lenders improperly accelerate demand notes,[13] (5) lenders substitute a stronger borrower for a weaker one in

---

[4] Id. One commentator has stated that "in almost all the situations I have seen, the lender had nearly always the right to do what it did. The issue was in the manner in which it exercised its rights." Cocheo & Clark, "Lenders, Better Watch Your Backs," *ABA Banking Journ.,* at 31–32 (November 1986).

[5] Thierbach, *Lender Liability: Should Lenders Be Required to Continue to Advance Credit to Marginal Borrowers?* 15 West. St. U. L. Rev. 631, 633 (1988).

[6] Id. at 633–34.

[7] Blogdgett, "Lender Liability Still Lurking: Borrowers Win Only One in Nine Cases But Banks Worry," *74 ABA Journal* 42(1) (May 1, 1988). It must be noted, however, that most lender liability actions are dismissed or settled prior to trial. J. Hubbell, "Defending Lender Liability Suits," 19 *Colorado Lawyer* 2409 (December 1990).

[8] See, e.g., *State Nat'l Bank v. Farah Manufacturing Co.*, 678 S.W.2d 661 (Tex. Ct. App. 1984) (holding the lender liable for $18,947,348.77 in damages); *K.M.C. Co., Inc. v. Irving Trust Co.*, 757 F.2d 752 (6th Cir. 1985) (holding the lender liable for $7.5 million); *Landes Constr. Co., Inc. v. Royal Bank of Canada*, 833 F.2d 1365 (9th Cir. 1987) (verdict awarding $18.5 million). Recently, however, courts have limited the circumstances under which borrowers may recover for claims against lenders. See, e.g., *Penthouse Int'l Inc. v. Dominion Federal Savings & Loan Ass'n*, 855 F.2d 963 (2d Cir. 1988), *cert. denied, 490 U.S. 1005 (1989)* (reversing $128.7 million judgment against lender) 17; *Kruse v. Bank of America*, 202 Cal. App. 3d 38, 248 Cal. Rptr. (1988), *cert. denied*, 488 U.S. 1043 (1989) (reversing $37.5 million judgment against lender).

[9] D. Shuller, "Techniques to Reduce Lender Liability Risk," 6 *Probate & Property* 16 (May/June 1992).

[10] *Farah Manufacturing Co., Inc. v. State Nat'l Bank*, 678 S.W.2d 661 (Tex. Ct. App. 1984).

[11] *999 v. C.I.T. Corp.*, 776 F.2d 866 (9th Cir. 1985).

[12] See *Universal C.I.T. Credit Corp. v. Shepler*, 164 Ind. App. 516, 329 N.E.2d 620 (1975).

[13] *K.M.C. Co. Inc. v. Irving Trust Co.*, 757 F.2d 752 (6th Cir. 1985).

connection with a loan for a failing business or property,[14] and (6) lenders are perceived to have broken promises or made untrue statements.[15]

Borrowers most often assert lender liability claims as counterclaims in response to collection actions brought by lenders.[16] As a legal cause of action, however, the term "lender liability" does not denote any particular theory of liability.[17] Rather, claimants against lenders employ traditional legal theories in a new fashion in an attempt to redress perceived injustices in the lending relationship. The legal theories under which borrowers commence litigation include various common law causes of action (including fraud, misrepresentation, economic duress, breach of contract, and tortious interference) and several statutory prescriptions (including environmental, antitrust, racketeering, and banking statutes).[18]

A key element in many of these theories is the concept of the lender's undue or unlawful "control" over a borrower.[19] Although it is virtually impossible to draw a clear line between permissible and unlawful control,[20] lenders are often sued as a result of the power they exert over borrowers' disbursements, income, sales, or equity.[21] It has been held that in order to be found liable for such undue control, a lender must exercise sufficient authority over a borrower so as to dictate the borrower's corporate policy and dispossession of assets.[22]

---

[14] J. Hubbell, "Defending Lender Liability Suits," 19 *Colorado Lawyer* 2409, 2410 (December 1990).

[15] *Id.*

[16] J. Hubbell, "Defending Lender Liability Suits," 19 *Colorado Lawyer* 2409 (December 1990).

[17] For example, in the case of *Sanchez-Corea v. Bank of America*, 38 Cal. 3d 892, 701 P.2d 826, 215 Cal. Rptr. 679 (1985), bank customers brought an action against their bank under the legal theories of breach of contract, fraud, breach of implied covenant of good faith and fair dealing, disparagement of credit, interference with prospective economic advantage, promissory estoppel, negligence, and intentional infliction of emotional distress.

[18] The "flawed" application of these theories to lender liability cases has, according to one commentator, "occasionally resulted in both disaster and confusion." Granoff, "Emerging Theories of Lender Liability: Flawed Application of Old Concepts," 104 *Bank. L. Journ.* 492, 493 (1987).

[19] For example, in the case *A. Gay Jenson Farms Co. v. Cargill, Inc.*, 309 N.W.2d 285 (Minn. 1981), a lender was held liable for the debts of a borrower when it was determined that the lender was an "active participant in [the borrower's] operations rather than simply a financier." Id. at 292.

[20] A. Cappello and F. Komoroske, "Lender Liability Based on Undue Control over a Borrower," 28 *Trial* 18, 19 (December 1992).

[21] More specifically, lenders are subject to liability upon findings that they maintained a security interest over most of a borrower's assets; placed their own employees in the borrower's business; subjected a borrower's decision-making to lender approval; participated in the daily business operations of the borrower; made the borrower's personnel decisions; and conducted regular audits and visits of the borrower. See A. Cappello & F. Komoroske, "Lender Liability Based on Undue Control over a Borrower," 28 *Trial* 18, 19-20 (December 1992).

[22] *In re Aluminum Mills Corp.*, 132 B.R. 869, 895 (N.D. Ill. 1991). See also "Creditor Liabilities Resulting from Improper Interference with the Management of a Financially Troubled Debtor," 31 *Bus. Law.* 343 (1975).

COMMON LAW CAUSES OF ACTION

Lenders have been held liable to borrowers under a variety of common law causes of action. Among these, claimants have successfully proceeded under the theories of fraud and misrepresentation.[23] To commence an action based on fraud, a borrower must allege that the lender made a material misrepresentation that, when made, the lender was aware that it was false, or recklessly made it as a positive assertion without any knowledge of its validity. Moreover, the borrower must allege that the lender made the representation with the intention that it be acted on by the borrower and that the borrower acted in reliance on it to its detriment.[24]

An action for misrepresentation will lie when a lender with knowledge superior to that of the borrower (or a means of knowledge not open to the borrower) is silent,[25] or where the lender knows that the borrower is acting under a mistake of material fact and fails to correct the error,[26] or if lender's disclosure to the borrower is only partial.[27] Thus, lenders have been found liable under this tort for creating a false impression regarding the lender's decision (or lack of decision) to declare a default,[28] and by making representations that, although the lender has in fact decided not to extend further loans, promise further financing if the accounts receivable are assigned,[29] and by the creation of the false impression to a third party of the borrower's financial soundness.[30]

A lender was held liable for the tortious nondisclosure of material facts when it undertook to provide information about a customer's financial position but failed to disclose acts suggesting the instability of that position.[31]

---

[23] See *Danca v. Taunton Sav. Bank*, 385 Mass. 429 N.E.2d 1129 (1982); *Stirling v. Chemical Bank*, 382 F. Supp. 1146 (S.D.N.Y. 1974), *aff'd*, 516 F.2d 1396 (2d Cir. 1975).

[24] *Custom Leasing, Inc. v. Texas Bank & Trust Co. of Dallas*, 516 S.W. 2d 138, 142-43 (Tex. 1974); see also Restatement (Second) of Torts §527 (1977).

[25] *Mullin v. Bank of America*, 199 Cal. App. 3d 448, 245 Cal. Rptr. 66 (1988); *Noved Realty Corp. v. A.A.P. Co, Inc.* 250 A.D. 1, 5, 293 N.Y.S. 336, 340 (1st Dep't 1937).

[26] *Aaron Ferrer & Sons, Ltd. v. Chase Manhattan Bank, N.A.*, 731 F.2d 112, 123 (2d Cir. 1984); *Beth Israel Medical Center v. Smith*, 576 F. Supp. 1061, 1071 (S.D.N.Y. 1983); *Fund of Funds, Ltd. v. Arthur Andersen & Co.*, 545 F. Supp. 1314, 1359-60 (S.D.N.Y. 1982).

[27] *Southeastern Financial Corp. v. United Merchants & Manufacturers, Inc.*, 701 F.2d 565, 567 (5th Cir. 1983); *Sheridan DriveIn, Inc. v. State*, 16 A.D.2d 400, 228 N.Y.S.2d 576, 585 (4th Dep't 1962).

[28] *State Nat'l Bank v. Farah Manufacturing Co.*, 678 S.W.2d 661 (Tex. Ct. App. 1984).

[29] *Sanchez-Corea v. Bank of America*, 38 Cal. 3d 892, 701 P.2d 826, 215 Cal. Rptr. 679 (1985).

[30] *General Motors Acceptance Corp. v. Central Nat'l Bank*, 773 F.2d 771, 780 (7th Cir. 1985).

[31] *Central State Stamping v. Terminal Equip. Co.*, 727 F.2d 1405, 1409 (6th Cir. 1984). In the case of *Richfield Bank & Trust Co. v. Sjogren*, 244 N.W.2d 648 (Minn. 1976), the court held that it is the "moral duty of banks to the community in which they do business to use reasonable care in seeing that their depositors are not committing a fraud on the public." Id. at 651.

Borrowers have prevailed against lenders on the theory of constructive fraud as well.[32] In one case, a bank was held liable when a bank officer failed to inform a loan customer of the officer's involvement in the purchase of the customer's ranch and failed to consider the customer's best interest. The court determined that a fiduciary relationship existed between the bank and the loan customer on the bases that the customer had dealt with the lender for 24 years and the bank officer had acted as a financial advisor to the customer.[33]

A lender also incurred liability under the theory of negligent misrepresentation when it failed to exercise reasonable care in making promise that it would loan money on a corporation's purchase order. The court noted that the lender had

> permitted the corporation to solicit orders, establish production lines, commence the manufacture of products, and exhaust its cash reserve in the process thereof, without once issuing a word of warning or caution that the known necessary financing would not be forthcoming. These defendants were led down a primrose path of promised financing and were impaled on the thorns of improvident investments and personal guarantees en route.[34]

Borrowers have successfully proceeded against lenders under the theory of "tortious interference," both in connection with contractual relationships and economic advantage.[35] This theory is based on a line that the law has draw beyond which it prohibits members of the community to intentionally intermeddle with the business affairs of others.[36] Interference is considered unlawful unless justified or privileged in some way,[37] but is actionable only if such

---

[32] Constructive fraud arises from a breach of a legal or equitable duty, trust, or confidence resulting in damages to another. *Barrett v. Bank of America, N.T. and S.A.*, 183 Cal. App. 3d 1362, 1368-69, 229 Cal. Rptr. 16, 20 (1986).

[33] *Deist v. Wachholz*, 108 Mont. 207 678 P.2d 188 (1984). See also *Whitney v. Citibank, N.A.*, 782 F.2d 1106, 1116 (2d Cir. 1986).

[34] *Banker's Trust Co. v. Steenburn*, 95 Misc. 2d 967, 409 N.Y.S.2d 51, 66 (Sup. Ct. 1978). Interestingly, the court in *First City Bank v. Global Auctioneers, Inc.*, 708 S.W.2d 12 (Tex. 1986), upheld an award of actual and punitive damages against a lender for inducing the transfer of funds through misrepresentations about the financial soundness of the transferee, even though the jury concluded that the plaintiff could have discovered the falsity through a reasonable investigation. The court's reasoning was grounded on the proposition that a person committing fraud cannot avoid liability by proving that the other party could have uncovered the fraud through reasonable diligence.

[35] *Leonard Duckworth Inc. v. Michael L. Field & Co.*, 516 F.2d 952 (5th Cir. 1975); *Nordic Bank PLC v. Trend Group Ltd*, 619 F. Supp. 542 (S.D.N.Y. 1985); *Black Lake Pipe Line Co. v. Union Constr. Co.*, 538 S.W.2d 80 (Tex. 1976); *Delcon Group v. Northern Trust Corporation*, 135 Ill. Dec. 212, 543 N.E.2d 595, 187 Ill. App. 3d 635, *app. den.*, 139 Ill. Dec. 511, 548 N.E.2d 1067, 128 Ill.2d 672 (1989); *State Nat'l Bank of El Paso v. Farah Manufacturing Co.*, 678 S.W.2d 661 (Tex. Ct. App. 1984).

[36] 45 Am. Jur. 2d *Interference* §1 (1969).

[37] *State Nat'l Bank v. Farah Manufacturing Co.*, 678 S.W.2d 661 (Tex. Ct. App. 1984). See *Frank Colson, Inc. v. Buick v. General Motors Corp.*, 488 F.2d 202, 206 (5th Cir. 1974) (holding that even where a justifiable business interest exists for the lender to so interfere, there is no absolute privilege for a lender to interfere with borrower's contractual relationships with others).

interference is motivated by legal "malice."[38] A lender was held liable for interference in the contractual relations of a borrower when it violated a nonencumberance provision in an asset sale agreement between the borrower and the seller of assets by taking a security interest in such assets.[39] A lender was found to have interfered in a borrower's business when it imposed a 13-point program to help "salvage whatever is possible from the debtor's situation," which included the reduction of the salary of borrower's president, the replacement of the borrower's accountant with one chosen by the lender, and having all of the borrower's disbursements approved by the lender.[40] In another case, however, a lender was held not to have tortuously interfered when it sent letters to a borrower's customers requesting that they send the money they owed the borrower directly to the lender.[41]

Courts have held that once a lender undertakes to process a loan application, it has a duty to do so with the exercise of reasonable care or be liable in tort for negligence.[42] One court held a lender liable for negligence on the basis that the lender "failed in its responsibility to exercise reasonable care and diligence" after several of its officers made conflicting statements to the borrower (which were, however, not severe enough to constitute fraud).[43] Lenders have also been held liable on the basis that they intentionally sought to inflict emotional distress on borrowers[44] and under prima facie (or general) tort principles.[45]

Borrowers in response to collection actions instituted by lenders have also employed the theory of "economic duress."[46] Under this theory, a borrower claims that a lender is threatening it with costly situations, including bankruptcy or loss of credit rating.[47] Borrowers seek to be relieved from an obligation

---

[38] Restatement (Second) of Torts, Introductory Note to Chapter 37 (1979).

[39] *First Wyoming Bank, Casper v. Mudge*, 748 P.2d 713 (Wyo. 1988).

[40] *Melamed v. Lake Country Nat'l Bank*, 727 F.2d 1399, 1403-04 (6th Cir. 1984).

[41] *Delcon Group v. Northern Trust Corporation*, 135 Ill. Dec. 212, 543 N.E.2d 595, 187 Ill. App. 3d 635, *app. den.*, 139 Ill. Dec. 511, 548 N.E.2d 1067, 128 Ill.2d 672 (1989).

[42] *Jacques v. First Nat'l Bank*, 307 Md. 527, 515 A.2d 756 (1986); *First Federal Sav. & Loan Ass'n v. Caudle*, 425 So.2d 1050 (Ala. 1983).

[43] *Champion Int'l Corp. v. First Nat'l Bank of Jackson*, 642 F. Supp. 237, 242 (S.D. Miss. 1986). In the case of *United States & Carnegie Pension Fund, Inc. v. Orenstein*, 557 F.2d 343 (2d Cir. 1977), however, a lender was held not to be liable for furnishing incorrect information to the borrower when the lender had acted in good faith and expressly disclaimed any intent to give investment advice. Id. at 345-46.

[44] See *Sanchez-Corea v. Bank of America*, 38 Cal. 3d 892, 701 P.2d 826, 215 Cal Rptr. 679 (1985).

[45] See *State Bank of Commerce v. Demco of Louisiana, Inc.*, 483 So. 2d 1119 (La. 1986).

[46] *Federal Deposit Ins. Co. v. Linn*, 671 F. Supp. 547, 556 (N.D. Ill. 1987); *Nordic Bank PLC v. Trend Group, Ltd.*, 619 F. Supp. 542, 560 (S.D.N.Y. 1985); *Citibank, N.A. v. Real Coffee Trading Co.*, 566 F. Supp. 1158, 1162 (S.D.N.Y. 1983); *Union State Bank v. Weaver*, 526 F. Supp. 29, 33 (S.D.N.Y. 1981); *805 Third Ave. Co. v. M.W. Realty Assoc.*, 58 N.Y.2d 450, 448 N. E. 2d 15, 461 N.Y.S.2d 778 (1983); *First Texas Sav. Ass'n v. Dicker Center Inc.*, 631 S.W.2d 179 (Tex. App. 1982).

[47] See Restatement (Second) of Torts §871 comment F (1977).

assumed from the lender.[48] Borrowers must show more, however, than mere "pressure of business circumstances, financial embarrassment or economic necessity."[49] Liability under economic duress has been imposed on a lender where such lender, in bad faith, threatened to declare a default, bankrupt the borrower, and "padlock his doors,"[50] and where it refused to provide financing to a mortgagor and would not transfer its financing commitment to another lender unless the mortgagor paid the lender's $12,000 debt.[51]

As opposed to actions sounding in tort, breach of contract claims have afforded many borrowers recovery against lenders for both oral and written contracts.[52] Lenders have been found liable under this theory for a failure of a lender to finance the purchase of farm animals despite a prior agreement,[53] the failure of a lender to disclose funds under an irrevocable line of credit,[54] and the lender's breach of an implied obligation of good faith where it discounted the borrower's financing without prior notice.[55]

STATUTORY CAUSES OF ACTION

In addition to the application of common law theories of liability, borrowers have managed to forge a myriad of federal statutes into powerful liability weapons against lenders. In recent times, the Federal Comprehensive Environmental Response, Compensation and Liability Act[56] (also known as CERCLA or Superfund) has become one of the most potent federal statutory weapons asserted against lenders. Under CERCLA, lenders have been held liable to share in damages and environmental cleanup costs where hazardous or toxic materials are discovered on mortgagors' property.[57] CERCLA assigns

---

[48] *State Nat'l Bank v. Farah Manufacturing Co.*, 678 S.W.2d 661, 683 (Tex. Ct. App. 1984).

[49] *First Texas Sav. Ass'n v. Dicker Center, Inc.*, 631 S.W.2d 179, 186 (Tex. App. 1982).

[50] *State Nat'l Bank v. Farah Manufacturing Co*, 678 S.W.2d 661 (Tex. Ct. App. 1984).

[51] *Pecos Constr. Co. v. Mortgage Investment Co.*, 80 N.M. 680, 459 P.2d 842 (1969).

[52] *Landes Constr. Co., Inc. v. Royal Bank of Canada*, 833 F.2d 1365, 1371 (9th Cir. 1987). The advantage, however, of using a tort theory, rather than one in contract, against a lender is that a plaintiff recovers all damages proximately caused by the lender's conduct, instead of those merely foreseeable at the time the contract was entered into. Proximately caused damages are generally easier to prove and produce higher recoveries. *Sanchez, Symposium: Lender Liability Introduction*, 15 West. St. U. L. Rev. 177 (1988).

[53] *National Farmers Organization, Inc. v. Kinsley Bank*, 731 F.2d 1464 (10th Cir. 1984).

[54] *Shaughnessey v. Mark Twain State Bank*, 715 S.W.2d 944 (Mo. App. 1986).

[55] *K.M.C. Co. Inc. v. Irving Trust Co.*, 757 F.2d 752 (6th Cir. 1985). See also *Brown v. Aveco Inv. Corp.*, 603 F.2d 1367 (9th Cir. 1979); *First Nat'l Bank in Libby v. Twombley*, 213 Mont. 66, 689 P.2d 1226 (1984).

[56] Pub. L. No. 96-510, 94 Stat. 2767 (codified as amended at 42 U.S.C. §§9601–9675 (1988)). CERCLA was amended by the Superfund Amendments and Reauthorization Act of 1986 (SARA), Pub. L. No. 99-499, 100 Stat. 1613.

[57] See *United States v. Maryland Bank & Trust Co.*, 632 F. Supp. 573 (D. Md. 1986).

liability for cleanup costs (1) to the current owners or operators of a contaminated facility, (2) to those who were owners or operators at the time of the waste disposal, (3) to the transporters of the hazardous waste, and (4) to the generators of the hazardous waste.[58]

It is generally alleged that lenders fall within the categories of "owners or operators." For example, a lender may be considered to be an "owner" of a contaminated facility if it foreclosed on a security interest and took title to such a property. A lender may be considered an "operator" if its involvement with the borrower's business goes beyond what is regarded as necessary to protect its security interest. The CERCLA law holds responsible parties strictly liable for all costs and damages[59] and will apportion all such damages and cleanup costs jointly and severally if allocation cannot be made among individual responsible parties.[60]

As a result of government's failure to articulate a clear national environmental policy balancing economic interests and environmental concerns, legal precedent applying CERCLA to make a claim against lenders is unstable and frequently inconsistent.[61] Recently, for example, developing case law had provided that, prior to foreclosure, a secured lender was exempt from CERCLA liability so long as it did not participate in the day-to-day management of a borrower's operations.[62] In 1991, however, a federal appeals court put this rule into doubt, holding that a lender could be held liable under CERCLA if the lender had the "capacity to influence" hazardous substance disposal decisions through its participation in the facility's financial management, regardless of whether the lender had actually ever exercised that capacity.[63]

---

[58] 42 U.S.C. §9607(a)(1)-(4).

[59] See *County Line Inv. Co. v. Tinney*, 933 F.2d 1508, 1515 (10th Cir. 1991); *United States v. Monsanto Co.*, 858 F.2d 160, 167 & n.11 (4th Cir. 1988), *cert. denied*, 490 U.S. 1106 (1989).

[60] *County Line Inv. Co. v. Tinney*, 933 F.2d at 1515 & n.11 (10th Cir. 1991). In other words, if a reasonable basis cannot be found to apportion costs and damages, any one defendant could become liable for the entire harm. This will tend to result in a lender having to bear a larger percentage of the cleanup costs than its proportionate contribution to the environmental harm. N. Toulme & D. Cloud, "The Fleet Factors Case: A Wrong Turn for Lender Liability under Superfund," 26 *Wake Forest L. Rev.* 127, 129 (1991).

[61] G. Wolf, "Lender Liability under the Federal Superfund Program," 23 *Ariz. St. L. J.* 531 (1991). See R. Mayes, *Secured Creditors and Superfund: Avoiding the Liability Net*, 20 Env't Rep. (BNA) 609 (July 28, 1989 ("The liability net created by CERCLA is like a mile-long net behind a modern a modern fishing trawler: it is wide, deep, and dangerous to anything that gets caught up in it.")

[62] See N. Toulme and D. Cloud, "The Fleet Factors Case: A Wrong Turn for Lender Liability Under Superfund," 26 *Wake Forest L. Rev.* at 133.

[63] *United States v. Fleet Factors Corp.*, 901 F.2d 1550, 1557-58 (11th Cir. 1990), *cert. denied*, 111 S. Ct. 752 (1991). But see *In re Bergsoe Metal Corp.*, 910 F.2d 668, 672 (9th Cir. 1990) (opining that "some actual management of the facility" is required before a lender loses the secured creditor exemption).

That decision had caused a wave of panic among lenders, who petitioned Congress for legislative action to clarify lenders' exposure under Superfund.[64] In April 1992, the U.S. Environmental Protection Agency (EPA) ended the "nightmare"[65] for lenders, as presented by CERCLA liability, by issuing a regulation that defined the parameters of the security interest exemption set forth in the CERCLA statute.[66] Under the EPA regulation, lenders can be held liable only if they participate in and exercise decision-making control over the management and operations of borrowers.

Borrowers have asserted claims against lenders under a myriad of other federal statutes as well. For example, lenders have been held responsible for a borrower's unpaid withholding taxes under the Internal Revenue Code,[67] or liable as a "controlling person" or "aider and abettor" of borrower under federal securities laws.[68] Moreover, under the Federal Bankruptcy Code, a lender's claims could be equitably subordinated to a debtor's other claimants on the basis that the lender was in control of the debtor and should be treated as an "insider" who owes a fiduciary duty to such other claimants.[69]

In addition, the Racketeer Influenced Corrupt Organizations Act (RICO)[70] has been interpreted to permit private borrowers to hold lenders

---

[64] N. Toulme and D. Cloud, "The Fleet Factors Case: A Wrong Turn for Lender Liability under Superfund," 26 Wake Forest L. Rev. at 128.

[65] A. Cappello and F. Komoroske, "Lender Liability Based on Undue Control over a Borrower," 28 *Trial* 18, 21 (December 1992).

[66] 57 Fed. Reg. 18344 (1992) (codified at 40 C.F.R. §300.1100). *See* P. Quentel, *EPA Issues Long-Awaited Lender Liability Rule*, 22 E.L.R. 10637 (October 1992).

[67] 26 U.S.C. §§3505, 6672 (1988). Section 6672 of the Internal Revue Code provides that: 1. [a]ny person required to collect, truthfully account for, and pay over any tax imposed by this title [employment withholding taxes] who willfully fails to collect such tax, or truthfully account for and pay over such tax, or willfully attempts in any manner to evade or defeat any such tax or the payment thereof, shall . . . be liable to a penalty equal to the total amount of the tax evaded . . . . 2. ??????? 3. 26 U.S.C. §6672(a). *See United States v. First Nat'l Bank of Circle*, 652 F.2d 882 (9th Cir. 1981); *United States v. McMullen*, 516 F.2d 917 (7th Cir.), *cert. denied*, 423 U.S. 915 (1975); *Mueller v. Nixon*, 470 F.2d 1348 (6th Cir. 1972), *cert. denied*, 412 U.S. 949 (1973). Lenders can be liable for a borrower's withholding taxes simply on the knowledge that the borrower was unable to pay such taxes.

[68] *Metge v. Baehler* 762 F.2d 621 (8th Cir. 1985), *cert. denied sub. nom.*, *Metge v. Bankers Trust Co.*, 474 U.S. 1057 (1986); *Technology Exch. Corp. of Am. v. Grant County State Bank*, 646 F. Supp. 179 (D. Colo. 1986).

[69] *United States v. Kayser-Roth Corp., Inc.*, 910 F.2d 24, 27 (1st Cir. 1990), *cert denied*, 111 s> ct. 957 (1991). A lender's new status of "insider" may result in the subordination of its claim through the doctrine of equitable subordination. 11 U.S.C. §510(c) (1988). The mere ability to exercise control is, however, insufficient to invoke this doctrine. The lender must have exercised control in such a way as to result in actual injury to the borrower. *Porter v. Yukon Nat'l Bank*, 866 F.2d 355 (10th Cir. 1989). *See In re Clark Pipe & Supply Co.*, 87 B.R. 21, 23-24 (E.D. La. 1988), *mod'f*, 893 F.2d 693 (5th Cir. 1990) (bank considered to be insider as a result of its sole control of a borrower's accounts receivable and disbursement of operating funds).

[70] RICO, 18 U.S.C. §§1961 *et seq.* The RICO statute prohibits a "person" from furthering an "enterprise," or his interests in such an enterprise, through a "pattern" of "racketeering activity."

liable for treble damages in connection with loans received from lenders. Borrowers have asserted RICO-based liability claims on the bases of fraudulent interest charges,[71] fraudulent efforts by lenders to protect existing loans,[72] refusals by lenders to extend promised financing,[73] and unlawful attempts by lenders to acquire control of the borrower's assets, customers, or control of operations.[74]

Borrowers have asserted lender liability actions under federal antitrust statutes, primarily under the authority of the Sherman Antitrust Act[75] and the Clayton Antitrust Act.[76] Lender liability actions under these statutes have not increased materially in recent years, however, predominately due to the heavy burden of proof imposed on the plaintiff[77] and because the scope of such laws has been declining. Consequently, there have been relatively few plaintiff victories utilizing antitrust laws and include cases primarily where a lender's decision to terminate a borrower's credit was sudden and unsubstantiated,[78] where there was evidence of a conspiracy to drive a borrower out of business,[79] and where several banks conspired in an unlawful combination to illegally fix a high prime rate.[80]

The Bank Holding Company Act[81] has also been applied against lenders. This act prohibits improper and anticompetitive tying arrangements[82] by

---

[71] *Wilcox v. First Interstate Bank of Oregon, N.A.*, 815 F.2d 522 (9th Cir. 1987); *NCNB National Bank of North Carolina v. Tiller*, 814 F.2d 931, 936 (4th Cir.) *petition denied* 484 U.S. 974 (1987); *Atkinson v. Anadarko Bank and Trust Co.*, 808 F.2d 438 (5th Cir. 1987), *cert. denied*, 483 U.S. 1032 (1987).

[72] *Lawaetz v. Bank of Nova Scotia*, 653 F. Supp. 1278 (D.V.I. 1987); *Hatherley v. Palos Bank and Trust Co.*, 650 F. Supp. 832 (N.D. Ill. 1986); *Heritage Insurance Company of America v. First National Bank of Cicero*, 629 F. Supp. 1412 (N.D. Ill. 1986).

[73] *Runnemede Owners, Inc. v. Crest Mortgage Corp.*, 861 F.2d 1053 (7th Cir. 1988); *Dunham v. Independence Bank of Chicago*, 629 F. Supp. 983 (N.D. Ill. 1986); *LSC Assoc. v. Lomas & Nettleton Financial Corp.*, 629 F. Supp. 979 (E.D. Pa. 1986).

[74] *Citibank v. Data Lease Financial Corp.*, 828 F.2d 686 (llth Cir.), *cert. denied*, 484 U.S. 1062 (1987).

[75] 15 U.S.C. §§1 and 2.

[76] 15 U.S.C. §§14 and 15.

[77] A complainant must, *inter alia*, furnish proof that the lender's actions have had an anticompetitive effect and must produce evidence establishing a conspiracy or monopoly.

[78] *Neel v. Waldrop*, 639 F.2d 1080 (4th Cir. 1981).

[79] *Id.*

[80] *Michaels Building Co. v. Ameritrust Co., N.A.*, 848 F.2d 674 (6th Cir. 1988).

[81] See 12 U.S.C. §§1971 *et. seq.* The purpose of the Bank Holding Company Act is to prohibit anticompetitive banking practices, in which borrowers accept or provide some other service or product or refrain from dealing with other parties in order to obtain the bank product or service that they desire. *Lancianese v. Bank of Mount Hope*, 783 F.2d 467, 469 (4th Cir. 1986).

[82] A tying arrangement is one in which a supplier of a given product conditions the sale of the product on the purchase of a different (less desirable) product, or requires that the purchaser not buy the product from any other supplier.

lenders[83] and entitles borrowers who have been injured by an unlawful tying arrangement to maintain a private cause of action permitting the recovery of both general and treble damages. Unlike antitrust laws, the Bank Holding Company Act does not require proof of market power or impact on competition.[84]

CONCLUSION

The litigious nature of American society, coupled with the tenuous condition of many sectors of the country's economy, has resulted in a plethora of liability suits against lenders. As shown, these suits find their basis in imaginative uses of traditional state common law and federal statutory law. Of course, many defenses are available to lenders also within this same body of law.[85] Nevertheless, there is no substitute, legal or otherwise, for ordinary prudence and discretion on the part of lenders to avoid litigation in the first place.

Lenders could avert lawsuits, or mitigate their effects, if they follow a few basic, precautionary steps. Lenders should avoid any types of oral understandings with borrowers that are not set forth within the loan documentation. Lenders should avoid intruding into the day-to-day operation of a borrower's business and avoid of any type of conduct that might lend support to a legal claim of malice or ill will. Borrowers should be afforded as much advance written notice as possible should lenders decide to terminate a loan or refuse further credit.[86] In addition, potential lender liability exposure can be reduced through the inclusion of contractual provisions in the loan documentation that seek to avoid jury trials. [87]

To ensure against sharing in potentially crushing environmental cleanup costs, lenders should require borrowers to complete an environmental questionnaire or conduct their own due diligence assessment. Loan documentation should cover present and potential environmental matters and should specifically leave

---

[83] *Sharkey v. Security Bank & Trust Co.*, 651 F. Supp. 1231 (D. Minn. 1987); *Nordic Bank PLC v. Trend Group, Ltd.*, 619 F. Supp. 542 (S.D.N.Y. 1985).

[84] *Bruce v. First Federal Sav. & Loans Ass'n of Conroe, Inc.*, 837 F.2d 712 (5th Cir. 1988).

[85] For example, lenders may assert a waiver or estoppel defense if it can be shown that the borrower requested the lender to control the business or failed to object when the lender did. *Citibank v. Data Lease Financial Corp.*, 828 F.2d 686 (llth Cir.), *cert. denied*, 484 U.S. 1062 (1987). Lenders may also assert the defenses of justification or privilege, where lender's have the right to intermeddle in the borrower's business if the lender's financial interests are at stake. *Riquelme Valdes v. Leisure Resource Group, Inc.*, 810 F.2d 1345 (5th Cir. 1987).

[86] Granoff, "Emerging Theories of Lender Liability: Flawed Applications of Old Concepts," 104 *Bank. L. Journ.* 492, 51315 (1987).

[87] It is believed that in connection with lender liability litigation, juries are more likely than judges to err in favor of borrowers in finding lenders liable and in determining the amount of damages. See D. Shuller, Techniques to Reduce Lender Liability Risk, 6 Probate & Property 16 (May/June 1992).

control of all such environmental matters to borrowers.[88] The proliferation of actions against lenders only underscores the importance of lenders to use guidelines such as these (and those prescribed in the chapter), and follow the basic precepts of caution and common sense in their lending and workout policies.

[88] G. Wolf, "Lender Liability under the Federal Superfund Program," 23 *Ariz. St. L. J.* 531, 551–52 (1991).

10

ESTABLISHING A RISK MANAGEMENT AREA

As with all other areas of a bank's activities, the board of directors has a critical role to play in overseeing the credit granting and credit risk management functions of the bank. Each bank should develop a credit risk strategy or plan that establishes the objectives guiding the bank's credit granting activities and adopt the necessary policies and procedures for conducting such activities. The credit risk strategy, as well as significant credit risk policies, should be approved and periodically reviewed by the board of directors. The board needs to recognize that the strategy and policies must cover the many activities of the bank in which credit exposure is a significant risk.[1]

A credit risk strategy should include a statement of the bank's willingness to grant credit based on type (for example, commercial, consumer, real estate), economic sector, geographical location, currency, maturity, and anticipated profitability. This would include the identification of target markets and the overall characteristics that the bank would want to achieve in its credit portfolio (including levels of diversification and concentration tolerances).

---

[1] "Principles for the Management of Credit Risk," consultative paper issued by the Basel Committee on Banking Supervision, Basel, July 1999.

The credit risk strategy should recognize the goals of credit quality, earnings, and growth. Every bank, regardless of size, is in business to be profitable and, consequently, must determine the acceptable risk/reward trade-off for its activities, factoring in the cost of capital. A bank's board

> The bank's board of directors is responsible for overall strategic planning, which, most important, includes setting the bank's tolerance for risks. The board should also ensure that management establishes a measurement system for assessing the various risks, develops a system to relate risk to the bank's capital level, and establishes a method for monitoring compliance with internal policies. It is likewise important for the board of directors to adopt and support strong internal controls and written policies and procedures and ensure that management effectively communicates these throughout the organization.

of directors should approve the bank's strategy for selecting risks and maximizing return. The board should periodically review the financial results of the bank and, based on these results, determine if changes need to be made to the strategy. The board must also determine if the bank's capital level is adequate for the risks assumed throughout the organization.

LOAN POLICY

> A cornerstone of safe and sound banking is the design and implementation of written policies and procedures related to identifying, measuring, monitoring, and controlling credit risk. Credit policies establish the framework for lending and guide the credit granting activities of the bank. Credit policies should address such topics as target markets, portfolio mix, price and nonprice terms, the structure of limits, approval authorities, exception reporting, etc. Such policies should be clearly defined, consistent with prudent banking practices and relevant regulatory requirements, and adequate for the nature and complexity of the bank's activities. The policies should be designed and implemented within the context of internal and external factors such as the bank's market position, trade area, staff capabilities and technology. Policies and procedures that are properly developed and implemented enable the bank to: (i) maintain sound credit granting standards; (ii) monitor and control credit risk; (iii) properly evaluate new business opportunities; and (iv) identify and administer problem credits.[2]

Loan administration policies and (loan) review procedures are critical to long-term success. Before granting credit, a bank's objectives, loan policies, and procedures must be established. Key objectives are (1) to grant loans on a sound, collectible basis, (2) to invest funds profitably for the benefit of shareholders and protection of depositors, (3) to serve the legitimate credit needs of the community. The maintenance of prudent lending policies, effective internal systems and controls, and loan documentation make up the essential fabric of any loan administration.3

[2] Ibid.
[3] Federal Reserve Board (FRB).

As a matter of record, the Officer of the Comptroller of the Currency (OCC),[4] one of a number of governmental regulators, stressed that it is imperative, even in times of plenty, to stay focused on credit/portfolio issues. In a position document,[5] the OCC asked banks to continue being vigilant not only in tracking individual loans but in viewing risk management from a broader perspective—that is, espousing a more effective portfolio credit risk management process. "Such a process," the OCC has stated, "should enable bank management to identify, measure, monitor, and control loan portfolio credit risk."

> Flexibility must exist to allow for fast reaction and early adaptation to changing conditions in the bank's earnings/assets mix and within its service area. The written loan policy is the cornerstone for sound lending and loan administration. An adequate loan policy promotes a bank's business and lending philosophy despite changes in management and stability as it provides a reference for lenders, clarity to minimize confusion concerning lending guidelines, and sound objectives for evaluating new business opportunities. Excerpts of a Bank's Risk Management Policy appear in Appendix 2 to Chapter 10.

The following are the essential elements of a portfolio risk-management process:[6]

1. Assessing the credit culture of an institution
2. Setting portfolio objectives and risk tolerance limits
3. Establishing a portfolio management information system
4. Formulating portfolio segmentation and risk diversification objectives
5. Analyzing adequately loans originated by other lenders
6. Establishing aggregate policy and underwriting exceptions systems
7. Subjecting portfolios to stress tests
8. Maintaining independent controls
9. Analyzing portfolio risk/reward trade-offs

The Federal Reserve takes a similar view and promotes a portfolio approach to credit-risk management.[7] Implicit is the need to put forth a more proactive,

---

[4] Comptroller of the Currency (OCC), Advisory Letter 97-3, 1996.

[5] The document in the form of an advisory letter followed a speech given in late 1996 by Comptroller Eugene Ludwig, during which he voiced concern about evidence of an easing in underwriting standards.

[6] OCC document.

[7] Federal Reserve Manuals (1) "Examination Manual for U.S. Branches and Agencies of Foreign Banking Organizations" and (2) "Framework for Risk-Focused Supervision of Large Complex Organizations." The first manual, printed in September 1997, is 441 pages and is devoted to a comprehensive set of procedures to provide a uniform framework to examine branches and agencies of foreign banking organizations. The second manual, printed in August 1997, describes the Federal Reserve framework for the supervision of large complex institutions. Both manuals are included on the CD: Library/Federal Reserve Systems Manuals subdirectory.

dynamic approach to the whole business of managing credit risk. How well a bank scores on this front will influence the regulators' opinion of the effectiveness of senior risk management, a view that is certain to end up in the Fed's CAMELS bank rating (see Appendix 1 to Chapter 10).

It follows that the loan policies must include pragmatic underwriting standards reviewed by a bank's directors and channeled to all levels of management including lower-echelon staff through appropriate data-gathering and reporting systems (more on this later; see also Chapter 17, "Global Exposure Tracking Systems: Application and Design"). The institution's credit risk stratagem should include, as well, internal limits on exposure, pricing standards, a capital adequacy benchmark on microlevels as well as portfolio levels, an effective credit review and classification process, and methodologies like risk-adjusted return on capital (RAROC) for ensuring that the allowance for loan losses is maintained at appropriate levels. The scope of risk management policies and procedures should be appropriate to the bank's size and loan activities and consistent with prudent banking practices and regulatory requirements.

While lending policy and procedures differ, both agendas require utmost attention. Credit policies deal with the framework for consistent credit decisions directed toward attaining the goals established by the bank for the credit function.[8]

> In the process of decision-making, credit policy is constantly interpreted and applied to concrete situations, with the help of specific guides or procedures. The policy serves as a guide in determining how to handle given kinds of problems, but it never offers a definitive solution. It presents a range of solutions, within which the credit executive is free to exercise his judgment.[9]

Lending policies should clearly delineate the scope of the bank's credit facilities and the body of practices, procedures, and rules whereby loans are made, serviced, and collected. Loan policy should be broad in scope and not disproportionately restrictive. Formulation and enforcement of inflexible standards stifles creativity and initiative and hampers lenders from properly servicing clients and the community at large. A lending policy should provide an environment that encourages finding ways to submit deals the line believes are creditworthy, though the deals themselves may not conform with certain aspects of the bank's written lending policy.

Setting Up Broad Statements of Broad Loan Policy[10]

- Loans should be made for constructive purposes consistent with the best interests of the bank, its customers, its shareholders, and the community.

---

[8] See Chapter 19, "Risk Rating Models: Design and Application."

[9] *FRB Commercial Bank Examination Manual.*

[10] A major New York bank, Manufacturers Hanover Trust, set up these "rules" many years ago. They are appropriate still.

- Loans should have a sound plan of repayment and be predicated upon sound lending principles.
- Loans should be priced fairly and competitively and should compensate the bank for risks assumed.
- Loans must comply with applicable laws and regulations.
- Loans of a speculative nature and situations where the bank is subordinate to other creditors should be avoided.
- Irrespective of established individual lending authorities, wherever possible, the extension of credit will have the approval of more than one officer.
- Lending authorities established herein apply to loans originating only in divisions to which the officers are assigned (except general loan officers).
- Wherever practicable, lines of credit shall be established annually (either confirmed to the customer or for internal guidance as the case may be) as soon as possible after the receipt of fiscal statements. All lines of credit automatically expire one year from date of approval.
- Loans, lines, and commitments will be approved according to established lending authorities always based on total credit exposure to any one borrower.

Many banks funnel risk management policy through a *Policy Committee.* The committee may designate a *chief credit officer* or a loan committee to administer policy. The chain of command can filter down to decentralized structures ending up at the branch level, where line lenders are endowed with approval authority up to a predetermined amount. Conversely, some banks operate with a centralized structure whereby loan committees have lending authority and line officers do not. There are a number gradient structures in between, some listed as follows:

1. *Centralized structure.* This structure is characterized by banks delegating lending authority to loan committees. Line lenders do not have approval limits per se—there is a low level of line accountability, formal procedures, policies, and underwriting standards. Centralized structures are more commonly found in small banks. Centralized structures and loan committees have become more infrequent.

2. *Highly decentralized.* Lending authority is delegated to line officers up to approval limits. Examples include JPMorgan Chase, and Citibank. As loan amounts increase, higher levels of approval are required. A decentralized structure assumes that sound lending policies and procedures are in place. Lenders at these banks are highly trained, up to date, and respond quickly to changes in loan policy. Thus, executive-level bankers seldom have to ride herd to ensure line areas comply with policy. A highly decentralized organization fosters increased market opportunities and encourages prudent risk taking (i.e., greater due diligence).

The example presented for the most part in item 2 is typical and was initiated by a large East Coast bank. Things to think about:

- Strong leadership means taking an active role in identifying new lending skills required by credit officers and in developing the training programs needed to make prudent lending decisions.
- Credit administrators should ensure that the review function is independent of the marketing or line lending areas and that it is staffed adequately to provide management with needed information.
- Management should identify loan review functions that are critical and follow through with updates.
- Likewise, management should get involved in customer calls and marketing, identify and track deficiencies, and never take anything for granted by tracking credit documentation and collateral.

3. *Au fond decentralized.* A senior credit policy officer is assigned to each lending unit. This lending structure is basically equivalent to the highly decentralized structure, except that, due to the persistent high level of loan problems, some banks have adjusted their strategy to include a structure that enforces adherence to policy throughout the underwriting process and life of the loan.

4. *Dual system strategies.* Many banks separate the origination function from the loan administration role. Dual system strategies can be simple, whereby a credit department assesses creditworthiness, or highly complex, as in the following example: Here a complex dual structure takes shape through which both line and credit groups take joint responsibility at the initial evaluation point and jointly monitor the credit until it is retired. Each lending unit is fully equipped with a credit department, industry specialists, and senior credit officers. The process provides for continuous review of underwriting standards and compliance to policy. Unlike a highly decentralized structure, the credit staff drives the bank, not the line. Dual structures are prevalent, and they separate marketing and credit functions.

The following conspectus was collected from annual reports and depicts the range of diversity inherent in the loan policy of money centers and regional banks. Because loan policies are never static, we will not use real names.

1. *Bank A.* This bank is driven by elaborate credit standards, with line marketing distinctly relegated to a secondary role. A dual approval structure forms the backbone to the bank's credit process. Tight control is exercised through an initial underwriting phase continuing throughout the life of the loan, a highly structured credit process. The credit structure incorporates internal industry specialists who not only sign off on transactions but are involved in monitoring exposures over time.

2. *Bank B.* This bank uses a highly decentralized process fostering a go-go spirit at the line level. An elaborate set of checks and balances controls under-

writing standards that work well in an expanding economy, but in a recession, the credit culture becomes problematic. Problem loans are mounting.

3. *Bank C.* This bank promotes a dynamic response to a changing lending/economic environment by separating underwriting and analysis functions. The approval and decision to sell assets are removed from the origination function. Standardization of risks allows for equating trading risks to lending risks. *Bank C* enjoys a gamely reputation owing to the fact that it develops and monitors risk (well before competitors) through sophisticated computerized techniques.

4. *Bank D.* This bank changes its bearings depending on the level of standardization within the product type. For example, consumer loans and mortgages (its targeted growth area) are processed at a central loan center that assures uniformity in underwriting standards and enhances control. Other areas function under a decentralized process, using policies and procedures to control underwriting quality. The Policy Committee actively reviews portfolio concentrations using computer simulation models.

5. *Bank E.* This bank is decentralized with an elaborate centralized monitoring system. The Credit Policy Committee identifies and quantifies all risks. It sets trading, borrower, and industry limits.

6. *Bank F.* Highly decentralized, this bank emphasizes a diversified portfolio to assure quality-underwriting standards.

7. *Bank G.* This bank uses a centralized process whereby all credit authority is vested in a loan committee. The process does not promote accountability or risk taking. *Bank G* had a tendency toward safe, low-margin business, where the bank traditionally enjoyed industry strength.

8. *Bank H.* This bank moved from a centralized process to a decentralized process in the early 1990s. Known for a clublike network that prevails to this day, the bank established a "formal" credit administration area later than comparative banks setting policies, procedures, and underwriting standards. A senior credit officer assigned to each lending unit enforces adherence to policy. The officer reports jointly to credit administration and a lending unit officer-in-charge. Risk management review has limited authority including loan downgrades.

CREDIT POLICIES AND PROCEDURES: FORMAL AND WRITTEN

The Federal Reserve and other supervisory authorities stress the importance of formal written credit policies. Such policies promote discipline, especially when the institution's standards are under assault owing to intense loan competition. A written loan policy acts as the cornerstone for sound lending, promotes business, and fosters the bank's reputation. A well drawn up policy enshrines lending philosophy in stone despite changes in management, points in time, and most important, a bank's operating environment. Providing a reference for lenders, written policies clarify levels of responsibilities, thus minimizing the confusion that

Loan administration and review: Section 112 of the FDIC Improvement Act (FDICIA)

Section 112 requires senior management to describe in writing the bank's loan review and administrative processes as part of an annual management letter. This management report gives senior management and the board of directors an opportunity to assess the adequacy of the loan review and loan administration functions.

The audit and reporting requirements of Section 112 of the Federal Deposit Insurance Corporation Improvement Act (Section 36 of the Federal Deposit Insurance Act) became effective July 2, 1993. The regulation requires banks with assets of more than $500 million to have annual audits performed by independent public accountants, to form audit committees, and to render annual reports that include, among other things, audited financial statements and a management report. Part 363.2 states that the management report should contain the following:

- Statement of management's responsibilities for preparing the institution's annual financial statements, for establishing and maintaining an adequate internal control structure and procedures for financial reporting, and for complying with laws and regulations relating to safety and soundness, which are designated by the FDIC and the appropriate federal banking agency;
- Assessments by management of the effectiveness of such internal control structure and procedures as of the end of such fiscal year and the institution's compliance with such (safety and soundness) laws and regulations during such fiscal year.

The appendix of the regulation gives guidance for structuring the narrative of the management report about loan underwriting and documentation. This appendix emphasizes the importance of effective loan underwriting and documentation procedures. Therefore, the management report should discuss the bank's loan underwriting policies and the internal control procedures used to ensure both adherence to loan policies and that the loan-loss reserve is adequate, given the overall condition of the portfolio.

often accompanies ad hoc guidelines, and sound objectives for evaluating new business opportunities. An excellent and concise set of "rules" for writing up lending guidelines is offered by the FDIC in section 112 of the FDIC Improvement ACT entitled "Loan Administrating and Review."

Formal policies include the type of covenants imposed on specific loans. When designed and enforced properly, loan covenants help lower losses by communicating clear thresholds for financial performance and potentially triggering corrective or protective action at early stages when exposures are salvageable.

Sound banks are not precluded from approving deals that do not meet all written standards. While creativity is encouraged, management should approve and monitor policy exceptions. Formal reporting that describes exceptions to loan policies, by type of exception and organizational unit, can be extremely valuable for informing management and directors of the number and nature of material deviations from the policies that they have designed and approved.

POLICY AND PRACTICE

Aside from annual report disclosures (Exhibit I), credit policy is more effective as a day-to-day guide for general credit decision making, and it should be spelled out in very specific language. These disclosures take many forms and they are referred to as practices, methods, procedures, directives, and so on. They state in detail exactly how credit personnel are to go about carrying out the credit policy.

As noted earlier, many banks promote a quasi-independent environment by encouraging and rewarding business development and supporting branch-level credit areas when possible and appropriate. Considerable leeway is given for individual judgment calls, though credit administration guidelines prescribe degrees of responsibility for clearly defined lending situations. The effectiveness of the credit approval and booking processes are always under scrutiny—actual approvals, loan documentation, review of credits once booked, follow-up calls, and the appropriate information systems that allow ongoing tracking of exposures.

THE LENDING FUNCTION DEPARTMENTALIZED

The vast body of deal structures, not to mention rules set by the bank and regulators, calls for a large body of specialized knowledge not likely to be possessed, to an topmost degree at least, by any one individual. In larger banks the lending function is organized by departments—real estate, consumer credit, highly leveraged transactions, and so on. Many large banks, serving businesses nationally and across international borders, organize the lending function into country groups or industry groups as well, thus providing clients with the best service from lenders experienced and knowledgeable with the market.

Let's review a sampling of the responsibilities credit administrators are charged with.

Credit Risk Management at JPMorgan Chase

Credit risk management embodies practices embraced by both heritage firms (Chase and JPMorgan) as followed:

1. Processes in place are intended to ensure credit risk instruments are accurately assessed, properly approved, and continuously monitored.
2. Independent credit risk management functions exist within each major business unit.

Credit risk is the risk of loss due to borrower or counterparty default. The risk is managed at both the transaction and portfolio levels. Credit risk management processes are highly disciplined and are designed to preserve the independence and integrity of the risk assessment process, as well as integrate effectively with business management.

LIMITATION ON AGGREGATE OUTSTANDING LOANS

As a guide to limiting the total amount of loans outstanding, a bank's exposure system calls up data on the entire relationship—direct and indirect exposures, settlements, global RAROC, and account balances (main accounts to the entire family of accounts internationally. Portfolio exposures, including industry along with exogenous influences, are factored into the formula as well. These include the credit demands of the community, the volatility of deposits, macroeconomic conditions, and so on.

LOAN CONCENTRATIONS

Loan policy strives to develop diversification within the portfolio (a big concern with regulators) and to obtain some optimum balance between maximum yield and minimum risk (see Chapter 12, "Portfolio Maintenance: An Overview," for a fuller treatment of this subject). At the very least, policy should evaluate additional risks incurred when new deals are booked and it should examine how the new approvals influence existing concentrations (covariance). Loan policy also should require that loan concentrations be reviewed and reported frequently to determine concentrations to be worked down, increased, or shunned altogether.

Institutions moderate portfolio risk by lending across different industries and among a broad client base. Operating within industry thresholds, management generally limits credit exposure, and in doing so aims to achieve an optimal mix between portfolio risk and return—generally along the "efficient frontier." While many bankers believe that loan portfolio concentration in similar industries should be avoided, others still suggest that specialization produces superior results by concentrating expertise in a few industries: media, defense, health care, real estate, and so on. This policy can pay off handsomely when teams of industry-knowledgeable loan originators solicit, analyze, and sell off pieces of industry portfolios they do not want.

Loan administrators stress that reviews be conducted often on industry trends, particularly the cyclical ones, along with exposures that may be overly sensitive to adverse external factors. Industries that appear on many bankers' watch lists include transportation, real estate, defense, and electronic data processing.

LOAN AUTHORITY

The lending policy should establish limits for lending officers. Officer limits are influenced by position, experience, training, track record, and tenure. Approval limits are provided for lending teams as well, allowing a combination of officers or a group committee to approve larger loans than the bankers would be allowed to approve individually. The reporting procedures and the frequency of committee meetings are generally defined in a policy/procedures manual. A documented approval process for exceptions to normal loan policy is important. It should include requirements for the approval of exceptions by specific levels of loan authority. Exposure systems at a number of banks report loan exceptions to credit administration[11] and, when serious, to the full board of directors.

CAPITAL ADEQUACY

While they don't make the rules, the loan administration department is deeply concerned with capital adequacy issues.[12]

> Banks must be able to demonstrate that chosen internal capital targets are well founded and these targets are consistent with the bank's overall risk profile and its current operating environment. In assessing capital adequacy, bank management needs to be mindful of the particular stage of the business cycle in which the bank is operating. Rigorous, forward-looking stress testing that identifies possible events or changes in market conditions that could adversely impact the bank should be performed. Bank management clearly bears primary responsibility for ensuring that the bank has adequate capital to support its risks.[13]

Bank capital must be sufficient to protect depositors and creditors from potential financial distress. Allocating sufficient capital against specific loan exposures is on everyone's mind these days—regulators, the board of directors, and, of course, those responsible for loan policy. Capital requirements have so far tended to be simple mechanical rules rather than applications of sophisticated risk-adjusted models, although moves are afoot to change this in the near term.[14]

REPRESENTATIVE CONTENTS OF A BANK LOAN POLICY[15]

Indeed, there have been important new developments for framing internationally acceptable capital adequacy standards. The Basel Committee on Banking

---

[11] See Chapter 17, "Global Exposure Tracking Systems: Application and Design."

[12] See Chapter 11, "Capital Adequacy."

[13] Basel Committee on Banking Supervision Consultative Document Pillar 2 (Supervisory Review Process) Supporting Document to the New Basel Capital Accord issued for comment by 31 May 2001; January 2001.

[14] Discussed further in Chapter 11, "Capital Adequacy."

[15] Board of Governors of the Federal Reserve System Division of Banking Supervision and Regulation, SR 99-18 (SUP), July 1, 1999: Subject—Assessing Capital Adequacy in Relation to Risk at Large Banking Organizations and Others with Complex Risk Profiles.

Supervision plans to introduce a new capital adequacy framework to replace the 1988 Accord. This new capital framework consists of three pillars: minimum capital requirements, a supervisory review process, and effective use of market discipline. The Federal Reserve Bank (FRB) is also concerned with capital adequacy. Over the past several years, FRB supervisors have placed increasing emphasis on banking organizations' internal processes for assessing risks and for ensuring that capital, liquidity, and other financial resources are adequate in relation to the organizations' overall risk profiles. This emphasis has been motivated in part by the greater scope and complexity of business activities at many banking organizations, particularly those activities related to ongoing financial innovation. In this setting, one of the most challenging issues faced by loan administration is how to integrate the assessment of an institution's capital adequacy with a comprehensive view of the risks it faces, particularly in global lending areas.[16] Simple ratios—including risk-based capital ratios—and traditional rules of thumb no longer suffice in assessing the overall capital adequacy of many banking organizations, especially large institutions and others with complex risk profiles such as those significantly engaged in securitization or other complex transfers of risk.

POLICY DEALING WITH MANAGEMENT AND LOAN INFORMATION SYSTEMS

As developed in Chapter 17, "Global Exposure Tracking Systems: Application and Design," the objective of loan information systems is to evaluate the effectiveness of the corporation's management information system in providing the board of directors and senior management committees with the timely, relevant, and accurate information that is necessary to monitor and manage risks and make informed decisions. As a result, the target management information systems (MIS) inspection utilizes a "top-down" approach, which focuses on the information used by the board and senior management committees and the overall MIS architecture. MIS that supports levels of management below those addressed in the inspection should continue to be reviewed during the appropriate examination.[17]

The loan information system function includes review of the loan policy and loan administration procedures, maintenance of loan documentation for borrowers, reports prepared for the benefit of senior management or the board of directors, adequacy of a loan review system, and a system to manage problem loans. Loan information and documentation is a computer-based network of documents that demonstrate that the borrower has the willingness and ability to repay the

---

[16] Federal Reserve System Report on the Target Inspections of Management Information Systems, September 1995

[17] *FRB Loan Examination Manual.* The complete Commercial Bank examination manual is available on the CD in the Federal Reserve System Manuals subdirectory.

loan. These documents also verify that the lender has adhered to sound lending policies and acted prudently to safeguard the bank's funds and ensure repayment of the loan by all reasonable means.

FRB LOAN EXAMINATION: INTERNAL LOAN REVIEW

FRB examiners are guided by a number of objectives depending on the reviewed bank's size, lending activities, and management philosophy. However, regardless of how the loan review is structured, there are several essential areas of responsibilities and communication goals starting with the examination and ending with reports to the bank's management, including the following:[18]

- Provide an objective grading system for loans.
- Provide current information regarding portfolio risk to management and the board on a timely basis.
- Place problem credits under additional scrutiny.
- Evaluate trends in the loan portfolio.
- Cite loan policy exceptions and noncompliance with procedures.
- Cite documentation exceptions.
- Cite violations of laws and regulations.
- Assist in the development and revision of policy and procedures.
- Act as an information source concerning emerging trends in the portfolio and the bank's economy.
- Ensure that the portfolio conforms to the bank's loan policy,
- Ensure that executive management and the board are informed on the bank's asset quality and ensure that credit standards are met in all lending activities.
- Allow lenders sufficient freedom to operate with imagination and resourcefulness without fear of censure.

RISK RATING SYSTEMS

Few methodologies work better safeguarding the integrity of credit exposures than a well-designed and documented risk-rating system. The majority of financial institutions employ internal systems (along with external ones like KMV) to measure the credit risk of both individual loans and the portfolio in general. Grades are assigned from low risk (i.e., remote chance of loss), to doubtful, to likely loss (see Chapter 19, "Credit Risk Rating: Design and Application").

Ratings are also useful in the credit monitoring process once the loan is placed on the books. For example, if the credit review officer determines that a

---

[18] *FRB Loan Examination Manual.*

The list below mirrors a typical profile of loan policy. Specific loan classifications defined by management are included along with loan quality control functions and a committees hierarchy.

General Policy

Management

Trade area

Balance loan portfolio

Portfolio administration

Loan-to-deposit ratio

Legal loan limit

Lending authority

Loan responsibility

Interest rates

Loan repayment

Collateral

Credit information and documentation

Delinquency ratios

Loan-loss reserves

Charge-offs

Extensions or renewals of past-due installment loans

Consumer laws and regulations

Specific Loan Categories

Business development opportunities

Desirable loans by loan category:

1. Commercial loans
2. Agricultural loans
3. Mortgage loans
4. Installment and branch bank loans
5. VISA and revolving credit
6. Mortgage-banking subsidiary
7. Letters of credit
8. Loan commitments
9. Undesirable loans

Miscellaneous Loan Policies

Loans to executive officers, directors, 10% shareholders and companies they control, employee loans, mortgage-banking subsidiary, conflict of interest

Quality Control

1. Credit department
2. Loan review
3. Recovery department

Committees

Directors loan committee of the board of directors

Officers loan committee

Loan review committee

> Some institutions have introduced credit scoring techniques in their small business lending in an effort to improve credit discipline while allowing heavier reliance on statistical analysis rather than detailed and costly analysis of individual loans. Institutions should take care to make balanced and careful use of credit scoring technology for small business lending, and in particular should avoid utilizing this technology exclusively for loans or credit relationships that are large or complex enough to warrant a formal and individualized credit analysis.
>
> Source: Federal Reserve Bank

grade 3 loan has deteriorated to grade 4 levels, the bank may enter into what is often euphemistically called a "dialogue" with the borrower. In some cases, this discussion can be held well before the loan is in danger of becoming a classified asset.

Assigning a risk grade to each loan during the approval process is a useful means to identify the overall level of risk associated with the loan, so long as the risk rating structure and assignment procedures provide a meaningful and consistent indication of the risk of a loan. Risk rating analysis can also provide a valuable reference point for assessing the appropriate degree of trade-off among various loan terms and characteristics and, in particular, in determining appropriate loan pricing.

LOAN PRICING AND RISK-ADJUSTED RETURN ON CAPITAL (RAROC)

Few loan administrators fault the relationship between pricing and credit risk (see Chapter 18, "Pricing Models: Design and Application"). Effective pricing models are designed to interact with return on equity (ROE), return on assets (ROA), and RAROC (objective variables) and to underscore pricing in key, if not all, lending areas. Loan pricing is less an art than a science working in concert with global exposure, an essential tool for credit administration areas. There has been a lot written recently about the increasing inability of lenders to make money on commercial loans due to narrowing spreads, looser covenants, and too much competition. One hears a lot about inadequate returns for the risk, banks cutting back on commercial lending, and even regulators' repeated warnings against the lowering of credit standards. Most of the dire statements about the inadequacy of loan pricing to compensate for risks are based on the narrowing of spreads. Lenders frequently complain that spreads relative to prime have narrowed and their current customers don't warrant the prices being offered. In the old days, the prime rate was associated with a bank's most creditworthy customers. Today, pricing for risk is proving to be the most important and daunting challenge for the future. Commercial lenders will have to learn to apply technology in new and innovative ways to capture and deliver actionable information.

They will have to learn to embrace new, complex, and sophisticated analytics and deliver the results in a clear, intuitive, and actionable format to users. Furthermore, to the extent that there are increased risks, the industry is arguably better positioned to absorb losses without a significant number of failures than it has been in quite a long time.

Risk-adjusted return on capital equates to valuing risk-based performance. Bankers Trust first applied RAROC to the financial services business more than a decade ago. Since that time, several banks have experimented with variants of this approach. RAROC is fundamentally a top-down procedure that tries to align objectives of management with those of shareholders. It attempts to distribute down to products, businesses, customers, or even individual loans the risk costs that the finance function calculates for the entire firm. RAROC uses funds-transfer pricing and capital allocation in apportioning aggregate risk. RAROC ties the firm's overall appetite for capital to solvency risk. As commonly applied today, RAROC starts with a desired credit rating translated into an annual default rate.

IDENTIFYING, CLASSIFYING, AND COMMUNICATING MAIN CAUSES OF LOAN PROBLEMS

If a bank's delinquency rates are consistently below average, its credit policies may be too strict and good business likely was turned away. Effective loan policy gets this message across: carefully review every credit request and try conscientiously to make it work; secondly, search actively for opportunities to promote local growth, and this means through the community at large. It's easy to turn business away, but with the prestige that goes with *constructive lending,* a bank will not need to do much searching before business comes knocking at the door. But this pristine state of affairs applies to constructive lending, and constructive lending is bred through sound loan policies. As implied throughout this chapter, a major cause of loan problems stems from the loan administration's inability to establish a sound lending policy, failure to set up adequate written procedures, and ineptitude when it comes to administrating all aspects of the lending function within established guidelines.[19] Indeed, write-offs are expected as the price of doing business and are just plain unavoidable when clients fail to survive economic or business shocks, such as the loss of a major contract or adverse macroeconomic/industry conditions. But when losses are the result of sloppy lending policies, that's another matter.

---

[19] Ibid.

Federal examiners underscored the following points as "major sources and causes of problem credits."[20] These disclosures reflect harshly on culpable senior administrators along with their directors. Loan policy, in the final analysis, requires a certain amount of prudence, wisdom, and common sense. As the following points show, these attributes are lacking in more than a few institutions.

1. *Self-dealing loans.* This situation is found in a significant number banks that are facing serious problems in the form of an overextension of credit on an unsound basis to directors or large shareholders, or to their interests, who have improperly used their positions as owners to obtain funds in the form of unjustified loans (or sometimes as fees, salaries, or payments for goods or services). Officers who hold their positions at the pleasure of the board and shareholders may be subject to influence and, therefore, may not be in a position to evaluate and reject such credits on the same basis as credit requests of other customers. In that situation, management will often vigorously defend the unsound loans or other self-dealing practices perpetrated upon the bank by the owners. In a self-dealing situation, both the source and the cause of the problem may originate within the bank.

2. *Anxiety for income.* The loan portfolio is usually the most important revenue-producing asset. The earnings factor, however, must never be permitted to outweigh that of soundness so that credits that carry undue risks or unsatisfactory repayment terms are granted. Unsound loans usually cost far more than the revenue produced.

3. *Compromise of credit principles.* Bank management, for various reasons, may grant loans carrying undue risks or unsatisfactory terms with full knowledge of the violation of sound credit principles. The reasons these banks are willing to compromise basic credit principles may include timidity in dealing with individuals having dominating personalities or influential connections, or there may be friendships or personal conflicts of interest involved. Self-dealing, anxiety for income in appropriate salary incentives and bonuses based on loan portfolio growth, and competitive pressures also may lead to a compromise of credit principles.

4. *Incomplete credit information.* Character and capability may be determined by many means, but complete credit information is the only acceptable and reasonably accurate method for determining a borrower's financial capacity. The lack of supporting credit information is an important cause of problem credits. Adequate and comparative financial statements, operating statements, and other pertinent statistical support should be available. Other essential information (such as the purpose of the borrowing and the intended plan and source of repayment), progress reports, inspections, and memoranda of outside information and

---

[20] Board of Governors of the Federal Reserve System Division of Banking Supervision and Regulation, SR 99-24 (SUP), September 29, 1999, "Loan Write-Up Standards for Assets Criticized During Examinations."

loan conferences should be contained in the bank's credit files. Proper credit administration and accurate credit appraisal is not possible without such information.

5. *Failure to obtain or enforce repayment agreements.* This failure constitutes a very important cause of loan trouble. Loans granted without a clear agreement governing repayment are, at the very least, in violation of a fundamental banking principle. Such loans are likely to become problems at a subsequent date. More common and generally as bad is the case where the bank has an agreement with the borrower regarding the repayment or progressive liquidation of the loan but fails to collect the principal payments when and how it should. A study of loan losses will show that, in many cases, amortization never equaled the principal payments the borrower agreed to make. It is a sound axiom that good lending and good borrowing both require consistent liquidation.

6. *Complacency.* The following items manifest complacency and should always be guarded against:
   a. Lack of adequate supervision of old and familiar borrowers
   b. Dependence on oral information furnished by borrowers in lieu of reliable financial data
   c. Optimistic interpretation of known credit weaknesses based on past survival of recurrent hazards and distress
   d. Ignoring warning signs pertaining to the borrower, economy, region, industry, or other related factors

7. *Lack of supervision.* Many loans that are sound at their inception develop into problems and losses because of a lack of effective supervision. Ineffective supervision is almost invariably the result of a lack of knowledge of the borrower's affairs over the lifetime of the loan.

8. *Technical incompetence.* The technical ability to analyze financial statements and to obtain and evaluate other credit information, thereby protecting the bank in the placement and supervision of loans, is possessed by all able and experienced bankers. When it is not, unwarranted losses are certain to develop. The credit incompetence of management should be discussed promptly by the board of directors.

9. *Poor selection of risks.* A majority of banks have some large loans or a rather large number of small loans that are insignificant to the bank in the aggregate. The bank may regard these as not only warranted loans, but also as exceptions to the bank's general credit policies, which contain inherent weaknesses. Because these loans are recognized as a departure from sound credit principles, and because their aggregate amount is moderate, the examiner need not be unduly concerned. However, when exceptions become the rule—recognized or unrecognized—significant loan problems can develop. The following is a list of general loan types that may fall within the category of poor selection risks:

a. Loans wherein the bank advances an excessive proportion of the required capital relative to the equity investment of the borrowers.

b. Loans based more on the expectation of successfully completing a business transaction than on existing net worth and repayment capacity.

c. Loans for the speculative purchase of securities or goods.

d. Collateral loans carried without adequate margins of security.

e. Loans made because of other benefits, such as the control of large balances on deposit in the bank, and not based on sound net worth or collateral.

f. Loans resting solely on the nonmarketable stock of a local corporation in conjunction with loans directly to that corporation. The bank is placed in an awkward position. It may consider itself forced to finance the corporation far beyond warranted limits to avoid loss on the loans that rest on the stock of the corporation.

g. Loans predicated on collateral of problematical liquidation value. A moderate amount of such loans, when recognized by bank management as subject to inherent weakness, may cause few problems. However, the bank can encounter trouble if this practice begins to reflect the rule rather than the exception.

10. *Overlending.* In one sense, this point should be joined with technical incompetence. However, it is a weakness found in some bankers who are otherwise competent. It is almost as serious, from the standpoint of ultimate losses, to lend a fundamentally sound financial risk too much money as it is to lend to an unsound risk. Loans beyond the reasonable capacity of the borrower to repay are unsound. Nowhere is technical competence and credit judgment more at a premium than in determining a sound borrower's safe, maximum loan level.

11. *Competition.* Competition among banks for size and community influence may result in the compromise of credit principles and the acquisition of unsound loans. The ultimate cost of unsound loans always outweighs temporary gains in growth and influence.

Credit administration executives take classified loans very seriously, not only because internal auditors have reviewed statistics on these loans, but because external examiners are involved as well. The Federal Reserve Bank requires examiners to prepare a full loan write-up for institutions rated composite 3, 4, or 5 (see Appendix 1 to Chapter 10, Uniform Financial Institutions Rating System also known as the CAMELS bank rating system). The write-ups are used to support respective classifications to management and, in the case of problem banks, to support any necessary follow-up supervisory actions. Items adversely classified or listed as special mention are critiqued in sufficient detail to support the bank examiner's judgment concerning the bank rating that will be assigned.

Since loan administrators must respond to the following factors, they must be both prepared and knowledgeable. Written reports focus on these points:[21]

- A general description of the obligation
- Amount of exposure (both outstanding and contingent or approved lines yet to be drawn)
- Location of obligor and type of business or occupation
- Description and value of collateral
- Notation if borrower is an insider or a related interest of an insider
- Guarantors and a brief description of their ability to act as a source of repayment, especially if their financial strength has changed significantly since the initial guarantee of the credit facility
- Amounts previously classified
- Repayment terms and historical performance, including prior charge-offs, and current delinquency status (with notation if currently on nonaccrual status)
- Summary listing of weaknesses resulting in classification or special-mention treatment
- Reference to any identified deficiencies in the item that will support loan administration or violation comments elsewhere in the report
- A concise description of management action taken or planned to address the weakness in the asset

THE ROLE AND RESPONSIBILITIES OF LOAN OFFICERS

If lending policies have been clearly stated and are thoroughly understood, line officers will be granted a reasonable amount of authority. Borrowers want to deal with individuals who can make decisions, not dispatch-bearers who refer loans and show savvy only in the paperwork they send to the head office. And response delays are only icing on the cake. Customers who are declined usually feel that had they negotiated with the bank's major players instead, they might have been more persuasive and the deal would have been approved. Unreasonable limits on the lending authority of junior officers hampers business development, results in less than optimal customer relations, and constrains the development of those officers. Training line officers means providing the latitude to allow them to exercise their own judgments and work through mistakes that are bound to happen. To be sure, today's relationship managers are jacks-of-all-trades—salesperson, compliance officer, credit administrator, documentation specialist, and business consultant. For this reason, credit policies and procedures must state *explicitly* the framework guiding lower echelons of responsibilities (and follow through to

---

[21] *Commercial Lending Review,* Karin S. Turpin, **13**(1), no. 1 (Winter 1997/1998), 67–71.

ensure that the bank's personnel administration uses this framework as the basis for job descriptions).

Karin S. Turpin, an expert in the field, offers practical advice for balancing credit and business development responsibilities. Turpin suggests that credit officers regard their respective loan portfolios in relation to the area's entire loan portfolio. Furthermore, each individual officer's portfolio needs to be reasonably consistent with the department's goals and objectives for credit quality, industry concentrations, and profitability. This not only ensures continuity but also contributes to the department's efforts to meet annual goals. She believes loan officers should raise and respond to the following questions:

1. Is the assigned group of assets consistent with the department's total group of assets by loan type, borrower, industry, and geographical location?
2. Are pricing, profit margins, and return on equity (ROE) consistent with department goals and objectives?
3. Is the risk profile of each asset consistent within the department and among loan categories (as measured by the risk ratings or grades assigned to each asset)?
4. Do loans comply with underwriting guidelines and credit policy?
5. With what types of exceptions has the loan been underwritten (high loan to value, tight advance rate, long loan tenor)?
6. How tight are collateral coverage, debt-service coverage, and financial ratios? (Will this demand greater and more frequent monitoring of the loan?)
7. Does the credit/loan agreement provide adequate downside protection throughout the life of the loan?
8. Most important, bank management must ask, how does each individual account officer contribute to a material difference between a well-managed portfolio and a poorly managed one?

CREDIT REVIEWS AND THE QUALITY OF FINANCIAL ANALYSIS

In order to make sound lending decisions, lending officers must have all the pertinent information at hand. Loan procedures should determine the frequency of financial information for various types of exposures along with external credit checks—litigation records, agency credit reports, and so on. Even experienced lenders on occasion become overconfident about the prospects of their customers or take for granted facts that should be carefully checked and verified. That's one reason loan procedures should be defined in such a manner that any *serious* credit data gap found in communiqué supporting new or existing loan facilities is judged a clear violation of lending policy. As the earlier chapters infer, data gaps arise because, lenders (1) don't bother asking clients for timely financial information, (2) are afraid to ask, and (3) do not take the trouble visiting with clients to "peek around."

> Modeling tools are not black boxes that ignore or inhibit wisdom or mechanize the decision-making process but instead foster creativity and requisite skills (including communicative) to participate in strategic decision making at the highest level.
>
> Glantz, M. Scientific Financial Management New York, AMACOM, 2000, pg xii.

While it may be tempting to avoid the financial analysis of old, established, reputable borrowers, in the aggregate these so-called "easy" deals often represent a significant portion of the area's or bankwide portfolio. Yet modern analytics and financial statement analysis go hand in hand; the process is easy, because computerized systems are more the rule than the exception and, of course, customer's appreciate it when they deal with lenders who know their business.

Over a few short years, the approach to financial statement analysis has evolved from casual disciplines of ratios and cash flow to rigorous quantitative and qualitative decision making. Loan valuation techniques like stochastic optimization, simulation, and data mining were still largely exploratory and at best quite tentative. Loan administrators and line officers now have a much richer bag of tricks at their disposal, whose effectiveness can be realized using readily available database and desktop computer technologies. These new techniques offer the banks a broad set of tools capable of addressing problems that are much harder or virtually impossible to solve using the more traditional techniques of analysis still common in some lending areas.

The formal presentation of simulations and stochastic optimization based loan proposals, or other forms of forward-looking analysis, is important in making explicit the conditions required for a loan to perform and for communicating the strengths and weaknesses of the transaction to headquarters. These simulations, along with other advanced financial tools, provide an additional useful benchmark against which management fosters loan sales and syndications that further the objectives of reducing loan concentrations and optimizing a bank's portfolio mix. Modeling tools provide the means to stress-test sensitive sectors of the portfolio but have the most value in maintaining credit discipline when, rather than only describing the single "most likely" scenario for future events, they characterize the range of events that might impair collection of a single or a basket of loans.

BASIC CREDIT REVIEW GUIDELINES

Behind any credit review is the credit file, the bank's written record of each borrower and the business conducted. Bank supervisors have for years been urging even the smallest banking institutions to establish and maintain at least simplified forms of credit files. These files should contain, as a minimum, an analysis of the borrower's latest financials, agency reports, pertinent new clippings, a brief history of the borrower's business and relationship with the bank, and the loan officer's memos regarding the purpose of each loan along with the repayment program agreed upon. The file should include as well copies of correspondence concerning the borrower and records of credit inquiries and interviews both at the bank and at the customer's place of business.

As for credit reviews, the primary goal of these reports is simply to reduce loan losses. Credit reviews reduce to manageable size the vast amount of written credit material, which must be read. Reviews critique the quality and administration of loans after they are booked. They help loan officers strengthen their loans because these documents force lenders to really think about their exposures—they represent the main channel of communication (oral and written) between line and administration, whereby management is kept aware on a regular basis of both the condition of borrowers and the general loan portfolio. Aside from annual requirements, credit reviews are sent up whenever a new loan proposal sheet is required, when loans become marginal, when loans are classified, or upon special request by senior administrators.

A Generic Credit Review Outline

A credit review should be a comprehensive, unbiased, and independent analysis of key credit issues.

1. Provide all sources of information.
   a. Summarize the work completed
   b. Examined financial statements only
   c. Personal visits with company management
   d. Talked with other banks
   e. Consulted with bank industry experts
   f. Researched other relevant sources
2. Organize your credit review under the following headings. Weed out unnecessary information. Look at what's important.
   a. Name and address
   b. Purpose of the review
   c. Business background
      i. Company background and bank relationship. The information provided in this section should be factual, not open to individual interpretation. A description of the borrower's business, its products or services, markets served, and its main competitors should be developed accurately.
      (1) Nature of business
      (2) Management and control
      (3) Industry, macroeconomic sensitivities, and/or company problems

    d. Financial reporting

    e. Fiscal year and noteworthy trends

        i. Analysis of material fiscal changes in the financial statements, including balance sheet, income statement, and cash flow

           (1) Explanation of material changes

        ii. Analysis of collateral or "second way out" protection

    f. Projections

        i. Develop critical assumptions for most likely and conservative cases or run simulation, critical assumption, or value drivers.

        ii. What could happen that would affect the borrower's ability to repay?

    g. Debt capacity and financial strategies (including sources of repayment)

    h. Conclusions

        i. List clearly and concisely the positive and negative factors of the credit deduced from your analysis.

        ii. Present recommendations (where required).

3. Back up each finding by reference to text, statistical exhibits, or computer printout.

A REPORT CARD FOR THE BANK'S MANAGEMENT: UNIFORM FINANCIAL INSTITUTION'S RATING SYSTEM (CAMELS)

The Federal Financial Institutions Examination Council (FFIEC) adopted the Uniform Financial Institution's Rating System (UFIRS) in November 1979.[22] Over the years, the UFIRS has proven to be an effective internal supervisory tool for evaluating the soundness of financial institutions on a uniform basis and for identifying those institutions requiring special attention or concern. A number of changes, however, have occurred in the banking industry and in the federal supervisory agencies' policies and procedures, which have prompted a review and revision of the 1979 rating system. The revisions to UFIRS include the addition of a sixth component addressing sensitivity to market risks, the explicit reference to the quality of risk management processes in the management component, and the identification of risk elements within the composite and component rating descriptions.

SUMMARY

A key function of senior management, in concert with the board, is to design, implement, and support the bank's strategic objectives. Strategic planning takes

---

[22] See Appendix 1 to Chapter 10 and CAMELS spreadsheet included in the CD-ROM.

a long view, rather than a day-to-day perspective, and is aimed at integrating asset deployment, funding, capital adequacy, management, marketing, operations, and information systems to achieve balance between shareholder value objectives and regulatory restraints. Inadequate planning is an obstacle to meeting strategic objectives such as changing bank direction, expansion of current activities, and anticipated asset mix. A poorly formed risk management area is disruptive and will likely hinder future strategic goals.

REVIEW QUESTIONS

1. What is a function of credit policies? What topics should those policies address? What can well-developed policies enable a bank to do?
2. What are the essential elements of a portfolio risk-management process?
3. Explain the following statement: A policy does not offer a definitive solution. What are the broad statements of a broad loan policy? Enumerate them.
4. What are two opposite types of structure? Describe them and state their main advantages and disadvantages.
5. Why is it important to departmentalize the lending function? How do the credit administrators deal with the limitation on aggregate outstanding loans and loan concentration?
6. What is a function of MIS in credit management?
7. What are the role and responsibilities of loan officers? Why is it important to push the decision-making process down to the line officers?
8. What are three reasons why a lender may fail to perform a financial analysis of a borrower? Why is a financial analysis so important?
9. What is a credit file and what information should it contain? What is a function of the credit reviews?

SELECTED REFERENCES AND READINGS

Aspinwall, R. C., and R. A. Eisenbeis. (1985). *Handbook for banking strategy*. New York: Wiley.

Bank Administration Institute. Bank Management.

Corns, M. C. (1962). *The practical operations and management of a bank*. Boston: Bankers Publishing.

Datta, Mitra, J., and World Bank. (1997). *Fiscal management in adjustment lending*. Washington, DC: World Bank.

Diamond, W., V. S. Raghavan. (1982). *Aspects of development bank management*. Baltimore, Published for the Economic Development Institute of the World Bank by the Johns Hopkins University Press.

Donaldson, T. H. (1989). *Credit risk and exposure in securitization and transactions*. New York: St. Martin's Press.

Fair, D. E., F. L. d. Juvigny, *et al.* (1982). *Bank management in a changing domestic and international environment: The challenges of the eighties.* The Hague: Boston.

Hingham, M.A., M. Nijhoff; distributor for the U.S.A. and Canada Kluwer, Boston.

Giroux, G. A., and P. S. Rose. (1981). *Financial forecasting in banking: Methods and applications.* Ann Arbor, MI: UMI Research Press.

Greuning, H. v., and S. Brajovic Bratanovic. (2000). Analyzing banking risk: A framework for assessing corporate governance and financial risk management. Washington, D.C.: World Bank.

Hayes, D. A. (1977). *Bank lending policies, domestic and international.* Ann Arbor, MI: Division of Research Graduate School of Business Administration, University of Michigan.

Hempel, G. H., and D. G. Simonson. (1991). *Bank financial management: Strategies and techniques for a changing industry.* New York: J. Wiley.

Hempel, G. H., D. G. Simonson, *et al.* (1998). *Bank management: Text and cases, 5th edition.* New York: Wiley.

Hester, D. D., and J. L. Pierce. (1975). *Bank management and portfolio behavior.* New Haven, CT: Yale University Press.

Kammert, J. L. (1981). *International commercial banking management.* New York: Amacom.

Mauri, A. (1998). A new approach to institutional lending and loan administration in rural areas of LDCs. *Rivista Internazionale Di Scienze Economiche E Commerciali = International Review of Economics and Business,* 707–715.

Rhyne, E. (1988). *Small business, banks, and SBA loan guarantees: Subsidizing the weak or bridging a credit gap?* New York: Quorum Books.

Stigum, M. L., and R. O. Branch. (1983). *Managing bank assets and liabilities: Strategies for risk control and profit.* Homewood, IL: Jones-Irwin.

Vasconcellos, G. M., and M. J. Lynge, Jr. (1988). Loan loss reserve decision in large commercial banks." *University of Illinois At Urbana-Champaign. Bureau of Economic and Business Research. College of Commerce and Business Administration, Bebr Faculty Working Paper No. 1479,* 1–[28].

INTERNET LIBRARY

1. Supervision and regulation letters, commonly known as SR Letters, address significant policy and procedural matters related to the Federal Reserve System's supervisory responsibilities. Issued by the Board of Governors' Division of Banking Supervision and Regulation, SR Letters are an important means of disseminating information to banking supervision staff at the board and the Reserve Banks and, in some instances, to supervised banking organizations; http://www.federalreserve.gov/boarddocs/SRLETTERS/

2. FRB Commercial Bank Examination Manual, November 2000, Analytical Review and Income and Expense, effective date May 1996. Helps the examiner develop an overview of a bank's financial condition and results of operations through the use of analytical review techniques, among others; http://www.federalreserve.gov/boarddocs/supmanual/cbem/cb4000.pdf

3. Bank for International Settlement publication: Sound Practices for Loan Accounting and Disclosure (July 1999), http://www.bis.org/publ/bcbsc142.pdf

4. The Basle Committee consultative paper on loan valuation, loan loss provisioning, and credit risk disclosure (October 1998), http://www.bis.org/press/p981014.htm#pgtop

5. Federal Reserve Report on the Target Inspections of Management Information Systems, http://www.federalreserve.gov/boarddocs/SRLETTERS/1995/sr9545.htm#exhibit%

6. FRB Uniform Financial Institutions Rating System, http://www.federalreserve.gov/boarddocs/SRLETTERS/1996/sr9638.htm

7. FRB Lending Standards for Commercial Loans (1998), http://www.federalreserve.gov/board-docs/SRLETTERS/1998/SR9818.HTM

8. Federal Reserve System, Framework for Risk-Focused Supervision of Large Complex Institutions (August 1997), pdf file http://www.federalreserve.gov/boarddocs/SRLETTERS/1997/ sr9724a1.pdf

UNIFORM FINANCIAL INSTITUTION'S RATING SYSTEM COMMONLY REFERRED TO AS THE CAMELS RATING SYSTEM

The Uniform Financial Institution's Rating System is an internal supervisory tool currently used by the federal supervisory agencies as follows: (1) the Board of Governors of the Federal Reserve System (FRB), (2) the Federal Deposit Insurance Corporation (FDIC), (3) the Office of the Comptroller of the Currency (OCC), (4) the Office of Thrift Supervision (OTS), and (5) the National Credit Union Association (NCUA).

In addition, state banking departments, as well as the Farm Credit Administration, use the rating system. The supervisory agencies use the rating system to evaluate the soundness of financial institutions on a uniform basis and to identify those institutions requiring special supervisory attention or concern. The CAMELS rating system workbook CAMELS is in the subdirectory Models-Demos\Chapter 10. The model has been augmented and can be used to rate financial institutes.

TABLE 10A.1   Descriptions of Composite CAMELS Ratings

Rating	Description
1	Institutions in this group are basically sound in every respect; any critical findings or comments are of a minor nature and can be handled in a routine manner. Such institutions are resistant to external economic and financial disturbances and are more capable of withstanding the vagaries of business conditions than institutions with lower ratings. As a result, such institutions give no cause for supervisory concern.
2	Institutions in this group are also fundamentally sound, but may reflect modest weaknesses correctable in the normal course of business. The nature and severity of deficiencies, however, are not considered material and, therefore, such institutions are stable and also able to withstand business fluctuations quite well, While areas of weakness could develop into conditions of greater concern, the supervisory response is limited to the extent that minor adjustments are resolved in the normal course of business and operations continue satisfactorily.
3	Institutions in this category exhibit a combination of financial, operational, or compliance weaknesses ranging from moderately severe to unsatisfactory. When weaknesses relate to financial condition, such institutions may be vulnerable to the onset of adverse business conditions and could easily deteriorate if concerted action is not effective in correcting the areas of weakness. Institutions that are in significant noncompliance with laws and regulations may also be accorded this rating, Generally, these institutions give more cause for supervisory concern and require more than normal supervision to address deficiencies. Overall strength and financial capacity, however, are still such as to make failure only a remote possibility.
4	Institutions in this group have an immoderate volume of serious financial weaknesses or a combination of other conditions that are unsatisfactory. Major and serious problems or unsafe and unsound conditions may exist, which are not being satisfactorily addressed or resolved. Unless effective action is taken to correct these conditions, they could reasonably develop into a situation that could impair future viability, constitute a threat to the interests of depositors, and/or pose a potential for disbursement of funds by the insuring agency. A higher potential for failure is present but is not yet imminent or pronounced. Institutions in this category require close supervisory attention, financial surveillance, and a definitive plan for corrective action.
5	This category is reserved for institutions with an extremely high immediate or near-term probability of failure. The volume and severity of weaknesses or unsafe and unsound conditions are so critical that they require urgent aid from stockholders or other public or private sources of financial assistance. In the absence of urgent and decisive corrective measures, these situations will likely require liquidation and the payoff of depositors, disbursement of insurance funds to insured depositors, or some form of emergency assistance, merger, or acquisition.

Source: *Commercial Bank Examination Manual*, A, 5020. 1, pp. 3–4: Uniform Financial Institution's Rating System, effective March 1984. The workbook CAMELS was developed by the author.

TABLE 10A.2   Components of the CAMELS Ratings

Component	Description
Capital adequacy	A bank's Tier 1, total capital, and leverage ratios in relation to its peer group are the most important factors in assigning a prelimi-

nary rating. Peer groups are based on bank asset size, number of offices, and location in a metropolitan or nonmetropolitan area. More capital is required for banks with deficiencies in any other area of the examination, particularly in asset quality. Examiners also pay close attention to how equity and asset growth affect the capital ratios, and they look at retained earnings as a ratio of average total equity to determine whether a bank's equity growth is through retained earnings or an unsustainable outside source. They also look at the size of the dividend payout.

Asset quality

The asset quality rating is an indicator of future losses to the bank and affects the ratings of other areas of examination, which must be considered in light of their adequacy to absorb anticipated losses. The most important factor in the asset quality rating is the bank's weighted classified asset ratio, which is computed as [15% *substandard assets +50%*doubtful assets + 100%*loss assets]/[Tier I capital + allocation for loan and lease losses]. Examiners also consider the level, trend, and composition of classified assets and nonaccrual and renegotiated loans, loan concentrations, lending policies, and effectiveness in monitoring past-due loans, insider loans, and the types of risks inherent in the bank's on- and off-balance sheet portfolios.

Management

Management is evaluated on a number of criteria, including compliance with applicable laws and regulations, whether there is a comprehensive internal or external review audit, internal controls to safeguard bank assets, and systems for timely and accurate information. Examiners also consider the other components of the CAMELS rating, shareholder return, and the extent to which the bank is serving all sectors of its community.

Earnings

Earnings are assessed for ability to absorb future losses, so this rating is affected by asset quality, a bank's level, trend, and relation to peer of net interest income, noninterest income, overhead expense and provision for loan and lease losses, extraordinary items, additional required provision for loan and lease losses or other nonrecurring items, and dividend payouts.

Liquidity

The liquidity rating is a determination of a bank's ease in obtaining money cheaply and quickly, and a bank's management of interest rate risk, Considerations include the bank's loan commitments and standby letters of credit, the presence of an "unstable core" of funding, access to capital markets, the ratios of federal funds purchased and brokered deposits to total assets and the ratios of loans to deposits.

Sensitivity to market risk

Rating is based on based on, but not limited to, assessments of the sensitivity of the financial institution's earnings or the economic value of its capital to adverse changes in interest rates, foreign exchange rates, commodity prices, or equity prices, the ability of management to identify, measure, monitor, and control exposure to market risk given the institution's size, complexity, and risk profile, the nature and complexity of interest rate risk, exposure arising from nontrading positions where appropriate, the nature and complexity of market risk exposure arising from trading and foreign operations.

TABLE 10A.3   Classified Asset Categories

Component	Description
Special mention	This category includes loans that are potential problems but that are currently of adequate quality. Loans with inadequate documentation and loans particularly vulnerable to a change in economic conditions may be classified as such. Loans to borrowers with deteriorating but still acceptable financials are another example.
Substandard	Loans in this category are judged to have a well-defined weakness that may result in losses to the bank if left uncorrected. Characteristics include significant deviations from scheduled payments, delinquency, carried over debt, numerous extensions or renewals without statement of source of repayment, decreased borrower profitability, or poor borrower cash flow.
Doubtful	Doubtful loans have problems similar to those of substandard loans, but they also have a loss exposure considered severe enough to jeopardize full collection of the loan highly unlikely. However, the loan is not yet considered a loss due to the possibility of mitigating circumstances, such as a proposed merger, capital injection, or refinancing plans. A loan should not be classified as doubtful for two consecutive exams, since it is assumed the status of the loan should be resolved during the time between exams.
Loss	A loan considered uncollectible is classified as a loss. Although some probability of partial recovery may exist, it is considered preferable to write off the loan in the current period. Such loans are characterized by severe delinquency.
Management	Management is evaluated on a number of criteria, including compliance with applicable laws and regulations, whether there is a comprehensive internal or external review audit, internal controls to safeguard bank assets, and systems for timely and accurate information. Examiners also consider the other components of the CAMEL rating, shareholder return, and the extent to which the bank is serving all sectors of its community.
Liquidity	The liquidity ratings is determination of a bank's ease in obtaining money cheaply and quickly, and a bank's management of interest rate risk. Considerations include the bank's loan commitments and standby letter of credit, the presence of an "unstable core" of funding, access to capital markets, the ratios of federal funds purchased and brokered deposits to total assets and the ratios loans to deposits.

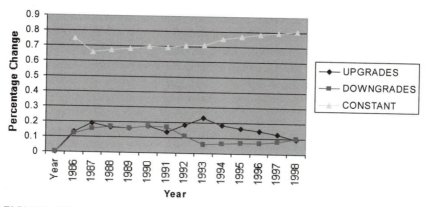

FIGURE 10A.1   Changes between Examinations in CAMELS Ratings

TABLE 10A.4   Changes between Examinations in CAMEL Ratings

Year	Banks	Upgrades	Downgrades	Constant
1986	472	13.1%	11.9%	75.0%
1987	3,816	18.7%	15.5%	65.8%
1988	5,426	16.1%	16.8%	67.2%
1989	7,258	15.7%	15.8%	68.5%
1990	7,905	17.4%	17.5%	69.8%
1991	8,072	13.5%	17.1%	69.4%
1992	8,729	18.2%	11.3%	70.6%
1993	9,364	23.0%	6.0%	71.0%
1994	8,777	18.2%	6.3%	75.5%
1995	7,754	16.4%	6.7%	76.9%
1996	7,194	14.9%	6.6%	78.4%
1997	6,217	12.7%	7.9%	79.4%
1998	5,422	9.5%	10.0%	80.5%

Appendix 10.2

FORMAL CREDIT POLICIES

EXAMPLE OF A LOAN POLICY[1]

Policy Committee

(Date)

Secretary

The secretary of the credit policy committee (officer-in-charge of the credit and finance group) will maintain the minutes of any meeting of the committee and keep current records of all lending authorities of $250,000 or more individually or in combination granted to officers of the institution. Senior loan officers will advise the secretary, in writing, of all such authorities extended to officers under their jurisdiction and all subsequent changes.

---

[1] This example was drawn on the loan policy of an anonymous bank many years ago. Recent loan policies are generally proprietary.

General

1. Irrespective of established individual lending authorities, wherever possible, the extension of credit will have the approval of more than one officer.
2. Lending authorities established herein apply to loans originating only in divisions to which the officers are assigned (except general loan officers).
3. Wherever practicable, lines of credit shall be established annually (either confirmed to customer or for internal guidance as the case may be) as soon as possible after receipt of fiscal statements. All lines of credit automatically expire one year from date of approval.
4. Loans, lines, and commitments will be approved according to established lending authorities always based on total credit exposure to any one borrower. Total credit exposure shall be defined as the following facilities, whether domestic or overseas, and whether made by the bank, subsidiaries or affiliates: loans, lines, revolving credits, term loans, overdrafts, uncollected lines, letters of credit, acceptances, mortgages, formal and informal guarantees, direct or indirect lease arrangements and any other secured loans (except loans to government bond dealers made by the portfolio and investment banking division).
5. Established lending authorities will not apply to "unusual" loans which require specific approvals outside of normal lending authorities.

Classes of Lending Officers

1. General loan officers: chairman, president, vice chairmen, and executive vice presidents in charge of the international, metropolitan, national and portfolio and investment banking divisions.
2. Deputy general loan officers: senior vice presidents designated by the president, and the vice chairmen.
3. Senior loan officers: senior vice presidents of the international, metropolitan and national divisions, and other officers as designated by the president and the vice chairmen, on the recommendation of the general loan officer in charge of the respective divisions
4. Supervisory loan officers: certain vice presidents of the international, metropolitan, national, and portfolio and investment banking divisions, and the real estate and mortgage department designated by a general loan officer or a deputy general loan officer on the recommendation of a senior loan officer in the respective divisions or departments.
5. Loan officers: other officers of the bank who have been granted lending authorities in accordance with the limits established elsewhere in this memorandum:

   a. Individual lending authorities of $250,000 and below will be established by a senior loan officer and a supervisory loan officer
   b. A general loan officer or a deputy general loan officer on the recommendation of a senior loan officer or a supervisory loan officer will establish individual lending authorities above $250,000, but not in excess of $1 million.
6. Records: the executive vice president of each division will keep current records of all lending authorities established within his or her division. Senior loan officers will keep current records of all lending authorities granted to officers under their jurisdiction.

Limits of Lending Authority

General

1. The authorities of deputy general loan officers and senior loan officers extend to all loans within their respective divisions or departments.
2. The authorities of supervisory and other loan officers extend to the respective region, district, territory, corporate banking center, branch, or department to which they are assigned.
3. Senior loan officers are charged with the responsibility for the effective control and review of all loans made within their region and will establish such procedures as they deem necessary to assure (a) the implementation of bank loan policy, (b) the maintenance of current and complete credit files on all borrowers, and (c) that each loan carries the approvals prescribed in this memorandum on the appropriate proposal sheets or notes.
4. Limits:
   a. Over $15 million—two general loan officers
   b. Up to and including$15 million—a general loan officer with either a deputy general, senior, supervisory, or loan officer
   c. Up to and including $10 million—a deputy general loan officer with either a senior, supervisory, or loan officer or two senior loan officers
   d. Up to and including $5 million—a senior loan officer with either a supervisory or loan officer
   e. Up to and including $2.5 million—a supervisory loan officer and a loan officer
   f. Up to and including $1 million—a vice president and a loan officer
   g. Up to and including$250,000—an assistant vice president and a loan officer
   h. Up to and including$50,000—an assistant secretary and a loan officer

Specific dollar lending authorities for loan officers are not to be combined, and the authority of one of the approving officers must be sufficient to cover the full amount of the loan, line or commitment.

Exceptions to the Loan-Authority Dollar Limitations

1. Day loans to "street houses," "street loans" secured by marketable collateral and loans to government bond dealers may be approved by two of the vice presidents in the Wall Street Department within the lines established by the executive vice president of the portfolio and investment banking division.
2. Lines for the sale of federal funds may be approved by the executive vice president of the portfolio and investment banking division or a senior vice president of the international, metropolitan or national divisions together with a supervisory or loan officer.
3. Foreign exchange lines may be approved by a senior loan officer of the international, metropolitan or national divisions together with a supervisory or loan officer. Approval of daily settlement limits, however, must conform to normal approval requirements.
4. A supervisory loan officer together with a loan officer may approve secured loans to correspondent banks up to and including $5 million. Loans above that amount shall be approved in accordance with normal lending authorities.
5. Any two loan officers may approve offerings under established lines for day loans or the sale of federal funds. Any two loan officers may approve offerings under established current lines of credit or under term and revolving credit commitments.

Unusual Loans Requiring Special Approvals

1. The following loans require the approval of a deputy general loan officer together with a senior, supervisory, or loan officer for amounts up to and including $500,000. The approval of a general loan officer together with a deputy general, senior, supervisory, or loan officer is required for amounts up to and including $2 million, and the approval of two general loan officers is required for amounts of more than $2 million:
   a. Lines, loans, and commitments to real estate investment trusts (REITs)
   b. Loans for unfriendly acquisitions.
   c. Loans in which the bank's compensation involves equity kickers and/or warrants.
   d. Loans to political candidates and political organizations.

e. Loans secured by blanket assignments (except in the United Kingdom, where taking of fixed and floating charges over a company's assets is normal banking practice).

2. The following loans require the approval of a senior loan officer together with a supervisory or loan officer for amounts up to and including $250,000. The approval of a deputy general loan officer together with a senior, supervisory, or loan officer is required for amounts up to and including $1 million. The approval of a general loan officer together with a deputy general, senior, supervisory, or loan officer is required for amounts up to and including $5 million, and the approval of two general loan officers is required for amounts of more than $5 million:

   a. Revolving credits and term loans with maturities of seven years or with a balloon payment greater than one-half of the loan.
   b. Evergreen (no payout) revolving credits.
   c. Loans that have the effect of replacing a material portion of net worth with debt.
   d. Loans to not-for-profit organizations.
   e. Loans collateralized by a 50% or greater concentration of one security.
   f. Loans secured by other than cash equivalents, cash surrender value of life insurance, or readily marketable collateral. (Loans secured by accounts receivable and inventories are not subject to the required approvals of this paragraph).
   g. Standby letters of credit.

3. Loans in excess of $50,000 to officers of correspondent banks secured by that bank's capital stock require the approval of a general loan officer together with a deputy general, senior, supervisory, or loan officer.

4. New or increased lines, loans or commitments to finance companies or leasing companies up to and including $5 million require the approval of a senior loan officer together with a supervisory or loan officer. All lines, loans, or commitments above that amount shall be approved in accordance with normal lending authorities. Concurrence of the finance company section of the corporate finance department is also required on all new or increased facilities to finance companies and leasing companies.

5. Unsecured loans to individuals require approvals (not described here).

6. $75 million "house limit." Any extensions of credit, whether temporary or otherwise, above $75 million, or any increases of credit extensions above this amount (more than a $500,000 increase), must be approved by either the president, or a vice chairman. In this case, total extension of credit shall mean our total exposure to any one borrower or related borrowers such as subsidiaries, affiliates, joint ventures, or other borrowers where there exists a common ultimate financial

responsibility. The total credit exposure shall be defined as the following facilities, whether domestic or overseas, whether made by the bank, subsidiaries, or affiliates: loans, lines, revolving credits, term loans, overdrafts, uncollected lines, letters of credit, acceptances, mortgages, formal and informal guarantees, any other secured loans (except loans to government bond dealers made by the portfolio and investment banking division), direct or indirect lease arrangements, and any affiliated loan arrangement. the secretary shall keep a list of such loans in excess of the "House Limit," and this list shall be updated biannually for the president and the vice chairmen.

LOAN REVIEW COMMITTEES

International, Metropolitan, National Divisions, and the Real Estate and Mortgage Department

1. The general loan officers are ex-officio members of all Loan Review Committees.
2. Each committee will meet on a regular basis (not less than twice monthly).
3. Each committee will establish appropriate procedures for the continuous review of all outstanding loans with advice to the Credit Policy Committee of the procedures that have been established.

Members of the Loan Review Committees

1. Members of the International Division Loan Review Committee shall be the senior vice presidents in the international division and other officers designated by the executive vice president in charge of the international division.
2. Members of the metropolitan division loan review committees shall be as follows: the corporate banking group committee members shall be the executive vice president in charge of the division and the senior vice presidents in charge of the respective regions. The branch banking group committee members shall be the senior vice president and deputy general manager in charge of the group and the senior vice presidents in charge of the respective areas. Chairman of both committees shall be the senior vice president in charge of credit policy.
3. Members of the National Division Loan Review Committee shall be the senior vice presidents in the national division, the heads of each district, and other officers designated by the executive division. Chairman of the committee shall be the vice president in charge of loan review.

11

CAPITAL ADEQUACY

Bank capital fosters public confidence and provides a buffer for contingencies involving large losses, thus protecting depositors from failure. Capital funds provide time to (1) recover, so that losses can be absorbed out of future earnings rather than capital funds, (2) wind down operations without disrupting other businesses, and (3) ensure the public that the bank has positioned itself to withstand new hardships placed on it. As the Basel Committee has

Bank management clearly bears primary responsibility for ensuring that the bank has adequate capital to support its risks. This chapter covers the assessment of capital adequacy, the Basel 1988 accord, and the new capital adequacy framework. The chapter also presents a supervisory review of capital adequacy and establishes the appropriate levels of capital and Federal Reserve examination procedures known as the "assessment of capital adequacy."

Functions and Growth of Bank Capital

- Banks utilize much higher financial leverage than does almost every other industry.
- Equity capital accounts for about 7% of total capital.
- Capital rules foster confidence.
- Capital must be sufficient to protect against on- or off-balance sheet risks.
- Minimum capital standards are vital for reducing systemic risk.
- Bank capital reduces risks borne by the FDIC.
- Adequate capital allows absorption of losses out of future earnings rather than capital funds.
- Bank capital affects regulatory functions.
- Bank capital influences other functions (e.g., it supplies the working tools of the enterprise).

---

noted, "Capital is an important indicator of a bank's overall condition, for financial markets, depositors and bank regulators."[1]

> Banks must be able to demonstrate that chosen internal capital targets are well founded and these targets are consistent with the bank's overall risk profile and its current operating environment. In assessing capital adequacy, bank management needs to be mindful of the particular stage of the business cycle in which the bank is operating. Rigorous, forward-looking stress testing that identifies possible events or changes in market conditions that could adversely impact the bank should be performed. Bank management clearly bears primary responsibility for ensuring that the bank has adequate capital to support its risks.[2]

The protective function of bank capital has been viewed not only as assuring that depositors are paid in full in case of liquidation, but also as helping to maintain solvency by providing a cushion so that a bank threatened with losses might continue operating. Unlike most firms, only a portion of bank capital contributes to solvency. Banks are generally considered solvent as long as capital is unimpaired—that is, asset values are at least equal to adjusted liabilities[3] and, significantly, bank assets are diligently appraised, marked-to-market, and cushioned to a high degree against unexpected risks (risk adjusted). Bankwide risks falling under protective capital include the following:[4]

---

[1] Basel Committee on Banking Supervision is a committee of banking supervisory authorities that was established by the central bank governors of the Group of Ten countries in 1975. It consists of senior representatives of bank supervisory authorities and central banks from Belgikum, Canada, France, Germany, Italy, Japan, Luxembourg, the Netherlands, Sweden, Switzerland, the United Kingdom, and the United States. It usually meets at the bank for International Settlements in Basel, where its permanent secretariat is located.

[2] Basel Committee on Banking Supervision Consultative Document Pillar 2 (Supervisory Review Process) Supporting Document to the New Basel Capital Accord issued for comment by May 31, 2001; January 2001.

[3] Liabilities excluding subordinated capital notes and debentures, plus capital stock.

[4] Basel Committee on Bank Supervision, Basel, Switzerland.

- *Credit risk* refers to the potential that a borrower or counterparty will fail to perform on an obligation. Because most earning assets are in the form of loans, poor loan quality is the major cause of bank failure. As a result, risk exposures are assessed, whether on or off the balance sheet to include typical loans, receivables under derivative and foreign exchange contracts, and lending-related commitments (e.g., letters of credit and undrawn commitments to extend credit). Using statistical techniques, estimates are made of both expected losses (on average, over a cycle) and unexpected losses for each segment of the portfolio. These estimates usually drive the *credit cost along with capital allocations* to each business unit and are incorporated into each unit's "value added." As a result, the credit risk profile of each business unit becomes an important factor in assessing performance. First and second lines of protection against credit losses for purposes of capital adequacy are earnings and loan loss reserves.

First Line of Defense Against Credit Losses for Capital Adequacy Purposes	Second Line of Defense Against Credit Losses for Capital Adequacy Purposes
Current earnings. The appropriate focal relationship is the ratio of current earnings, after taxes, provisions for loan losses and dividends, to actual loss expectations.	Reserve for loan losses and other capital accounts after the reserve has been charged and exhausted. The second line of defense of capital adequacy (from a historical perspective) holds that if the principal preconditions are satisfied, loan loss reserves and other capital accounts must aggregate to 20 times the level of historical loss, to provide a reasonable margin of safety.

- *Market risks* refers to risks arising from adverse movements in market price or rate, for example, interest rates, foreign exchange rates, or equity prices. Traditionally, management and regulators focused strictly on credit risk. In recent years, another group of assets have come under scrutiny—assets typically traded in financial markets. These assets form the "trading book," in contrast to the "banking book," and are associated with *traditionally* nontraded assets—loans (though today there is a big play in the secondary loan market). For most large banks, while the trading book is relatively small compared with the banking book, its rising prominence makes market risk an important regulatory concern. In January 1996, rules were adopted[5] to regulate market exposures setting risk-based capital requirements for the trading book of banks and securities houses. Basel Capital Accords require commercial banks with significant trading activity to provide regulators with value-at-risk (VAR) estimates from internal risk-measuring models; this is because VAR estimates a bank's market risk capital requirements better than most other models. VAR addresses aggregating market exposures across disparate asset classes helping to calculate a portfolio-level measure of market risk.

---

[5] European Union (EU).

- *Basis risk* refers to the difference in the pricing characteristics of two instruments—for example, when market rates for different financial instruments change at different times or by different amounts.

- *Liquidity risk* refers to the possibility that an institution will be unable to meet obligations when due because assets cannot be liquidated, required funding is unavailable (referred to as "funding liquidity risk"), or specific exposures cannot be unwound without significantly lowering market prices because of weak market depth or market disruptions ("market liquidity risk"). Capital position has a direct bearing on an institution's ability to access liquidity, particularly during periods of crisis, which is why internal systems for measuring, monitoring, and controlling liquidity risk are frequently evolving. Weak liquidity might cause a bank to liquefy assets or acquire liabilities to refinance maturing claims. Banks typically evaluate capital adequacy in terms of their liquidity profile and the fluidity of the markets in which they operate.

- *Operational risk* refers to the risk that inadequate information systems, operational problems, breaches in internal controls, fraud, or unforeseen catastrophes will result in unexpected losses. Frequently, operating risks account for a substantial fraction (20% or more) of large banks' total risk. Thus, assessing capital for credit and market risks, while excluding operating risks, could easily understate overall capital requirements. The requirements problem is complicated by the fact that, while operating risks are viewed as quite important, models for quantifying these risks are not in widespread use.

- *Legal risk* refers to the potential that unenforceable contracts, lawsuits, or adverse judgments can disrupt or otherwise negatively affect the operations or condition of a banking organization.

- *Reputation risk* refers to the potential that negative publicity regarding an institution's business practices, whether true or not, will cause a decline in the customer base, costly litigation, or revenue reductions.

A HISTORICAL PERSPECTIVE: TRADITIONAL ASSET CATEGORIES

From a historical perspective, bank assets traditionally were divided into six groups, each associated with a specific capital requirement. Although these allocations may appear a bit arbitrary, they were consistent with bank policies at the time (at least before the 1988 Basel Accords) and were supposed to be ample to absorb losses. The six categories that follow required capital levels sufficient to satisfy regulators and keep banks functional:

- *First category: Required reserves and highly liquid assets.* Cash, bank balances, U.S. government securities maturing within five years, bankers' acceptances, and federal funds sold. No capital was required against these essentially riskless assets. While remote market risk

> The Basel Accord is not a static framework but is being developed and improved continuously. The Basel Committee neither ignores market participants' comments on the Accord nor denies that there may be potential for improvement. More specifically, the Committee is aware that the current treatment of credit risk needs to be revisited so as to modify and improve the Accord, where necessary, in order to maintain its effectiveness.
> Source: Tom de Swaan

exists even in short-term U.S. government securities, earnings easily absorb any exposures.

- *Second category: Minimum risk assets.* Loans and investments with very low risk, U.S. government securities with maturities over five years, government-guaranteed loans and government agencies' securities, loans secured by similar assets or by savings passbooks, cash value of life insurance, prime commercial paper, brokers, loans, and other assets of similar quality.

- *Third category: Portfolio assets.* Traditionally included usual banking risk assets, for example, the remaining loan portfolio free from regulatory classification, along with the remainder of investment-grade (rated Baa or above) securities (other than U.S. government bonds) maturing in more than five years.

- *Fourth category: Substandard assets.* Assets with more than normal banking risk, obligors with a weak financial condition or unfavorable record, risky exposures backed by marginal collateral quality or insufficient or below-margin securities.

- *Fifth category: Work-out assets.* Loans auditors classified as doubtful, such as weak credits backed by dubious common stock, defaulted securities, or real estate assets not legally acquirable except by foreclosure.

- *Sixth category: Asset losses along with fixed assets.* Fixed assets are working basics but not considered bank investments in a real sense. Elaborate premises attract business, but offer depositors little protection in the event of bank failure. Bank facilities can be disposed of only when a bank goes into liquidation and likely will return little value during economic downturns.

The Basel Accord

Capital rules changed with the 1988 Basel Accord. Basel was instrumental in reversing a protracted downward trend in the capital adequacy of international banks, increasing the attention the financial markets paid to the quantity and quality of bank capital.

> The Accord effectively contributed to enhanced market transparency, to international harmonization of capital standards, and thus, importantly, to a level playing field within the Group of Ten (G-10) countries and elsewhere. . . . Virtually all non-G-10 countries with international banks of significance have introduced, or are in the process of introducing, arrangements similar to those laid down in the Accord. These are achievements that need to be preserved.[6]

Since the 1988 Basel Accord, banking and financial markets have changed markedly, following in the wake of new innovative credit risk measurement and management tools, as well as sophisticated bank products. Yet the Basel Accord failed to keep pace with the new playing field of the 1990s and was thus ripe for revision.

Post-1988 proposed amendments offer a lot more plasticity. Capital standards are less subject to excessive reinterpretations, dampening chances that regulatory burdens will prove unproductive. This means, the argument goes, that large spreads between regulator-perceived risks (and capital) and bank-perceived risks are easier resolved, reducing the odds of "misguided" capital allocations. For example, if management felt that a bank had far more capital than needed, paring down allocations might encourage the bank to pursue riskier loans within a certain risk category (chasing higher returns on capital).

The 1988 Basel Accord focused a great deal on credit risk.[7] Basically, the accord provided a framework for capital weightings according to risk: 0%, 10%, 20%, 50%, and 100%. For example, Organization for Economic Cooperation (OECD)-government debt and cash are zero-weighted loans to banks set at 20%; loans fully secured by mortgages on residential property are weighted at 50%; claims on the private sector or on banks incorporated outside the OECD with a residual maturity of over one year are weighted at 100% (see the left column in Table 11.1).

The 1988 Basel Accord will be replaced by a system using external credit ratings. As it stands now, the debt of an OECD country with an A rating will risk-weight 20% as depicted in Table 11.2, while AAA debt will receive a zero capital weighting. Corporate debt will be marked with graduated weightings so that an AA-rated loan will be risk-weighted at 20%, while an A-rated loan will be risk-weighted at 100%. (See the right column in Tables 11.1 and 11.2).

VALUE DEFINED BY ACCOUNTING, ECONOMIC, AND REGULATORY FACTORS

Capital adequacy is measured three ways: book value (via generally accepted accounting principles, or GAAP), economic (market value), and regulatory defined value (RAP). The contrasts between the three methods can be noteworthy.

---

[6] Tom de Swaan, former chairman of the Basel Committee on Banking Supervision.

[7] International Convergence of Capital Measurement and Capital Standards (1988).

TABLE 11.1   Existing and Proposed Capital Guidelines

	Existing Bank for International Settlements (BIS) capital adequacy guidelines	Proposed new guidelines
0%	Cash Claims on central governments and central banks denominated in national currency and funded in that currency Other claims on OECD and central governments and central banks Claims collateralized by cash of OECD central-government securities or guaranteed by OECD central governments	AAA- to AA- rated sovereigns
0%, 10%, 20%, or 50%	At national discretion Claims of domestic public-sector entities, excluding central government, and loans guaranteed by such entities	Not applicable
20%	Claims on multilateral development banks and claims guaranteed by, or collateralized by, securities issued by such banks Claims on banks incorporated in countries outside the OECD with a residual maturity of up to one year and loans with a residual maturity of up to one year guaranteed by banks incorporated in countries outside the OECD Claims on nondomestic OECD public-sector entities, excluding central government, and loans guaranteed by such entities Cash items in process of collection	A+ to A-rated sovereigns AAA to AA- rated banks AAA to AA- rated corporates
50%	Loans fully secured by mortgage on residential property that is or will be occupied by the borrower or that is rented	BBB+ to BBB-rated sovereigns A+ to A-rated banks (risk weighting based on that of the sovereign in which the bank is incorporated) A+ to A-rated banks (risk weighting based on the assessment of the individual bank) BBB+ to BBB-rated banks Unrated banks (risk weighting based on the assessment of the individual banks) Loans fully secured by mortgage on residential property that is or will be occupied by the borrower or that is rented
100%	Claims on the private sector Claims on banks incorporated outside the OECD with a residual maturity of over one year	BBB+ to BBB-rated banks (risk weighting based on that of the sovereign in which the bank is incorporated)

TABLE 11.1   Continued

	Existing Bank for International Settlements (BIS) capital adequacy guidelines	Proposed new guidelines
	Claims on central governments outside the OECD (unless denominated in national currency and funded in that currency) Claims on commercial companies owned by the public sector Premises, plant and equipment, and other fixed assets Real estate and other investments (including nonconsolidated investment participations in other companies) Capital instruments issued by other banks (unless deducted from capital) All other assets	BB+ to B-rated sovereigns BB+ to B-rated banks (risk weighting based on that of the sovereign in which the bank is incorporated) BB+ to B-rated banks (risk rating based on the assessment of the individual bank) BBB+ to BBB-rated corporates BB+ to B-rated corporates Unrated banks (risk weighting based on that of the sovereign in which the bank is incorporated) Unrated corporates Commercial mortgages
150%	Not applicable	Below B-rated sovereigns Below B-rated banks (risk weighting based on that of the sovereign in which the bank is incorporated) Below B-rated banks (risk weighting based on the assessment of the individual bank) Below B-rated corporates Securitization tranches rated below BB- and BB-bbb

Source: JPMorgan, Special Corporate Study, Financial Institutions; The Basel Committee's New Capital Adequacy Framework—Market Implications; page 5, Table 3: BIS capital adequacy rules—A comparison of existing and proposed guidelines, June 8, 1999.

TABLE 11.2   Claims and Assessments

Claim	Assessment					
	AAA to AA-	A+ to A-	BBB+ to BBB-	BB+ to B-	Below B-	Unrated
Sovereigns	0%	20%	50%	100%	150%	100%
Banks: Option 1[1]	20%	50%	100%	100%	150%	100%
Banks: Option 1[2]	20%	50%[3]	50%[3]	100%[3]	150%[3]	50%[3]
Corporates	20%	100%	100%	100%	150%	100%

[1] Risk weighting based on risk weighting of sovereign in which the bank is incorporated.
[2] Risk weighting based on the assessment of the individual bank.
[3] Claims on banks of a short original maturity, for example, less than six months, would receive a weighting that is one category more favorable than the visual risk weight on the bank's claims.

When book and economic values diverge markedly, bankers and regulators alike can walk away with a distorted view of capital coverage. Consider a money-center bank's book and market (equity) values prior to and just after the international debt crisis, the height of the crunch in commercial real estate lending, or a saving and loan institution's book net worth vis-à-vis market worth during the height of the thrift crisis and just after the government bailout. Expressed in terms of economic value to book value, we see at once that ratio falls below 1. In practice, if book accounting is to have any relevance to the science (and art) of capital apportionment, then devalued assets, whether in the form of underwater mortgages or questionable loans, must be marked-to-market—and frequently. We need not be reminded of Enron and the other recent financial reporting debacles.

Economic or Market-Denominated Capital

The market value of capital represents the real net worth suitable for settling claims. Banks can be book solvent but insolvent when the same assets are priced in the marketplace. The situation might arise if auditors failed (by error or design) to adjust loan-loss reserves to match the quality of a bank's loan portfolio, or if assets were not marked-to-market following adverse interest or exchange rate movement. Remember, economic values are influenced by market-perceived, *risk-adjusted* earning power, while book value follows historical cost. It is not surprising, in times of stress, to find significant differences between the two methods. Banks, after all, operate in a dynamic and uncertain world.

An offshoot of market value is a concept the literature calls fair or reasonable value (known also as intrinsic value). While the market value of listed security can be identified at the time, the stock's fair value as viewed by different investors (or, for that matter, internal auditors, management, or regulators at large) can differ. Graham, Dodd, and Cottle defined fair value as "that value which is justified by the *facts; for example, assets, earnings, and dividends.*"[8] The computed (fair) value is likely to change at least from year to year as the factors governing that value are modified.

In practice, investors holding stock in the financial services look to financial strength, sustainable liquidity and earnings quality, and growth. To banks and their investors, earnings quality is practically synonymous with loan quality. Why is loan quality both a fundamental and paramount concept? Reasoning holds that investors believe that although lower-quality loans may temporarily bring in abnormally high income, in the long run this ill-advised policy will statistically result in abnormal losses negating the higher income that was temporarily booked. Also factored in are historical loan loss provisions, actual losses incurred, the relative size of annual provisions for losses, and reserves for losses,

---

[8] Graham, Dodd, and Cottle were authors and leading gurus in the investments field. See *Security Analysis: The Classic 1934 Edition,* New York, McGraw-Hill Professional Publishing (1996).

together with the tally of nonperforming assets—all disclosed in annual reports and reports published by investment houses.

Regulatory Denominated Capital (Regulatory Accounting)

Regulatory capital, under existing and proposed amendments to the Basel 1988 Accords, deals with three capital "tiers"—Tier 1 (core) capital serves as the most basic form of permanent capital; Tier 2 includes various forms of capital not qualifying as Tier 1 capital; and Tier 3 capital, a new concept, calls for capital that may be allocated only against market risks of inherently short duration.

REGULATING CAPITAL FEATURE

An Overview of Tier 1 Capital

Tier 1 capital (core capital) is a bank's most valuable form of capital and must comprise at least 50% of total regulatory capital. Included are common equity, qualifying noncumulative perpetual preferred shares (these instruments have the perpetual characteristics of equity and rank at the bottom of the capital structure, just ahead of common stock, but offer a fixed rather than variable rate of return), and qualifying noncontrolling interests in subsidiaries arising on consolidation from Tier 1 capital instruments (see the Table 11.3 for a detailed breakdown of Tier 1 capital characters). Goodwill and other intangible assets are deducted from Tier 1 capital, and the resulting figure is then compared to total risk-weighted assets to determine the risk-weighted Tier 1 capital ratio.

While common equity is the most prevalent form of Tier 1 capital, it is also the most expensive. In practice, the issuing bank could be required to guarantee some level of return on capital or face constraints from existing shareholders fearful of stock dilution and other negative consequences. But the issue remains—Tier 1 is increasingly recognized as a way of balancing the often divergent concerns of *regulators*, whose overriding objective is to preserve balance sheet integrity, and *shareholders,* whose interests are directed toward strong investment returns. For banks, the issuance of Tier 1 capital, while certainly not cheap, offers an attractive means to address the needs of two important constituencies—supervisors and investors.

Capital adequacy guidelines mandate that,[9] for banks domiciled in OECD countries, Tier 1 capital must amount to a minimum of 4% of total risk-weighted assets; in practice, however, most commercial banks target a Tier 1 ratio in the range of 6 to 7%. Still other banks carry significantly higher capital ratios,

---

[9] Capital adequacy guidelines were established under the Basel Accord: an agreement reached under the auspices of the Bank for International Settlements.

reflecting a combination of factors such as strength and sustainability of earnings, availability of hidden reserves, unrealized gains on securities, and management's conservatism toward earnings and capital retention.

Tier 1 Leverage Ratio

Behind Tier 1 leverage benchmarks are limits regulators like to place on an institution leveraging up its equity capital base. Dividing Tier 1 capital by average total consolidated assets brings us to Tier 1 leverage. Average total consolidated assets equal quarterly average total assets reported on the bank's recent regulatory report, less goodwill, certain other intangible assets, investments in subsidiaries or associated companies, and certain excess deferred-tax assets that are dependent on future taxable income.

The Federal Reserve has adopted minimum Tier 1 leverage as 3% for highly rated banks. For state member banks, the same holds as long as these banks operate with well-diversified risk portfolios, little unhedged interest-rate-risk exposure, solid asset quality, high liquidity, and good earnings (derived based on the risk-adjusted return on capital, or RAROC, of course)—in other words, they must be ranked composite 1 under the CAMELS[10] rating system.[11] Other state member banks are expected to have a minimum Tier 1 leverage ratio of 4%. Bank holding companies rated a composite 1 under the BOPEC rating system and those that have implemented regulators' risk-based capital measure for market risk must maintain minimum Tier 1 leverage of 3%.[12] Other bank holding companies are expected to have a minimum 4% Tier 1 leverage. Of course, there are exceptions, but in the final analysis, supervisors will require that regulatory capital is commensurate with both the level and nature of risks.

How is regulatory denominated capital broken down? How will new capital pillars change the notion of capital adequacy? Will banks need to establish new structures to cope with the amended capital accords? We address these issues in the next section.

BREAKDOWN OF TIER CAPITAL COMPONENTS

Tier I Capital

Common Shareholders' Equity

Included are common stock, capital reserves, and retained earnings, as well as adjustments for the cumulative effect of foreign currency translations, less stock

---

[10] A rating system of the Federal Reserve Board used to rate bank holding companies. Acronym for capital adequacy, asset quality, management, earnings, liquidity, and sensitivity to market risk.

[11] The CAMELS rating system in electronic form is included on the CD: Demos_Models/Chapter 11.

[12] The Basel Committee on Banking Supervision affirmed this view in a release issued in October 1998, which stated that common shareholders' funds are the key element of capital.

held in treasury. A capital instrument deemed not permanent or that has prefer-ence with regard to liquidation or payment of dividends is not considered (regu-latory defined) common stock, regardless of what investors call the instrument. Regulators take special note of terms that look for common stock issues that have more than one class. Preference features may be found in a class of common stock, and if so that class will be pulled out of the common stock category. When adjustments are completed, the remaining common stock becomes the dominant form of Tier 1 capital.

Accordingly, capital guidelines discourage over-reliance on nonvoting equity elements in Tier 1 capital. Nonvoting equity attributes arise in cases where a bank has issued two classes of common stock, one voting and the other non-voting. Alternatively, one class may have so-called super-voting rights, which entitle the holder to more votes than other classes. Here, super-voting shares may have the votes to overwhelm the voting power of other shares. Accordingly, banks with nonvoting, common equity along with Tier 1 perpetual preferred stock in excess of their voting common stock are "clearly over relying on nonvoting equity elements in Tier I capital." The important point is that in such cases, reg-ulators are likely to reallocate some nonvoting equity elements from Tier 1 to Tier 2 capital.

Perpetual Preferred Stock

Risk-based capital guidelines define perpetual preferred stock as preferred stock with no maturity date, stock not redeemable at the holder's option, and preferred issues with no other provisions requiring future redemption. Perpetual preferred qualifies as Tier 1 capital only if it can absorb losses while the bank operates and only if the bank has the inclination and legal right to defer or eliminate preferred dividends altogether.

Perpetual preferred stock allowing redemptions at the option of the financial institution may qualify as Tier 1 capital only if the redemption is subject to the prior approval of regulators. Stock convertible at the option of the bank into another issue of perpetual preferred stock or subordinated debt is subject to prior regulatory approval as well.

Noncumulative Preferred Stock

Banks may include perpetual preferred stock in Tier 1 only if the stock is non-cumulative. Noncumulative issues must not permit accruing or payment of unpaid dividends, period. On the other hand, perpetual preferred stock calling for accumulation and future payment of unpaid dividends is regulatory cumula-tive, regardless of what the issue says, and will end up in Tier 2 supplemental capital.

Preferred issues with reset dividend rates conditional on the bank's financial condition or credit standing are excluded from Tier 1, but may be acceptable Tier 2 capital.

The obligation under such instruments to pay out higher dividends when a bank's condition deteriorates is inconsistent with the essential precept that capital should provide both strength and loss absorption capacity to a bank during periods of adversity.[13]

Embedded Special Features in Preferred Issues

Some preferred issues embed features that raise questions as to whether these issues are acceptable as any manner of permanent capital. In this category, regulators may see the so-called exploding rate or a similar feature where, after a specified period, the dividend rate automatically increases to a level that promotes or even triggers redemption. Higher dividend requirements could be forced on a bank trying to work out problems, thus ruling out the possibility for inclusion in Tier 1 capital.

Convertible Perpetual Preferred Stock

Convertible issues allow investors to convert bank preferred stock into a fixed number of common stock at a preset price. Because the conversion feature reduces capital structure risk, the stock will generally qualify as Tier 1 capital (provided, of course, that it is noncumulative). However, preferred issues, which investors are able to convert into common stock at current market prices, raise concerns. If the bank is performing poorly, the conversion ratio may trigger conversion into a large number of low-priced common shares. This could result in serious common dilution. The concern here is that the threat of dilution could make the bank reluctant to sell new common stock or place the bank under strong market pressure to redeem or repurchase the convertible preferred. Thus, convertible preferred stock will likely not qualify as Tier 1 capital.

Minority Interest in Equity Accounts of Consolidated Subsidiaries

Minority interest in equity is included in Tier 1 capital because, as a general rule, it represents equity freely available to absorb losses in operating subsidiaries. Banks are expected to avoid using minority interest as an avenue for introducing elements that do not otherwise qualify as Tier 1 capital (such as cumulative or auction-rate perpetual preferred stock) or that would, in effect, result in an excessive reliance on preferred stock within Tier 1 capital. Should a bank use minority interest in these ways, regulators might require reallocation of a portion of the bank's minority interest to Tier 2 capital. The characteristics of Tier 1 capital are summarized in Table 11.3.

Tier 2 Supplemental Capital

Tier 2 capital includes allowance for loan and lease losses on (general reserves only; some countries, but not the United States, permit "undisclosed" reserves)

---

[13] Quote from the Federal Reserve Board.

TABLE 11.3 Summary Characteristics of Tier I Capital

Meaning	Tier 1 capital, often called "core" capital, represents the most basic form of permanent capital supporting a bank's operations.
Importance	Tier 1 capital is a bank's most valuable form of capital and must comprise at least 50% of total capital, as per Basel Accord guidelines.
	Tier 1 capital is an important focus of interest for determining investment analysts' and rating agencies' views on a given bank's capital strength.
	Like other forms of capital, Tier 1 provides operating and strategic flexibility for bank managements in pursuing performance objectives.
	While common equity is the most common type of Tier 1 capital, it is also the most expensive form of capital to raise.
	Tier 1 capital is increasingly recognized as a means of balancing the often divergent interests of banking industry regulators, whose overriding objective is to preserve or strengthen the integrity of a bank's balance sheet, and shareholders, who are demanding high returns on their equity investments.
	For banks, the issuance of Tier 1 qualifying debt is an attractive means to address the needs of both of these important constituencies.
Maturity	None
Restrictions	Minimum of 4.0% of total risk-weighted assets ("Total Capital"); most banks target 6.0% Tier 1 capital ratios.
Provisions	Noncumulative, interest deferral. Full loss absorption.

Source: Bank for International Settlements.

nonqualifying cumulative perpetual, long-term and convertible preferred stock; nonqualifying perpetual debt and other hybrid debt-equity instruments; intermediate-term preferred stock, and term subordinated debt, "upper" and "lower." The total of Tier 2 capital is limited to 100% of Tier 1, although amounts in excess of this limitation are permitted but do not qualify as capital. There are other limits as well. For instance, to qualify as supplementary capital, subordinated debt and intermediate-term preferred stock must have an original average maturity of at least five years.

Upper Tier 2 subordinated debt must be less than 50% of total capital while lower Tier 2 debt must be less than 50% of Tier 1 capital or 25% of total capital. The characteristics of Tier 2 capital are summarized in Table 11.4.

One caveat for inclusion of subordinated debt in Tier 2 capital deals with terms that permit investors to accelerate payment of the principal upon specific events. As far as regulators are concerned, the only acceleration clauses acceptable in a subordinated debt issue are those triggered by insolvency (i.e., appointment of a receiver). Terms permitting accelerated payment other than insolvency allow investors to bail out of a troubled bank before depositors. Also, debts with accelerated payment terms that do not meet the minimum five-year maturity requirements for debt capital instruments do not qualify.

TABLE 11.4   Summary Characteristics of Tier 2 Capital

Meaning	Tier 2 subordinated debt consists of two elements: upper and lower	
	Upper Tier 2 subordinated debt	**Lower Tier 2 subordinated debt**
Maturity	Undated in structure, but coupon stepups allowed after 5, 7, or 10 years to provide economic maturity/call date to maturity	Dated. Minimum tenor of 5 years but often at least 10 years, given required amortization starting five years prior
Amortization	None, unless issued in dated form	Typically 20% per annum in the 5 years prior to maturity
Provisions	Interest deferral triggered at option of management, if predetermined test is breached, loss absorption occurs under certain circumstances	No interest deferral No loss absorption
Status	Junior subordinated, usually ranking below lower Tier 2	Subordinated to senior claims; senior to upper Tier 2 capital and always senior to all equity providers
Event of default	Failure to pay interest or principal when due Acceleration limited to winding up and liquidation	Limited to winding up and liquidation
Lock-in	Yes, on interest, typically linked to nonpayment of	No dividends or breach of capital ratio; interest accumulates on deferred interest and principal payments
Restrictions	Must be less than 50% of total capital	Must be less than 50% of Tier 1 capital or 25% of total capital

Source: Bank for International Settlements.

Another limitation is when an event of default is defined too broadly. A regulator's scrutiny goes into high gear when subordinated debt terms are inconsistent with safe and sound banking practice. In a case like this, the issue will likely be pulled out of regulatory denominated capital altogether.[14] Also there is the disquieting possibility that an event of default might allow investors to accelerate payment ahead of other issues containing cross-default clauses. This could restrict day-to-day operations.

Other events of default, such as change of bank control or a disposal of subsidiaries, may restrict or even curtail the turnaround strategies of a troubled bank. Still other events of default, such as failure to maintain certain capital ratios or rates of return or to limit the amount of nonperforming assets or charge-offs to specific thresholds, may allow subordinated debt holders to recoup their investment before a deteriorating institution turns into a full-fledged failure.

---

[14] FRB Loan examination guidelines.

Supervisors have long recognized two shortcomings in the Basel Accord's risk-based capital framework. First, the regulatory measures of "capital" may not represent a bank's true capacity to absorb unexpected losses. Deficiencies in loan loss reserves, for example, could mask deteriorations in banks' economic net worth. Second, the denominator of the revised risk-based capital (RBC) ratios, total risk-weighted assets, may not be an accurate measure of total risk. The regulatory risk weights do not reflect certain risks, such as interest rate and operating risks. More important, they ignore critical differences in credit risk among financial instruments (e.g., all commercial credits incur a 100% risk weight), as well as differences across banks in hedging, portfolio diversification, and the quality of risk management systems.

Source: The Federal Reserve System Task Force on Internal Credit Risk Models, May 1998.

Tier 3 Capital

A key difference between Tier 3 and Tier 2 capital is that Tier 3 capital may only be allocated against market risks, which are inherently short term. In contrast, risks comprising the "familiar" banking book are intermediate or long term. In practice, the banking book is matched up with appropriately tenured capital instruments. The trading book, in comparison, is more liquid. Should problems arise, corrective action can be taken more quickly owing to the expected liquidity and mark-to-market nature of the underlying risks. While Tier 3 is limited in its availability to support trading book risk, a bank's ability to access this form of capital can have a positive impact on its capital planning strategies.

Assuming the trading book is large enough to accommodate the use of Tier 3 capital, a longer dated Tier 3 issue may serve as a viable capital financing alternative for banks fully peaked on lower Tier 2 capital but reluctant to issue upper Tier 2 because of the cost or (possibly) investor resistance. For example, investors may be turned off to certain features—perpetual nature, deep subordination, unattractive stepup, liquidity, and so on. Despite the relatively onerous lock-in provision, Tier 3 capital still ranks *pari passu* with lower Tier 2 capital in bankruptcy, affording it some degree of substitutability with lower Tier 2 capital. The characteristics of Tier 3 capital are summarized in Table 11.5. See also the placement of Tier 3 capital in Table 11.6.

Drawbacks

While the groundbreaking 1988 Basel Accord established minimum capital levels for international banks, incorporating off-balance-sheet exposures and a risk weighting system, some imperfections became obvious. First, applying the bank's risk weightings, as they were set by the Basel Accord, did not always provide the default risk measurement precision supervisors called for. Another had to do with the problem banks had in arbitraging their regulatory capital requirements to exploit divergences between true economic risk and risks delineated by the Basel Accord. Another concern had to do with credit risk as

TABLE 11.5   Summary of Tier 3 Capital

Meaning	Tier 3 capital includes certain forms of fully paid, subordinated debt, which carry unique characteristics with regard to maturity, payment interest and principal, and structure; Tier 3 capital can only be allocated against market risk, primarily the bank's trading activities
Maturity	No less than two years and one day in tenor
Amortization	None
Provisions	Interest deferral, at option of management, if predetermined test is breached; loss absorption may occur under certain circumstances
Status	Subordinated to senior, but *pari passu* with lower Tier 2 instruments
Events of default	Limited to winding up and liquidation
Lock-in	Allowed for interest and principal, with regulatory approval, provided that minimum capital adequacy ratios are breached; upon interest deferral, interest on interest does not accrue
Restrictions	Tier 3 capital cannot exceed 250% of the Tier 1 capital allocated toward market
BIS Amendment	Amount of Tier 3 that can be used by a bank is limited to 250% of the Tier I capital, which is allocated against market risks, although bank regulators in certain countries may apply more stringent restrictions
S&P View	The S&P indicated that it will review each Tier 3 issue individually, but will likely rate such instruments three notches below senior debt.
	Its justification for this approach is that the decision about a potential default is left (to a large extent) to the bank's regulators.
	The S&P argues that because the "pay or don't pay" decision is in the hands of the bank's regulators and not management (as in the case of upper Tier 2 debt instruments), Tier 3 instruments may carry greater repayment risk, particularly with regard to the timeliness of interest or principal payments.
	Thus, the S&P has taken the view that the certainty that interest and principal will be paid on Tier 3 obligations is less than that for upper Tier I2 instruments and, interestingly, even less than that for a bank's preferred shares.

Source: Bank for International Settlements.

the predominate focus to the exclusion of risks associated with a broad range of bank products.[15] As a result, amendments calling for updates to the 1988 Basel Accord were placed in motion.

As we noted earlier, the new amendments are much broader and are designed to sharpen regulatory capital's role in measuring other risks beyond credit. These risks include interest rate risk in the banking book; operational, liquidity, legal and reputation risks; and a host of other risks not explicitly addressed in the earlier Basel Accord.

---

[15] Other risks were certainly a functional part of capital allocation, but with the new amendments a much more inclusive risk awareness will be required by regulators.

TABLE 11.6   A Typical Commercial Bank's Capital structure: Supplementary Core Capital

Classification	Structure	Fundamentals	Capital ratio
	Senior debt	Funding, not capital	Capital ratio of 8%
Supplementary capital	Subordinated debt (dated)	Lower Tier 2 (up to 50% of Tier I)	
	Subordinated debt	Tier 3 trading book only	
	Subordinated debt (qualifying dated)	Upper Tier 2	
	Junior subordinated debt (perpetuals)	(Up to 100% of Tier 1)	
Core capital	Tier I qualifying debt	Tier 1 capital ratios of 4%	
	Preference shares	Tier 1	
	Common shares	Tier 1	
	Retained earnings	Tier 1	

Source: JPMorgan

The essence of the matter here is that new amendments call for "three pillars." The first pillar is designed to set up minimum capital requirements (already highlighted in this chapter) and to develop and expand on standardized 1988 rules *but replace the risk-weighting system with a system that uses external credit ratings* (see the right column of Table 11.1). The second pillar sets up methodology dealing with *supervisory* review of capital adequacy ensuring that a bank's capital position is consistent with its risk profile and overall strategy. The amendments encourage early supervisory intervention if a bank falls below established capital adequacy thresholds. The third pillar, market discipline, encourages high disclosure standards and augments the role of market participants (investors) so that they will do more to encourage banks to hold adequate capital. Let's review the second and third pillars in some detail.

THE SECOND PILLAR: SUPERVISORY REVIEW OF CAPITAL ADEQUACY

The second pillar establishes a supervisory review explicitly as a central piece in the proposed capital allocation structure. Rather than being a discretionary pillar, the supervisory review process acts as a fundamental complement to both the minimum regulatory capital requirements (pillar 1) and market discipline (pillar 3). Supervisors are to take on an increased role, not only reviewing a bank's capital position and strategy, but also ensuring that capital is in accord with a bank's overall risk profile and, furthermore, that the bank is in compliance with regulatory capital minimums. If capital falls below threshold levels, the second pillar invites quick, early supervisory action.

Following are four basic "rules" for regulators:[16]

Pillar 2: Supervisory Review of Capital Adequacy

- Seeks to ensure that the bank's position is consistent with its overall risk profile and strategy, otherwise early supervisory intervention will be likely
- Supervisors want the ability to require banks to show greater degrees of risk to hold capital in excess of 8% minimum

---

1. Regulators will expect banks to operate above the minimum regulatory capital ratios and require banks to hold capital in excess of the minimum.
2. Banks should have processes for assessing overall capital adequacy in relation to their risk profile, as well as strategies for maintaining capital levels.
3. Supervisors should review and evaluate a bank's internal capital adequacy assessment and strategy, as well as its compliance with regulatory capital ratios.
4. Supervisors should seek to intervene at an early stage to prevent capital from falling below prudent levels.

With regard to establishing appropriate capital levels, a variety of "qualitative" factors fall into place, including the following:

1. Experience and quality of management and key personnel
2. Risk appetite and track record in managing risk
3. Nature of the markets in which a bank operates
4. Quality, reliability, and volatility of earnings
5. Quality of capital and access to new capital
6. Diversification of activities and concentration of exposures
7. Liability and liquidity profile
8. Complexity of legal and organizational structure
9. Adequacy of risk management systems and controls
10. Support and control provided by shareholders
11. Degree of supervision by other supervisors

The Federal Reserve Board (FRB) also has developed a framework for "a sound internal analysis of capital adequacy" (the board's language) calling for four fundamental elements: identifying and measuring all material risks, relating capital to the level of risk, stating explicit capital adequacy goals with respect to risk, and assessing conformity to the institution's stated objectives. Recognizing

---

[16] Source: Federal Reserve Board.

the significance of pillar 2, the following extracts are from the FRB's four-point framework:[17]

1. *Identifying and measuring all material risks.* A disciplined risk-measurement program promotes consistency and thoroughness in assessing current and prospective risk profiles, while recognizing that risks often cannot be precisely measured. The detail and sophistication of risk measurement should be appropriate to the characteristics of an institution's activities and to the size and nature of the risks that each activity presents. At a minimum, risk-measurement systems should be sufficiently comprehensive and rigorous to capture the nature and magnitude of risks faced by the institution, while differentiating risk exposures consistently among risk categories and levels. Controls should be in place to ensure objectivity and consistency and to make certain that all material risks, both on and off the balance sheet, are adequately addressed. Measurement should not be oriented to the current treatment of these transactions under risk-based capital regulations.

When measuring risks, institutions should perform comprehensive and rigorous stress tests to identify possible events or changes in markets that could have serious adverse effects in the future.[18] Institutions should also give adequate consideration to contingent exposures arising from loan commitments, securitizations programs, and other transactions or activities that may create these exposures for the bank.

2. *Relating capital to the level of risk.* The amount of capital held should reflect not only the measured amount of risk, but also an adequate cushion above that amount to take account of potential uncertainties in risk measurement. A banking organization's capital should reflect the perceived level of precision in the risk measures used, the potential volatility of exposures, and the relative importance to the institution of the activities producing the risk. Capital levels should also reflect that historical correlations among exposures can rapidly change. Institutions should be able to demonstrate that their approach to relating capital to risk is conceptually sound and that outputs and results are reasonable. An institution could use sensitivity analysis of key inputs and peer analysis in assessing its approach.

One credible method for assessing capital adequacy is for an institution to consider itself adequately capitalized if it meets a reasonable and objectively determined standard of financial health tempered by sound judgment—for exam-

---

[17] *FRB Trading and Capital-Markets Activities Manual,* April 2000, Capital Adequacy, Section 2110.1.

[18] As part of evaluation process, rigorous stress testing is called for, which should center on unexpected downturns in market conditions that might adversely impact capital. This is particularly important in the trading area to ensure market risk is sufficiently covered by capital. Stress testing on the market side includes material interest rate positions, repricing and maturity data, principal payments, (interest) reset dates, maturities, and the rate index used for repricing and contractual interest rate ceilings or floors for adjustable-rate instruments. This assessment is based largely on the bank's own measure of *value at risk.*

ple, a target public-agency debt rating or even a statistically measured maximum probability of becoming insolvent over a given time horizon. In effect, this latter method is the foundation of the Basel Accord's treatment of capital requirements for market foreign-exchange risk.

3. *Stating explicit capital adequacy goals with respect to risk.* Institutions need to establish explicit goals for capitalization as a standard for evaluating their capital adequacy with respect to risk. These target capital levels might reflect the desired level of risk coverage or, alternatively, a desired credit rating for the institution that reflects a desired degree of creditworthiness and, thus, access to funding sources. These goals should be reviewed and approved by the board of directors. Because risk profiles and goals may differ across institutions, the chosen target levels of capital may differ significantly as well. Moreover, institutions should evaluate whether their long-run capital targets might differ from short-run goals based on current and planned changes in risk profiles and the recognition that accommodating new capital needs can require significant lead time.

An institution's internal standard of capital adequacy for credit risk could reflect the desire that capital absorb "unexpected losses"—that is, some level of potential losses in excess of that level already estimated as being inherent in the current portfolio and reflected in the allowance. In this setting, an institution that does not maintain its allowance at the high end of the range of estimated credit losses would require more capital than would otherwise be necessary to maintain its overall desired capacity to absorb potential losses. Failure to recognize this relationship could lead an institution to overestimate the strength of its capital position.

4. *Assessing conformity to the institution's stated objectives.* Both the target level and composition of capital, along with the process for setting and monitoring such targets, should be reviewed and approved periodically by the institution's board of directors.

Capital compliance is, of course, a large factor in the Uniform Financial Institutions Rating System CAMELS).[19] Recall that regulators assign CAMELS *capital adequacy ratings rating 1 and 2* respectively, if a bank under audit exhibits a strong capital level relative to its risk profile (rating 1) or satisfactory capital level (rating 2). *Rating 3* is assigned to banks with a less than satisfactory capital level relative to risk. As we saw in an appendix to the previous chapter, *rating 3* implies a need for improvement, even though a bank's capital level exceeds minimum regulatory and statutory requirements. But *ratings 4 and 5* are troublesome to say the least, with *rating 4* indicating deficient capital levels with the institution's economic soundness threatened. A *rating 5* is given to a bank

---

[19] See Appendix 2 to Chapter 10 for a review of CAMELS. Recall that this internal supervisory tool is used by the federal supervisory agencies including the Board of Governors of the Federal Reserve System, the Federal Deposit Insurance Corporation, the Office of the Comptroller of the Currency, the Office of Thrift Supervision, the National Credit Union Association, and the Farm Credit Administration.

critically deficient in regulatory capital such that the institution's viability is more than just threatened. In other words, regulators reporting a CAMELS capital adequacy rating of 5 are saying that *immediate assistance from shareholders or other external sources of financial support is required.*

THE THIRD PILLAR: MARKET DISCIPLINE

The third pillar deals with the role market discipline plays in promoting bank capital adequacy. Basically, one could argue, a bank should disclose summary information about its *entire* capital structure, both normal capital (stock, subordinated notes, and so on) and the more esoteric capital (innovative, complex, and hybrid capital instruments). To encourage further compliance with the third pillar, banks will be required to disclose reserves for credit losses, maturity, level of seniority, stepup provisions, interest or dividend deferrals, use of special-purpose vehicles (SPVs), and terms of derivatives embedded in hybrid capital instruments, to mention a few. The disclosure requirements will offer a much cleaner, more unclouded view of a bank's loss-absorbing capacity.

CAPITAL RATIOS

Basel's position is that requisite capital ratios should include enough information to enable banks, regulators, and investors to improve their capital assessment abilities. Capital ratios have long been a valuable tool for evaluating the safety and soundness of banks with trends especially meaningful (Figures 11.1 and 11.2). The informal use of ratios by bank regulators and supervisors goes back well over a century. In the United States, minimum capital ratios have been required in banking regulation since 1981, and the Basel Accord has applied capital ratio requirements to banks internationally since 1988. Although bank regulators have relied on capital ratios formally or informally for a very long time, they have not always used the ratios in the same way. For instance, in the days before explicit capital requirements, bank supervisors would use capital ratios as rules of thumb to gauge capital adequacy; there was no illusion that the simple ratios (for example, capital to total assets or capital to deposits) could provide an accurate measure appropriate for capital levels.

As we saw earlier, the Basel Accord of 1988 applied different credit risk weights to different positions and included in the base for the capital ratio a measure of the off-balance-sheet exposures of the bank. Despite these calibrations, the intent was not to determine an exact appropriate level of capital for the bank, "but rather to provide a more flexible way of determining the minimum required level."[20]

---

[20] Basel Committee on Banking Supervision, 1988.

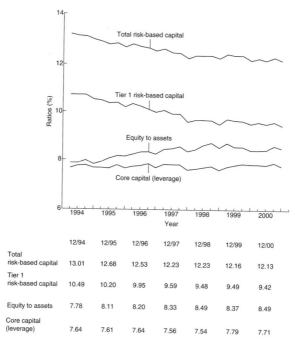

	12/94	12/95	12/96	12/97	12/98	12/99	12/00
Total risk-based capital	13.01	12.68	12.53	12.23	12.23	12.16	12.13
Tier 1 risk-based capital	10.49	10.20	9.95	9.59	9.48	9.49	9.42
Equity to assets	7.78	8.11	8.20	8.33	8.49	8.37	8.49
Core capital (leverage)	7.64	7.61	7.64	7.56	7.54	7.79	7.71

FIGURE 11.1   Capital Ratio Trends: 1994–2000

The degree of supervisory intervention in specific banks is now guided by a formula driven largely by the Basel ratios and by a simple leverage ratio. Banks are classified as "adequately capitalized" if they meet Basel requirements plus a leverage ratio requirement, but additional distinctions are made among levels of capital. For example, a bank is "well capitalized" if it holds a certain buffer above predetermined adequacy levels. In contrast, a bank falling well below the pre-arranged threshold, set somewhat below a minimum adequate level, is labeled "critically undercapitalized" and will likely be closed by regulators. At the lower threshold, a bank is either a de facto failure or is in imminent danger of becoming one. So then, regulators choose a threshold highly correlated with failure. Some of the other ratios implicitly or explicitly linked to capital adequacy include the following:

1. Return on assets
2. Return on equity
3. Loan loss coverage
4. Net charge-offs to loans
5. Equity capital to assets
6. Valuation reserve to loans

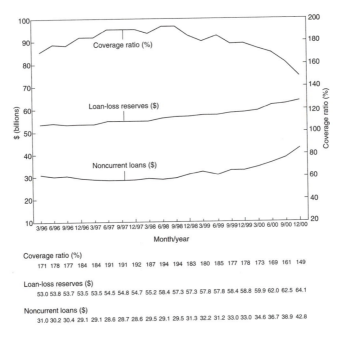

Coverage ratio (%)
171 178 177 184 184 191 191 192 187 194 194 183 180 185 177 178 173 169 161 149

Loan-loss reserves ($)
53.0 53.8 53.7 53.5 53.5 54.5 54.8 54.7 55.2 58.4 57.3 57.3 57.8 57.8 58.4 58.8 59.9 62.0 62.5 64.1

Noncurrent loans ($)
31.0 30.2 30.4 29.1 29.1 28.6 28.7 28.6 29.5 29.1 29.5 31.3 32.2 31.2 33.0 33.0 34.6 36.7 38.9 42.8

FIGURE 11.2 Reserve Coverage Ratio: 1996–2000

7. Ratio of provision for loan losses to net charge-offs (This indicates whether provisions are in line with actual charge-offs.)
8. Ratio of nonperforming assets to total loans and other real estate loans (This ratio indicates the proportion of total loans in default and the amount of real estate that had to be foreclosed and assumed. Some banks do not include loans until they are 90 or even more days in default.)
9. Ratio of long-term subordinated debt to total capital accounts (For "all insured commercial banks" the ratio is very low, since usually large banks sell these debt issues.)
10. Earnings per share
11. Ratio of cash and U.S. government securities to assets and deposits
12. Ratio of capital accounts and equity accounts to assets and deposits
13. Ratio of capital accounts to loans (risk assets)

Critically Undercapitalized Banks and Bank Failures: Four Examples

Under the Federal Deposit Insurance Corp (FDIC) Improvement Act of 1991, Congress expanded the FDIC's authority to appoint itself receiver of insured institutions if they become critically undercapitalized. An institution is considered critically undercapitalized when its tangible equity capital falls below 2%. Consider the following examples:

1. The comptroller of the currency closed National State Bank in Metropolis, Illinois, in December 2000 when it found that the bank was critically undercapitalized—that is, it had less than 2% tangible equity capital. Inadequate control of the credit and transaction risks and inadequate supervision by the board of directors resulted in a high volume of losses. These losses and subsequent provisions to absorb additional losses depleted capital and threatened the bank's liquidity. The OCC determined that closure and the appointment of the FDIC as receiver were necessary to protect the interests of the bank's insured depositors.

2. Monument National Bank in Ridgecrest, California, which was serving as a branch of Israel Discount Bank of New York, was closed in June 2000. The failed bank received a national bank charter in March of 1984. The OCC used its receivership authority after finding that Monument National was "critically undercapitalized"—that is, the bank's tangible equity capital was less than 2% of its total assets. The bank never fully recovered from the poor credit administration practices and the high volume of classified assets experienced in 1998. As a result, the bank incurred losses that depleted substantially all of its capital. In light of these findings, the OCC determined that the closure of the bank and appointment of the FDIC as receiver was necessary to protect the interests of the bank's insured depositors.

3. The FDIC closed Victory State Bank Columbia, South Carolina, and took possession of the bank in its capacity as receiver. On January 5, 1999, Victory State Bank was determined to be critically undercapitalized. The main problems the bank faced were poor management, excessive insider compensation, operating losses, and a burdensome volume of problem assets. The bank has been unprofitable since 1995, and its operating losses totaled $1.3 million over its last two years.

4. In 2000, Hawaii regulators closed the Bank of Honolulu. The bank was shut down after operating under a Federal Deposit Insurance Corp. (FDIC) cease and desist order for nearly two years. In December 1998, the FDIC cited the bank for inadequate management, insufficient equity capital, bad loans, and lax collection practices. The FBI arrested the bank's majority stockholder, who had also been its chief executive officer until removed by the FDIC. Authorities accused the CEO of hiding assets before filing for bankruptcy. The FDIC estimated that the failure would cost the Bank Insurance Fund (BIF) approximately $2.5 million. This was the fifth failure of a BIF-insured institution that year and the second over a two-week period. The FDIC has decided to pay uninsured depositors 65% of their verifiable claims.

Capital Adequacy: Establishing a Technical Framework

It should be clear at this point that many regulators have come to believe that at a minimum, banks should have a credible internal capital allocation methodology[21]—small wonder, considering the global volatility in financial markets, heightened international competition and the rapid growth of technology. Naïve, ad hoc methods are of little use dealing with exposures that have the potential to drain serious capital. It's reasonable to deduce that the extent to which the output of a risk model is incorporated into a bank's decision-making processes is highly suggestive of management's confidence in that model.[22] For those banks having the most sophisticated systems for allocating capital, output from these models are embedded not only for capital adequacy, but throughout the institution's risk management and incentive systems as well. For example, determining break-even prices on credit instruments, setting client exposure limits, deciding on broad portfolio concentration limits, and actively managing overall portfolio credit risk are all part of the day-to-day business of managing the capital structure.

The problem with any model is, of course, gathering data. Sophisticated risk models require good information (though this has become less of a problem with the advent of data mining and neural network technologies). Models also tend to be limited due to their somewhat conceptual drawbacks. For example, if we look behind some models, "correct" credit data are often sparse (try asking a privately held small-cap apparel manufacturer for credit information), correlations may not be easily observed or deciphered, credit returns are often skewed, and, because of statistical problems, back testing may be infeasible with results seriously flawed. To make matters worse, statistics, assumptions, and techniques differ across borders—thus, bank-to-bank comparisons turn out skewed with dissimilarities in required capital resulting. Alas, if we compared output from JPMorgan Chase's highly sophisticated VAR models and those employed by small regional banks, VAR measures will likely differ along with allocated capital vis-à-vis market risk.

In spite the strong case for quantitative analysis, when all is said and done, it's Tom de Swaan's keen insight that reaches the core of what risk modeling is all about: "risk models only provide an edge; a banker's experience, judgment, and common sense will never be replaced by models . . . If credit risk models are to be used for regulatory capital purposes, they should not be judged in isolation. Supervisors should also carefully examine and supervise the qualitative factors in a bank's risk management and set standards for those factors."

---

[21] Federal Reserve System Task Force on Internal Credit Risk Models, May 1988

[22] The CD includes a 58-page document "Credit Risk Models at Major U.S. Banking Institutions: Current State of the Art and Implications for Assessments of Capital Adequacy." The report is courtesy of the Federal Reserve System Task Force on Internal Credit Risk Models. The report is located in the directory Library\Federal Reserve System Manuals.

CASE STUDY JPMorgan Chase Capital Management Framework

Let's examine how this world-class financial institution utilizes statistical and nonstatistical risk measures in administering market risk (which is key to managing capital adequacy). The following was extracted from the firm's 2000 annual report.

Background

JPMorgan Chase employs a comprehensive approach to market risk management for its trading, investment and asset/liability management ("A/L") portfolios. Trading portfolios are exposed to market risk because the values of trading positions are sensitive to changes in market prices and rates. Investment and A/L portfolios are affected by market risk because revenues derived from these activities, such as securities gains and losses and net interest income, are sensitive to changes in interest rates. Interest rate risk at JPMorgan Chase arises from a variety of factors, including differences in timing between the maturities or repricing of assets, liabilities and derivatives. For example, the repricing characteristics of loans and other interest-earning assets do not necessarily match those of deposits, borrowings or other liabilities.

Basis risk is another type of risk to which JPMorgan Chase is exposed in its trading, investment and A/L activities. For example, when prime-priced commercial loans are funded with LIBOR-indexed liabilities, there is exposure to the difference between changes in prime and LIBOR rates.

Market risk is managed on a daily basis at JPMorgan Chase and is supervised by the Market Risk Management Group, which functions independently from the business units and consists of professionals located in major markets around the world. Market risk is primarily controlled through a series of limits, which are used to align corporate risk appetite with risk taking activities. The Board of Directors approves Value-at-Risk (VAR) limits and stress-loss advisory limits. VAR limits apply at the aggregate corporate and business unit levels. Statistical and nonstatistical limits and stress-loss advisories apply at the trading desk level, along with designations of authorized instruments and maximum tenors. The use of nonstatistical measures and stop-loss advisories, together with VAR limits, reduces the likelihood that potential trading losses will reach daily VAR limits under normal market conditions.

Risk limits are set according to a number of criteria, including relevant market analysis, market liquidity, prior track record, business strategy, and management experience and depth. Risk limits are reviewed regularly to maintain consistency with trading strategies and material developments in market conditions and are updated at least twice a year.

Risk Measurements

Because no single risk statistic can reflect all aspects of market risk, the Firm utilizes several statistical and nonstatistical risk measures. Combining the two approaches is key to enhancing the stability of revenues from market risk activities because, taken together, these risk measures provide a more comprehensive view of market risk exposure than any single measure. Risk measures include:

- Value-at-Risk (VAR)

- Stress Testing—Economic Value; Net Interest Income (NII); Basis Point Value (BPV) and Vulnerability Identification (VID)

The methodologies used at Chase and JPMorgan, Value-at-Risk and stress testing, were generally consistent. Certain aspects of their implementation differed, such as the length of time used, the weighting of historical data and the statistical confidence levels employed (VAR at Chase was calculated at the 99% confidence level, while the comparable measure used at JPMorgan was calculated at the 95% confidence level). During 2001, the statistical measures used by JPMorgan Chase will combine the best practices of both heritage firms. VAR and stress testing will remain the predominant risk measurement tools of JPMorgan Chase.

Value-at-Risk is a measure of the dollar amount of potential loss from adverse market moves in an everyday market environment. The VAR methodology used at JPMorgan Chase is based on historical simulation, which assumes that actual observed historical changes in market indices, such as interest rates, foreign exchange rates, and equity and commodity prices, reflect possible future changes. Historical simulation methodology permits consistent and comparable measurement of risk across instruments and portfolios.

VAR calculations are performed for all material trading and investment portfolios and for all material market risk-related A/L activities. All statistical models have a degree of uncertainty associated with the assumptions employed. The use of historical simulation for VAR calculations is not as dependent on assumptions about the distribution of portfolio losses as are other VAR methodologies that are parameter based. Since the VAR methodology is dependent on the quality of available market data, diagnostic information is used to continually evaluate the reasonableness of the VAR model. This information includes the calculation of statistical confidence intervals around the daily VAR estimate and daily "back testing" of VAR against actual financial results.

Daily Earnings at Risk (DeaR), a variation of the VAR methodology, was the statistical measure used at JP Morgan to estimate the Firm's exposure in normal markets to market risk and to credit risk in the trading derivatives portfolio. Table 10 Combined JPMorgan Chase VAR presents VAR information for JPMorgan Chase at December 31, 2000. The disclosure of Chase VAR and JT Morgan DEaR information for periods prior to December 31, 2000, is presented separately below.

Although no single risk statistic can reflect all aspects of market risk, the tables that follow provide a meaningful overview of the market risk exposure at each heritage firm for the dates presented.

In 2000, Chase posted positive daily market risk-related revenue for 254 out of 259 days, with 88 days exceeding positive $20 million. In 1999, Chase posted positive daily market risk-related revenue for 250 out of 260 days, with 62 days exceeding positive $20 million. Chase incurred no daily trading losses in excess of $20 million in either 2000 or 1999.

TABLE 11.7   Combined JPMorgan Chase VAR

Combined JPMorgan Chase VAR at December 31, 2000 (in millions)	
Trading portfolio	$501
Market risk-related A/L activities	102
Less portfolio diversification	(35)
Aggregate VAR	$118

TABLE 11.8   Chase Aggregate VAR

Chase Aggregate VAR (in millions)	Year Ended December 31, 2000			December 31, 2000 VAR	December 31, 1999 VAR
	Average VAR	Minimum VAR	Maximum VAR		
Trading portfolio	25	20	31	24	23
Market risk-related A/L activities					
(Substantial all risk interest related)	72	60	107	101	67
Less: Portfolio diversification	(19)	NM	NM	(23)	(16)
Aggregate VAR	$78	$68	$105	$102	$74

NM = Not meaningful.

AN EXAMPLE OF A BANK'S CAPITAL STRUCTURE

JPMorgan Chase's long-term capital target is a Tier 1 capital ratio in the range of 8% to 8.25%. The Capital Committee reviews capital targets and policies regularly in light of changing economic conditions and business needs. The total required economic capital for the firm is compared with available capital to evaluate overall capital utilization. JPMorgan Chase's policy is to maintain an appropriate level of capital to provide for growth and protection against unanticipated losses. Exhibit I shows JPMorgan Chase's capital generation and regulatory use during the past three years.

> **JPMorgan Chase & Co Capital Structure**
>
> JPMorgan Chase's capital management framework helps to optimize the use of capital by determining (1) the optimal amount of capital commensurate with internal assessments of risk estimated by an economic capital allocation model, targeted regulatory ratios and credit ratings, business strategies, protection against losses even under stress conditions, and liquidity management; (2) capital investment for activities with the most favorable returns, and (3) the most efficient composition of the firm's capital base.

EXHIBIT I   Sources and Uses of Free Cash Flow Year Ended December 31 (in billions)

Sources of free cash flow	2000	1999	1998
Cash operating earnings less dividends	$4.0	$5.6	$3.3
Plus: Preferred stock and equivalents/special items	($0.1)	$0.2	($0.7)
Less: Capital for internal asset growth	$0.1	$0.3	$0.3
Total sources of free cash flow	**$4.0**	**$6.1**	**$2.9**

Uses of free cash flow

Increases (decrease) in capital ratios	($0.1)	$1.1	$1.3
Acquisitions	$7.0	$1.1	$1.6
Repurchases net of stock issuances	($2.9)	$3.3	$0.0
Total uses of free cash flow	**$4.0**	**$5.5**	**$2.9**

The sources of free cash flow shows that the primary source of JPMorgan Chase's free capital is cash operating earnings (less dividend requirements). As risk-weighted assets grow in the normal course of business, the firm is required to retain additional capital in order to maintain its capital ratios within targeted levels. Therefore, the sources of free cash flow equal the total retained earnings generated, less the additional capital needed to support new assets in order to maintain targeted capital ratios. This total amount is the firm's "free cash" or capital in excess of target ratios.

The uses of free cash flow shows that capital has been used to support goodwill and other assets acquired through acquisition and for share repurchase. The line "Increases (decreases) in capital ratios" represents the amount of capital retained, causing the firm's capital ratios to rise (or fall) from targeted levels.

During 2000, $4 billion of free cash flow was generated, 27% less than in 1999 due to lower cash operating earnings. During 2000, less capital was needed to support internal growth or to bolster capital ratios. The cash flow generated in 2000 was principally earmarked to support the Flemings acquisition.

• *Dividends.* In the first quarter of 2000, JPMorgan Chase raised the quarterly cash dividend on its common stock to $0.32 per share from $0.27 per share. The firm's current dividend policy is to pay common stock dividends equal to approximately 25% to 35% of operating earnings, less preferred stock dividends. The board of directors will determine future dividend policies after taking into consideration the firm's earnings and financial condition and applicable governmental regulations and policies.

• *Buybacks.* During 2000, each heritage firm repurchased, under previously announced authorizations, an aggregate of almost $3 billion (73 million shares) of their common equity. Both companies terminated their share repurchase programs in 2000 (JPMorgan in September and Chase in October). During 2000, approximately 60 million shares (from the treasury) were issued under various employee stock option and other stock-based plans. Additionally, 69 million shares were issued (from the treasury) in connection with acquisitions, and 22 million shares were issued (from the treasury) for the accelerated distribution of JPMorgan stock as a result of the merger.

• *Regulatory capital.* JPMorgan Chase is subject to regulation under state and federal law, including the Bank Holding Company Act of 1956. This act was amended by the Gramm-Leach-Bliley Act, which allows financial holding companies (a defined term) to engage in activities that are "financial in nature" and to own, to a greater extent than previously permitted, securities of companies engaged in nonbanking activities. The firm was granted financial holding company status on March 13, 2000.

The firm's primary federal banking regulator, the Federal Reserve Board, establishes minimum capital requirements and leverage ratios for the consolidated financial holding company and for state-chartered bank subsidiaries, including The Chase Manhattan Bank and Morgan Guaranty Trust Company of New York. Management anticipated that these bank subsidiaries would merge in the third quarter of 2001. The Office of the Comptroller of the Currency establishes similar capital requirements and leverage ratios for national bank subsidiaries, including Chase Manhattan Bank USA, N.A.

These risk-based capital ratios are determined by allocating assets and specified off-balance sheet financial instruments into categories, with higher levels of capital being required for categories perceived as representing greater risk. Capital is divided into two tiers: Tier 1 capital and Tier 2 capital. In addition to retained earnings, the Federal Reserve permits the firm to raise Tier 1 and Tier 2 capital by issuing different types of financial instruments to the public. These financial instruments then are classified as either Tier 1 or Tier 2, depending on their terms and the types of conditions or covenants they place on the issuer.

Tier 1 capital includes securities with no fixed maturity date, such as common stock, nonredeemable perpetual preferred stock, and the minority interest of unconsolidated affiliates (which may include securities commonly referred to as "trust preferreds"). Tier 2 capital includes subordinated long-term debt and similar instruments and "qualified loan loss reserves," such as the allowance for loan losses. The amount of subordinated long-term debt that may be included in Tier 2 capital may not exceed more than 50% of the issuer's Tier 1 capital. In addition, the capital treatment accorded long-term subordinated debt is reduced as it approaches maturity. Qualified loan loss reserves may be included in Tier 2 capital up to 1.25% of risk-weighted assets. Total Tier 2 capital is limited to 100% of Tier 1 capital.

Exhibits II and III, along with Figure 11.3 show the risk-based capital ratios of JPMorgan Chase over the past five years.

EXHIBIT II   JPMorgan Chase & Co.: Tier I and 2 Capital December 3 I (in millions)

Tier 1 capital	2000	1999
Common stockholders' equity	$41,062	$34,863
Nonredeemable preferred stock	$1,271	$1,372
Minority interest[a]	$4,662	$4,451

Less: Goodwill and investments in		
certain subsidiaries	$8,783	$3,628
nonqualifying intangible assets	$631	$80
Tier 1 capital	*$37,581*	*$36,978*
Tier 2 capital		
Long-term debt and other instruments		
Qualifying as Tier 2	$12,833	$12,855
Qualifying allowance for credit losses	$3,955	$4,059
Less: Investment in certain subsidiaries	$917	$472
Tier 2 capital	*$15,871*	*$16,442*
Total qualifying capital	**$53,452**	**$53,420**

[a]Minority interest includes trust preferred stocks of certain business trust subsidiaries and the preferred stock of a Real Estate Investment Trust subsidiary of JPMC.

EXHIBIT III   JPMorgan Chase & Co.: Risk-Based Capital Ratios at December 31

	1996	1997	1998	1999	2000
Total capital	12.3%	11.7%	11.9%	12.3%	12.0%
Tier 1 capital	8.5%	7.9%	8.2%	8.5%	8.5%
Tier 2 capital	5.8%	5.4%	5.3%	5.9%	5.4%

CLOSING THOUGHTS

As part of the process for evaluating capital adequacy, a bank should be able to identify and evaluate its risks across all its activities to determine whether its capital levels are appropriate. The process should adequately differentiate risk exposure among various risk categories, providing a complete overview of an institution's banking book risk profile. This includes identifying credit risk concentrations, noticing trends in the portfolio (i.e., low-quality loans, as a percentage of the loan portfolio trend over time), including controls to ensure the objectivity and consistency of internal risk assessment, and finally, providing analysis to support the accuracy risk measurement process. Recent years have seen the refinement and acceptance of credit risk models as a commercial banking risk-management tool.

Exposure risk management is bound to improve in breadth and refinement across institutions, jostled in no small part by the proposed accords reviewed in this chapter. Increased awareness will be given to the interdependencies that some bankers ignore—between atypical risks, different types of lending, and the whole business of capital adequacy. As this happens, we will see practically uni-

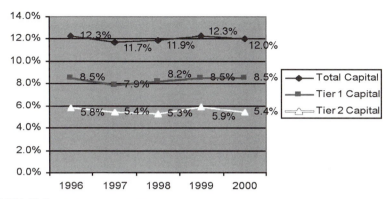

FIGURE 11.3   Risk-Based Capital Ratios Graph

versal use of sophisticated risk measuring tools whether we're looking at a commercial or a consumer loan, a derivative, or simply transactions involving settlements.

REVIEW QUESTIONS

1. What is the protective function of bank capital? Describe the bankwide risks falling under protective capital.
2. What are the six traditional bank asset categories from a historical perspective, and which assets do they include?
3. Explain the difference between capital adequacy measured by book value (GAAP) and economic (market) value. What is the Tier 1 capital, and which assets does it include? Explain the Tier 1 leverage ratio.
4. What is the Tier 2 capital? Explain the key differences between Tier 2 and Tier 3 capital.
5. Describe the major drawbacks in the current Basel Accord's risk-based capital framework. What is the purpose of the proposed new amendments called "three pillars"?
6. What are the four basic "rules" for regulators according to the second pillar? What qualitative factors are considered in establishing appropriate capital levels? Describe the Federal Reserve Board's four-point framework for "a sound internal analysis of capital adequacy."
7. Explain the bank classifications "adequately capitalized," "well capitalized," and "critically undercapitalized."
8. List some of the ratios that are implicitly or explicitly linked to capital adequacy.
9. What are, in your opinion, major advantages and disadvantages of sophisticated risk models?

SELECTED REFERENCES AND READINGS

Abayaratna, G. M., and South-East Asian Central Banks, Research and Training Centre. (1990). *Capital adequacy and banking risks in the SEACEN countries*. Kuala Lumpur, Malaysia: South East Asian Central Banks Research and Training Centre.

Adhikary, G. P. (1988). *Capital adequacy of banks in the SEACEN countries: An overview*. Kuala Lumpur, Malaysia: South East Asian Central Banks Research and Training Centre.

Federal Home Loan Bank of San Francisco. (1980). *New sources of capital for the savings and loan industry: Proceedings of the fifth annual conference, December 6–7, 1979. San Francisco, CA.*

Federal Home Loan Bank of San Francisco. (1986). *Thrift financial performance and capital adequacy: Proceedings of the twelfth annual conference, December 11–12, 1986. San Francisco, CA.*

Maisel, S. J. (1981). *Risks and capital adequacy in commercial banks*. Chicago: University of Chicago Press.

Matten, C. (1996). *Managing bank capital: Capital allocation and performance measurement*. Chichester; New York: Wiley.

Talley, S. H., and Board of Governors of the Federal Reserve System (U.S.). (1983). *Bank capital trends and financing*. Washington, DC: Board of Governors of the Federal Reserve System.

United States. Congress. House. Committee on Banking Finance and Urban Affairs. Subcommittee on Financial Institutions Supervision Regulation and Insurance. (1991). *Financial Industry Reform and Capital Enforcement Act (H.R. 192): Hearing before the Subcommittee on Financial Institutions Supervision, Regulation and Insurance of the Committee on Banking, Finance, and Urban Affairs, House of Representatives, One Hundred Second Congress, first session, February 28, 1991*. Washington, U.S. G.P.O. For sale by the Supt. of Docs. Congressional Sales Office U.S. G.P.O.

United States. Congress. House. Committee on Banking Finance and Urban Affairs. Subcommittee on General Oversight and Investigations. (1988). *Capital adequacy in the savings and loan industry: Field hearing before the Subcommittee on General Oversight and Investigations of the Committee on Banking, Finance, and Urban Affairs, House of Representatives, One-hundredth Congress, first session, Santa Ana, CA, August 10, 1987*. Washington, U.S. G.P.O. For sale by the Supt. of Docs. Congressional Sales Office U.S. G.P.O.

United States. Congress. House. Committee on Banking Finance and Urban Affairs. Subcommittee on General Oversight and Investigations. (1988). *Risk-based capital requirements for banks and bank holding companies: Hearing before the Subcommittee on General Oversight and Investigations of the Committee on Banking, Finance, and Urban Affairs, House of Representatives, One-hundredth Congress, second session, April 21, 1988*. Washington, U.S. G.P.O. For sale by the Supt. of Docs. Congressional Sales Office U.S. G.P.O.

United States. Congress. House. Committee on Banking Finance and Urban Affairs. Subcommittee on International Development Institutions and Finance. (1988). *The proposed general capital increase for the World Bank: Hearings before the Subcommittee on International Development Institutions and Finance of the Committee on Banking, Finance, and Urban Affairs, House of Representatives, One-hundredth Congress, second session, May 4, 11, 18, and 24, 1988*. Washington, U.S. G.P.O. For sale by the Supt. of Docs. Congressional Sales Office U.S. G.P.O.

United States. Congress. House. Committee on Government Operations. Commerce Consumer and Monetary Affairs Subcommittee. (1986). *Capital forbearance for agricultural banks: Hearing before a subcommittee of the Committee on Government Operations, House of Representatives, Ninety-ninth Congress, second session, June 17, 1986*. Washington, U.S. G.P.O. For sale by the Supt. of Docs. Congressional Sales Office U.S. G.P.O.

United States. Congress. Senate. Committee on Banking Housing and Urban Affairs. (1990). *Banking regulators' report on capital standards: Hearing before the Committee on Banking, Housing, and Urban Affairs, United States Senate, One Hundred First Congress, second session, September*

10, 1990. Washington, U.S. G.P.O. For sale by the Supt. of Docs. Congressional Sales Office U.S. G.P.O.

United States. General Accounting Office. (1986). *Deposit insurance: analysis of reform proposals: Staff study*. Washington, D.C., The Office.

SELECT INTERNET LIBRARY

CD Internet Links

(1) A New Capital Adequacy Framework Consultative Paper Issued by the Basel Committee on Banking Supervision issued for Comment by 31 March 2000; Adobe Document.

(2) Basel Committee on Banking Supervision Consultative Document Pillar 2 (Supervisory Review Process) Supporting Document to the New Basel Capital Accord; Adobe Document.

(3) Basel Committee on Banking Supervision Bank for International Entitlements Ch-4002 Basel, Switzerland Update on Work on a New Capital Adequacy Framework Issue 1 November 1999; Adobe Document.

(4) Board of Governors of the Federal Reserve System Instructions for Preparation of Consolidated Financial Statements for Bank Holding Companies Reporting Form FR Y-9C, Reissued March 1999, Adobe Document. http://www.federalreserve.gov/boarddocs/reportforms/forms/FR_Y-9C19991231_i.pdf http://www.bis.org/publ/bcbs34.pdf

(5) Basel Committee February 1999 Capital Adequacy Principles paper, http://www.bis.org/publ/bcbs47.pdf

(6) A new Capital Adequacy Framework, supplementary documents 18 January 2000, http://www.bis.org/press/p000118.htm#pgtop

(7) Basel Committee: A New Capital Adequacy Framework: Pillar 3, Market Discipline, January 2000, http://www.bis.org/publ/bcbs65.pdf

(8) Basel Committee: A New Capital Adequacy Framework: Pillar 3, Market Discipline (Basel Committee Publications No. 65), http://www.bis.org/publ/bcbs65.htm

CD

Name	Size	Type
Basel Committee on Banking Supervision Consultative Document Pillar 2 (Supervisory Review Process)	90KB	Adobe
Basel Committee on Banking Supervision Bank for International Settlements, Ch-4002 Basel, Switzerland Update on work on a New Capital Adequacy Framework Issue 1 November 1999	21KB	Adobe
A New Capital Adequacy Framework Consultative paper issued by the Basel Committee on Banking Supervision Issued for comment by 31 March 2000 Basel June 1999	212KB	Adobe
Trading and Capital-Markets Activities Manual April 2000; Capital Adequacy Section 2110.1	272KB	Adobe
Credit Risk Models at Major U.S. Banking Institutions: Current State of the Art and Implications for Assessments of Capital Adequacy Federal Reserve System Task Force on Internal Credit Risk Models	145KB	Adobe

12

PORTFOLIO MAINTENANCE

An Overview

Portfolio managers in the banking industry face a higher level of risk/reward decisions than their counterparts in the equity markets—institutional investors. For example, most bank loans provide a fixed return to lenders over fixed periods that are dependent on interest rates and the borrower's ability to pay. A good loan will be repaid on time and in full. It is hoped the bank's cost of funds will be low and will permit attractive returns. If the borrower's business excels, the bank will not participate in upside growth (except for a vicarious pleasure in the firm's success). However, if business failure results, lenders share much, perhaps most, of the pain. The limited upside risk and unlimited downside risk of bank lending was a major cause of innumerable problems in the late 1980s.

One solution is to price "riskier" loans differently from "safe" loans. However, recurring overcapacity in the banking industry has made this somewhat difficult. Alas, if a bank wants to add to its book, it must sometimes be willing to compete with low-bid bankers who usually have the least understanding of risk. There is an inevitable organizational bias toward optimism. Unlike the stock market, few banks "bottom fish" by loaning to troubled companies, with the exception of debtor-in-possession (DIP) financing.

Traditional credit analysis has always focused on the borrower's financial risk more so than the firm's sensitivity to macroeconomic events (arbitrage pricing theory, or APT, factors, discussed later). The result is that compensating for pricing risk in the highly competitive banking environment is difficult and perhaps unrealistic. A perverse problem arises when a bank acquires superior origination skills in a particular region or industry. As a bank builds expertise, it usually increases exposure to that area in its loan portfolio. A portfolio of loans to various nonoil drilling companies in Oklahoma in the early 1980s suffered because these businesses depended on the dominant industry in the state. Likewise, a lender who developed a niche in the motion picture industry was vulnerable to cycles affecting that business. To sum it up, lenders are vulnerable to two disadvantages: (1) pricing that fails to compensate for risk and (2) overconcentrations in a region or industry. This chapter explores the portfolio question and offers ways bankers can ameliorate some of these problems.

In practice, the risk of individual credits is measured by *microanalysis*: analyzing cash flow patterns, financial ratios, and pro forma financial statements. Cash flow patterns are a strong indicator of the firm's ability to generate and spend wisely funds needed to run the business. Ratios are trended and compared to industry standards to get a sense of a firm's liquidity, financial leverage, cash flow coverage, and its ability to use assets to generate sales and profits. Lastly, pro forma statements allow lenders to gauge possible future direction and needs of the firm, as well as to test the firm's sensitivity to assumptions about its economic and managerial environment. If only because of the availability and compelling logic of these analyses, it is unlikely that their use will ever be diminished by any of the recent "objective" tools supplied by portfolio management vendors or rating agencies.

Think of microanalysis as the evaluation of unsystematic or company-specific risks. *Macroanalysis*, or analysis on the portfolio level, is no less important. This entails structuring policies and procedures that tend to portfolios of risky assets so that the amalgamation of exposures are adequately diversified, are set in line with target markets, and aim for an optimal portfolio return (e.g., along the Efficient Frontier; see Appendix 2 to Chapter 12). The relatively new awareness—portfolio management at the highest, most sophisticated level—has moved many bankers to implement loan exposure tracking systems, credit rating, and loan pricing models for the express purpose of managing portfolio risk. Bankers, however, are not equipped to "do it alone."

Bank reform legislation and Federal Reserve audit standards are immeasurably important (and helpful) to banks trying to put portfolios in order. Regulatory standards ensure that, for banks, exposure diversification is foremost on the mind of portfolio managers—to spread loans among dissimilar business lines preventing homogenous firms from borrowing excessive amounts (loan concentrations), to manage capital efficiently, and to find the optimal balance between risk and reward.

THE CASE FOR LOAN PORTFOLIO MANAGEMENT

In a nutshell, portfolio management calls for special attention to fallout from macroeconomic shocks and industry declines, risk and profit volatility, excessive exposure limits, geographically depressed regions, and obsolete products. Let's take a closer look at concentrations. Exposure concentrations occur when direct, indirect, or contingent obligations exceed 25% of the bank's capital structure.[1] Included are the aggregate of the following:

- Overdrafts
- Securities purchased outright or under resale agreements
- Sale of federal funds
- Suspense assets
- Leases
- Acceptances
- Letters of credit
- Placements
- Loans endorsed, guaranteed, or subject to repurchase agreements and any other actual or contingent liability
- Concentrations involving one borrower, an affiliated group of borrowers, or borrowers engaged in or dependent on one industry

Banks generally operate within industry thresholds, limiting credit exposures to attain the best mix of individual and portfolio safety. While most bankers believe that heavy concentrations in homogeneous industries are best avoided, others regard industry concentrations as a big plus, arguing that specialization promotes high-caliber loans by focusing the bank's expertise in a few industries. To be sure, banks are inclined to assign loans to officers by industry (media, defense, health care, real estate, and so on), providing the proper gestation time for these bankers to become experts in the industries they represent. This strategy often pays handsomely, as teams of expert loan originators solicit, analyze, and sell off portions of industry portfolios they don't want.

Periodic reviews are choreographed on industry and economic factors, particularly in highly cyclical segments of the portfolio. Historically, economic forces have been manifest in transportation, real estate, defense, and retailing. However, some of these concentrations are acceptable—even necessary if the institution is to act on the mandate for which it was chartered. For example, banks located in

---

[1] *The Federal Reserve Examination Manual for Commercial Banks.*

farming, dairying, or livestock areas develop a very close relationship with their clients and over time have built up considerable expertise servicing these markets.

One type of concentration involves credit extensions to foreign governments, governmental agencies, and majority-owned or majority-controlled entities. Portfolio selection focuses on the performance and structure of the economy, the profitability of export markets, the ability to service debt, and the debtor country's ability to develop natural resources. An important variable deals with economic growth, particularly the question of broad-based growth versus growth concentrated in certain sectors. Deciding the dimensions of governmental influence on the economy is a matter of fiscal policy, specifically policies influencing savings and investment. The current revenue base may be insufficient to support expenditures impeding savings and investment. One large U.S. bank pointed to its economic concerns across borders:

> Because multinational companies and private domestic companies are often sensitive to changes in national policy environments and because they can often portend shifts in a country's creditworthiness, shifts in foreign direct investment patterns and patterns of nongovernment long-term capital flows deserve close attention. Similarly, short-term capital outflows on the part of domestic residents, which are often sensitive to the domestic outlook, may also be important indicators of changes in a country's creditworthiness.

A further example of concentration involves clusters of borrowers who handle the same manufacturer's product. For example, a bank may have financed a large concentration of dealers' floor planning of a particular brand of recreational vehicle, in addition to agreeing to discount large customer's conditional sales contracts. Any one dealer could form a concentration if direct obligations are combined with the indirect paper.

Additional concentrations surface when product defects are discovered and generate adverse publicity. Sales and profits may decline if governmental agencies impose restrictions until the product defects are corrected. In turn, customers whose paper was discounted by the bank may halt payments in protest until they are personally satisfied. The problem may be only temporary, but a large portion of the portfolio may be of questionable collectability or in outright default. A bank might hold in portfolio a large block of exposures to firms (and employees) representing the dominant business establishment(s) in a small city or town. It may seem right as the bank's civic duty, as the repercussions from a dominant small-town business closing impacts suppliers, unemployment levels, and the town's economic well-being.

Regarding this last point, banks with geographically concentrated operations are potentially vulnerable to local economic contractions because of an inherent concentration of loan and deposit customers.[2] Researchers found that a bank's

---

[2] Andrew P. Meyer and Timothy J. Yeager, "Are Small Rural Banks Vulnerable to Local Economic Downturns?" *Review, Federal Reserve Bank of St. Louis* (March/April 2001).

location significantly influences its choice of borrowers because monitoring costs increase as the distance between lender and borrower increases. Hence, banks tend to make loans to the people and businesses that are geographically nearby.

In addition, there is an empirical relationship between the performance of geographically concentrated banks and local economic activity firms in the area because if they become distressed at the same time, the bank's credit quality will likely suffer more than credit quality at a bank with credit dispersed across economic markets. In addition, liquidity risk is likely to be higher at geographically concentrated banks because such banks often rely on deposits from fewer entities. In contrast, a more geographically diversified bank can attract deposits from a larger base of individual and business customers; therefore, large swings in deposits and withdrawals are less likely.

> Bank examiners review an institution's internal controls, policies, practices, and procedures dealing with credit concentrations. According to examination guidelines, a bank's system should be documented in a complete and concise manner and should include, where appropriate, narrative descriptions, flowcharts, copies of forms used, and other pertinent information.

As we can see, without effective policies and procedures in place, loan concentrations can significantly increase portfolio risk—only one of a number of reasons regulators search out clues to verify compliance. Some issues raised include whether controls were instituted to monitor various aspects of the lending relationship, such as the exposure concentrations of a single borrower and affiliates, loans to a company dominant in the local economy, the company's employees and major suppliers, loans dependent on one crop or one industry group, and loans out of the bank's normal territory.

To drive this point home, let's examine the Basel Committee position on loan concentrations. The Basel Committee issued a set of directives dealing with risk concentrations and large exposures.[3] Principle 9 is chronicled here:

> Banking supervisors must be satisfied that banks have management information systems that enable management to identify concentrations within the portfolio and supervisors must set prudential limits to restrict bank exposures to single borrowers or groups of related borrowers. Banking supervisors must set prudential limits to restrict bank exposures to single borrowers, groups of related borrowers and other significant risk concentrations. These limits are usually expressed in terms of a percentage of bank capital and, although they vary, 25% of capital is typically the most that a bank or banking group may extend to a private sector non-bank borrower or a group of closely related borrowers without specific supervisory approval.
>
> It is recognized that newly established or very small banks may face practical limits on their ability to diversify, necessitating higher levels of capital to reflect the resultant risk. Supervisors should monitor the bank's handling of concentrations of risk and may

---

[3] Core Principles for Effective Banking Supervision: Principle 9 (Basel Core Principles), September 1997.

require that banks report to them any such exposures exceeding a specified limit (e.g., 10% of capital) or exposures to large borrowers as determined by the supervisors. In some countries, the aggregate of such large exposures is also subject to limits.

Modern Portfolio Theory and Systematic Exposure Risk

Modern portfolio theory is very well developed and used in practice with most investment research and financial academic literature focusing on investment decision making (e.g., asset allocation, stock selection, portfolio construction and management, risk analysis, and performance attribution analysis). There is an abundant amount of literature and commentary dealing with the decision-making process for investment decisions (e.g., equities, bonds, cash, and derivative products) as well as ample university courses, texts, seminars and conferences, models, and decision-making tools.

Furthermore, these quantitative and mathematical techniques and models have been thoroughly studied, developed, tested, and revised for evaluating, comparing, and selecting the most attractive investment opportunities. All of these advanced portfolio techniques are based on the preferences, goals, and objectives of investors. While much of the methodology works extremely well, how can a bank benefit? One key factor is for bankers to realize that for them, out of the entire body of portfolio theory/research and quantitative analysis, two issues remain open: predicting and monitoring *systematic risk* (macroeconomic cycles or industry shocks) and hedging down risky positions within segments of the portfolio with properly designed hedge strategies. The remainder of this chapter deals with these two issues.

MONITORING SYSTEMATIC RISK IN THE PORTFOLIO: MACROECONOMIC AND INDUSTRY EXPOSURES

Economic (Systematic Risk) Analysis of the Loan Book

Bank performance is more likely to be correlated with local economic data in rural rather than urban areas because rural banks tend to lend to a relatively high percentage of firms and residents in their own counties. If enough of those firms or residents are faring poorly, local economic data should reflect the poor performance. In contrast, banks located in metropolitan areas usually lend to a smaller fraction of all the firms and individuals in their area. Poor performance by individual small businesses and households will likely have less effect on measures of aggregate economic activity in urban areas than in rural areas. Let's review how fallout from macroeconomic turbulence affects investments (the loan book is, after all, a bank's biggest investment). *Arbitrage pricing theory (APT)* presents an appropriate framework for this discussion. However, we acknowledge that APT is an active *portfolio management method for institutional investors*. Hence, the discussion is not as much about econometric modeling as it is about grasping the quantitative significance of systematic risk via APT factors, thinking about what makes them tick, and applying macroeconomic and industry sensitivities to the right portfolio analytics.

Arbitrage Pricing Theory

> The arbitrage pricing theory (APT) has survived several years of fairly intense scrutiny. Most of the explanations and examinations have taken place on an advanced mathematic and econometric level, which means that few persons outside academia have had the time to read them. Nevertheless, APT has gained the notice of the investment community, and their curiosity will no doubt grow considerably during the next few years as the logical appeal and, more importantly, practical implications of APT become apparent.[4]

At the core of APT is the notion that a few systematic factors affect the long-term average returns of financial assets. APT does not deny myriad factors that influence the daily price variability of individual stocks and bonds; rather it focuses on major forces that move aggregates of assets in large portfolios. By identifying these forces, we can gain an intuitive appreciation of their influence on portfolio returns. The ultimate goal is to acquire a better understanding of portfolio structuring and evaluation, thereby improving overall portfolio design and performance.

The APT, developed by Richard Roll and Stephen Ross (1976), propagated from the capital asset pricing model and has evolved as a major tool to probe systematic risk. The methodology (run through APT computer models) assimilates fundamental economic factors common to all securities, not just one (beta) to explain stock returns. Current APT research concentrates on multivariate statistical techniques such as factor analysis to decompose an investment's total return into separate pieces explainable by exogenous factors, each of which explains a unique amount of the variance of the investment's total returns. The fundamental factors are macroeconomic and include but are not restricted to the following:

1. Industrial production (or the market portfolio)
2. Changes in a default risk premium (measured by the differences in promised yields to maturity on AAA versus Baa corporate bonds)
3. Twists in the yield curve (measured by the differences in promised yields to maturity on long- and short-term government bonds)
4. Unanticipated inflation
5. Changes in the real rate (measured by the Treasury bill rate minus the consumer price index)

Underlying variables of economic logic make sense. For instance, common stock prices represent the present value of discounted cash flows or industrial production relates to profits. Other APT variables relate to the discount rate.

---

[4] Richard Roll and Stephen Ross, "The Arbitrage Pricing Theory Approach to Strategic Portfolio Financial," *Analysts Journal* (January/February 1995).

Because APT partitions economic factors, portfolios having disparate sensitivities to these systematic factors can be constructed. For example, a portfolio consisting of rental properties (with the loan portfolio included) would be downside sensitive to unanticipated inflation, since rents cannot be raised overnight to compensate for an *unanticipated* jump in home heating oil prices. Choosing investments with upside sensitivities to *unanticipated* inflation would conceivably reduce the portfolio's risk. Thus, returns of securities are influenced by several principal factors that affect economy. Changes in these factors affect stock returns in several ways depending on how sensitive the stock's return is to each of these factors. The sensitivity of a stock's return to a factor (e.g., interest rates) is the factor's beta. If three factors affect stock returns, there will be three factor sensitivities or factor betas. In addition to systematic factors, asset returns are affected by factors unique to the firm in question (unsystematic risk). However, if large portfolios are constructed, unsystematic risks cancel out through the process of diversification.

Multivariate statistical techniques such as factor analysis decompose an asset's total return into separate pieces, which explains a unique amount of the variance of the asset's total return. The formula for the arbitrage pricing model is as follows:

$$E(Rj) = Rf + \beta j_1 [E(R_1) - Rf] + \beta j_2 [E(R_2) - Rf] + \beta j_3 [E(R_3) - Rf]$$

where

$E(Rj)$ = expected return on stock j

Rf = risk-free rate

$\beta j_1\ \beta j_2\ \beta j_3$ = sensitivities of stock j to factors 1, 2, 3

Factor 1 might be the stock's sensitivity to industrial production; factor 2 might refer to sensitivity to changes in the default risk premium, factor 3 may measure the stock's reaction to unanticipated inflation or twists in the yield curve.

$E(R_1)\ E(R_2)\ E(R_3)$ = Average returns on factors 1, 2, 3

Example

Let's assume APT factor sensitivities on a particular security, stock k, is 1.3, 0.9, and −1.2 with factors 1, 2, and 3, respectively. Thus, βk_1 = 1.3, βk_2 = 0.9, and βk_3 = −1.2. Assume the average response to factors 1, 2, and 3 market wide is 11%, 7%, and 3%, respectively. We can set $E(R_1)$ = 11%, $E(R_2)$ = 7%, and $E(R_3)$ = 3%.

Lastly, let's set the long-term government bond rate Rf = 6%. The expected return on stock k, E(Rk), is

$$E(Rk) = .06 + 1.3\,(.11 - .06) + 0.9\,(.07 - .06) - 1.2\,(.03 - .06) = 17.0\%$$

Shareholders demand a return of 17%. But what return is "right" for banks electing to finance this business?

Risk Analysis and Management of Bank Loan Portfolios[5]

Modern portfolio theory states that investors will be rewarded only for nondiversifiable risk. A portfolio comprising 100% IBM stock will be risky, but the investor should only expect rewards that would accrue to a diversified IBM investor. Finance theory states that diversified investors set prices in the equity market; all investment eggs are not in one basket. The capital asset pricing model and arbitrage pricing theory postulates that the investor will be compensated only for the systematic risk that remains in his or her diversified portfolio. Given that an IBM position adds to a portfolio's exposure, if the economy surges, the investor can expect to outperform the market.

APT suggests that investors will be rewarded for accurately forecasting economic (systematic) events and positioning their equity portfolios accordingly. In the best scenario, the bank portfolio manager creates a portfolio with high spreads, low cost of funds, and minimal defaults. In the worst case, the portfolio and the bank are under water. As the 1980s demonstrated, the worst case was often the most likely case. But clearly, banks took risks that were not priced appropriately (refer to Chapter 18, "Pricing Models: Design and Application" and Chapter 16, "Overview of RAROC and CreditMetrics"). Even loans supported by superior credit analysis often defaulted because of damaging macroeconomic events and pricing pressure caused by overcapacity. Given that loans cannot be priced to adequately compensate for risk, it is appropriate to minimize risk through diversification. Knowledge of APT and related techniques can help bank managers identify those risks.

Risk Diversification

As we saw earlier, the principal benefit of advances in investment theory for bank management is risk reduction. This implies a commitment to diversification and risk measurement. Data from the equity markets can theoretically be used within APT style models to gauge concentrations of industry, geographic, and systematic risk. Provided with the appropriate mandate along with the right information, a portfolio manager can structure the bank's portfolio to diversify away as much risk as possible.

It might serve well to keep in mind that a rose's aroma is always more arresting than its photo. In practice, APT analysis of commercial loans is uncommon, albeit rare, and is rather difficult to implement because there was until recently little or no public information on the past or future economic sensitivities of most privately held companies. KMV models discussed in Chapters 13 and 14 have significantly allayed this problem and are the preferred modeling tool to proxy

---

[5] The author wishes to thank Andrew C. Robertson for his invaluable assistance in developing this section on equity portfolio management.

private firms. So too are the tools of Roll and Ross Asset Management Corp., represented as the world leader in APT portfolio applications.

Alternatively, to a lesser extent it is possible to proxy companies from the bank's existing loan portfolio or the public equity markets to calculate a borrower's APT risk profile. Following are steps along this trail that will either improve loan portfolio quality per se or clear up the notion of credit-sponsored systematic risk.

Step 1: Calculate Company Systematic Risk

If a company has publicly traded equity or debt, price history can be analyzed using APT modeling provided by Roll and Ross Asset Management Services for Institutional Investors (*http://www.rollross.com/*). Roll and Ross Asset Management is an investment advisory firm that uses the proprietary arbitrage pricing technique to contain risk and enhance return with a high degree of consistency. Incorporated in 1986, the principals have conducted research for more than 20 years on the practical uses of their investment approach, the APT.

The firm's APT portfolio is designed to deliver results superior to any specified benchmark. Roll and Ross analysts monitor a large number of individual assets traded in major world markets and calculate quantitative characteristics of these assets in the APT context. Portfolios can be selected from approximately 15,000 common stocks in 17 countries. Client portfolios are currently under management in Brazilian, Dutch, French, Japanese, and U.S. equities, as well as internationally diversified equities.

If the company's securities are lightly traded or closely held, it may be necessary to calculate APT factors on a case-by-case basis.[6] In many cases, firms that were publicly traded before a leveraged transaction have price histories. These data may be helpful in understanding the company's reaction to past economic shocks such as the oil shocks of the 1970s. In most cases, it will be necessary to choose a proxy company or industry to estimate APT factors. For example, Milky Way candy bars can be expected to have economic sensitivities similar to those of Hershey or Three Musketeers. Portfolio managers can use either company's APT risk factors or an average of all candy manufacturers. Geographic concentration is rarely an issue that affects equity risks (one exception, however, was the effect of Hurricane Andrew on Florida companies in 1992). However, the location of a small company's operations can be critically important and should be considered as a systematic risk.

Step 2: Aggregate Systematic Risk at the Portfolio Level

The end result of this exercise should be factored sensitivities for each company that can be applied to various APT risks outlined previously in Richard Ross's

---

[6] These are not necessarily the views of Roll and Ross Asset Management Services.

original model and more. Besides sensitivities to interest rates, inflation, and economic growth, macroeconomic factors may also include influences such as oil prices, investor confidence, and geography. Certain regional banks may wish to calculate specific systematic risks pertinent to their market areas (e.g., peso devaluation in Mexico or earthquakes in California). These APT and custom systematic risk factors should be calculated or estimated for every current and prospective loan in the portfolio.

The weighted risk contribution of each loan should then be calculated. This requires an understanding of the company's capital structure and the position of the loan in the hierarchy of debt obligations. A simple way to weight these risks is to use the debt-to-equity ratio. The risk contribution of a senior debenture to an established company with a strong balance sheet is much less than that of a bridge loan to a new, highly leveraged company. Of course, the risks should be weighted by absolute size as well.

A matrix showing the various factor risks, capital structures, and loan sizes can be constructed using standard financial software. The total portfolio risk can be calculated using a weighted approach such as that outlined here:

	Interest Rate Risk	Inflation Risk	Debt/Equity Ratio	Percentage of Portfolio	Adjusted Interest Rate Risk	Adjusted Inflation Risk
Acme	1.2	2	50.00%	10.00	6.00%	10.00%
Sunshine	0.75	0.8	90.00%	60.00	40.50%	43.20%
Zero	2	0.85	10.00%	30.00	6.00%	2.60%
Portfolio				100.00	52.50%	55.80%

The portfolio in the example consists of three loans to companies with widely varying risks and capital structures. While Sunshine Company is the most highly leveraged, its risk factors are below average. Acme and Zero are each particularly sensitive to a risk factor, but because they represent smaller parts of the portfolio and their financial leverage is lower, they contribute less risk to the overall portfolio. The loan portfolio's adjusted factors are below the market average, as can be expected. This means the diversified portfolio has no particular exposure to any single risk factor.

Step 3: Eliminate Unwanted Factor Risk

Once the loan portfolio's risks have been identified, the bank could determine whether any factor risks are over or underrepresented. A diversified portfolio should have equal risk exposure to all factor risks. If the factor risks approach 1 or the equity market average, the portfolio managers will realize that the portfolio is as risky as that of an *equivalent stock portfolio*. As noted previously, it is unlikely that the returns will compensate for the risk. The next task is to eliminate unwanted factor risks and to reduce the overall level of the risk. Reviewing individual loans applying data mining techniques will flag loans contributing the most risk to the portfolio. This risk could be the result of high factor sensitivity or thin balance sheet protection. In either case, the manager might elect to divest the most risky loans or protect loans with credit derivatives. Clearly, this implies a liquid market for loans under question. Difficulty selling off these loans in the secondary market raises another warning signal. Conversely, the bank may elect to purchase loans in the secondary markets with characteristics that are under-represented in its portfolio.

APT tools can be used to quickly and accurately (as accurate as the current technology permits) diversify away systematic risk. APT databases can be reviewed to identify firms or industries with factor risks opposite to those in the current portfolio. A more direct approach uses equity price data to spot companies that move counter to those in a portfolio. For example, a portfolio manager with a large exposure to the auto industry will avoid loans to companies in industries with risks that are highly correlated with autos and add loans to negatively correlated industries. However, he or she should be aware that risks change over time, as do company's sensitivities to particular risks. The auto industry's problems in the late 1980s reflected sensitivity to GDP shocks (i.e., recession and, recently, extremely high oil prices). However, the industry is also sensitive to interest rates. If those economic factors become prevalent, a different set of industries could easily be identified to hedge unwanted macroeconomic risk.

If this process is successful, the resulting loan portfolio will have substantially reduced particular exposure to any systematic risk with an overall reduction in risk. Note that the projected profitability of a loan is not considered. We know that even a well-structured loan can provide unwanted systematic risk. But if it is good paper and large enough, it might be profitably sold in the secondary loan market.

Industry Analysis of the Loan Book

Industries are composed of companies with similar risk characteristics shaped by the nature of a shared or closely related economic function. The economic function influences the industry life cycle, the rapidity of change, and the degree of capital intensity. In addition, competition within the industry greatly determines the success or failure of firms. Therefore, changes in the environment or competitive structure can have an impact on a broad range of companies within an industry. An industry's sensitivity to environmental or "systematic" factors, such as changes in demand, regulations, taxation, and the cost of key inputs, periodically contributes to surges in business failures. Successful companies adapt their capital structure to suit the challenges of their industry and manage the uncertainty of future profitability.

The economic *attributes* of an industry are an important basis for the analysis of industry risk. For example, does technological change play an important role in software development or in borrowers' ability to maintain a competitive advantage? Is the firm operating in an industry driven by intellectual capital needs, as in firms located in Silicon Valley? Or does the industry include a small number of competitors selling specialized products, as in the case of large oil companies?

One money center bank set up an *industry specialists/market intelligence group* operating under its Loan Risk Policy Division. The group is charged with measuring industry risk and tracking industry concentrations. Industry specialists are assigned specific industries—chemical, drug, aerospace, automobile, steel, paper, and so on. They identify the economic characteristics of their industry and determine optimal strategies that borrowers need to pursue to gain competitive advantage.

The bank's industry specialists matured into in-house experts on issues ranging from financial reporting unique to the industry to prospectus writing on success/failure criteria. Specialists coordinate closely with line lenders and advise senior management on important developments and overall exposures—particularly how the industry outlook affects the borrower's industry risk grade. The industry grade, provided by the industry specialists, combined with an assessment of the obligor's competitive tier and provided a reference point for risk grading (see Chapter 19, "Risk Rating Models: Design and Application").

Industry specialists also provide general guidelines dealing with specific industry characteristics. A few of their rhetorical questions, along with industry characteristics (Table 12.1) are listed here:

- Does the borrower operate in a strong and growing industry?
- Is the borrower a significant factor in the industry or market?
- Are legal or regulatory climates favorable?
- Do barriers to entry exist?
- Is the industry minimally affected by cyclical changes?
- Is the industry seasonal?
- Is the industry vulnerable to sudden economic or technological change?
- Is the industry's operating leverage modest?
- Are labor problems minimal?
- Is regulatory the environment satisfactory?
- Is product liability an industry issue?
- Are long-term prospects favorable?
- Does the borrower rank in the first tier of the industry?
- Is the borrower industry "focused," enjoying a meaningful market share?
- Are performance ratios generally better than industry peers?

Industry Analysis of Bank Regulators and Examiners

Federal Reserve Board (FRB) examiners categorize industry analysis into five stages, or levels: (1) identification of loans by industry, (2) analysis of industry

TABLE 12.1   Industry Characteristics

Emerging phase

Key words	Technology and production.
Product	Emphasis now on adding bells and whistles to basic products in order to enhance market appeal, distinguish the product from an increasing number of imitators, and reach into new markets.
Management	Very technology, engineering, or detail oriented. Hands on management with very centralized reporting structure.
Financing	Initially from management resources or venture capital. Later in this phase, some banks and stock underwriters enter the picture. Critical bottleneck.
Distribution	Limited by production capabilities. Tend to use outside distributors.
Regulation	Incidental or generic to general legislation.
M&A deals	M&A. Some astute large firms acquire firms operating in this phase to gain access to patent or technology skills.

Growth phase

Key words	Marketing and distribution.
Product	New product with technological edge. Product significantly improves customer's situation by reducing labor or other input costs or improving standard of living. Emphasis is on developing the production capabilities that bring the technology to market in volume and at a price that makes it viable.
Management	Focus shifts from technological, entrepreneurial qualities of founding fathers to executives (probably outside hires) with marketing and financial skills.
Financing	At this phase, internal capital growth rates are good, return on equity is good; outside funds can be had from stock market or banks. But outside lenders place a financial reporting discipline on these companies.
Distribution	Emphasis shifts from outside distributors to internally controlled sales and distribution organizations.
Regulation	As these companies get more into the public realm, Security and Exchange Commission regulations come into play. Also, a body of case law emerges that has a quasi-regulatory influence. Oftentimes specific legislation regulating or governing the product begins to emerge.
M&A Deals	M&A picks up, particularly on a horizontal basis, as companies seek distribution capability (market share). Occasionally vertical acquisitions are used to protect availability or price of raw materials or components.

Mature phase

Key words	Price competition and cost cutting.
Product	Technology is well established, markets are saturated, and long-term growth is in line with general economy. Companies compete for market share on price basis.
Management	Old management reflects hereditary culture, usually clubby in nature by now. Difficult to do cost cutting necessary to maintain at least average return on equity. In the emerging phase, production was the management goal; in the growth phase, distribution was the goal; in the mature phase, management of the corporation itself becomes the goal.

Financing	Price earnings ratio is down, therefore the equity market is less attractive to the company. Because of increased size and long-term operating records, debt markets are still open. Generally reduced need for financing.
Distribution	Smart management is trying to add on related products with higher margins to utilize distribution network.
Regulation	Nuisance level. Regulatory cultures change even more slowly than corporate cultures.
M&A deals	M&A activity takes place with view to (1) reduce administrative costs, (2) more fully utilize production and distribution capacity, or (3) acquire emerging companies.

fundamentals, (3) reporting industry concentrations, (4) quantifying industry risk, and (5) incorporating industry analysis into the loan portfolio. It might be a good idea for bank portfolio officers to internalize the following FRB stages of industry analysis:

Level 1: Identify Loans by Industry[7]
1. Attach an Standard Industry Code (SIC) to every loan.
2. Define industry groups.
3. Assign a credit risk rating to every loan.
4. Distinguish between the credit rating for a borrower and the credit rating for a loan transaction.

Level 2: Analyze Industry Fundamentals
1. Prepare industry studies for loan officers and credit committees.
2. Evaluate credit risk exposure in relation to the industry.
3. Identify borrowers by industry.
4. Analyze individual bank credits by industry.
5. Perform comparative analysis of industries:
   a. Analyze financial ratios.
   b. Compare operating characteristics.
   c. Understand financial and operating risks.
6. Establish industry credit standards (loan structure, collateral coverage, documentation requirements).
7. Achieve functional independence but avoid isolation:
   a. Remove responsibility for industry studies and analysis from the loan officers.
   b. Organize industry analysis under chief economist or senior credit officer, but preserve intelligence lines with lending personnel.

---

[7] *1994 Federal Reserve Loan Examination Manual* dealing with the nuts and bolts of an industry audit.

Level 3: Report Industry Concentrations
1. Aggregate industry concentrations:
    a. Use weighted average or percentiles of credit ratings aggregated by the industry.
    b. Analyze risk of portfolio by industry.
2. Establish an industry credit policy committee:
    a. Review industry studies.
    b. Analyze concentrations in relation to capital or loans.
    c. Set loan limits.
    d. Use for strategic planning purposes.
    e. Identify growth industries and problem industries.

Level 4: Quantify Industry Risk
1. Develop industry risk ratings for industry analysis:
    a. Use an external model from an outside vendor.
    b. Develop an internal model.
    c. Use economic or industry data.
    d. Use financial or bond market data as indicators of industry risk.
    e. Compare industry risk ratings with the weighted average credit rating of the bank's exposure by industry.
    f. Run scenarios (commodity price changes, interest rate changes) to determine the sensitivity of the loan portfolio to outside shocks.
    g. Determine covariance of industries or interrelationships among industries.

Level 5: Incorporate Industry Analysis into the Loan Portfolio
1. Diversify the loan portfolio to reduce industry risk and industry concentrations.
2. Distinguish between the decision to originate a loan and the decision to retain it for the portfolio.
3. Use loan sales to reduce concentrations in the portfolio.
4. Sell loans to organized secondary markets.
5. Use industry risk systems:
    a. To influence loan pricing.
    b. To develop risk-adjusted rates of return measures.
    c. To assign capital or loan loss reserves.
    d. To conceptualize the loan portfolio like a securities portfolio.

A Few Pointers on Stress Testing Loan Portfolios

Portfolio stress testing measures an industry's vulnerability to economic downturns and other adverse systematic events. How should banks go about developing methodology for stress-testing exposures? The acting banking commissioner's position on the subject is clear: he encourages banks to conduct their own loan portfolio stress testing but is not afraid to take action if they don't:[8]

> Stress testing starts by asking rhetorical "what if" questions dealing with loan portfolio composition, loss history, management expertise, capital protection, asset quality, and other factors. Next run sample credits pulled from the bank's exposure network to determine how both systematic and unsystematic adverse events might affect loan performance. Adverse events are anything beyond bank management's control that could jeopardize loan repayments. In addition, the borrower's entire debt structure is examined, not just individual loans booked at the bank. Common adverse events include economic recessions, interest rate increases, stock market declines, foreign market downturns, contract losses, and curtailed defense spending.

> Take this recommendation to stress portfolios seriously: Portfolio managers who have their own analyses in place may be able to avoid having bank examiners do it for them. Policy memorandum 1016 expressly provides that the banking department's regional director can waive the requirement for bank examiners to conduct the stress analysis if "it is believed that the results will be minimally beneficial."

For example, an economic downturn is assumed to result in all the following risk factors for the loan under review: 15% loss of sales, 15% collateral devaluation, 15% accounts receivable write-off, largest account receivable write-off, 15% inventory losses, 15% increase in overhead, and 15% increase in cost of goods sold.[9]

Results can then be sorted into three broad risk categories: low risk, normal risk, and high risk, with descriptions of each category included in a policy memorandum. *The policy memorandum includes the magnitude and number of high-risk loans (ex parte stress test) and the amount of Tier 1 capital represented.* Stress-test analyses should also include contingency plans regarding actions management might take given certain scenarios. These include techniques or products that actualize hedges or reduce the size of exposures.[10]

HEDGING DOWN RISKY EXPOSURES

Hedging reduces a portfolio's risk by actually offsetting one risk against another. With diversification, risk is reduced because uncorrelated risks do not behave in lockstep. For example, a single security portfolio will tank if just one security price crashes. Investors holding multiple uncorrelated securities seldom experience calamities. How portfolio hedges are constructed will vary according to specific goals established by a bank.

---

[8] Acting banking commissioner Randall James.
[9] Ibid.
[10] Basel Committee.

Conventional Loan Sales (see Exhibit 12.1 "Common Definitions: Loan Sales")

Until the mid-1980s, banks expanded portfolios by approving loans and keeping the assets on their books until borrowers repaid. Banks have reversed course, getting loans off their books by selling them directly to other banks or unloading positions in the secondary loan market. Loan sales provide a valuable portfolio tool, minimizing risk through diversification. From the standpoint of smaller banks, buying portions of loans booked at larger institutions has two advantages: improving portfolio diversification and earning a higher rate of return than could be obtained by selling federal funds or investing in commercial paper and government securities with comparable maturities. Loan sales allow management to control the overall size of bank assets. Other advantages include the following:

- Loan sales provide increased return on assets by reducing assets on the bank's balance sheet and providing more fee-generated income.
- Capital/asset ratios are examined closely as banks are restricted by asset growth and legal lending limits.
- As a form of risk management, loan sales allow banks to originate large commitments and sell down these commitments ending with relatively small commitments.
- As a fee generator, loan sales provide greater than proportional up-front fees on the bank's net commitment.
- Loan sales enable banks to tap a wider investment base, including the following:
  - *Foreign banks.* These banks may have a lower funding base and thereby accept a lower return on assets. Foreign banks often want to diversify their portfolios and to create contacts with potential U.S. customers.
  - *Regional banks.* Like foreign banks, regionals have lower funding costs and can accept a lower return. The greater proportion of core deposits is the primary reason regional banks enjoy lower funding costs. Loan purchases provide regionals with adequate returns, develop relationships with money center banks, and introduce the banks to a new customer base. Also, the regionals may have no other access to the deals being shopped by the larger money center banks.
  - *Insurance companies.* These companies generally buy because of their large investment needs. They also have adequate credit review skills to participate.
  - *S & Ls and thrifts.* These institutions generally participate in higher-yielding deals.

While loan sales have not changed that much over the past few years, there have been significant modifications in the nature of many credits being sold. Particular emphasis has been placed on approving loans to quality borrowers for very short or relatively long maturities with the intent of selling virtually all of these loans in the marketplace. Short-term investments consist of under-90-day paper executed by investment-grade or high-quality, nonrated borrowers, or "strips" of revolving credits to this same class of borrower. Yields are thin; usually there is a small basis point spread between these investments and government securities. Medium-term investments involve underlying transactions greater than a one-year tenor with both investment and noninvestment-grade transactions. These investments generally require a fully documented credit facility. Medium-term loan sales usually carry an attractive rate of interest. These types of loan participations are referred to by the investment bankers as "story paper" since the loans do not carry a national credit rating and must be "reviewed" prior to purchase. Bankers who buy paper with only a story attached are playing the game at their own risk. Clearly, due diligence, including responsible credit investigations, rests with investors. The loan sale process includes several variations.

Syndications

Investors commit to a primary position in a transaction prior to closing and sign for such at closing. Syndication may represent distribution of either a "best effort" syndication amount or an underwritten syndication amount. The deal sponsor provides the structure and runs his or her own analysis. The syndication process may include the following arrangement: Assume the borrower wants to raise $100 million with bank A as agent. In the example, bank A will negotiate the documents with the borrower and then solicit a group of investors offering them pieces of the $100 million loan at $20 million each (Figure 12.1).

The Key Issues from the Borrower's Perspective
1. Speed and simplicity are essential.
2. The participating banks negotiate one document, not four.
3. The lead bank, bank A, acts as an agent/intermediary with the banks. The borrower is close to bank A and has no relationship with the other banks.
4. Pricing tends to be more aggressive.
5. The arrangement eliminates market risk.

The Key Issues from the Agent Bank's Perspective
1. Bank A continues to maintain a senior relationship with the borrower.
2. The bank has its points represented in all of the loan documentation.
3. The bank is rewarded with an up-front fee.

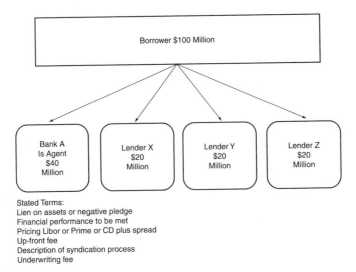

Stated Terms:
Lien on assets or negative pledge
Financial performance to be met
Pricing Libor or Prime or CD plus spread
Up-front fee
Description of syndication process
Underwriting fee

FIGURE 12.1 The Syndication Process

Novations

Novation involves an assignment by the seller (originating bank) to the buyer, whereby the borrower has consented all seller rights and responsibilities to the borrower. The seller is released from its responsibilities and the buyer (investor) is situated as if it were an original signing party to the loan agreement (Figure 12.2). Overseas, a novation is commonly accomplished through a transferable loan certificate.

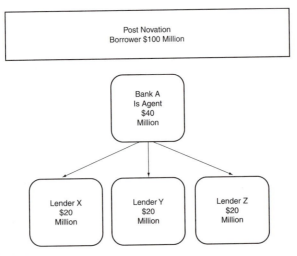

FIGURE 12.2 The Novation Process

Participations

An agreement whereby a selling bank transfers to investors the right to receive a pro rata share of the payments from the borrower. Generally, participation imposes limitations on the rights of a seller to agree, without buyer approval, to changes in principal, interest, payment schedule, collateral, guarantors, and possibly the advance rate formula. Such an arrangement, which does not transfer voting rights, is generally completed without the borrower's direct approval (Figure 12.3).

Up-Front Fees

Originating banks receive higher than proportional up-front fees. For example, assume the deal called for a $500 million exposure carrying a 1% up-front fee. If the bank kept the loan in its portfolio, it would earn $5 million: $500 million (1%) = $5 million. Selling parts of the loan would reduce the bank's investment. However, generated income would increase to 1.75%.

Banks	Amount	Total	Fee	Fee Income (in millions)
Six banks	$50,000	$300,000	1%	$3.000
Six banks	$25,000	$150,000	.75%	$1.125
Bank A (hold)	$50,000	$50,000	1.75%	$.875
Total		$500,000		$5,000

Securitization

Securitization is a prominent form of loan sale in which securities are backed by pools of mortgage loans, auto loans, credit card balances, boat loans, computer equipment leases, airplane leases, high-yield bonds, life insurance policy loans, and commercial real estate loans, among other types of collateral. The key to securitization is finding assets that generate a predictable cash flow stream—like loans.

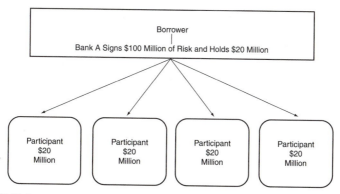

FIGURE 12.3 The Participation Process

The securitized loans are relatively homogenous as to rates, terms, and collateral. A commercial bank, or its subsidiary, books car loans and then sells the loans to another entity who restructures the assets into a loan pool. The pool retains the loans as collateral for its own obligations, which, in turn, can be sold to third-party buyers. Typically, an investment banker would structure the deal for a smaller bank and the originating bank, or its subsidiary, would continue to service the loans.

Typically, asset-backed securities are not issued by banks but by limited-purpose entities (such as trusts or single-purpose corporations) created by the banks. The bank sells the loans to the issuing entity; the issuer sells securities backed by the pool of loans to investors and pays the bank for the purchased loans with the proceeds from the sales of the securities. The bank usually retains the right to service the loans for the issuer of the securities, for a fee. If the transactions pass certain legal and accounting tests, they are considered to be a true sale of assets from the originator of the loans to the issuer of the securities.

Originators of asset-backed securities usually want to sell loans without recourse. Thus, generally three methods protect investors: overcollateralization, senior/subordinated structures, and credit enhancement. Overcollateralization simply involves collateral whereby scheduled cash flow exceeds the cash flow needed to pay the principal and interest on the securities. As long as the actual losses in the collateral pool are less than the excess cash flow built into the collateral pool, there should be enough cash flow to make all required payments to investors.

In the senior/subordinated structure, the issuer of a pass-through security sells two distinct classes of certificates, both of which are secured by the single pool of collateral. The senior certificates are offered to investors, whereas the originator usually purchases the subordinated certificates. At the time the senior and subordinated certificates are issued, the scheduled cash flow from the collateral pool must be enough to support the scheduled principal and interest on both the senior and junior certificates. However, the cash flow from the collateral is allocated first to pay principal and interest to the owners of the senior certificates. The holders of the subordinated certificates only receive payments from cash flow above and beyond that needed to pay the senior certificate holders. As long as actual losses in the collateral pool do not exceed the scheduled payments on the subordinated certificates, there should be enough cash flow to pay the senior certificates holders. The larger the subordinated class relative to the total issue, the greater the protection for the senior class holders.

Asset-backed securities can be enhanced by a letter of credit, which the issuing entity draws on to cover losses in the collateral. The letter of credit is obtained from a bank (other than the originating bank) or insurance company. Typically, credit enhancement covers a certain percentage of the first loss on the total pool. This is at a level comparable to historical losses plus a margin. Banks receive fees for providing a letter of credit (as long as they are not the originator) that adds to bank income.

The following list summarizes key reasons why securitization improves loan portfolios and provides additional fee-based income.

- *Liquidity.* Traditional credit produces illiquid assets. While some loans can be sold to other banks and insurance companies, there is presently still no real hot secondary market for most commercial loans, and many banks can do little to adjust their portfolios to changing interest rates or market conditions. Securitization provides the necessary liquidity for such adjustments.
- *Credit risk.* The traditional credit system concentrates credit risk both geographically and within weak institutions. Banks can geographically diversify their portfolios by purchasing securitized credit from all parts of the world. The ability to sell these securities internationally diversifies the institution's funding base, reducing dependence on local economies. For example, in a properly structured securitized credit transaction, credit risk is spread among the originator, a credit enhancer (either another commercial bank, foreign bank, or insurance company, domestic or foreign), and the investor. Most important, the removal of an asset from an institution's portfolio reduces capital requirements and reserve requirements on deposits funding the asset.
- *Interest risk.* Commercial banks are highly sensitive to interest rate risk. Securitization may be used to reduce interest rate risk by improving the institution's asset-liability mix. This is especially true if the institution has a large investment in fixed-rate, low-yield assets. Securitization places interest risk with investors more willing and able to take such risk, such as pension funds, insurance companies, and mutual funds. A securitized credit system allows banks to offer fixed-rate loans and to choose whether to take the interest risk.
- *Money velocity and earnings.* Banks can improve their profitability through the increased velocity of money flowing through the bank. Banks earn fees from (1) issuing entities for servicing securitized loans and issuing letters of credit and (2) reduced costs and through management of a smaller and more diversified loan portfolio. In addition, by removing assets, the institution enhances its return on equity and assets.

Risks Financial Institutions Encounter

Risks faced in the securitization process are identical to those in traditional lending transactions. These involve credit risk, concentration risk, and interest rate risk—including prepayment risk, operational risk, liquidity risk, moral recourse risk, and funding risk. However, since the securitization process separates the traditional lending function into several limited roles such as originator, servicer, credit enhancer, trustee, and investor, the types of risks that a bank may encounter will differ depending on the role it assumes.

Investors in asset-backed securities, as noted earlier, are exposed to credit risk—the risk that obligers will default on principal and interest payments.

Investors are also subject to the risk that the various parties, for example, the servicer or trustee, in the securitization structure will be unable to fulfill their contractual obligations. Moreover, investors may be susceptible to concentrations of risks across various asset-backed security issues through overexposure to an organization performing various roles in the securitization process or as a result of geographic concentrations within the pool of assets providing the cash flows for an individual issue.

Also, since the secondary markets for certain asset-backed securities are thin, investors may encounter greater-than-anticipated difficulties when seeking to sell their securities. Furthermore, certain derivative instruments, such as stripped asset-backed securities and residuals, may be extremely sensitive to interest rates and exhibit a high degree of price volatility, which, therefore, may dramatically affect risk.

Banking organizations that issue asset-backed securities may be subject to pressures to sell only their best assets, thus reducing the quality of their own loan portfolios. On the other hand, some banking organizations may feel pressures to relax their credit standards because they can sell assets with higher risk than they would normally want to retain for their own portfolios.

Compliance with Regulations

To ensure that portfolio managers involved in asset-backed securities are in compliance with regulatory requirements, the FRB issued a set of objectives, questions, and standards, which are summarized here:[11]

1. The bank is required to comply with laws, regulations, and policy statements.
2. Securitization activities should be integrated into the overall strategic objectives of the organization.
3. Bank portfolio managers should have an appropriate level of experience in securitization activities.
4. Institutions should not hold any asset-backed securities that are inappropriate, given the size of the bank and the sophistication of its operation.
5. Policies and procedures governing securitization should ensure that all asset-backed securities owned and any assets sold with recourse are properly accounted for in the bank's books and on regulatory reports.
6. Sources of credit risk should be fully understood, and properly analyzed and managed, without excessive reliance on credit ratings by outside agencies.

---

[11] FRB Asset Securitization Examination Objectives, effective date September 1992.

7. Credit, operational, and other risks should not only be recognized but addressed through appropriate policies, procedures, management reports, and other controls.

8. Portfolio officers are required to operate in conformance with established bank policies and procedures.

9. Liquidity and market risks need to be properly understood so that the bank is not excessively dependent on securitization as a substitute for funding or as a source of income.

10. Procedures should be in place to ensure that steps have been taken to minimize the potential for conflicts of interest due to securitization.

11. Banks need to foretell possible sources of structural failure in securitization transactions, and they must ensure that the institution has adopted measures to minimize the impact of such failures should they occur.

12. Banks must be aware of the legal risks and uncertainty regarding various aspects of securitization.

13. Portfolio managers should avoid concentrations of exposure in the underlying asset pools, in the asset-backed securities portfolio, or in the structural elements of securitization transactions.

14. All sources of risk are evaluated at the inception of each securitization activity and are monitored on an ongoing basis.

15. Corrective action must be taken if policies, practices, procedures, or internal controls are deficient, or when violations of law, regulation, or policy statements are disclosed.

EXHIBIT 12.1   Common Definitions: Loan Sales

1. *Underwritten amount.* The amount that the bank formally "commits" to a transaction. This is the amount for which the bank is at economic risk and for which it must sign if syndication is not completed.

2. *Downstream correspondent bank.* This usually refers to small or medium-sized banks that purchase loan participations from larger regional banks.

3. *Best-efforts syndication amount.* The difference, if any, between the total facility amount and the selling bank commitment amount. Generally, risks with respect to syndication amount relate to reputation risk or arrangement/syndication fees. The seller performance is on a best-efforts basis.

4. *Repo clause.* An agreement in which the seller of a participation promises to repurchase the participation at a higher price on a specific date.

5. *Resyndication.* The process undertaken when one or more banks underwrite an entire loan and then syndicate to a group of primary lenders.

6. *Underwriting liability.* The general reference to any seller liability to the buyer arising before, during, or slightly after the completion of a loan sale transaction. Risks generally relate to misrepresentation or nondisclosure of information.

7. *Latent liability.* The general reference to any ongoing seller liability to the buyer arising from either underwriting liability or from ongoing seller responsibilities to the buyer.

8. *Bid loan.* A loan to a borrower for a particular maturity date and generally for an absolute interest rate.

9. *Loan part.* The commonly used term in the investor marketplace for the economic transaction in which an investor purchases a participation in a bid note or a grid bid note.

10. *Skim/scalp.* The part of a loan's yield that sellers of participations retain for their own profit.

11. *Competitive bid option.* When a borrowing company wishes to draw all or part of its funds under an existing loan, it puts that piece of the credit up for bid among the primary syndicate members. The bank bidding lowest wins the right to finance that piece.

12. *Drop dead fee.* A fee paid by a borrower to compensate lenders for committing funds to finance a takeover bid that never takes place.

13. *Upstream correspondent bank.* Refers to money centers and other major banks that sell loan participations to regional banks.

14. *Signing amount.* The amount for which the originator or seller bank intends to sign. The amount may be no more than the originator bank commitment amount nor less than the portfolio hold amount and is most often between those amounts.

15. *Strips*: The sale to investors of specific rollovers under a committed credit facility, the duration of which is longer than the specific rollover (e.g., a 30-day advance under a 3-year revolving credit).

CREDIT DERIVATIVES

Credit derivatives (see Chapter 15, "Credit Derivatives") enable banks to improve their balance sheets by buying the risk of some other institution's exposure or, conversely, selling the risk of loans included in their portfolios. By engaging in these strategies, banks diversify lending risk by hedging or adding to exposures. The growth of credit derivatives looms from the substantial flexibility associated with this credit strategy. The ability of portfolio managers to create custom-made assets (exposures) of the optimal risk, tenor, and currency has elevated this tool to the apex of risk management.

CONCLUSION

Until recently, the means to deal with credit exposures were meager. Some banks engaged in the practice of setting aside excessive loan provisions and allocating capital that in many cases was unwarranted. Some banks flatly turned old and established customers down, which not only proved expensive and inflexible but also sacrificed the institution's reputation in the process. Others imposed arbitrary facility limits, effectively putting a cap on business development. Granting credit involves accepting risks, but banks have new ways to manage their portfolios. This chapter reviewed a few of these mechanisms such as loan sales and securitization programs (credit derivatives will be covered in Chapter 15). But as a first step, systematic (macroeconomic and industry) shocks to exposure concentrations must be clearly identified and controlled.

We revisit loan portfolios again in Chapter 13, "Portfolio Management of Default Risk," and Chapter 14, "EDF Credit Measure." Peter Crosbie and Jeffrey Bohn at KMV authored both chapters. KMV, now part of Moody's, is the world's leading provider of market-based quantitative credit risk products for credit risk investors. KMV's products are widely used around the globe by credit risk investors to assess the risk and return characteristics of portfolios of corporate bonds, commercial and industrial loans, and credit derivatives. The major challenge facing bankers and other credit risk investors is identifying the dynamics of the default risk of the entire portfolio. After all, credit risk is a portfolio problem. In the final analysis, portfolio risk and return is driven by the connection between changes in default risk and changes in credit spreads.

Appendix 1 to Chapter 12 introduces the quantitative side of loan portfolio management on more or less a basic level. We review how portfolio hedges are constructed with statistics by examining a "deal" that illustrates economic cycle risk/hedge strategies and portfolio risk assessment methods. Appendix 2 introduces deterministic optimization within a loan portfolio (see Chapter 7, "Projections and Risk Assessment," specifically the section on stochastic optimization, for a more advanced survey of optimization).

REVIEW QUESTIONS

1. What are the essential elements of a portfolio risk-management process?
2. What are the roles and responsibilities of loan portfolio officers?
3. What are the advantages of diversification in the loan portfolio?
4. Assume that the poultry industry is countercyclical to the economy in general and to beef production in particular. Does this negative correlation between poultry and beef mean that a bank whose returns tend to move in concert with beef production would run less risk if it diversifies by making more loans to poultry producers?

5. Many larger banks set up industry specialists. They operate under loan risk policy, providing guidelines on specific industry characteristics. Explain how these specialists measure industry risk and track industry concentrations?

6. Define the following terms, using examples to illustrate your answer.
   a. Systematic and unsystematic risk
   b. Arbitrage pricing
   c. Microanalysis
   d. Syndications
   e. Notations
   f. Participations

7. Loan sales allow a bank's management to control the overall size of bank assets. Describe five other benefits of loan sales.

8. Explain the following statement: "Securitization is a prominent form of loan sales, in which securities are backed by pools of mortgage loans. The key to securitization is finding assets on a bank's books that generate a predictable cash flow stream."

9. Why do limited-purpose entities, rather than the banks that originated the loans, typically issue asset-backed securities?

SELECTED REFERENCES AND READINGS

Aja-Nwachukwu, I. (1990). Risk factor in the management of the loan portfolio of commercial banks. *Nigerian Financial Review* **3**, 21–32.

Albert, H. W. (1991). Asset securitization: Benefits for all banks. *Bankers Magazine* **174**, 16–20.

Arnold, I. J. M., and J. Lemmen. (1999). The vulnerability of banks to government default risk in the EMU. *London School of Economics and Political Science. Lse Financial Markets Group. Special Paper Series* No. 115, 1–28. Examines the vulnerability of banks in European Monetary Union (EMU) countries to shocks to default risk premiums on public debt. This vulnerability depends on (1) the total amount of public debt in bank portfolios, (2) the extent to which the default risk of public debt of EMU member states is diversifiable, and (3) the degree of actual geographical diversification of public debt holdings by banks.

Asia Law & Practice Ltd. (1997). *Securitization: A global guide. Securitization.* Hong Kong, China: Asia Law & Practice Ltd.

Barbour, D., T. W. Slover, *et al.* (1998). *Asset securitization in emerging market economies: Fundamental considerations.* London: International Finance & Tax Law Unit Centre for Commercial Law Studies Queen Mary & Westfield College University of London in cooperation with the London Centre for International Banking Studies and the London Institute of International Banking Finance & Development Law.

Becketti, S., and C. S. Morris. (1987). Loan sales: Another step in the evolution of the short-term credit market. *Economic Review/Federal Reserve Bank of Kansas City* **72**, 22–31.

Bennett, P. (1984). Applying portfolio theory to global bank lending. *Journal of Banking & Finance* **8**, 153–169.

Blåvarg, M., and P. Lilja (1998). Securitisation: A future form of financing? *Quarterly Review/Sveriges Riksbank* (3), 25–49.

Boemio, T. R., and G. A. Edwards, Jr. (1989). Asset securitization: A supervisory perspective. *Federal Reserve Bulletin/Board of Governors of the Federal Reserve System* **75**, 659–669.

Calem, P., and R. Rob. (1999). The impact of capital-based regulation on bank risk-taking."*Journal of Financial Intermediation* **8**(4), 317–352.

Cantor, R., and R. Demsetz. (1993). Securitization, loan sales, and the credit slowdown. *Quarterly Review/Federal Reserve Bank of New York* **18**, 27–38.

Carey, M. (2000). Dimensions of credit risk and their relationship to economic capital requirements. *National Bureau of Economic Research. Working Paper Series* No. 7629, 1–[39].

Carlstrom, C. T., and K. A. Samolyk. (1995). Loan sales as a response to market-based capital constraints. *Journal of Banking & Finance* **19**, 627–646. With "Comments on papers presented by Carlstrom and Soamolyk, and Jagtiani, Saunders, and Udell," by George S. Oldfield, pp. 659–660.

Chirinko, R. S., and G. D. Guill. (1993). Portfolio diversification and global credit risk management. *International Journal of Development Banking* **11**, 3–12.

"Credit risk: A *Risk* special report. (1999). Risk 12 (10, Suppl.), 1–40.

Christy, G. C. (1988). Problem loan prevention and management from a portfolio point of view. *Journal of Commercial Bank Lending* **71**, 4–13.

Dannen, F. (1989). Failed promise of asset-backed securities. *Institutional Investor* **23**, 261–264.

Das, A. (1998). Portfolio risks and scale economies in banking: The Indian case. *International Journal of Development Banking* **16**(2), 3–12.

Demsetz, R. (1993). Recent trends in commercial bank loan sales. *Quarterly Review/Federal Reserve Bank of New York* **18**, 75–78.

Demsetz, R. S. (1994). Economic conditions, lending opportunities, and loan sales. *Federal Reserve Bank of New York. Research Paper* No. 9403, 1–36.

Euromoney Publications. (1993). *Securitization: An international guide.* London: Euromoney Publications.

Gjerde, Ø., and K. Semmen. (1995). Risk-based capital requirements and bank portfolio risk. *Journal of Banking & Finance* **19**, 1159–1173.

Globecon Group. (1995). *Active bank risk management: Enhancing investment & credit portfolio performance.* Burr Ridge, IL: Irwin.

Gorton, G., and G. Pennacchi. (1990). Banks and loan sales: Marketing non-marketable assets. *National Bureau of Economic Research. Working Paper Series* No. 3551, 1–[41]. Uses a sample of more than 800 individual loan sales to investigate the nature of loan sales contracts.

Hancock, D., A. J. Laing, *et al.* (1995). Bank capital shocks: Dynamic effects on securities, loans, and capital. *Journal of Banking & Finance* **19**, 661–677. With "Comment on Hancock. Laing and Wilcox and Peek and Rosengren," by Robert B. Avery, pp.713–715.

Hassan, M. K. (1993). Capital market tests of risk exposure of loan sales activities of large U.S. commercial banks. *Quarterly Journal of Business and Economics* **32**, 27–49.

Henderson, J., and ING Barings. (1997). *Asset securitization: Current techniques and emerging market applications.* London: Euromoney Books.

Hendry, S., and G.-J. Zhang (1999). Liquidity effects and market frictions. *Nederlandsche Bank. Dnb-Staff Reports* No. 29,1–42.

Hess, A. C. (1995). Portfolio theory, transaction costs, and the demand for time deposits. *Journal of Money, Credit and Banking* **27**(Pt. 1), 1015–1032.

Hill, C. A. (1998). Latin American securitization: The case of the disappearing political risk. *Virginia Journal of International Law* **38**(3), 293–329.

Hirota, S. I., and Y. Tsutsui. (1999). Do banks diversify portfolio risk? A test of the risk-cost hypothesis. *Japan and the World Economy* **11**(1), 29–39.

Jacques, K,. and P. Nigro. (1997). Risk-based capital, portfolio risk, and bank capital: A simultaneous equations approach. *Journal of Economics and Business* [533]–547.

Jones, J., W. W. Lang, and P. Nigro. (2000). Recent trends in bank loan syndications: Evidence for 1995 to 1999. *United States, Office of the Comptroller of the Currency. Economics Working Paper* No. 2000–10, 1–26.

Kavanagh, B., T. R. Boemio, *et al.* (1992). Asset-backed commercial paper programs. *Federal Reserve Bulletin, Board of Governors of the Federal Reserve System* **78** [107]–116.

Kendall, L. T., and M. J. Fishman. (1996). *A primer on securitization.* Cambridge, MA: MIT Press.

Ketkar, S., and D. Ratha. (2001). Securitization of future flow receivables: A useful tool for developing countries." *Finance and Development, a Quarterly Publication of the International Monetary Fund* **38**(1), 46–49. During financial crises, developing countries cannot obtain low-cost, long-term loans. Securitization of future flow receivables can help investment-grade public and private-sector entities in these countries to obtain credit ratings higher than those of their governments and raise funds in international capital markets." Also published in Arabic, Chinese, French, and Spanish.

Ketkar, S., D. Ratha, *et al.* (2001). *Development financing during a crisis: Securitization of future receivables.* Washington, DC: World Bank, Economic Policy and Prospects Group. Market placements by future receivables can allow public and private-sector entities in a developing country to escape the sovereign credit ceiling and raise lower-cost financing from international capital markets. If planned and executed ahead of time, such transactions can sustain external financing even during a crisis.

Kravitt, J. H. P. I. R. C., and C. M. Nicolaides. (1991). Coping with cross-border securitisation. *International Financial Law Review* **10**(11), 34–38.

Kwan, S. H., and E. S. Laderman. (1999). On the portfolio effects of financial convergence: A review of the literature. *Economic Review/Federal Reserve Bank of San Francisco* No. 2, [18]–31.

McMillin, W. D. (1996). Monetary policy and bank portfolios. *Journal of Economics and Business* **48**, 315–335. Examines "the existence of the bank lending channel for monetary policy over the period 1973:1–1994:11."

Miller, S. M., and A. G. Noulas. (1997). Portfolio mix and large-bank profitability in the USA. *Applied Economics* **29**, 505–512.

Morgan, J. B. (1989). Managing a loan portfolio like an equity fund. *Bankers Magazine* **172**, 28–35.

Mori, A., M. Ohsawa, *et al.* (1996). A framework for more effective stress testing. *Institute for Monetary and Economic Studies. Bank of Japan. Discussion Paper Series* No. 96-E-2, 1–31.

Nachane, D. M., and S. Ghosh. (2001). Risk-based standards, portfolio risk and bank capital: An econometric study. *Economic and Political Weekly* **36**(10), 871–876.

Ocampo, J. M. (1989). ABCs of asset securitization. *Bankers Magazine* **172**, 5–9.

Pecchenino, R. A. (1998). Risk averse bank managers: Exogenous shocks, portfolio reallocations and market spillovers. *Journal of Banking & Finance* **22**, 161–174.

Pederson, G. D. (1992). Agricultural bank portfolio adjustments to risk. *American Journal of Agricultural Economics* **74**, [672]–681.

Pennacchi, G. G. (1988). Loan sales and the cost of bank capital. *Journal of Finance* **43**, 375–396. Considers a model where banks may improve the returns on loans by monitoring borrowers. An explanation is also given as to why some banks might buy loans and why loan sales volume has recently increased.

Ramaswamy, S. (1998). Portfolio selection using fuzzy decision theory. *Bank for International Settlements, Monetary and Economic Dept. Bis Working Papers* No. 59, 1–20.

Rendell, R. S. (1983). *International financial law.* London: Euromoney.

"Securitisation in Asia: A market of growth and innovation. (2000). *Asiamoney* **11** (3, Suppl.), 1–28.

"Securitization: The Asian guide. (1997). *Asiamoney* **8** (Suppl.), 1–40.

Shashikant, U., and B. Ramesh. (1997). Benefits from diversification into emerging markets: Theories and evidence. *Journal of Foreign Exchange and International Finance/National Institute of Bank Management* **11**, 47–60.

Stanley, T., C. Roger, *et al.* (1996). The logic of strategic management of your loan portfolio. *Bankers Magazine* **179**, 51–57.

Steele, F., Jr. (1987). Credit exposure reporting: Where we are and where we want to be. *Journal of Commercial Bank Lending* **69**, 33–43.

Swegle, R. W., Jr. (1989). Accounting for asset securitization. *Bankers Magazine* **172**, 22–24.

Szegö, G. P. (1980). *Portfolio theory: With application to bank asset management.* New York: Academic Press.

Tennekoon, R. C. (1991). *The law and regulation of international finance.* London: Butterworths.

Twinn, C. I. (1994). Asset-backed securitisation in the United Kingdom. *Bank of England, Quarterly Bulletin* **34,** 134–143.

Walker, D. A. (1997). A behavioral model of bank asset management. *Journal of Economic Behavior & Organization* **32,** 413–431.

Wilson, T. C. (1998). Portfolio credit risk. *Economic Policy Review/Federal Reserve Bank of New York* **4,** 71–82. Presented during "Financial Services at the Crossroads: Capital Regulation in the Twenty-first Century," a conference hosted by the Federal Reserve Bank of New York in partnership with the Bank of England, the Bank of Japan, and the Board of Governors of the Federal Reserve System, and held in New York on February 26–27, 1998.

World Bank. (1993). *Portfolio management: Next steps: A program of actions.* Washington, DC: The Operations Policy Department.

Yu, H. (1992). Bank portfolio risk and interest rate spread of risky loans: A methodological analysis. *Journal of Financial Management and Analysis* **5,** 1–12.

SELECT INTERNET LIBRARY AND CD

CD Includes

ChasePort.xls: Bank Portfolio Analysis. Deterministic optimization of industries in a loan portfolio

PortProblem.xls: Potfolio covariance—financing an acquisition

Solvjpe.xls: The Perfect Portfolio Ltd. Deterministic optimization of a stock portfolio with beta constraint of one.

AN INTRODUCTION TO THE STATISTICS OF PORTFOLIO MANAGEMENT

Product Cyclical Inc. operates as a producer of expensive watches. During economy expansion, returns are excellent reflecting increased top-of-the-line watch purchases. When economic downturns occur, earnings are dismal as consumers cut back purchases of this luxury in favor of less expensive alternatives. Product Cyclical's CFO is reviewing a possible takeover of a negatively correlated (countercyclical) business to soften the risk of macroeconomic shocks on existing operations.

The most likely acquisition candidate, Countercyclical Corp., is a low-priced custom jewelry manufacturer. The custom jewelry industry is countercyclical. Recessions provide excellent returns as diminished disposable income triggers higher demand for this product. Conversely, during good economic times, Countercyclical suffers dearly as consumers cut back custom jewelry purchases, shifting consumption to high-end watches.

Backing into portfolio theory for a minute, let's assume Product Cyclical considered a host of acquisition candidates beforehand and plotted each set (Countercyclical Corp. together with candidates X, Y, Z, etc.) on *Markowitz's Efficient Frontier* (Figure 12A.1) Specifically, we plot the minimum variance set

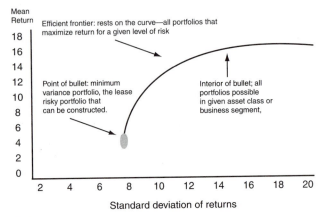

FIGURE 12A.1 Markowitz's Efficient Frontier

(a set of two investment portfolios that, for each level of return, have the least risk). The minimum variance set of portfolios has a quadratic form and graphs as a parabola. We employ the quadratic equation and only focus on those portfolios that lie above the minimum variance portfolio in order to map a typical efficient set. The efficient set appears on the left, plotted in the risk/return (standard deviation/expected return) space.

Continuing, a well-behaved utility function gives rise to indifference curves. An indifference curve displays the entire set of risk/return combinations that provides exactly the same utility. Thus, the risk/return combination associated with portfolio A and the risk/return combination associated with portfolio B provide the same satisfaction (utility) because they lie along the same indifference curve. But we want to know the optimal portfolio. By superimposing the firm's indifference map on the efficient set of available (acquisition) portfolios, we can determine which portfolio maximizes the firm's utility. This point reflects the perfect balance between expected returns and risk. The portfolio that maximizes Cyclical's utility is called the optimal portfolio. It occurs at the point of tangency between the CFO's indifference map and the efficient set of portfolios.

Before results are plotted on a portfolio map, Product Cyclical's financial team determined each firm's return sensitivities to the business cycle. The team assumed economic conditions over five years.

MEAN AND STANDARD DEVIATION CALCULATIONS FOR PRODUCT CYCLICAL INC.

Since decision making involves ex ante returns, the team quantified uncertainty associated with these returns under varying economic conditions. Here we look at the entire probability distribution of returns.

TABLE 12A.1   Cyclical's Expected Return

State of economy	P_s	R_a	P_sR_a
Down	17.0%	−17.0%	(0.0289)
Average	50.0%	18.0%	0.0900
Up	33.0%	51.0%	0.1683
			$\underline{Ra} = 0.2294$

In Table 12.A1 the central tendency of the distribution is captured in its expected value (the weighted average of all possible outcomes where the probability of each outcome is used as weights). The variability or risk of the distribution is summarized by its variance. An equivalent risk measure is the standard deviation of the distribution, which is the square root of the variance. For the special case of a normal distribution, the standard deviation takes on special significance (see Table 12A.2).

Before results are plotted on a portfolio map, Product Cyclical's financial team determined each firm's return sensitivities to the business cycle. The team assumed economic conditions over five years. Since decision making involves ex ante (expected) returns, they quantified the uncertainty of these returns.

The first significant number is the expected return of Cyclical, $\underline{Ra} = 22.94\%$. From the example we see that $\underline{Ra}$ is the sum of each return multiplied by its respective probability associated with expected economic conditions.

To make this clearer, let's look at an example: We visit a casino and flip a coin. The casino offers you $1,000 if the coin comes out heads; tails pay nothing. The expected payoff on the toss is $500 (50% heads multiplied by $1,000 plus 50% tails multiplied by zero). However, let's say the casino offers you $300 if you agreed not to chance the coin toss. The $300 payoff represents a certainty return. A bank financing this "transaction" would charge the risk-free rate. The difference between $500, the expected risky return and the $300 certainty return is the risk premium that's required chancing a loss.

We extend the table analysis in Table 12A.2.

Table 12A.2 Product Cyclicals's Variance and Standard Deviation

State of economy	P_s	R_a	P_sR_a	$(R_a - R_a)$	$(R_a - R_a)^2$	$P_s(R_a - R_a)^2$
Down	17.0%	−17.0%	(0.0289)	(0.3994)	0.1595	0.0271
Average	50.0%	18.0%	0.0900	(0.0494)	0.0024	0.0012
Up	33.0%	51.0%	0.1683	0.2806	0.0787	0.0260
			$\underline{Ra} = 0.2294$			

Variance = $\sigma a^2 = 0.0543$
Standard deviation = $\sigma a = 0.2331$

Product Cyclical operates in a nonequilibrium environment. Because $\underline{Ra}$, the expected risky return, ignores variability, we look to the standard deviation, $\sigma_a = 0.2331$. When data are tightly clustered around a steep bell-shaped curve, the standard deviation is small. When data are sprawled out along a wide bell curve, the standard deviation will be larger. One standard deviation in either direction of the mean accounts for 68% of the area under the curve. Two and three standard deviations on either side represent 95% and over 99%, respectively, of areas under the curve.

While in this example the standard deviation measures the variability or uncertainty of returns, uncertainty is not necessarily risk. Risk is a relative measure and though financial analysts associate a large standard deviation with probability of losses, what constitutes an unacceptable loss or shortfall is subjective. As modern portfolio theory suggests, only volatility beyond the firm's target return counts as undue risk. Most important, assets (and investments) are held not in isolation but jointly with other assets.

Thus, risk associated with an asset is influenced by interaction of the pattern of its return with the *patterns* of return of the other assets held in combination. This is correlation, which can be defined as the linear association between two random variables X and Y. One measure of correlation is the covariance—the standard measure of how returns relate to each other. Before we examine covariance, let's run through Countercyclical's expected return $\underline{Rb}$ and standard deviation σb.

CALCULATIONS OF THE MEAN AND STANDARD DEVIATION FOR COUNTERCYCLICAL CORP.

Recall that both the custom jewelry and high-priced watch producers generate similar returns, except that patterns are reversed. Countercyclical's returns are highly negative during peak economic vitality, but turn around during recessions. The reverse holds for Product Cyclical. While this example is somewhat far-fetched, it's not totally unrealistic. There are plenty of cyclical businesses out there, for example, finance companies (such as high-yield credit card issuers)

TABLE 12A.3   Countercyclical's Return, Variance, and Standard Deviation

State of economy	P_s	R_b	P_sR_b	$(R_b - R_b)$	$(R_b - R_b)^2$	$P_s(R_b - R_b)^2$
Down	17.0%	51.0%	0.0867	0.3927	0.1542	0.0262
Average	50.0%	18.0%	0.0900	0.0627	0.0039	0.0020
Up	33.0%	−18.0%	(0.0594)	(0.2973)	0.0884	0.0292
$R_b = 0.1173$						

$\sigma b^2 = 0.0573$
$\sigma b = 0.2395$

TABLE 12A.4   Covariance of Returns: Product Cyclical with Returns of Countercyclical

State of economy	P_s	$(R_a - R_a)(R_b - R_b)$	$P_s(R_a - R_a)(R_b - R_b)$
Down	17.0%	−0.157	−0.027
Average	50.0%	−0.003	−0.002
Up	33.0%	−0.083	−0.028
Cov(Ra,Rb) = −0.056			

who perform well in economic downturns, when consumers need to borrow to replace lost disposable income.

The covariance of Cyclical's return with Countercyclical's is negative, suggesting that, given specific economic conditions, the returns of the two firms move in opposite directions.

Since the expected return, standard deviation, and covariance are all tied together, let's combine results by assuming each firm contributes 50% to total assets. The expected return of the combined business (or this two-investment portfolio) is as follows:

The expected return on this two investment portfolio is: $Rp = wa\underline{Ra} + wb\underline{Rb}$,

Assume product cyclical represents	50.0% of assets
Assume countercyclical represents	50.0% of assets
Expected return for this portfolio	17.3%

$Rp = 0.5(.2294) + 0.5(0.1173) = .173$

Where wa is the investment weight of Product Cyclical Inc. (50%) and wb represents the investment weight of Countercyclical Corp. (50%).

Recall, Product Cyclical. realizes a premerger expected return of 11.73%. However, post-merger return falls to 17.3%. The standard deviation of returns of the combined entity is determined by:

$$SD_2 = [w_a^2\sigma_a^2 + w_b^2\sigma_b^2 + 2w_aw_bCOV(R_a,R_b)]^{\frac{1}{2}}$$

$$SD_2 = [(.5^2)(.233^2) + (.5^2)(.239^2) + 2(.5)(.5)(-.056)]^{\frac{1}{2}} = 0.007$$

With a standard deviation of just 1%, the portfolio's risk has been reduced to an insignificant level. The outcome is as follows:

	Stand-alone Return	Merged return	Stand alone risk	Merged risk
Product Cyclical Inc	22.9%	17.3%	23.3%	0.7%
Product Countercyclical Corp.	11.7%	17.3%	23.9%	0.7%

Countercyclical Corp shareholders are clear winners. Increased returns combine with reduced risk.

Recall that the standard deviation of returns of the merged companies approached zero meaning variability was infinitesimal. We confirm this with another statistic, the correlation coefficient derived by dividing the covariance by the product of the two standard deviations of each firm's returns. It's measured by Pearson's r, such that the value of the coefficient ranges from -1 to $+1$. A positive value of r means that the association is positive (i.e., if X values increase, Y values increase linearly and vice versa). A negative value of r means that the association is contrary, minus one means the association is diametric. Positive one correlation coefficient means a perfect positive relation exists between two variables. Correlation factors near zero point to little or no relationship between sets of data.

In our hypothetical example, the correlation coefficient of expensive watch returns with returns of low priced custom jewelry is close to minus one indicating an almost perfect negative relationship between the returns of Product Cyclical and Countercyclical:

$$Cov(Ra,Rb) = \rho ab\ (\sigma a\sigma b)$$

Solving for the correlation coefficient: $\rho ab = Cov(Ra,Rb)/\sigma a\sigma b$.
In our example using Product Cyclical and Countercyclical:

$$\rho ab = -.056/(.2331)(.2395) = -.9987$$

The standard deviation of the two-investment portfolio and the correlation coefficient yielded identical results. This portfolio is perfectly hedged against macroeconomic fluctuations.

OPTIMIZING A BANK PORTFOLIO USING EXCEL'S SOLVER

Any problem having decision variables and an objective function to be maximized or minimized is considered a linear programming or optimization problem (see Chapter 7, "Cash Flow Projections, Stochastic Optimization"). If the problem is bounded by constraints, it's called "constrained optimization"; otherwise, the term used is "unconstrained optimization." A factory may be limited in size or able to produce only so much of a given product per day; a bank's risk policies may preclude increasing an industry exposure beyond a specific volatility measure; capital costs might be constrained by systematic and unsystematic risk factors. The question is, of course, how do you combine these thousands of constrained variables in a way that produces maximum value within these set boundaries? We shall try to answer that question, albeit on a fundamental level employing a deterministic optimization model.

OPTIMIZATION MODELS

Optimization models have three essential components: decision variables, objective function, and constraints. The first phase in the process is to define decision variables.

Decision Variables

Each decision variable specifies the level of activity over which someone has control, like production scheduling, capital investment allocations, and industry concentrations within a bank's loan portfolio. There should be enough decision variables to describe all possibilities associated with a financial or operational problem.

Objective Function

The objective function is a numerical benchmark associated with the problem—for instance, maximize profits, minimize costs, optimize shareholder value, or maximize returns on a loan portfolio. The purpose of the decision maker is to select that course of action.

Constraints

Constraints are limitations or restrictions on the possible choices and combinations of decision variables, mentioned earlier. Constraints describe the logical or physical conditions the decision variables must obey. Constraint functions may be linear or nonlinear. For example an airline's passenger load factor is limited by the seat capacity on its airplanes. Bank loan policy may reject all loans falling below investment grade.

CHASE BANK: A DETERMINISTIC OPTIMIZATION SOLUTION

Deterministic optimization models contain no random variables and can only produce single-valued results, which means they actuate under the implicit assumption of certainty. While this procedure will usually lead to simplistic results, one way around the problem might be running different values for select uncertainty variables to see how the output changes. While this sensitivity approach might resolve small levels of uncertainty, the extent and range of uncertainty conditions is often too significant for any well-reasoned amount of sensitivity trials, not to mention online time. In the real world, analysts favor stochastic models—for example, Decisioneering's OptQuest is a leader in stochastic optimization software.

The Problem

You are a senior vice president in charge of Chase Bank's loan portfolio. Your function is to monitor industry concentrations to clients to follow conservative investment strategies. The bank's loan portfolio is made up of five industries: Industry A: agriculture production (22.0%), Industry B: trucking (20%), Industry C: building construction (10%), Industry D: tobacco (10%), and Industry E: forestry (38%). The portfolio's yields a 15.4% return and is constrained by a 5.3% variance.

Chase Bank has recently changed its strategy to a more aggressive position along the efficient frontier; specifically the bank wants to increase its loan portfolio variance from 5.3% to 7.1%. Your assignment is to increase the bank's return by changing the industry concentrations given its new variance constraint.

Open the workbook ChasePort located in the subdirectory Models_ Demos/Chapter 12. Set up the titles for each of the rows and columns. Put these in an italic or bold font to make them easier to find on the spreadsheet. It is also a good idea to highlight the cells that will contain the decision variables in a different color. These are the cells that Solver will alter. The decision cells are E$10: E$14, the weights of each industry concentration with respect to the total loan portfolio.

Next, insert the given values, the betas of each industry,[1] and ResVar, a measure of "errors" along the security markets line. Now call up the Excel's add-in, the Solver, by selecting Tools/ Solver. The Solver dialog box consists of three main areas: *"Set Target Cell," "By Changing Cells,"* and *"Subject to the Constraints."* Our first cell entry is next to *"Set Target Cell."* Enter E18 the target cell you want to maximize—Portfolio Return. Next enter E10: E14 under *"By Changing Cells."*

Finally, allocate cells for the constraints in the box *"Subject to the Constraints."* Constraints are fundamental to Solver. Excel's constraint specifies an upper or lower limit, or an exact value that a calculated function of the decision variables must satisfy for any solution found by the Solver. The *primary* constraint, or the main decision cell, will be, of course, G$18. The limit on portfolio variance is 7.1%. The other constraints we set in Solver will prevent illogical solutions from occurring: (1) total portfolio equals 100%, and(2) industry concentrations will be equal to zero or better—that is, no industry represents a "negative" investment. The basket of securities held must be greater than or equal to zero. Solver parameters are depicted in Figure 12A.1.

Click on the *Solve* button. Solver performs the calculations and changes the values in the spreadsheet to show the results of the solution. You are then

---

[1] We use betas to keep the problem simple. In reality, betas measure the volatility of a stock with respect to a portfolio. This statistic is not very meaningful in measuring the risk of a loan portfolio. Covariance is more meaningful.

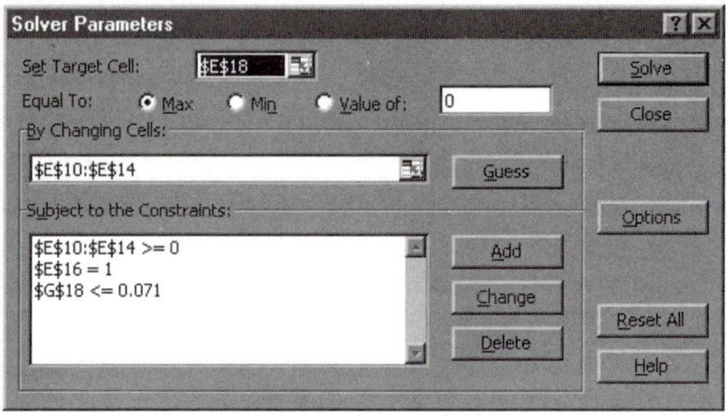

FIGURE 12A.1 Solver Parameters

presented with another dialog box asking if you want to return the values to their original state or leave them as is. Additionally, you can select which reports of the analysis you need to generate. Use the mouse to select any or all of the reports.

If you call for reports, Solver creates three reports: *Answer, Limits and Sensitivity. Click on OK.*

Answer Report

This report lists the target cell and adjustable cells with their original and final values, constraints, and information about the constraints. This report also includes information about the status of and slack value for each constraint. The status can be binding, not binding, or not satisfied. The slack value is the difference between the solution value of the constraint cells and the number that appears on the right side of the constraint formula. A binding constraint is one for which the slack value is 0. A nonbinding constraint is a constraint that was satisfied with a nonzero slack value. The bank's portfolio return increased to 17.4% the result of new industry concentrations.

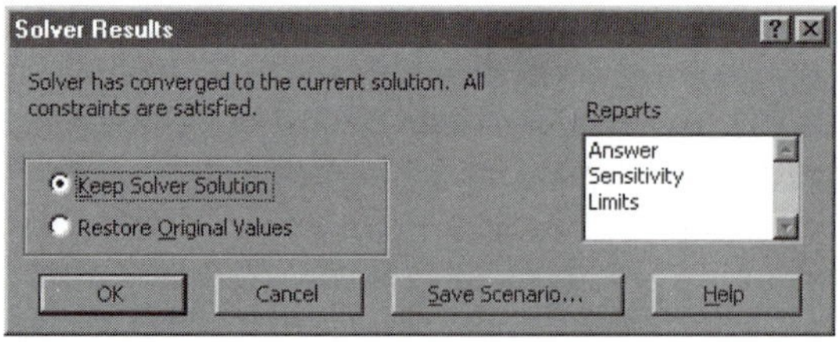

FIGURE 12A.2 Solver Results

EXHIBIT I Solver Answer Report Microsoft Excel 9.0 Answer Report
Worksheet: [ChasePort.XLS]

Target Cell (Max)

Cell	Name			Original value	Final value
E18	Portfolio Totals: Return			15.4%	17.4%

Adjustable Cells

Cell	Name			Original value	Final value
E10	Industry A: Agriculture production weight			22.0%	28.0%
E11	Industry B: Trucking weight			20.0%	8.1%
E12	Industry C: Building construction weight			10.0%	30.7%
E13	Industry D: Tobacco weight			10.0%	11.6%
E14	Industry E: Forestry weight			38.0%	21.6%

Constraints

Cell	Name	Cell Value	Formula	Status	Slack
E16	Total weight	100.0%	E16=1	Binding	0
G18	Portfolio Totals: variance	7.1%	G18<=0.071	Binding	0
E10	Industry A: Agriculture production weight	28.0%	E10>=0	Not binding	28.0%
E11	Industry B: Trucking weight	8.1%	E11>=0	Not binding	8.1%
E12	Industry C: Building construction weight	30.7%	E12>=0	Not binding	30.7%
E13	Industry D: Tobacco weight	11.6%	E13>=0	Not binding	11.6%
E14	Industry E: Forestry weight	21.6%	E14>=0	Not binding	21.6%

Limits Report

The limits report lists the target cell and the adjustable cells with their respective values, lower and upper limits, and target values. This report is not generated for models that have integer constraints. The lower limit is the smallest value that the adjustable cell can take while holding all other adjustable cells fixed and still satisfying the constraints. The upper limit is the greatest value.

EXHIBIT II Solver Limits Report Microsoft Excel 9.0 Limits Report
Worksheet: [ChasePort.XLS]

Cell	Target name	Value
E18	Portfolio Totals: Return	17.4%

Cell	Adjustable	Value	Lower limit	Target result	Upper limit	Target result
E10	Industry A: Agriculture production weight	28.0%	28.0%	17.4%	28.0%	17.4%
E11	Industry B: Trucking weight	8.1%	8.1%	17.4%	8.1%	17.4%
E12	Industry C: Building construction weight	30.7%	30.7%	17.4%	30.7%	17.4%
E13	Industry D: Tobacco weight	11.6%	11.6%	17.4%	11.6%	17.4%
E14	Industry E: Forestry weight	21.6%	21.6%	17.4%	21.6%	17.4%

Sensitivity Report

This report provides information about how sensitive the solution is to small changes in the formula in the set. This report has two sections: one for your variable cells and one for your constraints. The right column in each section provides the sensitivity information.

EXHIBIT III Solver Sensitivity Report Microsoft Excel 9.0 Sensitivity Report Worksheet: [ChasePort.XLS]

Adjustable cells Cell	Name	Final Value	Reduced Gradient
E10	Industry A: Agriculture production weight	28.0%	0.0%
E11	Industry B: Trucking weight	8.1%	0.0%
E12	Industry C: Building construction weight	30.7%	0.0%
E13	Industry D: Tobacco weight	11.6%	0.0%
E14	Industry E: Forestry weight	21.6%	0.0%

Constraints Cell	Name	Final Value	Lagrange Multiplier
E16	Total weight	100.0%	1.3%
G18	Portfolio Totals: Variance	7.1%	71.2%

13

PORTFOLIO MANAGEMENT
OF DEFAULT RISK

Corporate liabilities have default risk. There is always a chance that a corporate borrower will not meet its obligations to pay principal and interest. For the typical high-grade borrower, this risk is small, perhaps one-tenth of 1% per year. For the typical bank borrower, this risk is about one-half of 1%.

Although these risks do not seem large, they are, in fact, highly significant. First, they can increase quickly and with little warning. Second, the margins in corporate lending are very tight, and even small miscalculations of default risks can undermine the profitability of lending. But most important, many lenders are themselves borrowers, with high levels of leverage. Unexpected realizations of default risk have destabilized, de-capitalized, and destroyed lenders. Banks, finance companies, insurers, investment banks, lessors—none have escaped unscathed.

Default risk cannot be hedged away, or "structured" away. The government cannot insure it away. It is a reflection of the substantial risk in companies' futures. Various schemes exist, and more are coming, which can shift risk, but in the end, someone must bear this risk. It does not "net out" in the aggregate.

Default risk can be reduced and managed through diversification. Default risk, and the rewards for bearing it, will ultimately be owned by those who can diversify it best. Every lender knows the benefits of diversification. Every lender works to achieve these benefits. However, until recently lenders have been reluctant to, or unable to, implement systems for actually measuring the amount of diversification in a debt portfolio. Portfolios have "concentrations"; ex post we see them. Ex ante, lenders must look to models and software to quantify concentrations. Until recently, these types of models have not been generally available. Thus, it should not come as a surprise that there have been many unexpected default events in lenders' portfolios in the past.

Quantitative methods for portfolio analysis have developed since Markowitz's pioneering work in 1950. These methods have been applied successfully in a variety of areas of finance, notably to equity portfolios. These methods show the amount of risk reduction achievable through diversification. They measure the amount of risk contributed by an asset, or a group of assets, to a portfolio. By extension, they also show the amount of diversification provided by a single asset or group of assets. The aim of these methods is to maximize the return to a portfolio while keeping the risk within acceptable bounds. This maximization requires a balancing of return to risk within the portfolio, asset by asset, group of assets by group of assets.

This logic can be illustrated by imagining that it was not the case. If a low-return-to-risk asset is swapped for a high-return-to-risk asset, then the portfolio's return can be improved with no addition to risk. The process is equilibrated by changes in risk. As an asset is swapped out of the portfolio, it changes from being a source of concentration to being a source of diversification (i.e., its risk contribution falls). The reverse applies as an asset is swapped into the portfolio. Thus, the return to risk increases for the low return asset and decreases for the high return asset, until their return-to-risk ratios are equal. At that point, no further swap can raise return without also raising risk. This then characterizes the optimal portfolio or, equivalently, the optimal set of holdings.

This conceptual model applies to the default risk of debt as surely as it applies to equities. Equity practitioners, however, have used the past 25 years to develop techniques for measuring the asset attributes that are necessary for an actual portfolio management tool. The same development has not occurred for debt portfolios because of the greater analytical and empirical difficulties. In particular, it is necessary to quantify the level of default risk in a single asset and to quantify the relationship between the default risks of each pair of assets in the portfolio.

Due to a variety of technical developments in finance, it has become both possible and feasible to make these measurements. KMV has pioneered the development of these methods for the past 12 years in its practice with commercial banks. The fruits of this development effort are several products designed to address the quantification and management of credit risk. KMV estimates an expected default frequency (EDF™) for firms with publicly traded equity and delivers this estimate via a PC-based viewer called Credit Monitor™ or an Internet-based viewer called CreditEdge™. Both of these software products cover nearly 30,000 firms globally and come bundled with a variety of analysis tools. For firms without publicly traded equity, KMV offers the Private Firm Model (PFM™), which also produces an EDF credit measure. The PFM EDF values are housed in a software product called the Private Firm Analyst™, which works in tandem with Credit Monitor. KMV's EDF values combined with facility-specific data can be used together with KMV's Global Correlation Model™ and Portfolio Manager™ to analyze and manage portfolios of credit-risky assets. The result is that practical and conceptually sound methods exist for measuring actual diversification and for determining portfolio holdings to minimize concentrations and maximize return in debt portfolios.

The remainder of this chapter introduces the methods and approaches of quantitative debt portfolio management underlying KMV's products and models, and their implications for bank management.

THE MODEL OF DEFAULT RISK

A corporation has fixed obligations. These may be no more than its trade obligations, although they could just as well include bank loans and public debt. At one time, there was no legal means to escape the fulfillment of such obligations; a defaulter fled or was jailed. Modern treatment allows the defaulter to escape the obligation, but only by relinquishing the corporation's assets to the obligee. In other words, a firm owing a single creditor $75 million fulfills the obligation by either paying the $75 million or by transferring the corporation's assets to the lender.

Which action the borrower will take is an economic decision. And the economic answer is straightforward: if the corporate assets are worth more than $75 million, the borrower will meet the obligation; if they are worth less, the borrower will default. The critical point is that the action depends on the market value of assets; book or accounting value will not suffice. Note that the "option to default" is valuable. Without it, the corporation could be forced to raise additional capital with the benefit accruing not to its owners but instead to its prior lender.

A lender purchasing a corporation's note can be thought of as engaging in two transactions. In the first it is purchasing an "inescapable" debt obligation (i.e., one that cannot be defaulted on). In the second, it is selling a "put" option to the borrower that states that the lender will buy the corporation's assets for the amount of the note at the option of the borrower. In the event the assets turn out to be worth less than the amount of the note, the borrower "puts" the assets to the lender and uses the proceeds to pay the note.

The lender owns a risk-free note and is "short" the default option. The probability of default is the same as the probability of the option being exercised. If the probability of default goes up, the value of the option goes up, and the value of the lender's position (because it is "short" the option) goes down.

The probability of exercising the default option can be determined by application of option valuation methods. Assume for a moment that the market value of the corporation's assets is known, as well as the volatility of that value. The volatility measures the propensity of the asset value to change within a given time period. This information determines the probability of default, given the corporation's obligations. For instance, if the current asset market value is $150 million and the corporation's debt is $75 million and is due in one year, then default will occur if the asset value turns out to be less than $75 million in one year.

If the firm's asset volatility is 17% per year, then a fall in value from $150 million to $75 million is a three standard deviation event with a probability of 0.3%. Thus, the firm has a default probability of 0.3%. (Keep in mind that 17% of 150 is 25. This is the amount of a one standard deviation move. The probability calculation assumes that the assets have a lognormal distribution.)

The market value of the firm's assets in one year is unknown. Based on firm characteristics including past performance, the expected asset value is determined to be $150 million, with a standard deviation of $25 million. This information makes it possible to represent the range of possible asset values and their frequencies in Figure 13.1.

The firm has obligations due in one year of $75 million. If the market asset value turns out to be less than $75 million, then the owners of the firm will prefer to default. If the asset value is greater than $75 million, then the owners will prefer to pay the debt, since they will retain the residual value.

The probability of default is thus represented by the shaded area. It represents the frequency of outcomes where the asset value is less than $75 million.

The shape of the frequency distribution is often simply assumed, given the expected value and standard deviation. For many purposes this is satisfactory, but practical experience with default rates shows that this shape must be measured, rather than assumed, to obtain sufficiently precise estimated default rates.

ASSET MARKET VALUE AND VOLATILITY

Just as the firm's default risk can be derived from the behavior of the firm's asset value and the level of its obligations, the firm's equity behavior can be similarly derived. The shareholders of the firm can be viewed as having a call option on the firm's asset value, where the exercise price is equal to the firm's obligations. If the market asset value exceeds the obligation amount at the maturity date, then the shareholders will exercise their option by paying off the obligation amount.

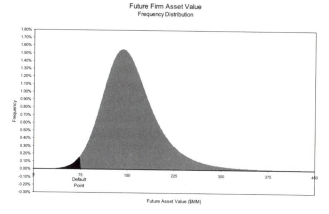

FIGURE 13.1 Future Firm Asset Value

If the asset value is less, they will prefer to default on the obligation and relinquish the remaining asset value to the lenders.

Using this framework, the equity value and volatility can be determined from the asset value, asset volatility, and the amount and maturity of obligations. What is actually more important is that the converse is also true: the asset value and volatility can be inferred from the equity value, equity volatility, and the amount and maturity of obligations. This process enables us to determine the market characteristics of a firm's assets from directly observable equity characteristics.

Knowing the market value and volatility of the borrower's assets is critical, as we have seen, to the determination of the probability of default. With it we can also determine the correlation of two firms' asset values. These correlations play an important role in the measurement of portfolio diversification.

The market value of assets changes unpredictably through time. The volatility in the historical time series is measured by the asset standard deviation, which was used in Figure 13.1 to describe the range of possible future asset values.

The liabilities of the firm including equity represent a complete set of claims on all the cash flows produced by the assets. Thus, the market value of the assets exactly equals the market value of the liabilities including equity. As the market value of assets changes, the market value of liabilities changes, but the changes are not evenly apportioned across the liabilities due to differences in seniority.

The equity value changes close to dollar-for-dollar with the asset value. The vertical distance between the asset and equity values in Figure 13.2 is the market value of obligations senior to the equity ("debt"). The difference (i.e., the debt value) is shown below the axis. If the asset value falls enough, the probability of default on the debt increases and the market value of the debt also falls. A $1 fall

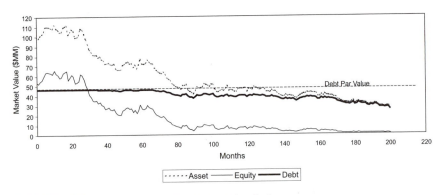

FIGURE 13.2   Asset, Equity, and Debt Values: Time Series

in the asset value leads to perhaps a \$0.10 fall in the debt value and a \$0.90 fall in the equity value.

In percentage terms, the changes in the equity value are always larger than the changes in the asset value, because the equity value is a fraction of the total asset value. As the asset value, and thus equity value, falls, the equity volatility increases dramatically. The relationship between the asset and equity value is described by option theory. This theory makes it possible to infer the asset value and volatility by knowing the level of fixed obligations and the equity value and volatility.

MEASUREMENT OF PORTFOLIO DIVERSIFICATION

Defaults translate into losses (depicted in Figure 13.3). The loss associated with a single default depends on the amount recovered. For the purposes of this exposition, we will assume that the recovery in the event of default is known, and that this recovery is net of the expenses of collection including the time value of the recovery process. Thinking of the recovery as a percentage of the face value of the loan, we can also specify the "loss given default" as one minus the expected recovery.

Using this structure, the expected loss for a single borrowing is the probability of default times the loss given default. Interestingly, the unexpected loss depends on the same variables as the expected loss. (It equals the loss given default times the square root of the product of the probability of default times one minus the probability of default.) The unexpected loss represents the volatility, or standard deviation of loss. This approach raises the question of how to deal with

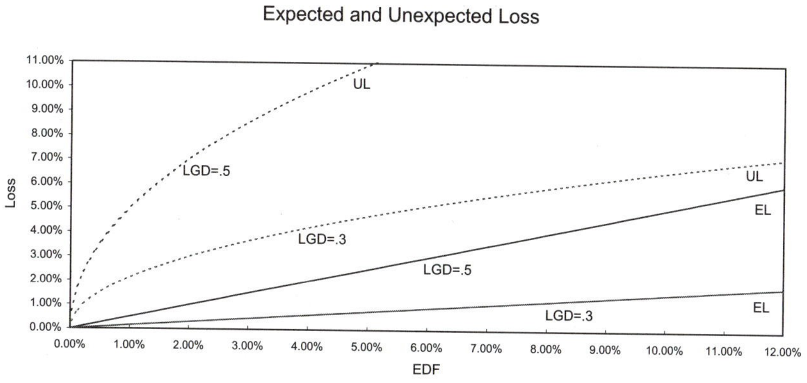

Expected and Unexpected Loss

FIGURE 13.3 Expected and Unexpected Loss

instruments of different maturities. The analysis here uses a single time horizon for measuring risk. Establishing one horizon for analysis forms the basis of a framework for comparing the attractiveness of different types of credit exposures on the same scale. The risk at the horizon has two parts: the risk due to possible default and the risk of loss of value due to credit deterioration. Instruments of the same borrower with different maturities (as long as the maturity is at or beyond the horizon) have the same default risk at the horizon, but the value risk (i.e., uncertainty around the value of the instrument at horizon) depends on the remaining time to maturity. The longer the remaining time, the greater the variation in value due to credit quality changes.

For simplicity of presentation, the following analysis will assume that the maturity of all instruments is the same as the horizon. While this will eliminate maturity as an aspect of credit risk, it will not change the qualitative nature of any of the results. Although maturity effects are important in practice, they are generally of lesser importance than the risk due to default.

$EDF \equiv$ probability of default

$LGD \equiv$ loss given default (percentage of face)

$EL \equiv$ expected loss $= EDF \times LGD$

$UL \equiv$ unexpected loss $= LGD \sqrt{EDF \, (1 - EDF)}$

Measuring the diversification of a portfolio means specifying the range and likelihood of possible losses associated with the portfolio. All else equal, a well-diversified portfolio is one that has a small likelihood of generating large losses.

The average expected loss for a portfolio is the average of the expected losses of the assets in the portfolio. It is not a simple average but rather a weighted average, with the weights equal to each exposure amount as a percentage of the total portfolio exposure.

It would be convenient if the volatility, or unexpected loss, of the portfolio were simply the weighted average of the unexpected losses of the individual assets, but it is not. The reason is that portfolio losses depend also on the relationship (correlation) between possible defaults.

A simple example illustrates this point. Consider an island on which it always rains on one side or the other in a given year, but never on both, with each side equally likely to receive rain. Consider two farms, one on each side of the island, each with debt on which it will default if it doesn't rain. A portfolio holding both loans in equal amounts, and nothing else, will have an expected default rate of 50%. Each borrowing will have an unexpected default rate of 50% $(= \sqrt{0.5 \times (1 - 0.5)}$. In other words, each of the portfolio assets is quite risky. But the portfolio as a whole has an unexpected loss rate of zero. The actual default rate and the expected default rate for the portfolio are identical. In each year, one and only one borrower will default, though which one is uncertain. There is a perfect negative correlation.

The alternative extreme is that it only rains half of the years on average, but when it rains, it always rains on both sides. This is perfect positive correlation; the farms will default in exactly the same years. Holding one loan is equivalent to holding both loans: there is no risk reduction from diversification.

An intermediate case is that raining on one farm makes it no more likely or less likely that it will rain on the other. The events of rainfall are independent. In this case, in one-fourth of the years both loans will default, in one-fourth neither will default, and one-half the time only one will default. There is now substantial diversification versus the perfect positive correlation case, since the likelihood of both defaulting is reduced by half.

Now let us extend this notion of diversification to the more general case of a portfolio with multiple risky securities. The portfolio loss measures can be calculated as follows:

$X_i \equiv$ face value of security i

$P_i \equiv$ price of security i (per \$1 of face value)

$V_p \equiv$ portfolio value $= P_1 X_1 + P_2 X_2 + ... + P_n X_n$

$w_i \equiv$ value proportion of security i in portfolio ("weight") $= P_1 X_1 / V_p$

$\rho_{ij} \equiv$ loss correlation between security i and security j

Note that $w_1 + w_2 + ... + w_n = 1$.

$EL_i \equiv$ expected loss for security i

$EL_p \equiv$ portfolio expected loss $= w_1 EL_1 + w_2 EL_2 + ... w_n EL_n$

$UL_i \equiv$ unexpected loss for security i

$UL_p \equiv$ unexpected loss for portfolio

$$= \sqrt{\begin{aligned} & w_1w_1UL_1UL_1\rho_{11} + w_1w_2UL_1UL_2\rho_{12} + w_1w_nUL_1UL_n\rho_{1n} + w_2w_1UL_2UL_1\rho_{21} + w_2w_2UL_2UL_2\rho_{22} + \ldots \\ & + w_2w_nUL_2UL_n\rho_{2n} + \ldots + w_nw_1UL_nUL_1\rho_{n1} + w_nw_2UL_nUL_2\rho_{n2} + \ldots + w_nw_nUL_nUL_1\rho_{nn} \end{aligned}}$$

Note that if $\rho_{ij} = 1$ if $i = j$, and $\rho_{ij} = \rho_{ji}$. The portfolio's expected loss is the weighted average of the expected losses of the individual securities, where the weights are the value proportions. On the other hand, the portfolio's unexpected loss is a more complex function of the ULs of the individual securities, the portfolio weights, and the pairwise loss correlations between securities.

In practice, actual defaults are positively but not perfectly positively correlated. Diversification, while not perfect, conveys significant benefits. Unfortunately, negative default correlations are rare to nonexistent.

Calculating portfolio diversification means determining the portfolio's unexpected loss. To do this, default correlations and, ultimately, correlation in instrument values are required.

MODEL OF DEFAULT CORRELATION

Default correlation measures the strength of the default relationship between two borrowers. If there is no relationship, then the defaults are independent and the correlation is zero. In such a case, the probability of both borrowers being in default at the same time is the product of their individual probabilities of default.

When two borrowers are correlated, this means that the probability of both defaulting at the same time is heightened (i.e., it is larger than it would be if they were completely independent). In fact, the correlation is just proportional to this difference. Thus, holding their individual default probabilities fixed, it is equivalent to say either that two borrowers are highly correlated or that they have a relatively high probability of defaulting in the same time period.

The basic default model says that the firm will default when its market asset value falls below the face value of obligations (the "default point"). This means that the joint probability of default is the likelihood of both firms' market asset values being below their respective default points in the same time period.

This probability can be determined quite readily from knowing (1) the firms' current market asset values; (2) their asset volatilities, and (3) the correlation between the two firms' market asset values. In other words, the derivatives framework enables us to use the firms' asset correlation to obtain their default correlation.

This may not seem to be all that helpful, but in fact it is critically important to the empirical determination of default correlations. The correlation, for example, between equity returns can be directly calculated because the histories of firms' stock returns are easily observable. Default correlations cannot be successfully measured from default experience.

The historically observed joint frequency of default between two companies is usually zero. Exxon and Chevron have some chance of jointly defaulting, but nothing in their default history enables us to estimate the probability since n either has ever defaulted. Grouping firms enables us to estimate an average default correlation in the group using historical data, but the estimates so obtained are highly inaccurate.

No satisfactory procedure exists for directly estimating default correlations. Not surprisingly, this has been a major stumbling block to portfolio management of default risk.

The derivatives approach enables us to measure the default correlation between two firms, using their asset correlation and their individual probabilities of default. The correlation between the two firms' asset values can be empirically measured from their equity values, as was described in the previous section.

Figure 13.4 illustrates the ranges of possible future asset values for two different firms. The two intersecting lines represent the default points for the two firms. For instance, if firm 1's asset value ends up being below $180 million (the point represented by the vertical line), then firm 1 will default. The intersecting lines divide the range of possibilities into four regions. The upper right region represents those asset values for which neither firm 1 nor firm 2 will default. The lower left region represents those asset values for which both will default.

The probabilities of all these regions taken together must equal 1. If the asset values of the two firms were independent, then the probabilities of the regions could be determined simply by multiplying the individual probabilities of default and nondefault for the two firms. For instance, suppose that firm 1's default probability is 0.6% and firm 2's is 0.3%. Then the probability of both defaulting, if they are independent, is the product of the default probabilities, or 0.0018%.

If the two firms' asset values are positively correlated, then the probability of both asset values being high or low at the same time is higher than if they were independent, and the probability of one being high and the other low is lower. For instance, using the previous default probabilities, the probability of both defaulting might now be 0.01%, if their asset values are positively correlated.

By knowing the individual firms' default probabilities, and knowing the correlation of their asset values, the likelihood of both defaulting at the same time can be calculated. The time series of a firm's asset values can be determined from its equity values. The correlation between two firms' asset values can be calculated from their respective time series.

We can calculate default correlation as follows:

$JDF \equiv$ joint default frequency of firm 1 and firm 2 (i.e., actual probability of both firms defaulting together)

$$\rho_D \equiv \text{default correlation for firm 1 and firm 2} = \frac{JDF - EDF_1 EDF_2}{\sqrt{EDF_1(1 - EDF_1)EDF_2(1 - EDF_2)}}$$

The numerator of this formula represents the difference of the actual probability of both firms defaulting and the probability of both defaulting if they were

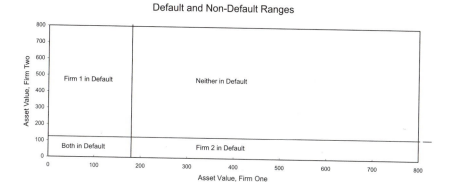

Default and Non-Default Ranges

FIGURE 13.4　Default and Nondefault Ranges

independent. Note that if the asset values are independent, then the default correlation is zero.

In practice, we extend this model to consider the correlation in the value of claims such as loans or bonds within a portfolio. The default state corresponds with a particularly low value realization for the loan or bond issued by the defaulted firm. This extension requires estimation of the joint value distribution between each pair of credit risky assets in the portfolio. KMV's Portfolio Manager™ incorporates this richer approach to determine the value correlation among all securities in a portfolio. In this way, the correlated credit migration over time can be captured to determine a more accurate measure of possible losses in the future.

MODEL OF VALUE CORRELATION

An important strength of the structural model of default presented here and implemented in KMV technology is the ability to generalize relationships in a way to create a comprehensive credit portfolio model. In addition to the EDF values for each firm, the joint default frequency (JDF) must be calculated to determine a value correlation. In the context of the structural model explained earlier, the JDF can be calculated by focusing on the relationship between a firm's market asset value and its respective default point. EDF values embed this information on an individual firm level. The remaining piece of the puzzle is the correlation between each firm's market asset value.

Mathematically we can write down the following function for the JDF:

$N_2\,(\ ) \equiv$ bivariate normal distribution function

$N^{-1}\,(\ ) \equiv$ inverse normal distribution function

$\rho_A\,(\ ) \equiv$ correlation between firm 1's asset return and firm 2's asset return

$JDF = N_2\,(N^{-1}\,(EDF_1),\ N^{-1}(EDF_2),\ \rho_A)$

Estimating pair-wise asset correlations for publicly traded firms can be done in a number of ways. One method would be to calculate a time series of asset values for each firm and then calculate a sample correlation between each pair of asset value series. While this method may seem reasonable in theory, in practice it is the least effective way to calculate correlations for credit portfolio modeling. We are most interested in the systematic co-movement and work to estimate efficiently this co-movement over a subsequent time horizon. Because the movement in a typical firm's asset value is mostly driven by factors idiosyncratic to that firm, sample correlations will reflect co-movement that is unique to that sample period—not very useful for predicting ex ante correlation over a subsequent time horizon. Given the weakness in this approach (not to mention the problems associated with insufficient observations needed to even calculate sample correlations), we turn to factor modeling to calculate correlations.

A factor model relates the systematic or nondiversifiable components of the economy that drive changes in asset value. For example, the entire economy may follow a business cycle that affects most companies' prospects. The impact may differ from company to company, but they are affected nonetheless. Determining the sensitivity of changes in asset values to changes in a particular economic factor provides the basis for estimating asset correlation.

Changes in a firm's asset value constitutes an asset value return or firm return. We can decompose this return as follows:

$$\begin{bmatrix} Firm \\ return \end{bmatrix} = \begin{bmatrix} Composite \\ factor \\ return \end{bmatrix} + \begin{bmatrix} Firm \\ specific \\ effects \end{bmatrix}$$

The composite factor return proxies for the systematic risk factors in the economy. We can further decompose this composite factor return as follows:

$$\begin{bmatrix} Composite \\ factor \\ return \end{bmatrix} = \begin{bmatrix} Country \\ factor \\ returns \end{bmatrix} + \begin{bmatrix} Industry \\ factor \\ returns \end{bmatrix}$$

$$\begin{bmatrix} Country \\ factor \\ return \end{bmatrix} = \begin{bmatrix} Global \\ economic \\ effect \end{bmatrix} + \begin{bmatrix} Regional \\ factor \\ effect \end{bmatrix} + \begin{bmatrix} Sector \\ factor \\ effect \end{bmatrix} + \begin{bmatrix} Country \\ specific \\ effect \end{bmatrix}$$

$$\begin{bmatrix} \text{Industry} \\ \text{factor} \\ \text{return} \end{bmatrix} = \begin{bmatrix} \text{Global} \\ \text{economic} \\ \text{effect} \end{bmatrix} + \begin{bmatrix} \text{Regional} \\ \text{factor} \\ \text{effect} \end{bmatrix} + \begin{bmatrix} \text{Sector} \\ \text{factor} \\ \text{effect} \end{bmatrix} + \begin{bmatrix} \text{Industry} \\ \text{specific} \\ \text{effect} \end{bmatrix}$$

Firm asset correlation can then be calculated from each firm's systematic or composite factor return. In this way, we relate the systematic component of changes in asset value, which produces a better estimate of future co-movements in asset values. In KMV's Global Correlation Model, industry and country indices are produced from a global database of market asset values (estimated from the traded equity prices together with each firm's liability information) for nearly 30,000 publicly traded firms. These indices are used to create a composite factor index for each firm depending on its country and industry classifications.

Mathematically, the following relationship is constructed:

$w_{kc} \equiv$ weight of firm k in country c

$w_{ki} \equiv$ weight of firm k in industry i

Note that $\displaystyle\sum_{c=1}^{\bar{c}} w_{kc} = \sum_{i=1}^{\bar{i}} w_{kc}$ where $\bar{c}$ is currently 45 countries and $\bar{i}$ is 61

industries for KMV's Global Correlation Model (as more data become available this coverage increases):

$r_c \equiv$ return index for country c (estimated from publicly traded firms)

$r_i \equiv$ return index for industry i (estimated from publicly traded firms)

$\phi_k \equiv$ composite (custom) market factor index for firm k

$$\phi_k = \sum_{c=1}^{\bar{c}} w_{kc}r_c + \sum_{i=1}^{\bar{i}} w_{ki}r_i$$

Once the custom index is calculated for a particular firm, the sensitivity (i.e., beta) to the market factors reflected in this index can be estimated. The relationship used for this estimation is written as follows:

$r_k \equiv$ return for firm k

$\beta_k \equiv$ beta for firm k

$\epsilon_k \equiv$ firm-specific component of return for firm k

$r_k \equiv \beta_k\phi_k + \epsilon_k$

We can similarly estimate the sensitivity or beta ($\beta_{Country, \ Common \ Factor}$ and $\beta_{Industry, \ Common \ Factor}$) of countries and industries on factors we specify. In KMV's model, we have chosen two global factors, five regional factors, and seven sectoral factors. Since we may have effects unique to industries and countries (i.e., not linked through the 14 common factors), we also have country (45 countries) and industry (61 industries) specific factors. An example of calculating the sensitivity of firm k to a global factor is written as follows:

$$\beta_{kG} = \beta_k \left(\sum_{c=1}^{45} w_{kc}\beta_{cG} + \sum_{i=1}^{61} w_{ki}\beta_{iG} \right)$$

These calculations produce the parameters necessary to estimate the firm asset value correlation. We construct this calculation as follows:

$\sigma(j,k) \equiv$ covariance between firm j and firm k

$\rho_{jk} \equiv$ correlation between firm j's and firm k's asset value returns

$\sigma_j \equiv$ standard deviation of firm j's asset value return

$$\sigma(j,k) = \sum_{G=1}^{2} \beta_{jG}\beta_{kG}\sigma^2_G + \sum_{R=1}^{5} \beta_{jR}\beta_{kR}\sigma^2_R + \sum_{S=1}^{7} \beta_{jS}\beta_{kS}\sigma^2_S + \sum_{i=1}^{61} \beta_{ji}\beta_{ki}\epsilon^2 + {}_i\sum_{c=1}^{45} \beta_{jc}\beta_{kc}\epsilon^2_c$$

$$
\begin{bmatrix} Return \\ covariance \\ j\ and\ k \end{bmatrix}
=
\begin{bmatrix} Global\ (G) \\ economic \\ factors \end{bmatrix}
+
\begin{bmatrix} Regional\ (R) \\ economic \\ factors \end{bmatrix}
+
\begin{bmatrix} Industry\ (S) \\ sector \\ factors \end{bmatrix}
+
\begin{bmatrix} Industry\ (i) \\ specific \\ factors \end{bmatrix}
+
\begin{bmatrix} Country\ (c) \\ specific \\ factors \end{bmatrix}
$$

$$
\begin{bmatrix} Return \\ correlation \\ j\ and\ k \end{bmatrix}
=
\frac{\begin{bmatrix} Return \\ covariance \\ j\ and\ k \end{bmatrix}}{\begin{bmatrix} Return \\ volatility\ j \end{bmatrix} \times \begin{bmatrix} Return \\ volatility\ k \end{bmatrix}}
$$

$$\rho_{jk} = \frac{\sigma(j,k)}{\sigma_j\sigma_k}$$

The covariance calculation depends on the sensitivities or betas ($\beta_{Company,\ Factor}$) for each firm combined with the factor variances (σ^2_{Factor}). To arrive at the correlation, we must scale the covariance by the standard deviation of the returns as shown in the final equation of the preceding group.

Simply said, the factor model focuses attention on the components driving co-movements. These components can be separated into the effects listed earlier; however, the important aspect of this process is identifying the total systematic component. To the extent that is correctly estimated, the subsequent decomposition into constituent effects is only necessary for gaining intuition behind the source of correlation between any two firms. This approach relies on the embedded systematic components reflected in the data on publicly traded firms around the world.

Returning to the JDF calculation, we combine this asset value correlation with the individual firm EDF values to arrive at a default correlation. Default correlation is sufficient if we do not model possible credit migration over our horizon of analysis. If we plan to consider the possibility of credit migration at the horizon, we need to calculate the joint distribution of values among the loans made to the firms being analyzed. Explicitly calculating this relationship requires calculation of a double integral (over all possible firm asset values) for each pair of firms in the portfolio. For most sizable credit portfolios, this approach is cost prohibitive from a computational perspective.

Instead we can make use of the factor structure explained earlier to construct a Monte Carlo simulation, which draws the individual factors over and over again to determine the possible portfolio value realizations. Each of these portfolio value realizations embeds the loan value correlations since each loan value is calculated based on the relationship feeding back to each firm's asset value. These asset values derive from the sensitivity to each of the risk factors.

A simple example will make this process clearer: Assume we are analyzing a portfolio of three loans to three different companies. We determine that the asset values of company A and company B increase (decrease) whenever interest rates decline (rise). Company C is unaffected by changes in interest rates. In this economy, we have only one factor—interest rate movement. We then simulate this one factor. Whenever this interest rate factor is high, A's and B's asset values are small. These low asset values result in the loans to A and B being valued at a discount; C's loan value is unchanged, since C is not affected by the interest-rate factor. If the interest rate factor is low, A's and B's loans will be valued at a premium. The key to the correlation arises from the similar behavior in loan value whenever a particular factor level is drawn.

Clearly, the movement in the value of A's and B's loans are correlated while C's loans are uncorrelated with the rest of the portfolio. The process of simulating different factor realizations generates a variety of portfolio value realizations. These value realizations can then be transformed into a loss distribution. The extent to which loan values move together links back to the sensitivities to the different risk factors in the factor model.

THE LIKELIHOOD OF LARGE LOSSES

We are all familiar with the bell-shaped or normal distribution. If portfolio losses had such a bell-shaped distribution, we could accurately specify the likelihood of large losses simply by knowing the expected and unexpected loss for the portfolio. The problem is that individual debt assets have very skewed loss probabilities. Most of the time the borrower does not default and the loss is zero. However, when default occurs, the loss is usually substantial.

Given the positive correlation between defaults, this unevenness of loss never fully smoothes out, even in very large portfolios. There is always a large probability of relatively small losses and a small probability of rather large losses.

This "skewness" leads to an unintuitive result: a very high percentage of the time (around 80%), the actual losses will be less than the average loss. The reason is that the average is pulled upward by the potential for large losses. There is a great danger of being lulled by a string of low losses into believing that the portfolio is much better diversified than in fact it is.

Fortunately, the frequency distribution of portfolio losses can be determined using the information we have already discussed. Knowing this distribution for a given portfolio gives an alternative characterization of diversification:

> Portfolio A is better diversified than portfolio B if the probability of loss exceeding a given percentage is smaller for A than for B, and both portfolios have the same expected loss.

Figure 13.5 contrasts the loan loss distribution for a portfolio with a bell-shaped loss distribution having the same expected loss and unexpected loss. There are two striking differences. The most obvious is that the actual loan loss distribution is asymmetric. There is a small probability of large losses and a large probability of small losses.

If losses were determined as per the bell-shaped distribution, then losses would exceed the expected loss about half the time, and the other half of the time they would be less than the expected loss. For the actual loss distribution, realized losses will be less than the expected loss approximately 75% of the time. There is a significant likelihood that even a risky portfolio will generate consecutive years of low realized losses.

The second major difference is that the probability of very large losses approaches zero much more quickly for the bell-shaped distribution than for the skewed distribution. In fact, for a portfolio with a skewed loss distribution there is an economically significant chance of realized losses that are six to eight standard deviations in excess of the expected loss. For the bell-shaped distribution, there is virtually no chance of a four standard deviation event occurring.

Figure 13.6 contrasts two loan loss distributions for different portfolios. The two portfolios have the same level of expected loss, but portfolio A has a higher unexpected loss. There is a significantly higher chance of incurring a large loss in portfolio A than in portfolio B. These probabilities can be seen by looking at the areas under the respective curves. For instance, the probability of a 4% loss in portfolio A is 0.1%, but the probability of a 4% loss in portfolio B is only 0.05%. The implication of this difference for the two portfolios in debt rating terms is the difference between a single B rating and a single A rating.

This view of diversification has an immediate concrete implication for capital adequacy. Given the frequency distribution of loss, we can determine the like-

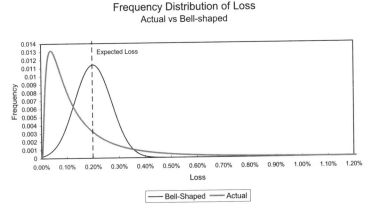

FIGURE 13.5   Frequency Distribution of Loss: Actual versus Bell-Shaped

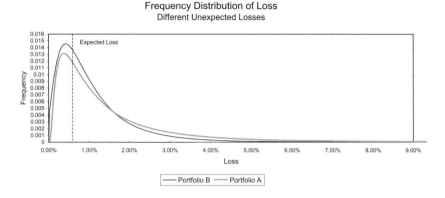

FIGURE 13.6 Frequency Distribution of Loss: Different Unexpected Losses

lihood of losses that exceed the amount of capital held against the portfolio. This probability can be set to the desired level by varying the amount of capital.

To illustrate how this can be done in practice, it is necessary to consider the market value, rather than the book value, of the portfolio. To do that, we need to be able to determine the market value of a security. Ideally, we want to use data from a deep and liquid market in the security we are modeling. In the case of credit risky securities, the markets are typically neither deep nor liquid. Consequently, we must rely on models to determine a mark-to-market value. Let us consider the case of determining the market value of a loan.

VALUATION

The market value of a loan is simply the price for which it can be bought or sold. Although there is a loan sales market, loans by and large are not actively transacted for extended periods. The result is that current market prices do not exist for most loans.

The objective of valuation is to determine what a loan should sell for, were it to trade. The value cannot be determined in the abstract or in some absolute sense, but only by comparison to the market prices of financial instruments that are traded. Valuation consists of extrapolating actual market prices to nontraded assets, based on the relationship between their characteristics. In the case of loans, the process involves consideration of the borrower's traded equity and traded debt should it exist.

Bank assets have a variety of complexities: default risk, utilization, covenants, priority, and so forth. Many of these complexities can be viewed, and valued, as options belonging to the borrower or lender. Some of these complexities are addressed subsequently in this chapter.

For this exposition, one of the simplest cases will suffice, namely a fixed-term, fixed-rate corporate loan. If this loan were not subject to default risk, then it could be valued readily by comparison with the pricing on similar term AAA-rated notes. The level of default risk in AAA-rated notes is very small, making them a good market benchmark. On the other hand, Treasury notes, which literally have no default risk, are not as good a benchmark for corporate liabilities, due to persistent and unpredictable differences between corporate and government issues.

The so-called pricing on a loan is the set of fees and spreads, which determines the promised cash flows between borrower and lender. This is the equivalent of the coupon rate on a bond. The value of the loan is obtained by discounting the loan cash flows by an appropriate set of discount rates. The discount rates, in the absence of default risk, would simply differ by increments of term, according to the current term structure.

In the presence of default risk, the discount rates must contain two additional elements. The first is the expected loss premium. This reflects an adjustment to the discount rate to account for the actuarial expectation of loss. It is based on the probability of default and the loss given default. The second is the risk premium. This is compensation for the nondiversifiable loss risk in the loan.

If the loan did not contain a risk premium, then on average it would only return the risk-free base rate. The key point is the qualifier, "on average." In years when default did not occur, the loan would return a little more due to the expected loss premium. However, in the event of default, it would return much less.

Since an investor could obtain the risk-free base rate not just "on average," but all the time by buying the risk-free asset, the risky asset must provide additional compensatory return. This would not be the case if default risk were completely diversifiable, but (as we have discussed) it is not. The market will provide compensation for unavoidable risk bearing (i.e., the portion of the loan's loss risk that cannot be eliminated through diversification).

The amount of nondiversifiable risk can be determined from knowing the borrower's probability of default and the risk characteristics of the borrower's assets. The market price for risk bearing can be determined from the equity and fixed income markets. This approach, based on option valuation methods, can be used to construct discount rates, specific to the borrower, which correctly account for both the time value of money and the expected and unexpected loss characteristics of the particular borrower.

There are only two possible outcomes for a loan. Either it is repaid, or the borrower defaults. The loss distribution for a single loan is simply:

Event	Probability
Default	EDF
No default	1-EDF

In the event of default, we expect to lose a percentage of the face value of the loan equal to LDG. If the yield on the loan is Y and the risk-free base rate is R_f, then the return distribution can be characterized as follows:

Event	Probability	Return
Default	EDF	$R_f - LDG$
No default	1-EDF	Y

The expected return is the probability weighted average of the returns:

$$E(R) = EDF\,(R_f - LGD) + (1 - EDF)Y$$

The required compensation for the actuarial risk of default is equal to $(LDG \times EDF)\backslash(1 - EDF)$. This is called the expected loss premium. If the loan yield equaled the risk-free base rate plus the expected loss premium, then

$$Y = R_f + \frac{LGD \times EDF}{(1 - EDF)},\text{ and}$$

$$E(R) = EDF\,(R_f - LGD) + (1 - EDF)\left(R_f + \frac{LGD \times EDF}{(1 - EDF)}\right)$$

$$E(R) = R_f$$

The expected loss premium provides just enough additional return when the borrower does not default to compensate for the expected loss when the borrower does default.

However, this is not the end of the story. What the previous calculation shows is that if the only additional compensation were the expected loss premium, then the lender on average would receive only the risk-free base rate. It would be much better for the lender to just lend at the risk-free base, since it would get the same average return and would incur no default risk. There must be additional compensation for the fact that the realized return is risky even for a large, well-diversified portfolio of loans. That additional compensation is called the risk premium.

The required pricing on a loan is thus the risk-free base rate plus the expected loss premium plus the risk premium.

$$Y = R_f + EL\ premium + Risk\ premium$$

The required risk premium in the market can be determined by taking the credit spread on debt securities and subtracting the appropriate EL premium. The remainder is the market risk premium.

If we think of the yield on a loan as being an average of these various discount rates (as "yield-to-maturity" is for a bond), then the value of the loan is simply its promised cash flows discounted at its yield. If the yield exceeds the loan rate, then the loan will be at a discount. An increase in the probability of default will push up the yield required in the market and push down the price of the loan. Other factors remaining the same, loan value moves inversely to changes in default probability.

ECONOMIC CAPITAL AND FUND MANAGEMENT

Consider now a bank. Think of the bank as being divided into two parts. One part is the actual portfolio of assets; the second is an amalgam of all other bank functions. Let us call the part containing the portfolio "the fund," and think of the fund as containing a portfolio management function but no other bank functions.

The fund is leveraged. It borrows from the rest of the bank at the appropriate market rate; we may think of it also as borrowing directly in the bond or money markets. Equity supporting the fund is owned by the rest of the bank, although in principle some or all could be owned outside of the bank. In essence, the fund is an odd sort of leveraged money market fund. The fund's assets have a market value, either because the individual assets have actual market prices or because we can value them as was discussed in the previous section.

The fund has fixed obligations (i.e., its borrowings). These borrowings also have determinable market values. The value of the fund's equity is exactly equal to the excess of the market value of its assets over the market value of its obligations. The economic capital of a bank is closely related to the market value of its equity. Rather than being the excess of the market value of assets over the *market* value of liabilities, economic capital is the excess of the market value of assets over the market value of liabilities, *assuming the liabilities had no default risk*. For a bank with low default risk, these values are virtually identical. However, for a distressed bank, economic capital can be zero or negative, whereas market equity is always positive.

The "economic capital" fluctuates with the market value of assets. The fund can raise more equity or more debt and invest it in additional assets, or it can make payouts to debt or equity, reducing its assets.

The objective of fund management is to maximize the value of the fund's equity. In a hypothetical world of frictionless markets and common information (i.e., a world without institutional constraints), this would be achieved by purchasing assets at or below market; selling assets at or above market.

Regardless of circumstance, this is a desirable policy, and its implementation requires rigorous measurement of default risk and pricing that by market standards at least compensates for the default risk. However, institutional constraints do exist, and markets are not frictionless nor information symmetrically dispersed. In fact, it is the existence of these market "imperfections" that makes intermediation a valuable service. There is no need for banks or mutual funds to exist in a world of perfect capital markets.

In practice, equity funding is "expensive." This may be because equity returns are taxed at the fund level, or because the "opaqueness" of bank balance sheets imposes an additional "risk" cost (agency cost). The result is that banks feel constrained to use the minimal amount of capital consistent with maintaining their ability to freely access debt markets. For wholesale banks, that access is permitted only to banks with extremely low default probabilities (.10% or less per year).

Finally, the fund is an investment vehicle. In a world where transactions are costly, one of the fund's functions is to minimize those costs for final investors. It does this by providing competitive return for its risk. Failure to do this makes it a secondary rather than primary investment vehicle; in other words, if it is less than fully diversified, another layer of investment vehicles, and another round of transactions costs, is required to provide diversification to the investor.

Both of these considerations add two additional objectives:

- Obtain maximal diversification.
- Determine and maintain capital adequacy.

As previously discussed, capital adequacy can be determined by considering the frequency distribution of portfolio losses. Maintaining capital adequacy means that the desired leverage must be determined for each new asset as it is added to the portfolio. This leverage must be such as to leave the fund's overall default risk unchanged. Assets that, net of diversification, add more than average risk to the portfolio must be financed (proportionately) with more equity and less debt than the existing portfolio.

Capital adequacy means using enough equity funding that the fund's default risk is acceptably low. A conventional measure is the actual or implied debt rating of the fund; the debt rating can be interpreted as corresponding to a probability of default. For instance, an AA-rated fund typically has a default probability less than 0.05%.

The fund will default if it suffers losses that are large enough to eliminate the equity. Figure 13.7 shows the loss distribution of the fund's portfolio. For any given level of equity funding, it is possible to determine the probability of losses that would eliminate the equity. For instance, if this portfolio were 4% equity funded, then the probability of depleting the equity is 0.10%. This is equivalent to a single A debt rating.

Maximal diversification means the lowest level of portfolio unexpected loss, conditional on a given level of expected return. Note that this is different than minimizing risk without regard to return. The latter can be accomplished by holding U.S. Treasuries.

For each level of return, and for a given set of possible assets, there is a unique set of holdings that gives the minimum unexpected loss. When we depict the expected return and unexpected loss associated with each of these portfolios, the resulting graph is called the "efficient frontier."

The process for determining how much "economic capital" (equity) to use in financing an asset and the process for maximizing diversification both require measuring how much risk an individual asset contributes to the portfolio, net of risk reduction due to diversification.

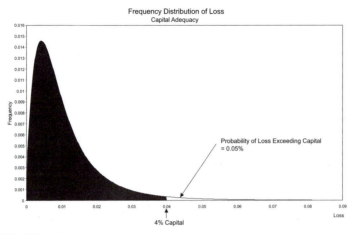

FIGURE 13.7 Frequency Distribution of Loss: Capital Adequacy

RISK CONTRIBUTION AND OPTIMAL DIVERSIFICATION

Diversification means that the risk in the portfolio is less than the average of each asset's stand-alone risk. Some part of each asset's stand-alone risk is diversified away in the portfolio. Thinking of it in this way, we can divide the stand-alone risk of an asset into the part that is diversified away and the part that remains. This latter part is the risk contribution of the asset to the portfolio, and the risk of the portfolio is the holdings-weighted average of these risk contributions.

The residual risk contribution of an asset changes as the composition of the portfolio varies. In particular, as the holding of the asset increases, its risk contribution increases. The percentage of its stand-alone risk that is not being diversified away increases at the same time as the value weight of the asset in the portfolio increases.

Figure 13.8 shows the loss risk of a single asset. The total height of the bar represents the unexpected loss of the asset.

The bottom segment of the bar represents the portion of the unexpected loss that could not be eliminated through diversification even in the broadest possible portfolio. This is called the nondiversifiable, or systemic, risk of the asset. When one speaks of the "beta" of an asset, one is referring to this portion of an asset's risk.

In the context of an actual portfolio, diversification will generally be less than optimal, and some portion of its risk that could be diversified away has not been. This portion is represented by the second segment of the bar.

The sum of the bottom two segments is the risk contribution of the asset to the portfolio. It represents the risk that has not been diversified away in the portfolio. Some has not been diversified away because it cannot be (the systemic por-

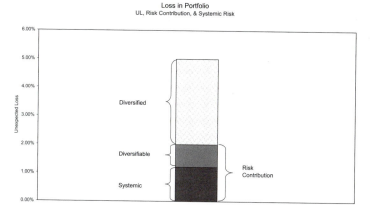

FIGURE 13.8   Loss in Portfolio: Unexpected Loss, Risk Contribution, and Systemic Risk

tion); some has not been diversified away because the portfolio is less than optimally diversified.

The portfolio's unexpected loss is simply the holdings-weighted average of the risk contributions of the individual assets. Risk contribution is the appropriate measure of the risk of an asset in a portfolio because it is net of the portion of risk that has been diversified away.

As the holdings change, the risk contributions change. For instance, if the proportionate holdings of this asset were increased in the portfolio, less of its risk would be diversified away, and the risk contribution would go up.

Systemic risk is measured relative to the whole market of risky assets. Risk contribution is specific to a particular portfolio: the particular set of assets and the particular proportions in which the assets are held. In a typical portfolio, there are assets whose returns are large relative to the amount of risk they contribute; there are also assets whose returns are small relative to the amount of risk they contribute to the portfolio. These assets are mispriced relative to the portfolio in which they are being held.

In some cases, this "mispricing to portfolio" simply reflects that the assets are mispriced in the market, and it is ultimately fixed as the market price adjusts. More often, however, it reflects that the portfolio has too much or too little of the particular assets. If an asset that has too little return for its risk is partially swapped for an asset that is generously compensated for its risk, two things happen. First, the portfolio improves: without any increase in risk, the portfolio return improves. Second, as the holding of the former asset decreases, its risk contribution goes down; similarly, the risk contribution of the latter asset increases. As the risk contributions change, the return-to-risk ratios change for each asset. The former asset is no longer so under-rewarded, the latter is no longer so over-rewarded. Continuing the swap will continue to improve the portfolio until the return-to-risk ratios for each of the assets are brought into alignment with the overall portfolio.

This process, applied to all assets in the portfolio, leads to the maximization of diversification for any given level of return. Thus, a key part of the portfolio management process is to measure the risk contribution of each asset, and its return relative to that risk. The optimized portfolio will not contain the same amount of all assets; the holdings will be based on the risk contribution of each asset relative to its return. In fact, an optimized portfolio is one where all assets have the same return-to-risk ratio. Any deviation would imply the existence of a swap that could improve the overall portfolio.

A portfolio is optimized by swapping low return-to-risk assets for high return-to-risk assets. To do this requires identifying which are the high and low return-to-risk assets.

Figure 13.9 is taken from KMV's Portfolio Manager software. It illustrates for a bond portfolio the return-to-risk characteristics of all the assets in the portfolio. The return to each asset is measured by its spread adjusted for expected loss. The risk is measured by the risk contribution to the portfolio.

The assets represented by the noninverted triangles all have average return-to-risk ratios. Assets lying above have high values; assets lying below it have low values. As the holding of a low return-to-risk asset is decreased, its risk contribution falls and its return-to-risk ratio improves. The reverse happens for high return-to-risk assets whose holdings are increased. This mechanism serves to move assets into the average range as the portfolio diversification is improved. No further improvement is possible when all assets lie within the band.

It is vitally important to note that the results of portfolio optimization depend on the set of potential assets that the fund can hold. In the final analysis, it will not make sense to maximize diversification over the existing set of assets in the portfolio without considering the effect of adding new assets into the portfolio. Because of the relatively low default correlations between most borrowers, the gains from broad diversification are substantial and do not decrease quickly as portfolio size increases.

An equity mutual fund would be poorly diversified if it were limited to only holding those equities that it had underwritten itself. This is much more the case for debt portfolios, because there are larger and more persistent benefits to diversification in debt than in equity. The implication is that funds will want to hold the broadest possible set of assets and must be prepared to buy them when it benefits the fund. The approach described here can be used to identify which assets are desirable additions at which prices.

Different holdings of assets in the portfolio result in portfolios with different risk and return characteristics. This is illustrated in Figures 13.10 and 13.11 (note that Figure 13.11 is a rescaled version of Figure 13.10).

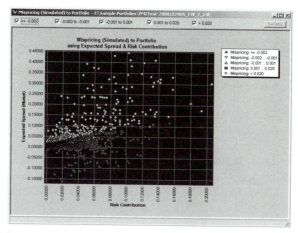

FIGURE 13.9   Simulated Mispricing to Portfolio Using Expected Spread & Risk Contribution

The square points (■) represent the expected spread, unexpected loss pairs of individual assets. A portfolio that consisted 100% of a single asset would have the same risk and return as that asset.

An actual portfolio constructed from these assets, depending on its proportions, will have a specific risk/return combination. The cross (✚) represents one such actual portfolio.

Because the assets are positively correlated, all portfolios will have some risk. For a given level of return there must therefore be a portfolio with minimum but still positive risk. The diamond (◆) represents the portfolio with the same expected spread as the actual portfolio (✚) but the least possible risk.

Similarly, there is an upward bound on achievable return at any level of risk. The portfolio represented by the gray circle (●) illustrates the maximal return portfolio with the same risk as the actual portfolio.

The light line passing through these portfolios is the "efficient frontier." It represents the expected spread/UL values for those portfolios that have the smallest possible unexpected loss for a given level of expected spread. The unexpected loss of these portfolios lies far to the left of the ULs of the individual assets. This reflects the amount of risk that is eliminated through diversification.

The inverted triangle (▼) is the global minimum risk portfolio. The triangle (▲) above it represents the portfolio on the efficient frontier with the highest return-to-risk ratio.

RISK CONTRIBUTION AND ECONOMIC CAPITAL

We have already seen that overall leverage in a managed fund can be determined from considering the frequency distribution of loss for the portfolio. For instance,

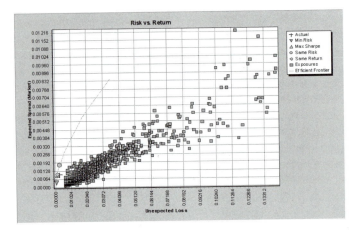

FIGURE 13.10   Risk versus Return

if a fund has assets of $100 million and a given loss distribution, then we can determine the likelihood that within one year the fund's assets will have a value less than $95 million. Let us suppose that this probability is 0.3%. If the firm has fixed obligations of $95 million due in one year, then this probability corresponds to the probability that the asset value will be insufficient to pay the obligations. In other words, the fund's obligations would have a default probability of 0.3%.

An annual default probability of 0.3% corresponds to the default risk of triple-B rated debt. If the fund wished to have a higher rating, it would have to reduce this probability. It could either reduce the probability of large unexpected losses (i.e., change its loss distribution by getting better diversified), or it could

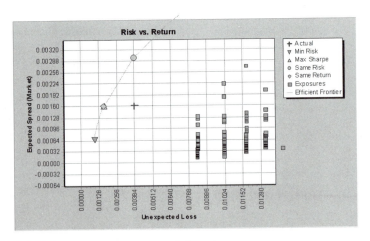

FIGURE 13.11   Risk versus Return (Rescaled View)

use more equity to fund itself given its loss distribution. By referring to the loss distribution, we can find the combination of equity and fixed obligations for any desired debt rating.

Let us suppose that a fund has, in fact, found the level of equity that gives it the rating that it desires. As it adds a new asset, it will want to fund it with sufficient equity so that the default risk of the fund's obligations remains unchanged. The amount of equity required depends on the risk contribution of the new asset. An asset whose risk contribution, percentage-wise, is equal to the risk of the existing portfolio will require, percentage-wise, the same amount of equity funding as the existing total portfolio. A riskier asset will require proportionately more, and a safer asset will require proportionately less.

In actual loan portfolios, there is tremendous variation in risk contribution. The least risky assets are generally a hundred times less risky than the most risky. Required equity allocations will also vary by the same magnitudes.

Equity allocation is dynamic. The goal of equity allocation is to create an automatic stabilizer so that the fund's probability of default remains constant as the portfolio's composition and condition change. This requires (1) appropriate funding of new assets, (2) monitoring of the market value of the portfolio in order to know the level of equity capital at all times, and (3) continuing assessment of the portfolio's frequency distribution of loss.

As the discussion to this point indicates, determination of the loss risk of an exposure is the foundation of portfolio analysis. The discussion to this point has emphasized the role of default probability. The amount of the exposure and the loss given default are also required to determine the loss risk of an exposure. Due to the option characteristics of bank assets, both of these characteristics can be difficult to quantify. A method is needed to determine the loss risk implied by undrawn commitments with risk-reducing covenants.

COMMITMENTS, COVENANTS, AND EXPOSURE

Bank assets grant a variety of options to bank customers. They also contain terms and provisions known as covenants, which are options that the bank reserves to itself. Two major examples are committed borrowing arrangements and covenants that allow the bank to take action when a borrower's default risk increases. To determine the loss risks of a bank's portfolio, it is necessary to translate these options into their implications for loss.

As previously discussed, a term loan can be thought of as an unconditional obligation of the borrower to repay, less a default option that allows the borrower to deliver its assets in lieu of payment in the event the borrower's performance is sufficiently bad. The totality of the credit problem is the default option.

Consider now a committed facility without covenants. The commitment amount is $X. The bank has committed to lending, at the behest of the borrower, up to $X. Should the borrower get into financial difficulties, it is definitely in its interest to borrow the full amount of the facility. If it does sufficiently poorly, it will default. Thus, the undrawn commitment represents the pure default option. It will be exercised at the same time to the same extent and produce the same loss as the default option that is bundled with a *term* loan with a face value equal to the commitment amount. From the standpoint of managing the default risk of the portfolio, an unrestricted commitment of $X represents the same exposure as a term loan of $X.

Consider now the committed facility with covenant restrictions. The covenants are options. Should certain triggering events occur, the bank can take certain actions. The effect of the covenants depends on (1) the timeliness and relevance of the triggering events, (2) the actions that can actually be taken as a result, (3) the skill with which the bank actually executes on the opportunity, and (4) the degree of mitigation of loss that is possible.

These issues are conceptual, empirical, and operational. A perfectly designed condition is of no use if the bank executes poorly. Similarly, the degree of mitigation in practice depends on the alternatives available to the borrower.

At a conceptual level, three types of loss mitigation are available. The covenants may permit (1) reduction of the maximum amount of borrowing under the commitment, (2) increase in seniority of the borrowing, and (3) increase in collateral. Each one of these effects can be incorporated into the model of loss. Covenants may also permit repricing. Conditional pricing can and should be incorporated into the assessment of expected return rather than loss.

In particular, if covenants exist that will increase seniority or collateral in the event of deterioration, then the "loss given default" for the exposure should be based on the expected recovery, assuming the increase in seniority or collateral. This assumes that the covenant would be triggered and used prior to default.

If covenants exist that would limit the ability to access the facility, then these covenants would result in an effective exposure that was less than the maximum amount of the commitment.

Ultimately, the empirical quantification of these effects requires analysis of experience and operational performance. In recent years, banks have begun to embark on this process of analysis, and early results provide some guidance for the assessment of covenant effects. Much work remains to be done, however.

SUBPORTFOLIO AND PORTFOLIO

The techniques described in this chapter represent an accurate and detailed approach to the determination of portfolio loss risks. In practice, the applicability of this approach depends on not just how well it works, but also on the quality of answer that is required.

There are different "subportfolios" within the typical bank: large corporate, middle market, small business, commercial real estate, consumer, residential mortgage, and so on. Some of these portfolios have relatively stable and predictable loss characteristics. These are generally subportfolios with very large numbers of relatively equal-sized exposures, relatively high default rates, and low correlations. By contrast, other subportfolios contribute a disproportionate amount of loss risk, notably large corporate and commercial real estate. These are generally subportfolios with large individual exposures, smaller total numbers of borrowers, and uneven exposure amounts. They also have high internal correlations and generally lower default rates.

The general framework of analysis, while developed to analyze corporate loan portfolios, has many elements that can be used to measure and manage loss risk for any type of borrower, as long as a quantifiable method of measuring default probability exists. The major limitation on integrating noncorporate exposures into the portfolio is the timely measurement of default risk.

RELATIONSHIP AND CUSTOMER PROFITABILITY

Banks, as a rule, are poorly organized to be fund managers. Portfolio decisions are not actively made, but are rather the passive outcome of credit, origination, and syndication decisions. The current "new view" is to manage portfolios by way of constraints (i.e., "limits" on exposures) by industry, geography, and so forth. This is also not active management but an attempt to mitigate the costs of the existing dysfunctional processes.

The problem is that fund management is not viewed as a profit center. It is a back-office function, a staff function, and a reporting function. The solution lies in putting fund management on an independent basis.

Consider a fund manager who "posts" bid and ask prices for assets. He or she is willing to buy them or sell them at those prices. A loan officer in originating an asset would have the option of either selling it to the fund, syndicating it to the market, or both. The lending officer makes money from the underwriting spread. The portfolio manager is rewarded based on the performance of the fund. The two functions can be performed independently.

Suppose that there is other profitable business that the bank does with a borrower, which is considered to be dependent on the existence of a borrowing relationship. This does not necessarily imply a price concession to the borrower, but assume it does. This is irrelevant to the fund manager. The fund manager is only interested in the performance of the fund and requires certain pricing to obtain it.

Thus, the underwriter will have to book the loss on origination in order to sell the loan into the portfolio (or into the market). Suppose this loss is $50,000. The underwriter will only be willing to underwrite the loan if the other group at the bank, which has the profitable business with the borrower, is willing to make a $50,000 transfer to the origination unit.

If the other unit is unwilling to pay the cost to keep the customer, then that is not a profitable customer. The bank will be better off without it. It is not necessary to have either a centralized decision-making process or an aggregate "customer profitability system" in order to make the right decision.

In fact, the main problem is information—the true cost and true benefit to each unit of dealing with a particular customer. The bank is currently organized in a way that these costs and benefits cannot be accurately measured. Effectively separating functions makes it possible to determine the costs and benefits.

For instance, if a bank cannot profitably underwrite certain loans because its underwriting costs are too high, that is a business opportunity that can be addressed by figuring out how to do it more cheaply, not necessarily by abandoning the business. The incentive to identify and seize such opportunities requires independent behavior at the level of specific businesses, including the business of fund management.

The challenge to bank management is to permit this independence while ensuring that it gets the information it needs to maintain its overall desired risk profile, to motivate behavior that raises overall bank value, and to capture synergistic opportunities between business segments. The methods that have been discussed here address these objectives. They can be used explicitly by a portfolio or subportfolio manager to manage a portfolio. They can also be used separately from the portfolio manager in order to monitor the portfolio manager and to measure the performance of the portfolio.

CONCLUSION

Bank portfolio management has two central features: the measurement of diversification at the portfolio level and the measurement of how individual assets or groups of assets affect diversification. These measurements require estimates of (1) probabilities of default for each asset, (2) expected recovery in the event of default for each asset, and (3) default correlations between each pair of borrowers.

This chapter has described a consistent conceptual framework and actual methods for determining these quantities. The relevance and feasibility of the methods are best illustrated by simply noting that they are currently being used to assess bank portfolios in practice. In particular, these methods enable the bank to assess the following:

- The overall frequency distribution of loss associated with its portfolio
- The risk and return contribution of individual assets or groups of assets
- The risk/return characteristics of its existing portfolio and how to improve it
- Overall economic capital adequacy
- The economic capital required for new and existing assets

- How to maximize diversification and minimize the use of economic capital

In short, these new methods provide the means by which a bank can implement a rigorous program to manage its portfolio for maximum return while maintaining risk at a desirable level.

14

EDF™ CREDIT MEASURE

Default risk is the uncertainty surrounding a firm's ability to service its debts and obligations. Prior to default, there is no way to discriminate unambiguously between firms that will default and those that will not. At best we can only make probabilistic assessments of the likelihood of default. As a result, firms generally pay a spread over the default-free rate of interest that is proportional to their default probability to compensate lenders for this uncertainty.

Default is a deceptively rare event. The typical firm has a default probability of around 2% in any year. However, there is considerable variation in default probabilities across firms. For example, the odds of a firm with an AAA rating defaulting are only about 2 in 10,000 per annum. A single A-rated firm has odds of around 10 in 10,000 per annum, five times higher than an AAA-rated firm. At the bottom of the rating scale, a CCC-rated firm's odds of defaulting are 4 in 100 (4%), 200 times the odds of an AAA-rated firm.

The loss suffered by a lender or counterparty in the event of default is usually significant and is determined largely by the details of the particular contract

---

or obligation. For example, typical loss rates in the event of default for senior secured bonds, subordinated bonds, and zero coupon bonds are 49%, 68%, and 81%, respectively.

Cross default clauses in debt contracts usually ensure that the default probabilities for each of the classes of debt for a firm are the same. That is, the default probability of the firm determines the default probability for all of the firm's debt or counterparty obligations. However, the loss in the event of default for each of the classes of obligations can vary widely depending on their nature (security, collateral, seniority, etc.).

Although in general a poor investment strategy, it is possible to be rewarded for taking on large concentrations of risk in equities because these concentrations at times produce large returns. However, overwhelming evidence of the ineffectiveness of this *stock-picking* strategy has been available since the early 1970s and, as a result, the majority of equity investments are managed in diversified portfolios. Unlike equities, debt has no upside potential and thus the case for managing default risk in well-diversified portfolios is even more compelling. The limited upside potential of debt spreads means that there are no possible circumstances under which an investor or counterparty can be rewarded for taking on concentrations of default risk. Like other rare events with high costs, default risk can only be effectively managed in a portfolio.

In addition to knowing the default probability and loss given default, the portfolio management of default risk requires the measurement of default correlations. Correlations measure the degree to which the default risks of the various borrowers and counterparties in the portfolio are related. The elements of credit risk can therefore be grouped as follows:

Stand-alone Risk
- *Default probability*. The probability that the counterparty or borrower will fail to service its obligations.
- *Loss given default*. The extent of the loss incurred in the event the borrower or counterparty defaults.
- *Migration risk*. The probability and value impact of changes in default probability.

Portfolio Risk
- *Default correlations*. The degree to which the default risks of the borrowers and counterparties in the portfolio are related.
- *Exposure*. The size, or proportion, of the portfolio exposed to the default risk of each counterparty and borrower.

While each of these items is critical to the management of credit portfolios, none is more important or more difficult to determine than the default probability. The remainder of this chapter focuses on the determination of default probability using information from a firm's financial statements and the market price of its equity.

MEASURING DEFAULT PROBABILITY: THE PROBLEM

There are three main elements that determine the default probability of a firm:

- *Value of assets.* The *market value* of the firm's assets. This is a measure of the present value of the future free cash flows produced by the firm's assets discounted back at the appropriate discount rate. This measures the firm's prospects and incorporates relevant information about the firm's industry and the economy.
- *Asset risk.* The *uncertainty or risk* of the asset value. This is a measure of the firm's business and industry risk. The value of the firm's assets is an estimate and is thus uncertain. As a result, the value of the firm's assets should always be understood in the context of the firm's business or asset risk.
- *Leverage.* The extent of the firm's contractual liabilities. Whereas the relevant measure of the firm's assets is always its market value, the book value of liabilities relative to the market value of assets is the pertinent measure of the firm's leverage, since that is the amount the firm must repay.

For example, Figure 14.1 illustrates the evolution of the asset value and book liabilities of Winstar Communications, a New York telephone company that filed for Chapter 11 bankruptcy protection in April 2001.

The default risk of the firm increases as the value of the assets approaches the book value of the liabilities, until finally the firm defaults when the market value of the assets is insufficient to repay the liabilities.

In our study of defaults, we have found that in general firms do not default when their asset value reaches the book value of their total liabilities. While some firms certainly default at this point, many continue to trade and service their debts. The long-term nature of some of their liabilities provides these firms with some breathing space. We have found that the *default point*, the asset value at which the firm will default, generally lies somewhere between total liabilities and current, or short-term, liabilities.

The relevant net worth of the firm is therefore the market value of the firm's assets minus the firm's default point:

[*Market value of assets*] − [*Default point*]

A firm will default when its market net worth reaches zero.

Like the firm's asset value, the market measure of net worth must be considered in the context of the firm's business risk. For example, firms in the food and beverage industries can afford higher levels of leverage (lower market net worth) than high-technology businesses because their businesses, and consequently their asset values, are more stable and less uncertain.

For example, Figure 14.2 shows the evolution of asset values and default points for Compaq Computer and Anheuser-Busch. Figure 14.3 shows the

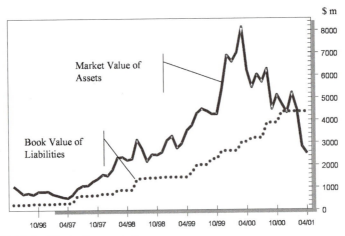

FIGURE 14.1   Winstar Communications

corresponding evolution of the annual default probabilities. The default probabilities shown in this figure are the one-year default rates, the probability that the
firm will default in the ensuing year, and are displayed on a logarithmic scale.

The effect of the relative business risks of the two firms is clear from a comparison of the two figures. For instance, as of April 2001, the relative market values, default points, asset risks, and resulting default probabilities for Compaq
and Anheuser-Busch were as shown here:

	Anheuser-Busch	*Compaq Computer*
Market value of assets	44.1	42.3
Default point	5.3	12.2
Market net worth ($b)	38.8	30.1
Asset volatility	21%	39%
Default probability (per annum)	.03%	1.97%

The asset risk is measured by the asset volatility, the standard deviation of
the annual percentage change in the asset value. For example, Anheuser-Busch's
business risk is 21%, which means that a one standard deviation move in its asset
value will add (or remove) $9 billion from its asset value of $44.1 billion. In contrast, a one standard deviation move in the asset value of Compaq Computer will
add or remove $16.5 billion from its asset value of $ 42.3 billion. The difference
in their default probabilities is thus driven by the difference in the risks of their
businesses, not their respective asset values or leverages.

As you would expect, asset volatility is related to the size and nature of the
firm's business. For example, Figure 14.4 shows the asset volatility for several
industries and asset sizes.

Asset volatility is related to, but different from, equity volatility. A firm's
leverage has the effect of magnifying its underlying asset volatility. As a result,

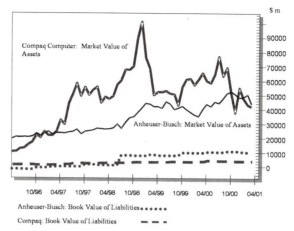

FIGURE 14.2   Market Net Worth

industries with low asset volatility (for example, banking) tend to take on larger amounts of leverage, while industries with high asset volatility (for example, computer software) tend to take on less. As a consequence of these compensatory differences in leverage, equity volatility is far less differentiated by industry and asset size than is asset volatility.

Asset value, business risk, and leverage can be combined into a single measure of default risk, which compares the market net worth to the size of a one

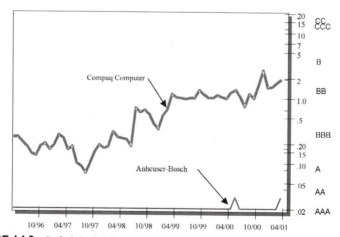

FIGURE 14.3   Default Probability

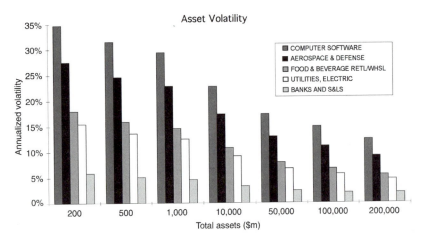

FIGURE 14.4   Asset Volatility

standard deviation move in the asset value. We refer to this ratio as the *distance-to-default,* and it is calculated as follows:

$$\text{Distance to default} = \frac{[\text{Market value of assets}] - [\text{Default point}]}{[\text{Market value of assets}][\text{Asset volatility}]}$$

For example, in April 2001 Anheuser-Busch was approximately 4.2 standard deviations away from default while, in contrast, Compaq Computer was only 1.8 standard deviations away from default. That is, it would take a 4.2 standard deviation move in the asset value of Anheuser-Busch before it will default, while only a 1.8 standard deviation move is required in Compaq's asset value to result in its default.

The distance-to-default measure combines three key credit issues: the value of the firm's assets, its business and industry risk, and its leverage. Moreover, the distance-to-default measure also incorporates, via the asset value and volatility, the effects of industry, geography, and firm size.

The default probability can be computed directly from the distance-to-default measure if the probability distribution of the assets is known or, equivalently, if the default rate for a given level of distance-to-default is known.

MEASURING DEFAULT PROBABILITY: A PRACTICAL APPROACH

There are three basic types of information available that are relevant to the default probability of a firm: financial statements, market prices of the firm's debt and equity, and subjective appraisals of the firm's prospects and risk. Financial statements, by their nature, are inherently backward looking. They are reports of the past. Prices, by their nature, are inherently forward looking. Investors form debt and equity prices as they anticipate the firm's future. In determining the market prices, investors use, among many other things, subjective appraisals of the firm's prospects and risk, financial statements, and other market prices. This information is combined using each investor's own analysis and synthesis and results in the investor's willingness to buy and sell the debt and equity securities of the firm. Market prices are the result of the combined willingness of many investors to buy and sell, and thus prices embody the synthesized views and forecasts of many investors.

The most effective default measurement, therefore, derives from models that utilize both market prices and financial statements. There is no assertion here that markets are perfectly efficient in this synthesis. We assert only that, in general, it is difficult to do a better job than they are doing—that is, it is very difficult to consistently beat the market. Consequently, where available, we want to utilize market prices in the determination of default risk because prices add considerably to the predictive power of the estimates.

Oldrich Vasicek and Stephen Kealhofer have extended the Black-Scholes-Merton framework to produce a model of default probability known as the Vasicek-Kealhofer (VK) model. This model assumes the firm's equity is a perpetual option with the default point acting as the absorbing barrier for the firm's asset value. When the asset value hits the default point, the firm is assumed to default. Multiple classes of liabilities are modeled: short-term liabilities, long-term liabilities, convertible debt, preferred equity, and common equity. When the firm's asset value becomes very large, the convertible securities are assumed to convert and dilute the existing equity. In addition, cash payouts such as dividends are explicitly used in the VK model. A default database is used to derive an empirical distribution relating the distance-to-default measure to a default probability. In this way, the relationship between asset value and liabilities can be captured without resorting to a substantially more complex model characterizing a firm's liability process.

KMV has implemented the VK model to calculate an Expected Default Frequency™ (EDF™) credit measure, which is the probability of default during the forthcoming year or years for firms with publicly traded equity (this model can also be modified to produce EDF values for firms without publicly traded equity.) The EDF value requires equity prices and certain items from financial statements as inputs. EDF credit measures can be viewed and analyzed within the context of a software product called Credit Monitor™ (CM). CM calculates EDF values for years 1 through 5, allowing the user to see a term structure of EDF values. KMV's EDF credit measure assumes that default is defined as the nonpayment of any scheduled payment, interest, or principal. The remainder of this section describes the procedure used by KMV to determine a public firm's probability of default.

There are essentially three steps in the determination of the default probability of a firm:

1. *Estimate asset value and volatility.* In this step the asset value and asset volatility of the firm are estimated from the market value and volatility of equity and the book value of liabilities.
2. *Calculate the distance-to-default.* The distance-to-default (DD) measure is calculated from the asset value and asset volatility (estimated in the first step) and the book value of liabilities.
3. *Calculate the default probability.* The default probability is determined directly from the distance-to-default measure and the default rate for given levels of distance-to-default.

Estimate Asset Value and Volatility

If the market price of equity is available, the market value and volatility of assets can be determined directly using an options pricing based approach, which recognizes equity as a call option on the underlying assets of the firm. For example, consider a simplified case where there is only one class of debt and one class of equity (see Figure 14.5).

The limited liability feature of equity means that the equity holders have the right, but not the obligation, to pay off the debt holders and take over the remaining assets of the firm. That is, the holders of the other liabilities of the firm essentially own the firm until those liabilities are paid off in full by the equity holders. Thus, in the simplest case, equity is the same as a call option on the firm's assets with a strike price equal to the book value of the firm's liabilities.

The VK model uses this option nature of equity to derive the underlying asset value and asset volatility implied by the market value, volatility of equity, and the book value of liabilities. This process is similar in spirit to the procedure used by option traders in the determination of the implied volatility of an option from the observed option price.

For example, assume that the firm is actually a type of levered mutual fund or unit trust. The assets of the firm are equity securities and thus can be valued at

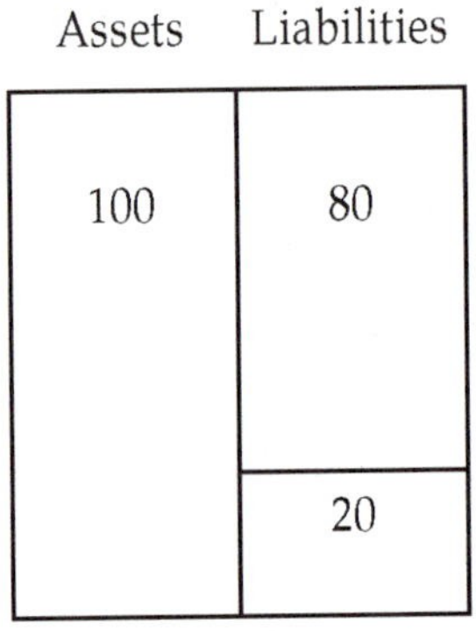

Assets   Liabilities

100	80
	20

FIGURE 14.5   Capital Structure: One Class of Debt and One Class of Equity

any time by observing their market prices. Further, assume that our little firm is to be wound up after five years and that we can ignore the time value of money (discounting adds little to our understanding of the relationships and serves only to complicate the picture). That is, in five years time, the assets will be sold and the proceeds divided between the debt and equity holders.

Initially, assume that we are interested in determining the market value of the equity from the market value of the assets. This is the reverse of the problem we face in practice but provides a simpler perspective to initially understand the basic option relationships (see Figure 14.6).

To be specific, assume that we initially invest $20 in the firm and borrow a further $80 from a bank. The proceeds, $100, are invested in equities. At the end of five years, what is the value of equity? For example, if the market value of the assets at the end of year 5 is $60, then the value of equity will be zero. If the value of the assets is $110, then the value of the equity will be $30, and so on. Thus, in Figure 14.6, the lines from $0 to $80 and from $80 to point B represent the market value of the equity as a function of the asset value at the end of year 5.

Assume now that we are interested in valuing our equity prior to the final winding up of the firm. For example, assume that three years have passed since the firm was started and that there are two years remaining before we wind the firm up. Further, we have marked the equities to market and their value is determined to be $80. What is the value of the equity? Not zero. It is actually something greater than zero because it is the value of the assets two years hence that really matters and there is still a chance that the asset value will be greater than $80 in two years time. In Figure 14.6, the value of the equity with two years to go is represented by the curve joining $0 and point B.

The higher the volatility of the assets, the greater is the chance of high asset values after two years. For example, if we were dissatisfied with our fund's performance after three years because it has lost $20 in value, dropping from $100 to $80, we may be tempted to invest in higher-potential, higher-risk, equities. If we do, what is the effect on the equity value? It increases. The more volatile assets have higher probabilities of high values and, consequently, higher payouts

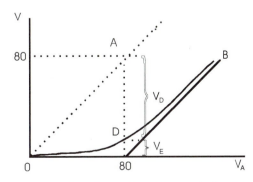

FIGURE 14.6 Deriving Underlying Asset Value and Asset Volatility: An Example

for the equity. Of course, there are accompanying higher probabilities of lower asset values, because volatility works both ways, but with limited liability this does not affect the equity value. At the end of the five years, it makes no difference to the equity if the final asset value is $79 or $9; its payout is the same, 0.

Where did the increase in the equity's value come from? It did not come from an increase in the asset value. We simply sold our original portfolio for $80 and purchased a new portfolio of higher-risk equities for $80. There was no value created there. The value, of course, came from the bank holding our firm's debt. In Figure 14.6, the value of the firm can be divided between the debt and equity holders along the line joining the points $80 and A, where the line 0 to A plots the asset value against itself. Thus, the only way the value of equity can increase while the asset value remains constant is to take the value from the market value of the debt. This should make sense. When we reinvested the firm's assets in higher-risk equities, we increased the default risk of the debt and consequently reduced its market value.

The value of debt and equity are thus intimately entwined. They are both really derivative securities on the underlying assets of the firm. We can exploit the option nature of equity to relate the market value of equity and the book value of debt to determine the implied market value of the underlying assets. That is, we solve the reverse of the problem described in our simple example. We observe the market value of the equity and solve backward for the market value of assets (see Figure 14.7).

In practice, we need to take account of the more complex capital structures and situations that exist in real life. For example, we need to consider the various terms and nature of debt (for example, long- and short-term debt and convertible instruments), the perpetuity nature of equity, the time value of money, and, of course, we have to solve for the volatility of the assets at the same time. Thus, in practice, we solve the following two relationships simultaneously:

$$[Equity\ value] = Option\ function\left([Asset\ value][Asset\ volatility][Capital\ structure][Interest\ rate]\right)$$

$$[Equity\ volatility] = Option\ function\left([Asset\ value][Asset\ volatility][Capital\ structure][Interest\ rate]\right)$$

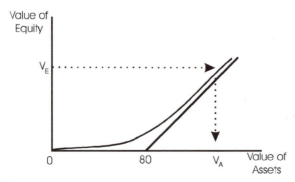

FIGURE 14.7   Relating the Market Value of Equity to the Market Value of Assets

Asset value and volatility are the only unknown quantities in these relationships and thus the two equations can be *solved* to determine the values implied by the current equity value, volatility, and capital structure.

Calculate the Distance-to-Default

There are six variables that determine the default probability of a firm over some horizon, from now until time H (see Figure 14.8):

1. The current asset value
2. The distribution of the asset value at time H
3. The volatility of the future assets value at time H
4. The level of the default point, the book value of the liabilities
5. The expected rate of growth in the asset value over the horizon
6. The length of the horizon, H

The first four variables—asset value, future asset distribution, asset volatility, and the level of the default point—are the really critical variables. The expected growth in the asset value has little default discriminating power and the analyst defines the length of the horizon.

If the value of the assets falls below the default point, then the firm defaults. Therefore, the probability of default is the probability that the asset value will fall below the default point. This is the shaded area (EDF value) below the default point in Figure 14.8.

Figure 14.8 also illustrates the causative relationship and trade-off among the variables. This causative specification provides analysts with a powerful and reliable framework in which they can ask what-if questions regarding the model's various inputs and examine the effects of any proposed capital restructuring. For example, the analyst can examine the effect of a large decrease in the stock price or the effects of an acquisition or merger.

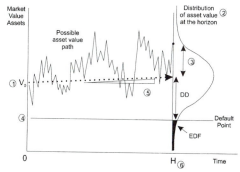

FIGURE 14.8 Default Probability Values

If the future distribution of the distance-to-default measure were known, the default probability (expected default frequency, or EDF value) would simply be the likelihood that the final asset value was below the default point (the shaded area in Figure 14.8). However, in practice, the distribution of the distance-to-default is difficult to measure. Moreover, the usual assumptions of normal or log-normal distributions cannot be used. For default measurement, the likelihood of large adverse changes in the relationship of asset value to the firm's default point is critical to the accurate determination of the default probability. These changes may come about from changes in asset value or changes in the firm's leverage. In fact, changes in asset value and changes in firm leverage may be highly corre-lated. Consequently, KMV first measures the distance-to-default as the number of standard deviations the asset value is away from default and then uses empir-ical data to determine the corresponding default probability. As discussed in a previous section, the distance-to-default is calculated as

$$[Distance\ to\ default] = \frac{[Market\ value\ of\ assets] - [Default\ point]}{[Market\ value\ of\ assets][Asset\ volatility]}$$

and is marked as DD in Figure 14.8.

Calculate the Default Probability

We obtain the relationship between distance-to-default and default probability from data on historical default and bankruptcy frequencies. KMV's database includes more than 250,000 company-years of data and more than 4,700 incidents of default or bankruptcy. From these data, a lookup or frequency table can be generated which relates the likelihood of default to various levels of distance-to-default.

For example, assume that we are interested in determining the default prob-ability over the next year for a firm that is seven standard deviations away from default. To determine this EDF value, we query the default history for the pro-portion of the firms, seven standard deviations away from default, that defaulted over the next year. The answer is about five basis points (bp), 0.05%, or an equiv-alent rating of AA.

We have tested the relationship between distance-to-default and default fre-quency for industry, size, time, and other effects and have found that the rela-tionship is constant across all of these variables. This is not to say that there are no differences in default rates across industry, time, and size but only that it appears that these differences are captured by the distance-to-default measure. Our studies of international default rates are continuing, but the preliminary results of studies by KMV and some of its clients indicate that the relationship is also invariant across countries and regions.

Putting It All Together

In summary, three steps are required to calculate an EDF credit measure: (1) esti-mate the current market value and volatility of the firm's assets, (2) determine how far the firm is from default, its distance-to-default, and (3) scale the distance-to-default to a probability. For example, consider Philip Morris Companies Inc., which at the end of April 2001 had a one-year EDF of 25 bp, close to the median EDF of firms with a A rating. Table 14.1 illustrates the relevant values and calculations for the EDF.

A CLOSER LOOK AT CALCULATING EDF CREDIT MEASURES

Merton's general derivative pricing model was the genesis for understanding the link between the market value of the firm's assets and the market value of its equity. It is possible to use the Black-Scholes (BS) option-pricing model, as a special case of Merton's model, to illustrate some of the technical details of estimating EDF values. The BS model is too restrictive to use in practice but is widely understood and provides a useful framework to review the issues involved. As explained before, KMV actually implements the VK model to calculate KMV's EDF credit measure. This section works an example of the calculation of an EDF value using the BS option-pricing model. The section also discusses some of the important issues that arise in practice and, where necessary, highlights the limitations of the BS model in this context.

Equity has the residual claim on the assets after all other obligations have been met. It also has limited liability. A call option on the underlying assets has the same properties. The holder of a call option on the assets has a claim on the assets after meeting the strike price of the option. In this case the strike of the call option is

TABLE 14.1   EDF Values and Calculations

Variable	Value	Notes
Market value of equity	$110,688 MM[a]	(Share price) × (Shares outstanding)
Book liabilities	$64,062 MM	Balance sheet
Market value of assets	$170,558 MM	Option-pricing model
Asset volatility	21%	Option-pricing model
Default point	$47,499 MM	Liabilities payable within one year
Distance-to-default	3.5	Ratio: $\dfrac{170 - 47}{170 \times 21\%}$
		(In this example, we ignore the growth in the asset value between now and the end of the year.)
EDF (one year)	25 bp	Empirical mapping between distance-to-default and default frequency.

[a] Million.

equal to the book value of the firm's liabilities. If the value of the assets is insufficient to meet the liabilities of the firm, then the shareholders, holders of the call
option, will not exercise their option and will leave the firm to its creditors.

We exploit the option nature of equity to derive the market value and volatility of the firm's underlying assets implied by the equity's market value. In particular, we solve backward from the option price and option price volatility for
the implied asset value and asset volatility.

To introduce the notation, recall that the BS model posits that the market
value of the firm's underlying assets follows the following stochastic process:

$$dV_A = \mu V_A dt + \sigma_A V_A dz \tag{1}$$

where

V_A, dV_A are the firm's asset value and change in asset value,

μ, σ_A are the firm's asset value drift rate and volatility, and

dz is a Wiener process.

The BS model allows only two types of liabilities, a single class of debt and
a single class of equity. If X is the book value of the debt which is due at time T,
then the market value of equity and the market value of assets are related by the
following expression:

$$V_E = V_A N(d1) - e^{-rT} XN\ (d2) \tag{2}$$

where

V_E is the market value of the firm's equity,

$$d1 = \frac{In\left(\dfrac{V_A}{X}\right) + \left(\dfrac{r + \sigma^2{}_A}{2}\right)T}{\sigma_A \sqrt{T}}$$

$d2 = d1 - \sigma_A \sqrt{T}$, and

r is the risk free interest rate.

It is straightforward to show that equity and asset volatility are related by the
following expression:

$$\sigma_E = \frac{V_A}{V_E} \Delta \sigma_A \tag{3}$$

where

σ_E is the volatility of the firm's equity, and

Δ is the hedge ratio, $N(d1)$, from (2).

Consider the example of a firm with a market capitalization of $3 billion, an
equity volatility of 40% per annum, and total liabilities of $10 billion. The asset
value and volatility implied by the equity value, equity volatility, and liabilities
are calculated by solving the call price and volatility equations, (2) and (3),

simultaneously. In this case[1] the implied market value of the firm's assets is $12.511 billion, and the implied asset volatility is 9.6%.

In practice, it is important to use a more general option-pricing relationship as characterized by the VK model that allows for a more detailed specification of the liabilities and that models equity as a perpetuity. KMV's EDF credit measure currently incorporates five classes of liabilities: short-term, long-term, convertible, preferred equity, and common equity.

The model linking equity and asset volatility given by equation (3) holds only instantaneously. In practice the market leverage moves around far too much for (3) to provide reasonable results. Worse yet, the model biases the probabilities in precisely the wrong direction. For example, if the market leverage is decreasing quickly, then (3) will tend to overestimate the asset volatility and thus the default probability will be overstated as the firm's credit risk improves. Conversely, if the market leverage is increasing rapidly, then (3) will underestimate the asset volatility and thus the default probability will be understated as the firm's credit risk deteriorates. The net result is that default probabilities calculated in this manner provide little discriminatory power.

Instead of using the instantaneous relationship given by (3), KMV's EDF credit measure is produced using a more complex iterative procedure to solve for the asset volatility. The procedure uses an initial guess of the volatility to determine the asset value and to *de-lever* the equity returns. The volatility of the resulting asset returns is used as the input to the next iteration of the procedure that in turn determines a new set of asset values and hence a new series of asset returns. The procedure continues in this manner until it converges. This usually takes no more than a handful of iterations if a reasonable starting point is used. In addition, the asset volatility derived here is combined in a Bayesian manner with country, industry, and size averages to produce a more predictive estimate of the firm's asset volatility.

The probability of default is the probability that the market value of the firm's assets will be less than the book value of the firm's liabilities by the time the debt matures. That is,

$$p_t = \Pr[V^t_A \le X_t | V^0_A = V_A] = \Pr[\ln V^t_A \le \ln X_t | V^0_A = V_A] \tag{4}$$

where

p_t is the probability of default by time t,

V^t_A is the market value of the firm's assets at time t, and

X_t is the book value of the firm's liabilities due at time t.

The change in the value of the firm's assets is described by equation (1), and thus the value at time t, V^t_A, given that the value at time 0 is V_A, is

---

[1] All liabilities are assumed to be due in one year, $T = 1$, and the interest rate r is assumed to be 5%.

$$In\ V^t_A = In\ V_A + \left(\mu - \frac{\sigma^2_A}{2}\right)t + \sigma_A\sqrt{t}\epsilon \tag{5}$$

where

μ is the expected return on the firm's asset, and

ϵ is the random component of the firm's return.

The relationship given by equation (5) describes the evolution in the asset value path that is shown in Figure 14.8. Combining (4) and (5), we can write the probability of default as

$$p_t = \Pr\left[In\ V_A + \left(\mu - \frac{\sigma^2_A}{2}\right)t + \sigma_A\sqrt{t}\epsilon \le X_t\right] \tag{6}$$

and after rearranging,

$$p_t = \Pr\left[-\frac{In\ \dfrac{V_A}{X_1} + \left(\mu - \dfrac{\sigma^2_A}{2}\right)t}{\sigma_A\sqrt{t}} \ge \epsilon\right] \tag{7}$$

The BS model assumes that the random component of the firm's asset returns is normally distributed, and as a result we can define the default probability in terms of the cumulative normal distribution:

$$p_t = N\left[-\frac{In\ \dfrac{V_A}{X_1} + \left(\mu - \dfrac{\sigma^2_A}{2}\right)t}{\sigma_A\sqrt{t}}\right] \tag{8}$$

Recall that the distance-to-default is simply the number of standard deviations that the firm is away from default and thus in the BS world is given by

$$DD = \frac{In\ \dfrac{V_A}{X_1} + \left(\mu - \dfrac{\sigma^2_A}{2}\right)t}{\sigma_A\sqrt{t}} \tag{9}$$

Continuing with our example, assume that the expected return on the assets, μ, is equal to 7% and that we are interested in calculating the one-year default probability. The distance-to-default, DD, in this case,[2] is 3.0, and the corresponding default probability from equation (8) is 13 bp.

In practice, we need to not only adjust the distance-to-default to include not only the increases in the asset value given by the rate but also adjust for any cash outflows to service debt, dividends, and so on. In addition, the normal distribution is a very poor choice to define the probability of default. There are several reasons for this, but the most important is the fact that the default point is in reality also a random variable. That is, we have assumed that the default point is described by the firm's liabilities and amortization schedule. Of course, we know

---

[2] The distance-to-default is calculated by equation (9), $DD = \dfrac{In\ \dfrac{12.511}{10} + \left(0.07 - \dfrac{0.0092}{2}\right)}{.096}$.

that this is not true. In particular, firms will often adjust their liabilities as they near default. It is common to observe the liabilities of commercial and industrial firms increase as they near default, while the liabilities of financial institutions often decrease as they approach default. The difference is usually just a reflection of the liquidity in the firm's assets and thus its ability to adjust its leverage as it encounters difficulties.

Unfortunately ex ante we are unable to specify the behavior of the liabilities, and thus the uncertainty in the adjustments in the liabilities must be captured elsewhere. We include this uncertainty in the mapping of distance-to-default to the EDF credit measure. The resulting empirical distribution of default rates has much wider tails than the normal distribution. For example, a distance-to-default of four, four standard deviations, maps to a default rate of around 100 bp. The equivalent probability from the normal distribution is essentially zero.

CALCULATING LONG-TERM EDF CREDIT MEASURES

The extension of the model to longer terms is straightforward. The default point, asset volatility, and expected asset value are calculated as before except they take into account the longer horizon (see Figure 14.9). For example, suppose we are interested in calculating the EDF value for a three-year horizon. Over the three years, we can expect that the default point will increase as a result of the amortization of long-term debt. This is a conservative assumption that all long-term debt is refinanced short term. We could just as easily model the asset value decreasing as the debt is paid down, but in practice debt is usually refinanced. In any case, it really doesn't matter whether the assets go down by the amount of the amortization or the default point increases by the same amount; the net effect on the default point is the same.

In addition to the default point changing, as we extend the horizon the future expected asset value is increasing, as is our uncertainty regarding its actual future value. The expected asset value increases at the expected growth rate and the total asset volatility increases proportionally with the square root of time.[3]

The distance-to-default is therefore calculated using the relevant three-year asset value, asset volatility, and default point. The scaling of the default probability again uses the empirical default distribution mapping three-year distance-to-defaults with the cumulative default probability to three years. That is, the mapping answers the question, what proportion of firms with this three-year distance-to-default actually default within three years? The answer to this question is the three-year cumulative default probability. EDF values are annual default probabilities, and the three-year EDF value is calculated as the equivalent

---

[3] The asset variance is additive and therefore increases linearly with time. The asset volatility is the square root of the variance and therefore increases with the square root of time.

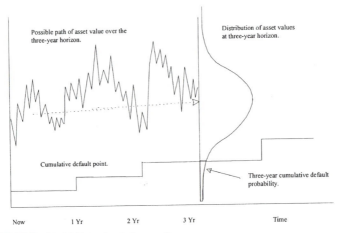

FIGURE 14.9   Model Extension to Longer Terms

average annual default probability.[4] For example, suppose the three-year cumulative probability is 250 bp, then the three-year EDF value is 84 bp.

SOME FREQUENTLY ASKED QUESTIONS ABOUT KMV'S EDF CREDIT MEASURES

How Does the Model Deal with Off-Balance-Sheet Liabilities?

This is a critical question for many firms, particularly financial institutions where these liabilities can obviously be quite significant. Fortunately, the model is surprisingly robust to the precise level of the liabilities.

For example, consider the firm used previously in our BS example. Assume that in addition to the $10 billion in liabilities the firm has a further $5 billion in off-balance-sheet commitments. That is, the true default point is actually $15 billion not $10 billion. The *actual* EDF value of the firm can therefore be calculated using the BS model as follows. The firm's market capitalization remains $3 billion, and its equity volatility is still 40% per annum. The implied asset value and volatility, with liabilities of $15 billion, are calculated again by solving the call price and volatility equations, (2) and (3), simultaneously. In this case,[5] the implied market value of the firm's assets is $17.267 bn, and the implied asset

---

[4] The EDF is calculated from the cumulative default probability using survival rates. For example, the three-year cumulative probability of default and the three-year EDF are related by the following expression: $1 - CEDF_3 = (1 - EDF_3)^3$. The probability of not defaulting within three years, $1 - CEDF_3$, and the average annual probability of not defaulting, $1 - EDF_3$.

[5] All liabilities are assumed to be due in one year, $T = 1$, and the interest rate r is assumed to be 5%.

volatility is 6.9%. The asset value is about $5 bn higher and the asset volatility is lower reflecting the higher leverage of the firm. (Recall the equity volatility was kept the same but we increased the leverage; as a result the implied asset volatility must be lower.)

The corresponding distance-to-default is 2.7 and the implied EDF value is still approximately 13 bp.

Obviously, if you have more complete or up-to-date information on the firm's liability structure, it should be used in the model. Credit Monitor includes an add-on product called EDF Calculator™ (EDFCalc™) that enables the user to enter a more complete, or more recent, statement of the firm's liabilities.

Does the Model Incorporate the Possibility of Large Changes in the Market Value of the Firm?

Yes. In addition to incorporating the uncertainty in the liability structure of the firm, the empirical distance-to-default to EDF value distribution captures the possibility of large jumps, up or down, in the firm's market value. The empirical distribution includes data from several serious market downturns including the crash of October 1987.

Can the Model Be Used to Simulate Market Downturns or Crashes?

The EDF credit measure already includes the effects of market downturns and crashes weighted by their appropriate probabilities. However, it is quite straightforward to ask questions such as in the event of a 30% drop in the market, what will be the effect on a firm's, or a portfolio of firms', EDF values? The effect of a market downturn on the equity value of any particular firm can be estimated using the firm's equity beta:

$$\Delta V_E = \beta_E \Delta V_m \qquad (10)$$

Should EDF Values Be Averaged or Smoothed to Remove Their Variation over Time?

No. It is certainly true that the EDF value of a firm can vary over time, but these variations are reflecting changes in credit quality as perceived by the equity market. Therefore, any smoothing or averaging is simply masking the signals from the market.

The volatility in an EDF credit measure over time can pose problems for some bank's credit processes where the EDF value directly determines the grade. However, this issue is usually simply overcome by determining actions by range of EDF values. That is, action triggers are attached to grades that are defined in terms of EDF value ranges. As a result, small, economically insignificant movements within a grade do not trigger any action and movements between grades trigger an appropriate review.

A related question is whether or not there is any trend information in EDF value. There is not. EDF values are driven by market prices and thus are directly analogous to prices. If there isn't any trend information in the equity price, there isn't any in the EDF credit measure.

Why Isn't Information from the Bond or Credit Derivatives Market Included?

There is a whole class of models, usually called reduced-form models, that relate credit spreads and default probabilities. Our experience implementing these approaches has not been successful to date. There is nothing wrong with the models per se, indeed in theory they hold the promise of some advantages over the causal model described in this chapter. However, the data required to calibrate and implement reduced-form models are not yet widely available. In most cases, credit risk simply is not as actively and cleanly traded as equities at the moment. This situation will undoubtedly change as the credit derivative and other markets grow, but to date we have not found credit spread information to be of sufficient quality to support the estimation of individual-level default probabilities.

To date, the most successful use of credit spread data that we are aware of has been in the cross-sectional[6] estimation of credit spread curves. These curves describe the typical market spread for a given level of credit quality.

Are the Default Probabilities Applicable across Countries and Industries?

The distance-to-default measure incorporates many of the idiosyncrasies of different countries and industries. For example, the business risk, as measured by the asset volatility, varies for a given industry across countries. Volatilities tend to be the lowest in Europe and the highest in the United States with Asian countries usually in-between. With the exception of the difficulty posed by differing accounting standards, the default point can be measured appropriately for each firm regardless of its country of incorporation. The different economic prospects for countries are obviously captured by the individual equity and asset valuations. As a result, we believe that the distance-to-default captures most of the relevant intercountry differences in default risk. However, the question does remain whether differences in bankruptcy codes, culture, and so on may result in different default rates for a given distance-to-default. That is, is the distance-to-default to EDF value mapping constant across countries?

---

[6] Cross-sectional in this context means combining data from many different firms and issues. This is in contrast to the problem tackled in this chapter—the estimation of the default probability for each individual firm.

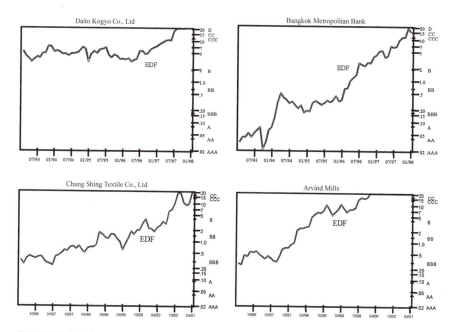

FIGURE 14.10 Daito Kogyo, a Japanese construction company, defaulted in July 1997; Bangkok Metropolitan Bank (Thailand) was taken over in January 1998; Chung Shing Textile Co., Ltd, a Taiwanese Thread Mill company, defaulted in April 2001; Arvind Mills, an Indonesian Fabric Mill, defaulted in February 2001

KMV's empirical default distribution that is used to map distance-to-default to EDF credit measures is built from publicly listed defaults in the United States. As a result, its translation to other countries should be questioned. However, we believe that the default probabilities resulting from this U.S.-based mapping are good measures of economic default risk. That is, it is possible as a result of political or other intervention that a firm will be saved from default in say Europe when in the United States it might have been left to fail. However, these interventions are not free and are costly to someone, often the taxpayer, or in the case of Asia, more commonly the shareholders of related firms. It seems unwise to us to measure default risk incorporating a reliance on the uneconomic behavior of another group. The uneconomic behavior may well continue, but it certainly seems unwise to institutionalize it in a measure of default risk. We do not believe it is possible to reliably model uneconomic behavior and thus we aim to provide a hard economic measure of default and allow analysts to factor in their own measure of implied government or other support.

Philosophy aside, our experience with EDF values internationally has been very good. More than half the users of KMV's EDF credit measures operate outside of the United States. During the Asian credit problems in 1997, the model performed extremely well; see examples in Figure 14.10. More recent credit difficulties in a number of countries around the world have been foreshadowed by appropriate increases in the EDF credit measures of firms in distress. The model has also been tested anecdotally in most European countries. We continue to collect default data internationally and continue to release studies of the KMV EDF credit measure's performance as these data accumulate.

Does the EDF Credit Measure Contain Any Measure of Country (Translation) Risk?

It is likely there is some measure of country risk impounded in the EDF credit measure; but exactly how much we don't know. The calculations for KMV's EDF credit measures are done in the firm's local currency and therefore the country risk measure comes from the discount in the local equity price as a result of international investors' concerns regarding the convertibility of the currency. Obviously it is impossible to separate this influence from all the others, and as a result we do not know how much country risk, if any, is present in the EDF value. The amount is likely to vary by country as a function of the accessibility of the country's equity market and of the interest of international investors.

How Well Does the EDF Credit Measure Work on Thinly Traded or Closely Held Firms?

Surprisingly well. This question often arises in connection with efficient markets and the culture of Anglo-Saxon markets. While the results of the international default studies will have to speak for themselves, we already actually know quite a lot about the performance of the model in thinly traded markets.

Our experience with these firms is drawn from the bottom end of the U.S. equity market where the companies are smaller and less actively traded than most of the firms on international exchanges. Our coverage of the United States is comprehensive, and the bottom 2,000 or so companies have market caps of less than $20 million (almost 1,000 have a market capitalization of less than USD 7 m). Most of these companies are not even listed on an exchange and are traded instead over the counter. Obviously, trading in these companies is going to be thin and many are likely to be very closely held.

This is also a group of firms that default often and thus we have a large body of evidence on the model's performance on these firms. It is very good. It appears that it doesn't seem to take many economically motivated investors to move the equity price to reflect the risk of the firm.

Does the Model Assume That the Equity Market Is Efficient?

No. The efficiency of a market usually refers to the degree to which the current price reflects all the relevant information about a firm's value. While we do not necessarily assume that the price reflects all the relevant information about a

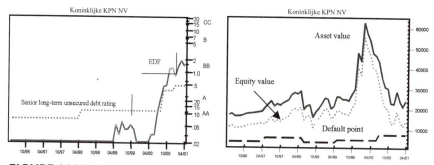

FIGURE 14.11   Koninklijke KPN NV, a Dutch telephone company surprised the market with it's differences.

firm, we do know that it is difficult to consistently beat the market. For example, over 90% of managed funds were unable to outperform the market in 1998. That is, it is difficult to pick stocks consistently and difficult to know when the market is under- or overvaluing a firm. The market reflects a summary of many investors forecasts and it is unusual if any one individual's, or committee's, forecast is better. Consequently, we believe that the best source of information regarding the value of a firm is the market.

The market though can be caught by surprise, as in Figure 14.11. Koninklijke KPN NV, a Dutch telephone company, caught the market and rating agencies by surprise although some credit analysts undoubtedly worried that it was overvalued.

Fraud is often the cause of extremely large and sudden changes in credit quality. For example, in Figure 14.12 it is not hard to spot when the announcement regarding the improprieties in the reporting of Mercury Finance's assets was made.

However, most of the time the market will be well aware of problems, or opportunities, and this information will be fairly reflected in the EDF value (see Figure 14.13).

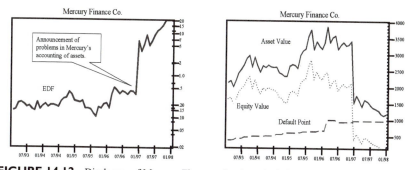

FIGURE 14.12   Disclosure of Mercury Finances fraud results in its sudden change in value.

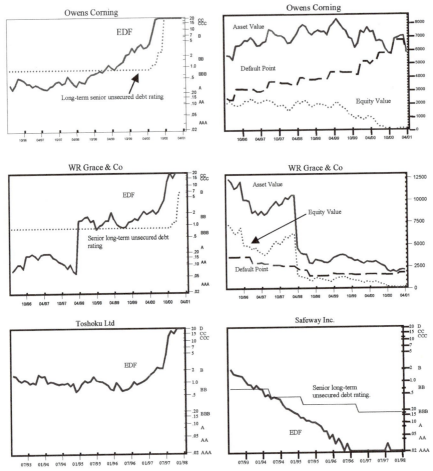

FIGURE 14.13 Owens Corning, an American Construction Materials company, failed in November 2000; the equity value of WR Grace, a U.S. Chemical products company, dropped significantly in May 1998 and the company failed in October 2000; Toshoku, a Japanese food trading company, failed in December 1997. The equity value of Safeway, a U.S. food retailer, increased by $12.5 bn over the years 1994 to 1997, while its liabilities increased by only $1.5 bn

How Well Does the Model Work on Financial Institutions?

The credit risk of financial institutions is notoriously difficult to assess. Financial institutions are typically very opaque and thus judging the quality of their assets and determining the extent of their liabilities is almost always very difficult. In

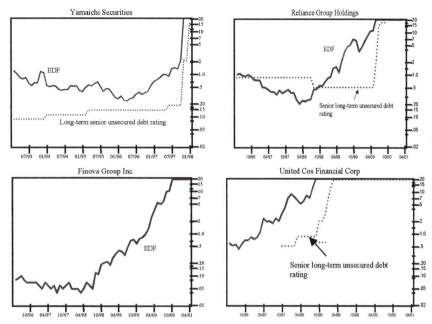

FIGURE 14.14   Yamaichi Securities defaulted during November 1997 and Reliance Group Holdings, the property and casualty insurance company, has been in default on its payment obligations since November 2000; Finova Group Inc., the financial services company, filed for Chapter 11 protection in March 2001; United Companies Financial Group, the mortgage banker and loan company, filed for bankruptcy in March 1999

addition, the liquidity of their assets means that their true size is sometimes difficult to judge. The window dressing of balance sheets at reporting dates is commonplace.

The equity market is well aware of these issues and no doubt does better than most at sorting them out. In addition, we are fortunate that EDF values are relatively robust to the understatement of a firm's liabilities (see our earlier discussion on this issue). However, it is undoubtedly true that many financial institutions stretch this property of the model to its limits. In addition to these challenges, most financial institutions are tightly regulated and thus the appropriate definition of default may not be the point when their asset value falls below their liabilities. Unfortunately, there are very few financial institution that default, and thus testing and calibrating the model on just financial institutions is difficult.

Overall, despite these challenges we believe that the model performs very well on financial institutions, certainly better than any alternative approach that we know of. The lack of actual defaults means it is difficult for us to determine if the level of the EDF value is as precise as it is for commercial and industrial firms, but the anecdotal evidence is clear; the model provides a timely and reliable early warning of financial difficulty (see Figure 14.14).

How Does This Apply to Firms That Do Not Have Publicly Traded Equity?

One of the themes of this chapter has been that the equity value of the firm conveys a considerable amount of information regarding the firm's credit quality. When this information is not available, we are forced to fall back on peer comparisons to determine the asset value and asset volatility. We do this analysis in a companion product to Credit Monitor (CM) called the Private Firm Analyst™ (PFA). CM enabled with PFA provides the tools for calculating and analyzing an EDF value for firms without publicly traded equity. These EDF values are calculated using KMV's Private Firm Model™ (PFM).[7]

PFM uses a similar framework to the VK model except that the asset value and asset volatility are estimated using financial statement data and industry and country comparables. The estimation of the asset volatility is relatively straightforward. As we have seen, size, industry and country can explain asset volatility quite well. Estimating the asset value is much more challenging. PFM uses a broad set of comparables and essentially determines an appropriate EBITDA multiple.[8] That is, given the set of comparables, what is a reasonable multiple to apply to the private firm's EBITDA to determine its asset value?

In spite of the obvious challenges that the absence of market data poses, overall the PFM does rather well. For example, in Figure 14.15 we plot the EDF values from CM and PFM along with the senior unsecured debt rating for two public firms: Marvel Entertainment, a U.S. publishing company that defaulted in December of 1996, and Ben Franklin Retail Stores, a U.S. retail company that defaulted in July 1997. As you would expect, at any one point in time, the correspondence between the public and private EDF credit measures is far from perfect. However, longitudinally the correspondence can be quite remarkable as it is in both of these cases.

PFM's performance on truly private companies has been tested extensively in the United States and efforts are underway to extend this testing to Europe and Asia. There are some sectors in which the PFM does not do well at all. Most notably, it cannot be used on financial institutions. The operating cash flow for these firms is a very poor indicator of asset value.

The public market comparables tie the PFM's EDF credit measure into the credit cycle. That is, because the EBITDA multiples adjust to reflect the current

---

[7] The PFM is discussed more fully in other publications available from KMV.

[8] We use EBITDA, earnings before interest, taxes, depreciation, and amortization, as a proxy for the firm's free cash flow.

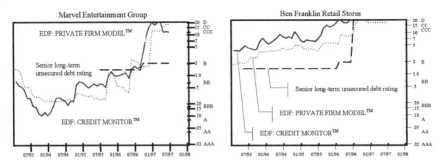

FIGURE 14.15   Private Firm Model Plotting EDF

market conditions and outlook, the EDF credit measures from the PFM change over time, even if the financial statements of the firm remain stable. This is obviously a key property of the model and, within the limitations of financial statement data, keeps the EDF values as forward looking as possible (see Figure 14.16 for another example).

TESTING THE DEFAULT MEASURE'S PERFORMANCE

Determining the performance of a default measure is both a theoretical and an empirical problem. For example, what exactly do we mean by performance or predictive power? In practice, we can only hope to estimate probabilities of

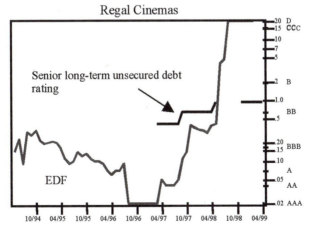

FIGURE 14.16   Regal Cinemas, a U.S. motion pictures company, went private in May 1998 after a leveraged buyout; the Private Firm Model ® EDF credit measure on the LBO debt came out at 20% in August 1998; Regal Cinemas defaulted in September 2000

default. That is, we will not be able to definitively classify firms into *will default* and *will not default* categories. As a result, in assessing the performance of a model, we face the task of assessing its ability to discriminate between different levels of default risk.

For example, consider the policy of never lending to firms with an EDF value greater than 2%, around a B rating. The benefit of this policy is that we avoid lending to firms that have a relatively high probability of default and thus avoid lending to a lot of firms that do eventually default. The cost of this policy is that we do not lend to any firms below a B rating and many of these firms, about 98%, do not default. Thus, one measure of a model's performance is the trade-off between the defaulting firms we avoid lending to and the proportion of firms we exclude. This trade-off is commonly called the power curve of a model.

For example, in Figure 14.17 we plot the power curves for EDF credit measures and the senior unsecured debt rating from a major bond rating agency. The cutoff points for the population are plotted along the horizontal axis and the proportion of defaults excluded at each cutoff point is plotted on the vertical axis. If we rank all firms by their EDF credit measures and impose a cutoff at the bottom 10%, then we avoid lending to 73% of the defaulting firms. That is, by not lending to the bottom 10% as ranked by the EDF credit measure, we can avoid 73% of all defaulting firms. At a cutoff of 30% we are able to avoid lending to 97% of defaulting firms and, of course, if we do not lend to anybody, a cutoff of 100%, we avoid lending to all of the defaulting firms. Thus, for a given cutoff, the larger the proportion of defaults that are excluded, the more powerful is the model's ability to discriminate high-default-risk firms from low-default-risk firms.

The overall default rate, and thus the default probability of firms, varies considerably over time. Figure 14.18 plots the default history for the United States from 1973 through 2001. The chart shows that as a general rule of thumb we can

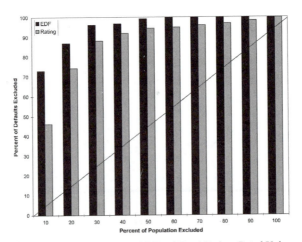

FIGURE 14.17   Default Predictive Power EDF and Bond Ratings Rated Universe

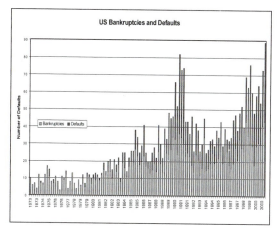

FIGURE 14.18   U.S. Bankruptcies and Defaults

expect the default rate to double or triple between the high and low of the credit cycle. Thus, an effective measure of default risk cannot average default rates over time; instead, it must reflect the changes in default risk over time. Because KMV's EDF credit measure incorporates asset values based on information from the equity market, it naturally reflects the credit cycle in a forward-looking manner. For example, Figure 14.19 shows the median EDF value for US A, BBB, BB, and B-rated firms from April 1996 through April 2001, and Figure 14.20 shows the EDF value quartiles for financial institutions in Thailand and Korea from February 1993 through January 1997.

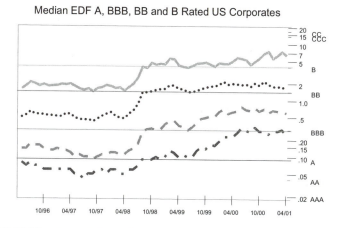

FIGURE 14.19   Median EDF A, BBB, BB, and B-Rated U.S. Corporates

Thai Financial Institutions

Korean Financial Institutions

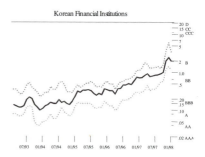

FIGURE 14.20   EDF Value Quartiles

At the individual firm level, the model's ability to reflect the current credit risk of a firm can be assessed by observing the change in the EDF value of a firm as it approaches default. Figure 14.21 plots the medians and quartiles of the EDF values for five years prior to the dates of default for rated companies. Default dates are aligned to the right such that the time moving to the left indicates years prior to default. EDF values are plotted along the vertical axis. The level of EDF values is sloping upward, toward increasing levels of default risk, as the date of default draws closer. Moreover, the slope increases as the date of default approaches.

Five years prior to default, the median EDF value of defaulting companies is approximately 1%, around BB. One year prior to default the median has increased to over 6%. During the time of this sample, the median EDF value for

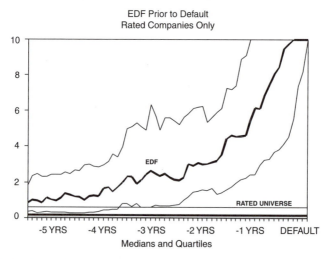

EDF Prior to Default
Rated Companies Only

FIGURE 14.21   EDF Prior to Default: Rated Companies Only

all rated companies, both default and nondefault, was around 0.16%. (The median and percentiles for the rated universe are the straight lines running parallel to the horizontal axis at the bottom of the chart.) Two years prior to default, the lower quartile of EDF values (the riskiest 25%) of the defaulting firms breaks through the upper quartile of the rated universe (the safest 25% as measured by the rating agency). Thus, two full years prior to default 75% of the defaulting firms had EDF values in the bottom quartile of the universe.

There is no single measure of performance for default measures such as KMV's EDF credit measure. Performance must be measured along several dimensions, including discrimination power, ability to adjust to the credit cycle, and ability to quickly reflect any deterioration in credit quality. The EDF value generated from the equity market and financial statement information of a firm does all of these things well. The dynamics of the EDF credit measure come mostly from the dynamics of the equity value. It is simply very hard to hold the equity price of a firm up as it heads toward default. The ability to discriminate between high and low default risks comes from the distance-to-default ratio. This key ratio compares the firm's net worth to its volatility and thus embodies all of the key elements of default risk. Moreover, because the net worth is based on values from the equity market, it is both a timely and a superior estimate of the firm's value.

SUMMARY AND DISCUSSION

A three-step process is used to calculate KMV's EDF™ credit measure:

1. Estimate the market value and volatility of the firm's assets.

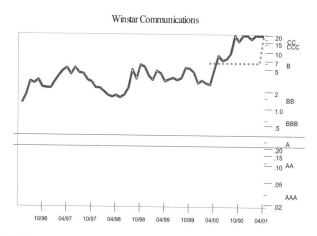

FIGURE 14.22 Winstar Communications

2. Calculate the distance-to-default, the number of standard deviations the firm is away from default.

3. Scale the distance-to-default to an expected default frequency (EDF) using an empirical default distribution.

Because EDF credit measures are based on market prices they are forward looking and reflect the current position in the credit cycle. They are a timely and reliable measure of credit quality. As a final example of the forward-looking strength of EDF values, Figure 14.22 shows the EDF for Winstar Communications, which filed for bankruptcy in April of 2001. (Winstar Communications was presented in our first example, Figure 14.1.) The first sign of a serious deterioration in the credit quality is in August 1998 when the EDF jumps from 1.7% to 2.3% (BB to B). The EDF value climbed as high as 6% in October 1998, recovering a little as Winstar secured additional financing before finally reaching 20% (D) in September 2000, eight months prior to filing for bankruptcy.

EDF credit measures are an effective tool in any institution's credit process. Accurate and timely information from the equity market provides a continuous credit monitoring process that is difficult and expensive to duplicate using traditional credit analysis. Annual reviews and other traditional credit processes cannot maintain the same degree of vigilance that EDF values calculated on a monthly or a daily basis can provide. Continuous monitoring is the only effective early warning protection against deteriorating credit quality. EDF values are also often used to help focus the efforts of traditional credit processes. They provide a cost-effective method to screen credits quickly and to focus credit analysis where it can add the most value. Further, because EDF values are real probabilities, they are the key data items in many institutions' provisioning, valuation, and performance measurement calculations.

15

CREDIT DERIVATIVES

New Instruments to Trade Credit Risk

Credit derivatives are similar to other derivatives that transfer risk between parties; the difference is that credit derivatives transfer credit risk rather than price or interest rate risk. These contracts permit, say, a small bank to separate or allocate risk tied to specific debt structures and transfer that exposure to an investor or a larger bank better equipped to manage or absorb that risk. For example, a Midwest bank located in the farm belt has explicit portfolio risk that is highly correlated to macroeconomic sensitivities and adverse climactic changes. It is nigh impossible to diversify portfolio risk with dissimilar loans made in its geographic region. From the perspective of the bank, risk repositioning adds value when the opportunity cost of managing a concentrated portfolio exceeds the cost of hedging it. If the guarantor investor or bank can hold the risk position at a cost lower than the cost of spreads paid by the risk-transferring institution associated with a higher perception of risk, the contract adds value on the other end. There are two winners here and no losers.

To see this a little more in perspective, the agriculture bank holding the original position has three alternatives: (1) the bankers can continue to maintain the loan facility in-house, taking a loss provision on the expected loss and allocating capital on the unexpected loss portion; (2) the bank can work out a loan sale for a full or partial amount, absorbing costs associated with negotiating the loan sale; and (3) it can hedge fully or partially against loss by structuring a credit derivative. In choosing the optimal strategy, the bank will likely use a risk-adjusted measure and may well find the least-cost, highest return course is the credit derivative.

Credit derivatives are often more efficient than direct loan sales because some investors not active in the loan sales market are more willing to acquire credit derivatives. "Offloading" credit in the credit derivative market is less visible to the borrower and to other competing banks, and it imposes fewer administrative obligations on the selling bank than loan sales (in which participants typically require the selling bank to pass on information from the borrower and obtain consent of the participants to amendments to the credit documents).

Credit derivatives can lower exposures within industry or macroeconomic concentrations or to large borrowers since the contracts offer an alternative to traditional methods of distribution such as assignments and participations. Unlike an assignment, however, the protection guarantor (derivative buyer) retains the reference obligation if the contract is structured as a default swap. The protection guarantor may use a default swap to avoid selling the reference security for relationship, tax, accounting, or regulatory purposes or simply because it is the least expensive option.

As the exposure, but not the asset itself, is sold, credit derivatives help bank protection buyers manage internal limits while maintaining client goodwill. Some bank customers are sensitive to having their obligations sold off.

Like other financial contracts, such as interest-rate contracts or currency contracts, credit derivatives come in various types and forms and may include forwards, swaps, and options. In that regard, the innovative character of credit derivatives primarily lies in the choice of the underlying index rather than in the formal characteristics of the contracts traded.

Credit derivatives allow banks to generate income where direct lending opportunities are not available. For example, consider a Midwest bank with particular expertise in exposures to furniture makers. The bank has relationships with all creditworthy furniture makers in location A. As a part of its industry underwriting, the bank also follows a number of attractive location B firms. However, the bank does not have the ability to lend directly to these companies due to its restrictive regional calling effort. By selling protection in the default swap market, the bank can gain exposure to these out-of-market firms quickly and efficiently.

One of the most appealing applications of default credit derivatives deals with the loan book portfolio. Banks are continuously repositioning loan portfolios along the efficient frontier, strategizing the risk-return profile. In other words, banks analyze direct and indirect exposures globally to assess the economic capital at risk against returns associated with portfolio exposures. When viewed in this way, most loan books do not represent an optimal portfolio because of industry, geographic, or credit quality concentrations. Banks naturally develop expertise in particular target markets and, therefore, do not always have the ability to originate a truly diversified mix of assets.

The resulting concentrations leave many banks overexposed to particular economic sectors. However, the advent of credit derivatives allows these same banks to efficiently alter their portfolio without undermining client relationships. For example, like agriculture exposures considered earlier, take the case of a Long Island midsized bank with heavy concentrations in service industry and apparel loans and a Massachusetts bank with large concentrations in technical industry exposures. The two agree to swap certain positions to improve the mix in their respective portfolios, opting to contract a low-cost portfolio default swap whereby they trade an amount of similar risk (covariance) assets at offsetting premiums.

In a further example, a bank may commit to large shares in new credits or approve deals to older relationships and then "hedge down" shares in each newly approved facility, reducing credit exposure and altering capital allocations associated with specific exposures. Moreover, small community banks or those with higher funding costs can employ credit swaps to purchase exposures at more attractive spreads than might be available if loans were approved directly. Other exposure purchases are nonbank institutions, investment funds, and some insurance companies who act as counterparties to credit derivative transactions with banks. These institutions either do not lend, are unwilling to absorb pickup ancillary costs, or lack the means to administer loan portfolios. As a result, these investors gain access to traditional loan markets previously unavailable.

CREDIT EVENTS

Credit events represent the nuclei of almost all credit derivatives. Credit derivatives are generally structured so that a payout only occurs when a predefined event of default or credit downgrade takes place. Other contracts may require payment when a predetermined loss threshold is breached. Default payments may be based on an average of dealer prices for the reference asset during some time period after default using prespecified sampling procedures or a set percentage of the notional amount of the reference asset. One problem may arise if durations or terms do not coincide—that is, the guarantee may be shorter than maturities of underlying assets, creating a gap in protection to beneficiaries. Credit events are typically defined to include a material default, bankruptcy, or debt restructuring for a specified reference asset. If such a credit event occurs, the guarantor (protection seller) makes a payment to the beneficiary (protection buyer) and the swap then terminates. The size of the payment is usually linked to the decline in the reference asset's market value following the credit event.

Some transactions provide for only two credit events: *a payment default on a reference credit or an insolvency of the obligor on a reference credit.* While these credit events are simple and relatively easy to verify, other transactions include a list of a half dozen or more credit events. These range from a credit rating downgrade to a default by the same obligor on a different credit (a "cross default") to the restructuring of the agreements relating to the reference credit. While this expanded set of credit events may provide greater protection to the "beneficiary" of a credit default product, the occurrence of these events may be difficult to verify, and the description of the events in the agreement is often vague and may require subjective judgments (i.e., did the restructuring have a material adverse effect on the credit?)

MATERIALITY REQUIREMENT

If a materiality requirement is part and parcel to the contract, two events must occur before a payment is triggered: (1) a credit event and (2) a significant change in the price of the reference security. The logic behind a materiality requirement is that a "technical" default by the reference entity, which does not alter the value of the reference security, should not trigger the default swap. The most common materiality requirement is spread materiality. If spread materiality is specified, then the spread between the reference security's yield and the interpolated swap rate must increase by some predetermined amount, for example, 250 basis points, before the default swap is triggered.

MARKET GROWTH

The credit derivative market is rapidly evolving and has grown 50-fold since the end of 1996 (Figure 15.1). The expansion is due to an increasingly broader understanding of the product along with growing interest from bank portfolio managers and the investment community. In addition, reduced transaction costs and improved methods in quantifying and managing credit risk have helped, along with a vast improvement in structures. For example, recently a market developed for put options on specific corporate bonds or loans. While the payoffs of these puts are expressed in terms of a strike price, rather than a default event, if the strike price is sufficiently high, credit risk effectively is transferred from the buyer of the put to the writer.

During the early stages of this product's life, contract negotiation was often a tedious affair due to the lack of general acceptance or, alas, rudimentary understanding of many features including the lack of standardized documentation, pricing characteristics, and the unique terms of reference assets. As the market broadened, the negotiation process improved. Unlike traditional guarantees, credit derivative transactions are structured and documented with master agreements similar to those governing traditional swaps or options. The International

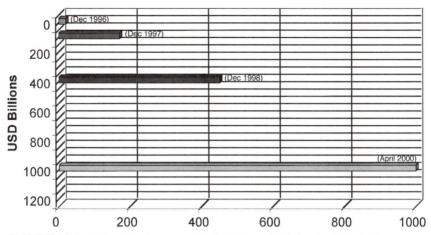

FIGURE 15.1   Volume Development in Nominal Values of Existing Credit Derivatives

Swaps and Derivatives Association (ISDA) has been instrumental in developing credit derivative agreements, which are now used internationally.

ISDA DOCUMENTATION

The ISDA published the first standardized confirmation for credit derivative transactions. The ISDA confirmation is a long-form confirmation that provides a menu of choices for parties to use in structuring credit default derivatives. For instance, parties may use any or all of the credit events listed in the document, select physical or cash settlement, and incorporate concepts such as materiality, payment default thresholds, and the need for publicly available information. The ISDA confirmation may be used with an ISDA master agreement or by itself as a separate, stand-alone contract. In any case, the 1999 ISDA master agreement is recognized as the central precondition for development of the market. (The CD includes an earlier version of the ISDA multicurrency and Cross Border Master agreement with permission to publish. The 1999 agreement can be obtained at the ISDA Web site, www.ISDA.org for a small charge.) The agreement and its contract specifications currently form part or all of almost all credit derivatives contracts. ISDA standards provide criteria that trigger credit default events, including bankruptcy, obligation default, failure to pay, repudiation/moratorium, and restructuring.

In addition, there are at least two Internet trading platforms for credit derivatives: CreditTrade (www.credittrade.com) and Creditex (www.creditex.com). These sites bring some transparency to the credit derivatives market. In addition, the European Credit Swap Index, launched in March 2000 by J.P. Morgan, tracks default-swap premiums on about 100 European corporations. In April 2000, Standard and Poor's launched a series of U.S. corporate credit-spread indexes that could form the basis for a more generic and useful style of credit spread put option.

At the heart of the ISDA confirmation are the following four terms:

- *Reference entity.* The entity against which credit protection is sold (the corporate bank loan or a high-yield bond).
- *Obligation.* Defines the scope of the *reference entity's* obligations covered by a credit event. An obligation can be defined narrowly (e.g., obligations under a specified corporate bond issued by the reference entity) or broadly (e.g., any obligations of a reference entity for the payment of money).
- *Credit event.* An event occurring with respect to the *reference entity* that calls into question its creditworthiness. A credit event can either occur with respect to the reference entity or with respect to an obligation of the reference entity (which may or may not be a specified reference obligation).
- *Reference obligation.* An obligation of the reference entity used for determining the cash settlement amount in connection with a cash-settled trade.

The methods used to determine the amount of the payment triggered by the occurrence of a credit event vary by transaction. For a cash-settled credit swap transaction, the cash settlement amount may be based on the difference between a specified value of a reference obligation and the market value of the reference obligation at the time of settlement, or it may be a predetermined fixed amount. In calculating the market value of the reference obligation for cash settlement, the parties may specify one of a number of valuation methods, such as dealer quotations on a single day (market) or an average over some period (average market), and they must also elect a quotation method (bid, offer, midmarket).

For a physically settled credit-swap transaction, parties may have the buyer deliver to the seller either the reference obligation in a specified principal amount or any deliverable obligations in a specified principal amount. The definition of *deliverable obligations* often includes a wide range of obligations, including allegations under derivatives contracts.

Due to the subjective nature of some credit events, whether or not a credit event has actually occurred may be controversial. The ISDA document incorporates the concept of publicly available information and the concept of materiality to address that challenge.

To avoid disputes in certain circumstances and to limit payment to true credit events, the ISDA confirmation permits the parties to require that the public have knowledge of the applicable credit event. The optional condition of publicly available information contained in the ISDA confirmation requires that information describing the credit event must be published by a specified number of internationally recognized news sources. However, it does not require that a party be identified as the sole source of the information reported. Also, the information does not need to prove the existence of the credit event; it only needs to be a reasonable indication that a credit event has occurred. This concept may also help to eliminate difficult issues with respect to the disclosure of confidential, nonpublic information.

The ISDA confirmation also includes materiality as an optional condition. This allows the parties to require that, in addition to the occurrence of a credit event, there has been *a significant drop in the price of a reference obligation (price materiality) or a significant widening of the spread applicable to a reference obligation (spread materiality)*. The materiality concept protects parties to an ISDA confirmation against nominal defaults that inadvertently may have caused a credit event or interest rate effects on the reference obligation(s).

PRICING CREDIT DERIVATIVES AND THE REFERENCED CREDIT

Most bonds and widely syndicated loans enjoy a recognized market whereby quotations are readily available. Brokers provide quotes and vendors offer prices for numerous bonds and loans. However, for many loans or privately placed debt issues, no active, transparent market exist, though benchmarks are often structured for similar firms with public issues. These comparatives may not be perfect—events of default may differ along with terms, tenors, and credit structures (senior versus subordinated, secured versus unsecured, medium term versus long term). In any case, pricing credit derivatives are driven by the credit profile of the reference entity. The lower the credit quality and rating of the reference security, the higher the price. Many credit derivative dealers and some software vendors have developed quantitative pricing models; however, no widely accepted method exists.

Valuation providers such as the market quotation method under an ISDA master agreement rely on price quotations from dealers or a calculation agent in the credit derivative market. Agreements ensure—either as primary valuation methods or as a firewall if dealer price quotations are unavailable—that the calculation agent will value the reference credit. Note that if the calculation agent is the counterparty—that is, a dealer in credit derivatives—the nondealer counterparty should seek some protection against an unfavorable valuation by the calculation agent.

For example, the agreement could prescribe the method that the calculation agent should use to value the asset when dealer quotations are not available or are not used. The dealer price is generally determined either by referring to a market quotation source or by polling a group of dealers and reflects *changes in the credit profile of the reference obligor and reference asset*. If it is not feasible to specify the method of valuation such as default probabilities or option pricing, an alternative might be to require the calculation agent to use a time-honored method of valuing this class of the referenced credit and to provide a detailed report outlining the valuation methodology, which should include formulas, assumptions, and models. If periodic valuations are required in the agreement, the language should make it clear: valuation methods should at least be consistent over the duration of the contract.

CREDIT DERIVATIVES: BASIC STRUCTURES

Loan Portfolio Swap

Commercial banks use these swaps to diversify loan exposures. Bank A lends mostly to midsized apparel producers, while bank B lends primarily to small-cap technology companies. Bank A and bank B agree to swap with each other payments received on a basket of each bank's exposures, thereby diversifying the industry concentration risk and optimizing the return/volatility matrix of their respective loan portfolios. Loan portfolio swaps effectively trade risks and returns from one basket of credits for risks and returns from another basket of credits.

Total Rate-of-Return Swap

In this case, two parties enter an agreement whereby they swap periodic payments over the agreement's life. One party makes payments based on the total return (coupons plus capital gains or losses) of a specified reference asset. The second party makes fixed or floating payments much like a vanilla interest rate swap. Both parties' payments are based on the same notional amount. Recall, the reference asset can be almost any asset, index, or basket of assets. The beneficiary pays the total return on a reference asset, including *appreciation* in the asset's value, to a guarantor in exchange for a spread over funding costs plus *depreciation* in value and thus the protection.

Example: Total Rate-of-Return (TROR) Swap

In a total rate-of-return (TROR) swap, illustrated in Figure 15.2, the beneficiary (bank A) agrees to pay the guarantor (bank B) the "total return" on the reference asset, which consists of all contractual payments, as well as any appreciation in the market value of the reference asset. To complete the swap arrangement, the guarantor agrees to pay LIBOR (London Interbank Offered Rate) plus a spread and any depreciation to the beneficiary. The guarantor in a TROR swap could be viewed as having *synthetic* ownership of the reference asset since it bears the risks and rewards of ownership over the term of the swap.

The protection seller not only assumes credit risk, but also receives a risk premium for bearing the risk. The greater the credit risk, the higher the risk premium.

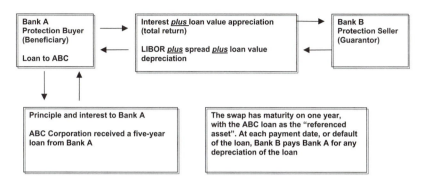

FIGURE 15.2 Total Rate-of-Return Swap

At each payment exchange date (including when the derivative matures), or upon a specified credit event, like default, the contract may terminate. Any depreciation or appreciation in the amortized value of the reference asset, in this case a loan, is calculated as the difference between the notional principal balance of the reference asset and the dealer price.

If the dealer price is less than the notional amount (i.e., the hypothetical original price of the reference asset) of the contract, then the guarantor must pay the difference to the beneficiary, absorbing any loss caused by a decline in the credit quality of the reference asset. Thus, a TROR swap differs from a standard direct credit substitute in that the guarantor is guaranteeing not only against default of the reference obligor, but also against a deterioration in that obligor's credit quality, which can occur even if there is no default.

Credit Default Swaps

The purpose of a credit default swap, as its name suggests, is to provide protection against credit losses associated with a default on a specified reference asset. The swap purchaser (i.e., the beneficiary) "swaps" the credit risk with the provider of the swap (i.e., the guarantor). While the transaction is called a "swap," it is very similar to a guarantee or financial standby letter of credit. *The fundamental difference between a credit default swap and a total return swap is the fact that the credit default swap provides protection against specific credit events.* The total return swap provides protection against loss of value irrespective of cause, for example, a default, market sentiment causing credit spreads to widen, or a formal application of valuation pricing and default risk models.

Basically, two parties enter into an agreement whereby the protection buyer pays the protection seller a fixed periodic coupon for the specified life of the agreement. The protection seller makes no payments unless a specified credit event occurs.

Since credit default options and swaps are generally viewed as the functional equivalent of a credit guarantee, they can have considerable regulatory significance. For example, suppose party A pays party B a fixed premium (in a lump sum or periodic payments) for the right to receive a payment from party B if, at any time during the next year, a specified event (a "credit event"), such as a default, occurs on the reference credit. If a credit event occurs and the value of the reference credit declines below a threshold, party B pays the difference between the principal amount of the credit and its market value and another amount specified in the agreement.

Example: Credit Default Swap

In a credit default swap illustrated in Figure 15.3, the beneficiary (bank A) agrees to pay to the guarantor (bank B) a fee, typically amounting to a certain number of basis points on the par value of the reference asset either quarterly or annually. In return, the guarantor agrees to pay the beneficiary an agreed-upon, market-based, post-default amount or a predetermined fixed percentage of the value of the reference asset if there is a default. The guarantor makes no payment until there is a default. A default is strictly defined in the contract to include, for example, bankruptcy, insolvency, or payment default, and the event of default itself must be publicly verifiable. In some instances, the guarantor is not obliged to make any payments to the beneficiary until a preestablished amount of loss has been exceeded in conjunction with a default event; this is often referred to as a materiality threshold.

The swap is terminated if the reference asset defaults prior to the maturity of the swap. The amount owed by the guarantor is the difference between the reference asset's initial principal (or notional) amount and the actual market value of the defaulted reference asset. The methodology for establishing the post-default market value of the reference asset should be set out in the contract.

Credit-Linked Notes

In its simplest form, a credit-linked note (CLN) is a standard note with an embedded credit default swap. By virtue of the embedded credit default swap, the note has a risk/return profile that depends on the performance of a third-party reference credit in addition to the performance of the issuer of the note. The link to the performance of the reference credit occurs via the redemption value of the note. The note will redeem at par, on a specified date, if the third party has not defaulted. An event of default will cause the note to be redeemed early at the post-default price of the reference credit.

Credit-linked notes are typically issued by a trust or special-purpose entity. While there are various structures, credit risk is generally moved from a bank to the trust using some form of credit derivative. For example, the trust then issues notes, and the total return of the notes is linked to the market value of the underlying pool of debt securities. From the issuer's perspective, credit-linked notes

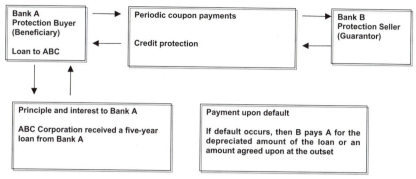

FIGURE 15.3 Credit Default Swap

often are used to reduce regulatory capital. In addition, they provide an efficient way to adjust quickly the credit risk profile of the loan portfolio. From the investor's perspective, credit-linked notes provide access to a pool of securities, often on a leveraged basis, without the need for the investor to buy or sell derivatives directly. As with other derivatives, credit-linked notes can be structured to meet the specific requirements of a particular class of investors.

Example: Credit Linked Note

Citigroup, a major Enron Corporation creditor, hedged its exposure by creating credit-linked securities. The securities provided investors with a steady stream of return. Under prearranged terms and triggers, if Enron could not repay its loans to Citigroup, Citigroup would (1) cease paying returns to investors, (2) take possession of investor's principal and (3) in exchange for principle, transfer Enron debt to investors. The securities, totaling $1.4 billion, were issued from August 2000 to May 2001. The securities covered a large percentage of Citigroup's potential losses from Enron, which filed for bankruptcy protection in December 2001 (Figure 15.4).

In setting up the derivative, Citigroup established paper companies incorporated as trusts. The trusts offered five-year credit linked notes providing investors with a steady stream of fixed payments. In turn, Citigroup invested funds received from investors in government securities and highly rated corporate bonds. If the notes' five-year terms elapsed without incident, Citigroup pledged to return the investor's principles. If Enron went bankrupt, Citigroup would take possession of the highly rated securities and in return hand investors Enron's unsecured debt.

Credit-linked notes are typically the product of a negotiating process involving the sponsors of the trust and potential investors. Investors thought they were

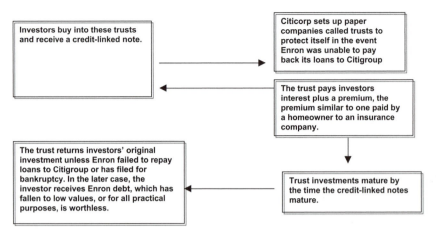

FIGURE 15.4 Credit linked note

realizing a great deal. On the other hand, Citigroup, upon completing its due diligence, was more than willing to pay investors a premium in order to reduce loss exposure on the Enron exposure. The institution's higher risk adjusted return on capital (RAROC) more than offset premiums paid to investors.

Overall Risk Management

For an investor, lender, or issuer, credit derivatives call for risk management policies that combine characteristics of existing procedures likened to standard derivatives, settlements, debt obligations, and other exposures. Overall, risk management policies, in varying degrees, deal with several forms of risk, which are, of course, assuaged by recovery rates (Figure 15.5).

Credit Risk

As we saw earlier, for a lender, the purpose of credit derivatives is to diversity or transfer credit risk; an investor may be seeking to obtain exposure to credit risk to which it does not otherwise have direct access or which it could not fund efficiently as a lender. Assessing credit risk by careful due diligence is an integral part of structuring a credit derivative.

Operational Risk

Are controls in place to ensure that credit derivatives transactions are being used in accordance with established policy? Are positions correctly valued and reported? Many internal controls suggested by regulators and industry groups to limit operational risks arising from derivatives can be adapted to apply equally well to credit derivatives. These include fine-tuning risk management policies to

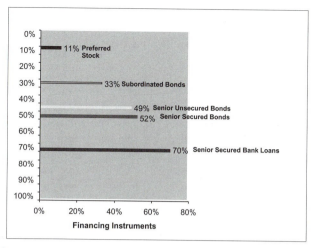

FIGURE 15.5   Recovery Rates

accommodate credit derivatives, developing high-end risk management systems including value-at-risk or simulation/sensitivity analysis, promoting and updating hedging policies, and segregating front-office trading activities and decision making from middle-office risk management and back-office verification and settlement.

Liquidity Risk

Though the market has expanded rapidly, credit derivatives do not yet have the liquidity held by many interest-rate and currency derivatives. In part this is due to unique structures or privately held debt placements and bank loans. This represents a definite risk that should be understood and dealt with when derivatives are structured and monitored afterward; they are likely to be discharged before expiration. Timing also affects the swap's liquidity. For example, a counterparty purchasing an existing credit derivative will likely perform due diligence on the underlying asset. Thus, it may take time or prove arduous to enter into an offsetting derivative or to hedge exposure to a particular credit derivative. Liquidity will likely improve as the market becomes more widespread.

Market Risk

Investors implicitly factor market risk into the structure and pricing of credit derivatives. Market risk management controls should adjust for price risk arising from changes in the value of derivatives, which are naturally affected by the value of underlying bonds or loans. This means end users, dealers, and other investors typically have in place well-fortified policies, procedures, and systems that monitor market exposure. Market exposures usually fall within limits set by senior management or even the board of directors. The problem is credit derivative risk pricing is often more complicated than is pricing for typical derivative products because of limited historical data on correlations between loans of a borrower and more widely traded bonds of the same company.

Basis Risk

A bank that holds a loan or a privately placed security may seek to reduce its risk by entering into a credit derivative in which the reference credit is a widely traded bond of the same obligor. However, the credit risk and trading characteristics of the widely held bond may be different from a loan or privately placed security of the same obligor. In addition, the maturity of a credit derivative may be shorter than the maturity of the credit hedged by the derivative, creating a risk that the derivative cannot be rolled over when it matures or can only be rolled over at a higher cost than the initial derivative. As will be discussed later, mismatches between the default risk of a hedged asset and the default risk of a derivative's reference credit, and between maturities of a hedged asset and the derivative, have posed difficult issues for regulatory authorities. Most credit derivatives entail two sources of credit exposure: one from the reference asset and the other from possible default by the counterparty to the transaction.

Regulartory Concerns

The Federal Reserve Bank has published documentation dealing with management and structures of credit derivatives For internal credit risk management purposes, "banks are encouraged to develop policies to determine how credit derivative activity will be used to manage credit exposures." [1] For example, a bank's internal credit policies may determine when it is appropriate to reduce credit exposures through credit derivative transactions. Policies should address when credit exposure is reduced and how all credit exposures will be monitored, *including those resulting from credit derivative activities*.

In reviewing a credit derivative entered into by a beneficiary banking organization, bank examiners often review several factors:

- The bank's credit exposure to both the guarantor and the beneficiary.
- The referenced asset, if the beneficiary owns the asset.
- The degree by which a credit derivative transfers the credit risk of an underlying asset from the beneficiary to the guarantor (is transfer uncertain or limited?). The degree of risk transference depends on the terms of the transaction.

Bank examiners are usually required to ascertain whether the amount of credit protection a beneficiary receives (by entering into a credit derivative) is sufficient to warrant treatment of the derivative as a guarantee for regulatory cap-

---

[1] Federal Reserve Bank publications, memos, and the *Commercial Bank Examination Manual*.

ital and other supervisory purposes. Those arrangements that provide virtually complete credit protection to the underlying asset will be considered effective guarantees for purposes of asset classification and risk-based capital calculations. On the other hand, if the amount of credit risk transferred by the beneficiary is severely limited or uncertain, then the limited credit protection provided by the derivative should not be taken into account for these purposes.

Some credit derivative transactions provide credit protection for a group or basket of reference assets and call for the guarantor to absorb losses on only the first asset in the group that defaults. Once the first asset in the group defaults, the credit protection for the remaining assets—covered by the credit derivative— ceases. If internal bank auditors or bank examiners determine that the credit risk for the basket of assets has effectively been transferred to the guarantor and the beneficiary banking organization owns all of the reference assets included in the basket, then the beneficiary may assign the asset with the smallest dollar amount in the group—if less than or equal to the notional amount of the credit deriva- tive—to the risk category appropriate to the guarantor. Conversely, a banking organization extending credit protection through a credit derivative on a basket of assets must assign the contract's notional amount of credit exposure to the highest risk category appropriate to the assets in the basket.

According to Federal Reserve Bank documentation,[2] a bank should not enter into credit derivative transactions unless its management has the ability to under- stand and manage the credit and other risks associated with these instruments in a "safe and sound manner." Accordingly, bank examiners are asked to determine the appropriateness of these instruments on an institution-by-institution basis. Such a determination takes into account *management's expertise in evaluating these instruments; the adequacy of relevant policies, including position limits; and the quality of the institution's relevant information systems and internal controls.*[3]

Risk-Based Capital Treatment of Credit Derivatives

For purposes of risk-based regulatory capital, credit derivatives generally are treated as off-balance sheet direct credit substitutes. The notional amount of the contract should be converted at full value to determine the credit equivalent amount to be included among the risk-weighted assets of the guarantor. A bank risk guarantor will generally assign its credit exposure to the risk category appro- priate to the obligor of the reference asset reduced by any collateral.

One major issue is regulatory capital. Loan loss provisions are an important component of Tier 2 regulatory capital. Proponents of the new risk-adjusted methods of managing bank capital such as risk-adjusted return on capital (RAROC) argue that, on a correctly risk-adjusted basis, Tier 2 capital levels

---

[2] Ibid.

[3] Ibid.

should be around 5%. This implies that institutions that currently have excess balances of liquid assets are bearing a large cost for holding these balances. Some banks looking to lower capital costs will favor regulations permitting substitution of credit derivative contracts for loan loss provisioning (which could improve RAROC). Thus far, the more conservative regulatory response has focused on the possibility that banks will use credit derivatives to increase rather than hedge risk.

Whether the credit derivative is considered an eligible guarantee for purposes of risk-based capital depends on the degree of credit protection actually provided. Also, the amount of credit protection actually provided by a credit derivative might be limited depending on the terms of the arrangement. In this regard, for example, a relatively restrictive definition of a default event or a materiality threshold that requires a comparably high percentage of loss to occur before the guarantor is obliged to pay could effectively limit the amount of credit risk actually transferred in the transaction.[4]

If the terms of the credit derivative arrangement significantly limit the degree of risk transference, then the beneficiary bank cannot reduce the risk weight of the "protected" asset to that of the guarantor bank. On the other hand, even if the transfer of credit risk is limited, a banking organization providing limited credit protection through a credit derivative should hold appropriate capital against the underlying exposure while it is exposed to the credit risk of the reference asset.

Banking organizations providing a guarantee through a credit derivative may reduce the credit risk associated with the transaction by entering into an offsetting credit derivative with another counterparty, a so-called back-to-back position. Banks entering into such a position may treat the first credit derivative as guaranteed by the offsetting transaction for risk-based capital purposes. Accordingly, the notional amount of the first credit derivative may be assigned to the risk category appropriate to the counterparty providing credit protection through the offsetting credit derivative arrangement.

In some instances, the reference asset in the credit derivative transaction may not be identical to the underlying asset for which the beneficiary has acquired credit protection. For example, a credit derivative used to offset the credit exposure of a loan to a corporate customer may use a publicly traded corporate bond of the customer as the reference asset, whose credit quality serves as a proxy for the on-balance sheet loan. In such a case, *the underlying asset will still generally be considered guaranteed for capital purposes as long as both the underlying asset and the reference asset are obligations of the same legal entity and have the same level of seniority in bankruptcy.*

In addition, banking organizations offsetting credit exposure in this manner would be obligated to demonstrate to internal auditors and examiners that there

---

[4] Ibid

is a high correlation between the two instruments; the reference instrument is a reasonable and sufficiently liquid proxy for the underlying asset so that the instruments can be reasonably expected to behave in a similar manner in the event of default and, at a minimum, the reference asset and underlying asset are subject to mutual cross-default provisions. A bank using a credit derivative, which is based on a reference asset that differs from the protected underlying asset, will often be required to document the credit derivative being used to off-set credit risk and link it directly to the asset or assets whose credit risk the transaction is designed to offset.

The main point is that the documentation and effectiveness of the credit derivative transaction are subject to audit requirements. Banks providing credit protection through these derivatives must hold capital against the risk exposures that are assumed. When doubtful about risk-based capital allocation, the rule goes, it's best to err on the side of conservatism.

> Until recently, the treatment of credit derivatives under bank capital guidelines was not clear. In SR 96-17, the Federal Reserve Bank clarified the capital treatment of credit derivatives for bank holding companies and state banks that are members of the Federal Reserve System. When it reviews a credit derivative, the FRB views the party that has transferred the credit risk as the "beneficiary" and the party that has assumed this risk as the "guarantor." The guarantor should maintain capital against its exposure to a reference credit in the same manner as if the guarantor had exposure under other off-balance sheet direct credit substitutes. Under FRB risk-based capital guidelines, one hundred percent of the face amount of direct credit substitutes, such as a guarantee, is assigned to the appropriate risk category according to the obligor. Guarantors may also be exposed to credit risk of a counterparty, which generally is measured in a manner similar to that mandated for other derivatives by the FRB's risk-based capital guidelines, i.e., the current exposure (mark-to-market replacement cost) of the transaction plus an estimate of the potential future exposure of the transaction to market price changes.[5]

Another potential downside of credit derivatives, particularly with respect to credit derivatives on bank loans, concerns loan-monitoring incentives. For any given loan, the originating bank is usually in the best position to monitor the ongoing creditworthiness of the borrower. The bank's incentive to perform this monitoring function, however, will be significantly reduced if the bank subsequently purchases credit protection on this loan via a credit derivative. Whereas loan sales and securitizations are structured so that the originator retains monitoring incentives, credit derivatives typically are not.

SHORT EXAMPLES OF CREDIT DERIVATIVES UTILIZATION

1. Bear Stearns focuses its effort on repackaging loans and custom-tailoring transactions for clients. Credit Suisse First Boston links

---

[5] Ibid.

credit derivatives with its asset swap capabilities to generate business. On the other hand, Merrill Lynch, which lumps credit derivatives and most other debt businesses into a huge global credit group, takes the kitchen-sink view: not only do default or total return swaps fall into its credit derivatives bailiwick, but so do asset swaps and collateralized bond and loan transactions.

2. UBS has crafted notes that give investors exposure to pools of emerging market debt from Latin America and Eastern Europe. Investors earn leveraged returns at ratios as high as 10 to 1 in the deals. The UBS deals were ultimately sold to offshore investors.

3. Rabobank issued medium-term notes that carry convertibility trigger events linked to Chile and Brazil. If restrictive currency measures are imposed in those countries, the counterparties to the related transactions must make payments to Rabobank to cover its losses.

4. Merrill Lynch looks for credit derivative applications in its bond underwriting transactions or even in mergers and acquisitions. It has introduced issuers to spread options—puts or calls carrying strike prices at specified credit spreads—which have enabled the company to lock in financing costs at low, prevailing prices for funding it will do several months down the road. Merrill also designed credit-sensitive notes that recently enabled Hilton Hotels to sell $300 million of 10-year notes to investors worried about the balance sheet impact of a possible ITT takeover. The yield adjusts upward if Hilton makes a big acquisition or is downgraded to junk-bond status within three year's time.

5. J.P. Morgan sold $1 billion of credit-linked notes referenced to Wal-Mart and Walt Disney debt. Those two deals, though, involved total return swaps between the issuing trust and Morgan; the dealer will pay interest and principal in exchange for the proceeds but won't be liable to continue those payments should the reference securities default.

According to Joyce Frost, head of marketing, credit derivatives at Chase Securities Inc., banks thinking of using credit derivatives to manage credit risk should evaluate their readiness to use these tools. To do so, bankers can ask themselves the following questions:[6]

- Do you have concentrated credit exposure, either through lending, cash management, or trust business?
- Are your clients sensitive to your reducing credit risk to them through loan assignments?
- Are your cash distribution capabilities limited?
- Are you willing to forgo income, and how much? If you sell off exposure without taking on other exposure, net-interest income will be reduced.

---

[6] "Is Your Bank Ready for Credit Derivatives?" *Commercial Lending Review* **14,** no. 1 (Winter 1998/1999), 1.

- Do you understand the product? Walk through the transaction to make sure you fully understand the structure and documentation.
- Have you explored the system requirements to reflect the reduction or addition of credit risk?

SUMMARY

Credit derivatives have become significant risk-reduction and investment products. They enable bankers to parcel out to outsiders credit risk in all exposure areas including the trading portfolio. Credit derivatives are financial contracts that allow one party (the "beneficiary") to transfer to another party (the "guarantor") the credit risk of a "reference asset" that the beneficiary actually owns. These over-the-counter derivatives enable the guarantor to assume the credit risk associated with the reference asset without directly purchasing it. Credit derivative contracts between protection buyers and sellers arise out of payment obligations of a debt issuer as basis for the derivative. These obligations include bonds, mezzanine securities, loans, or any other forms of debt. Depending on the derivative, the entire spread risk or only the default risk can be transferred to the protection seller.

During the past few years, many of the obstacles to growth in the credit derivatives market have been swept away, and in the near term investors and bankers will see other favorable developments. Dealers, industry groups, and particularly the International Swaps and Derivatives Association have moved swiftly to create standardized documentation that can be applied to new credit derivatives. As documentation continues to be perfected, this will have a positive effect on streamlining the negotiation process, enhancing liquidity, and providing greater certainty regarding regulatory treatment and reducing the concerns of regulators. One reason for the optimistic outlook, particularly pertaining to some unresolved legal and regulatory issues, is that regulatory authorities have come to a (conditionally) favorable view that credit derivatives, if properly used, can contribute to sound credit risk management.

Software products such as J.P. Morgan's CreditMetrics and Credit Suisse Financial Products' CreditRisk+ offer banks the analytical tools to do just that. Various financial industry lobby groups such as the International Swaps & Derivatives Association and the Institute of International Finance are lobbying for these kinds of changes.

REVIEW QUESTIONS

1. What is a credit derivative? Discuss the effect of the use of credit derivatives on a bank's exposures or other macroeconomic factors.

2. Define overall risk management. Given this definition, explain the nuances associated with credit risk? Operational risk? Liquidity risk? Market risk? Basis risk? Should the aspects be considered equal in importance? If not, which would you consider the most important?

3. Describe the five different types of risk associated with risk management. Which are more efficient, credit derivatives or direct loan sales? Why is this the case? Be sure to include in your answer the concepts of administrative obligations and the degree of exposures. Why are both these aspects considered important?

4. What is a credit event? Explain in detail one such event. Include in your answer what generally happens when a credit event occurs with relation to guarantor and beneficiary?

5. Explain the reasons for the rapidly evolving growth of the credit derivatives market since 1996.

6. What is the logic behind a materiality requirement in a credit derivative contract? What two events must occur before a payment is triggered? What is the most common materiality requirement?

7. What is an ISDA confirmation? What four items are at the heart of the ISDA confirmation? How has the ISDA standardized credit derivative transactions?

8. Discuss the different types of credit derivative structures. Compare and contrast total return swaps with credit default swaps?

9. What are two possible downsides of credit derivatives, especially those associated with bank loans? In the same scenario, what would be two possible incentives?

10. What questions should bankers ask themselves before making the decision to use credit derivatives in their loan portfolio?

11. For the purposes of risk-based capital, what would you consider an acceptable degree of credit protection? Give a brief example of a scenario where you might be forced to choose the acceptable degree of risk protection.

SELECTED REFERENCES AND READINGS

Ammann, M. (1999). *Pricing derivative credit risk: Manuel Ammann.* New York: Springer.

An overview of credit derivatives. (1997, July). Harvard Business School (Case study # 9-297-086).

Caouette, J. B., E. I. Altman, and P. Narayanan. (1998). *Managing credit risk: The next great financial challenge.* New York: Wiley.

Das, S. (1998). *Credit derivatives: Trading & management of credit & default risk.* Singapore; New York: Wiley (Asia).

Das, S. (2000). *Credit derivatives and credit linked notes.* New York: Wiley.

Das, S. R., and R. K. Sundaram. (1998). *A direct approach to arbitrage-free pricing of credit derivatives.* Cambridge, MA: National Bureau of Economic Research.

Duffee, G. R., and C. Zhou. (1997). Credit derivatives in banking: Useful tools for managing risk? United States. Board of Governors of the Federal Reserve System. Division of Research and Statistics. *Finance and Economics Discussion Series* **No. 1997-13**, 1–30.

Francis, J. C., J. Frost, and J. G. Whittaker. (1999). *Handbook of credit derivatives.* New York: McGraw-Hill.

Neal, R. S. (1996). Credit derivatives: New financial instruments for controlling credit risk. *Economic Review/Federal Reserve Bank of Kansas City* **81**(2), 15–27.

Nirenberg, D. Z., and S. L. Kopp. (1997). Credit derivatives: Tax treatment of total return swaps, default swaps, and credit-linked notes. *Journal of Taxation* **87**, 82–96.

Parsley, M. (1996). Credit derivatives get cracking. *Euromoney* **323**, 28–34.

Pierides, Y. A. (1997). The pricing of credit risk derivatives. *Journal of Economic Dynamics & Control* **21**, [1579]–1611.

Tavakoli, J. M. (1998). *Credit derivatives: A guide to instruments and applications*. New York: Wiley.

CD INCLUDES

(1) ISDA Multicurrency Cross Border Master Agreement (1992)

(2) The Market Commentary, an invaluable analysis of the credit derivatives market on a worldwide basis.http://www.credittrade.com/

(3) Creditex tradestation, an online credit derivatives trading site. http://www.creditex.com/creditex/ SilverStream/Pages/Index.html

16

AN OVERVIEW OF RISK-ADJUSTED RETURN ON CAPITAL (RAROC) AND CREDITMETRICS

RISK-ADJUSTED RETURN ON CAPITAL (RAROC)

A risk management group at Bankers Trust initiated the risk-adjusted return on capital (RAROC) methodology in the late 1970s. The bank wanted to improve the risk/return tradeoff of exposures and raise to a more desirable level the accuracy of allocating capital against all but extreme loss possibilities—from business and credit risk to operational risk. Building on the value-at-risk (VAR) concept, Bankers Trust's RAROC model locked into the range and diversity of the institution's loss experience.

The aim of RAROC then was to keep the bank "whole" by limiting exposure risk to specified loss probabilities. This was achieved by a capital allocation matching the maximum *potential* loss at a strategically predetermined confidence level after taxes—for example, 99%. RAROC methodology, thus, assessed the transaction's value in equilibrium in a worst-case (unexpected) event.

The model has evolved since its early days. Today RAROC strategy plays an important role in bank risk management, mainly in establishing performance

> Value at risk sets out to calculate on a probabilistic basis with a given degree of confidence the maximum loss that an institution is likely to sustain on its open positions.

targets and allocating capital resources.[1] RAROC systems allocate capital for two reasons: (1) risk management and (2) performance evaluation. For risk-management purposes, one major objective centers around capital allocation directed to individual business units for performance evaluation. The process involves estimating the amount of risk (volatility) each business unit contributes to bankwide risk and, hence, capital requirements. Another way of putting it is that RAROC assigns capital to business units as part of a process to determine the risk-adjusted rate of returns and, ultimately, the economic value added of each business unit.

For example, *business unit RAROC* goals/targets influence annual profit plans helping department managers determine compensation for bank officers assigned to loan centers, branches, and business units. Performance is measured in terms of *both* profits accruing to departments and capital levels required, with results compared to internal and external benchmarks. Because RAROC addresses the magnitude of risks and returns in equilibrium with those risks, the methodology is a big improvement over traditional performance-benchmark ratios like return on equity and return on assets. These two ratios cannot deal with exposures with atypical risk profiles that must be evaluated on an equal footing.

What are the risk measurement criteria of individual transactions and the portfolio the transaction(s) resides in? It's volatility of the return provided by the asset, or the volatility of the asset value itself, or both. The greater the volatility, the more capital is required to cover transactional exposures. The more ancillary capital (equity) required to "protect" exposures, the more cash flow is needed to balance off volatility associated with returns. The denominator of RAROC, allocated capital, is equal to the loan amount, or fractional exposure (in the case of

---

Risk-adjusted return does not tell a bank which transactions to approve or how to price them; it is merely one input among several. Risk-adjusted return on capital allows bankers to be cognizant of the risk associated with their returns while deciding for themselves which transactions to do. By understanding the dynamics of a transaction's risk-adjusted profitability, bankers using this technique can evaluate the extent to which

- the transaction's return exceeds the bank's hurdle rate, or
- other business done with the client justifies pricing below the hurdle rate, or
- potential business justifies pricing below the hurdle rate, or
- there are ways to increase or manage the risk-adjusted return (by altering the transaction itself or using portfolio management techniques).

Source: The Globecon Group, Ltd.

---

[1] As important as the RAROC concept is, it is just one of many inputs lenders use to make decisions.

derivatives), in dollars multiplied by some estimate of the potential (*unexpected*) loss the bank wishes to reserve against. It is noteworthy that *expected* loss, not *unexpected* loss, is tied to a bank's income statement. Knowledge of expected loss helps to determine loan spreads, fees, and loan loss provisions. Expected losses are long-run average losses, the mean of a distribution, whereas with unexpected losses, the tail of a distribution is set at a precise exposure-loss confidence level. See Chapter 13 for a more detailed discussion of expected and unexpected losses.

As the risk of an asset increases, so does the denominator of RAROC. Thus, if two assets have the same return but one is riskier, the RAROC calculation will show that the riskier asset is inferior. As we saw earlier, riskier assets must generate higher returns in order to compare favorably in RAROC terms with more stable assets. By identifying and measuring risk, the decision-making process becomes more structured and consistent, and by recognizing the cost of capital assigned to cushion risk, a bank can relate the expected returns provided by its investment to capital costs required to service it.

Over what time should risks be measured? A bank might use volatility measurements over 5-year or even 10-year intervals, with the aim of capturing "full cycles" in risk. However, it is often not easy to obtain reliable data for extended periods, especially true of rapid growth firms and emerging industries. However, reasonably precise measurements may be possible using implied volatility over shorter periods. In any case, banks try to ensure that risk measures are as timely and forward-looking as possible, so updating risk measures and capital assignments quarterly is often a good idea. In any case, the important input variable is not historical but implied future volatility. By assigning levels of capital based on anticipated future risks rather than on the exposure's historical volatility, RAROC systems allow the lender to appropriately adjust the exposure mix of the credit portfolio and by doing so improve the risk-reward profile of the bank.[2]

In their book *Managing Credit Risk,* Caouette, Altman, and Narayanan offer readers a procedural four-step strategy to arrive at RAROC in a specific example:[3]

1. Analyze the activity or product and determine the basic risk categories it contains.
2. Quantify the risk in each category by a market proxy.
3. Using the historical price movements of the market proxy to compute the RAROC risk factor, *apply calculation 1 as follows:*

RAROC risk factor = 2.33 (weekly volatility) $(52^{1/2})$ $(1 - t)$

Where t = tax rate; $(1 - t)$ yields an after-tax solution

2.33 = standard deviations under a normal distribution representing a 99% confidence level

Square root of 52 annualizes weekly volatility.

---

[2] See Chapters 13 and 14.
[3] Caouette, Altman, and Narayanan, *Managing Credit Risk.* New York: Wiley, 1998.

4. Using the RAROC risk factor (RRF), we can determine the capital allocation required for a given risk category, using calculation 2:

Capital required = RRF (Exposure or position size)

With required capital known, RAROC then is derived as the ratio: profit/capital required. Let's determine risk adjusted return on capital on a foreign exchange position.

Determining RAROC Application: Foreign Exchange Position

Currency Y with Respect to the Dollar

Assume Bank ABC's foreign exchange department's required RAROC on a $5,762,000 foreign exchange position is 28.5%. The position is expected to yield a 1.75% after-tax profit margin. The average change in currency Y: $ is -0.057%. The standard deviation of the average change is 0.58%, which means that on most days the distance to the left of the mean is -0.637% and to the right the distance is 0.523%. The short-term volatility annualizing factor is 7.2111, the square root of 52. A 99% confidence level can be found 2.33 standard deviations from the mean, while 95% confidence is located 2 standard deviations out. The assumed tax rate is 32%. Determine the following:

1. The profit accruing to the position
2. The RAROC risk factor at 99% and 95% confidence
3. The capital required at each confidence level
4. The RAROC at each confidence level

Was profit sufficient to meet the department mandated (required) transaction RAROC at each confidence level? The spreadsheet in Exhibit I solves for the RAROC risk factor. Once the RAROC risk factor is known, Excel finds the solution easily.[4]

EXHIBIT I   ABC Bank Foreign Exchange Department Calculation of Risk Adjusted Return on Capital on Foreign Exchange Trading Exposure ABC

Details	Input	Explanation
Department's required RAROC on exposure Y: Dollar	28.5%	
Foreign exchanged exposure	5,762,000	

---

[4] While the author developed the Excel model, real credit accrues to Caouette, Altman, and Narayanan for their excellent and insightful RAROC risk factor example. The model derived from their example is also included in the CD.

After-tax profit margin on exposure	1.75%	
Average change in currency Y with with respect to the dollar	−0.057%	Mean of normal distribution
Standard deviation of average change	0.580%	
99% confidence level as measured by SD	2.33	2.33 standard deviations beyond mean
95% confidence level as measured by SD	2.00	2.00 standard deviations beyond mean
Range of change: Left of mean	−0.637%	On most days rates changed between −0.057%, −0.58%, and −0.057% + 0.58%
Range of change: Right of mean	0.523%	
Adjustment to annualize	7.2111	Square root of 52
Tax rate	32.0%	

	Output	
Profit	100,835	Profit margin X exposure
RAROC risk factor at 99% confidence: capital allocation sufficient to cover unexpected loss	6.627%	2.33 (weekly volatility) $(52^{\frac{1}{2}})$ $(1-t)$,
RAROC Risk Factor at 95% confidence: capital allocation sufficient to cover unexpected loss	5.688%	2 (weekly volatility) $(52^{\frac{1}{2}})$ $(1-t)$,
Capital required at 99% confidence	381,828	RAROC risk factor at 99% confidence X exposure
Capital required at 95% confidence	327,749	RAROC risk factor at 95% confidence X exposure
RAROC at 99% confidence Was profit sufficient to meet transaction RAROC requirement?	26.4% NO	Profit/Capital required at 99% confidence =IF(B6>B30, "NO," "YES")
RAROC at 95% confidence Was profit sufficient to meet transaction RAROC requirement?	30.8% YES	Profit/Capital required at 95% confidence =IF(B6>B33,"NO," "YES")

Loss Distribution Skewness

In figuring RAROC, the two most important measures of distribution shape are measures of skewness and measures of kurtosis. Skewness describes the lack of symmetry in a loss distribution and kurtosis describes the distribution's peakedness. A loan portfolio's skewness (or that of a single loan) directly relates to the magnitude of required capital. Loan portfolios characterized, for example, by large skewness usually necessitate higher amounts of capital to reduce default probabilities to strategically acceptable levels.

The familiar normal distribution does not fit credit default probabilities. Rather, credit default risks map closer to a beta distribution, as illustrated in

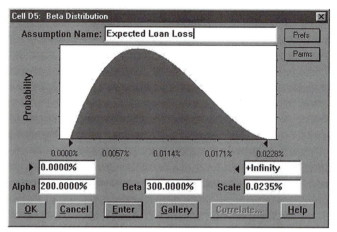

FIGURE 16.1   A Beta Distribution (Source: Decisioneering's CB Pro. Reproduced with permission.)

Figure 16.1. A beta distribution depicts asymmetry associated with a typical loan's payoff structure. In a best-case scenario, a bank is paid in full—principal, fees, and interest. At worse, the loan is written off. If we were to picture a beta distribution of portfolio risk, the loss distribution captures a high probability of low losses but a low probability of heavy charge-offs—for example, hurricanes hitting the Florida Keys, crashes in oil prices, or dot-com bankruptcies wiping out big loan concentrations in that sector. Just how skewed the right tail becomes in a beta distribution is conditional on correlations; on one hand, too many concentrations of correlated credit risk deepen credit risk. Conversely, well-managed portfolios consisting of a sufficient number of negatively correlated (industry or economically sensitive) concentrations reduce risk, as well as the capital required to protect it. Thus, it is not uncommon for banks to reduce RAROC requirements on individual positions if a new loan, for example, "helps" assuage portfolio risk. Figure 16.2 illustrates such an occurrence.

As we see in Figure 16.2, the risk of the portfolio—represented by the cross—is much less than the average of the risks in the portfolio—depicted by dots—because of diversification. Diversification means a large fraction of each individual asset's stand-alone risk does not contribute to portfolio risk but is eliminated, partially or completely, via interaction with the risks of other assets (the argument is that RAROC requirements can conceivably be reduced for a select basket of large individual loans with strong negative covariances). The amount of risk remaining after diversification, the "risk contribution" of the asset, depends on the sizes of holdings in the portfolio. Changing the portfolio changes the risk contributions.

Market risk, in contrast to risks associated with lending, is seldom skewed and is, for the most part, distinguished by a (symmetric) normal distribution, as Figure 16.3 shows.

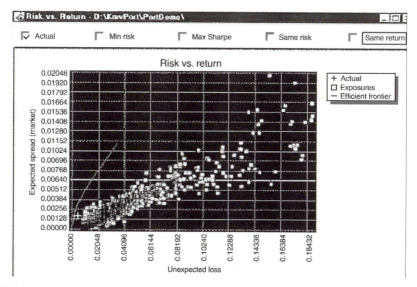

FIGURE 16.2   KMV Risk versus Return (Source: KMV. Reproduced with permission.)

If distributions capturing credit write-offs were to fit into a nonskewed or normal distribution, capital requirements covering a specific level of losses would much reduce. For example, in a normal distribution, the probability of a four standard deviation write-off statistically approaches zero. Not so, given a beta distribution: probabilities of a four standard deviation chance of write-offs increase to an economically significant level necessitating a capital allocation likely to be just as economically significant.

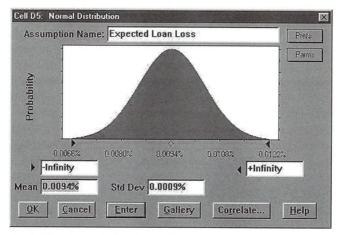

FIGURE 16.3   Normal Distribution: Expected Loan Loss (Source: Decisioneering's CB Pro. Reproduced with permission.)

RAROC 2020

RAROC 2020, a variant of the original model developed by Banker's Trust, uses sensitivity analysis to show how a portfolio is affected by moves in market indexes. The sensitivity function enables users to view a portfolio's profit or loss exposures to a 1% change in market conditions. RAROC 2020 can also create what-if scenarios that show users whether they would profit by changes in market conditions. Based on this and capital risk numbers, a CFO can look at the company's portfolio and determine whether the level of risk is appropriate for his or her organization.

RAROC 2020 helps portfolio managers determine risk/return characteristics of each constituent of their portfolio. The system searches through large databases of historical correlations and volatilities for each of a number of risk characteristics or factors. Drawing on the historical characteristics of risk factors allows RAROC 2020 to describe the risk profile of an asset portfolio, which is then inputted to a simulation model. The result makes it possible to correlate risks to returns, providing a basis for investment, RAROC, and capital allocation decisions between assets within the portfolio.

CREDITMETRICS

CreditMetrics is a set of analytical methods and databases used to measure portfolio value and risk released by J. P. Morgan in April 1997. J. P. Morgan published the model was published as a technical document, and it is currently handled by the RiskMetrics Group, which is also responsible for the software implementation of CreditManager. CreditMetrics is described in a 17-page document. The following overview is based on that document.[5]

CreditMetrics models changes in portfolio value that result from significant credit quality changes. That is, CreditMetrics builds on the notion that asset (loan) or portfolio values are viewed not only on principles of default probabilities, but also in terms of changes in credit quality over periods, of which default is just a special-case credit phenomenon. Starting from its initial risk rating, a loan may end up in one of eight future states, categories, or baskets, each state representing a bond rating to which the exposure may finally migrate. The "basket" an asset can migrate to is described by a transition probability, for example, a transition matrix for the seven bond-rating grades.

CreditMetrics inputs information on individual credits, producing output—the distribution of portfolio values at some future fixed horizon. From this distri-

---

[5] Section 5, CreditMetrics with Contributions from the RiskMetrics Group: A Portfolio Approach to Credit Risk, The J. P. Morgan Guide to Credit Derivatives. The author, a retired member of the JPMorganChase family, is proud, as always, to bear witness to this fine banking institution's innovative contributions to the credit literature. The above reference is just one of many examples of the Institution's contributions.

bution, the model generates statistics, which quantify the portfolio's absolute risk level, such as the standard deviation of value changes or the worst-case loss at a given level of confidence, say 99%, which we reviewed earlier in the opening section of this chapter dealing with RAROC.

While this gives a picture of a portfolio's total risk, risks are analyzed at a finer level by examining the risk contribution of each exposure to the portfolio, identifying concentration risks or diversification opportunities (e.g., loan sales, acquisitions, and securitizations) or evaluating the impact of a potential new exposure. In short, CreditMetrics provides a systematic approach to do the following:

1. Quantify total credit risk—losses associated with credit events
2. Identify risk sources—credit exposures specifically, and how credits are affected by specific and often unanticipated events
3. Investigate risk inflows – correlation of a credit position with respect to a loan portfolio (e.g., incremental risk to the portfolio)
4. Employ risk limits—limiting concentrations
5. Determine capital allocation—protecting the portfolio against unexpected losses by the appropriate capital protection
6. Improve the risk-reward tradeoff—increasing returns at the same level of risk

Being able to quantify the degree of concentration by name, industry, geography, and sector is a powerful methodology. For example, portfolio managers can set credit limits with help from industry specialists offering as criteria industry macroeconomic sensitivities, exposure amount, covariances, and rating, to name a few. As judicious as this may be, in the end, this type of limit is arbitrary.[6]

CreditMetrics calculates marginal risk contributions according to the amount of diversification or concentration that each name brings to the portfolio. It thus offers a more reasoned approach to credit risk limits.[7]

Methodology

Estimating credit value volatilities is not easy; risk-rating migration and defaults occur infrequently (certainly at the higher grade level). Thus, observing bond spreads or prices over a short historical period will probably not capture the workable price volatilities associated with all possible changes in credit quality. To overcome this, CreditMetrics methodology constructs the full process of possible credit quality changes. The methodology is designed as three interlinking parts:[8]

---

[6] Ibid
[7] Ibid
[8] Ibid

1. The definition of the possible "states" for each obligor's credit quality and a description of how likely obligors are to be in any of these states at the horizon date
2. The interaction and correlation between credit migrations of different obligors
3. The revaluation of exposures in all possible credit states

The first step in this process is to obtain a bond rating or risk grade.[9] CreditMetrics determines the probabilities that the obligor migrates to any of the states between now and a future date (horizon). A transition matrix characterizes a rating system by providing probabilities of migration (within a specified horizon) for all of the system's states.

Among the most widely available transition matrices are those produced by the major rating agencies. These matrices depict the average annual transition rates over a long history (typically 20 years or more) for a particular class of corporate bonds, commercial paper, and other debt instruments. The problem is that while agency default rates are benchmarks for describing individual categories, the use of average transition matrices for credit portfolio modeling fails to capture the credit cycle. Since agency matrices only represent averages over a long-term horizon, they fail to account for the current year's credit transitions that might range from mild to highly problematic.

The methodology offers ways to address this—for example, selecting smaller periods of the agency history and creating matrices based, say, on only the transitions in two or three increments. A second way is to explicitly model the relationship between transitions and defaults, and macroeconomic/industry variables, such as spread levels or industrial production. Regardless of the transition matrix ultimately chosen as the "best," users are advised to examine the portfolio under the variety of transition assumptions illustrated in Table 16.1.

Revaluation

While the first step deals with description of the migrations of individual credits, the next step determines the value implied in the exposure's migration. Consider a Baa-rated, three-year, fixed 6% coupon bond, currently valued at par. With a one-year horizon, the revaluation step consists of estimating the bond's value in one year under each possible transition. For the transition to default, CreditMetrics values the bond given an estimate of the likely recovery value.

Many institutions use their own recovery assumptions here, although public information is available. For the nondefault states, CreditMetrics obtains an estimate of a debt instrument's horizon value by utilizing the term structure of bond spreads and risk-free interest rates.

---

[9] We cover this in Chapter 19, "Introduction to Credit Risk Grading."

TABLE 16.1   One-Year Transition Matrix—Moody's Rating System

	Aaa	Aa	A	Baa	Ba	B	Caa	D
Aaa	93.35%	5.94%	64.00%	0.00%	2.00%	0.00%	0.00%	0.02%
Aa	1.61%	90.53%	74.60%	0.26%	9.00%	0.01%	0.00%	0.04%
A	7.00%	2 28%	92.35%	4.63%	0.45%	12.00%	0.01%	0.09%
Baa	5.00%	0.26%	5.51%	88.46%	4.76%	71.00%	0.08%	0.15%
Ba	2.00%	0.05%	0.42%	5.16%	88.48%	5.91%	0.24%	1.29%
B	0.00%	0.40%	0.13%	0.54%	5.16%	84.22%	1.91%	6.81%
Caa	0.00%	0.00%	0.00%	0.62%	0.62%	4.08%	69.19%	24.06%

In the end, users arrive at the values depicted in Table 16.2. With the information in Table 16.2 they have sufficient information on the instrument in the example to calculate the expected value (mean) and standard deviation of the bond's value at the horizon.

Incorporating other variations of exposures is relatively simple, involving defining the values in each possible future rating state of the underlying credit. This amounts to constructing a table similar to Table 16.2. For some exposure types (for example, bonds and loans), building a table calls for a few inputs that are not hard to assign: recovery assumptions and spreads. Other exposure classifications—commitment lines or derivative contracts—require additional information.

TABLE 16.2   Values at Horizon for Three-Year 6% Baa Bond

Rating at horizon	Probability	Accrued coupon	Bond value	Bond plus coupon
Aaa	0.05%	6.0%	100.4	106.4
Aa	0.26%	6.0%	100.3	106.3
A	5.51%	6.0%	100.1	106.1
Baa	88.48%	6.0%	100.0	106.0
Ba	4.76%	6.0%	98.5	104.5
B	0.71%	6.0%	96.2	102.2
Caa	0.08%	6.0%	93.3	99.3
D	0.15%	6.0%	40.1	46.1
		Mean	99.8	105.8
		Standard deviation	2.36	2.36

Building Correlations

The final step is to construct correlations between exposures. Identifying the exposure's risk contribution requires users to come up with an estimate of correlations of credit quality changes between each pair of targeted constituents or names.

Several firms within the same industry often will be downgraded simultaneously owing to systematic events that hit across the board: high fuel costs affecting airlines, poor real estate prices affecting local mortgage lenders, and plant layoffs striking out at retail establishments dependent on local disposable income. But as obvious as the concepts of correlations are, it is difficult to estimate their magnitude statistically with a high precision. CreditMetrics requires users to consider correlations across all possible changes in credit quality. All considered, there are four possible approaches to correlation according to the modelers of CreditMetrics:

1. *Uniform correlation.* Simply set correlations to be equal across all firms. This approach is an improvement over having no portfolio model to start with and can later be used for stress testing.
2. *Bond spread correlations.* Drawing correlations from bond prices were quickly rejected because of the sparse and low-quality data available (for example, matrix prices rather than prices based on actual trades).
3. *Credit rating joint likelihood tables.* Just as the rating agencies have tabulated transition matrices for single names, they can tabulate joint likelihood changes for two names together. New and promising research on this topic should be published in 2002.
4. *Equity price correlations.* For public firms, the relative value of firms and their joint movements in value are readily observable in their stock prices. This information can be summarized by industry and country and then applied to all firms.

CreditMetrics assumes that changes in asset value produce credit migrations, or are at least the main force behind migrations. The approach is both conceptually and intuitively well founded in options theory that presumes that default occurs when the value of a firm's assets falls below the market value of its liabilities. However, CreditMetrics methodology does not use asset information directly to predict defaults:

> The stand-alone information for each name (in particular the name's probability of default) is provided as a model input through the specification of the transition matrix. Rather, assets are used only to build the interaction between obligors.[10]

To begin the construction of correlations, CreditMetrics assumes that asset value changes are normally distributed. The asset change distribution is then par-

---

[10] Section 5, CreditMetrics with Contributions from the RiskMetrics Group referenced above.

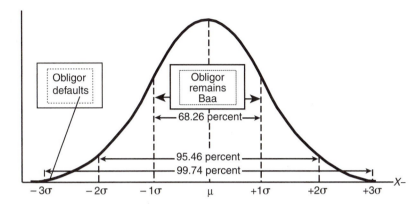

FIGURE 16.4 Partition of Asset Change Distribution for a Baa Obligor

titioned for each name according to the name's transition probabilities. Figure 16.4 describes a Baa-rated obligor with default probability equal to 0.15%. In this example, the default partition (which conceptually can be thought of as the obligor's liability level) is chosen as the point beyond which lies 0.15% probability; the CCC partition is then chosen to match the obligor's probability of migrating to CCC, and so on. The result is illustrated in the following table:

Asset return	< -3.0	-3.0 to 2.8	-2.8 to –2.4	-2.4 to –1.6	-1.6 to 1.5	1.5 to 2.7	2.7 to 3.3	>3.3
New rating	Default	Caa	B	Ba	Baa	A	Aa	Aaa
Value	40.1	93.3	96.2	98.5	100.0	100.1	100.3	100.4

From this framework of individual exposure volatilities and pair-wise correlations, CreditMetrics directly calculates the volatility of individual loans, a segment of the portfolio, or the entire exposure portfolio.

REVIEW QUESTIONS

1. What evidence exists to suggest that RAROC strategy plays an important role in bank risk management.
2. As important as the RAROC concept is, it is just one of many inputs lenders use to make decisions. Discuss fully.
3. Describe the methodology behind CreditMetrics methodology and how CreditMetrics constructs the full process of possible credit quality changes.

SELECTED REFERENCES AND READINGS

Caouette, J. B., E. I. Altman, and P. Narayanan. (1998). *Managing Credit Risk: The Next Great Financial Challenge*, New York: John Wiley & Sons, Inc.

CreditMetrics–Technical Document, Morgan Guaranty Trust Co., New York, ... http://www.bis.org/pub/bcbs49.pdf.

James, C. *RAROC Based Capital Budgeting and Performance Evaluation: A Case Study of Bank Capital Allocation* This paper was presented at the Wharton Financial Institutions Center's conference on "Risk Management in Banking," October 13–15, 1996. #96–40.

McGuire, C. *RAROC on the Rise* Wall Street & Technology; New York; Sep 1999; Volume: 17, Issue: 9, Start Page: 44.

Sesit, M. R. J.P. *Morgan's Risk Analysis Gains Support—Backing May Help Create Standard for Measuring, Managing Credit Risk, Wall Street Journal*; New York; Jun 30, 1997; Edition: Eastern edition; Start Page: A10D.

Shearer, A. T., and R. F. Forest. *Improving Quantification of Risk-Adjusted Performance Within Financial Institutions* Commercial Lending Review; Boston; Summer 1998; Volume: 13 Issue: 3 Start Page: 4857.

Spinner, K. *Value-for-Systems* Wall Street & Technology; New York; Nov 1995; Volume: 13, Issue: 12, Start Page: 31.

Spinner, K. *Measuring Credit Exposures The JP Morgan Way* Wall Street & Technology; New York; Winter 1998; Supplement: Product Digest; Start Page: 16–20.

Taylor, J. *Rethinking the credit-loss distribution: The implications for RAROC modeling* Commercial Lending Review; Boston; Winter 2000/2001; Volume: 16 issue: 1, pg 7–12.

Stoughton, N. M., and J. Zechner. (1999). "Optimal capital allocation using RAROC and EVA." *Centre For Economic Policy Research*. Discussion Paper Series No. 2344: 1–33.

CD

RAROCRiskFactorMain.xls: ABC Bank Foreign Exchange Department: Calculation of Risk Adjusted Return On Capital On Foreign Exchange Trading Exposure ABC

17

GLOBAL EXPOSURE TRACKING SYSTEMS

Application and Design

The risk management process is a part of risk control. The former is responsible for controlling exposure risks. Risk control deals with the policies, procedures, and systems banks require to administer lending areas and ensure that loans fall within preset exposure-risk parameters. A bank's global exposure tracking system (GES) is the epicenter of risk control. Highly interactive and computerized, an exposure data network facilitates loan approvals and provides data for a wide range of credit related operations.

For example, bank managers use exposure systems to set facility limits, shape credit policy, review targets and controls, and make capital allocation, pricing, and portfolio decisions. A GES can be structured around coordinators partitioning into three responsibility units: (1) customer responsibility, (2) family responsibility, and (3) facility responsibility. Data flow begins at the customer (unit) relationship level, combines at the family level (parent and subsidiaries/affiliates), and ends up at the senior coordination level (senior management who set family facility limits).

An effective internal control system requires a major commitment to

- Hire, support and retain employees throughout the management system with appropriate training and background in trading, modeling, information technology and other required skills.
- Invest in global risk-monitoring systems, encompassing both sophisticated risk models and sufficient computer and communications capacity to handle high-volume, high-speed transactions in all their financial and legal complexity.
- Establish a management structure with appropriate checks and balances, between front and back office, for example, and with more direct responsibility to the respective audit committees.
- Adopt a more sophisticated approach to credit risk, operational risks, and management of collateral and related disciplines.

Source: Basel Committee, "Framework for the Evaluation of Internal Control Systems," October 1998.

CUSTOMER RESPONSIBILITY (COORDINATION) UNITS

Customer responsibility begins with relationship bankers. Line officers complete data sheets on new facilities and renewals, including much of the following:

Basic Information

- Name of relationship manager
- Location/division/credit area
- Statements received
- Memo distributed
- Maximum exposure, including derivatives and letter of credit exposures
- Amount of facility requested and facility type
- Outstandings
- Terms
- Last credit committee review including date, committee, and summary

Company Background

- Customer
- Address
- Form of organization
- Date established
- Customer since
- Name and address or parent (if any)
- Name and address of guarantor (if any)
- Industry code (SIC)
- Geographic market area
- Market strategy/niche

- Major competitors
- Industry/economic summary
- Assessment of principal customers, suppliers, and product lines
- Competition
- Problems to which company is most vulnerable
- Fiscal sales and profits—dollar and percentage change from previous year
- Key "payback" ratios—cash flow coverage and leverage
- Management summary
- Principal/officers
- S&P (or similar) debt rating
- Name and address of accountant
- Accounting changes or qualifications
- Fiscal date

Other Information Supporting Facility

- Guarantors (if any)
- Collateral (if any)
- Date previous credit review filed
- Previous risk grade
- Loan pricing
- Risk-adjusted return on capital (RAROC)
- Documentation on file and updated
- Subordination agreements, uniform commercial code filings, etc.
- Total bank lines (dollar amount)
- Lead bank
- Other lenders
- Present rating
- Recommended rating
- Report including Dun and Bradstreet, TRW, and litigation records
- Trade experience

It might be useful at this point to compare data sheets completed by line officers to information requested by regulators during bank examinations. The Federal Reserve established the minimum documentation required on bank examination reports. The following information is normally entered onto computer-based loan review systems:[1]

- Name and location of borrower
- Notation if the borrower is an insider or a related interest of an insider
- Business or occupation

---

[1] Memo to The Officer in Charge of Supervision at Each Federal Reserve Bank: April 24, 1996, Subject: Minimum Documentation Standards for Loan Line Sheets, Richard Spillenkothen, director.

- Loan terms
- Purpose of loan
- Repayment source
- Collateral summary and value
- Loan officer assigned to the credit and internal rating of the credit
- Total commitment and total outstanding balances
- Examination date
- Past due/nonaccrual status
- Amounts previously classified
- Loan disposition (pass, special mention, or adverse classification)
- Rationale for examiner's conclusions (preferably in bullet form)
- Name or initials of the examiner reviewing the credit
- Any significant comments by, or commitments from, management (including management's disagreement with the disposition of the loan, if applicable)
- Any noted documentation exceptions or loan administration policy or procedural weaknesses and any contravention of law, regulation, or policy

FAMILY RESPONSIBILITY (COORDINATION) UNIT

The unit family responsibility area usually located at the main office, pools and decomposes exposures to the family: parent or holding company, subsidiaries, and affiliates. For purposes of establishing an aggregate family, total credit exposure is expressed as (1) *primary* and (2) *settlement*. *Primary* exposures include *direct* exposures and *indirect* exposures; direct exposures are further categorized into *full value* and *replacement* (Figure 17.1).

Primary/Direct/Full Value Exposures

Examples of full value exposures include but are not restricted to, the following:

- *Own paper borrowing.* Short-term unsecured borrowings that do not fall under a line of credit.
- *Lines of credit.* Short-term lines usually established with a bank letter stating the approved advances and maximum amount allowed.
- *Joint credit lines.* The parent, together with each of its subsidiaries, may borrow singly, or collectively, so that the aggregate amount of loans outstanding does not exceed the confirmed line.
- *Overlines.* A line of credit granted to the customer of a correspondent bank.
- *Revolving commitments.* Legally binding obligations to extend credit for which a fee or other compensation is received. The credit risk of

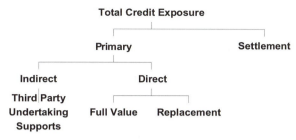

FIGURE 17.1   GES Perspectives: Total Credit Exposure

loan commitments stems from the possibility that the creditworthiness of the customer will deteriorate between the time the commitment is made and the time the loan takedown occurs.

- *Term loans.* Nonrevolving commitments with maturities beyond one year. These loans generally contain periodic (annual, semiannual, or quarterly) amortization provisions.
- *Check or business credit.* Credit services provided by three basic methods: overdraft system, cash reserve system, and special draft system.
- *Commercial letters of credit.*
- *Acceptances.* Exposures arising when letters of credit mature but have not been retired.
- *Discounted Bills or Notes Receivable (B/Rs).* Loans are reduced at the time of each collection and liquidated when all the B/Rs are collected.
- *Construction loans.* Loans to be used for a designated time period for construction projects with repayment contingent on the borrower obtaining permanent financing.
- *Secured loans.* Factoring, loans secured with accounts receivables, inventory, or marketable securities.

Primary/Direct/Replacement Exposures

Replacement exposure (or fractional exposure) represents the unhedged cost of replacing defaulted parties when banks guarantee performance under derivative contracts. In a manner of speaking, replacement exposure represents the maximum loss possible on these contracts. For example, consider a simple (vanilla) interest rate swap. These are two ways of looking at default risk: actual exposure and potential exposure. Actual exposure is the measure of the loss if the counterparty were to default. Actual exposure is based on the movement in swap market rates between the inception of the agreement and the current date. Potential exposure is based on a forecast of how market conditions might change between the present and the swap's maturity date, including in some manner the probability of default by the counterparty. Exposures on derivatives and similar contracts are managed so that they generally net out at day's end.

With traditional instruments, loans typically, the amount the counterparty is obliged to repay is the full or principal amount of the instrument. For these instruments, the amount at risk equals the principal amount. Derivatives are different. Because they derive value from an underlying asset or index, credit risk is not equal to the principal amount of the trade, but rather to the cost of replacing the contract if the counterparty defaults. This replacement value fluctuates over time and is made up of current replacement and potential replacement costs.

It is relatively straightforward to measure current replacement cost. The Basel Committee for Banking Supervision recommends using the current mark-to-market value of the contract. Potential replacement value is not as easy to estimate because it is a function of remaining maturity as well as the expected volatility and price of the underlying asset, both of which can fluctuate a great deal. The Basel Committee recommends multiplying the notional principal of a transaction by an appropriate percentage, which it calls the "add-on," to arrive at a potential replacement value.

Others dealing in derivatives champion Monte Carlo simulation, probability analysis, and option valuation models as the best ways to derive potential replacement cost. Their analysis generally involves modeling the volatility of underlying variables and their effect on the value of the derivative contracts. These methods, drawing on data stored within a GES warehouse (discussed later), can be used to derive average or "expected" exposure and maximum or "worst case" exposure.

Primary/Indirect/Third-Party Undertaking and Supports

Indirect exposures include loans or obligations endorsed, guaranteed, or subject to repurchase agreements. Bank guarantees might be in the form of standby letters of credit or commercial paper backup lines. They may be negotiated to cover performance under construction contracts or serve as assurance that obligations will be honored under warranties.

Total Credit Exposure/Settlements

Settlement risk is the risk that a settlement in a transfer system fails to take place as expected. Three examples of settlement risk are foreign exchange, securities settlements, and over-the-counter derivatives. The risk that transactions cannot be settled can affect almost any type of asset (and instrument) that requires a transfer from one party to another. Settlement risk figures most prominently in currency trading because the daily settlement flows in foreign exchange clearing dwarfs just about any other exposure risk.

The Bank for International Settlements estimates the average daily turnover of global currencies in spot, outright forward, and foreign exchange swap contracts is US $1,230 billion. Since each trade involves two or more payments, daily settlement flows are likely to amount, in aggregate, to a multiple of this figure, especially on standard expiration dates. Significantly, a report prepared by the Committee on Payment and Settlement Systems (CPSS) of the central banks of the G-10 countries maintains that a bank's maximum foreign exchange settlement exposure could equal, or even surpass, the amount receivable for three days' worth of trades, so that at any point in time, the amount at risk to even a single counterparty *could exceed a bank's capital.*

GES AND LOAN CONCENTRATIONS

Loans within the system are grouped so that exposures with similar risk characteristics are combined. Significant and imprudent concentrations can arise in relation to individual borrowers, the family of related borrowers, particular economic or industry sectors, or country and regional exposures. Concentrations involving excessive or undue risks are, for the most part, micromanaged: loans are sold and purchased, credit derivatives negotiated, and so on. For all the right reasons, banks train exposure systems to optimally process and warehouse concentrations data. It is equally important that lenders familiarize themselves with their institution's internal policies, data producing systems, and controls placed to monitor and manage concentrations.

Liquidity Concerns

GES is an integral part of sound funds (liquidity) control, helping to ensure liquidity requirements are monitored continuously. Thus, senior management is apprised of liquidity conditions that enable management to take corrective action under preestablished guidelines.[2]

- Limits on the loan-to-deposit ratio
- Limits on the loan-to-capital ratio
- General limits on the relationship between anticipated funding needs and available sources for meeting those needs (for example, the ratio of anticipated needs/primary sources shall not exceed a certain percentage).
- Quantification of primary sources for meeting funding needs
- Limits on the dependence on individual customers or market segments for funds in liquidity position calculations
- Flexible limits on the minimum/maximum average maturity for different categories of liabilities (for example, the average maturity of

---

[2] Federal Reserve Board.

negotiable certificates of deposit shall not be less than a preordained period)
- Minimum liquidity provision to be maintained to sustain operations while necessary longer-term adjustments are made

Customer Relationship and Marketing

Customer information data banks include outstandings under credit lines, loan high points, fees paid for cash management services, average deposit balances, outstanding letters of credits and acceptances, profitability analyses, and affiliated data such as customers' personal loans and investments. The immediate benefits derived from information systems are obvious to lenders preparing client calls: bank customers are alert to bankers taking time to become familiar with their business. Clients exhort lenders to provide real-time information *accessible on laptops*—not just on loans serviced, but on the aggregate account relationship, often globally. Only a short time ago, lenders had to rifle through paper files or ask colleagues in other departments to obtain customer information.

Loan Exposures and Accounting

The Basel Committee has produced a wealth of literature on this topic, and for good reason. Judicious auditing and reporting policies and practices are preconditions to risk management. From the Basel Committee's perspective, the most common causes of bank failures, by far, are poor credit quality and credit risk management (including auditing and loan valuation standards). "Failure to identify and recognize deterioration in credit quality in a timely manner can aggravate and prolong the problem."[3]

Discern this quote like you might fancy a fine wine:

> Unless deterioration is identified and losses recognized by the establishment of adequate allowances or charge-offs in a timely manner, a bank might well persist in highly risky lending strategies or practices and thus accumulate significant loan losses, possibly resulting in failure. From a safety and soundness perspective, therefore, it is important *that both exposure data gathering capabilities and accounting principles capture and reflect realistic measurements* of assets, liabilities, equity, derivative contracts, off-balance sheet commitments, and related profits and losses. Insufficient disclosure the result of poor exposure information systems increases chances that misleading or wrong information is passed along to senior officials setting exposure limits.[4]

On the contrary, disclosure of reliable information based on sound accounting principles and internal GES strengthens confidence in an institution.

---

[3] The Basel Committee on Bank Supervision.
[4] Ibid.

GES and Disclosure to Outsiders

Banks are, of course, charged with proper disclosure to certain outsiders, mainly regulators and auditors of impaired and past-due loans. Examples of important disclosure include but are not restricted to the following:[5]

- Information dealing with accounting policies and methods used to document loans and allowance for impairment
- Disclosure regarding methods used to determine specific along with general allowances and key assumptions
- Information on significant concentrations of credit risk
- Loan balances when interest accruals in accordance with the terms of the original loan agreement have ceased due to deterioration in credit quality
- Reconciliations of movements in the allowance for loan impairment ("continuity schedule") showing separately various types of allowances
- Balances and other information when loans have been restructured
- Contractual obligations with respect to recourse arrangements and the expected losses under those arrangements

Exception Reports

In addition to constituents forming the foundation for sound lending policies, banks often place in service GES processes that target exceptions to that policy. Before a bank grants credit, GES source information, reports, established line limits, and a host of other credit communications are disseminated at appropriate levels. If requisite information is missing or loan data systems are incapable of providing management with enough information and a loan is granted nonetheless, examiners will assuredly cite the "guilty" party. If the exposure is large enough, "the buck may stop here," meaning regulators may charge the board of directors for failing to properly discharge its duties and responsibilities.

GES can provide exception reports sorted by loan exposure criteria, portfolio concerns, collateral categories, and loan officer performance rankings. If loan officers are responsible to follow up on exceptions marked for their area. they can correct the problem more readily if required information is downloaded onto the system.

Regulatory Reporting and GES

Submitting accurate, complete reports to regulators is serious business. Section 8 of the Bank Holding Company Act provides for the assessment of penalties for

---

[5] Federal Reserve Board.

submission of late, false, or misleading reports filed by bank holding companies required by Regulation Y.[6] Banks with adequate loan information systems that unintentionally file incorrect information can be fined up to $2,000 per day. If the error was not inadvertent (the burden of proof rests with the bank via its GES), a penalty of up to $20,000 per day can be assessed until the errors are corrected. If the submission was done with "reckless disregard" for the law,[7] a fine of up to $1 million or 1% of the institution's assets can be assessed *for each day* of the violation. Accordingly, regulators expect banks to develop the quality systems and procedures required to prepare accurate detailed regulatory reports and maintain clear, concise records with an emphasis on documenting adjustments.[8]

How do quality exposure information systems bolster chances that reports to bank regulators are filed in accordance with the law? The system's real-time attributes and apt design are two answers. A sampling of the reports required by Federal Reserve Board (FRB) regulators includes the following:

1. FR Y-9C Consolidated financial statements for top-tier bank holding companies with total consolidated assets of $150 million or more and lower-tier bank holding companies that have total consolidated assets of $1 billion or more. In addition, these FR Y-9C quarterly reports are filed by all multibank bank holding companies with debt outstanding to the public or that are engaged in certain nonbank activities, regardless of size.

2. All loan exposures we saw earlier are included in Schedule HC-B and HC-L, and then some: mortgage-backed and asset-backed securities, loans to foreign governments, futures and forwards, forward rate agreements, interest-rate swaps, foreign exchange, currency swaps, options (interest-rate, currency), and index-linked activities.

3. The Federal Reserve Board and Federal Financial Institutions Examination Council require financial institutions to summarize their gross positions outstanding in traded products on the *Report of Condition and Income* as well as on the *Report of Assets and Liabilities* (referred to collectively as the call reports).[9] These regulatory reports vary according to the size and type of institution.

4. Federal Financial Institutions Examination Council reports include 002 reports for U.S. branches and agencies of foreign banks and a series of reports for domestic banks, while the FRB requires the Y-series to cover bank holding companies.

---

[6] *Federal Reserve Board 2000 Supervisory Policy and Issues and Trading and Capital-Markets Activities Manual,* April 2001. The complete page document is included on the CD.

[7] Ibid.

[8] Exposures arising from new bank products are automatically updated on advanced GES in real time.

[9] Ibid

5. Regulation T Sec. 220.1 Authority, purpose, and scope. Regulation T (this part) is issued by the board of governors of the Federal Reserve System pursuant to the Securities Exchange Act of 1934 (15 U.S.C.78a et seq.). Its principal purpose is to regulate extensions of credit by brokers and dealers; it also covers related transactions within the board's authority under the act. It imposes, among other obligations, initial margin requirements and payment rules on certain securities transactions.
6. Regulation O, Sec. 215.8 records of member banks governing extension of credit to insiders of the bank or the bank's affiliates.

GES and Reports to the Board of Directors

The board generally approves the *Annual Schedule for Loan Review* during the first meeting of each year. The schedule documents loan size, structure, performance, and type of loan, borrower affiliations, and portfolio concentrations. Information must be complete enough to enable the board to draw conclusions concerning the portfolio's quality, along with the capital adequacy needed to cushion unexpected losses. The schedule for loan review allows sufficient time to prepare reports so information gained from the loan review is available to management. Let's review other GES actualized and accounting reports that a bank's board of directors will typically address:[10]

1. A monthly statement of balance sheet condition and statement of income. Those statements, according to regulators, should be in reasonable detail, and compared to the prior month, the same month of a prior year, and to the budget. The directors receive explanations for all large variances, very difficult to attain without proper information systems.
2. Monthly statements of changes in all capital and reserve accounts. These statements detail, again, variances.
3. Investment reports that group the securities by classifications and reflect the book value, market value, yield, and a summary of purchases and sales.
4. Loan reports that list significant past due loans, trends in delinquencies, rate reductions, nonincome producing loans, and large new loans granted since the last report.
5. Audit and examination reports. Deficiencies in those reports produce a prompt and efficient response from the board. The reports reviewed and actions taken are reflected in minutes of the board of directors' meetings.
6. A full report of all new executive officer borrowing at any bank.

---

[10] Federal Reserve Board, duties and responsibilities of directors, examination procedures.

7. A monthly listing of type and amount of borrowing by the bank.
8. An annual presentation of bank insurance coverage.
9. All correspondence addressed to the board of directors from the Federal Reserve and any other source.
10. A monthly analysis of the bank's liquidity position.
11. An annual projection of the bank's capital needs.
12. A listing of any new litigation and a status report on existing litigation and potential exposure.

Country Exposure Reporting

Country risk exposure GES tabulations and management-denominated exposure limits are important portfolio constituents. Country exposure risks include exposures influenced by economic structures, policies, sociopolitical institutions, geography, and currencies. See Chapter 19 "Risk Rating Models: Design and Application."

GES and FAS 114 and FAS 119

FAS 114, "Accounting by Creditors for Impairment of a Loan" (Issued May 1993)

The Financial Accounting Standards Board addresses accounting by creditor for impairment of certain loans. It is applicable to all creditors loans, covering uncollateralized along with collateralized positions. Exceptions include large groups of smaller-balance homogeneous loans that are collectively evaluated for impairment, loans that are measured at fair value or at the lower of cost or fair value, leases, and debt securities as defined in FASB Statement No. 115 and "Accounting for Certain Investments in Debt and Equity Securities." FAS 114 applies to all loans that are restructured in a troubled debt restructuring involving a modification of terms.

GES Daily Reports
- Foreign exchange
- Derivatives
- Treasury
- Funds transfer

Weekly Monthly and Quarterly Reports
- Exception reports
- Special reports for users
- Management reporting
- Credit administration reports
- Communication with senior management

Furthermore, FAS 114 requires that impaired loans be measured based on the present value of expected future cash flows discounted at the loan's effective interest rate. Alternatively, the impaired loan, as a practical expedient, can be measured at the loan's observable market price or the fair value of collateral if the loan is collateral dependent.

FAS 119, "Disclosures about Derivative Financial Instruments and Fair Value of Financial Instruments" (October 1994)

This statement requires disclosures about derivative financial instruments-futures, forward, swap, and option contracts, and other financial instruments with similar characteristics. It also amends existing requirements of FASB Statement No. 105, "Disclosure of Information about Financial Instruments with Off-Balance-Sheet Risk and Financial Instruments with Concentrations of Credit Risk," and FASB Statement No. 107, "Disclosures about Fair Value of Financial Instruments."

FAS 119 requires disclosures about amounts, nature, and terms of derivative financial instruments that are not subject to Statement 105 because they do not result in the off-balance-sheet risk of accounting loss. It requires that a distinction be made between financial instruments held or issued for trading purposes (including dealing and other trading activities measured at fair value with gains and losses recognized in earnings) and financial instruments held or issued for purposes other than trading. It also amends Statements 105 and 107 to require that distinction in certain disclosures required by those statements.

EXPOSURE INFORMATION SYSTEMS: DESIGN

Money center banks domicile robust forms of GES that tick around the clock and around the world. With few exceptions, officers and staff have little idea of how these recursive computational procedures and algorithms fit together, let alone how raw loan data are mined, warehoused, sorted, and filtered throughout the organization. So much for JP Morgan Chase's GES, a wonderfully encyclopedic chain of systems, albeit well beyond this chapter's scope. Nevertheless, perfectly acceptable loan exposure models can be built around a body of applications, procedures, and rules easily obtainable from the existing computer-technological literature. Let's begin our review with a brief overview of control factors required in the placement of any computerized information system.

Exposure data systems and information technologies have risks that banks try vigorously to control because they can disrupt day-to-day operations or cause the bank to lose valuable customers and accrue losses arising out of slow or faulty data processing. Controls over information systems and their attendant technology can be categorized as *general* and *application. General controls* are controls over a computer system that hopefully ensure its smooth operation. For example, general controls include backup systems and recovery procedures, changes in GES software design and updates, maintenance procedures, and access security controls. *Application controls* are computerized steps within software applications and other manual procedures that control the processing of GES transactions. Banks have choices designing several different data architectures. A few, discussed in the following section, are by no means the alpha and omega of this specialized technology.

DATA ARCHITECTURE

Data Mining

Data mining is the automated extraction of hidden predictive information from databases. Once an exposure system has been created in a data mining environment, the system makes predictions like forecasting "family" exposures or by providing the raw data that senior bankers use to set guidelines—for example, exposure limits, limits on loan-to-deposit ratios, limits on loan-to-capital ratios, or general limits on the relationship between anticipated funding needs and funding sources. Some of the characteristics associated with a data mining system include those discussed here:

- *Response speed.* A major factor in any GES, response speed is the time it takes for the system to complete analysis or submit data at a desired level of accuracy. *Real time* is the standard response speed, not the exception.
- *Compactness.* For smaller banks facing budget constraints, an exposure system's compactness can be a key budgetary issue. Compactness refers to how small, byte-wise, the system can function without compromising portfolio objectives. In addition, compactness refers to the ease by which the system can be encoded into a compact portable format, whether embedded in a spreadsheet, coded into a specific computer language like Visual Basic, or carved on a silicon chip. If a system is too "bulky" to easily embed itself into a format that will make usable where and when needed, the system itself may not be very useful.
- *Flexibility.* Another concern GES designers face is flexibility, which refers to the ease with which the relationships among the variables or their domains can be changed or the goals of the system modified.
- *Embeddability.* An additional attribute still, embeddability refers to the ease by which the bank's exposure system can be coupled with the infrastructure of the organization, particularly when banks merge or divest operations. After a reorganization or merger, for example, a formally localized system may be drafted as a component within a larger system or form part of other databases. In this case, the localized system must be able communicate with other components within the larger infrastructure. If the original system was outsourced, it may contain proprietary hardware or software that could result in time delays or the additional cost of renegotiated license agreements.

- *Friendliness.* Related to embeddability is the system's "friendliness" and tolerance or noise. Friendliness, or ease of use, refers to how complicated a GES's mining system appears to users: line officers to senior bankers. A mining system's tolerance for data noise is a measure of its overall proficiency and accuracy.
- *Tolerance for complexity.* The degree to which a system is affected by interactions among various components of the process (e.g., the prodigious GES information network). Complex processes involve many, often nonlinear, interactions between variables. A quintessential example is default prediction, which involves a host of nonlinear systematic and unsystematic factors: industry growth/decline rates, macroeconomic factors, financial and operating leverage, market demographics, and so on. These variables interact in complex ways, which is why default prediction is high art and science, often requiring the service of specialists like Moody's KMV (Chapters 13 and 14).

Data Warehousing

Data mining and data warehousing are related, albeit different, methodologies. A data warehouse is an architecture for organizing data: a subject-oriented, integrated, time-variant, nonvolatile collection of data in support of, for example, a credit area decision-making process. A data warehouse stores tactical information answering "who?" and "what?" questions. A query submitted to a data warehouse might be: "What were aggregate construction loan outstandings between February 3 and April 14 for the ten largest branches in the third lending district?"

Typically, data warehouse systems consist of a set of programs that extract data from the global exposure environment—a database that maintains exposures throughout the bank—and systems that provide data to users—senior management for example.

Three Prime Attributes of Data Warehousing: Time Series Data, Data Administration, and Systems Architecture

- *Time series data.* A bank's data warehouse will support analysis of loan trends over time and compare data, current versus historical.
- *Data administration.* Another critical factor is senior management's commitment to maintain the quality of exposure data. Data administrators (e.g., unit family) are responsible for proactively managing how data are applied in tracking family exposures.
- *Systems architecture.* Databases supporting decision making should be able to retrieve large sets of aggregate and historical data within a quick response time, as mentioned earlier. A defining characteristic of data warehousing is separation of operational and decision support

functionality. By separating these two very different processing patterns, the data warehouse architecture enables both operational and decision support applications to focus on what they do best and therefore provide better performance and functionality.

Architecture is a design completed early in a project that encompasses (but does not necessarily detail) all aspects of the finished product. It includes the following features:

- A description of the credit-related, exposure-related problems the system is designed to address
- Local and global (bankwide) objectives, constraints, and critical success factors for the system
- Project participants and the role of each participant—relationship bankers, family unit responsibility and senior-level facility approvals, and portfolio management, as described earlier
- Major system components and the interfaces, connections, or communication paths among the components
- Anticipated GES system enhancements, migration paths, and modifications
- Cadre required to develop the system on schedule and maintain it over the long term

In conclusion, in-house designers of data warehousing, along with a bank's outside consultants, should organize teams that start by seeking to understand a data warehouse system's components and interfaces, as well as how it fits into the lending area's infrastructure, and what the potential is for meeting portfolio objectives set by senior management.

Online Analytical Processing (OLAP)

In contrast to a data warehouse, *online analytical processing* takes a multidimensional view of aggregate data to provide quick access to strategic information for further analysis. Online analytical processing (OLAP) is a breed of software technology that allows users to gain insight from information transformed from raw data into real dimensionality.

A data warehouse stores and manages data for data access, whereas online analytical processing metamorphoses warehouse data into tactical information. OLAP ranges from basic navigation and browsing (often known as "slice and dice"), to calculations, to more serious analyses such as time series and complex modeling. One important characteristic is multidimensional analysis: analysis reaching beyond conventional two-dimensional scrutiny to different dimensions of the same data, thus allowing for analyses across boundaries. For example, one possible query coming from a credit area vice president might be: "What is the effect on the covariance of family exposure with respect to the general loan portfolio if operating segment A reduced its outstanding loan by $45 million while the portfolio's standard deviation increased by X basis points?" Or from a producer's perspective the question might be: "What will be the change in widget production cost if metal prices increased by 25 cents per pound and transportation costs went down by 15 cents per mile?"

OLAP's analytical and navigational activities include but are not limited to the following:

1. Calculations and modeling applied across dimensions, through hierarchies, or across members
2. Trend analysis over sequential time periods
3. Slicing subsets for onscreen viewing
4. Drill-down to deeper levels of consolidation
5. Reach-through to underlying detail data
6. Rotation to new dimensional comparisons in the viewing area

Data Marts

A data mart is a simple form of a data warehouse that locks onto a single subject (or functional area), such as accountants in lending district XYZ that rendered clean opinions on deals that turned out bad, or the number of loan facilities Mary Smith approved this quarter over $4 million. Data marts are often built and controlled by a single department within a banking organization. Given its single-subject focus, a data mart typically draws data from limited sources. The information flow could come from internal operational systems, a central data warehouse, or external data. A data warehouse, in contrast, deals with multiple subject areas and is typically implemented and controlled by a central organizational unit such as the unit family coordinators we reviewed earlier. Typically, a data warehouse assembles data from multiple source systems.

Data marts are generally smaller and less complex than data warehouses; hence, they are typically easier to build and maintain. Table 17.1 summarizes the basic differences between a data warehouse and a data mart.

TABLE 17.1 Data Warehouses versus Data Marts

	Data warehouse	Data mart
Realm	Senior-level loan risk management, global	Small bank letters of credit department
Fields	Multiple	Single field/subject
Data sources	Numerous	Sparse
Normal size	100 gigabytes to more than a trillion bytes	Less than 100 gigabytes
Time to realization	Months to years	Weeks to months

The three types of data marts are *dependent, independent,* and *hybrid.* Categorization is based primarily on the data source feeding into the data mart. *Dependent data marts* draw loan exposure data from a central data warehouse that has already been created. *Independent data marts,* in contrast, are stand-alone systems built by drawing loan data directly from operational or external sources of data or both. *Hybrid data marts* can draw loan data from operational systems or data warehouses.

A dependent data mart allows an operating unit, say a local bank's department D, to combine its data in one data warehouse providing all the advantages that arise from centralization. An independent data mart can be created without the use of a central data warehouse to, say, smaller units within department D. A hybrid data mart allows department D to combine input from sources other than a data warehouse. This could be useful if the department required ad hoc integration—for example, if a new loan product were added to the Department "D" product mix.

Neural Networks

Neural networks processes data by altering the states of networks formed by interconnecting enormous bits of elemental data, which interact with one another by exchanging signals—as neurons do in the body's nervous system. Indeed, the best way to visualize neural networking is to think of the human nervous system. The basic processing element in the human nervous system is the neuron. Within the human brain dwell treelike networks of nerve fiber that connect to the cell body, where the cell nucleus is located. Extending from the cell body is a single long fiber called the axon, which eventually branches into strands and substrands and connects to other neurons through junctions.

In a simplified mathematical model of the neuron, the effects are represented by "weights," which modulate the effect of the associated input signals, and the nonlinear characteristics exhibited by neurons are represented by a transfer function. The neuron impulse is computed as the weighted sum of the input signals, transformed by the transfer function. The learning capability of an artificial neuron is achieved by adjusting the weights in accordance to the chosen learning algorithm, since it is arduous to accurately determine multiple values.

This involves creating a network that randomly determines parameter values. The network is then used to carry out input-to-output transformations for actual problems. The correct final parameters are obtained by modifying the parameters in accordance with the errors that the network makes in the process.

Rating agencies, banks consider a spectrum of factors before assigning an objective, algorithmic rating.[11] Here, while input factors—sales, operating margins, working capital, cost of capital, net fixed asset requirements, and other crit-

---

[11] In contrast to the interactive risk rating system featured in Chapter 19, which is subjective in nature.

ical assumptions—might be assignable as input variables, others are questionable. For example, how do you input a borrower's willingness to repay? That's where neural networks come in. Rather than working out a payment history regression (thereby judging the borrower's ability to repay), risk-rating functions might be appropriately solved by training a network using back-propagation. Why? Traditional statistical regression is quite difficult to use in translucent dimensions since it is ambiguous what factors the dependent variable "willingness" relates to. Neural networks, on the other hand, overcome problems related to translucent dimensions.

Rule Induction

Rule induction is another complementary approach for revealing patterns in the data. This approach may be applied to the same data analyzed by neural networks. The data should include both positive and negative examples, for example, a borrower table, where each record refers to another borrower, and the fields are various features, such as income, profit, address, industry, key ratios, and whether the firm paid the loan on time. If the last field is selected as the dependent variable, the rule induction software will reveal if-then rules such as: "If the firm's cash flow coverage ratio is between 15% and 25%, and the industry credit grade is below 5, the probability that the loan is not paid is 0.8. (There are 1,500 customers."

On top of revealing if-then rules, the software may find if-and-only-if rules, such as: If the profit is less than 200, or industry is food manufacturing, the probability that the loan is not paid is 0.9, and if these two conditions do not hold (That is, the profit is at least 200, and the field of business is not food manufacturing), then the probability that the loan is paid is 0.85." Contrary to if-then rules, that sufficient conditions, if-and-only-if rules present necessary and sufficient conditions. Obviously when an if-and-only-if rule such the above-mentioned is discovered, we can say that we found a theory explaining almost all the cases in the data.

Either the if-then rules or the if-then-only-if rules can then be used for the following purposes:

1. Issuing predictions for new cases: For example, when a new customer asks for a loan the software calculates the probability that the customers will not pay the loan by applying the rules on the customer's data.
2. Revealing cases to be audited: Cases in the data that deviate from strong rules might be data errors or cases of fraud.
3. Revealing interesting phenomena: unexpected rules denote interesting phenomena in the data.

WizWhy—analyzer & predictor and WizRule—business rules detector for data auditing, by WizSoft, Inc. are using the technology described above. WizWhy and

WizRule comprehensive demos are included on the CD along with User Guides and a White Paper. The models are located in the directory Models_Demos/Chapter 17\WizRule, and Models_Demos\Chapter 17\WizWhy Demo.

FINAL THOUGHTS

The dictionary defines evolution as "a gradual process in which something changes into a different and usually more complex or better form." What a fitting description of GES! Over the short term, exposure-tracking networks have evolved to become indispensable assets, on par with R&D or any "hard" asset in the premises and equipment category.

Lightning-paced exchange of loan data will accelerate even still, particularly at small-cap bank levels. Indeed, GES has redefined the very nature of the banking industry. But keep in mind that beneath the silver lining is a degree of uncertainty, prototypical among emerging technologies. That is, before advancing systems can deliver the goods, they require an extended phase of learning by those who use them. Computerization upgrades without the appropriate knowledge base needed to support and use them have the potential to backfire.

Even so, a GES's potential payoff is worth the price of the lottery. No matter how much time and energy an institution is prepared to invest in commercial loan tracking systems, almost any *well-thought-out* system will bring benefits in accuracy, productivity, security, and compliance. Exposure data systems are like finely tuned watches, designed to meet the challenges of rigorous risk-adjusted return on capital pricing standards, intensive bank audits, often-stressed systematic (economic/industry) exposures, and volatile markets. Though bankers may never have to pull a GES emergency cord or face the somber task of micromanaging an imperiled loan portfolio through an economic crisis, the investment in efficient exposure and management information systems will pay for itself in language bankers understand: increases in shareholder value.

SELECTED REFERENCES AND READINGS

Adamo, J. -M. (2001). *Data mining for association rules and sequential patterns: Sequential and parallel algorithms*. New York: Springer.

Altman, E. I., and M. J. McKinney. (1987). *Handbook of financial markets and institutions*. New York: Wiley.

Basel Committee on Banking Supervision. (1998). Sound Practices for Loan Accounting, Credit Risk Disclosure and Related Matters. Consultative paper October 1998.

Consultative Committee of Accountancy Bodies. Auditing Practices Committee. (1982). *Auditing guidelines: Auditing in a computer environment*. London: The Committee.

Della Riccia, G., R. Kruse, *et al.* (2000). *Computational intelligence in data mining*. Wien; New York: Springer.

Fayyad, U. M. (1996). *Advances in knowledge discovery and data mining*. Menlo Park, CA: AAAI Press Cambridge MA.: MIT Press.

Federal Deposit Insurance Corporation and United States Office of Thrift Supervision. (1997). *Bank & thrift branch office data book*. Washington, DC: Federal Deposit Insurance Corporation Public Information Center.

Federal Reserve Board.. (2000). Supervisory Policy and Issues; Recognition and Control of Exposure to Risk Section 2160.0.

FRB. (1996). Memo to the Officer in Charge of Supervision at Each Federal Reserve Bank: April 24, 1996. Subject Minimum Documentation Standards for Loan Line Sheets, Richard Spillenkothen, director.

FRB. (2001). 2000 *Supervisory Policy and Issues and Trading and Capital-Markets Activities Manual*, April 2001.

FRB. Duties and Responsibilities of Directors: Examination Procedures.

Ferdinandi, P. L. (1999). *Data warehousing advice for managers*. New York: Amacom.

Financial Accounting Standards Board. (1994). *Accounting by creditors for impairment of a loan-income recognition: An amendment of FASB statement no. 114*. Norwalk, CT: The Board.

Graves, S. C., W. H. Hausman, *et al.* (1977). *Scheduling automatic warehousing systems: Simulation results*. West Lafayette, IN: Institute for Research in the Behavioral Economic and Management Sciences, Krannert Graduate School of Management, Purdue University.

Han, J., and M. Kamber. (2001). *Data mining: Concepts and techniques*. San Francisco: Morgan Kaufmann.

Hewitt, J. R., United States Office of the Comptroller of the Currency, Multinational Banking Division., *et al.* (1986). *Computerized loan origination networks and traditional mortgage lenders*. Washington, DC: Comptroller of the Currency Administrator of National Banks: Federal Home Loan Bank Board.

Kambayashi, Y. (1999). *Advances in database technologies: ER'98 Workshops on Data Warehousing and Data Mining, Mobile Data Access, and Collaborative Work Support and Spatio-Temporal Data Management, Singapore, November 19–20, 1998: Proceedings*. Berlin; New York: Springer.

Kandel, A., M. Last, *et al.* (2001). *Data mining and computational intelligence*. Heidelberg; New York: Physica-Verlag.

Kaplan Smith & Associates and United States Federal Home Loan Bank Board. (1985). *[Financial viability monitoring system]*. Pasadena, CA: Kaplan Smith & Associates.

McGee, R. W., and National Association of Accountants. (1984). *The effects of software accounting policies on bank lending decisions and stock price*. New York: National Association of Accountants.

Moeller, R. A. (2001). *Distributed data warehousing using Web technology: How to build a more cost-effective and flexible warehouse*. New York: Amacom.

Mohania, M., and A. M. Tjoa (1999). *Data warehousing and knowledge discovery: First International Conference, DaWaK'99, Florence, Italy, August 30–September 1, 1999: Proceedings*. Berlin; New York: Springer.

Reinartz, T. (1999). *Focusing solutions for data mining: Analytical studies and experimental results in real-world domains*. Berlin; New York: Springer.

Rud, O. (2001). *Data mining cookbook: Modeling data for marketing, risk and customer relationship management*. New York: Wiley.

Shim, J. *An intelligent cache manager in data warehousing environment and its application to the web caching*. 1 v.

Sullivan, D. (2001). *Document warehousing and text mining*. New York: Wiley.

United States General Accounting Office. (1997). *Guaranteed loan system checklist systems reviewed under the Federal Financial Management Improvement Act of 1996: Exposure draft*. Washington, DC, Gaithersburg, MD (P.O. Box 6015, Gaithersburg 20884-6015), The Office.

United States General Accounting Office and United States. Small Business Administration (2000). *SBA loan monitoring system: Substantial progress yet key risks and challenges remain. Report to the Administrator, Small Business Administration.* Washington, DC (P.O. Box 37050, Washington 20013), The Office.

United States Joint Financial Management Improvement Program. (1999). *Direct loan system requirements.* Washington, D.C. (Room 3111, 441 G St., N.W. Washington, D.C. 20548-0001), The Program.

Willemssen, J. C. (1998). *Small Business Administration planning for loan monitoring system has many positive features but still carries implementation challenges: Statement of Joel C. Willemssen, Director, Civil Agencies Information Systems, Accounting and Information Management Division, before the Subcommittee on Government Programs and Oversight, Committee on Small Business, House of Representatives.* Washington, DC, Gaithersburg, MD (P.O. Box 6015, Gaithersburg 20884-6015).

Zaki, M. J., and C.-T. Ho (2000). *Large-scale parallel data mining.* Berlin; New York: Springer.

18

PRICING MODELS

Design and Application

Loan pricing within a risk-return framework is one of the most basic concepts of managing credits. When banks operated in a forgiving environment, lending mainly to investment-grade credits, default risk was low and pricing was just about automatic. But as disintermediation proliferated, banks lent to more vulnerable clients, raising the volatility of returns while diminishing the quality of loan portfolios. In addition, loan values declined, cost containment and capital requirements across the spectrum of many banks were ignored, and an optimal asset mix was difficult to attain:

> A bank acquires funds through deposits, borrowing, and equity, recognizing the cost of each source and the resulting average cost of funds to the total bank. The funds are allocated to assets, creating an asset mix of earning assets such as loans and non-earning assets such as a bank's premises. The price that customers are charged for the use of an earning asset represents the sum of the cost of the bank's funds, the administrative costs (e.g., salaries, compensation for non-earning assets, and other costs), and a profit objective that compensates the bank for bearing risk. If pricing adequately compensates for these costs and all risks undertaken, bank value is created. Customer value is created if

the price is perceived by the customer to be fair, based on the funds and service received.[1]

As this quotation suggests, naive loan pricing hurts bank value, particularly in a tense credit environment. Conversely, well-defined pricing policies provide risk-adjusted returns to cover exposure risk and provide a platform to maintain and foster additional business—deposits, fee-based services, investment banking, cash management, trade finance, and trust, to mention a few. Angling the portfolio, loans are priced in line with an entire family of related accounts to position the institution for both additional business and optimal capital returns—thus, neither underpricing the relationship with a diminution in risk-adjusted returns nor overpricing it only to lose the entire business to competitors (see Chapter 16).

An adept loan policy covers all aspects of the (banking) relationship, consolidating many disparate accounts, related businesses, and the multitude of other factors into a single, coherent risk/return analysis.

> Most banks embrace the concept of relationship banking as a means of differentiating themselves from capital market or nonbank competitors. No longer is the deal a single loan, but a series of ongoing loans and services delivered to meet a wide range of customer needs. Although the most prominent element of the relationship is often the loan, the interaction of all parts of the relationship injects complexities into the pricing model. Relationship profitability becomes the primary focus, often replacing loan profitability.[2]

Due to the nature of this highly competitive business, pricing loans has traditionally been drawn into the so-called relationship parameter. Lending, by definition, serves as the foundation for broader corporate business, aiming to maximize the profitability of the entire client relationship, rather than focusing on one or two individual loans (see Chapter 17, "Global Exposure Tracking Systems"). As a result, lower deal pricing may be offset by revenue producing products in other departments (or locales), allowing institutions to earn target returns on a consolidated client basis—in other words, the loan may well serve as the cost of developing broader client relationships. Into the bargain, an effective pricing strategy means developing a price buildup methodology (Figure 18.1). The methodology works itself through all pricing components—obligor risk, facility structure, ancillary costs, global exposure network, and competition.

PRICING ERRORS

Naive pricing can lead to pricing traps and errors including the following:

---

[1] Robert Kemp and Laurence Pettit, Jr. "Loan Pricing's Effect on Bank Value" Excerpted with permission from *The Bankers Magazine,* July/August 1992.
    [2] Ibid.

1. *Meeting the competitor's price.* If the lender cites competition to justify a lower price, the banker fails to understand risk, has poorly structured the credit to minimize risk, or has ignored the need for an adequate return for the bank.

2. *Volume is more important than risk-adjusted pricing.* Volume does not, discretely, add value. Risk-based pricing transmits value. Lenders sometimes confuse volume and risk-adjusted returns, neglecting fundamentals that contribute to bankwide utility because they simply believe loan volume is the solution to all problems.

3. *Pricing based on marginal cost. The problem*: Deal profit is sometimes insufficient to cover overall funding costs. So how will the bank compensate stakeholders? A bank may find it difficult to survive long-term with its pricing policy grounded exclusively on marginal cost, particularly the marginal cost of a bank's cheapest funds (i.e., demand deposits).

4. *Price can compensate for default risk.* Because of competitive pressures, the lure of wider margins from riskier credits is tempting. The fact is that *no price compensates a lender for a bad loan.*

5. *Stability of price/risk relationships over time.* The quickest way to price a loan is to look at the price on the last similar successful deal to the customer. This practice fails to recognize three siblings of credit risk: business, industry, and macroeconomic variability. Price is influenced by future risk, not past conditions. Second, risk premiums are not necessarily market stable. This is true for banks and their customers. In volatile economic times (for example, 2001), it is harder to acquire funds, leading to higher risk premiums. In less volatile times, the 1990s, for example, funds were easier to acquire, with resulting lower risk premiums, demonstrated by looking at returns of noninvestment-grade securities. In good economic times, it is easy to sell securities at relatively low yields. Price/risk relationships are not stable over time, so loans should be priced to reflect the future price/risk interrelationships associated with clients and markets.

6. *Future pricing can compensate for underpricing current risk.* Some banks justify low spreads by assuming that future client business compensates today's underperforming/underpriced loan. In other words, as the argument goes, banks can overcharge borrowers tomorrow to make up for low rates charged today.

7. *Loan risk equal to default risk.* Lenders often measure loan risk solely as default risk. Default risk is the risk of nonpayment, whereas loan risk adds up to more than default risk. The loan risk premium must also cover uncertainties of late payments and restructuring costs due to cyclical or other unforeseen developments. As the primary earning assets of the bank, loans play a significant role in determining risk premiums required to cover hurdle rates associated with capital costs.

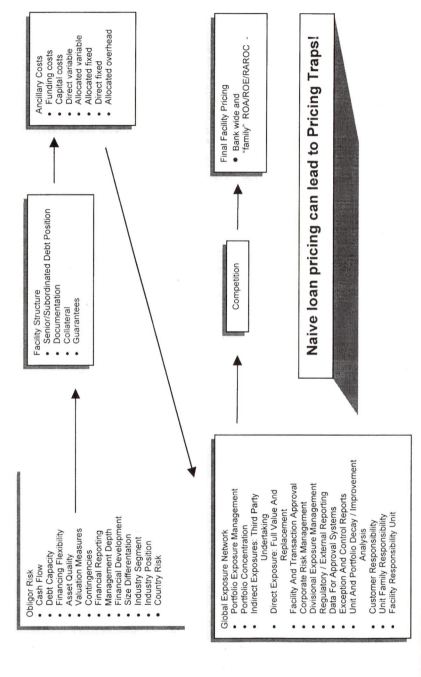

FIGURE 18.1 Price Buildup Methodology

Simply stated, pricing loans solely on default risk will diminish corporate value.

DEFAULT RATES AND LOAN PRICING

Few bankers argue the need to satisfactorily price deals and thus avoid value-destroying pricing traps. But accomplishing this magic is easier said than done: risk-adjusted or actuarial approaches to loan spreads and "pricing traps" represent, in a sense, reverse polarity (Figure 18.2). The process requires survival and recovery. With the right statistical estimates (no information is entirely foolproof), loan returns will generally provide enough of a margin to compensate for default risk (for immediate loan areas and globally). But without default and recovery estimates across a broad range of risks, risk-adjusted pricing regresses to an exercise in academia. See the chapters on KMV (Chapter 14 and 15), RAROC (Chapter 16), and Risk Rating (Chapter 19).

Historical survival and recovery rates are available for a wide range of credits. In degrees, the lower the credit rating, the more attentive the pricing. When loan quality deteriorates, default rates do not increase linearly; there is little difference between a credit grade 1 or 2, or between AAA and AA deals. But there are noticeable differences between a Baa credit and a single-B credit, where default spread widens significantly.

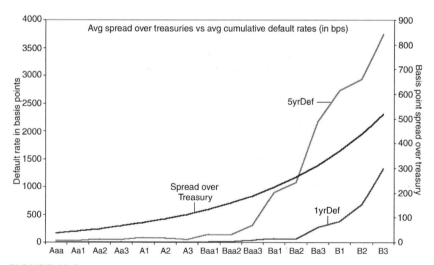

FIGURE 18.2 Average Spread over Treasurer versus Average Cumulative Default Rates (in bps) *Source: Moody's Investor Service, Global Credit Research,* "Historical Default Rates of Corporate Issuers, 1920–1997" (February 1998). "Explaining Yields on Identically Rated Bonds; OLS Regression with White (1980) corrected standard errors, Dependent Variables: Spreads over Treasuries."

The best way to develop an internal pricing model is to start with a very simple model and then extend it in stages, doing so in ways that appear to be most important. With this approach, the department will have a usable model early on. Moreover, you can analyze the sensitivities of the simple model to find out where key gaps are and use this to set priorities for expanding the model. If, instead, you try to create a large model from the start, you run the risk of running out of time or computer resources before you have anything usable. Also you may end up putting much work into creating an elaborate module for an aspect of the problem that turns out to be of little importance. Here are some hints:

- Identify ways to expand and improve the model.
- Add pricing variables that you think are important.
- Add objectives or criteria for evaluating outcomes.
- If you are developing an optimization pricing model, expand the number of decision options specified for a decision variable, or the number of possible outcomes for a discrete chance variable.
- Expand a single decision into two or more sequential decisions, with the later decision being made after more information is revealed.
- For your dynamic model, expand the time horizon to include ten-year maturates (from five years, though five-year loans may be more typical) or reduce the time steps (say, from annual to quarterly time periods).

Beyond statistical default rates, pricing requires a profound understanding of borrowers, along with the ability to judge the qualitative factors on which every risk-return relationship takes root. As we saw in the previous chapters, bank value and its ascendant, bankwide risk-adjusted return on capital, not loan spreads alone, govern loan policy and pricing decisions. The forces of competition and the overriding need to foster relationships apart from overall loan values have clouded the whole issue of loan pricing, creating an ever-increasing number of pitfalls for banks. Bankers are in the business of making loans, but the fiduciary responsibility of bankers is value creation as well, meaning paying special attention to all the costs of bearing risk. Pricing models focus on this aspect, and when linked to bankwide exposure systems and risk-rating procedures they help bankers realize value-creating opportunities.

LOAN PRICING MODELS

Pricing models include key (assumption or independent) variables that combine to produce return on assets, return on equity, or risk-adjusted return on capital (forecast or dependent variables). Models should be able to define trade-offs among rate spreads, fees, deposit balances, fixed and variable costs, and a host of other variables to produce the appropriate return (i.e., provide correlations between assumption variables and rank correlations between assumption variables and target forecast variable). Whether the bank chooses to build its own model internally or to buy into a commercial vendor (such as KMV or Loan Pricing Corporation), the bank will incur costs for the model's design, evaluation, training, and systems support. But the cost is well worth the trouble (or price), because computer-based loan pricing models, particularly the stochastic ones, markedly improve ways in which bankers manage returns on their portfolios. Characteristics of a good pricing model includes the following:

1. Easy to install, use, and administer
2. Available on a wide variety of platforms
3. Computes risk-adjusted returns
4. Computes yields-to-maturity
5. Provides multiperiod analysis
6. Accounts for all relevant variables
7. Supports the negotiating process
8. Provides full relationship profitability
9. Provides comprehensive, context-sensitive help

The basic idea is to develop a unique target price for each loan, including adjustments for identifiable risks and costs. Returns are compared to target pricing established by area or bank policy. To illustrate, consider the following stochastic spreadsheet model developed by the author employing the net borrowed funds approach. In calculating the loan yield, the net borrowed funds approach assumes a company borrows its own funds first and the bank supplies the difference between the deposit and the loan amount, with yield calculated on the net difference. While deterministic models rely on single sets of assumptions, our stochastic (i.e., simulation) model involves an entire range of results and confidence levels feasible for a given run. This model is included in the CD the subdirectory Models_Demos/Chapter 18/LoanPricMod/Input. You are encouraged to open the spreadsheet as you read the text. The text and Excel worksheet are cross referenced: (A), (B), (C), and so on. Shaded cells represent assumption cells that you define. Recall from Chapter 7, cash flow projections, that an entire range of results and confidence levels is feasible for any given forecast run.

STOCHASTIC NET BORROWED FUNDS PRICING MODEL

Second City Bank prices an unsecured $1,000,000 line of credit to Picnic Furniture Manufacturing Company. Details of the transaction are presented in Exhibit I.

EXHIBIT I   Picnic Furniture Manufacturing Company Line of Credit Information

Facility information

Borrower: Picnic Furniture Manufacturing Company

Lenders: Second City Bank

Amount: $1,000,000 five-year unsecured facility

Purpose: Expansion

Bank ROA Guideline: 1.25%

Note: Random variables are used in stochastic computer run on the CD.

Input screen: Schedule 1: Facility and deposit information

Facility information

Enter unsecured line of credit (assumed to be fully utilized)	1,000,000
Enter base rate (prime of LIBOR) rate (B)	10.5%
Enter spread over base: Influence by hurdle rate (F)	1.71%
Enter funding costs (D)	8.41%
Enter servicing: Enter percentage of complete schedule three (E)	
Enter loan loss expense (function of expected risk)	1.50%
Enter percentage equity reserve requirement (function of unexpected risk)	7.00%
Enter taxes	35%

Deposit information

Enter activity costs as percentage of balances	4.10%
Enter balance requirement	7.00%
Enter reverse requirement	10.00%
Net borrowed funds (Facility less balance requirement)	930,000
Interest rate: base rate plus spread	12.21%
Fees in lieu of balances	5,3000

Input screen: Schedule 2: Facility fees [C]

Commitment fees on the unused portion of the loan	0.50%
Facility fee—fee for making credit facility available	0.78%
Management free—managing banks in a syndicated credit	
Miscellaneous fees	1.22%

Input screen: Schedule 3: Servicing costs (E)

Do not complete schedule if percentage was entered	
Direct variable (enter percentage facility)	1.30%

Allocated variable (enter percentage of facility)	1.50%
Direct fixed (enter amount)	6,167
Allocated fixed (enter percentage of facility [variable component])	0.10%
Plus amount (fixed component)	200
Total servicing costs	35,367

Fees in lieu of balances (A)

(1) Percentage of base rate (prime or LIBOR) fee   Balances on deposit at the Federal Reserve

(2) (2) Line facility fee

(3) Percentage of prime fee = $\dfrac{\text{(Balance arrangement)}(1 - \text{Reserve requirement)(Cost of funds)}}{\text{Prime rate}}$

To determine percentage of prime fee the following information copied from schedule 1

Balance requirement as a percentage of facility	**7.00%**
Reserve requirement	10.00%
** Cost of funds as percentage	8.41%
Prime or LIBOR rate	10.50%
Facility amount	1,000,000

Output: Fees in lieu of balances

Facility	1,000,000
Percentage of balance requirement	7.00%
Balances required	70,000
Percentage of LIBOR (prime) fee	5.05%
Fee in lieu of balances	5,300.02

= Facility amount × percentage if LIBOR (prime) fee × LIBOR (prime rate)

Line Facility Fee
Line facility fee = (Balance arrangement)(1 - Reserve requirement)(Cost of funds)

To determine line facility fee enter the following information

Balance requirement as a percentage of facility	7.00%
Loan loss reserve as a percentage of facility	7.00%
**Costs of funds as a percentage	8.25%
Facility amount	1,000,000

Output: Line facility fee

Facility	1,000,000
Percentage of balance requirement	7.00%
Percentage line facility fee	0.5477%
Line facility fee	0.5300%
Facility amount × Line facility fee	5,300.02

(A) Fees in Lieu of Balances (see Cell F5 for cross referencing)

Compensating balance requirements, sometimes consigned to loan agreements, obligate the borrower to hold demand or low-interest deposits as additional compensation for the loan. Balances can be expressed as a component of the loan commitment, a portion of the actual amount borrowed, or a fixed dollar amount. Fees are paid in advance or in arrears. Since it is part of the pricing mechanism, deficiency fees are charged retroactively if the agreed upon balance arrangement is not honored. Deficient balances are treated as borrowed funds and the fee is calculated like interest usually at the borrowing rate or earnings credit rate.

Compensating balances have been criticized in some circles as being an inefficient pricing mechanism because, though they raise effective borrowing costs, banks must hold idle reserves against the additional deposits and, therefore, cannot fully invest them in earning assets. Among banks that have moved toward unbundled and explicit pricing, balance requirements are thought to obscure the true returns on lending, which is one reason balances have been replaced by fees in lieu of balances or simply higher loan rates. Conversely, since balances replace funds that the bank would otherwise purchase, balances "earn" income at the lending institution's cost of funds rate. As the cost of funds fluctuates with market interest rates, balances will be worth more when the cost of funds increases and less when funding cost falls.

Fees in lieu of balances should reflect these changing rates, yet it is impracticable to reprice a loan every time the bank's funding costs change. Thus, the interest rate environment influences the setting of fees. Fees in lieu of balances are expressed as a *percentage of prime fee, line fee,* or *facility fee.* Since the prime rate includes a spread over the lenders' cost of funds, the *percentage of prime fee* in lieu of balances will keep the bankers "whole" despite fluctuations in the cost of funds. Therefore, the primary contribution of customer-supplied balances (net of effects of the reserve requirement) is reduced funding costs. As long as the balances are provided at a rate that is less than other funds available from the market, they will reduce funding costs.

The *line/facility fee* may undercompensate lenders if interest rates rise, since the fee was calculated based on a lower cost of funds. Cells G26 and G44 illustrate and compare the percentage of prime fee to the line facility fee. You will see that both fees work out to the identical number.

(B) Rate

Prime Rate

During the late 1970s, as much as 90 % of money center bank loans were linked to the prime rate. Now money center banks generally use a money market base. The prime rate is simply a benchmark by which rates for other borrowers are set. Prime is a floating rate, established by each bank based on its overall cost of obtaining funds to support loans. The bank's spread is already included in the rate, and any market fluctuations during the term of the loan are passed on to the borrower directly. An additional increment added to or subtracted from prime reflects the creditworthiness of the borrower—the greater the perceived credit risk of the borrower, the greater the price.

What should be obvious at this point is that a bank's loan-pricing decision should not be driven solely by the prime rate or any other base rate benchmark, as the whole notion of loan pricing involves complex decision making with a multiplicity of factors at play. The myth of prime rate lending has come to us from the misconstrued notion that prime is the lowest rate available to the bank's best corporate customers.

In any case, a common banking practice is to price loans based on spreads over prime. The standard procedure calls for an additive—that is, borrowers are quoted something like "prime + 2," which means prime plus 200 basis points. An alternative to prime-plus pricing is prime-times pricing, calling for a multiplicative formula rather than an additive one. This pricing is expressed as

Quoted rate = Multiplicative adjustment factor × prime rate

where the adjustment factor can be greater (premium) or less than (discount) the prime rate. For example, if the prime is 8.5% and the adjustment factor is 1.35, then the borrower is quoted a rate of 11.475% (8.5% times 1.35).

Some banks abandoned their use of prime because of publicity from court cases challenging this rate and associated lending practices during the early and mid-1980s. Plaintiffs claimed that banks misled customers by implying that the prime rate was the interest rate charged to their most creditworthy customers when in fact some loans were actually made below the prime rate.

LIBOR

Floating rates are based on the London Interbank Offering Rate (LIBOR). LIBOR is a widely quoted rate on short-term European money market credits. For some time, it has influenced the overseas lending rates of large U.S. banks, particularly when the spread between U.S. money market base rates and LIBOR rates favored the latter. Also, access to overseas sources of funds has recently made LIBOR an increasingly popular base rate among borrowers of regional and smaller banks.

Example

A manufacturer of plumbing equipment negotiates with its bank a $10 million loan, which can be priced at either prime plus 50 basis points or at three-month LIBOR plus 250 basis points. Assume that at current levels switching to a LIBOR-based facility reduces the borrower's loan costs by 25 basis points. Why would the prime option be higher in this case? A number of factors are in play. For example, LIBOR fluctuates along with uncertainties inherent in the market, while prime is an administered rate, unresponsive to whims and rumors, LIBOR fluctuates on either side of 25 basis points, while prime holds constant.

Based on the demand for alternative pricing structures, many corporate borrowers now have the option of tying their loan rates to the Eurodollar market. Eurodollars are U.S. dollar deposits held anywhere outside of the United States (actually, the Eurodollar market gives rise to LIBOR). LIBOR is an index or snapshot of the Eurodollar market at a particular point of time. At each business day at 11 a.m. London time, London's major banks are asked where Eurodollars are trading. These rates become LIBOR. After LIBOR is set, Eurodollars continue to trade freely, above and below LIBOR. LIBOR more accurately reflects the bank's marginal cost of funds than prime. However, as with prime loans, an incremental percentage above or below LIBOR is usually assessed to address the relative creditworthiness of the borrower.

Should the LIBOR option be chosen simply because the rate is lower? Although prime-based loans carry a higher price, they give borrowers flexibility to increase the loan amounts or pay down their lines as their cash flow situations permit. This is not true of LIBOR-based deals as the bank cannot set the price of a loan unilaterally but must negotiate with the borrower until parties mutually accept a structure and settle on a price.

(C) Types of Facility Fees

Commitment Fee

When the bank makes a commitment to lend funds or issue credit facilities, the customer is charged a commitment fee. This per annum fee is charged (usually quarterly or at time of interest collection) from the time of acceptance of the commitment until draw down/issuance and on the unused portion of the commitment. A commitment fee is applied to the unused amount of the available portion (the portion that is periodically designated available or the amount the company projects it will need during a specified period). A lower commitment fee is applied to the unavailable portion.

Commitment fees on the unused portion of the loan are usually assessed in each accounting period (monthly or yearly) by calculating the average usage rate. Because the bank must set aside capital in support of the unused credit line, commitment fees should be set high enough to generate a desirable return on capital should the credit line not be fully used and to otherwise encourage use.

Facility Fee

This fee is charged to customers for making a credit facility available. Unlike the commitment fee, the facility fee applies to the entire facility regardless of usage. Facility fees are frequently used in lieu of balance arrangements and to increase the overall yield on the facility. Facility fees and commitment fees are usually disclosed explicitly in the loan agreement. For profitability analysis and pricing, facility fees are generally amortized over the life of the loan according to FASB 91.

Prepayment Penalty Fee

This fee is charged if a loan is partially or entirely repaid before the scheduled maturity. Prepayments, if permitted at all, could be subject to potentially costly premiums. Since the existing agreement cannot be opened up and increased, customers that want to increase the amount of outstandings must enter into a new LIBOR agreement. LIBOR loan facilities more so than prime-based facilities may subject the borrower to a prepayment premium if the loan is prepaid in whole or in part prior to maturity. The premium is often calculated by comparing the interest the bank would have earned if the loan were not prepaid to the interest earned from reinvesting the prepaid amount at current market rates.

Agent's Fee

For its efforts and expense in packaging a credit and performing loan servicing duties, the principal bank in a multibank credit charges an agent's fee. The fee may be stated either as a dollar amount or as a percentage of the facility.

Management Fees

Banks designated as managing banks in a syndicated credit collect this fee.

Miscellaneous Fees

Special financing transactions, such as leveraged buyouts, acquisition financing, or tax-exempt financing, often warrant fees for the extra costs involved in structuring the deal. *Up-front fees, arrangement fees, closing fees,* and *fees certain* (to be collected whether the loan is closed or not) are common fees collected for complex deals. These fees may be flat fees or a percentage of the loan. They can be collected in advance or over the life of the loan.

(D) Cost of Funds

This reflects the *marginal* cost of all funds used to support the loan. Conventional wisdom defines the incremental cost of funds as the rate paid on capital used for funding the loan. Some bankers believe this definition is narrow because it underestimates the true cost of funds (rate). According to some, the incremental cost of funds (rate) should be identified as the total incremental expense incurred in gathering $1 of investable funds. For example, some banks with a significant amount of demand deposits and branch networks might have higher operating costs, deposit insurance costs, and reserve requirements.

(E) Service and Administrative Costs

An additional and often ignored cost of risk is risk related overhead. Riskier loans tend to have higher administrative expenses because of incremental monitoring requirements together with the increased involvement of credit administration and supervisory personnel required on these deals. Collection and loan workout areas and a portion of legal costs represent risk-related expenses, and their costs could be apportioned to loans based on the relative risks. It is unfortunate that some banks approve poorly priced loans when they cannot or are unwilling to allocate their cost base accurately.

If a bank cannot allocate costs, then it will make no distinction between the cost of lending to borrowers that require little investment in resources and the cost of lending to borrowers that require a considerable amount of analysis and follow-up. As a result, commercial lenders have generally understood the need to reduce costs and redesign the credit process to improve efficiency, recognizing that the market will not permit a premium for inefficiency.

Service and administrative costs are based on functional-cost data, cost-accounting figures allocated to average assets, or the bank's best estimates of the costs. Bankers and auditors categorize costs as follows:

1. *Direct variable.* Expenses charged to the profit/cost center that are directly associated with the loan. Direct variable expense can easily be estimated either from the loan proposal or by the loan department.
2. *Allocated variable.* Allocated expenses are the expenses incurred by other cost centers in support of a product. These expenses can usually be derived from a bank's cost accounting system that includes variable support expenses for data processing, the customer phone center, and other support departments.
3. *Allocated fixed.* Direct and allocated fixed expenses are calculated according to the total capacity of each operation (cost center) rather than using the fully loaded costs. Otherwise, as volume rises, per-unit fixed costs will be overstated. These calculations are usually based on an operation research and capacity/unit cost study.
4. *Direct fixed and allocated overhead.* Allocated overhead is the portion of the bank's total overhead that should be considered supportive of this particular product.

(F) Hurdle Rate Influences Spread over Base Rate

While operating expenses factor into the pricing arithmetic, loan pricing involves three essential steps:

1. Estimate minimum target or hurdle rate. The appropriate hurdle rate incorporates both the funding costs and a specified profit target.
2. Estimate income, expenses, and yield associated with the loan.
3. Compare the estimated yield with the target or hurdle rate to determine loan profitability. If the yield is less than the hurdle rate, the loan should be either rejected or restructured so that it meets the target.

OUTPUT SCREEN AND YIELD CALCULATION

The underlying formulas used to compute a loan's yield should be consistent with and support the bank's strategic objectives, a requirement that results in yield values that are somewhat different from traditional and simplistic computations. A good pricing model should compute yields to maturity, from the moment of inception to the moment of maturity (YTM), whenever it may occur in the future (because of limited assumptions and in an effort to produce a more manageable net borrowed funds pricing model, YTM is ignored). Remember, not only does a plethora of pricing components determine loan returns, but each component changes value over time, adding even greater complexity.

For example, interest rates for purchased funds can change frequently, money borrowed fluctuates over time, deposit balances vary with the borrower's cash position, administrative costs change, and so on. Changes, especially in a volatile market, affect yields and must be included in any price analysis. Loan pricing systems must respond to frequent changes in the negotiating environment and must include variables affecting profitability (even factors not at issue for the customer). As expected, no lending officer can track and take into account all variables, each changing over time, which is one reason computer-based loan pricing has become sine qua non.

EXHIBIT II   Output Screen Yield Calculation

Interest	122,100		Loan × interest rate
Fees in lieu of balances	5,300		Fees × interest rate
Other facility fees	24,933		
Total loan revenue		152,333	
Expense before funding costs			
Loan servicing costs	0		Loan × servicing %
Loan service from schedule B	35,367		From schedule B
Loan loss expense	15,003		Loan × loan loss expense
Annual activity costs	(2,000)		12-month average balances × percentage of activity cost
Total expenses		48,370	
Income before funding costs		103,964	
Yield calculation—net borrowed funds basis			
Income before funding costs	103,964		
Net borrowed funds	930,000		Loan less balance
Yield	11.179%		Income before funding costs/Net borrowed funds

Net income before funding costs	103,964	
Funding costs	(84,127)	Funding cost as a percentage loan (line fully utilized)
Taxes	(6,943)	
Net income		12,894
Return on assets calculation		
Loan amount	1,000,000	
Net income	12,894	
Return of assets	1.289%	Forecast cell
Return on risk-adjusted capital calculation		
Percentage of equity reserve requirement (function of unexpected risk)		
Loan amount	1,000,000	
Dollar amount equity reverse allocation (function of unexpected risk)	70,000	Unexpected risk not derived in this model but if it were,
Net income	12,894	you would reference the
RAROC	18.24%	RAROC worksheet. See "unexpected" worksheet for study.

The estimated loan revenue is composed of fees in lieu of balances and facility fees. Facility is the face value amount of the loan being borrowed. Net income is income after all funding costs and administrative expenses have been deducted. ROA is net income divided by the loan amount. Due to the fact that the ROA hurdle rate is 1.25% and the actual ROA is 1.289%, the bank would theoretically accept this loan provided ROA was the only pricing benchmark the bank employed in approving this deal.

Summary: Base case

Borrower: Picnic Furniture Manufacturing Company	
Lender: Second City Bank	
Loan revenue	152,333
Facility	1,000,000
Net income	12,894
ROA	1.289%
Facility ROA hurdle rate	**1.25%**
Facility internal rate of return	
Option pricing generated hurtle rate (MortonMaryannMagazWorksheet)	
RAROC	18.42%

From Deterministic to Stochastic Pricing Solutions

Standard pricing models rely on single sets of assumptions that usually lead to limited outcomes. Stochastic models, on the other hand, produce an entire range of results and confidence levels feasible for the pricing run. Monte Carlo simulation fosters a much more realistic pricing environment and, as a result, involves elements of uncertainty too complex to be solved with deterministic pricing models. Stochastic models require a random number generator set against key variables in the pricing program. A simulation run in the pricing deal in Exhibits I and II is shown in Figure 18.3. Results are depicted as well in the Simulations worksheet included in our workbook LoanPricMod.

Simulation trials in Figure 18.3 predicted that there is a 39% chance that the pricing on a deal could fall below the hurdle rate. We are, however, 100% certain that ROA will not drop below 83 basis points. The average return on assets assuming a normal distribution would be 1.2863% with the strongest possibilities of ROA between 116 basis points and 142 basis points (one standard deviation).

The three distribution assumptions noted here correlate to the most likely range of the expenses associated with administering the loan. For the normal distribution curve, loan losses fall within a normal distribution based on past experiences. For variable expenses, the expected maximum and minimum are unknown (uniform distribution). Finally, for a triangular distribution, we are certain that fixed costs will not fall below $5,900 and will not exceed $6,600, with the most likely amount, $6,000.

Pricing Models Based on Price Buildup (based on cost plus profit)[3]

These models used in many banks, type traditional pricing whereby pricing is based on most of the constituents of risk rating (the model is included in the

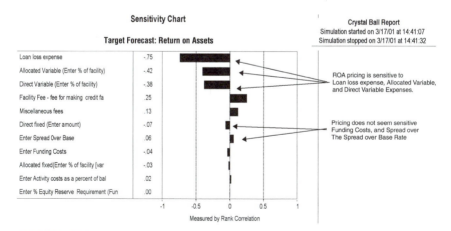

FIGURE 18.3 Crystal Ball Report (See Excel Model for Complete Report)

---

[3] Source: *Managing Credit Risk,* Caouette, Altman and Narayanan, Wiley. 1999. While this model is popular, the authors have provided an excellent condensed version. The author developed the Excel model and added a calculation column to the output section.

Forecast: Return on Assets

Summary: Cell: B84

| Certainty Level is 39.0333% |
| Certainty Range is from -Infinity to 0.0125 |

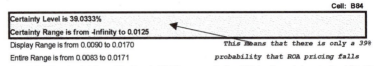

Display Range is from 0.0090 to 0.0170
Entire Range is from 0.0083 to 0.0171
After 3,000 Trials, the Std. Error of the Mean is 0.0000

This means that there is only a 39% probability that ROA pricing falls below 125 basis points required by the lending area.

Statistics:

	Value
Trials	3000
Mean ROA Pricing	**1.2870%**
Median ROA Pricing	**1.2863%**
Standard Deviation	0.0013
Skewness	-0.0241
Kurtosis	2.8592
Coeff. of Variability	0.1009
Range Minimum	0.0083
Range Maximum	0.0171
Range Width	0.0088
Mean Std. Error	0.0000

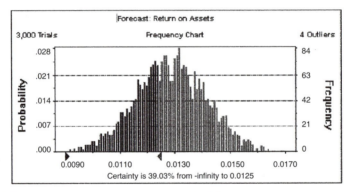

Forecast: Return on Assets (cont'd) Cell: B84

Percentile	Value
0%	0.8305%
10%	1.1184%
20%	1.1766%
30%	1.2181%
40%	1.2538%
50%	1.2863%
60%	1.3207%
70%	1.3552%
80%	1.3997%
90%	1.4549%
100%	1.7112%

This result is important. Pricing will not fall below 83 basis points ROA

The simulation indicates that there is a 50% probability that ROA will fall between 1.2863% and 0.8305% and 50% between 1.2863% and 1.7112%

FIGURE 18.3 Crystal Ball Report (continued)

Assumption: Loan loss expense

Normal distribution with parameters:

Mean	1.50%
Standard Dev.	0.15%

Selected range is from -Infinity to +Infinity

ROA pricing is very sensitive to loan less expense. Both the normal distribution and parameters should be verified to insure they are reasonable.

Assumption: Allocated variable (enter % of facility)

Uniform distributor with parameters:

Minimum	1.35%
Maximum	1.65%

Sensitive to ROA forecast variable. The uniform distribution along with parameters indicates that additional research needs to be completed to reduce volatility.

Assumption: Direct fixed (enter amount)

Triangular distribution with parameters:

Minimum	5,900
Likeliest	6,000
Maximum	6,600

Selected range is from 5.900 to 6.600

There should be little uncertainty here. The range should be narrowed in order to reduce the assumption's variability.

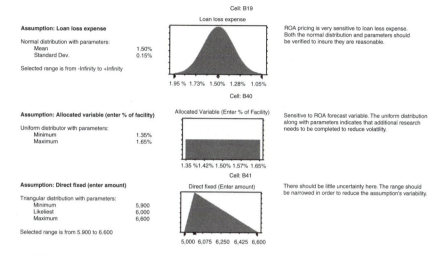

FIGURE 18.3 Crystal Ball Report (continued)

Workbook LoanPricMod/PriceModel2 and illustrated in Exhibit III). A charge to capital is influenced by the bank's minimum return (hurdle rate) and a capital ratio. Moody's supplied the historic loss rate for each risk-rating category (Figure 18.4) used to derive the expected loss frequency to be built into the price.

The two other inputs required are the capital ratio (7%) and the required capital return rate (14%). Using these assumptions, the rate to be charged for a four-year unsecured loan to a borrower with a rating of 4 comes to 8.63%, or a spread of 0.63 over the cost of funds.

EXHIBIT III Spreadsheet Example 1: Price Buildup Based on Cost plus Profit

Step 1: Determine historic loss rate by internal risk rating

Rating	**Historic five-year loss rate (%)**
AAA=1	0.01%
AA=2	0.19%
A=3	0.18%
BBB=4	**0.85%**
BBB=5	6.15%
B=6	18.38%

Step 2: Term structure of rates based on yield curve

Maturity (in years)	Cost of funds (%)
1	5.0%
2	5.5%
3	6.0%
4	**8.0%**
5	10.0%
10	12.0%

Step 3: Develop cost plus profit pricing model

Item	Amount	Calculation
Borrower risk rating	4	From your risk rating model
Loan maturity (years)	4	
Five-year loss rate (mortality)	0.85%	Historical five-year loss rate
Capital required as a percentage of the loan amount (capital ratio)	7.00%	Capital charge are based on "expected" losses and
Hurdle rate	14.00%	may not be sufficient. No unexpected losses set up here.
Loan amount	2,000,000	
Capital required	140,000	Capital ratio × Loan amount *but* model excludes unexpected losses **7% × 2,000,000**
Loan amount net of capital	1,860,000	Loan amount less capital required required **2,000,000 − 140,000**
Price buildup		
Annual capital charge	19,600	Hurdle rate × Capital required **14% × 140,000**
Annual funds cost	148,800	Cost of funds × Loan amount net of capital required **8% × (2,000,000 − 140,000)**
Annual loan loss allowance	4,250	Mortality rate % × Loan amount / Loan maturity in years **.85% × 2,000,000/ 4**
Break-even annual interest	172,650	Capital charge + funds cost + loan loss allowance income **19,600 + 148,800 + 4,250**
Loan interest rate	8.63%	Break-even annual interest income / Loan amount **172,650 / 2,000,000**
Minimum spread	0.63%	Loan interest rate − Cost of funds 8.63% − 8%

LOAN PRICING AND THE OPTION PRICING MODEL

An Example of Option Pricing: Black and Scholes Formula (1973)

The Black Scholes formula computes the value of an option based on the strike price, current stock price, risk free rate, the stock's volatility, and time to expiration. While these parameters can be successfully explained, Black Scholes merits a brush with statistics and probability theory. We'll employ a simple version of the model to value and price the corporate restructuring of a small-cap firm.

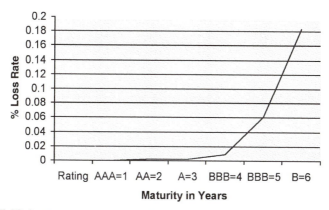

FIGURE 18.4   Historical Expected Loss Rate

CASE STUDY   Morton and Maryann Magazine Corp.

Morton and Maryann Magazine Corp. (M&M), a small-cap firm, has been in operation since May 1963. The firm grew from a small publisher to a respected and widely read Long Island publisher of high-end travel magazines. The firm produces a local monthly bulletin under the wings of its fully owned Huntington subsidiary. The suburban operation accounts for one-third of the combined business. Both M&M Publishing and the Huntington operation have loans with Dix Hills Bank:

Company	Loan amount	Years to maturity	Rate	Amortization
M & M Magazine Corp.	$8,000,000	5	9%	None: Due at maturity
Huntington subsidiary	$4,000,000	5	9%	None: Due at maturity

Its parent guarantees Huntington's obligations. Combined equity market value is $36 million; the standard deviation (σ) of percentage returns is .32. (Percentage returns equate to equity investors' market returns and in any one year represent increases in the investor's equity value plus dividends divided by the investor's equity value at the beginning of the year.) Without the Huntington operations, the standard deviation of percentage returns can be shown by $\sigma = .55$. Over the past few years, different demographics have resulted in a correlation coefficient of $-.5$ for the firm.

M&M opts to sell the Huntington operation. While the monthly travel bulletin is profitable, the firm recently felt the impact of a decreased circulation rate base and downward trends in advertising. Thus, management wants to redirect its focus to high-end travel magazines. Proceeds will be used to beef up the travel magazine operations, the backbone of the company. But diversification in both travel magazines and the bulletin reduces corporate risk, assuming demand for travel magazines will decline due to economic and demographic changes. Travel magazines are luxury items historically influenced by discretionary income. As the magazine industry has witnessed, the last recession hampered both advertising and circulation revenues, directly affecting the bottom line. The point is, the monthly diversifies total risk by providing a service to different segments of the readers' market.

M&M's travel magazine market is subject to the business cycle and changing demographics, including a larger ethnic population, and an increasing elderly population. Like many businesses, travel magazines face limited market share and competition. As the population matures, the medium for travel awareness changes. Time brings about oscillations in the needs, demands, and forms of leisure activities. Thus, the firm has planned operating strategies around a Darwinian philosophy in order to survive and will argue that the strategy pointing to divestment will be good for the firm.

The firm called a meeting with the bank to obtain the bank's approval to divest Huntington, as required by the loan covenants. While M&M's CFO, Oscar Zarchen, feels Dix Hills Bank will likely go along with the request, he wants to approach the bank prepared—that is, he wants to figure out how best to renegotiate the existing rate on the $12 million loan. Initially, the bank may not be agreeable to the proposed rate, but Zarchen hopes his strategy will convince loan officers that only a small rate increase is justified.

The bank may argue that the "value" of the bank's exposure will decline due to the higher default risk given the proposed sale of Huntington. In other words, based on the planned Huntington divestiture, both the firm's CFO and bank officers may derive a loan yield under option pricing conditions that leaves the bank no worse in terms of risk/reward pricing than before the sale. If Zarchen approaches the bank with a simplistic pricing scheme in hand, loan officers may say no deal, or if they make an offer, Zarchen may not know if the offer is fair.

By treating the two operations as a portfolio, management determines the risk of the "portfolio." The mean and standard deviation of percentage returns of two operations are examined separately and combined. If σp = zero before the planned divestiture, volatility of the combined returns of M&M's two operations (risk) approaches zero. Thus, the firm is immunized against macroeconomic shocks. If, on the other hand, after divestiture of Huntington, σp increases, percentage returns are more volatile giving the bank incentive to raise loan rates since the firm is no longer immunized (from the "all the eggs in one basket" syndrome). Default risk increases.

A fundamental aspect of portfolio analysis is that risk inherent in a single asset or business unit *contained* in a "portfolio" (similar to consolidated financials) is different from the riskiness of assets held in isolation (financials of unaffiliated individual firms). The covariance of the "portfolio" determines the correlation coefficient. Again, employing these techniques, management determines the combination of business units (within the portfolio) providing the highest return blended with the least risk. The issue facing M&M Magazine Corp. is essentially risk/return.

Thus, if stockholders own a single line of business-travel magazines, unique risk is very important. But once stockholders diversify into a portfolio (business combinations that sum to the consolidated entity), diversification has done the bulk of its work. The result is reduced corporate (and bank) risk. How will portfolio analysis, then, help the CFO and bankers determine the market value of debt, shareholder value, and, most important, the yields required on restructured loans once the firm executes its strategic plan to sell the monthly bulletin operation?

How Option Pricing Works to Complete This Deal

While the theory looks attractive, the value of combined operations is not easy to quantify. The general methodology for the analysis of divestitures requires a study of the results of breaking up the two organizations. This undertaking includes an estimate of the applicable cost of capital and expected returns and the application of valuation principles to formulate estimates of the value of the firms separately and combined. If the value of the combined firm is greater than the sum of the two operations taken separately, then M&M should not divest itself of its subsidiary.

The opportunity cost of capital is a weighted average of the cost of equity and debt capital. Further, it is the return on assets that firms must earn to increase shareholder wealth. Therefore, a study of the capital structure of the subsidiary should be undertaken by means of the option pricing model. With estimates of the cost of equity and cost of debt, the capital structures of both the combined firm and M&M on a stand-alone basis are analyzed to estimate the cost of capital. It's now time for M&M's CFO and the financial team to step up the analysis to the level of option pricing. Black & Scholes pointed out that common shares are call options, options to take (or retain) the firm's assets by paying off its debt. By put-call parity, we can also say that the value of debt is marked down by the value of a default put: stockholders can put the assets of the firm to its creditors and walk away without further liability. The exercise price of the put is the face value of the magazine company's debt. From this analysis, the financial team understood how to price the firm's liabilities.

When creditors place debt, shareholders receive cash by selling assets to creditors plus a call option. At maturity, if the firm's value exceeds the value of debt, stockholders will exercise their call by paying off the firm's $12 million obligation to the bank. However, if spinning off Huntington causes M&M to belly up, shareholders will not exercise their option. Investors in the firm will walk away as if they purchased stock or commodity options from their broker and stock or commodity values declined below the exercise price.

The bank ends up with the firm's assets, which will be valued below the face amount of the debt. In other words, regarding equity in a levered firm as a call option implies that investments increase the idiosyncratic or diversifiable risk of a firm without changing its expected return. This will benefit the firm's shareholders at the expense of the bank, even though the value of the firm is unaffected. Because idiosyncratic risk is independent of the market portfolio, an increase in this risk will increase the variance of returns for the firm without changing its beta or its expected return. Therefore, the value of the firm will not change.

However, a redistribution of wealth to shareholders at the expense of the bank may occur. The reason is that the higher variance will increase the value of the call option held by M&M shareholders. Therefore, increasing the riskiness of the firm's operations increases the value of equity but decreases the value of debt, as we will see next.

While Morton and Maryann Magazine Corp.'s bankers cannot be absolutely certain of the firm's new level of risk, Zarchen and the bank may wisely employ option techniques to derive the appropriate compensation for the bank to relax loan covenants pertaining to changes in the business.

Now let's assume projections were completed with support of simulation software. The results indicate within a 95% confidence level that the risk of percentage returns (standard deviation) has increased from 35% to 45%. Incorporating this information in our option pricing spreadsheet, the yield on the loan (from within the universe of option pricing) increases 248 basis points, compensating the bank for the higher level of risk. This translates into the bank receiving a 248 basis points compensation on the restructured term loan if it agrees to waive the loan covenant restricting divestment activity (if the company's risk level increases from .32 to .55).

EXHIBIT IV   Morton and Maryann Magazine Corp. (consolidated) Pricing Equity and Debt with Option Pricing the Model

Input assumptions: Low business risk	
Standard deviation in as a percentage	32.00
Risk free rate	9.00%
Combined days to maturity	1825
Face amount of debt	$12,000,000
Market value of the firm	$36,000,000
Commodity carrying cost or security dividend	$0.00
Output	
Value of common stock	$28,409,463
Call delta	$0.99

Put premium	$61,001
Put delta	$0.01
Value of debt	$7,590,537
(1 = Cash Commodities/2 = Futures/3 = Securities)	$3.00

The Morton & Maryann Magazine Company sells its Huntington Company subsidiary, thus increasing the standard deviation to 55%.

Input		Previous condition
Assumption: Risk of the business increases		
Standard deviation in percent	55.00	32.00
Risk free rate	9.00%	
Days to expiration	1825	
Face amount of debt: (Adjusted—Firm is now ⅓ smaller)	$8,000,000.00	
Market value of the firm: (Adjusted—Firm is now ⅓ smaller)	$24,000,000.00	
Commodity carrying cost or security dividend	$0.00	
Output		
Yield in equilibrium with higher variance	11.4750%	9.00%
Value of common stock	$19,492,725	
Call delta	$0.97	
Put premium	$593,751	
Put delta	$0.03	
Value of debt	$4,507,275	
Option pricing factor	$3.00	
Value increase (decrease) debt	($3,083,262)	
Change in debt value given higher volatility	$553,083	
Change in equity value given higher volatility	($553,083)	
Basis points to compensate for increased risk	247.5	
Elasticity yield factor: % Delta basis points / % Delta standard deviation	38.26%	

You can employ the Excel template if you want to verify the summary produced in Exhibit IV. The template MortonMaryannMagaz is in the subdirectory Models_Demos/Chapter 18.

Though default risk increased, the bank agreed to relax loan covenants, allowing the firm to proceed with the divestiture. A rate increase to 11.48% is reasonable compensation for incremental default risk. The $4 million loan to Huntington was repaid from the proceeds of the sale.

Option pricing is obviously not the only way to price debt and should never be used alone. But by estimating the probabilities that shareholders' call options finish "in the money," midsized firms and their capital providers (specifically banks) can arbitrate pricing issues on a level playing field, and *that's the important issue*—namely, the incremental cost of financing, which is loan yields in equilibrium with the volatility of a restructured business. For this reason, option pricing provides significant insight into the relationship between degrees of risk and returns demanded by key suppliers of capital.

REVIEW QUESTIONS

1. Although the quickest way to price a loan is to base it on the last successful deal, why is this not an effective method?
2. Describe and explain how loan pricing models are used and name four characteristics of proficient models.
3. Define the London Interbank Offering Rate (LIBOR) and explain how the Eurodollar market gives rise to it.
4. Discuss the difference between direct variable, allocated variable, direct fixed, and allocated fixed expenses. Why would a lender want to include these loan servicing costs in a pricing model?
5. Explain how the hurdle rate relates to ROA, ROE, and RAROC.
6. Define and explain the following:
   a. Commitment fee
   b. Prepayment penalty fee
   c. Facility fee
   d. Fees in lieu of balances
7. Why is the equity in a firm considered a call option on the value of the firm's assets?
8. How is the market value of a loan affected if the borrower decides to take on riskier projects, which increase the variance of the firm's assets?

SELECTED REFERENCES AND READINGS

Ahmad, K. M. (1989). Lending decisions and spreads: The syndicated Euro currency credit market. *Indian Economic Review* **24**, 83–100.

Angbazo, L. A., J. Mei, *et al.* (1998). Credit spreads in the market for highly leveraged transaction loans. *Journal of Banking & Finance* **22**, 1249–1282. Explores "the determinants of the required credit spreads on highly leveraged transaction (HLT) loans."

Best, P., A. Byrne, *et al.* (1998). What really happened to U.S. bond yields. *Financial Analysts Journal* **54**, 41–49.

Bielecki, T., and M. Rutkowski. (2000). "Term structure of credit: HJM with multiples." *Risk* **13**(4), 95–97. Presents a new approach to modeling credit risk, evaluating defaultable debt and pricing credit derivatives. The technique, based on Heath-Jarrow-Morton (HJM) methodology (1992), uses available information about credit spreads and recovery rates to model the intensity of credit migrations between various credit ratings classes.

Bielecki, T. R., S. R. Pliska, *et al.* (2000). "Risk sensitive asset allocation." *Journal of Economic Dynamics & Control* **24**(8), 1145–1177.

Brady, T. F. (1985). Changes in loan pricing and business lending at commercial banks. *Federal Reserve Bulletin/Board of Governors of the Federal Reserve System* **71**, 1–13.

Campbell, J. Y. (1993). Understanding risk and return. *National Bureau of Economic Research. Working Paper Series* No. **4554**, 1–[51].

Campbell, J. Y. (1998). Asset prices, consumption, and the business cycle. *National Bureau of Economic Research. Working Paper Series* No. **6485**, 1–[108].

Campbell, J. Y. (2000). Asset pricing at the millennium. *Harvard Institute of Economic Research. Discussion Paper Series* No. **1897**, 1–73.

Cantor, R., F. Packer, *et al.* (1997). Split ratings and the pricing of credit risk. *Federal Reserve Bank of New York. Research Paper* No. **9711**, 1–[27].

Chalmers, J. M. R. (1998). Default risk cannot explain the muni puzzle: evidence from municipal bonds that are secured by U.S. Treasury obligations. *Review of Financial Studies* **11**, 281–308.

Chen, A. H., S. C. Mazumdar, *et al.* (1996). Regulations, lender identity and bank loan pricing. *Pacific-Basin Finance Journal* **4**, 1–14.

Chew, W. (1999). Project bonds: key role of high-yield. *Global Finance* **13**, 76.

Chriss, N. (1997). *Black-Scholes and beyond: Option pricing models*. Chicago: Irwin.

Christensen, B. J. (1993). *Efficiency gains in beta-pricing models*. New York: New York University Salomon Center, Leonard N. Stern School of Business.

Crack, T. F., and S. K. Nawalkha. (2000). Interest rate sensitivities and bond risk measures. *Financial Analysts Journal* **56**(1), 34–43.

Crenshaw, A. (1989). Role of deposits in loan pricing. *Journal of Commercial Bank Lending* **71**, 21–27.

Daigler, R. T. (1994). *Advanced options trading: The analysis and evaluation of trading strategies, hedging tactics, and pricing models*. Chicago, IL: Probus.

Daniel, K. D., D. Hirshleifer, *et al.* (2000). Covariance risk, mispricing, and the cross section of security returns. *National Bureau of Economic Research. Working Paper Series* No. **7615**, 1–45.

Davis, E. P. (1992). Credit quality spreads, bond market efficiency and financial fragility. *Manchester School of Economic and Social Studies* **60**, Supplement.

Davis, E. P. (1993). VAR modeling of the German economy with financial spreads as key indicator variables. *London School of Economics and Political Science. Lse Financial Markets Group. Discussion Paper* No. **159**, 1–36. Evaluates the importance of the yield curve (public bond yield less money market rate), the credit quality spread (private bond yield less public bond yield), and the reverse yield gap (public bond yield less dividend yield on equities) as indicators of growth and inflation in Germany.

Duffee, G. R. (1996). Estimating the price of default risk. *United States. Board of Governors of the Federal Reserve System. Division of Research and Statistics. Finance and Economics Discussion Series* No. **96–29**, 1–[42].

Dym, S. (1997). Credit risk analysis for developing country bond portfolios. *Journal of Portfolio Management* **23**, 99–103.

Dziwura, J. R., and E. M. Green. (1996). Interest rate expectations and the shape of the yield curve. *Federal Reserve Bank of New York. Research Paper* No. **9631**, 1–40.

Elton, E. J. (1999). Expected return, realized return, and asset pricing tests. *Journal of Finance* **54**(4), 1199–1220. The presidential address to the American Finance Association.

Erb, C. B., C. R. Harvey, *et al.* (1999). New perspectives on emerging market bonds. *Journal of Portfolio Management* **25**, 83–92.

Faff, R. W., and P. F. Howard. (1999). Interest rate risk of Australian financial sector companies in a period of regulatory change. *Pacific-Basin Finance Journal* **7**(1), 83–101.

Fooladi, I. J., G. S. Roberts, *et al.* (1997). Duration for bonds with default risk. *Journal of Banking & Finance* **21**, 1–16.

Gertler, M., R. G. Hubbard, *et al.* (1990). Interest rate spreads, credit constraints, and investment fluctuations: an empirical investigation. *National Bureau of Economic Research. Working Paper Series* No. **3495**, 1–[39].

Golub, B. W., and L. M. Tilman. (1997). Measuring yield curve risk using principal components analysis, value at risk, and key rate durations. *Journal of Portfolio Management* **23**, 72–84.

Greenbaum, S. I., G. Kanatas, *et al.* (1989). Equilibrium loan pricing under the bank-client relationship. *Journal of Banking & Finance* **13**, 225–235.

Greenbaum, S. I., and I. Venezia. (1985). Partial exercise of loan commitments under adaptive pricing. *Journal of Financial Research* **8**, 251–63.

Helwege, J,. and C. M. Turner. (1999). The slope of the credit yield curve for speculative-grade issuers. *Journal of Finance* **54** (5), 1869–1884.

Ho, T. S. Y,. and A. Saunders. (1983). Fixed rate loan commitments, take-down risk and the dynamics of hedging with futures. *Journal of Financial and Quantitative Analysis* **18**, 499–516 December 4. The authors develop a normative model to analyze the hedging and fee-pricing decisions of a financial institution supplying fixed rate loan commitments to its customers.

Jarrow, R. A., D. Lando, *et al.* (1997). A Markov model for the term structure of credit risk spreads. *Review of Financial Studies* **10**, [481]–523.

Jarrow, R. A., and S. M. Turnbull. (2000). The intersection of market and credit risk. *Journal of Banking & Finance* **24**(1–2), 271–299.

Johnson, R. D., and J. O. Grace. (1990). Impact of deposit balances on loan pricing and profitability analysis. *Journal of Commercial Bank Lending* **73**, 31–39.

Johnson, R. D., and J. O. Grace. (1991). Can lenders rely on expected loan yields? *Bankers Magazine* **174**, 59–66.

Kamin, S. B., and K. v. Kleist. (1999). The evolution and determinants of emerging market credit spreads in the 1990s. *Bank for International Settlements. Monetary and Economic Dept. Bis Working Papers* **No. 68**, 1–32.

Kan, K. (1998). Credit spreads on government bonds. *Applied Financial Economics* **8**, 301–313. Estimates the credit spread for government bonds issued by Italy, France, Germany, and the United Kingdom.

Karagiannis, E. (1994). Credit spreads and fair value in the corporate market. *Financial Analysts Journal* **50**, 55–62. Presents an investment strategy designed to outperform a corporate credit market index while maintaining a neutral stance on interest rates and provides evidence that sector mispricings tend to self-correct.

Labadie, P. (1994). Term structure of interest rates over the business cycle. *Journal of Economic Dynamics & Control* **18**, 671–697.

Leibowitz, M. L. (1994). Interest rate- sensitive asset allocation.m*Journal of Portfolio Management* **20**, 8–15.

Madan, D., and H. Unal. (2000). A two-factor hazard rate model for pricing risky debt and the term structure of credit spreads. *Journal of Financial and Quantitative Analysis* **35 No. 1**, 43–65.

Madsen, C. (1997). Credit spreads. *Risk* **10**(Suppl.), 8–9. 1997 Risk Management Guide. (Nordic Markets)

Magee, B. (1999). Pay attention to interest. *Risk* **12**(10), 67–71.

Mattesini, F. (1996). Interest rate spreads and endogenous growth. *Economic Notes/Monte Dei Paschi Di Siena* **25**(1), 111–130.

Miranda, M. J., and J. W. Glauber. (1997). Systemic risk, reinsurance, and the failure of crop insurance markets. *American Journal of Agricultural Economics* **79**, 206–215.

Murphy, J. E. (1996). *Bond tables of probable future yields*. Minneapolis, MN. Crossgar Press,.

Platt, H. D., and M. B. Platt. (1992). Credit risk and yield differentials for high yield bonds. *Quarterly Journal of Business and Economics* **31**, 51–68.

Rasmussen, C. (1991). Danish view on loan pricing. *Bankers Magazine* **174**, 42–47.

Reisen, H., and J. v. Maltzan. (1998). Sovereign credit ratings, emerging market risk and financial market volatility. *Intereconomics: Review of International Trade and Development* **33**, 73–85. Commented on by Bernd Sehnatz, pp. 83–85.

Roberds, W., D. Runkle, *et al.* (1996). A daily view of yield spreads and short-term interest rate movements. *Journal of Money, Credit and Banking* **28**, 34–53. The authors "use daily observations from 1974 to 1991 on Federal funds and Treasury bill rates of maturities from one day to six months to sort out conflicts between the conventional wisdom and its qualifications and to better understand the relationship between the predictive power of the term structure and the stance of monetary policy.

Rogers, L. C. G., and D. Talay. (1997). *Numerical methods in finance.* Cambridge; New York: Cambridge University Press.

Roon, F. A. d., T. E. Nijman, *et al.* (1998). Pricing term structure risk in futures markets. *Journal of Financial and Quantitative Analysis* **33**, 139–57.

Rosen, L. R., and Dow Jones-Irwin. (1985). *The Dow Jones-Irwin guide to calculating yields.* Homewood, IL: Dow Jones-Irwin.

Slighton, R. L. (1982, Apr. 12). Wider LDC loan spreads ahead? *Chase Manhattan Bank, International Finance* **17**, 7–8.

Stanley, T., C. Roger, *et al.* (1995). Loan pricing: Desired return versus risk-based return. *Bankers Magazine* **178**, 37–41.

Wilmott, P., J. Dewynne, *et al.* (1996). *Option pricing: Mathematical models and computation.* Oxford: Oxford Financial Press.

Wu, C., and C.-h. Yu. (1996). Risk aversion and the yield of corporate debt. *Journal of Banking & Finance* **20**, 267–81.

Yawitz, J. B., and K. J. Maloney. (1983). Taxes, default risk, and yield spreads. *National Bureau of Economic Research. Working Paper Series* **No. 1215**, 1–25. The authors develop and test a model of interest rate spreads that incorporates both the effect of taxes and differences in default probabilities in a theoretically correct manner.

SELECT INTERNET LIBRARY AND CD

CD includes

M. Glantz: Stochastic Pricing Model

Internet Library

Loan Pricing Corporation Prices are available for approximately 1,800 bank loan tranches on a daily, weekly, or monthly basis at http://www.loanpricing.com/

19

RISK RATING MODELS
Design and Application

Risk grading provides bankers with a systematic methodology for uniformly analyzing risk across their portfolio. The principles underlying a risk rating system represent a common framework for assessing risk with a high degree of uniformity and providing a way to distinguish between levels of risk.

Credit ratings form the basis for a continuous loan review process, under which corporate credits are reviewed and regraded at least annually to focus attention on deteriorating credits so they can be classified in advance of reaching the point of no return. Just as important, credit grades form the basis upon which capital and loan provisions are calculated, developed, and assessed, allowing for determination of exposures through risk-adjusted returns on equity and other key bank benchmarks. These measurements serve as guides for resource allocation and active portfolio management and planning. In addition, ratings aid in determining the level of service and monitoring required. Grades indicating high-risk levels encourage managerial and accounting follow-up action.

The principles underlying a risk rating system are for lenders to take the following actions:

- Establish a common framework for assessing risk.
- Establish uniformity throughout the bank's units, divisions, and affiliates.
- Establish compatibility to regulatory definitions, which distinguish various levels of "poor" credit risk.
- Distinguish various levels of "satisfactory" credit risk.
- Promote common training through expanded definitions and risk rating guides.
- Initiate and maintain ratings on a continuous basis.
- Set criteria for review of ratings by the bank's auditing department to verify accuracy, consistency, and timeliness.
- Institute a systematic methodology for uniformly analyzing risk across the loan portfolio.

A rating scale should be established to effectively distinguish gradations of risk within the institution's portfolio, so that there is clear linkage to loan quality (or loss characteristics), rather than using the scale to simply serve an administrative function.

We define *risk* as the probability that an exposure loss will be sustained (Tables 19.1 and 19.2). Credit risk ratings reflect not only the likelihood or severity of loss but also the variability of loss over time, particularly as this relates to the effect of the business cycle. Linkage to these measurable outcomes gives greater structure and clarity to risk rating analysis and allows for more consistent assessment of performance against relevant benchmarks, for example, evaluating the interrelation between expected default frequency ranges and bond ratings (Table 19.1). Commercial loans expose banks to two types of risk: obligor risk and facility (or transaction) risk. Obligor risk is associated with economic and industry risks, industry structure risks, customer-specific risks, and the ever-present operating risks inherent in the lending business. Facility risks are risks inherent in a loan instrument or facility. If a bank feels that combined risk levels are unacceptable, it might sell the exposure or acquire other deals that are less exposed to these forces, thus reducing the risk of the portfolio.

Ratings begin with the risk of the obligor, then risks associated with the particular facility or transaction—variables that increase or decrease risk—are added, such as collateral, guarantees, terms, tenor, and portfolio impact. A single borrower would have only one obligor rating but might have several different facilities with different facility ratings, depending on terms, collateral, and so forth.

RISK RATING TUTORIAL: ROBFEL _NEW4.XLS

The ROBFEL risk rating tutorial is a 10-point interactive Industrial and Commercial Risk Grading workbook designed to reinforce the concepts in this chapter. You may navigate throughout the system by simply clicking "Risk" on the main menu. The workbook is menu driven and contains interactive dialog boxes that pop on the screen. A dialog appears (Figure 19.1), where initiating information is entered. The tutorial also includes caption callouts that reinforce concepts and help you traverse the various worksheets. The tutorial includes an extensive system of supporting macros, making it relatively simple to adapt the model into your bank's portfolio system. Following is a sample of the auditing macros:

1. The system (via Excels' Visual Basic programming language) tracks data entry from beginning to end, checking for missing information and errors.

TABLE 19.1   Comparing the Credit Grade to the Bond Rating and Expected Default Frequency

Credit grade	Bond rating	Key words	EDF high in basis points	EDF mean in basis points	EDF low in basis points
1	AAA to AA-	World-class organization	0.02	0.02	0.02
2	AA to A-	Excellent access to capital markets	0.13	0.02	0.02
3	A+ to BBB+	Cash flow trends generally positive	0.27	0.06	0.03
4	BBB+ to BBB	Leverage, coverage somewhat below industry average	0.87	0.16	0.08
5	BBB to BBB-	Lower-tier competitor; limited access to public debt markets	1.62	0.25	0.24
6	BBB- to BB-	Narrow margins; fully leveraged; variable cash flow	2.65	0.52	0.24
7	B	Cash flow vulnerable to downturns; strained liquidity; poor coverage	5.44	1.89	0.64
8	C	Special mention (1)	19.06	2.89	2.85
9	D	Substandard (2)			
10	D	Doubtful (3)			

TABLE 19.2 Definitions of Poor Credit Grades by the Authorities

Definitions issued by the regulatory bodies as of June 10, 1993	Comptroller of the Currency, Federal Deposit Insurance Corporation, Federal Reserve Board, Office of Thrift Supervision
Special mention	A special-mention asset has potential weaknesses that deserves management's close attention. If left uncorrected, these potential weaknesses may result in deterioration of the repayment prospects for the asset or in the institution's credit position at some future date. Special-mention assets are not adversely classified and do not expose an institution to sufficient risk to warrant adverse classification.
Substandard assets	A substandard asset is inadequately protected by the current sound worth and paying capacity of the obligor or of the collateral pledged, if any. Assets so classified must have a well-defined weakness or weaknesses that jeopardize the liquidation of the debt. They are characterized by the distinct possibility that the firm will sustain some loss if the deficiencies are not corrected.
Doubtful assets	An asset classified as doubtful has all the weaknesses inherent in one classified substandard with the added characteristic that the weaknesses make collection or liquidation in full, on the basis of currently existing facts, conditions, and values, highly questionable and improbable.
Loss assets	Assets classified as loss assets are considered uncollectible and of such little value that their continuance as viable assets is not warranted. This classification does not mean that the asset has absolutely no recovery or salvage value, but rather that it is not practical or desirable to defer writing off this basically worthless asset even though partial recovery may be affected in the future.

Macros prevent printing (including range printing) if the system finds omitted grades. By selecting the . . . Risk . . . Verify Data entry, you prompt the program to locate and disclose errors via a dialog box:

. . . "Missing Category Risk for: Debt Capacity/Financing Flexibility"

. . . "Missing Category Risk for: Microeconomic and Environment"

. . . "Enter Reason for Override in Financial Reporting Cumulative Grade"

. . . "Enter Reason for Override in Contingencies Cumulative Grade"

. . . "Enter Reason for Override in Industry Cumulative Grade"

and so on.

To view comments supporting ROBFEL Bank Tutorial:
- Select the Tools menu, click Options, and then click the View tab.
- In order to display both comments and indicators regardless of the mouse position, you will need to click Comments & indicator.

The system will accept override decisions, but will prompt you (via a dialog) to enter a reason for the override (inside the dialog) The system generates (prints) a new report . . . "Reasons for Override." The system will not print if explanations are not provided for overrides. Attempts to range print carry headings on all pages . . . "Data Not Verified."

2. If changes need to be made to the opening dialog box, you can select *Update Dialog Box* from the main menu.

3. If a guarantee does not support the credit, the system takes out the guarantee worksheet.

4. If collateral does not support the credit, the system takes out the collateral worksheet.

5. The system prints automatically. Select *Risk . . . Print . . . Entire System* to print the entire Risk Rating System. Select *Risk . . . Print . . . Summary Analysis* to print the Summary. If reports print "off the page," print macros may need adjustment to match the bank's printers. Simply locate the Zoom command inside the print macro (Module 1—unprotect the sheet first). Zoom is set at Zoom = 80. Change the Zoom to perhaps Zoom = 75. Experiment.

Getting Started

Open ROBFEL_New4.xls click "Enable macros." A dialog appears as depicted in Figures 19.1 and 19.2. Click "Start Tutorial Rating." The banker working a full-scale version (although this tutorial almost reaches that level) selects industry group, facility, maximum exposure, his or her name, name of the borrower, maximum ROBFEL Bank exposure, facility amount, previous credit grade (if any), and date.

The ROBFEL tutorial, to demonstrate to you how other macros work, is responsive to guarantees and collateral. If the boxes for guarantees or collateral supports the credit, please check the box labeled *Guarantees?* and/or *Collateral?* If guarantees or collateral are not checked, these items disappear from the system. Complete other information the dialog requests.

1. Enter individual credit grade for each category. The system will compute cumulative grades.
2. Worksheet *comment* and *text* boxes will provide guidance as you work through the system.

Click OK.

OBLIGOR GRADES

Module 1: Obligor Financial Measures (OFM Worksheet)

After you click "ok" in the dialog box (Figure 19.2), module I will automatically open in a few seconds. Examine each of the definitions corresponding to the

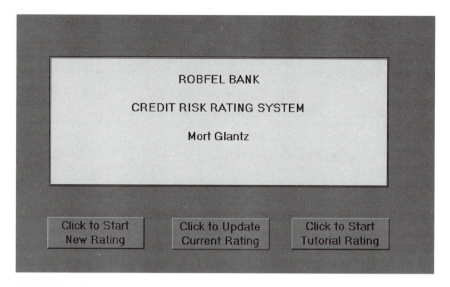

FIGURE 19.1   Credit Risk Rating Tutorial Opening Page

columns (grade, bond rating, expected default factor) and decide where the firm fits. Enter individual risks grades at the bottom of this worksheet (Table 19.3): *operating cash flows, debt capacity and financing flexibility, asset quality, valuation measures, contingencies, financial reporting, and management.* The tutorial workbook provides additional instructions. You can experiment by entering random numbers in red cells or your can elect to enter default grades appearing in the text.

First Column: Earnings and Operating Cash Flow

Recall from Chapter 6 that cash flow analysis is one of the banker's most important analytical tools. It raises questions about the way clients generate and absorb cash. As you review the risk rating boxes in the cash flow column, recall that borrowers taking on high debt levels to fund expansion may experience serious cash flow problems if their income stream is interrupted due to structural problems. Consider also firms neglecting their current assets. Sudden and problematic increases in receivables and inventories tie up large amounts of cash that otherwise would be used to fund "growth" strategies like investments, research, and essential expansion strategies—the sustaining force behind shareholder value. We pay particular attention to this column: what begins as the entry grade for cash flow could well end up the final obligor grade.

1. Are earnings stable, growing, and of high quality?
2. Are margins solid compared to the industry?
3. Is cash flow magnitude sufficient to fund growth internally?
4. Is operating cash flow strong in relation to present and anticipated debt?

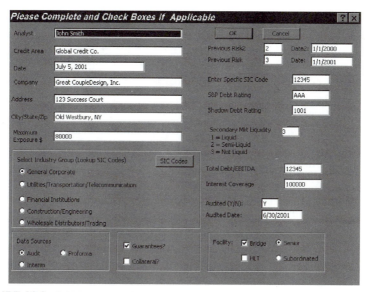

FIGURE 19.2   ROBFEL Bank Dialog Box

5. Is *net cash flow from operations* sufficient to cover most nondiscretionary outlays?

Cash flow	
Category risk grade	3
Cumulative risk grade	3.00

If the category risk grade is worse than 5, a warning appears on the page: "Warning/Grade Worse Than 5/View Essar Cash Flow Below/Is Your Cash Flow as Detailed?" Try entering a 6 in the cash flow category risk grade and follow up on "Warning" and "View" boxes that pop up on the spreadsheet.

Debt Capacity and Financial Flexibility

Since debt capacity is usually driven by cash flow, it is unusual for analysts to assign a higher grade to this column than the grade denoting cash flow—quality, magnitude, and trend. Debt entails a commitment to make cash payments, which

TABLE 19.3   Breakdown of Category, Cumulative Risk Grade, and Option to Accept or Override Preset Cumulative Grade Weights

	Operating cash flows	Debt capacity and financing flexibility	Asset/liability quality	Valuation measures
Category risk grade	3	4	4	4
Cumulative risk grade	3.00	3.33	3.43	3.71
Accept/override				

are contractually certain in timing and amount, under uncertain future financial and operating conditions. Because debt is used to maintain or expand operations, debt payments cannot be viewed in a vacuum; debt is only a subset of the many required cash inflows and outflows that contribute to value creation.

A borrower's ability to tolerate debt depends on the availability and volatility of future operating cash flows. Borrowers with relatively stable internal cash streams are less likely to become cash inadequate, debt burdened, or just flat insolvent. Firms with risky, volatile, or uncertain inflow streams are far less able to assume the fixed charges related to debt. Financial risk is not solely a product of debt levels: managers' fiduciary responsibility lies in managing debt with as much a discerning eye as they use to manage assets. Debt capacity comes to us in five shades: asset quality, cash flow coverage, product visibility and market strength, wide breadth of financial alternatives, and, of course, an established repayment track record. Lenders need to answer several questions when evaluating debt capacity:

1. Is leverage and coverage within the first quartile of the industry peer group?
2. What alternative sources of debt and capital exist?
3. Does the borrower have solid investment-grade ratings?
4. Can the borrower weather economic downturns?
5. Are debt maturities manageable?

Debt capacity	
Category risk grade	4
Cumulative risk grade	3.33

Balance Sheet Quality and Structure

Characteristically, current assets represent more than half the total assets of many businesses. Because they represent such a large investment and tend to be relatively volatile, current assets are worthy of a representative column in our risk rating tutorial.

1. Are assets solid and fairly valued?
2. Does the liability structure match the asset structure?
3. Do assets show concentration of location or use?
4. Are liquidity margins narrow?
5. Have asset turnover ratios been evaluated? These include average collection period, inventory turnover, and fixed asset turnover.
6. Is the bank lending where the assets are and does the bank have access to them?

Asset quality	
Category risk grade	4
Cumulative risk grade	3.43

Valuation

Corporate value is a function of the firm's future cash flow potential and the risks (threats) of those future cash flows. It is these perceived risks or threats that help define the discounting factor used to measure cash flows in present value terms. Cash flow depends on the industry and the economic outlook for the business's products, current and future competition, sustainable competitive advantage, projected changes in demand, and the business's capacity to grow in light of its past financial and operational performance. Risk factors include the business's financial condition (profitability, cash flows, the magnitude of financial and operational leverage, and ability to pay debt), management's ability to sustain operations and profitability, market and industry trends and outlook, competitive forces, the economic environment, legal and regulatory issues, and contingent liabilities. It is for these reasons that the valuation column acts as a fail-safe verification of cash flow performance. Thus, entering a cash flow grade of 2, for example, would be inconsistent with grade 8 entered in the valuation column. When assessing valuation, lenders should answer the following questions:

1. Will the bank develop a shareholder valuation from client projections?
2. Is there a healthy spread between the obligor's asset values—that is, cash flow value (also referred to as the *economic value* of assets, or the value of the firm)—and the market value of debt?
3. What is the spread between the obligor's operating profit margin and the threshold margin? The threshold margin is the minimum profit margin required to increase shareholder value.
4. Does the obligor have hidden liabilities that may result in a significant erosion of shareholder value? (Case in point: Enron Corporation.)
5. What are probabilities that shareholder value will fall below zero?

Valuation	
Category risk grade	4
Cumulative risk grade	3.71

Contingencies

These include litigation, guarantees of indebtedness, guarantees to repurchase receivables or property sold or otherwise assigned, and warranty/product liability obligations. Environmental laws are becoming increasingly complex with considerable governmental emphasis on compliance. Noncompliance can result in costly cleanups, fines, and penalties turning a creditworthy company into a financially distressed write-off.

If the risk grade falls below the preset threshold, 5, the cumulative grade defaults to the grade assigned to contingencies. Note the formula =IF(N106>5, N106,L107) in cell OPM!N107. Consider these questions when evaluating contingencies:

1. Are contingencies limited and easily controlled?
2. Is the potential impact on tangible new worth negligible?
3. Is the expected value of contingencies certain?
4. Are you familiar with the accounting for contingencies: SFAS No. 5, APB Opinion No. 22, "Disclosure of Accounting Policies," SEC requirements, FIN No. 34, the SEC's Financial Reporting Release (FRR) No. 23, SFAS No. 112, "Employers Accounting for Postretirement Benefits," and other accounting pronouncements?
5. Have you determined the amount to accrue for a loss contingency involving litigation?
6. Have you checked the nature and amount of large guarantees?
7. What are the borrower's obligations related to product liabilities, warranties, and catastrophic losses?
8. Have you assessed the probability that other parties will be able to pay their share of any apportioned liability?
9. Did you discount any long-term contingent liabilities net of related recoveries?
10. Did the borrower fail to record the costs of rectifying environmental problems?

Continue entering grades onto the electronic risk grading system as you read the chapter.

Contingencies

Category risk grade	5
Cumulative risk grade	3.71

Financial Reporting

Bankers should fully understand financial statements, budgets, projections, and other documents supporting loan exposures (see Chapter 2). They also have a responsibility to ensure that the audits the bank depends on are representational, faithful, verifiable, neutral, and consistent. Financial statements should not confuse users; rather, they should form a comprehensive, cohesive, and coherent body of financial disclosure that spells out the truthful story. In the words of the former chairman of the Securities and Exchange Commission, Arthur Levitt, "Transparent financial reporting must reign supreme—not only in the U.S.—but around the world."

Truer words were never spoken. In the wake of the Enron and Worldcom collapse, it has become apparent that while accounting rules are written very specifically, clever accountants find ways to get around them.

If you determine the audit is unreliable or difficult to judge, or if the information is insufficient to judge creditworthiness, or if the business plan is poorly defined or inaccurate, your rating will fall below an acceptable threshold—in this case, category risk grade 5. The partial formula, =IF(P106>5,10,N108), denotes how the cumulative grade reads. If the unit grade provided in financial reporting falls below 5, the cumulative grade becomes 10; otherwise there is no change. Consider these questions when judging financial documents:

1. Does a reputable accounting firm regularly complete an audit?
2. Are financial reports promptly issued?
3. Are statements accurate and complete?
4. Have you analyzed business segments having a significant impact on the consolidated entity?
5. Did you verify the reliability of information in business reporting?
6. Did you check the accountant's file and can you confirm that past audits passed reliability and comparability tests?
7. How does the company or its auditors assess whether significant estimates and assumptions are based on the best information available?
8. Does the company use independent specialists or sophisticated quantitative techniques to validate or develop key estimates and assumptions?
9. What negative events or unsatisfactory outcomes occurred during the year and how are those presented in the financial statements?
10. How do the company's accounting policies, disclosures, format of financial statements, and other financial communications compare to the company's competitors?
11. What changes, if any, have there been in the company's accounting policies or in management's application of the policies and the use of estimates and judgments?
12. Does the audit contain significant disclaimers or an adverse opinion?
13. Is the timeliness of statements problematic?
14. Did you review the borrower's business plan carefully in terms of consistency with independent audits?

Financial reporting

Category risk grade	4
Cumulative risk grade	3.71

Management and Controls

What about the personal side of the firms bankers lend to? The company's attributes, management, and controls are as important as cash flow, debt capacity, security, and asset quality. Poor management lacks the driving commitment to maximize shareholder value. Management in the lower risk categories lack adaptability—they are not responsive and innovative in their approach to change. Management's lack of alertness to changes dealing with measuring and implementing economic, competitive, technological, and financial factors can become extremely detrimental for sustained growth and profitability and will affect default probabilities. High management ratings, on the other hand, reflect management's ability to capture the essence of strategy formulation—that is, to organize the combined disciplines of risk and valuation and to guide the corporation into a winning future.

As you review the grade, consider how well the firm's managers respond to changes in the external environment and how they creatively deploying internal resources to improve the firm's competitive position. The key to success is to be able to quantify these factors and integrate them into strategic planning and formulation.

1. Is management capable, tried, and tested now and for the foreseeable future?
2. Are strong operating and financial controls in place?
3. Does management have broad industry experience, good continuity, and depth?
4. Do senior managers keep changing?
5. Is there a succession plan in place?
6. In the case of a closely held firm, is there a buy/sell agreement to facilitate ownership transfer upon the death of a principal?
7. Have the owners and managers taken salary cuts during difficult times?
8. Is management meeting customer or marketplace expectations?
9. How efficiently is management running the firm's operations?
10. Does management set goals and provide a context for achieving them?

Management	
Category risk grade	4
Cumulative risk grade	3.71

Using Weights to Determine Cumulative Obligor Financial Measures

Weights assigned in Module 1 are set in default mode for illustration (Cell OPM1!L107).

The model derives the cumulative grade using a weighting system set by the bank's management and influenced by the industry and loan facility. For example, the formula set to derive the cumulative grade in the valuation measures column (L107) is

=IF(L106=0,0,IF(OR(L106>10,L106=0),"ERROR",(Y3*F106+Y4*H106+Y5*J106+ Y6*L106)/(Y3+Y4+Y5+Y6)))

In reality, algorithms programmed in the weighting grid are industry and facility specific and are designed to arrive at accurate obligor cumulative grades (see Weights!A1 and Table 19.4). However, you may still call the shots and enter cumulative grades directly to the worksheet, bypassing grids.

Example 1: Assume the operating cash flow grade is 3 while the debt capacity grade is 4. The bank set default weights in the sums column (7 and 2), respectively, reflecting the importance of cash flow to debt capacity—since much of the borrower's financing capacity is derived from cash flow. Based on the weights, the cumulative grade is $(3 * 7 + 4 * 2)/(7 + 2) = 3.2$.

Example 2: Assume the operating cash flow grade is 2, the debt capacity grade is 3, and the asset/liability quality grade is 4. You argue the default weights in the third column (5, 3, and 9) reflect the importance of operating cash flow and debt capacity to asset/liability. If weights are accepted, the cumulative grade is $(2 * 5 + 3 * 3 + 4 * 9)/(5 + 3 + 9) = 3.24$.

Module 2: Financial Situations and Recent Developments— Worksheet FinDev

This module considers important changes beyond the fiscal date that affect the obligor's financial measures grade (module 1). Module 2 factors into the system and serves as insurance that bankers acquire and analyze timely (particularly negative) information, which can strongly affect the course of events. The obligor grade adjustment and reason for the adjustment are carried over to the summary page. In our practice session, we assume no change to this module.

Module 3: Industry Grade—Worksheet Indus

This section examines two columns: *Industry Segment* and *Position within Industry*. We enter the industry grade and industry position. The system takes these two numbers, completes the industry cumulative rating, and enters the rating on the industry worksheet. Select Risk/Industry Measures/Industry– Position Grid and Risk/Industry Measures/Industry/Cumulative Weighting to review the operation. The grid shown in Exhibit I determines the cumulative grade, which may deteriorate but cannot improve. In effect, module 3 serves as a check that you were not too liberal completing module 1. Enter a grade of 6 and 5 in Industry Segment (cell F107) and Position within Industry (cell H107), respectively. The cumulative grade has defaulted to 4.00 from 3.71.

In rare cases, you may elect to override the industry cumulative grade. A dialog appears when you confirm data entry: "Enter Reason for Override in Industry Cumulative Grade." If you do not enter a reason for the override in the dialog, the system will not print. Range printing will carry a heading on all pages: "Reports Not Verified."

EXHIBIT I   Industry/Position Grid

Borrower rating	Expected bond rating	Industry grade									
		1	2	3	4	5	6	7	8	9	10
1: First tier											
Substantially risk free	AAA to A−							5	5	5	7
2: First tier											
Minimum risk	AA to A−							5	6	6	7
3: Second tier				no effect							
Modest risk	A+ to BBB+				on			5	6	6	8
4: Second tier				cumulative credit grade							
Average risk	BBB+ to BBB							5	7	7	8
5: Second tier											
Above average risk	BBB+ to BBB−						4	5	7	8	9
6: Third tier											
Management attention risk	BBB− to BB−	4	4	4	5	5	6	7	8	9	10
7: Third tier											
Special mention	B	5	5	5	7	7	7	8	9	9	10
8: Fourth tier											
Substandard	C	6	6	7	7	7	9	10	10	10	10
9: Fourth tier											
Doubtful	D	7	7	8	8	8	9	10	10	10	10
10: Fourth tier											
Loss	D	8	8	9	9	9	10	10	10	10	10

Industry analysis is crucial. You need to consider the impact industry risk and peer position have on obligor financial measures. Attributes include cyclicality, seasonality, regulatory issues, environmental issues, product liability, barriers to entry, technical obsolescence, commodity versus value added, manufacture versus service, domestic reliance versus international sales diversification, government contract–related issues, and industry life cycle (see Chapter 12, "Portfolio Management of Default Risk," for a more complete industry discussion). Consider these questions when analyzing and industry:

1. Does the borrower operate in a strong and growing industry?
2. Is the borrower a significant factor in the industry or market?
3. Are legal or regulatory climates favorable?
4. Is the industry cyclically minimal?
5. Is the industry vulnerable to sudden economic or technological change?
6. Is the industry's operating leverage modest?

TABLE 19.4   General Corporate and Utilities/Transportation/ Telecommunications Cumulative Grade Weights

General corporate: Cumulative grade weights

Operating cash flows	1	2	4	4
Debt capacity and financing capacity	1	2		5
Asset/liability quality		1		3
Valuation				2
Management depth/accept or enter		6 :1 Means relationship between cumulative grade and management depth		6

Utilities/transportation/telecommunications: Cumulative grade weights

Operating cash flows	1	2	4	4
Debt capacity and financing capacity	1	2		4
Asset/liability quality		1		3
Valuation				2
Management depth/accept or enter		6 :1 Means relationship between cumulative grade and management depth		6

7. Are labor problems minimal?
8. Is the regulatory environment satisfactory?
9. Are long-term prospects favorable?
10. Does the borrower rank in the first tier of the industry?
11. Is the borrower "industry focused"? Does it enjoy a meaningful market share?
12. Are the borrower's performance ratios generally better than its industry peers?

The computer converts the industry/position grid (Exhibit I); its algorithms are shown in Exhibit II, and the equations that follow:

EXHIBIT II   Industry Grid Conversion Methodology

Cumulative OFM and FinDev before industry	3.71	1	2
Industry grade transfer		N/A	N/A
Cumulative grade before considering obligor's tier position		N/A	N/A
Industry grade selected from worksheet	6		
Industry position grade	5		
Matrix industry and tier grade		N/A	N/A
		N/A	N/A
Computer-generated cumulative grade	4.00		

Equation 1: Industry Grid Conversion Methodology Cumulative Grade before Considering Obligor's Tier Position: Example Grade 10

=IF(Y3="N/A","N/A",FINDEV!$C106)

Equation 2: Industry Grid Conversion Methodology—Matrix Industry and Tier: Example Grade 9

=IF(O7=1,5,IF(O7=2,6,IF(O7=3,6,IF(O7=4,7,IF(O7=5,8,IF(O7=6,9,IF(O7=7,9,IF(O7>7,10))))))))

Equation 3: Computer Generated Cumulative Grade

=MAXA(P9:Y9)

Module 4: Country Risk—Worksheet COUNTRYRISK

When loan exposures occur across international borders, they may carry additional risks not present in domestic lending. These risks, called country or cross-border risks, typically include risks arising from a variety of national differences in economic structures, policies, sociopolitical institutions, geography, and currencies. Country risk rating identifies and puts into perspective the potential for these risks to increase expected default probabilities—that is, to find imbalances that increase the risk of a shortfall in the expected return of a cross-border investment. Cross-border risks usually include but are not restricted to the following:

1. *Economic risk.* The significant change in the economic structure or growth rate that produces a major change in the expected return of an investment.
2. *Transfer risk.* The risk arising from a decision by a foreign government to restrict capital movements. Restrictions could make it difficult to repatriate profits, dividends, or capital.
3. *Exchange risk.* An unexpected adverse movement in the exchange rate. Exchange risk includes an unexpected change in a currency regime such as a change from a fixed to a floating exchange rate.
4. *Location risk.* The spillover effects caused by problems in a region, in a country's trading partner, or in countries with similar perceived characteristics.
5. *Sovereign risk.* The risk associated with whether a government will be unwilling or unable to meet its loan obligations, or is likely to renege on loans it guarantees. Sovereign risk can relate to transfer risk in that a government may run out of foreign exchange due to unfavorable developments in its balance of payments.

6. *Political risk.* The risk of a change in political institutions stemming from a change in government control, a change in the social fabric, or some other noneconomic factor. This category covers the potential for internal and external conflicts, expropriation risk, and traditional political analysis.

When completing the rating, consider the following questions:

1. What is the country investment ranking?
2. What is the Interagency Country Exposure Review Committee (ICERC) rating?
3. Has the ICERC rating improved or deteriorated over the preceding six months?
4. What is the country's resource base in terms of natural resources, human resources, and financial resources?
5. What is the outlook for domestic political stability?
6. What is the quality of economic and financial management? Does the leadership have the political strength to implement decisions, particularly if they involve austerity measures?
7. What is the country's long-run development strategy?
8. Is industrial development based on efficiency, or in support of prestige projects or the economic interests of politically powerful groups?
9. Is economic growth financed largely by domestic revenues and savings or through foreign speculative investments?
10. Is inflation under control?
11. Are wage and price policies in line with productivity growth?
12. In looking at the outlook for the balance of payments, what is the prognosis of current account, capital account, and debt service account improvements?
13. How are capital account deficits financed? Through World Bank or bilateral aid programs? Through bank loans?
14. Does the bank regularly gather information as to the company's risk exposure in each country and compare this with the country limits?
15. Is there action to eliminate any exposure in excess of a particular country limit?

The cumulative grade assigned to cell F107 is set by the formula: =IF(F106> 5,F106,D107). If the category risk grade, Country/Transfer Risk, is worse than 5, the cumulative grade defaults to the country grade; otherwise the original grade stands. Enter 1 as illustrated below:

Country risk

Category risk grade	1
Cumulative risk grade	4.00

FACILITY GRADES

As we saw earlier, facility risk refers to risks inherent in an individual facility, commitment, or loan: the credit product, the tenor/maturity (long versus short), collateral and support, guarantees, purpose of facility, documentation quality and verification, and portfolio. Attentiveness to all aspects of the loan's structure can significantly reduce the possibilities of loan downgrades or write-offs. For example, a bank approves a revolving credit to a U.S. subsidiary of a German company secured by a borrowing base (75% receivables, 60% inventory). The bank relies on monthly borrowing base reports from the company. Although the borrower is profitable, its financial flexibility is limited by modest debt capacity. Ultimate repayment lies in the ability of the German parent to provide financing. As a result of the facility's structure, you suggest a -1 improvement in the grade.

Downgrades to obligor risk ratings are exceptions. However, you might decide to downgrade if the facility calls for unusual tenor, if documentation is weak, if the loan's marketability has deteriorated, or if the purpose of the loan is inappropriate.

Module 5: Documentation Matrix—Worksheet Docum6

There is no faster way for disaster to strike than for bankers to ignore the periodic and thorough review of loan documentation. This means knowing who the borrower and guarantor are, reviewing covenants and recent compliance or violations, checking and updating subordination agreements and corporate resolutions, and, as noted earlier, making sure that collateral requirements and documents are up to date. A fail-safe rule to follow is this: *Risk rating is not considered complete until the banker physically reviews loan documentation under his or her jurisdiction.*

Consider these downgrades: documentation may not conform to normal standards; updates are past due and may not be valid (uniform commercial code [UCC] filings, etc.), resulting in a downgrade from +1 to + 2. Documentation that clearly does not conform to normal standards will lead to a downgrade ranging from +3 to + 8. Documentation is satisfactory but lacks meaningful covenants can result in a +1 downgrade.

Documentation adjustment to grade	0 or left blank
Cumulative risk grade	4.00

Module 6: Guarantees—Worksheet GUAR3

A guarantee is a written contract, agreement, or undertaking involving three parties. The first party, the *guarantor*, agrees to guarantee that the performance of the second party, the obligor, is fulfilled according to the terms of the contract, agreement, or undertaking. The third party is the *creditor*. For example, B makes a loan through his bank. The bank desires a guarantor for this loan in case of default by B. B asks A to act as guarantor for his loan. A agrees and signs a guaranty. A is the guarantor, B the obligor, and the bank the creditor. Following is an example of a full, uncontested, and unconditional guarantee:

The bank issued a $35 million unsecured term loan to Howie and Judy Inc. to refinance long-term notes issued by Jan Baking Company in conjunction with Howie and Judy Inc.'s 2000 acquisition of Western Type and Supply Company. Howie and Judy Inc.'s obligor grade is 5. Howie and Judy Inc., a wholly owned subsidiary of the Jan Baking Company since 1965, is a wholesale distributor of graphic art supplies, equipment, and chemicals to the printing industry. Howie and Judy Inc. contributed 47% of Jan's consolidated revenues and 22% of its net income. Jan Baking Company was incorporated in 1914. It specializes in single-portion pies, cakes, and cookies. Jan purchased Howie and Judy Inc. in 1965 for diversification purposes.

While both companies have performed consistently, Jan Baking remains the stronger of the two companies, both on a balance sheet and profit-and-loss basis, and is graded a 2. On a consolidated basis, the company displays strong interest coverage, adequate debt service capacity, and a satisfactory leverage position. In addition, the unsecured term loan to Howie and Judy Inc. is guaranteed unconditionally and in full by Jan Baking Company. Furthermore, the guarantee is uncontested. Historically, Jan has generated sufficient cash flow to meet current maturities and payments of dividends. Cash flow from operations coupled with short-term borrowings are used to fund capital expenditures. Based on this information, the credit grade was improved to 2, the grade of the guarantor.

The assigned credit grade to loans partially supported by third-party undertakings will lie somewhere between the borrower's rating and the rating assigned to the guarantor. Unconditional guarantees of payment will have considerably more impact than a comfort letter or a "verbal assurance."

Bankers can complete a risk rating form or check the guarantor's bond rating before completing the guarantee worksheet. *Note:* If the loan is not supported by a guarantee, Excel removes the worksheet GUAR3 if you did not check the box "*guarantee?*" in the opening dialog box (Figure 19.2).

For partial guarantees, the worksheet calculates a weighted risk rating. The weighted risk rating depends on relative credit responsibility and the expected default frequency for the obligor and guarantor.

The expected default factor of the obligor in basis points corresponds to the cumulative risk grade. You need to enter the guarantor's grade, assumed to be 2 in Table 19.5, and the percentage of the facility under the guarantor's responsibility, 70%. The program derives the obligor's prorate responsibility, 30%, the expected default factors of guarantor and obligor, 6 and 37, the combined EDF, 15.09, and the weighted grade, 3.50.

Guarantees are only as good as supporting documents and are usually reviewed by legal counsel. The system includes a column that helps you evaluate

TABLE 19.5 Sample Cells in the GUAR3 Worksheet

Guarantors grade	2	
Enter percentage of obligation: Guarantor	70%	
Obligors percentage of obligation	30%	
Expected default factor /guarantor	6	
Expected default factor/obligor	37	15.09
Obligors cumulative grade	4	
Transaction weighted grade	3.50	

whether documentation is perfected and uncontestable (grades 1 through 4), documentation exists is perfected but may be questionable (grade 5), documentation exists and is perfected but clearly lacks strength (grade 6), or if serious deficiencies exists (grades 7 through 10). If you enter a grade worse than 5 in either the Guarantee or Documentation columns, the system reinstates the obligor grade absent of the guarantee.

Enter a grade 3 in cell F111 located in the Guarantee column, and grade 4 in the Documentation column, cell H111. The grades you entered have no affect on the cumulative grade.

Module 7: Collateral Matrix—Worksheet Coll4

A careful collateral check should be performed before the risk grading process is finalized, more frequently for credits that are either heavily reliant on collateral or are secured by unique collateral. Make sure the bank's Uniform Commercial Code financing statements and security agreements are valid, up to date, and consistent with approval documentation. *Risk rating time is time spent to insure your collateral is properly secured and all liens perfected.*

The grade assigned to secured loans depends on, among other things, the degree of coverage, the economic life cycle of the collateral versus the term of the loan, possible constraints of liquidating the collateral, and the bank's ability to skillfully and economically monitor and liquidate collateral.

For the purposes of risk grading, collateral is separated into three classification tiers. Classification I includes highly liquid and readily attainable collateral with differences secured by other less liquid assets. Classification I collateral includes cash, CDs banker's acceptances or commercial paper, and top investment-grade bonds.

Classification II represents independent audit/valuation–required security, including the highest accounts receivable quality, the highest inventory quality (liquid and diversified inventory) and prime and readily marketable fixed assets including commercial real estate, and finally collateral easily accessible by assignees' or participants' voting rights on collateral not abridged.

Classification III, or other collateral, includes leasehold improvements, stock of subsidiaries, stock on pink sheets, receivables and inventory of concentrated/questionable quality, and real estate of questionable quality and marketability.

Consider the following example: Subsidiary is well capitalized and continues to maintain capital above SEC capital requirements for insurance companies. For the nine-month period ending December 31, 1999, Subsidiary had excess net capital of $39 million. Net income for the nine-month period ending December 31, 2000, totaled $11.7 million compared to $11.0 million in the prior period and $11.4 million for financial year ending March 31, 2000. Revenues of $179 million are up 18% from the previous period.

Parent Mutual has more than $4 billion in assets and carries an A+ rating from Best, signifying a solid financial condition. Additionally, Parent Mutual has the capacity to provide additional financial resources to Subsidiary if necessary. Subsidiary's facilities are short term with risk minimized by a 125% side collateral position over the bank's exposure. Collateral consists of high-grade receivables. Based on this, you improve ratings by –2.

At worse, collateral has no impact on the cumulative grade. Superior quality collateral will improve the cumulative grade by as much as four grade levels. But be careful. If lender approves a loan to a grade 9 or 10 credit solely on the basis of collateral, the bank's secured position may be contestable in court.

Many lenders raise (and answer) important questions before they complete a collateral facility page; some of these questions are as follows:[1]

1. What is its value compared to credit exposure?
2. What is its liquidity, or how quickly may its value be realized and with what certainty?
3. Is negotiable collateral held under joint custody?
4. Has the customer obtained and filed for released collateral sign receipts?
5. Are securities and commodities valued and margin requirements reviewed at least monthly?
6. When support rests on the cash surrender value of insurance policies, is a periodic accounting received from the insurance company and maintained with the policy?
7. Is a record maintained of entry to the collateral vault?
8. Has the bank instituted a system which ensures that security agreements are filed, collateral mortgages are properly recorded, title searches and property appraisals are performed in connection with collateral mortgages, and insurance coverage (including a loss payee clause) is in effect on property covered by collateral mortgages?

---

[1] FRB Commercial Bank Examination Manual.

9. In mortgage warehouse financing, does the bank hold the original mortgage note, trust deed, or other critical document, to be released only upon payment?
10. Have standards been set for determining the percentage advance to be made against acceptable receivables?
11. Are acceptable receivables defined?
12. Has the bank established minimum requirements for verification of the borrower's accounts receivable and established minimum standards for documentation?
13. Are accounts receivable financing policies reviewed at least annually to determine if they are compatible with changing market conditions?
14. Have inquiries about accounts receivable financing loan balances been received and investigated?
15. Were payments from customers scrutinized for differences in invoice dates, numbers, terms, and so on?
16. Do bank records show, on a timely basis, a first lien on the assigned receivables for each borrower?
17. Do loans granted on the security of the receivables also have an assignment of the inventory?
18. Does the bank verify the borrower's accounts receivable or require independent verification on a periodic basis?
19. Does the bank require the borrower to provide aged accounts receivable schedules on a periodic basis?

Enter -1 in cell E43 as illustrated.

Collateral effect on grade	-1
Cumulative risk grade	2.50

Module 8: Purpose—Worksheet PURPOSE

Classification Standards

1. The facility is appropriate for business.
2. Match funding is appropriate.
3. The financing strategy is not appropriate for this obligor.
4. The obligor is borrowing on a short-term basis to finance capital requirements.
5. The facility is used to finance excessive dividends.
6. This is an unsecured facility, while other lenders have the best collateral.
7. The bank is the subordinated lender.
8. The loan structure is poor.

Enter a zero in cell E28 or leave it blank.

Purpose adjustment to grade	0
Cumulative risk grade	2.50

Module 9: Tenor—Worksheet Tenor

From time to time and for various reasons, a bank may extend credit on terms or for a tenor that for a given borrower subjects the bank to a greater level of risk than indicated by the obligor rating. The FRB audit guidelines, for example, look for established maximum maturities for various types of loans

Tenor incremental risk may be reflected in a higher or worse risk rating. For example, an unsecured line of credit to a company with a obligor rating of 4 would not usually warrant a change in grade (the grade may actually improve in some cases with maturities under one year); however, a term loan of longer than usual tenor or a loan with a seven-year bullet maturity or a credit supported by a weak loan agreement may warrant a 5 or worse. The tenor matrix serves as a guide and should be changed to conform to bank policy.

Founded as a dairy in 1954, Quickbuy entered the convenience store business in 1964 and currently operates 450 convenience stores in the Northeastern region of the United States. Quickbuy has demonstrated consistent earnings, strong and stable cash flow, liquidity, and capitalization. For the fiscal year ended December 31, 2000, Quickbuy generated $251 million in revenues and posted a net profit of $3.3 million. The company consistently generated more than sufficient cash flow from operations to cover current maturities and dividends. Quickbuy's market position in the Mid-Atlantic region remains quite strong. The company ranks number 1 in sales and profitability per store. Quickbuy also maintains a debt/capitalization ratio of 59%, which is lower than many of its competitors. However, *due to the unusual length of the term on an unsecured basis,* the obligor's grade of 4 ended up as a grade 6 final risk rating.

Enter a 1 in cell E28 as illustrated below.

Tenor adjustment to grade	1
Cumulative risk grade	3.50

Module 10: Portfolio Risk and Investment Factors— Worksheet Portfolio

The two main points of this section are (1) will the facility have a neutral effect on the bank's portfolio and (2) will the facility provide adequate opportunities in the secondary market (Table 19.6)? Small banks and banks located in industry/economic pockets (the agriculture Midwest belt, for example) may not have acknowledged credit concentrations within specific industries. A credit concentration generally consists of direct or indirect (1) extensions of credit and (2) contingent obligations exceeding 25% of the bank's capital structure (Tier 1 plus loan loss reserves). This definition does not simply refer to loans, but includes the aggregate of all types of exposures: loans and discounts, overdrafts, cash items, securities purchased outright or under resale agreements, the sale of federal funds, suspense assets, leases, acceptances, letters of credit, placements, loans endorsed, guaranteed, or subject to repurchase agreements, and any other actual or contingent liability.

Limitations imposed by bank management and regulators are intended to prevent a client from borrowing an undue amount of the bank's resources, thereby increasing risk by reducing the loan spread among a relatively large number of firms engaged in different businesses. Bankers should recognize the various types of concentrations identified in a loan portfolio before completing the worksheet:[2]

If exposure concentrations are material, the appropriateness of concentrations should be verified before or during the risk grading process. Concentrations that involve excessive or undue risks require close scrutiny by the bank and should be reduced over a reasonable period of time. Bank managers use credit derivatives (Chapter 15) and loan securitizations and loan sales (Chapter 12) to reduce concentrations. Enter a zero or leave cell E28 blank. The cumulative risk grade remains at 3.50.

TABLE 19.6   Sample Cells from the PORTFOLIO Worksheet

Classification standards	Maximum effect on grade
Facility has neutral effect on the bank's portfolio	None
Facility provides adequate opportunities in the secondary market	
Facility has a neutral or positive effect on the bank's portfolio and provides excellent opportunities in the secondary loan market	From 0 to –2
Facility significantly increases portfolio's exposure to systematic risk	From +1 to +8
Facility represents an illiquid asset providing few opportunities in the secondary loan market	
Portfolio adjustment to grade	0
Cumulative risk grade	3.50

---

[2] FRB *Commercial Bank Examination Manual.*

THE SUMMARY PAGE

The summary page is illustrated in Table 19.7 and the worksheet named Summary. This page synopsizes the entire risk rating process and is usually the document attached to a facility sheet, credit review, or otherwise reported through the system to senior officials.

Supporting Worksheets

Supporting worksheets include Verification, Default Factors, Weights, SIC Codes, S&P, and Macros.

The ROBFEL_New4 Risk rating model includes schematic worksheets that describes how the system was set up (Table 19.8). The worksheets provide design and programming code that will help you tailor your own interactive risk rating system. These worksheets follow the SUMMARY worksheet.

TABLE 19.7   Summary Page Highlights: Individual Grades, Cumulative Grades, and Changes

Summary risk rating

				General Corporate		John Smith
Great CoupleDesign, Inc.						
123 Success Court		Max Exposure:		80,000	Credit Area:	Global Credit Co.
City/State/Zip: Old Westbury, NY		Facility Type:		Senior	Data Source:	Audited
Date: July 5, 2001		Classification:		Bridge	Audit Date:	6/30/2001

Weights				Credit Rating	
Operating Cash Flows	29%	4.0		Obligor Grade:	4.0
Debt Capacity and Financing Capacity	36%	5.0		System Grade	3.5
Asset/Liability Quality	21%	3.0		Final Grade:	4.0
Valuation	14%	2.0			

Obligor Financial Measure
Industry Specific Cumulative Grade Weights

OBLIGOR GRADES	Unit Grade	Change	Cumulative Grade		Previous Rating		
Cash Flow	3.0		3.0		Previous Risk Grade2	2	1/1/2000
Debt Capacity/Financing Flexibility	4.0	0.3	3.3		Previous Risk Grade	3	1/1/2001
Asset Quality	4.0	0.1	3.4				
Valuation Measures	4.0	0.3	3.7		Industry SIC Code		12345
Contingencies	5.0	0.0	3.7		S&P Debt Rating		AAA
Financial Reporting	4.0	0.0	3.7		Shadow Debt Rating		1001
Management Depth	4.0	0.0	3.7		KMV Default		
Fin Development	0.0	0.0	3.7		Secondary Mk Liquidity		Not Liquid
Industry Segment	6.0	0.0	3.7		Total Debt/EBITDA		12345.0x
Industry Position	5.0	0.3	4.0		Interest Coverage		100000.0x
Country Risk	1.0	0.0	4.0				
					Summary Rating	Grade	Change
FACILITIES GRADES					Obligor Only Grade	4.0	NA
Documentation	0.0	0.0	4.0		Facility Risk Grade Adjustment	-0.5	-4.5
Guarantees	0.0	-0.5	3.5		System Risk (Rounded)	3.5	4.0
Guarantee Documentation	0.0	0.0	3.5		Adjustments (Comments Below):		
					Financial Development	0	
	Collateral	-1.0	-1.0	2.5	Other		
	Purpose	0.0	0.0	2.5			
	Tenor	1.0	1.0	3.5	Final Adjusted Rating		
	Portfolio	0.0	0.0	3.5			

TABLE 19.8 Risk Rating Schematic Worksheets

Verification	Verification summary section; get intro – dialog box tutorial response; get intro dialog box, tutorial responses
Default factors	Rating, default factor average, guarantors grade, obligors grade, obligor default factor, transaction weighted grade, default factor to grade chart
Weights	Suggested cumulative grade weights include in general corporate, utilities/trans/telecommunications, wholesale distribution/trading, financial institutions, and construction and engineering.
SIC Codes Codes	Standard industrial code ranges for 45 industries
S&P	S&P rating conversion to credit risk rating grades 1 to 10. S&P ratio ranges include EBITDA margin, pretax profit, EBITDA/interest, current ratio, and valuation.
Macros	Includes 1655 rows of visual basic code that activate and drive this risk rating model. The first nine rows of coding provide an example:

```
'Auto Open Macro
Sub Auto_Open()
  Goto Opening Screen
  Application.Goto Reference:= "Intro"
  'Invoke Risk Rating system Menus
  Set_RiskRating Menu
  'Set Print Headers to Not Verifies-The User has to Verify After Entering Data
  PrinterSettings
  End Sub
```

CONCLUSION

In the final analysis, a bank's risk rating system is a judgmental one. The skill and experience of lending personnel are the two key attributes vital to the process of accurately assessing risk and most importantly:

> Rating systems should take proper account of gradations in risk and the overall composition of portfolios in originating new loans, assessing overall portfolio risks and concentrations, and reporting on risk profiles to directors and management. Moreover, such rating systems also should play an important role in establishing an appropriate level for the allowance for loan and lease losses, conducting internal bank analysis of loan and relationship profitability, assessing capital adequacy.[3]

---

[3]Quote from Federal Reserve Board memo.

SELECTED REFERENCES AND READINGS

Altman, E. I. (1998). The importance and subtlety of credit rating migration. *Journal of Banking & Finance*, 1231–1247.

Buchanan, N. (1994). Rating Eastern Europe. *Banker*, 10–11. In Eastern Europe, the absence of some of the tools of credit management, such as credit rating services and industry statistics, will place more demands on bankers. They will need to take a more hands-on role when dealing with portfolios in order to identify opportunities or threats.

DeYoung, R., J. P. Hughes, *et al.* (1998). Regulatory distress costs and risk-taking at U.S. commercial banks. *United States, Office of the Comptroller of the Currency, Economics Working Paper* **No. 98-1**, 1–50.

Eisenbeis, R. A. (1978). *Problems in applying discriminant analysis in credit scoring models.* Washington, DC: Board of Governors of the Federal Reserve System.

English, W. B., and W. R. Nelson. (1998). Bank risk rating of business loans. *United States, Board of Governors of the Federal Reserve System, Division of Research and Statistics, Finance and Economics Discussion Series* **No. 1998-51**, 1–[46].

Greene, W. (1998). Sample selection in credit-scoring models. *Japan and the World Economy* (3), 299–316. With a comment by Yasuhiro Sakai, pp. 317–320.

Greene, W. H. (1992). Statistical model for credit scoring. *New York University, Leonard N. Stern School of Business, Department of Economics, Working Paper Series* **No. EC-92-29**, 1–38.

Hand, D. J., and W. E. Henley. (1997). Statistical classification methods in consumer credit scoring: A review. *Journal of the Royal Statistical Society. Series a, Statistics in Society* (Part 3), [523]–541.

Haque, N. U., D. Mathieson, *et al.* (1997). Rating the raters of country creditworthiness. *Finance and Development, a Quarterly Publication of the International Monetary Fund and the World Bank*, 10–13. Looks at what criteria rating agencies apply and what countries can do to improve their credit ratings. Also published in Arabic, Chinese, French, German, Portuguese, and Spanish.

Hiltebeitel, K. M., and J. P. Borden. (1988). Technology update . . . using Lotus to develop credit scoring models. *Journal of Commercial Bank Lending*, 30–40.

House, R. (1995). Rating environmental risk. *Institutional Investor, International Edition*, 80–86.

Jacobson, T., and K. Roszbach. (1998). Bank lending policy, credit scoring and value at risk. *Sveriges Riksbank, Working Paper Series* **No. 68**, 1–25.

Lascelles, D. (1995). Environmental risk rating. *Economic Affairs*, 33–35.

Matthews, G. J. (1993). *Overall creditworthiness as a tool for sustainable development.* Montevideo, Uruguay: Unesco.

Mayer, M. (1999). The ratings game. *International Economy*, 33–35. Moody's, Standard & Poor's, and the IMF confront the question: Is all risk created equal?

Mays, E. (1998). *Credit risk modeling: Design and application.* Chicago; New York: Glenlake; AMACOM American Management Association.

Monroe, A. (1992). Better a low rating than none at all. *Global Finance*, 46–52.

Oral, M. (1992). Estimation model for country risk rating. *International Journal of Forecasting*, 583–593. Proposes, and applies to a group of 70 countries, a procedure that employs a generalized logit model to link country risk rating and political-economic indicators.

Payne, B. (1999). Basle spotlights rating agencies. *Risk*: 27–29.

Shapiro, H. D. (1986, September). Rating country credit. *Institutional Investor, International Edition*, 245–264. In the *Institutional Investor's* survey, Japan has toppled the United States from the number 1 spot.

Thomas, L. C., and Institute of Mathematics and Its Applications. (1992). *Credit scoring and credit control: Based on the proceedings of a conference on credit scoring and credit control, organized by the Institute of Mathematics and Its Applications and Held at the University of Edinburg in August 1989.* Oxford; New York: Clarendon Press, Oxford University Press.

Vigano, L. (1993). Credit scoring model for development banks: an African case study. *Savings and Development* **12**(4), 441–482. Proposes a model to enable LDC banks to better evaluate the creditworthiness of their clients. The Caisse Nationale de Credit Agricole of Burkina Faso is used as a test case.

SELECT INTERNET LIBRARY AND CD

CD includes

Interactive (generic) Excel risk rating system: ROBFEL_New 4

Internet Links

(1) FRB Publication: Credit Risk Rating at Large U.S. Banks; Adobe Document http://www.federal-reserve.gov/pubs/bulletin/1998/1198leadw.pdf

(2) Parameterizing Credit Risk Models With Rating Data Mark Carey Federal Reserve Board; Adobe Document http://www.federalreserve.gov/pubs/feds/2000/200047/200047pap.pdf

(3) Basel Committee Publication Credit Risk Modeling: Current Practices and Applications—Apr 1999; Adobe Document http://www.bis.org/publ/bcbs49.pdf

INDEX